SPORT AND RECREATION IN CANADIAN HISTORY

Carly Adams

University of Lethbridge

Editor

HUMAN KINETICS

Library of Congress Cataloging-in-Publication Data

Names: Adams, Carly, editor. | Human Kinetics Publishers.
Title: Sport and recreation in Canadian history / Carly Adams.
Description: First Edition. | Champaign : Human Kinetics, Inc., 2021. |
   Includes bibliographical references and index.
Identifiers: LCCN 2020023940 (print) | LCCN 2020023941 (ebook) | ISBN
   9781492569497 (pbk) | ISBN 9781492599203 (ePub) | ISBN 9781492569503
   (PDF)
Subjects: LCSH: Sports--Canada--History. | Outdoor
   recreation--Canada--History.
Classification: LCC GV585 .S62 2021 (print) | LCC GV585 (ebook) | DDC
   796.0971--dc23
LC record available at https://lccn.loc.gov/2020023940
LC ebook record available at https://lccn.loc.gov/2020023941

ISBN: 978-1-4925-6949-7 (print)

The web addresses cited in this text were current as of August 2020, unless otherwise noted.

Acquisitions Editor: Diana Vincer; **Managing Editor:** Anna Lan Seaman; **Copyeditor:** Patricia MacDonald; **Indexer:** Michael Ferreira; **Permissions Manager:** Dalene Reeder; **Graphic Designer:** Dawn Sills; **Cover Designer:** Keri Evans; **Cover Design Associate:** Susan Rothermel Allen; **Photograph (cover):** 'National Pastimes', by Jim Logan courtesy of the Indigenous Art Collection, Crown-Indigenous Relations and Nothern Affairs Canada; **Photo Asset Manager:** Laura Fitch; **Photo Production Manager:** Jason Allen; **Printer:** Marquis

Printed in Canada   10 9 8 7 6 5 4 3 2 1

The paper in this book is certified under a sustainable forestry program.

Human Kinetics
1607 N. Market Street
Champaign, IL 61820
USA

United States and International
Website: **US.HumanKinetics.com**
Email: info@hkusa.com
Phone: 1-800-747-4457

Canada
Website: **Canada.HumanKinetics.com**
Email: info@hkcanada.com

E7353

Tell us what you think!
Human Kinetics would love to hear what we
can do to improve the customer experience.
Use this QR code to take our brief survey.

CONTENTS

TIMELINE

Note: This timeline is incomplete. It does not represent a comprehensive list of events in Canadian sport history. Rather, the timeline highlights significant moments and events that are discussed within the chapters of the book. For a discussion on alternative ways to think about time and the political implications of timelines, please refer to chapter 15.

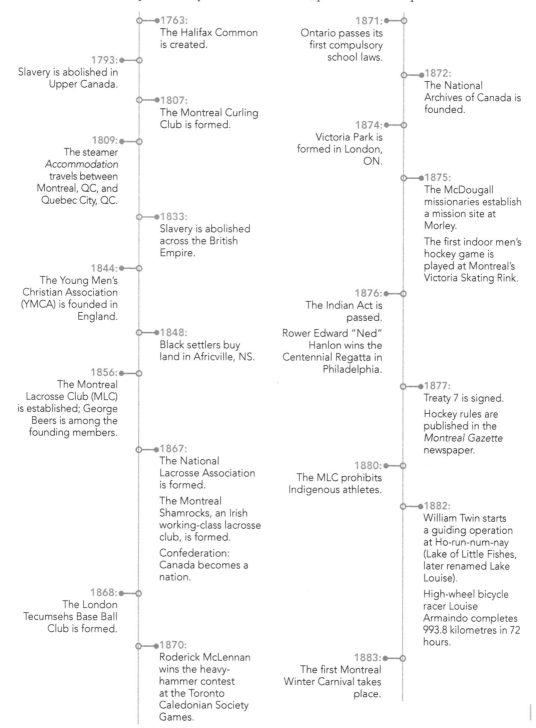

1763: The Halifax Common is created.

1793: Slavery is abolished in Upper Canada.

1807: The Montreal Curling Club is formed.

1809: The steamer *Accommodation* travels between Montreal, QC, and Quebec City, QC.

1833: Slavery is abolished across the British Empire.

1844: The Young Men's Christian Association (YMCA) is founded in England.

1848: Black settlers buy land in Africville, NS.

1856: The Montreal Lacrosse Club (MLC) is established; George Beers is among the founding members.

1867: The National Lacrosse Association is formed.

The Montreal Shamrocks, an Irish working-class lacrosse club, is formed.

Confederation: Canada becomes a nation.

1868: The London Tecumsehs Base Ball Club is formed.

1870: Roderick McLennan wins the heavy-hammer contest at the Toronto Caledonian Society Games.

1871: Ontario passes its first compulsory school laws.

1872: The National Archives of Canada is founded.

1874: Victoria Park is formed in London, ON.

1875: The McDougall missionaries establish a mission site at Morley.

The first indoor men's hockey game is played at Montreal's Victoria Skating Rink.

1876: The Indian Act is passed.

Rower Edward "Ned" Hanlon wins the Centennial Regatta in Philadelphia.

1877: Treaty 7 is signed.

Hockey rules are published in the *Montreal Gazette* newspaper.

1880: The MLC prohibits Indigenous athletes.

1882: William Twin starts a guiding operation at Ho-run-num-nay (Lake of Little Fishes, later renamed Lake Louise).

High-wheel bicycle racer Louise Armaindo completes 993.8 kilometres in 72 hours.

1883: The first Montreal Winter Carnival takes place.

1884:
George "Old Chocolate" Godfrey becomes the first Black heavyweight champion and first Canadian boxing champion.

1885:
The Canadian Pacific Railway is completed.

The pass system is implemented in Canada.

The Banff Hot Springs Reserve is formed.

1886:
The Whitcher report is released.

The Dominion Challenge hockey tournament is established.

The Amateur Hockey Association of Canada is established.

Siksika distance runner Api-kai-ees (Deerfoot) wins the Dominion Day one-mile race in Calgary, AB.

1887:
The Rocky Mountains Park Act is passed.

1888:
The Banff Springs Hotel is completed.

1890:
The district of Calgary fishery report calls for increased regulation.

George "Kid Chocolate" Dixon wins the world bantamweight boxing title and is the first Black world boxing champion.

The Ontario Hockey Association is formed.

1891:
The earliest written account of a women's hockey game is published in the *Ottawa Citizen*.

James Naismith invents basketball at Springfield College.

1893: Governor General Lord Stanley's donation, the Stanley Cup, is awarded for the first time.

1895:
The Coloured Hockey League of the Maritimes is established.

1898:
The Canadian Amateur Athletic Union (CAAU) is established.

1899:
The Canadian Amateur Hockey League is formed.

1900:
George Orton becomes Canada's first Olympic medallist.

1901:
The Winnipeg Victorias become Stanley Cup champions.

The playground movement is organized in Canada.

1902:
Rocky Mountains Park is expanded.

1903:
Major League Baseball is formed.

Florence Harvey wins her first Canadian Ladies' Golf Championship.

The first Royal Canadian Henley Regatta takes place.

1906:
The Lords Day Act is passed.

The Alpine Club of Canada is formed.

The Montreal Wanderers are crowned Stanley Cup champions.

The athletic war begins.

The Eastern Canada Amateur Hockey Association is formed.

1907:
The Manitoba Professional Hockey League is formed.

Robert Baden-Powell founds the Boy Scouts.

Tom Longboat wins the Boston Marathon.

1909:
The Amateur Athletic Union of Canada (AAUC) replaces the CAAU.

The National Hockey Association is formed.

The first Grey Cup is contested.

1911:
The Immigration Act is implemented.

1912:
John Armstrong "Army" Howard is the first Black Canadian Olympian.

The Pacific Coast Hockey Association is established.

The Maritime Professional Hockey League is formed.

Tom Three Persons wins the saddled bronco competition at the Calgary Stampede.

1913:
YMCA physical educators found the Far Eastern Championship Games.

1914:
The Asahi baseball club is formed in Vancouver, BC.

The Canadian Amateur Hockey Association is formed.

1915:
The Eastern Ladies Hockey League is formed.

The Edmonton Grads are formed.

1916:
The first international women's hockey match between Canada and the United States takes place.

The Montreal Canadiens become the first French-Canadian team to win the Stanley Cup.

1917:
The first Banff Winter Carnival is held.

The National Hockey League (NHL) is formed.

The first women's track and field championship is held in France.

1918:
The AAUC proposes a national sport and recreation program funded by the federal government.

1920:
The Winnipeg Falcons compete in the men's hockey competition at the Olympic Games.

1921:
The Toronto Ladies Athletic Club is founded in Toronto, ON.

1922:
The Gyro Club of Edmonton opens its first playground.

The Ladies Ontario Hockey Association is formed.

1923:
The first hockey games are broadcast on the radio.

1924:
Boston becomes the NHL's first U.S.-based franchise.

1925:
The Canadian Ukrainian Athletic Club is formed in Winnipeg, MB.

1926:
The Women's Amateur Athletic Federation is formed.

1928:
A Canadian team competes at the Olympic Games in Amsterdam, Netherlands.

The Workers' Sports Association of Canada (WSAC) is formed by the Young Communist League of Canada.

1930:
The first British Empire Games are held in Hamilton, ON.

Banff National Park is established under the National Parks Act.

1931:
Canadian heavyweight champion Lawrence "Larry" Gains is the first Black man to challenge for and win the British Empire heavyweight title.

The Preston Rivulettes are formed.

The Canadian Rugby Union adopts the forward pass.

Maple Leaf Gardens opens in Toronto, ON.

The Workers' Olympics in Vienna attract 76,245 worker-athletes from 23 countries.

1932:
High jumper Eva Dawes wins bronze at the Summer Olympics.

Ray Lewis becomes the first Black Canadian to win an Olympic medal.

1933:
The Dominion Women's Amateur Hockey Association is formed.

The Edmonton Rustlers are crowned the first national women's hockey champions.

1935:
Alfred Wilson, a pitcher and outfielder, is the first Black player to be integrated within Canadian high-level leagues in the Quebec Provincial League.

1936:
Dr. Phil Edwards wins the first Lou Marsh Award.

Andy Paull helps form the North Shore Indians lacrosse team.

The People's Olympiad in Barcelona, Spain, is cancelled.

Canadian and American cowboys go on strike and form the Cowboys' Turtle Association.

1938:
Barbara Howard is the first Black Canadian woman to represent Canada internationally.

1943:
The National Physical Fitness Act is passed.

1948:
Figure skater Barbara Ann Scott wins gold at the Winter Olympics.

1949:
The position Supervisor of Physical Education and Recreation is created at Indian Affairs.

1951:
The Indian Act undergoes major revisions.

The Tom Longboat Awards are established.

1952:
The first televised *Hockey Night in Canada* broadcast takes place.

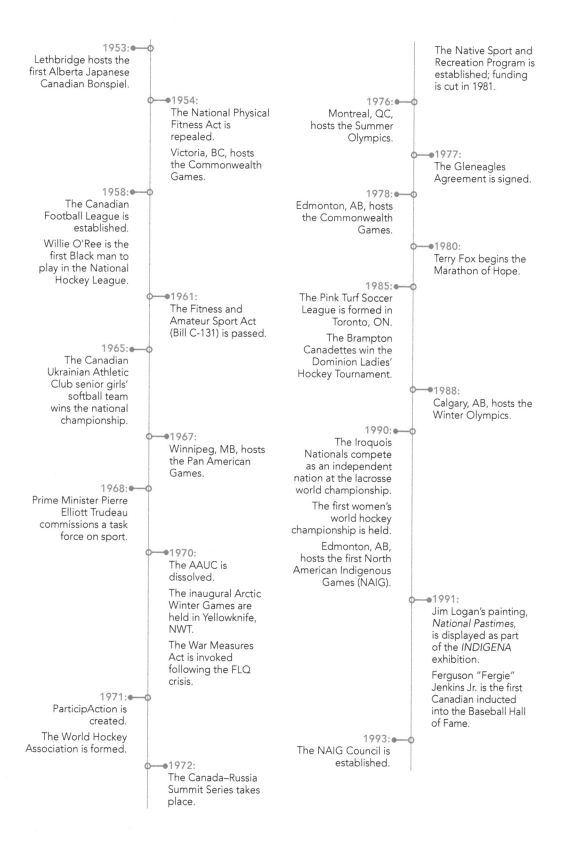

1953: Lethbridge hosts the first Alberta Japanese Canadian Bonspiel.

1954: The National Physical Fitness Act is repealed.

Victoria, BC, hosts the Commonwealth Games.

1958: The Canadian Football League is established.

Willie O'Ree is the first Black man to play in the National Hockey League.

1961: The Fitness and Amateur Sport Act (Bill C-131) is passed.

1965: The Canadian Ukrainian Athletic Club senior girls' softball team wins the national championship.

1967: Winnipeg, MB, hosts the Pan American Games.

1968: Prime Minister Pierre Elliott Trudeau commissions a task force on sport.

1970: The AAUC is dissolved.

The inaugural Arctic Winter Games are held in Yellowknife, NWT.

The War Measures Act is invoked following the FLQ crisis.

1971: ParticipAction is created.

The World Hockey Association is formed.

1972: The Canada–Russia Summit Series takes place.

The Native Sport and Recreation Program is established; funding is cut in 1981.

1976: Montreal, QC, hosts the Summer Olympics.

1977: The Gleneagles Agreement is signed.

1978: Edmonton, AB, hosts the Commonwealth Games.

1980: Terry Fox begins the Marathon of Hope.

1985: The Pink Turf Soccer League is formed in Toronto, ON.

The Brampton Canadettes win the Dominion Ladies' Hockey Tournament.

1988: Calgary, AB, hosts the Winter Olympics.

1990: The Iroquois Nationals compete as an independent nation at the lacrosse world championship.

The first women's world hockey championship is held.

Edmonton, AB, hosts the first North American Indigenous Games (NAIG).

1991: Jim Logan's painting, *National Pastimes*, is displayed as part of the *INDIGENA* exhibition.

Ferguson "Fergie" Jenkins Jr. is the first Canadian inducted into the Baseball Hall of Fame.

1993: The NAIG Council is established.

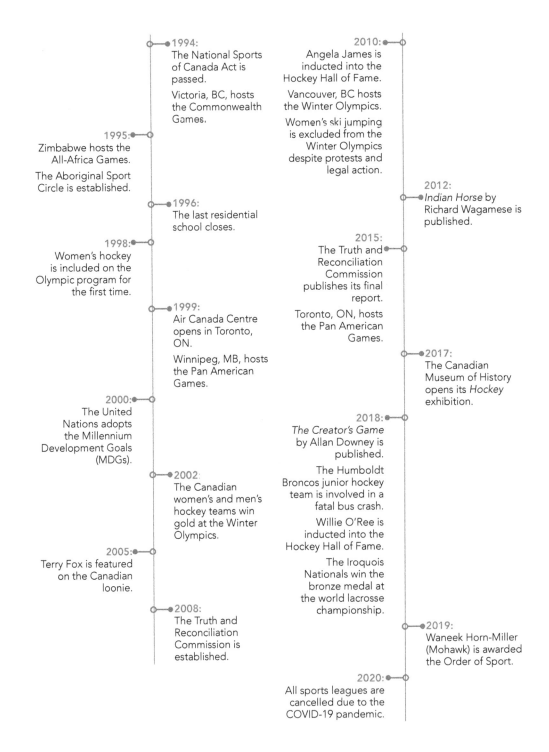

1994:
The National Sports of Canada Act is passed.

Victoria, BC, hosts the Commonwealth Games.

1995:
Zimbabwe hosts the All-Africa Games.

The Aboriginal Sport Circle is established.

1996:
The last residential school closes.

1998:
Women's hockey is included on the Olympic program for the first time.

1999:
Air Canada Centre opens in Toronto, ON.

Winnipeg, MB, hosts the Pan American Games.

2000:
The United Nations adopts the Millennium Development Goals (MDGs).

2002:
The Canadian women's and men's hockey teams win gold at the Winter Olympics.

2005:
Terry Fox is featured on the Canadian loonie.

2008:
The Truth and Reconciliation Commission is established.

2010:
Angela James is inducted into the Hockey Hall of Fame.

Vancouver, BC hosts the Winter Olympics.

Women's ski jumping is excluded from the Winter Olympics despite protests and legal action.

2012:
Indian Horse by Richard Wagamese is published.

2015:
The Truth and Reconciliation Commission publishes its final report.

Toronto, ON, hosts the Pan American Games.

2017:
The Canadian Museum of History opens its *Hockey* exhibition.

2018:
The Creator's Game by Allan Downey is published.

The Humboldt Broncos junior hockey team is involved in a fatal bus crash.

Willie O'Ree is inducted into the Hockey Hall of Fame.

The Iroquois Nationals win the bronze medal at the world lacrosse championship.

2019:
Waneek Horn-Miller (Mohawk) is awarded the Order of Sport.

2020:
All sports leagues are cancelled due to the COVID-19 pandemic.

PREFACE

Written by leading sport and recreation historians, *Sport and Recreation in Canadian History* serves as a foundation for critical discussions about how historical forces continue to shape 21st-century sport. Although the book focuses on sport and recreation practices on these lands now claimed by Canada, it is set within a larger historical context of interconnecting social and cultural practices to speak to the sustained tensions, complexities, and contradictions prevalent in Canadian society. The authors examine how gender, ethnicity, race, religion, ability, class, and other systems of oppression and privilege have shaped sport and recreation practices, and how Canadian sporting culture has reproduced, challenged, and reshaped these same systems.

Sport and Recreation in Canadian History facilitates research-based discussion by providing case studies of Canadian sport within broader social contexts. The book is a core text for university and college courses, but it is also useful for graduate students and as a resource for sport scholars and enthusiasts. For students in fields such as sport history, Canadian studies, gender studies, and Indigenous studies, the book encourages a critical understanding of how and why sport and recreation practices are intertwined with all areas of Canadian society.

This is not a comprehensive text; indeed, one of the key arguments running through this collection is that there is no such thing as a "complete" history. Rather, this text challenges readers to think about the past critically; to consider moments, practices, and groups who have been forgotten, silenced, or rendered invisible and how their contributions matter; and to think about how taken-for-granted assumptions about Canadian sport can be challenged and (re)storied.

How the Book Is Organized

Sport and Recreation in Canadian History contains 15 chapters. The chapters have been curated in this particular order, and I recommend you read them in this way. However, each of the chapters stands alone and can be read as individual contributions or in a different order depending on interest. Each chapter begins with learning objectives and concludes with discussion questions and suggested readings.

In chapter 1, I open the book with a discussion about why sport and recreation histories matter. In doing so, I discuss the role of historians in the historical process and the multiplicity of histories. I also discuss the significance of the text's cover image and how personal histories of sport connect to broader social, cultural, and political histories.

In chapter 2, Sarah Barnes and Mary Louise Adams offer a provocative discussion about how history is actively produced and not just a documentation of past events. They invite us to learn how to think historically and to consider the philosophical, political, and practical dimensions of "doing history." Focusing on archival research and oral history, Barnes and Adams encourage readers to think about power, inequality, accountability, and accessibility and why and how sport histories matter beyond the classroom.

In chapter 3, Braden Te Hiwi shares an approach to history that weaves together the past, present, and future in his exploration of the changing contexts of Indigenous peoples' cultures and physical activities. He discusses traditional Indigenous games, the Indigenous origins of lacrosse, the Arctic Winter Games, and the role of these activities in cultural exchange, cultural suppression, and cultural maintenance and revitalization. The chapter concludes with a discussion of the importance of conducting culturally relevant historical research.

In chapter 4, Janice Forsyth highlights three case studies—(1) sports in the residential school system, (2) the Tom Longboat Awards, and (3) the North American Indigenous Games—to discuss the way settlers have used sport to regulate and control Indigenous peoples and how Indigenous peoples have responded, rebuilding their lives and communities in a settler colonial state while resisting settler colonialism itself. She concludes by inviting readers to think about the purpose and impact of the Truth and Reconciliation Commission and the ways Canadian sport histories so often privilege settler ways of understanding and engaging in sport.

In chapter 5, Courtney W. Mason provides an overview of the development of national parks in Western Canada. Focusing on Banff National Park, he examines how Indigenous practices such as hunting, fishing, and gathering were deemed illegal in the park's system as part of the process of creating recreational and commercial opportunities for settlers and tourists. Mason invites us to reflect on how park policies were connected to larger colonial processes of land dispossession and cultural assimilation. Throughout the chapter, he highlights the roles of Nakoda people in local tourism, discusses why they were displaced from Banff, and details how some people resisted colonial regulations and policies.

In chapter 6, Robert Kossuth and David McMurray discuss the impact of industrialization and urbanization in Canada and the factors that led to the development of outdoor physical activities for adults and children as a way to offset the negative effects of urban-industrial living. They explain the notion of rational recreation and discuss how white middle- and upper-class urban Canadians attempted to recreate nature through the development of urban parks, supervised playgrounds, swimming facilities, and highly controlled wilderness adventures to improve the health and "morality" of those living in cities.

In chapter 7, Craig Greenham examines cricket and imperialism, lacrosse and nationalism, and baseball and continentalism to consider the ideological debates connected to the evolution of 19th-century Canadian sports. He concludes by encouraging us to think about the ideological struggles at the heart of sport today and the ways organized sport in contemporary Canada represents both a continuity of and a divergence from the past.

In chapter 8, Robert Kossuth builds on the previous chapter by exploring how sport in Canada today is a product of the professional sport model that emerged in the late 19th and early 20th centuries that privileged competitive, male-dominated, profit-oriented physical practices. He focuses on four individuals—Roderick McLennan, Ned Hanlan, Louise Armaindo, and Api-kai-ees—and the emergence of professional team sports such as lacrosse, baseball, football, and hockey to discuss the tensions between amateurism and professionalism in early organized sport in Canada.

In chapter 9, Russell Field, Michel Vigneault, and I explore the development of ice hockey to consider how some groups of people (predominantly white men) have maintained and exercised hegemony in the sport while others have been excluded from both full participation and our national stories. We encourage students to consider how hockey has become part of our national imagination and why our assumptions about the past are often accepted and sustained over time.

In chapter 10, Danielle Peers and Lisa Tink invite us to think about the difference between dominant and progressive histories and genealogy. To do this they explore three case studies: (1) the early 20th-century playground movement, (2) "inclusive" physical education in the early to mid-20th century, and (3) the mid-20th-century emergence of Paralympic sport. They challenge us to think about how we might tell histories differently as a way to recontextualize and critique injustices of the past and work towards more just futures.

In chapter 11, Ornella Nzindukiyimana and Kevin B. Wamsley discuss Black Canadian sporting experiences and how they have been shaped by racialization and racism. They emphasize the exclusive and discriminatory nature of Canadian sport and explore the complexities of Black Canadians' sport experiences, with a focus on how Black Canadians were framed differently by the media. To do this, they discuss changes in Black Canadians' participation in sport throughout the 19th and 20th centuries and how these complex experiences illustrate the intertwining of discrimination, acceptance, and empowerment.

In chapter 12, Stacy L. Lorenz and Jay Scherer introduce the sports–media complex and discuss the factors that contributed to the growth of sports coverage in Canadian daily newspapers and radio and television broadcasts. In so doing, they explore how media coverage of sport socially constructs cultural narratives that shape our understandings of gender, race, ethnicity, and local and national identities.

In chapter 13, Christine M. O'Bonsawin builds on previous chapters and critically situates colonialism in historical sport discourses. Rather than focusing on Indigenous peoples in Canadian sport history and Canada's organized sport structure, she shifts the point of intervention by positioning sport as a form of social organization that was (and remains) rooted in and reproductive of colonial power. In so doing, she considers the rise of Canadian sport and how the nation's international sport presence—as hosts of the Olympic Games, for example—circumvents legal processes concerning the rights of Indigenous peoples.

In chapter 14, Russell Field considers elite sport and grassroots initiatives to explore how the Canadian sport system both shaped and was shaped by Canada's involvement in international sport. As part of the discussion, he introduces and discusses the notions of sport-for-good and sport-for-development.

In chapter 15, I collaborate with Braden Te Hiwi to reflect on the field of sport history. In particular, we focus on time and timelines, as a way to de-centre settle colonial perspectives in historical knowledge.

On behalf of the contributors, I hope you enjoy engaging with the ideas, concepts, and histories in this text and that it provides you with a historical foundation from which to think critically about the past and to challenge often taken-for-granted assumptions about sport and recreation practices in Canada.

—Carly Adams

ACKNOWLEDGMENTS

A book project is a journey of collaboration, negotiation, joy, patience, and stamina. I am indebted to so many people in the roles they played in making this book a reality. First and foremost, I am grateful to all of the contributors: Mary Louise Adams, Sarah Barnes, Russell Field, Janice Forsyth, Craig Greenham, Robert Kossuth, Stacy L. Lorenz, Courtney W. Mason, David McMurray, Ornella Nzindukiyimana, Christine M. O'Bonsawin, Danielle Peers, Jay Scherer, Braden Te Hiwi, Lisa Tink, Michel Vigneault, and Kevin B. Wamsley. These contributors—who are also my friends, colleagues, and mentors—have shared their research and teaching expertise within the pages of this book. This book would not have been possible without all of you, and I am sincerely appreciative of your dedication, commitment, and enthusiasm for this project. Our students are fortunate to learn with you.

There are, of course, many others who have contributed to this book (directly and indirectly) in meaningful ways—through discussion, consultation, advice, and support. I am deeply grateful to Russell Field, Vicky Paraschak, Sam McKegney, Darren Aoki, Suzanne Lenon, Michelle Helstein, Julie Young, Kristine Alexander, Katie Misener, and Nancy Bouchier for generous discussions, insight, and support as well as friendship.

My heartfelt thanks, as well, to Debbi Adams, Jim Adams, Megan Adams, and Jared Adams for providing support and encouragement along the way. And a special thanks to my partner, Jay, who fills my life with love and adventure and who is also my mentor and editor extraordinaire.

I am especially grateful to Acquisitions Editor Diana Vincer for the support, guidance, and commitment to this project. You were a wonderful advocate for the book, and it has been a pleasure working with you. I also thank all the other folks at Human Kinetics who supported this project from beginning to end, especially Anna Seaman, Laura Fitch, Judy Park, Meghan Roney, Karla Walsh, Martha Gullo, and Dalene Reeder.

I thank artist Jim Logan for allowing us to use his painting *National Pastimes* on the cover of the book and in chapter 1. I am deeply grateful.

Finally, thank you to Jay, Quinn, and Avery for the unwavering encouragement, support, reassurance, strength, and love.

—Carly Adams

CHAPTER 1

SPORT AND RECREATION HISTORIES MATTER

Carly Adams, PhD
University of Lethbridge

LEARNING OBJECTIVES

In this chapter you will

- discover why sport and recreation histories matter;
- consider the importance of "silences" in the historical process;
- contemplate the role of historians and the multiplicity of histories;
- assess Jim Logan's painting on the front cover of the book; and
- consider how histories of sport connect to broader social, cultural, and political histories.

From February 14 to 16, 2020, the Lethbridge Curling Club in Alberta hosted the 68th annual Alberta Japanese Canadian Bonspiel. The weekend event included the curling tournament with more than 50 teams of men and women of all ages, a silent auction, Hall of Fame inductions, a banquet, and other social events. For an outside observer, the bonspiel celebrates excellence on the ice and promotes intergenerational physical activity for Japanese-Canadian curlers and their families (see figure 1.1). Yet when we look to the past and examine histories of the event, we see there is much more going on here.[1] How and why did Japanese Canadians in southern Alberta become involved in curling? The Alberta Japanese Canadian Bonspiel first started in 1953 as an eight-team event for mostly men; how did women become involved in the event, and what do their experiences tell us about changing attitudes and expectations for women's participation in sport and recreation during the second half of the 20th century? What seems, at first glance, to be a relatively simple story of a community bonspiel actually points to a constellation of other considerations both shaping and

Courtesy of Elsie Sasaki.

Figure 1.1   Elsie (Shigehiro) Sasaki and her three daughters Kendy, Linda, and Wanda. Elsie was involved in starting a ladies division in 1968 at the Alberta Japanese Canadian Bonspiel.

shaped by this relatively small sporting competition. For sport historians, this is the central task—to look at everyday events, processes, and representations and treat them as puzzles to be unpacked and considered from various perspectives.

To understand the Alberta Japanese Canadian Bonspiel, we must situate the event within the histories of Japanese Canadians in Canada. In what sense is this event connected to histories of incarceration, relocation, and resettlement during and following the Second World War? We must learn about how the Canadian government systematically incarcerated over 21,000 Japanese Canadians from British Columbia (most of whom were Canadian citizens) and sent them to internment camps.[2] Between 1942 and 1949, many Japanese Canadians were relocated to southern Alberta, and many of them remained to rebuild their lives following the war. The annual bonspiel "represents a site of agency and resistance as Japanese Canadians use this space to renew and create new friendships, to socialize, to challenge social exclusion and to share their sense of place, identity, and community."[3] For the men and women involved in the bonspiel, their participation in this seemingly innocuous sport event is complicated; it reflects the enduring trauma of internment and relocation while also acting as an expression of resiliency and renewal.

In the 21st century, sports are played, watched, and talked about by millions of people every day in Canada. We are inundated with stories and images of sport and recreation through social media, television, radio, news reports, and casual conversations with friends, family, and strangers. We hear stories of triumph, adversity, defeat, achievement, discrimination, and empowerment in all levels of sport, from grassroots activities to professional leagues. Yet how often do we stop and think about how we got to this moment? How are these stories, these decisions, actions, incidents, and institutions that make up sport built on histories and traditions? How do they connect us to past practices and bring certain perspectives to light, while leaving others in the shadows? How do they help imagine sporting futures?

Sport and recreation practices have always been a reflection of, response to, or change agent for social, cultural, political, and economic issues within Canada and globally. To fully understand the complexities of current moments in sport, how and why sport exists and functions as it does today, and to work towards more just futures, we need to understand the histories and the "silences" of Canadian sport and recreation practices. A historical analysis of sport and recreation provides the opportunity to ask questions that challenge taken-for-granted assumptions in and about Canadian sport.

For example, consider the following questions:

- How have British and American ideals influenced the development of Canadian sport?
- Why is hockey entrenched in Canada's national identity?
- Why has sport been traditionally male-dominated, and how has this affected women's sport participation?

- Why has the development of sport in Canada privileged some people over others?
- How can thinking historically about an event, sport governing body, or recreational practice change, challenge, or complicate our understanding of a current moment in Canadian sport?
- How has sport been used as a tool for the dispossession and assimilation of Indigenous peoples?
- Why were Black Canadians historically excluded from sport, and how are discriminatory attitudes embedded within Canadian sport institutions?
- How does media coverage of sport and recreation socially construct cultural narratives that shape our understandings of gender, sexuality, ability, race, ethnicity, and local and national identities?
- How have the political and corporate elite in Canada used the Olympic Games to circumvent legal processes concerning the rights of Indigenous peoples?
- Why did middle-class advocates in Canada believe that sport and physical activity would contribute to the acculturation of immigrants in the first half of the 20th century?
- Under what circumstances and for whom were the first municipal, provincial, and national parks in Canada created?
- Why is violence in some sports such as boxing and hockey attractive to spectators, and how have promoters used this to their advantage?

In this book, you will explore all of these questions. You will be asked to consider why sport and recreation histories matter. You will learn not only about enduring issues of inequality, discrimination, and colonial power that continue to structure sport practices but also how these forces have been resisted and challenged by some individuals and groups.

Histories and Historians of Sport

History as an academic discipline is a method of inquiry about the past. Not an act of uncovering an objective, knowable past. Rather, "history" is the work of historians, who play an active role in the making of history. As you will read in chapter 2, historians use many different historical methods and theoretical frameworks to understand the world around them. Some historians draw on social theories to understand their sources, while others are much more narrative in their approach. As with all research, this reinforces that one historian's interpretation of events may be very different from another historian's version of the same events. It depends on the questions asked and the perspective taken by the historian, as well as the historian's personal values and beliefs related to the topic. It is important to recognize that historians make choices about the questions they ask, the sources they choose to examine, and the approach they take to their research.

In everyday discussions, the term *history* refers to everything that has happened in the past. But we need to think about what that means. How do we know about what has happened in the past? Can we know everything? The answer, quite simply, is no. History is by definition constitutive of and by past events. As Historian E.H. Carr suggests, history is a "continuous process of interaction between the historian and [their] facts, an unending dialogue between the present and the past" and, I would add, the future.[4]

Sport history developed in the late 1960s as a subdiscipline of history. Some sport history experts emerged from physical education programs, while more traditional historians also took an interest in sport. Don Morrow and Kevin B. Wamsley suggest there are three generations of academic sport historians in Canada: The first generation researched and wrote comprehensive histories in the late 1960s and 1970s focused on Canadian history topics; the second generation explored issues of identity, community building, racism, gender, and other systems of oppression and situated their work within social, political, and economic histories of Canada; the third and current generation draws more on subject-centred methods, such as oral history (see chapter 2), and applies a more critical examination to earlier approaches.[5] Most of the authors contributing to this textbook could be categorized as third-generation sport historians.

Telling Stories

Historians, then, are storytellers. They must gather, analyze, and interpret traces of the past (evidence). Historians search for clues and solve puzzles and then they tell the story. The histories they write are derived from a process of interpretation and analysis of evidence. There are many ways historians do this and many histories that could emerge. It is important to consider every historian's perspective—their assumptions—because this shapes the questions they ask, the research they do, and the histories they write. What motivations does a historian have for doing this research and for telling this story? Why are they asking these questions? The story will be different depending on who tells it, and it will change as new evidence is discovered, new questions are asked, and new perspectives unfold. These stories and interpretations help us understand where we have come, how present events have come to be, and most important where Canadian sport might be headed in the future.

In 2003, Thomas King wrote: "Stories are wondrous things. And they are dangerous." He cautions: "So you have to be careful with the stories you tell. And you have to watch out for the stories you are told."[6] As we look to the past, it is important to recognize that no history is ever complete. We need to question the histories we read and hear and the stories we are told. Whose stories are they? Why are they being told in this way? And, perhaps most important, what stories are missing, silenced, or misrepresented? With King's words in mind, we need to think about the power of stories.

Although the title of this book is *Sport and Recreation in Canadian History* in reference to the academic field of sport history, it is important to consider the multiplicity of perspectives—the *histories* of Canadian sport. We must recognize that our understandings are both partial and fluid. Throughout this book you will read many different stories and perspectives about the histories of recreation and sport on the lands claimed by Canada. The intent within the chapters of this book is not to tell *the* history of sport and recreation in Canada, a definitive or comprehensive history, but to discuss ongoing research, perspectives, silences, and new directions for understanding our sporting past. Our task is to consider how one event, moment, experience, or set of historical data could be interpreted in different ways, with many different histories emerging. The intent of this book is to make you think about the histories of sport and recreation in Canada and how current sport and recreation moments can be placed *in their historical context*. All current events in Canadian sport have histories, histories that are important for understanding the present and imagining the future. As you read, I encourage you to think about Canadian sport, your practices and experiences and the images and representations you see around you, and the histories that have led to these moments.

National Pastimes by Jim Logan

The cover of this textbook features Cree Sioux Métis artist Jim Logan's painting *National Pastimes*. At first glance, the painting depicts a seemingly peaceful outdoor Canadian hockey rink in interior British Columbia. However, the image does not convey a single story; it contains multiple stories, sometimes competing and conflicting.

National Pastimes is one of seven paintings Logan did for the 1991 *INDIGENA* exhibition at the Canadian Museum of Civilization (now the Canadian Museum of History) in cooperation with the Indian Art Centre of Indian and Northern Affairs Canada, the Society of Canadian Artists of Native Ancestry, and the Canada Council. The *INDIGENA* project, a collection of essays, performances, paintings, installations, videos, and photographs, aimed to "engage indigenous Canadian[7] visual, literary and performing artists to address such issues as discovery, colonization, cultural critique and tenacity, from each of their perspectives."[8] In a book of the same name that accompanied the exhibition, Logan explains: "I see myself as a social commentator. I paint my life the way I see it lived."[9] The *National Pastimes* painting invites viewers to see multiplicity and complexity—not only to reflect on the poverty, oppression, and relentless colonial abuse in Indigenous communities but also to consider the resiliency, the joy found at the hockey rink. Regarding the intention behind his artistic works, Logan says: "So there is this dividing line in my work just like there is in the reality of living, there is a time to laugh and a time to weep. I always attempt to balance reality in my shows to give the viewer a chance to see the overall."[10]

Most recently, the painting was featured as part of the Canadian Museum of History's *Hockey* exhibition in Ottawa, Ontario, in 2017.

Revealing the Layers, Complexities, and Tensions

At this point, I invite you to turn to the front cover of the book. Look at the image from edge to edge. What do you see? The history of hockey, as represented through Logan's powerful painting, is complicated for many people, and yet we may not see the nuances in the painting at first glance because it does not fit with our popular understandings of hockey and Canada (see chapter 9). The cover of the textbook shows only a portion of Logan's painting, obscuring the edges and some of the intended social commentary, taking it out of context for the purposes of the front cover design and marketing the textbook.

Now examine the full painting (see figure 1.2). At the centre of the painting is a familiar winter scene of an afternoon game of pickup hockey—a scene that is often revered as quintessentially Canadian. Yet when viewing the whole painting, and seeing the multiple pastimes Logan draws attention to through the title of the painting, from the mountains to the houses, the church, the ice rink, we must consider all the vignettes of people and places as they work together to produce the scene. We must see the residential school, the priest with his arms around three young hockey players having their picture taken by another priest. The nun walking down the street. The men on the ice, the spectators, the people—hugging, fighting, playing music. The broken-down vehicles, the boarded-up windows on the homes, the chimneys piping out smoke into the cold air, and the partially hidden police car. On the very left, see the person who died by suicide swinging from the swing set. At a quick glance, the colourful painting gives the appearance of an idyllic community centred around a quintessentially Canadian outdoor ice rink. But upon closer inspection it is a complicated scene of joy, movement, and physical activity, layered with oppression, abuse, pain, hardship, and danger.

In reflecting on his uneasiness with this group of paintings, Logan explains:

> I realized I had grown up watching a lot of hockey, and I realized the one I watched a lot of hockey with was my dad. . . . Silent as our relationship may have been, we loved each other. My dad's interest in hockey naturally drew my interest and hockey became the dominant link between us, but our reasons for watching were so different. Hockey for my dad was an escape. He dreamed of being somebody important, somebody respected. He wanted to be a winner but fate wouldn't allow it. I watched hockey because it brought me closer to my dad. Hockey to me meant togetherness. On Saturday night for three whole periods we . . . were as close as we could ever get. The paintings in this series are an extension of my personal experiences. The social statement I am expressing here is that for many kids, Aboriginal or not, hockey is often more than just a sport, it's an escape.[11]

When we think about pastimes, we most often think of enjoyment and moments of camaraderie. But as Logan has explained, pastimes are also an escape for many people—from everyday life, from institutionalized and state-

Image: NATIONAL PASTIMES, by Jim Logan Collection of Crown-Indigenous Relations and Northern Affairs, Canada. Photo by Lawrence Cook.

Figure 1.2   *National Pastimes*, by Jim Logan, is displayed as part of the *INDIGENA* exhibition in 1991. Acrylic on canvas, 122 centimetres × 183.2 centimetres (48 × 72 inches).

sanctioned violence. The ice rink historically, presently, and undoubtedly into the foreseeable future, it is a space of celebration, achievement, and joy for some and escape, oppression, injustice, and discrimination for others. The ice rink also points to the silences in Canadian sport histories. As historians we must grapple with these silences. Logan's painting points to the ways in which the ice rink is a space of ongoing settler colonialism, racism, sexism, and ableism, and how our histories of this space are riddled with silences, privileging some stories and experiences over others. The authors in this book offer more nuanced understandings of sport and recreation to challenge dominant narratives that so often get told and retold in uncomplicated ways and to highlight some of the silences in our historical processes.

Interrogating Our Research Practices

In my May 2016 editorial for the journal *Sport History Review*, I suggested that as historians we need to interrogate our research practices, and the assumptions upon which they rest, to write histories differently, challenge dominant narratives of the past, and address the silences in our histories of Canadian sport.[12] The authors in this text, in many ways, have done just that—they are telling different stories, interrogating our research practices, and writing into the silences of Canadian sport histories.

I encourage you, as readers, to continue this process of interrogation and questioning as you read through the chapters. I also encourage you to think critically about the book as a whole. What do the authors tell us about sport and recreation histories on these lands we now call Canada? Whose stories are missing? As you engage with the material, think back to the questions I posed at the beginning of this chapter. Many of the chapters will push you to think about sport in new ways. I encourage you to continue to challenge taken-for-granted assumptions in and about Canadian sport histories.

Special Features in the Book

You'll find learning objectives at the beginning of each chapter and discussion questions at the end. What other questions can you ask based on what you have read in the chapter? The chapters also contain text boxes. I encourage you to think about why the authors have chosen to highlight these prominent people, moments, or events and why others have not been emphasized in this way.

On pages v-x, there is a timeline, a representation of Canadian sport histories based on dates and events through a Western Eurocentric chronological view of time. As you read the book, I encourage you not only to refer back to the timeline but also to think critically about how and why Canadian sport history can be represented in this way. What does it tell us about sport history and about how events are connected? What happens when we think differently about time? The very language of past, present, and future approaches to sport history are complicated. In chapter 15, Braden Te Hiwi and I offer a more in-depth discussion about the concept of time as it relates to opening up other possibilities to history by de-centring colonial knowledge. We encourage you to consider chapter 15 as you engage with the timeline.

In her work, sociologist Avery Gordon takes up the notion of haunting to consider how the past influences the present and the future, and how what is invisible or rendered silent is not necessarily "not there."[13] She calls for us to listen to and take notice of what is suspiciously absent as we "do" history and engage with the past. It could be argued that all the stories that make up Canadian sport history scholarship are haunted by other histories, looming presences that often remain masked, in large part because of taken-for-granted assumptions and sustained ways of understanding the Canadian sport system.

Let's go back to Canadian ice hockey. Hockey has long been linked to Canada's national identity. It is often part of conversations about the history of Canada as a nation (see chapter 9). Yet the stories that are shared are most often about men's professional hockey. Other stories such as those of local community games, or the experiences of girls, women, or non-white players, are often absent from our histories of hockey in Canada. Although this is changing as we continue to learn about the hockey experiences of girls and women, Black Canadians and Indigenous peoples, and other people of colour, for example, we have a long way to go in telling more inclusive and diverse Canadian sport histories.

Conclusion

All of you are practising historians. Historian Gerda Lerner suggests that although we do not think about it in this way, we are all "doing history" as we live our lives, tell our stories, and think critically about the world around us:

> As we go through life we present ourselves to others through our life story; as we grow and mature we change that story through different interpretations and different emphasis. We stress different events as having been decisive at different times in our life history and, as we do so, we give those events new meanings. . . . What we remember, what we stress as significant, and what we omit of our past defines our present . . . and affects our future.[14]

Every action, moment, and event has a history. Sport histories matter because they help us understand our present and make decisions about the future. As human beings we ask questions, we ponder, we reflect on our experiences, and we envision the future. Many of you will be headed into health, wellness, and sport-related professions. Whatever path you choose, you will be asked to think critically, to make decisions. Engaging with the past and understanding your actions and the actions of others within larger contexts will be of the utmost importance.

Sport and recreation are entwined with all aspects of Canadian history. It is a part of our social fabric as Canadians. As we listen to the news, participate in sport and recreation activities, or cheer on our favourite sports team, we must remember that these moments are represented and storied in particular ways. Each of these moments is connected to broader histories, some of which remain obscured or forgotten.

DISCUSSION QUESTIONS

1. Drawing on your own experiences and the arguments made in this chapter, why do sport and recreation histories matter?
2. Identify a current event in Canadian sport. As a historian, what questions could you ask to place this event in historical context?
3. Why is it important to consider the multiplicity of perspectives in Canadian sport histories?
4. How do silences enter the historical process? Why is it important to be aware of these silences?

SUGGESTED READINGS

Forsyth, Janice, and Audrey R. Giles, eds. *Aboriginal Peoples and Sport in Canada: Historical Foundations and Contemporary Issues.* Vancouver: UBC Press, 2012.

King, Thomas. *The Truth About Stories.* Toronto: House of Anansi Press, 2003.

Lerner, Gerda. *Why History Matters: Life and Thoughts.* New York: Oxford University Press, 1997.

Phillips, Murray, ed. *Deconstructing Sport History: A Postmodern Analysis.* Albany: State University of New York Press, 2005.

Trouillot, Michel-Rolph. *Silencing the Past: Power and the Production of History.* Boston: Beacon Press, 1995.

CHAPTER 2

METHODS AND THEORIES IN HISTORICAL RESEARCH

Sarah Barnes, PhD
Georgia Institute of Technology

Mary Louise Adams, PhD
Queen's University

LEARNING OBJECTIVES

In this chapter you will

- gain familiarity with some of the approaches that researchers have used to study histories of sport and recreation in Canada;
- learn about some of the methodological and theoretical considerations that shape how sport historians conduct their research;
- develop the skill of thinking historically;
- develop an understanding of the significance of archival research and oral history;
- explore how history is reflective of the social context in which it is produced; and
- consider the value and uses of history in the present day.

The only sporting moment that nobody quibbles about. If anything makes 1972 feel like yesterday, it's the memory of that instant in the Canada–Russia series, watched on clunky colour TVs wheeled into classrooms. The Cold War was in full force, the Summit Series absurdly freighted with meaning. It wasn't just hockey; it was an honest-to-goodness clash of competing world visions. The NHL versus the Red Army. Canada should have lost, really, because the Russians were so good. But that is not what history wrote. Through seven games, Canada had squeaked out three wins, Russia had three, and there was one tie. So, with 34 seconds left in a deadlocked series that had gone on for 27 nail-biting days, superstar goalie Vladislav Tretiak rebounded a poked shot from Phil Esposito, Henderson picked up the bounce and flicked the puck into the net. In a moment that became immortal, Henderson was a Canadian hero (see figure 2.1). He also scored the winners in the sixth and seventh games, keeping Canada in the series to that point. There are no contenders for a bigger moment in Canadian sports. It is hard to even imagine one.[1]

Figure 2.1   Paul Henderson celebrates Canada's last-minute goal during the 1972 Summit Series. Sport historians ask questions about why and how some sporting events, like the one captured in this image, are remembered while others are forgotten.

DENIS BRODEUR/NHLI/Getty Images

We have taken this quote from an article titled "The 15 Biggest Moments in Canadian Sports History," which was posted on the CBC website "in honour of Canada's 150th birthday." Many readers, like us, will not be surprised that Paul Henderson's last-minute goal in the 1972 Canada–Russia Summit Series topped the list. Almost 50 years after Henderson's goal was scored, journalists still promote its significance, Paul Henderson still appears on television talk shows, and Canadians of a certain age still compare notes on where they watched the game. As a grade seven student, the second author of this chapter, Mary Louise, watched the game in her school's gymnasium—the only time in her school career that she and her classmates were let out of class to watch television. What would make a sporting event so important that children would be let out of school to watch it? What would make something worthy of being called the biggest moment in Canadian sport? Which moments, which athletes, and which sports have the possibility of being framed in such terms? Which Canadian sport stories are repeated and valorized? Which are forgotten? What gets to be included in the history of sport in Canada?

In popular discussions of sport history, what comes to be part of the historical record can seem inevitable. An important event happens, and it is documented. Paul Henderson scores a last-minute goal in a game "absurdly freighted with meaning."[2] The facts of the event are recorded, the story of the goal is written, and voila! Sport history. But what makes it into the historical record is rarely inevitable. We suggest it is the product of cultural values, and of the techniques and approaches used by those who piece together historical narratives. The significance of Paul Henderson's goal was not in the goal itself, but in the 1970s Cold War context, in the mythologizing of hockey in Canada, and in the decisions made by journalists and others who, over the last four decades, have constantly replayed the story of the goal in print and other media. The principle aim of this chapter is to challenge the view that history is simply the documentation of events that happened in the past. History is produced not only by professional historians but also by journalists, novelists, filmmakers, students, and others who engage with materials from the past.

We open the chapter by defining what we mean by history and identifying some of the differences between popular history and history as an area of scholarly research. We then talk about the work that historians do and some of the issues they face as they do it. We focus on two specific methods that historians use to find out about the past: archival research and oral history. While the work of a historian might seem like it should be pretty straightforward—learn about the past and write about what you find—it can involve complex questions about power, inequality, accountability, and accessibility. Historical research and the writing of history can also have intended and unintended political implications and significant effects in the present.

By understanding the issues historians grapple with and the methods they use, we can learn how the broader social context shapes their research and the historical narratives they create. We can also learn a lot about what it means to think historically—and the benefits of doing so. In this way we can be better prepared to read history and to think critically about how history is used in popular culture and other aspects of everyday life.

Sport History Beyond Textbooks

When we think about history, it is common to think about books like this one you are reading. If someone were to tell you they received a history of tennis as a gift, you would assume they had received a book. The term *history* also refers to the academic discipline that is taught in universities and in schools. Professional historians are researchers and scholars who investigate the past and write the books and other texts that we call histories. This chapter looks at some of the issues historians face and some of the implications of the different methods they use to learn about the past. Our aim is, first, to help you understand and assess the historical materials you read and, second, to help you prepare to do your own primary research. We also hope that in learning to think like a historian, you will be able to critically evaluate the history you encounter outside of a university classroom or library. It is the ubiquity of history in our everyday lives that makes it important for everyone, not just historians, to develop the critical skill of historical thinking.

What does history look like outside of books and classrooms? We encounter it frequently not only in the media, as with the list we mentioned earlier, but also in a range of places and experiences that do not necessarily feel historical to us. Streets, public buildings, parks, and schools, for instance, are often named after famous athletes or important sports events. In St. Catharines, where Sarah grew up, there is a Royal Henley Boulevard, a Henley Drive, a Royal Henley retirement community, and a Henley Island, all named after the annual rowing regatta that has taken place in the city since 1903. In Maple, Ontario, an elementary school is named after hockey player Herb Carnegie, one of the greatest players of the 1940s, who was explicitly kept from playing in the NHL because of anti-Black racism. In Saint-Marc-des-Carrières, Quebec, a recreation centre is named after Chantal Petitclerc, 14-time Paralympic gold medallist in wheelchair racing. In Rossland, British Columbia, a lake, a highway, a provincial park, and a mountain summit are all named after 1968 Olympic gold medallist skier Nancy Greene.

Examples like these show how the achievements of certain athletes are kept visible and thus come to be part of a shared history of sport and, in some cases, a shared history of Canada. The athlete whose achievements are perhaps most visible in this regard is Terry Fox, a young runner who lost his leg to cancer at the age of 19. In 1980, at age 22, Fox undertook what he called the Marathon of

Hope, a run from the Atlantic to the Pacific to raise money for cancer research. Beginning in St. John's, Newfoundland, running on a prosthetic leg, Fox completed the equivalent of a marathon a day. He made it as far as Thunder Bay, Ontario, before his cancer returned. He passed away in 1981. Fox is remembered in annual Terry Fox Runs that attract thousands of people across the country and around the world. Roads, schools, fitness trails, and parks have been named after him. He has been the subject of biographies, made-for-TV biopics, and documentary films. His achievements and his legacy are commemorated with at least seven statues and three postage stamps. In 2005, Fox's image was featured on a loonie; he was the first Canadian ever to be featured on a circulating coin.

Sport history also appears in Hollywood films like *Chariots of Fire* and *Invictus*, in TV biopics, and on classic sport channels that broadcast old games. Some sports fans help shape sport history by collecting and trading cards, or by buying and preserving autographs or memorabilia associated with famous athletes. In many university and other athletic facilities, the history of sport is displayed in huge trophy cases full of engraved sterling cups. The cups themselves provide evidence about which sports and athletes have, over the years, been considered worthy of such visible and substantial (in cost and weight) rewards.

It is one of the aims of this chapter to give you tools and skills that will help you analyze and assess not only academic history but also the history you come across every day.

History Versus the Past

People often use the terms *history* and *the past* interchangeably. But in an important book called *Silencing the Past*, Haitian anthropologist and historian Michel-Rolph Trouillot argues that we need to distinguish between these two terms.[3] The past, Trouillot writes, is what actually happened in some earlier time period.[4] History, he continues, is the story we tell about the past. The 1972 Summit Series, eight hockey games between the Soviet Union and Canadian national teams, is the past—what actually happened. History is the narrative—or more precisely the narratives—that has been constructed about the series: in the original television broadcasts; in magazine and newspaper articles; in a book written by Paul Henderson himself; on a website (http://teamcanada1972.ca) dedicated to the series; in regular anniversary commemorations; and in scholarly articles. Trouillot's distinction between *the past* and *history* alerts us to the idea that it is not possible to simply go back and retrieve the past as it "really" was. Anyone who sets out to piece together a narrative about the past must make decisions about what to include, what to leave out, and how to present that information. The product of these decisions is what Trouillot calls history. History is *an interpretation* of what happened in the past.

Ample scholarship demonstrates that the process of turning the past into history is not a straightforward activity. History writing is an interpretive process that is influenced by the interests and background of the historian, by the accessibility of documents or other sources of information about the past, and by political, moral, and technical debates, some of which we discuss in this chapter. One of the differences between popular and more academic forms of history is that academic historians usually try to be explicit about the ideas and concerns that have shaped their decisions about how to interpret the past and what aspects of the past are worth studying. Many popular forms of history, like biographies of athletes or Hollywood films, take for granted that their subject matter is significant or worthy of being represented. More popular versions of history rarely spend time talking about the sources of historical information they have used. For academic historians, good sources of evidence are fundamental to high-quality historical work.

Primary and Secondary Sources

Historians love evidence—searching it out, studying it, making sense of it. When they talk about evidence, they are referring to the materials, or sources, they use to ground the narratives they write. There are two main categories of evidence: primary sources and secondary sources. For most of us who do historical research, primary sources are what we get most excited about. Sometimes the sources we need are obvious and easy to find—policy documents, government statistics, news articles about a scandal or controversy. But sometimes the search for sources can feel like a treasure hunt. Where might one look to find out about the history of LGBTQ sports leagues? Or the history of sport in a small rural town? Or the history of a sport like tug-of-war, which was once more mainstream (it was an Olympic event from 1900-1920)?

For her project on the history of ideas about sleep in sport, Sarah found some of her primary sources at the archives of the Harvard Fatigue Laboratory (1927-1947), considered to be the first exercise science lab in North America. At the archives, she got the chance to read handwritten notes about research experiments, unpublished manuscripts, and letters written to and from the scientists. She also got to look at collections of photographs, scrapbooks, and military reports. Although she had been looking for relevant work by the scientists, it was a letter from an athlete that ended up being her most important find. In Mary Louise's research on the history of gender in figure skating, she visited a number of archives in Europe and North America, never entirely sure what she might find or what might be useful. She watched films, listened to old interview recordings, and read books, magazines, newspapers, and other documents going back as far as the late 1700s. At the British Library in London, she got to read (and hold—with gloves on!) the oldest known book on skating, which was published in 1772. At the World Figure Skating Museum in Colorado, she read documents and took notes near displays of rhinestone-covered skating costumes.

Primary sources are documents, maps, images, and artifacts that were created in the past. Sport historians have used newspapers and magazines, government documents, organizational and club records, advertisements, photographs, letters, diaries, audio recordings, film footage, public monuments, and other artifacts that help shed light on how people played and competed in the past. Some historians use living memory as a primary source, interviewing people who witnessed or participated in an event or have first-hand knowledge of the topic the historian is studying. As we discuss in chapter 3, oral sources are also important for researchers working with Indigenous communities where knowledge is often passed on through stories and where mainstream written settler histories have long contributed to the justification of colonial practices.

Primary sources are the basis of academic research in history. The reliance on primary rather than secondary sources is one thing that distinguishes academic from popular history writing. Secondary sources describe, summarize, or analyze primary sources. Historians use secondary sources to learn more about their topics or to better understand the context of their own primary sources. Secondary sources include scholarly history books, journal articles, and reference materials. Historians read secondary sources to see what other historians have said about similar or related topics and to get a sense of the ideas, events, or social trends that might be important for their own work. In preparation for her research visit to the archives of the Harvard Fatigue Laboratory, Sarah read other people's histories of the lab and more general studies of the history of sport science. Reading the work of other scholars gave her an idea of what she might find in the archives and where she might direct focus at the Harvard lab to answer some of her research questions. The work of other scholars also allowed her to see how ideas about sleep and sport in the early 20th century fit into larger cultural discussions about athletic bodies and, even more generally, into discussions about race, gender, and good citizenship. The secondary sources helped put her project into context.

Providing context for our topics is an important part of developing an interpretation of the past. It is hard to get a deep understanding of an event or person without pulling our focus back to see how that event or person fits into the particular time and place in which they were situated. It would, for instance, be impossible to understand the fervent response to Paul Henderson's goal without an understanding of the cultural politics of the Cold War and the value Canadians saw in beating the communist Soviet Union team. Historians ask how it was that events, identities, experiences, and social relationships became possible in relation to particular social, economic, and political forces. By *context* we mean the background, or the social circumstances, that influences how people behave, make decisions, and understand their lives.

WORKING WITH PRIMARY SOURCES: WHY DIDN'T TABLE TENNIS BECOME CANADA'S NATIONAL SPORT?

Many sport historians turn to daily newspapers to gain valuable information about what happened in the past. Newspapers provide basic details of sporting events, including dates, competition results, statistics, player rosters, prize money, and much more. Beyond this type of factual data, newspapers highlight trends and offer commentary on controversies. Yet, like all written texts, newspapers are shaped by ideological and cultural forces. For instance, sensational headlines and dramatic photos purposefully designed to sell papers might distort local realities. Decisions about what stories to cover or what photos to run may reflect certain implicit biases, including concerns about offending advertisers.

Try to perform your own critical reading on an excerpt from "Table Tennis Growing to Large-Scale Sport," a newspaper article published in the *Globe and Mail* on December 25, 1946.

To help you get started, we provide the following questions:

- How do you think the historical context shaped the way this story was told?
- What can we learn from this story about how shared understandings of what counts as a sport change over time?
- What can we learn about the nature of public memory and how some sporting practices and traditions are lost or forgotten, while others are remembered and celebrated, by thinking about the popularity of table tennis in Toronto during the 1940s?

Table tennis has graduated from a recreation room pastime to a large-scale sport in Toronto with over 600 tournament players....The Ontario Table Tennis Association with headquarters in Toronto is the dominating organization in the country and includes the Canadian closed title holder, Lou Bredle, as its top-ranking star. In the women's division Miss Jean Smith holds top ranking. The game, which legend says was invented by a group of British Army officers in India in 1900, has been played for years in homes equipped with a recreation room. Here many people refer to it as ping pong, which irks the various table tennis associations. Played by almost every nation in the world, table tennis attracts thousands of spectators to its major tournaments. Over 65,000 spectators saw a world's championship in Alberta Hall, London. The last world's title was decided in Egypt in 1938. In Canada, the game has been played for many years with Toronto, Montreal and Vancouver the main centres. Only lack of playing facilities has prevented the game making more headway here. One of the few sports that remains strictly amateur, players must buy all of their own equipment and have been known to contribute to the trophies they play for....On the surface, the game strikes many as a "sissy sport" but after playing a few tournament games, the thought quickly vanishes. In the last Toronto and District tournament, Lou Bredle, the winner dropped five pounds. Although competitive play among the women is restricted to annual tournaments, there are about 200 active players in Toronto and district....The local association is endeavouring to create interest among the teen-agers and have approached the city with a view to having the sport played in the athletic curriculum of the city schools....Age is no barrier to playing. In the Toronto and District leagues, there are many men over 40 participating.[5]

Social Context

Context is made up of obvious and less obvious factors. The context of any particular event is shaped by big systems and institutions like religion, education, business, media, and government. It is also shaped by less visible or tangible factors like ideologies, attitudes, or moral belief systems and by social hierarchies based on identity categories like race, gender, class, sexuality, ability, and age. One of the important aspects of studying the context of our topics is that we are then better able to see how they are shaped by powerful dominant forces in our society, like capitalism. Attending to context lets us see that sport events and athletes do not exist in a vacuum.

McGill University historian Suzanne Morton recently made a video to explain the history of the men's varsity team name, the Redmen.[6] Based on research done by Morton and her upper-year Canadian history students, the video shows the changing meanings, including overtly racist, anti-Indigenous ones, of the term *Redmen*, the name that has been used by McGill men's teams since 1928. Using archival materials, including yearbooks, the McGill student newspaper, and other documents, the video challenges claims that the team name was never intended to insult or harm Indigenous people. While the initial motivation for the name may not have been racist, a colonial context in which Indigenous people would lose their status if they attended university, and in which most white people encountered Indigenous people only in the stereotypes of Hollywood films, brought racist meanings to the name over the decades. Although Morton is not a sport historian, her project shows that histories of sport can be used to shine light on problems in society at large, like racism, gender and class inequality, competitiveness, and nationalism. In this particular case, Morton's video, which she posted on Facebook, offers viewers a chance to learn more about the broader colonial and racist context in which university sport takes place, and in which Indigenous students undertake their studies. The project provided important historical evidence to support a successful campaign started by Indigenous students—and supported by a majority of McGill students—to force the university to change the name.[7]

Let's return to the example of game 8 of the 1972 Summit Series. The game took place at the height of the Cold War, a time when athletic victories were seen as important contributions to political conflict. For many Canadians, a win in hockey against the Soviets mattered a lot. It was an issue of national pride, of the ownership of hockey, of capitalism versus communism. As sport historian Russell Field explains, media coverage of the Summit Series and hockey—a game historically dominated by privileged white men—carried very specific and narrow ideas about what it meant to be Canadian.[8] Do you think a series of games in a different sport would have generated such passionate interest? What if women had played the games? What if the series had not been televised? Would a game today against the Russians (as opposed to the Soviets) generate the same kind of fervour?

As you try to develop answers to these questions, you are inevitably thinking about context. In what way are men's and women's hockey teams viewed differently? What social factors shape that difference? What is the importance of hockey in relation to Canadian identity? How are other sports framed in Canada in comparison to hockey? How and why would a series against the Russians be perceived differently today? As you think about context it becomes possible to see that the ongoing response to the Summit Series has been a product of a particular set of historical circumstances, shaped by the social, political, and economic situation in which it occurred. The "greatest moment in Canadian sport history" was shaped by international political events, nationalism, gender inequality, and, as historian Russell Field points out, technological developments that made it possible to broadcast the game via satellite.[9]

Conducting Sport History Research

One of the main ideas in this chapter is that history making is a process. But what are the steps involved in this process? How do historians do their work? Every historical research project has several essential activities: asking questions, collecting evidence, and interpreting evidence. Although we sometimes think about these activities separately, the research process is, like life, rarely linear. Researchers circle back, reassess, and adjust their plans as they think, reflect, and write.

Asking Research Questions

Sport historians often begin research projects because some minor thing piques their curiosity. Mary Louise's interest in the gender history of figure skating was sparked by a story about Kurt Browning in a magazine—it seemed like the author of the story was bending over backwards to assure readers that Browning is heterosexual. Why had that seemed so necessary? Would the writer have felt the need to make similar efforts on behalf of a male basketball player or runner? Sarah's research on the history of ideas about sleep and athletic performance was inspired by her part-time job as team manager of a basketball team. She often discussed sleep issues with athletes who were worried about feeling tired before big games. And then, at some point, it seemed like all of a sudden sport commentators in the media were constantly talking about athletes' sleep. Was this preoccupation with sleep new?

The first issue faced by anyone undertaking a piece of historical research is how to turn a research interest into a focused topic with an even more focused research question. The research question is the crux of the whole undertaking. The project needs to be designed to produce an answer to that question. The process of developing a research question involves reading the existing literature and poking around to find potential primary and secondary sources. A good grasp of the secondary literature tells scholars how other researchers have approached similar topics and what types of evidence they have marshalled to make their arguments.

What makes a good research question? There is no one answer. Perhaps most obvious is that the question might be answered through historical research. A good question is also one you do not yet know the answer to. The questions that interest us tend to reflect our assumptions and beliefs, our concerns and hopes about the future. As feminist sport researchers, for instance, we both tend to focus on gender as central to the experiences and understandings of sport we aim to document and analyze. Thus, in our work, we try to ask questions that help make gender (and its intersections with race, class, and sexuality) more visible. Other researchers might have other investments or concerns. Being aware of what is motivating our questions is a way of making sure we are actually asking something that matters.

Collecting Evidence

Once researchers have decided what to study, they need to figure out how to study it. What kinds of documents, artifacts, or other materials might help them answer their research questions? Do these kinds of evidence actually exist? Are they accessible to the researcher? If you were, for instance, interested in studying how Canadian players in the All-American Girls Professional Baseball League were discussed in the media during the Second World War era, you could look at reports in old newspapers. But if you wanted to know what the athletes themselves thought about their participation in the League, that would be more difficult. Did the women leave any written records of their views like letters or scrapbooks? Are there any photographs of them playing? Are any of the women still alive? Would it be possible to speak with them? Has anyone else ever interviewed them? Are the tapes or the transcripts of those interviews accessible? Sometimes very practical issues constrain or facilitate historical research projects.

Apart from the availability or accessibility of sources, researchers face other practical and philosophical challenges in their work. While historians who find their materials in archives might come away with a file folder of notes or photocopies, researchers who use online sources (e.g., digitized newspaper archives) might be facing hundreds of pieces of data. Scholars who are doing histories of more recent times, say, by analyzing Twitter or other social media reactions to an event, might be faced with thousands of pieces of data. How will they manage these? How will they organize their evidence so they can retrieve it as needed?

Formal ethical questions also shape how scholars treat their data. When researchers deal with sensitive information (e.g., historical medical or welfare records), they are often required to secure their data to protect the confidentiality of the records. This might require the use of encryption for digital sources or locked and secured filing cabinets for hard copies or interview recordings. University-based historians who do interviews or who use interview material gathered by previous researchers need to gain approval for their research from the ethics review boards at their institutions. This approval lays out the kinds of measures researchers are expected to take to minimize the risk of any harm faced by people who participate in research studies.

Interpreting Evidence

At a philosophical level, historians also face issues related to the nature of their evidence. What can we learn from it? What should we do about the fact that only certain voices are represented in the written record? For instance, English and French settlers, not Indigenous players themselves, wrote accounts of the Indigenous games that were turned into organized lacrosse.[10] We definitely learn something from reading these accounts, but it is more about colonial attitudes towards Indigenous people than it is about the meanings the original games may have held for those who played them. When history is primarily based on archival records, history reflects those who controlled the writing and collecting of the documents.

What is remembered, what is preserved, and what survives are all shaped by the collective values of the people who came before us. Not all people in previous eras—as in our own—were capable of reading or creating documents or of having their understandings of their experiences recorded in documents. Members of dominant groups—white people, the upper classes, the well-educated—are disproportionately represented in the historical record. The values of dominant groups have shaped what has been deemed significant, and thus it is these values that are more likely to be preserved. As an example, we can return to the old sterling trophies we mentioned earlier. Which sports and which athletes were seen as important enough to inspire the donation of an expensive silver cup? How visible are the sports and athletes who were not considered as worthy? What records of their prowess exist in the halls of present-day athletic facilities or sport halls of fame? Historical evidence is shaped by relations of power. Historians concerned with social justice and equality ask questions about how power relationships have produced presences and absences in the historical record. They try to stay attuned to the effects of power in the documents and other materials they study. They also try to think about the effects of such presences and absences today and in the future.

In the next sections, we discuss two of the methods historians use to answer their research questions: archival research and oral history. Our goal is to provide you with a better understanding of how history is made, and the types of dilemmas researchers face. We hope this discussion will help you to think more critically about the research you encounter in this and other textbooks and to be more prepared to conduct your own historical investigations.

Archival Research

Archival research is the most common method used by historians. An archive is simply a collection of records that have been kept because they are assumed to hold value. Sometimes the term *archive* refers to a particular institution or building or space where such collections of documents are housed (e.g., the Archives of Manitoba, the Alpine Club of Canada Library and Archives, the Archives and Special Collections of the University of New Brunswick). Archival collections range in size from a few file boxes stuffed away in a cupboard to massive national institutions. Searching out and then discovering the most appropriate archival collection for a project is often one of the most exciting parts of historical research.

When sport studies scholar Parissa Safai decided she wanted to better understand how sports medicine emerged in Canada during the second half of the 20th century, she turned to Library and Archives Canada.[11] Founded in 1872, this national repository contains 20 million books; 30 million photographic images; 3 million architectural drawings, plans, and maps; 90,000 films; 550,000 hours of audio and video recordings; 425,000 works of art; and more than 5 billion megabytes of information in electronic format.[12] Safai gathered more than 800 pages of archival materials during her project. She describes these in her article:

> Public archival records included, but were not limited to, such materials as minutes of meetings, administrative files, correspondence, committee and/or annual reports, brochures, government task force reports, and charters for sport medicine-related organizations. Federal/provincial-territorial policy documents included those on sport, on healthcare occupational groups, and those from relevant federal/provincial associations (including sport governing bodies, multi-sport organizations and medical/paramedical organizations).[13]

Sport historians also visit smaller provincial and territorial archives, as well as more regionally focused collections. As M. Ann Hall constructed a history of the Edmonton Commercial Graduates, the most successful basketball team in the history of the sport, and the winningest Canadian team in any sport, she consulted the City of Edmonton Archives, the Provincial Archives of Alberta, the Glenbow Archives in Calgary, and the Alberta Sports Hall of Fame.[14] In her book *The Grads Are Playing Tonight,* Hall lists an eclectic range of archival sources: scrapbooks, news clippings, souvenir booklets, game programs, photos, films, CBC radio broadcasts, the transcript of a speech by the Grads' coach, unpublished papers written by the players, and a player's diary. Hall's sister also did genealogical (family history) research to help fill in background information about the players' lives.[15]

Sport historians also benefit from the archival collections established by sport organizations (see figure 2.2). For instance, in her figure skating research Mary Louise was able to use materials from the archives of Skate Canada, the national governing body for the sport. For another project on feminism and sport, she used the collected papers of the Pink Turf Soccer League and the Notso Amazon Softball League, recreational leagues that started in the Toronto lesbian community in the 1980s. The papers of both organizations are housed in The ArQuives, Canada's LGBTQ2+ Archives.[16] Finding these types of small community collections can sometimes prove challenging.

Figure 2.2 Sport historians usually love working with primary sources, like the ones shown in this image. These file boxes might not look that exciting, but inside might be a letter, or a set of notes with a key piece of information that could change how the historian views the topic at hand.

Working in the Archives

Researchers who use archival records often work with materials that were never intended for this purpose by their creators. In Sarah's research, for example, she examined research notes that scientists made in their notebooks in the 1930s. The calculations, observations, and personal reminders they had quickly jotted down were likely not created with any sense that decades later there would be an audience for them. People who conduct archival research put a lot of work into figuring how to "read" or interpret documents that were never intended for the public. As with the overall project, historians try to put individual documents or artifacts into context. Who made the document? Who was the intended audience? How does it relate to the overall collection of documents? What assumptions lie behind what the document says? What types of things have been left out of the document? Questions of this nature show how the answers would be very different for a document prepared in an institutional context, like a list of regulations or a newspaper story, as opposed to a document written for more personal reasons, like a letter or a diary.

Archival research can have a romantic image: The historian sits in a quiet room carefully reading and taking notes from a dusty, leather-bound book or from a sheaf of handwritten letters. Surprising discoveries keep her focused and engaged with her work. As appealing as this image is, it's not the whole story. There are many social factors, or behind-the-scenes dynamics, that make archival research possible. Before researchers are able to consult materials in an archive, these materials need to be sorted and filed so they can be used effectively. Archives staff create finding aids or catalogues that help researchers know what they might find in a particular collection. Archivists also help researchers refine their topics and research questions and alert them to both primary and secondary sources they might not have known about. At smaller archives, archivists work hard to raise money and train volunteers to support and maintain their collections and to make them available to the public. At larger institutions, archivists are often the primary advocates for the importance of collecting and preserving materials from diverse groups and sources. While provincial and national archives are the official repositories for their respective jurisdictions, not all governments have allowed archival collections to flourish. Funding and staff cuts can put the accessibility and the preservation of collections at risk.

Archives are contested sites, by which we mean that people have competing views of how important they are, what they should do, and how. On the one hand, archives can allow historians to fill in gaps in the historical record. But on the other hand, archives reflect mainstream social systems that celebrate and circulate particular stories in our culture, while obscuring and making other stories less visible. Archives operate according to agreed-upon professional standards; they have rules that are meant to regulate access and availability. Such guidelines are intended to protect fragile original sources and to ensure their survival for future generations. But these guidelines can have unintended consequences, such as making it so that not everyone in our society shares equal access to important cultural artifacts.

The way a particular archival collection is organized will influence how researchers use it. Sport historian Fiona Skillen has written about the difficulty she had locating records related to women's sport in Scotland.[17] When she did track down documents relevant to her work, Skillen noticed they were often not carefully preserved or organized, as would have been comparable records associated with men's sport. The materials she found were "kept in boxes and bags in office cupboards and lofts; little if any were catalogued or ordered in any logical way."[18] The state of an archival collection can have a big influence on what topics get studied and what topics might be ignored and overlooked. A well-organized collection that preserves sources from marginalized groups in society can help challenge asymmetries in our shared public histories. A poorly organized collection, inaccessible documents, or a failure to collect documents from under-represented groups can make those asymmetries more pronounced.

Digitizing Archival Material

We would be remiss if we did not mention how archival research is changing in a digital era. The Internet and technological innovations are shifting where, when, and how sport historians gather archival evidence. New hardware (e.g., computers, cameras, and equipment), software (e.g., commercial apps and computer programs), and practices of digitization mean some researchers can now quickly amass great quantities of material. At the same time, diverse organizations are taking steps to make their archival collections available online. Gary Osmond and Murray Phillips explain:

> The days of research trips to libraries and archives; the anticipation of requesting items never seen before; of touching, feeling, and smelling archival material; of reading microfilm and microfiche records with strained eyes; and scribbling down personal and professional reactions to discoveries in the archives are not always mandatory anymore. It is now possible, and productive, for historians to sit at their desks requesting archival material from national and international institutions within hours, possibility even minutes, having a plethora of primary documents examined and sorted according to the search criteria, ready to be analyzed.[19]

Some sport historians might now face situations where they have access to too much material!

Many historians eagerly anticipate the positive outcomes that could be associated with these changes. Some hope that digitized sources will help redress historic imbalances and make archival collections more accessible. In theory, anyone with an Internet connection at a public library can go online and request digital copies of primary sources. But there also remain many questions and uncertainties about the implications of the digitization of documents from previous eras and the provision of access to digital material. Which experts and organizations will make decisions about which records are digitized, and in what order? Digitization is expensive. Will only bigger, more popular sports or professional sports be able to post digital collections online? Will digitized collections be open access or will access come with a fee? Which historians would be disadvantaged by financial barriers to online research? How will the availability of online databases shape the decisions historians make about what to study and what to ignore?[20]

Sport historians seem to agree on one point: Technological innovations do not automatically or inevitably make archival research more accessible or more inclusive. New hyperconnected realities could just as easily reinforce existing social hierarchies and inequities in sport history and public memory. Historians who are not based at universities might not have access to subscription-only databases. Community-level sports, nonmainstream sports, and emerging sports might still end up relatively undocumented, or documented in ways that make it difficult for researchers to find them. Men's professional sport with its massive media presence will likely continue to attract the majority of attention by scholars and others who write history. Women's sport could remain less studied than men's. If we want to fulfil the promise of online research, we need to develop ways of connecting researchers to small organizations, promoting the value of nondominant topics and sources, and making sure that data are open source and free to access.

While online and conventional archival research tends to be the most common method used by historians, it does not always allow historians to answer their questions. For example, archival records do not always yield information about the experiences or lives of those who have been excluded from dominant written records. Sometimes it is necessary to look beyond official narratives and the primary sources associated with dominant institutions. Oral history is one method that sport historians have turned to when archival holdings have failed to adequately highlight or address the complexities of life.

TRANSFORMATIVE MOMENTS: RESPONDING TO THE TRUTH AND RECONCILIATION COMMISSION

The Truth and Reconciliation Commission (TRC) was established in 2008 and was tasked with the job of giving voice to residential school survivors and of generating a history of Canada's state-funded, church-sponsored residential school system, which operated for more than 100 years. In 2015, the TRC published its final report, which included 94 calls to action. Five of these calls to action focus on sport. Number 87 encouraged non-Indigenous Canadians to learn more about the histories of Indigenous sport, as told from the perspectives of Indigenous peoples.

The work of Indigenous sport historians Janice Forsyth,[21] Christine M. O'Bonsawin,[22] and Allan Downey[23] provides an important starting point for understanding how sport has been both a tool of colonialism and a means of resistance for Indigenous peoples (see chapters 3, 4, and 13). These scholars have drawn on a variety of historical methods to collect, theorize, and share the meanings that Indigenous communities and residential school survivors attribute to their sport experiences.

The TRC calls to action have also prompted some non-Indigenous sport scholars to help broaden the Canadian public's awareness of Indigenous sport histories. For instance, in collaboration with Forsyth and other sport researchers, Vicky Paraschak, a non-Indigenous scholar who works at the University of Windsor, developed a public history project dedicated to making the achievements of Indigenous athletes more visible in Canadian society. Paraschak organized a group of colleagues, undergraduate and graduate students, and librarians to create 174 Wikipedia entries profiling the achievements of First Nations, Métis, and Canadian Inuit sportspeople. Paraschak and other researchers then went on to set up http://Indigenoussporthistory.ca, a website intended to give Indigenous sport history more public prominence. The website spotlights the achievements of Indigenous athletes, community sport programs, and the scholarship of Indigenous sport. It also provides links to resources that challenge Canadians to look at sport in terms that go beyond "good" or "bad." In the long history of colonialism in Canada, sport has advanced assimilationist policies, but it has also served as a vehicle of resilience and provided moments for achievement, freedom, and self-expression.

Oral History

Oral history is an approach to studying the past that is based on the voices of the living. Unlike archival research it does not centre printed materials or artifacts. It calls instead for people to talk about their experiences and to share their memories of the past. Oral history is based on relationship building and often has outcomes that go far beyond the collection of historical facts. For example, in 2013, Katrina Srigley, an academic historian, and Glenna Beaucage, a librarian and historian working for Nipissing First Nation (NFN), met with Elders, the Chief, and community members to develop a project on the history of Nbisiing Anishinaabeg, the people of NFN. The two historians were surprised when they were asked to focus on hockey and on the Nipissing Warriors, an Anishinaabeg team that had been very successful in the 1960s and 1970s. Srigley and Beaucage worked with Cree historian Lorraine Sutherland, to gather photographs and documents, and they used oral history methods, interviewing 15 former players and fans.[24] They shared what they learned in a community exhibit and in a short documentary called *The Nipissing Warriors*.[25] They also used the history project as the basis for a curriculum for local schools.

There are many different ways of collecting oral history, but the key goal is to listen to people who have first-hand experience of an event or situation. Sometimes interviewers might bring a photograph or an item such as a trophy or an old uniform to spark conversation or jog a narrator's memory. Researchers generally make audio or video recordings of their interviews and then transcribe them. A lot of preliminary research takes place before an interview. Oral historians hope that good preparation, well-developed questions, flexibility and openness, and good listening skills will elicit rich conversations. However, there are no guarantees with interviews. Even the best questions might fall flat. Like other forms of qualitative research, oral histories are unpredictable social activities. They involve trust, communication, and cooperation. In other words, oral histories depend on relationships.[26]

Self-reflexivity is a key aspect of oral history research. Researchers are encouraged to reflect on how their own identities, expectations, assumptions, backgrounds, and skills shape the conversations they have with their narrators. In a frank discussion about her research with Betty White, a Canadian track and field star from the 1930s, historian Carly Adams reflects on how her decisions as a researcher in real time shaped the story that she and White created together.[27] Adams identifies some of the seemingly small features of their conversation that might have opened up or constrained the dialogue, like the amount of time she gave White to respond to questions, or the moments she did or did not probe her for more information, or the times when she did not follow up on a specific question or ask more of White, or she followed up with a new topic too soon. Adams reflects on her own emotional responses to White's answers and how her preconceived notions, for instance about what it would have been like to be a woman in sport in the 1930s, sometimes got in the way of her being able to listen to what White was trying to say. Adams writes that while oral histories give us access to material about the past, they can also teach us about how historians and the people they interview make sense of the past. Trying to tease out our own assumptions and preconceived notions also teaches us something about the historical context that has shaped us and how it might influence the interpretations we make of the past.

Many historians who study the experiences of people from marginal groups favour the oral history approach. Its focus on relationship and collaboration, and on attention to process, has made it an attractive method to many feminist researchers. Feminists and other scholars who study marginalized groups have been drawn to this method because it centres the voices and experiences of those who tend not to be reflected in mainstream narratives about the past.[28] Feminist historians report being drawn to oral history because of its potential to weaken social hierarchies based on expertise and status and mainstream research practices that construct knowledge about rather than with and for others.[29] Oral history has the potential for interviewers and the people they are speaking with to be equal participants in knowledge creation—but historians note that this potential is not always fulfilled.[30] Together, narrators and interviewers try to reclaim experiences and identities that have been neglected or misrepresented in other forms of historical research and in institutional archives.[31] The accounts created through the process of oral history have the potential to speak back to cultural authorities and to disrupt official ways of remembering the past. They may also strengthen communities and build local knowledge.

Feminist oral histories are often guided by the principles of reciprocity and equality.[32] In other words, the goal is not to simply extract a story—or data—from someone. The objective is to produce a story in a way that advances social justice and affirms the narrator. Feminist oral historians routinely describe feeling a sense of responsibility to those with whom they work. Katrina Srigley says that before embarking on a project she asks herself the following:

> Why do I want to hear these stories? What do I plan to do with what I learn? Are there cultural protocols I should observe? Is there anything I might ask that would be upsetting or uncomfortable? How will I provide support if necessary? How will I thank the participant for their time?[33]

Feminist approaches encourage researchers to carry this attitude of self-reflection and respect through the entire research process, including as they make decisions about how to write up their narratives and present them to the public.

As with any research method, oral history has limitations. Even though oral historians generally want to create fair and equal conditions, there can be power imbalances between narrators and interviewers that are not always easy to address. And as with any research approach, good results come from practice. Oral history depends on a variety of skills, including the patience and willingness to foster relationships, the ability to listen carefully, and the resiliency to learn from mistakes.

Translating Findings

Sport historians use a variety of tools to communicate their findings to audiences. Books, peer-viewed journal articles, edited collections, textbooks, encyclopedia entries, and presentations at academic conferences are among the most common ways that university-based sport historians share their work. These kinds of scholarly forums allow sport historians to refine arguments, share insights, and receive feedback. As the chapters in this textbook show, there is considerable variety in form and style within academic writing. There is no one way for authors to draw out the historical significance and meaning of the topics they study. Collaboration and conversations with colleagues and students help historians hone their craft.

Sport historians also work hard to reach audiences outside the university. Some publish articles in newspapers or online outlets like HuffPost[34] or on sport-specific websites like The Allrounder,[35] or sport blogs like *Hockey in Society*[36] or *Engaging Sport*.[37] Academics also use Facebook, Twitter, and other social media sites to intervene in public debates and to link their work to community building and activism. For instance, as we mentioned earlier, McGill history professor Suzanne Morton posted the video *Colour, Colonialism, and the McGill Redmen: A Short History*[38] on Facebook, where it was widely shared. The video helped to support a campaign led by Indigenous students that forced the university to change the team name.

Sport history is also produced outside of academic settings. Novelists, visual artists, museum curators, documentary film makers, and engaged citizens conduct oral histories, consult archives, and collect historical sources in order to better understand current issues in sport and society. In an exhibit called *Muscle Panic*, Canadian visual and performance artist Hazel Meyer used historical photographs and textbooks to show how intersections of gender and sexuality in women's sport are shaped by enduring ideas about the vulnerability and fragility of white, middle-class women's bodies.[39] On a bigger scale, a 2017 exhibition at the Canadian Museum of History in Gatineau, Quebec, explores the relationship between hockey and Canadian history and identity. With more than 300 artifacts—including the jersey Paul Henderson wore when he scored his fateful goal—the exhibition provides an opportunity for visitors to reflect not only on famous moments and personalities but also on some of the less well-known aspects of the game, like the existence of leagues and teams for Black and Indigenous players, and the fact that women have been involved in hockey throughout its history.

Museum exhibits, art, novels, films, podcasts, social media, and other modes of creative expression are powerful vehicles for sport history because they can tap into peoples' emotions and embodied identities while creating a sense of historical empathy. Historical empathy is a process through which people learn to become more aware and sensitive to the complexities of the situations experienced by people living before us. Feminist historian Eve Kornfeld explains that historical empathy might be thought of as a tool for equality, inclusion, and social justice. It permits people to recognize connections between themselves and others and in doing so works against official narratives that often reproduce exclusionary or dehumanizing myths that maintain unequal social relations and marginalizing practices.[40]

Ojibway writer Richard Wagamese's novel *Indian Horse*, which has recently been turned into a feature-length film, is a particularly compelling example of how sport narratives can offer a route towards historical empathy.[41] Wagamese's story focuses on Saul Indian Horse, an Ojibway boy forced into a residential school. At the school Saul learns to play hockey. He excels at the game, and it becomes his way of coping with the abusive environment. Wagamese's descriptions of Saul's style of play and his sixth sense on the ice are exceptionally moving accounts of the physical experience of sport. As the book proceeds, the disjuncture between the pleasure Saul initially found in hockey and the crushing racism he faces as he starts to play with white people allows non-Indigenous readers to feel the impact of settler colonialism in a way they might not experience by reading a standard history text. In interviews, Wagamese said explicitly that part of the reason he wanted to write about hockey and to write about it well was that it would allow him to connect with an audience who might not otherwise read about or be moved by the history of residential schools or the persistent racism of white Canada.[42]

Impact of Sport History Research on Current Events

Throughout this chapter we attempt to show that history is useful, not only in academic settings but also in our everyday lives outside of the classroom. In this section, we highlight some of the ways that academics in our field have used different approaches to meet a variety of social, political, and intellectual objectives. We concentrate on three examples and encourage you to reflect on the objectives you might wish to accomplish through your own investigations of the past.

Exposing Hidden Histories

Some histories are specifically made to recover experiences that have been silenced and erased from public memory. The stories we tell about ourselves matter. When certain stories go untold, it implies that these stories are less important and less meaningful. Part of creating an inclusive and just society involves understanding and celebrating the histories, contributions, and struggles of all Canadians in the realm of sport and physical activity. A nice example of recovery is found in Ornella Nzindukiyimana's recent work, which reconstructs the experiences of John Armstrong "Army" Howard, Canada's first Black Olympian. Nzindukiyimana pieced together newspaper clippings, scrapbooks, and secondary sources, both to illuminate Armstrong's incredible athletic skill and to show

how his inclusion on the 1912 Canadian Olympic team contradicted the state's passage of racist immigration policies that positioned Black and South Asian people as unfit for citizenship at the turn of the 20th century.[43] By researching and recovering the story of the first Black Canadian Olympian, Nzindukiyimana creates a fuller, more representative historical record (see chapter 11).

Challenging Prejudices

Historical accounts can also be made in such a way as to challenge common-sense beliefs that maintain inequitable and exploitative social relations in our society. An example of this type of work is found in Robert Pitter's efforts to present the stories of Indigenous and Black hockey players who competed in the National Hockey League during the 1930s and 1940s.[44] By recounting the struggles and successes of athletes like George Armstrong, Jim Neilson, Willie O'Ree, Larry Kwong, and others, Pitter shows that enduring forms of systematic racism, as opposed to the absence of hockey traditions, help explain why the number of racialized men who play hockey today remains disproportionately low.[45] Pitter's work shows us that without a strong historical perspective, it can be difficult to fully diagnose the types of barriers that exist for many in sport and physical activity today (see chapter 10).

Contesting Policies

Historians have also used their work to hold the governing bodies of sport accountable to the principles of inclusion and equity. Historical research can illuminate how, for instance, social and structural barriers to sport operate. When the International Olympic Committee refused to allow women to compete in ski jumping in the 2010 Olympic Games in Vancouver, sport scholars Jason Laurendeau and Carly Adams undertook a project to better understand the historical context for this decision.[46] Their findings showed that ideas about gender difference and women's alleged athletic inferiority were central to the unequal treatment of male and female ski jumpers at the 2010 Olympic Games and in the decades prior. Using a range of documents including archival material, newspapers, and official IOC statements, they pieced together a history of women's involvement in ski jumping, which showed more than a century of women's participation in the sport as well as early mixed-sex competitions. The authors show that while 21st century gendered ideologies about risk in sport did not look exactly as they had a century ago, tired notions of women's fragility—which played a role in excluding women from competition in the 20th century—shaped the attitudes and beliefs of IOC officials in the years leading up to 2010 Olympic Games in Vancouver. Historical analysis offers us a way to think about the trajectory of ideas over time that may continue to shape and limit how we are able to understand ourselves and the world in the present day.

Conclusion

This chapter offers an overview of some of the methodological considerations of historical investigations of sport. More than providing a how-to guide, the chapter introduces some of the philosophical, political, and practical issues that shape how sport historians do their work. History making is a process that is wrapped up in power and politics. This chapter presents some of the approaches historians use as they ask questions, collect evidence, and evaluate data, and it notes some of the possibilities—and limitations—of archival research and oral history. Sport history can reproduce or challenge inequality. The analytical tools presented in this chapter are meant to help you reflect on how historical knowledge is made and what it might take to make public sporting histories that are more inclusive and equitable. Sport history matters beyond any classroom setting or textbook. By learning to think historically, you are better prepared not only to evaluate the historical narratives presented in this textbook but also to understand how history is used in popular culture and other aspects of everyday life.

The future is full of opportunities for people to study sport history in many ways and to apply what they find to their everyday concerns. By pursuing a variety of research questions and following different paths to answer them, sport historians can illuminate the past *and* the present in novel ways and can help to imagine a sports world that is more just. As the story about the McGill team name shows, sport history can also contribute to efforts to promote justice in the broader society.

DISCUSSION QUESTIONS

1. What are the most popular sporting myths in the community where you grew up? What or who do those myths celebrate? What groups of people are left out of these stories?

2. If you could study any sport-related historical problem or topic, what would you study? Why? How might you go about studying it? What kinds of sources would help you?

3. We have suggested that self-reflection is a part of the research process. Take a few minutes to consider how your own perspective as a researcher is shaped by your biography, social location, and life experiences.

4. Find a newspaper and flip through the sports section. In what ways and to what ends does history get used in discussions of present-day sport? Is history in the sports section different from how history appears in the national or international sections of the newspaper?

5. If you were to make an archive of your own history in sport, as a participant or spectator, what would you include? What would you leave out? Why? What are the assumptions guiding your collecting practices? What sense do you think a researcher in the future might make of your collection?

SUGGESTED READINGS

Adams, Mary Louise. *Artistic Impressions: Figure Skating, Masculinity, and the Limits of Sport.* Toronto: University of Toronto Press, 2011.

Forsyth, Janice. "Bodies of Meaning: Sports and Games at Canadian Residential Schools." In *Aboriginal Peoples and Sport in Canada: Historical Foundations and Contemporary Issues.* Edited by Janice Forsyth and Audrey Giles. Vancouver: UBC Press, 2013.

Gruneau, Richard, and David Whitson. *Hockey Night in Canada: Sport, Identities and Cultural Politics.* Toronto: Garamond Press, 1993.

Hall, M. Ann. *The Grads Are Playing Tonight! The Story of the Edmonton Commercial Graduates Basketball Club.* Edmonton: University of Alberta Press, 2011.

Kidd, Bruce. *The Struggle for Canadian Sport.* Toronto: University of Toronto Press, 1996.

CHAPTER 3

INDIGENOUS PEOPLES' CULTURES AND PHYSICAL ACTIVITIES

Braden Te Hiwi, PhD
University of British Columbia

LEARNING OBJECTIVES

In this chapter you will

- explore an approach to history that weaves together the past, present, and future;
- explore a framework for understanding the cultural importance of Indigenous peoples' physical activity;
- understand how Indigenous cultures and traditions enhance and support Indigenous peoples' participation in physical activities;
- learn how the dynamic nature of Indigenous cultures aids in interpreting Indigenous peoples' histories; and
- learn how, across periods of colonial change, Indigenous peoples' have always attempted to create their own approaches to physical activity.

The fern frond, figure 3.1, has a looping spiral shape that curls upon itself in reoccurring circles before it stretches out and opens up into a fern. It is possible to use the fern frond as a way to think about time and history. The fern frond conveys the seemingly contradictory ideas of perpetual growth and change over time through the extension of the loops, while at the same time it captures repetition and stability as the cycles return back into its centre.[1] The lessons within the spiral guide this chapter on exploring history that connects the past, present, and future. Some people think of the past, present, and future as separate dimensions of time. In some ways this is true. But in this chapter the past is reoccurring and cyclical, just like the fern frond, and thus the past and future are connected. The fern frond is a useful approach for coming to a greater understanding of Indigenous peoples' cultures and physical activities, and it guides the flow of this chapter.

Figure 3.1 The shape of the unfurled silver fern frond is important in *Māori* culture, the Indigenous peoples of Aotearoa (New Zealand). The shape is called the *koru* in the local language.

Pixabay/Pexels.com

The subfield of Indigenous sport history in Canada has expanded over the last 40 years. In the 1980s, a time when very few historians recognized any need for Indigenous sport history, Victoria Paraschak was a leader of Aboriginal research. Paraschak points out that Indigenous peoples' sport history is necessary for a more full and accurate understanding of Canada's past, and it also has the potential to enhance Indigenous peoples' efforts to revitalize their ways of life that have been restricted by colonial power.[2] Yet Indigenous peoples have been largely overlooked in Canadian sport history research, and when they are present, Indigenous voices—the perspectives, knowledges, priorities, and experiences of Indigenous peoples themselves—are too often ignored.[3] This matters because it can result in the belief that Indigenous peoples are of little importance to Canadian history. In the last 20 years Indigenous sport history has expanded. In addition, a small number of Indigenous scholars now make very important contributions to the field, including Janice Forsyth (Cree; see chapter 4), Christine M. O'Bonsawin (Abenaki; see chapter 13), and Allan Downey (Dakelh/Carrier).

In making her case for the importance of Indigenous sport history, Paraschak says that "history provides people with a sense of where they have come from, helps them better understand the present, and assists them in creating the future they might desire."[4] Uniting the past, present, and future can be a very fruitful way for understanding sport history research. In this chapter, we examine Indigenous cultures and physical activities by looking at three broad cycles of Indigenous cultural practice. The first is from a time long ago, including time immemorial, in which the cultural traditions flourished. The second cycle explores the changes caused by cultural exchange with settlers and the damages of colonial domination. And last, the third cycle looks at the vitality and strength of Indigenous cultures, as well as efforts to maintain and revitalize these cultures. Although much change exists across cycles, Indigenous peoples remain persistent in their commitment to their cultural beliefs and practices. To guide your interpretation of this history, interspersed sections of culturally relevant insight are provided, such as the continuum of past, present, and future, as well as the importance of thinking about cultures as being dynamic. To begin, this chapter provides an understanding of physical activity as a cultural activity and an introduction to Indigenous cultures.

A Note on Terminology

Using appropriate terminology can be thought of as a process of respect, self-determination, and understanding, rather than a search for a conclusive definition of Indigenous peoples. This section provides a brief, and necessarily incomplete, starting point for using terminology that may prompt more questions than answers, which is a normal part of learning. At a global level, there are many Indigenous peoples across the world. The Aborigines of Australia, Native Americans of the United States, and the *Māori* of Aotearoa (New Zealand) are some well-known terms that encapsulate many nations and communities.

In Canada, the terms *Aboriginal* and *Indigenous* share a similarity in meaning in that they are broad terms that encapsulate a great diversity of many groups of people, although *Indigenous* is often the preferred term when used by Indigenous peoples. The term *Aboriginal* was developed by, and is used by, the federal government of Canada and specifically refers to the grouping of Indigenous people into three categories: the Inuit, First Nations, and Métis. The Inuit are the Indigenous group in the Arctic, whose ancestral and contemporary connections to land include the areas known today as Nunavut, the Northwest Territories, and parts of Labrador, Newfoundland, and northern Quebec. First Nations, the largest Indigenous group in Canada, are made of many nations and hundreds of communities whose traditional territories span across the country (and into the United States). The Métis are another Indigenous group, including the Red River Métis, who trace their Nation's roots to the "history, events, leaders, territories, language, and culture associated with the growth of the buffalo hunting and trading Métis of the northern Plains," particularly during the community's development during the 19th century.[5]

First Nations, Métis, and Inuit—and the many communities that compose them—have their own cultures and histories as well as their own preferences for the terminology of their own people. The many terms used to identify Indigenous peoples can be overwhelming: An important point is not to attempt to remember them all but to appreciate the importance and power of being able to name and situate your own community. Learning about the local First Nations, Inuit, or Métis communities in the area you live, their preferences for terminology, the cultural features of those communities, and if there are Indigenous treaties in the area are good ways to begin developing your understanding of Indigenous communities in Canada.[6]

Physical Activities as Cultural Activities

One view of culture is that it is a way of life that groups of people share.[7] It is a broad and complex term that captures a lot about a group of people or a society. Each Indigenous nation has its own particular culture, which can include distinct languages, clothing, values, spiritual practices, philosophies, artwork, kinship patterns, and much more in their way of life. Physical activities are an example of a cultural practice because they pass down shared ideas and values as people participate and play.[8] Culture is always present during physical activity. Physical activities express the ideas, values, beliefs, customs, and traditions of the people who participate in them. It is not just Indigenous peoples who have a cultural dimension to their physical activities. All groups and societies have sporting cultures. If sport was not a cultural activity, then all communities across the world would engage in physical activity with the same ideals, pass down the same traditions, and share the same reasons for participation. But they do not. The common practice of spectators singing at English sporting matches, the spiritual dimension of Muay Thai kickboxing, and high school rugby teams in Aotearoa (New Zealand) beginning a game with a Māori haka are examples of culture and sport that are foreign to a Canadian way of life. In Canada, there are many communities (e.g., Indigenous, francophone) that have their own distinctive cultural practices.

Introduction to Indigenous Cultures

Although each Indigenous nation has its own distinct culture, there are common features among the vast number of Indigenous communities; perhaps the most central is the connection to land. Indigenous communities often express a deeply felt connection between themselves and the environments they live in, and as such their traditional territories are highly significant to them. Indigenous peoples have many expressions of their connection to their territories. It is common for Indigenous peoples to introduce themselves by sharing the peoples and territory where they are from; such is the importance of both the people and the land. The connection to land can help shape an entire way of life. The Dene Nation is a useful example.[9]

The Dene Nation is a large group who live in many communities across a huge area of North America. The traditional lands of the Dene extend from Alaska in the United States, across the Yukon and the Northwest Territories, out to Hudson Bay. To make a living in the cold and often harsh climate, Dene families and communities had to travel across their territories to access resources from different areas at different times of the year.[10] Some communities relied on the caribou for survival, and when the caribou herds undertook long journeys, so too did the Dene communities that relied on those animals. Dene communities had to travel to areas that were good for fishing, or that provided plants and berries for food and medicines. Many Dene communities would travel to sites in the summer, fall, and winter in order to thrive on their lands. The Dene people are therefore known to be travelling people, which requires fitness for their way of life. To be successful travellers, Dene communities needed to have a very close relationship with the lands—including the animals, plant life, rivers, mountains, and more—for the survival of the group. The close connection to the land was inherent to their way of life.

Oral traditions are another element common among Indigenous communities, such as speech making, song, discussion and debate, and storytelling. Indigenous stories are fundamental to passing down culture. Sometimes these stories are creation stories. Creation stories transfer knowledge about how the world was created, acts of supernatural beings (such as a Creator or god), and the nature of being within a culture. Passing down creation stories through the generations is a way to reaffirm the values, morals, and norms of a people's society and spirituality. By telling stories, the messages convey community belonging and identity, shared spiritual experiences, and practical as well as moral lessons about the appropriate ways to behave.[11] From this perspective, the stories say a lot about Indigenous communities. To view these stories as fiction, myths, or fairy tales for children misses their cultural importance. These stories reflect Indigenous realities, which is of the utmost priority in the preservation of oral traditions.[12] Oral traditions and connection to their environments are two commonalities Indigenous communities share in their ways of life, although the specifics of how these are practised and embodied vary from community to community and are presented here as a starting point for understanding Indigenous cultures.

Although Indigenous communities share many common features, Indigenous peoples are a highly diverse group. We must recognize these differences to gain a deep appreciation of Indigenous history. The cultural diversity found in Europe is a helpful example. Although Europeans have shared histories, geographies, and elements of culture, such as a widespread passion for soccer, Canadians have a great appreciation of the diversity within Europe. Seldom do Canadians confuse English food with Italian food, nor do Canadians typically believe that the Scots, Greeks, and Swedes share the same culture or history. This line of thinking can be applied to Indigenous peoples in Canada who share common features yet also have a wide variety of histories, works of art, customs, stories, physical activities, and more. Where possible, a greater understanding of what it is that unites Indigenous peoples should be supported by a deeper appreciation for the great diversity and distinctiveness of Indigenous nations.

Histories of Indigenous Cultures From Long Ago

While there is significant overlap in the traditional activities in Canadian and American Indigenous communities (indeed the Canada–United States border has territorially divided many Indigenous communities), this chapter puts emphasis on Canadian Indigenous communities.

Games of Chance

Games of chance are a type of activity that does not emphasize much physicality. Games of chance are recreational rather than about physical skill or strength, and they are often used as a way to have fun. One common activity was "dice" games, in which bones, sticks, and marked stones were tossed into the air and then counted depending on how they landed, similar to the commonplace use of dice today.[13] Dice games were played by many Indigenous communities in Canada, including the Salish communities of the Pacific Coast, the Inuit of the Arctic north, the Haudenosaunee (Iroquois) of central Canada, and the Mi'kmaq (Micmac) of the East Coast.[14]

Not all games of chance are simple luck, as many involve skill and are very complex, such as the moccasin game, the stick game, and the hand game.[15] A team of players is required for the hand game, in which a team takes small objects in their hands, conceals their hands under a blanket, robe, or something similar, and then hides the object in one of their hands. Then the players present their hands, with the objects concealed, to the other team for an opponent to predict or guess which hand holds the object. But this is not a game of pure chance because some players are better than others. The most skilled players are good at guessing where the object is hidden, and they are also good at deceiving the opposition. Thus the hand game contains elements of skill, strategy, intuition, psychology, and deception and also elements of a religious nature in which the ability to predict expresses a spiritual force beyond the human world.[16] Although dice games are played in quiet, it is common for activities like the hand game to be enhanced by singing and drumming. The type of singing and drumming during the hand game is similar to what takes place in modern-day powwows that are held across the country as physical, social, cultural, and spiritual gatherings for Aboriginal peoples.

Games of Strength, Speed, and Endurance

Many games of strength, speed, and endurance exist within Aboriginal cultures, including actions such as sprinting, running, throwing, wrestling, jumping, pushing, pulling, lifting heavy objects, and much more.[17] A very popular sport is running races, which are played across the country. Running games are of particular significance to the Dene Nation, which spend time moving and hunting on old trails throughout the seasonal cycle of the year. Races can be shorter and longer distances, and in the winter participants race on snowshoes.[18] Similar to a foot race, but requiring great strength as well, are backpack races. A backpack race simply requires participants to wear a heavy backpack, sometimes filled with rocks, while they race. Backpack races are traditionally played by Dene men and boys over shorter distances (e.g., from 70 to 170 metres [230-560 ft]).[19] The competitions of physical capacity are not just about winning or losing but have a larger purpose. An Elder, Joe Naedzo from Deline in the Northwest Territories, explains:

They would run side by side for some distance, before the one who was truly the fastest would pull ahead and leave the challenger behind. The person who outran the challenger would be the winner. Other racers would then replace them. The fastest racer was honored among the Sahtuotine [a regional group of the Dene Nation]. . . . The object of the competition was to see who was the fastest runner. Its real purpose was to identify who was to pursue game [animals for hunting]. This was necessary, because in those days hunting was done only with bow and arrow.[20]

As the Dene Elder noted, the skills promoted by running races are about being on the land and developing the endurance and strength for hunting, as well as a means for friendly athletic competition. Indigenous activities, and the way in which they are practised, are used to promote important skills and qualities that are deemed valuable to the way of life.

Games of Skill

Games of skill are also very popular in Indigenous cultures, including games that promote eye–hand coordination, agility, dexterity, and accuracy through a variety of types of activities such as ball games, ball and stick games, games with hoops and poles, and many others. One popular game of skill that also requires upper body power is snowsnake, which is played in Indigenous cultures across Canada. There are many varieties of this game involving darts or javelins that are either thrown in the air or on the ground along snow or ice in the winter.[21] In the 19th century, Reverend Peter Jones was the Chief of the Mississaugas of New Credit First Nation, whose community lies in the areas connected to Lake Erie and Lake Ontario. The Chief noted that the single most popular game of his community during the winter season was snowsnake.[22] A hard, smooth javelin of wood was crafted to be almost 2 metres (6 feet) in length for the event. Each participant would take the "snake" and throw it by the tail along a track of snow or ice as far as they could, as shown in figure 3.2. The

Courtesy of Kevin Redmond.

Figure 3.2 A child in an Indigenous community in Manitoba playing snowsnake.

Sahtu community, of the Dene Nation, plays another variation that focuses on accuracy rather than strength, in which a paddle is used to strike a smaller snowsnake to propel it towards a target while producing incredible speed.[23] This game is used to develop hunting skills on the land, as the snake can travel completely through the body of a moose.[24]

Indigenous Origins of Lacrosse

The sport now internationally known as lacrosse was adapted from the Kanien'kehá:ka (Mohawk) variation of a ball and stick game called tewaa:rathon, which combined skill, speed, and strength. Tewwa:rathon was not the only version of a ball and stick game, as they were popular throughout North America. Indigenous diversity is indicated in the dozens of variations of ball and stick games that involved a ball, a field, two teams, many participants (sometimes hundreds), a stick (or sometimes two) that could carry the ball (what we now call a lacrosse stick), and some form of goal. The Anishinaabe, Haudenosaunee, Huron, Mi'kmaq (Micmac), Aniyvwiya (Cherokee), and Mvskoke (Muscogee/Creek) communities of North America have long traditions in the game, and in British Columbia the Coast and Interior Salish nations picked up the game in the early 20th century. Traditionally, each community used its own style, rules, and equipment, guided by specific cultural beliefs and practices.

The variations of these ball and stick games were far from simply a form of exercise or an outlet for healthy competition but are best interpreted as a form of Indigenous culture.[25] Games of ball and stick often had a function larger than simply playing the game. Indeed, thinking about traditional activities as simply physical competitions that decide who wins or loses would be to impose cultural assumptions that limit an understanding of the games. Some of the most common functions for traditional variations of lacrosse were to prepare men for warfare, reduce warfare, reconcile with others, promote peace, and resolve disputes.[26] Sometimes the ball and stick games were used to honour the dead or to heal a person or community that was sick.[27] This cultural basis for ball and stick games is quite different from the sport of lacrosse as it is played in Canada today.

Indigenous Storytelling of Ball and Stick Games

Ball and stick games are deeply rooted in the great stories and oral histories of the communities that played these games, and the variety of stories is indicative of the diversity among Indigenous groups. Indigenous peoples tell stories that often feature animal characters, trickster characters, and elements of the environment to provide entertaining but meaningful teachings and experiences. Some stories are directly connected to physical activities.[28] One of the best-documented stories across North America of lacrosse centres around a mythical match between birds and land animals that provides lessons about the game, including the lesson that keeping the ball above the ground is the safest means to victory.[29] Indigenous communities told these stories to pass down knowledge and important teachings, and thus telling stories about ball and stick games was a cultural practice that helped sustain Indigenous cultures. A small excerpt from a story told in 1823 by the Eastern Aniyvwiya in the United States says that in the past the lacrosse game was played only during the full moon because it provided a reminder of fair play:

WORKING WITH PRIMARY SOURCES: THE GREAT GAME?

In *The Creator's Game*, Allan Downey, a Dakelh (Carrier) Nation scholar, stresses the importance of oral traditions.[31] Downey explores the history of lacrosse with a focus on Aboriginal identity and nationhood, and he uses evidence that focuses on Aboriginal, often Haudenosaunee, knowledge. Indigenous peoples have been excluded from the majority of written histories about Aboriginal peoples, and Downey privileges Indigenous peoples' knowledges and cultures as a respectful way to carry out the research. The first chapter retells one version of a Haudenosaunee creation story, as told to Downey by Jao De Dre (Delmar Jacobs) on the Six Nations Reserve in southwestern Ontario. The story involves the origins of the world in which the sky father and sky women were involved in the creation of the Earth on the back of a turtle, which is why some First Nations peoples refer to North America as Turtle Island.[32] The story connects to a ball and stick game that is used to solve the question of whether the Haudenosaunee people shall seek good or evil, and thus the game would be a method for resolving disputes.[33] Downey uses creation stories not as mere entertainment or as an interesting cultural relic from the past but to guide the audience's interpretation of the book through the lens and lessons of Indigenous knowledge. Indigenous peoples' physical participation in ball and stick games and the telling of stories about these games are ways for Aboriginal peoples to pass down their cultures through the generations.

Scholars can use Indigenous stories to understand the history and culture of sport, but stories can also be a culturally relevant way for researchers to write sport history. Stories are central in Downey's *The Creator's Game*, as he begins each chapter with a short story that centres around a traditional trickster figure from West Coast cultures named Usdas, whose antics and conversations are illustrative for the audience. The short stories provide a way for Downey to frame potential insights and priorities for the chapter that move beyond a chronological framing of history. In one example, Usdas has a telling and humorous conversation with George Beers, who was the Montreal sport enthusiast who institutionalized the contemporary sport of lacrosse in 1856 by colonizing its Indigenous past. After Usdas insists to Beers that lacrosse is an Indigenous game, an annoyed Beers snaps back, "It's Canada's game; it's 'Our Country and Our Game'!"[34] Usdas then replies:

> *"Nice premise, but 'Stolen Land and Stolen Game' has a better ring to it. And though it may be enshrined in folklore, we both know that lacrosse isn't Canada's national game. Parliament won't be meeting on that issue until 1994. But I like tricks, Beersie, so let's call it Canada's national sport. No one will know the truth, at least not for a while. What's the worst that could happen? It's not like Canadians are going to ban Indigenous athletes, appropriate their lacrosse identity, or use it to assimilate them."*[35]

Usdas, and the Indigenous perspective that he brings, literally speaks back to the authority of Beers by insisting on an Indigenous voice in interpreting the history of lacrosse, which includes a seamless weave of Canada in 1856 and 1994 as a present reality for the book's audience. Indigenous cultures are important not only to participation in physical activity and to traditions (e.g., storytelling) about physical activity but also for how sport historians conduct their research.

The contest between the parties was very severe for a long time, when one of them got the advantage by the superior skill of a young man. His adversary on the other side, seeing no chance of success in fair play, attempted to cheat, when in throwing the ball it stuck in the sky and turned into the appearance which the moon hath, to remind the Indians that cheating and dishonesty are crimes.[30]

This small snippet of Aboriginal culture uses the moon as a symbol to emphasize a clear relationship between history, oral traditions, ball and stick games, and the connection to the environment.

Reading Indigenous Histories

When reading Indigenous histories of games and activities, and Indigenous histories more broadly, we must recognize that Indigenous cultures today are deeply connected to Indigenous peoples' past. It is common for Indigenous peoples to talk about and practise their traditional ways, which often have long histories. But it is not so much that they are old that makes tradition inherently important, but that over time they have proven to be meaningful and successful ways to live life. To dismiss cultural practices as old, or from a time in history that does not seem relevant today, may in fact miss the key point from the perspective of Indigenous peoples. Therefore, the examination of Indigenous physical activities is not just relevant to the times and people of long ago, but, importantly, is also a platform for understanding modern-day (and future) physical activity practices that will be discussed towards the end of this chapter.

Indigenous Cultures Are Dynamic

To support an understanding of the connections between past, present, and future, it is helpful to appreciate that Indigenous cultures are dynamic and living. A culture that is dynamic means that over time parts of the culture remain stable while other parts change. Hunting is a physical and cultural activity that requires great accuracy, strength, and endurance, and it is a useful example for explaining stability and change in culture.[36] Many Indigenous communities relied on hunting (see chapter 5). The process of hunting included a cultural dimension, such that Indigenous customs to honour the animal's spirit, or the use of spiritual recitations and prayers, are an appropriate way to conduct a hunt. One example of a cultural tradition for northern Cree hunters is returning the dead animal through a doorway backwards in order to enable its spirit to leave frontwards. These types of practices continue today and are an example of cultural stability, and the maintenance of these practices is a testament to their importance to Indigenous communities.

Change and adaptations are normal processes for all hunting cultures. The developments in technology are one way that hunting has changed in Aboriginal communities. Historically, some Indigenous peoples have used hunting implements such as spears, knifes, traps, and bows and arrows to hunt, and many hunters continue to do so. Today, Indigenous peoples across Canada also sometimes use guns when hunting. The use of snowmobiles to hunt has also changed the hunting process. But these technological changes and adaptations should not be interpreted as the end of Indigenous hunting culture, or the weakening of Indigenous cultures. On the contrary, these technologies should be understood as Indigenous peoples adapting and changing to the modern context so that they maintain their hunting traditions and enhance the success of a hunt. Reading Indigenous history in ways that view Indigenous cultures as dynamic and living supports the connections between culture in the past, present, and future.

The approach to time that connects the past and present means that events of the past cannot easily be dismissed in the present. Some non-Indigenous peoples believe that Aboriginal communities should not live in the past, that colonization took place a long time ago and therefore does not matter now, and that Aboriginal people should move on and live in the present.[37] In some ways this is true and obvious; Indigenous peoples do not attempt to live their lives exactly as their ancestors did. Aboriginal peoples use social media, drive cars, and cook Chinese food. Yet Indigenous peoples place a very high priority on their traditions, such as the continued use of their languages, songs, kinship relations, and physical activities. Indigenous peoples reject the dismissal of their history, in part because it is also a dismissal of the ways they live their lives in the present. For instance, the attitude that the traditional sports and games outlined in this chapter are games of ancient cultures and are irrelevant to today can feel like an attack on Indigenous peoples' contemporary ways of life. History that supports Indigenous cultures as dynamic entities helps provide people with a sense of where they have come from, helps them better understand the present, and helps them create the future they might desire. The remainder of this chapter provides a brief overview of Indigenous efforts to maintain their culture in the context of cultural change and colonialism over time.

Cultural Exchange, Cultural Suppression, and Cultural Maintenance

From the 19th century through to the mid-20th century, Indigenous peoples experienced particularly significant cultural change and cultural suppression, arising from increased interaction with European settlers and the expansion of colonial domination. The trading posts used by Indigenous communities and fur traders in the Western Arctic between 1850 and 1940 are examples of cultural exchange with the Gwich'in peoples (of the Dene Nation). When communities from different cultures meet, live, work, and play together, the communities often change and adapt their cultures when interacting with others. In this instance the cultural exchange was brought about when European fur traders came to the Western Arctic, which includes the areas now known as the Yukon Territory and Alaska. European countries, including England and France, became involved in Canada's fur trade to access highly prized animal furs such as the beaver, squirrel, and mink, which were brought back to European markets.

To develop the marketplace of fur, summer gatherings at trading posts were organized for trading goods. In the early days of such gatherings in Canada's Western Arctic, trading meetings were frequent (e.g., 24 gatherings were held at the Fort Yukon Post between 1841 and 1852). Large groups of men, along with women and children, spent their time at the gatherings dancing.[38] Indigenous communities used traditional forms of dance as appropriate means to bring the various Indigenous communities together in peace during these events, as a culturally relevant way to manage the history of conflict between the communities.[39] Over time Gwich'in peoples were exposed to new European forms of dance, including the jigging and fiddling that the fur traders brought to the cultural exchange.[40] Adopting and adapting the jig was important to this particular community, and many other First Nations and Métis communities across Canada integrated European-style dances into their cultures through their exchanges with European immigrants.[41]

Not just dance was used to bring the communities together in peace at these trading posts; so too were activities like ball sports and wrestling, which provided a physical outlet between the sometimes hostile communities.[42] Other traditional activities of the Gwich'in that were popular at these intercultural gatherings included running races, tug-of-war games, and in the winter, events like snowshoeing and dogsled races.[43]

In the 20th century, with over 50 years of intercultural exchange at these trade gatherings, fur traders introduced the practice of providing prizes for the winner of matches or races. Prize money as reward for the victor may not sound like much of a change, but gambling for the explicit purpose of accumulating personal wealth from others was quite foreign to the Gwich'in communities. The use of prizes comes with a value set that suggests there should be a focus on winning in order to gain an additional reward from the sport, and this additional reward should be withheld from the losers. The value system promoted by this type of gambling had not been an important idea or practice in the Gwich'in people prior to this time, and as such it was a form of cultural change. The practice of prize money was a shift towards a non-Indigenous model of sport that is still dominant today and is reproduced in the emphasis placed on prize money, trophies at tournaments, and winning gold medals or baseball pennants. During these large gatherings, the Gwich'in had access to the benefits of this new model of sport, yet it also meant the older value system that emphasized the process of the activity (and not the external rewards of winning) became harder to practise.[44] The loss of opportunities to practise culturally relevant value systems is a negative result of intercultural exchange; this is an example of how elements of Indigenous cultures are not always easy to practise in mainstream sport.

Intercultural exchange enabled Gwich'in peoples and settlers of the Western Arctic to benefit from each other's knowledges, practices, cultures, and technologies. Historically, Indigenous peoples found many benefits from the newly arrived cultures, and at times enjoyed participating and engaging in foreign cultural practices and in the blending of cultural practices, as is seen in the trading post history. Today, Indigenous peoples continue to participate in nontraditional practices as is evidenced by their enthusiasm for all types of globally played sports and physical activities. However, the history of intercultural exchange is far from a simple story of mutual benefit. The relationship between Indigenous and settler societies became a very one-sided affair in which non-Indigenous peoples, organizations, and institutions sought to completely eradicate Indigenous cultures and peoples. There is sport history literature that covers cultural suppression and erasure in more detail than is provided in this chapter (see chapters 4 and 13), which, instead, emphasizes Indigenous peoples' resolve to maintain their ways of life as a strength of their communities over time.[45]

Cultural suppression of Indigenous games and sports was part of a broader process that sought to destroy Indigenous peoples' relationship to their land, language, spiritual practices, economic relations, kinship patterns, and more. The transformation of the game of tewaa:rathon to lacrosse is a case in point. The stories, cultural traditions, and ethos of tewaa:rathon were transformed by Beers and other Montreal anglophones through the establishment of the Montreal Lacrosse Club (MLC) in 1856, whereby a new set of rules and ideas for the sport of lacrosse were institutionalized.[46] Anglophone sport leaders of the time wanted to replace Indigenous culture with European culture, which was based on a very racist idea that Indigenous cultures of the past were inferior to the European cultures they believed should be Canada's future.[47] The MLC not only tried to eliminate Indigenous cultures but also began to limit Indigenous peoples' participation in the new game of lacrosse in 1857, and by 1880 the club barred Aboriginal athletes from participating at all.[48] The exclusionary practices of the MLC illustrate cultural suppression, often based on the supposed inferiority of Indigenous cultures, to enhance the dominance of European cultures in Canada.

There has been a significant focus on discrimination, racism, and colonialism in Indigenous sport literature.[49] In 1876, the federal government solidified its regulation of Indigenous peoples with the passing of the Indian Act as federal law; it remains the legal framework of the government in dealing with Indigenous affairs to the present day. Through the Indian Act, and its later additions, the federal government banned the cultural practices of Indigenous peoples. The banning of the Sundance ceremony on the Canadian plains and imposing fines on Indigenous peoples for dancing at powwows are examples of government attempts to eliminate and control Indigenous cultural practices.[50] In 1921, Duncan Campbell Scott, the director of the Department of Indian Affairs, expressed his unwavering commitment to replace Indigenous forms of recreation with more "reasonable" European activities, when he said, "It has always been clear to me that the Indians must have some sort of recreation, if our agents would endeavour to substitute reasonable amusements for this senseless drumming and dancing, it would be a great assistance."[51] The suppression of

Indigenous culture was not just the result of cultural exchange with Europeans but was a deeply racist and dedicated policy of the federal government.

Although Indigenous peoples adapt their cultures to the historical context they live in, the experiences of unwanted and enforced cultural change have been highly damaging. However, the goal of government-directed cultural termination never came to fruition; the existence of Indigenous peoples and their cultures today is based on an unwavering determination to maintain the integral elements of their cultures. The establishment of lacrosse and the efforts of the MLC to ban Indigenous peoples, for instance, was not the end of lacrosse for the Kanien'kehá:ka and other Haudenosaunee nations. In the 1920s, the Haudenosaunee communities in Akwesasne and at Grand River, both in Ontario, held many large community lacrosse matches that drew between 3,000 and 5,000 spectators.[52] These matches were held despite the efforts of government representatives (often Indian agents) and legislation (in this instance the Lords Day Act, 1906, was important) to control Haudenosaunee communities.[53] The federal government went so far as to replace the Indigenous leaders of these communities so they would not defy government demands about the sport.[54] The continuation of the sport was clearly political, in that the Haudenosaunee wanted to assert their own sovereignty and political control over their lives, including the sport of lacrosse. This is just one instance in which Indigenous peoples have sought to maintain, and at times revitalize, cultural activities as an expression of Indigenous peoples' way of life.

TRANSFORMATIVE MOMENTS: THE IROQUOIS NATIONALS

The Iroquois Nationals (a team made from players in the six Haudenosaunee Nations) played at the 1990 lacrosse world championship as an independent nation, in competition against countries such as the United States, Canada, England, and Australia. In 2018, the Nationals won the bronze medal in Israel. For this Indigenous team, the recognition and respect as a nation was of critical importance to the people and cultures of the Haudenosaunee. The team was developed to instil Haudenosaunee pride and to revitalize the culture, including promoting the traditional longhouse system, the traditional history of the sport, and the Haudenosaunee philosophy of the sport to community members. The Nationals are a contemporary assertion of Haudenosaunee nationhood, of which there is a long history that includes treaty to treaty relationships with the Crown. The Haudenosaunee affirm that the national and cultural aspects of the team are central to their efforts—it is not just about athletic success. The Nationals' claim to nationhood is remarkable, as the team uses Haudenosaunee passports (and not Canadian or American passports!) to cross international borders for competitions. Indigenous peoples' contemporary sport is connected to their political and cultural histories.

Indigenous Cultural Revitalization

Indigenous peoples' efforts to maintain their traditional cultures, knowledges, and practices make a strong connection between the present and the past. From the 1950s onward, Indigenous peoples have had increasing success in shaping their sporting lives against colonial imposition. This is explored in detail in the following chapter, through Janice Forsyth's analysis of the Tom Longboat Awards and the North American Indigenous Games. The 1970s is a powerful example of an era in which Indigenous peoples' efforts to shape their physical activities (and cultural practices, more broadly) highlight their fight to revitalize and restore their traditions and cultures into their contemporary lives.[55]

PROMINENT PEOPLE: ANDY PAULL (1892-1959)

Andy Paull was born in 1892 on the Mission Reserve in North Vancouver, British Columbia, to a prominent family. At a young age Paull was recognized as a potential leader among his community, the Skwxwu7mesh (Squamish) people. Paull was a descendant of Xwechtaal, a powerful serpent slayer from the Skwuxwu7mesh oral traditions, and later he grew to be a great athlete and political advocate for his people. During the early decades of the 19th century, Indigenous peoples' activities were highly regulated by the federal government. For example the Potlatch, a cultural ceremony common amongst the Indigenous Peoples of the pacific northwest, was outlawed by the Indian Act. The federal government condoned sports activities, such as large gatherings of social and athletic competition called Indian sport days, because the federal government believed it would help eliminate Indigenous cultures and replace them with European culture. Andy Paull, however, was able to use the sport of lacrosse to promote a sense of nationhood and the culture of his people.

In 1936, Paull, along with Skwxwu7esh and Haudenosaunee players, formed an all-Indigenous team called the North Shore Indians. The team played at the highest level of lacrosse in Canada and used their culture as a strength. The North Shore Indians would speak Skwxwu7mesh fluently during their games to promote their language and as a successful tactic on the field. After scoring a goal, Paull would get his team to line up and discuss the next play. Using their language out loud, in front of a league dominated by non-Indigenous peoples and at a time in which Indigenous cultures were belittled, was an outrageous way to reassert their culture as opposing teams waited for the midgame huddles to end. Many non-Indigenous peoples took umbrage at the use of the Skwxwu7esh language, but Andy Paull and the North Shore Indians took the government's idea that lacrosse will help eliminate Indigenous peoples' cultures and used it as a platform for defiance and to reaffirm cultural pride. Andy Paull's leadership is one example of Indigenous peoples' using sport to meet their needs and desires, which can include using their culture as a strength.

Indigenous Peoples Reshaped the Arctic Winter Games

A mainstream system of sport rapidly expanded during the 1960s and 1970s in Arctic Canada. Indigenous sport leaders worked to ensure their way of life was integral to sport and recreation development across the northern territories. The Arctic Winter Games (AWG) is a good example of the success of Indigenous leadership; to understand how Aboriginal communities have fought for their culture at the AWG, it is important to understand the beginning of this story. Sport in the Northwest Territories (NWT) and the Yukon (along with present-day Nunavut) in the 1960s had less capacity when compared with metrics of sport development in the larger Canadian provinces; for instance, the territories had less infrastructure (sports fields, courts, and so on), access to equipment, and capacity for high-level coaching. Politicians from the northern territories began to work towards a sport event for the Arctic north after they witnessed the territories' lack of competitive success at the 1967 Canada Games.[56] The efforts of territorial leaders resulted in the inaugural AWG held in Yellowknife, NWT, in 1970. The first AWG largely reproduced an event similar to the Canada Games, offering 10 events that were popular in larger Canadian cities, such as hockey, basketball, boxing, skiing, and volleyball. The AWG are still run every two years and now involve many circumpolar teams and athletes who come from Siberia, Norway, Alaska, and northern regions in Canada. The original vision was to take the model of sport that was popular in Canadian cities and use this to develop sport opportunities in the northern territories.[57]

Over time Aboriginal leaders were able to shape the AWG to meet the needs of the local cultures of the Arctic, specifically the Dene and Inuit communities, rather than simply reproduce the style of sport that came directly from the culture of urban sport experts. At the 1970 and 1972 AWG, none of the sports specifically reflected the large Indigenous population in the Canadian Arctic, and thus Indigenous Canadians were under-represented as participants in the AWG in the 1970s.[58] Nine different traditional sports of the Inuit were initially included as demonstration events rather than official sports in 1970. By 1974, Indigenous sport leaders successfully lobbied for Inuit sports to be official events and thus accorded the legitimacy of other sports. Snowshoeing was introduced in 1974, and in 1978 the snowshoe biathlon was added to better reflect the cultural activities in the Arctic.[59] Some of the Inuit sports require great skill, technique, power, and balance, such as the one-foot high kick, two-foot high kick (see figure 3.3), Alaskan high kick, and the kneel jump. Other games emphasize strength and pain resistance, such as the airplane, head pull, and knuckle hop.[60] By 1990, Dene leaders secured five Dene games as official events, three of which are variations on tug-of-war games, along with snowsnake and the hand game, which were described earlier.[61] Over time Indigenous leaders have drawn guidance from their sporting and cultural pasts to provide a successful platform for significant and successful Aboriginal participation at the AWG.

Indigenous peoples sought to change not only the specific activities but also many of the values and ideas that guide the AWG. Inuit athletes want to compete just like others at competitive sport events, yet there also exists a cultural emphasis on cooperation that is not common in many mainstream sports. For example, in the middle of AWG competition, in between contestant attempts at the various Inuit sports, it is common for Elders, competing athletes, and coaches of opposing athletes to voluntarily assist and help an athlete.[62] The cooperative dimension of supporting other athletes is remarkable and very different from the competitive model of sport. It would be highly improbable, for example, for an opposing coach of a Canadian university sport team to support an opposition player in full view of the fans during a match. For the Indigenous participants and supporters at the AWG, each individual's pursuit of winning remains, but there is also a cooperative logic that the enhanced performance of an individual is good for the sport and the participating communities. In this cultural context, it is logical for Indigenous peoples to

Figure 3.3 An athlete competes in the two-foot high kick event at the Arctic Winter Games.

Xander from Yellowknife, NT, Canada/Wikimedia Commons/CC BY 2.0

help others during competition. The cooperative approach of Indigenous communities is deeply rooted in a way of life that stresses the support of others for successfully living on the land.[63] Indigenous people have thus reshaped the AWG to better reflect their cultures and therefore pass down the activities, values, and ideas about appropriate behaviour that are very old and yet still practised to this day.

Conducting Culturally Relevant Historical Research

Sport historians have played a supporting role in the efforts of Aboriginal communities to maintain and revitalize their cultures through physical activities. One example is the work of Michael Heine, who, with the assistance of others, has developed resource manuals of traditional sports and games in Arctic Canada. To develop these resources, Heine undertook a series of culturally respectful processes to ensure the quality of the sporting manuals.[64] He used a community-based approach in which the participating communities helped guide the research and writing. By developing resources that could be used in the community, the research process was not just about collecting knowledge about Indigenous communities. Instead, the work was intended to have direct benefit to the participating communities, such as enhanced coaching resources. The knowledge recorded was from the stories told by Elders at community gatherings. Elders are of particular importance in Indigenous communities and often play an important role in passing down cultural teachings and knowledge through their stories. The approach used in the development of these training manuals to gather information thus privileged Indigenous knowledge and oral traditions, which is important not only to the physical activities but also to the ways in which historical research is conducted.

Past, Present, Future

The focus of this chapter is connecting the cultural dimension of Indigenous peoples' physical activity across time as a way to highlight the strength of Aboriginal cultures. In part, connecting the continuum of time in this way challenges harmful misconceptions about Indigenous peoples' cultures. Indigenous peoples challenge the idea that their cultures contradict life in the present. The connection between the past, present, and future requires an approach to understanding time that does not always follow a linear path. A linear approach to time assumes time happens in a sequential way, much like a straight line that connects a series of times or events. The timeline presented in this book represents a linear approach to time in which the years ascend; each year is distinct from the other years in the sequence, through the past to the present.

The influence of European cultures in Canada has resulted in this dominance of a linear conceptualization of time. This is a legitimate way to think about time, but it causes problems when it restricts knowledge about Indigenous history. Looking back at the history of Indigenous cultures in this way severs Indigenous traditions from the present because they are static and therefore locked in an era that can never repeat itself. Indeed, colonial thinking that places traditional cultures in a bygone era has been used by non-Indigenous peoples to explain a wide variety of negative social issues, such as poor outcomes for Aboriginal peoples' health, education, and lack of success in physical activity contexts.[65] This chapter focuses on the strengths of Indigenous cultures to counter such claims. The dismissal of Aboriginal cultural activities and priorities in the early years of the AWG provides evidence that a lack of respect for Indigenous cultures can result in a loss of culture and puts up barriers to Aboriginal participation.

Reading and interpreting Indigenous histories with a culturally respectful lens, which views the activities, actions, and cultures of periods in the past as connected to the present, provides clarity to Indigenous peoples' perseverance in maintaining their cultures. When Indigenous peoples are speaking their traditional language, telling traditional stories, playing traditional games, or bringing a set of values or ideals to organizing their sports, it is not evidence that Indigenous peoples are trapped, stuck, and living in the past. The revitalization of the hand game, dancing, drumming, or a cooperative value identified in the AWG, as discussed earlier, should be viewed as a strength of Indigenous peoples. It is precisely the cultural dimensions of traditional games, such as connection to land, connection to Elders, and the promotion of cultural pride that can enhance Indigenous peoples' participation in physical activity today.[66]

Contemporary research points to the many ways that Aboriginal peoples' cultures are valuable, such as to provide a basis for supportive and safe sport psychology and coaching, to foster appropriate ways to develop sport policy, to provide awareness of the role of gender in games participation, to guide health promotion in communities, or to improve the quality of physical education programming.[67] The future of Indigenous peoples' physical activity will rely on meaningful sport histories, which, when done well, preserve the stories about where they have come from, help them better understand the present, and assist them in creating the future they might desire.

Conclusion

The fern frond provides a symbol for thinking about history through patterns of change and stability; it helps us to see that growth and change can also, at the same time, be a return to the beginnings and origins. This chapter explores the changing contexts of Indigenous cultural traditions through periods of cultural strength, through cultural change and suppression, and in the revitalization of traditional activities for future generations. Through these periods of changing colonial relations, Indigenous peoples have persistently sought to maintain the integral elements of their cultures. The importance of culture in time immemorial, when Indigenous peoples used their traditions and culture to enhance their lives within physical activity contexts, remains equally relevant in the present. Indigenous peoples' cultures not only enhance their participation in physical activities but also can be very useful for reading, writing, and researching in the field of Aboriginal sport history.

DISCUSSION QUESTIONS

1. Can you identify one point of distinctiveness, and one point of commonality, across the Indigenous cultures discussed in this chapter?
2. How is culture an important feature of traditional Indigenous activities?
3. Why is it useful to think of Indigenous cultures as dynamic?
4. How have Indigenous peoples fought to promote and maintain their culture in physical activities?
5. Why is the connection to the past important to Indigenous peoples' perspectives?

SUGGESTED READINGS

Downey, Allan. *The Creator's Game: Lacrosse, Identity, and Indigenous Nationhood.* Vancouver: UBC Press, 2018.

Downey, Allan. "Playing the Creator's Game on God's Day: The Controversy of Sunday Lacrosse Games in Haudenosaunee Communities, 1916-24." *Journal of Canadian Studies* 49, no. 3 (2015): 111-143.

Forsyth, Janice, and Audrey R. Giles. *Aboriginal Peoples and Sport in Canada: Historical Foundations and Contemporary Issues.* Vancouver: UBC Press, 2013.

Heine, Michael. "Performance Indicators: Aboriginal Games at the Arctic Winter Games." In *Aboriginal Peoples and Sport in Canada: Historical Foundations and Contemporary Issues.* Edited by Janice Forsyth and Audrey Giles, 160-181. Vancouver: UBC Press, 2013.

Paraschak, Victoria. "Reasonable Amusements": Connecting the Strands of Physical Culture in Native Lives." *Sport History Review* 29, no. 1 (1998): 121-131.

CHAPTER 4

CASE STUDIES OF INDIGENOUS SPORT

Janice Forsyth, PhD
Western University
London, Ontario

LEARNING OBJECTIVES

In this chapter you will

- understand how colonialism shaped Indigenous involvement in Canadian sport;
- outline the ways Indigenous people responded to the imposition of sport in their lives;
- assess claims that support inequalities in sport participation for Indigenous people; and
- reflect on your own assumptions about the role of sport in society.

In Canada, organized sports are often described as empowering for different groups of people. This is especially true when referring to populations that are socioeconomically disadvantaged or marginalized, such as girls and women, people with disabilities, low-income youth, the LGBTQ2 community, new immigrants, and Indigenous people, all of whom have been targeted by governments, nonprofit organizations, schools, and corporations for special programming at one point or another. Even a cursory look online for such programs, typically framed as sport-for-development initiatives, gives some indication of the popularity of these programs as well as how the term *empowerment* is being used in relation to each group. Over time, Canadians have learned to make a positive causal connection between empowerment and sport participation, resulting in the notion that one automatically leads to the other.[1]

A problem with this causal connection is the silencing effect, wherein people believe so firmly in the positives of participation that it is hard for others to ask critical questions about the role of sport in our lives, perhaps out of concern for appearing negative or antagonistic. It also makes it hard for people to enact changes in the way sports are organized and funded because the people who are in charge of deciding what these activities should look like often believe the goodness of sport stems from the way it is structured. Many people involved in sports are thus resistant to change because they have the most to lose, socially, politically, and economically, if sports were organized in a way that did not reinforce their views.[2]

This brief introduction to empowerment ideology raises a number of questions for studying Indigenous sport histories: What if organized sports were used to break down the beliefs and practices that sustained Indigenous people instead of supporting them? What if they were used to instill a different set of cultural beliefs and practices among Indigenous people, ones that supported dominant interests? What if they helped sustain those unequal relationships over time? Could we still call sports empowering? For whom would they be empowering and under what conditions?

This chapter considers these questions from the point of view of history and colonization in Canada, focusing specifically on the way settlers used organized sports to regulate and subjugate Indigenous people and how Indigenous people responded to those efforts, using sports to rebuild their lives and their communities in a settler colonial state. Three case studies highlight this complicated history: sports in the residential school system, where organized sports were an integral part of the program of Indigenous assimilation; the Tom Longboat Awards, which was established in 1951 as a means to integrate Indigenous youth into mainstream society; and the North American Indigenous Games, a major multi-sport and cultural event that was developed by Indigenous people for Indigenous youth in an effort to create more opportunities and a positive space for sport participation than was provided in the mainstream system. Each case study is crafted as a separate segment, but it is important to note that all three histories are intertwined, with one feeding into the next. It is for this reason, and the linear confines of the written word, that some aspects of their shared histories are left until later. This will be most clear when discussing the National Indian Brotherhood and the Aboriginal Sport Circle, which appear briefly in the section on the Tom Longboat Awards but are discussed in more detail in the section on the North American Indigenous Games.

Whereas chapter 3, Indigenous Peoples' Cultures and Physical Activities, outlines the way Indigenous attachments to land, culture, identity, and politics are connected to sport from the precontact era to the present day, this chapter looks at organized sports in Indigenous contexts from the late 1800s onwards, focusing mostly on the post-1950 era. Although the two chapters are meant as stand-alone readings, together they help readers identify and appreciate the cultural basis of Indigenous sport practices in Canada, while providing a deeper understanding of how the Canadian sport system needs to change if it is to be inclusive and empowering for Indigenous people, especially the youth, which is the fastest growing population in Canada.[3] The central theme that links both chapters is colonialism, which remains the key factor that continues to limit and marginalize Indigenous ways of doing sport.

A note about terminology: For descriptions of people at the population level, the term *Indigenous* rather than *Aboriginal* will be used in all cases except where proper nouns are required, as in the case with the Aboriginal Sport Circle. The terms *First Nations*, *Métis*, and *Inuit* will be used when reference to cultural groups are needed. Specific place names that are normally also tied to nation-hood, such as the Mohawks of Kahnawá:ke, will be used where appropriate. These naming conventions represent current practices in Canada (see also the sidebar A Note on Terminology in chapter 3).

Processes of colonization have indelibly shaped the way Indigenous people participate in and think about organized sport in Canada. Of course, this logic also applies to Canadians more generally since colonization affected everyone, not just Indigenous people. However, that does not mean everyone struggled in the same way. Rather, through colonization, the dominant and powerful groups were able to build and secure their preferred vision for sport (and life more broadly) at the expense of others. That is why analyses of Canadian sport, especially those that take into account Indigenous sporting experiences, need to carefully attend to colonialism as an overarching framework worthy of analysis and reflection. In one sense, this chapter illustrates how the history of Canadian and Indigenous sport was (and remains) a struggle for control over the types of activities that were available to people, how they incorporated them into their lives, and the values and meanings they attached to them.[4] But it is also more than that. It illustrates the importance of understanding how Indigenous–settler relations in Canada shaped the way Indigenous people incorporated sports into their lives, sometimes by choice and other times by coercion.

Sport in the Indian Residential School System

The development of the nation-state in the latter half of the 1800s ushered in fundamental changes to Indigenous ways of life in Canada. During this time, the British Crown transferred its responsibility for managing its relationship with Indigenous people to the colonial government through the Department of Indian Affairs. Soon afterwards, in 1876, the newly established federal government consolidated all its policies on Indigenous people into the Indian Act, a powerful piece of legislation that regulated nearly every aspect of Indigenous life, from property ownership to child welfare.[5] Under the new regime, Indigenous people were viewed as impediments to progress, and the state enacted strategies that focused on Indigenous assimilation into mainstream society. From the beginning, the state embarked on a formal program to align Indigenous cultural practices and beliefs with dominant ideologies, working on the assumption that Indigenous ways of life were oppositional to and therefore a threat to the incipient capitalist economy.

In this rapidly changing era, Indigenous people were displaced onto reserves and into permanent settlements where the physical practices that once sustained their land-based lifestyles no longer served the same purpose or carried the same meaning (see chapter 5). As a result, many Indigenous physical practices fell to the wayside, while others, such as lacrosse, which had been appropriated and codified by Montrealer George Beers, were adapted by Indigenous people to fit their changing circumstances.[6] It was also during this era that settlers began to impose their own definitions of appropriate physical behaviour in the new state, using policies and legislation to enforce their views. In their estimation, everything from Indigenous subsistence lifestyles, such as fishing and hunting, to Indigenous religious and spiritual practices were viewed as problems needing to be curtailed and transformed.

Organized sports, which had taken hold in many regions of Canada by the late 1800s, were deployed on behalf of this broader strategy. Activities that fostered an appreciation for dominant understandings of thrift, work, and leisure were deemed highly suitable for Indigenous people, who, it was widely believed, needed to be taught how to use their leisure time wisely and to understand it as an extension of labour.[7] For example, in 1906, residents in southern Saskatchewan argued that Indigenous people would be more content and would make better progress on their farms if they would only participate in sports days.[8] Yet even when Indigenous people did participate in sports days, they still made little progress on their farms since Indian Affairs regularly set them up for failure by providing them with inadequate equipment and supplies, or settling them on non-arable land, making it impossible for them to provide for their families, let alone sell their products for income.[9]

Such sentiments about the value of sports were widespread in Canada and found their way into the Indian residential school system, which also emerged as an institutionalized practice in the late 1800s. Removing children and youth from their families and communities and placing them in schools that were sometimes far from home further ruptured Indigenous connections to their land, to their culture, and to their entire way of life. It is no wonder that the Truth and Reconciliation Commission of Canada, which was established in 2008 and tasked with the responsibility of investigating and documenting the history of the residential school system, concluded in 2015 that the policy on Indian schooling was a deliberate attempt at cultural genocide.[10] From the 1880s, when the federal government first began funding religious institutions to operate the schools, to the 1990s, when the last federally funded school was closed, more than 150,000 students passed through the system. At its high point in 1930, there were about 80 residential schools operating throughout most of Canada.[11] When the number of children and youth who attended the Indian day schools and chartered schools is factored into the equation, the impact caused by this official state policy is staggering.

Encouraging Cultural Conformity

In the residential schools, sports and other forms of physical activities were viewed as conversion activities that would facilitate Indigenous assimilation. The historical record is filled with official commentary about such potential. One illustrative example, from a 1926 report filed by the Anglican Church, explained how organized activities would contribute to its mission:

> Unlike their playmates of civilization, the Indian children's recreation must be cultivated and developed, as they lack the knowledge of creating their own amusements. Strange as it may seem, the average Indian cannot swim, so that their recreation becomes an education. Once taught, they become keen, and display good sportsmanship and courage.[12]

Likewise, a report filed by the United Church of Canada in 1927 stated that rational recreation was to occupy an important programmatic role at their schools since it could be used to wean students from their "savage" ways by introducing them to structured activities that would teach "obedience and discipline." The types of activities they had in mind were "football, cricket, baseball and above all hockey," although other sports would do just as well.[13] As shown in figure 4.1, in 1935, the students at Brandon Indian Industrial School were engaged in competitive football, softball, and athletics.

In spite of statements such as these, in reality, prior to the 1950s, neither the religious organizations nor Indian Affairs devoted much attention to this aspect of Indian administration. In terms of outdoor amenities, most schools lacked such basic playground equipment as swings and teeter-totters. Space and equipment, even for relatively inexpensive sports, such as softball, volleyball, basketball, and track and field, were also almost nonexistent. If sports were offered at school, it was usually through the efforts of individual instructors, who focused their attention almost exclusively on the boys. For instance, the codified game of lacrosse that Beers had popularized in the late 1800s, and which had been stripped of its Indigenous heritage, was played at various schools throughout

Figure 4.1   Students at Brandon Indian Industrial School in Brandon, Manitoba, in 1935. This is a photograph of the boys' football team (front row), the girls' softball team (second row), and the winners of the national athletic meet (third row).

the country.[14] By the early 1900s, however, hockey emerged as the most popular form of activity among Indigenous boys at school, even though most schools lacked the necessary hockey equipment to engage in regular competitive play.[15]

Increased Emphasis on Sport

In the 1940s, several factors led Indian Affairs to pay more attention to sports in its broader plan for Indian assimilation. One factor was the passing of the National Physical Fitness Act in 1943, which was an attempt to spur the nation to greater health. This was followed by the creation of the federal Department of National Health and Welfare in 1945, which was responsible for improving the health of all Canadians, using physical fitness as a cornerstone for achieving that goal. Also in that same year, the new Department of National Health and Welfare was given responsibility for the Indian Health Services Directorate, with the result that physical fitness became a prominent talking point at Indian Affairs. Then, in 1946, James Allison Glen, the Minister of Mines and Resources, which, at the time, was responsible for Indian Affairs, invited Indian agents to comment "directly and confidentially" to him on how to defuse the growing tide of Indigenous activism that emerged after their contributions to the Second World War.[16] The top three recommendations that field agents put forward were for more education, the development of sports and sports clubs, especially in the residential and day schools, and increased contact with white people—in that order.[17] Such was the response from Gifford Swartman, Indian agent for the Sioux Lookout region: "Athletic and other forms of recreation should also be encouraged—this should be stressed more in the Schools than it has been, in order that young people could carry the ideas back to their respective reserves."[18] In saying that, Swartman echoed comments made by religious authorities in previous decades. His suggestion to focus on the youth in the schools was consistent with the thinking at Indian Affairs, where plans were being made to move residential school students into the provincial school system.

Soon afterward, between 1948 and 1950, responsibility for Indian Affairs was transferred to the Department of Citizenship and Immigration, which prepared people for settlement by teaching them the values and behaviours that were desired in Canadians. Thus, organized sports helped address the government's concern for physical fitness and health among the Indians, while simultaneously facilitating their assimilation into white society. Taking all these issues into consideration, in 1949, Indian Affairs created a new position within its branch—that of Supervisor of Physical Education and Recreation, marking the first formal involvement of the federal government in Indigenous sport development.

The 1951 revisions to the Indian Act, which had not been amended since it was first created in 1876, resulted in organized sports becoming a more pronounced feature in the residential schools. The revised act called for the dismantling of the residential school system and included provisions that authorized the Minister of Indian Affairs to enter into agreements with mainstream school boards and provincial governments to school Indigenous children.[19] It also stated that residential schools were to follow provincial curricula, which included programs of physical education and extracurricular involvement in sports.[20] Thus, while sports had always been part of the residential school system, initially offered on an ad hoc basis, by the 1950s, they were a planned, integral part of the broader plan for assimilation.

The Tom Longboat Awards

In 1950, Indian Affairs hired Major Jan Eisenhardt as the first Supervisor of Physical Education and Recreation. One of his principal duties included developing and implementing a comprehensive program of physical education and recreation for students in residential and day schools and for people living on reserves, conducting courses in physical education and recreation for field agents and teachers of Indian schools, and cooperating with provincial authorities in joint programs of physical education and recreation.[21]

Within the first few weeks on the job, Eisenhardt took on the responsibility of evaluating the condition of organized sports and physical activities for First Nations under Indian Affairs' authority. Between April and October 1950, Eisenhardt visited 32 residential schools, 21 day schools, and 12 reserves in Quebec, Ontario, Saskatchewan, Alberta, and British Columbia. He created an inventory of activities and facilities at each location and reported on the general health standards, hygiene, clothing, and sanitation in each school, emphasizing the remedial concerns that shaped Indian Affairs' intentions, which was a common concern in the public school system as well.[22]

His detailed plan also included a brief recommendation that Indian Affairs supply prizes and trophies to increase participation in physical education, sports, and games. The purpose was to entice First Nations participants to better themselves through sport participation and physical education programs. In his report, he referred briefly to the Tom Longboat Awards (one of the most prestigious sport awards for Indigenous athletes in Canada) and to the famed athlete they are named after:

> I feel that throughout the years that our children go to school we could conduct many self-testing activities of benefit to child growth and development which finally would culminate in certain tests and certificates and medals to be given to those who pass them before leaving school. Encouragement would then be given to continue these activities on the reserves and eventually we might arrive at recognition being given to outstanding Indian athletes. Possibly someday a Tom Longboat medal for outstanding runners might be created.[23]

Soon after submitting his report, Eisenhardt contacted Colonel George C. Machum, prominent Montreal businessman and influential member of the Amateur Athletic Union of Canada (AAUC), the body that regulated amateur sport throughout the country, to request his assistance in the development and implementation of the awards (see chapter 7). Machum agreed and worked with Eisenhardt over the next several months to bring the awards to fruition. The AAUC arranged for a corporate sponsor to pay for the Longboat trophy and the initial start-up. The arranged sponsor, the Dominion Bridge Company, was a construction company and a major employer of steelworkers from the Mohawk community of Kahnawá:ke, Quebec. With the company's support, the program was implemented immediately and without much financial assistance from the federal government.[24]

From the start, Eisenhardt made it clear that the awards were intended for residential school students who, in his estimation, were "the most promising athletes" among the Indigenous population.[25] His view aligned with wider beliefs about the residential school system being the ideal training ground for instilling Indigenous children and youth with an appreciation for dominant cultural practices. Machum and the AAUC fully supported the emphasis on youth, seeing them as a source of untapped physical potential and a group who could be taught to appreciate the middle-class virtues of competitive amateur sport. With the exception of a few individuals, the majority of award winners between 1951 and 1974 were children and youth in either residential or day schools or in integrated schools that offered opportunities for organized sports.

Reproducing Gender and Race Ideology in Amateur Sports

In establishing the parameters for the awards, the AAUC made it clear that only amateur athletes could participate in the program, a restriction that eliminated a number of successful Indigenous athletes who, because they competed for money or prizes, were deemed professional and therefore ineligible. The amateur

PROMINENT PEOPLE: TOM LONGBOAT (1887-1949)

Born in 1887, Tom Longboat (see figure 4.2) was an Onondaga runner from the Six Nations of the Grand River, located in southern Ontario. He competed in various distances in "foot racing" in the early 1900s, rocketing to fame after winning the Boston Marathon in 1907 in a record time of 2:24:24. He went on to compete in the 1908 Olympic Games in London, England, where he was favoured to win the marathon but, similar to other competitors, collapsed late in the race presumably because of heat stroke. From 1906 to 1912, during the height of his career as an athlete, he was one of the most well-known athletes in the world. After Longboat passed away in 1949, he was inducted posthumously into the Canadian Sports Hall of Fame (1955), the Canadian Olympic Hall of Fame (1960), the Canadian Indian Hall of Fame (1967),

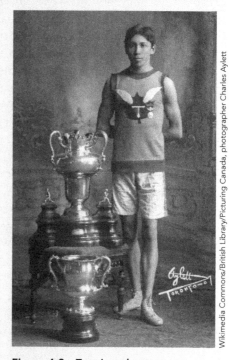

Figure 4.2   Tom Longboat.

and the Canadian Road Running Hall of Fame (1991). In 1999, *Maclean's* magazine named Longboat the top star of the 20th century,[26] and in 2000, Canada Post memorialized him by creating a commemorative stamp for its millennium collection. Few athletes have been remembered in so many ways.

rule was strictly enforced, as was demonstrated with the 1953 regional recipient for southern Ontario, Thomas Davey, a 19-year-old male athlete from the Six Nations Reserve.[27] When he was presented with his award at the annual sports day on the reserve he was also handed a cheque in the amount of $25 from the local band council. The matter caught the attention of the Superintendent of Indian Education, who promptly wrote to the Superintendent of the Six Nations Agency, informing him that Davey's amateur status was in jeopardy unless a detailed explanation as to the circumstances regarding the payment was given. The affair resulted in the Six Nations band council having to pass a resolution at a council meeting the following month stating the money was offered as a "scholarship" to Davey for his work at the Cadet Training School held in Banff, Alberta, earlier that year.

The two-tiered awards structure—at the provincial and territorial level and at the national level—revealed precisely who was selecting and celebrating Indigenous accomplishments.[28] At the provincial and territorial level, Indian agents, superintendents, local missionaries, and residential school staff were responsible for identifying the appropriate candidates. The regional directors for Indian Affairs were each directed to establish a selection committee to determine the most outstanding athlete in their area. By and large most committees were identical in terms of their representation, consisting primarily of Indian Affairs officials and leaders of the AAUC. The situation was different at the national level, where all the decision-making power rested with the Honors and Awards Committee of the AAUC, which generally met in private during their annual general assembly and then reported their results back to the main body. Not surprisingly, this chain of command excluded Indigenous involvement, ensuring that all the perspectives being forwarded from the regions and promoted at the top aligned with those of the three collaborating institutions: church, state, and sport. Soon after the awards were launched, Philip Phelan, Superintendent of Indian Education, wrote to Machum thanking him for his leadership and the contribution of the AAUC, emphasizing the importance of their combined agenda:

> As you know yourself the Canadian Indian is very interested in sports and games and has in many fields showed tremendous prowess, but the general participation of Indians in White men's competition is not as frequent as could be. The establishment of the Longboat Awards will bring to the fore Indians who probably would be able to compete on a par with the Whites.[29]

Here, ideas about integration were understood within a racialized context where "white" standards of achievement served as benchmarks for Indigenous accomplishments. This racial logic informed the awards' criteria, which were drawn heavily from the AAUC's approach to sporting excellence. Consequently, regional and national winners were evaluated on three areas that emphasized the ideals of white muscular Christianity: character, sportsmanship, and athletic achievement. Not surprisingly, gender was also a key issue. All male award winners, both regionally and nationally, displayed all three criteria. Meanwhile, female recipients need not be competitive athletes. In 1959, 19-year-old Donna Laura Pine from the Garden River Reserve was awarded the regional Longboat medal for northern Ontario for her dedication to the playground movement in the area. According to her nominator, she did not possess any athletic experience worth noting.[30]

Similar to their female contemporaries in mainstream sport, Indigenous women were playing and competing in an environment that celebrated and supported male athletic accomplishments.[31] When the Tom Longboat Awards program was launched in 1951 there were no formal stipulations against nominating females for either the regional or national award. Evidence from the annual reports of Indian Affairs and minutes of meetings of the AAUC show that female athletes were occasionally named as regional winners,[32] but only one woman, Phyllis Bomberry, was named as the national recipient in the first 17 years of the program.[33] Born in 1943, Phyllis was raised in Ohsweken, which is part of the Six Nations of the Grand River, where Tom Longboat was born and raised. She played many sports during her early years but excelled at softball. After moving to Toronto to complete her high school education, she was scouted by the Toronto Carpetland Senior A team, which won the senior Canadian Women's Softball Championship in 1967 and 1968. She won the national Tom Longboat Award for her outstanding contributions to these championship wins.

Though female athletes were not formally excluded from participating, the dominant model for sport that was being implemented on reserves and in residential schools, and on which the awards were organized, provided more opportunities for males than females. It was also based on gendered notions about which athletes were most deserving of public recognition and support: The category *athlete* meant *male athlete* to the nominators and selection committees. In this way, the awards reinforced dominant notions of gendered sport participation.

Moving Towards Indigenous Self-Determination

For nearly 25 years, from 1951 to 1972, the awards remained under the shared leadership of Indian Affairs and the AAUC. The dissolution of the AAUC in the early 1970s, combined with shifting priorities at Indian Affairs, resulted in the transfer of the awards to the Sports Federation of Canada (SFC), the new governing authority for sports in Canada, and the National Indian Brotherhood (NIB), the First Nations political body (now the Assembly of First Nations). Indian Affairs did not object to the transfer since it was looking to minimize its involvement in the awards anyway.

From 1973 to 1998, the NIB and SFC co-managed the awards, with the NIB directing activities regionally and the SFC managing activities nationally.[34] With NIB involvement, new political messages that called attention to Indigenous self-determination were layered onto the awards. Indigenous people had always used sport as a vehicle for social development, only now they were doing it openly and purposefully to address Canada's colonialism. Sport was one of the few socially acceptable areas where Indigenous people could gain widespread public attention for their accomplishments and still broadcast messages about who they were as people to mainstream audiences. The NIB was thus able to transmit a limited set of political messages to Indigenous people and Canadians by capitalizing on the symbolic power that the awards provided. To the NIB, the awards focused on and celebrated Indigenous cultural resurgence and pride, not assimilation. At the same time, however, the patterns that had been constructed during the first era of the awards were reinforced in the second, with the awards being a celebration of Indigenous male sporting excellence in the mainstream amateur sport system.

When the federal government shifted its priorities to high-performance sport in the early 1980s, it removed itself from Indigenous sport and dropped responsibility for the awards, leaving the NIB, which soon transitioned into the Assembly of First Nations (AFN), to assume full responsibility for the program. The AFN reshaped the awards by adding an educational component to the eligibility criteria and integrating them to the newly established Heroes of Our Time program. This change enhanced their goal of Indigenous self-determination by formally linking sport to educational attainment, but it also minimized the profile of the awards by incorporating them into a suite of other awards.

When the Aboriginal Sport Circle (ASC) was established in 1995, one of its first objectives was to seek responsibility for the awards and heighten their visibility within the Canadian sport system.[35] From 1999 onwards, the ASC set about transforming several long-standing traditions of the awards in order to meet the new political realities as determined by the Indigenous sport leaders. The emergence of a political awareness about Indigenous people led the ASC to adopt a wider definition of Indigeneity that was inclusive of the First Nations, Métis, and Inuit. No longer were the awards confined only to Indians as defined by the Indian Act. Contemporary politics surrounding issues of female representation in sport also shaped the structure of the awards with the establishment of a category for female athletes. Moreover, under ASC control, the awards became firmly rooted in the competitive sports model such that the criteria guiding the selection process focused on performance outcomes as the principal markers of success. This shift was most prominently expressed by a scoring grid that placed the highest value on podium finishes as well as participation in major mainstream international competitions. Finally, in seeking to elevate the profile of the awards and the accomplishments of Indigenous athletes in the mainstream sport system, the ASC made the considered decision to seek inclusion in the Canadian Sport Awards even though the Tom Longboat Awards were repeatedly positioned as adjunct to the mainstream awards program. The ASC's efforts speak to a determination to carve out a meaningful niche for Indigenous athletes in Canadian amateur sport, and to the challenges that Indigenous people continue to face in seeking inclusion in the dominant system.

The North American Indigenous Games

In the decades after the Second World War, Indigenous people in Canada and the United States began to be more assertive about changing the conditions under which they lived. A growing wave of organized activism swept across the continent as Indigenous people returned home only to be treated as second-class citizens. Everything from more control over education and child welfare, to suitable housing and drinking water, to the status of women under the Indian Act, as well as individual and community health issues, was in dire need of attention. Centuries of living under colonial rule needed to be addressed.

The 1960s saw the NIB emerge as the national political Indigenous organization pushing these issues forward in Canada, as well as international forums, such as the United Nations. From the outset, the NIB saw sport as an important mechanism that fed into their broader political aspirations because of the visibility it provided, especially having athletes compete on the national and international stage. As demonstrated with its involvement in the Tom Longboat Awards, the NIB also saw value in sport as a real and symbolic vehicle to foster individual and community pride and for broadcasting messages about Indigenous strength and unity to other Indigenous people as well as to the state.[36] Sport provided regularly occurring opportunities to support the development of a pan-Indigenous presence in Canada.

Indigenous interests in sport also dovetailed nicely with the government's growing concern about the fitness level of Canadians. In 1961, the federal government passed the Fitness and Amateur Sport Act, which provided the impetus for direct government involvement in sport and physical activity development. Soon after, the Canada Games were established in 1967, followed by the Arctic Winter Games in 1969 (see chapter 3). The federal government had clearly recognized sport as a way to build a healthier nation, as well as an important nation-building tool, and began investing significant dollars in competitive sports development, including the hosting of multi-sport events and major games.[37]

Indigenous Aspirations for Sport

One such program was the Native Sport and Recreation Program. Funded by the federal government through the national sport governing body, Fitness and Amateur Sport, the Native Sport and Recreation Program operated from 1972 to 1981.[38] It was as a five-year experimental project with the aim of increasing sport and recreation opportunities for First Nations people on reserves, and was administered by First Nations people. During this era, Indigenous sport leaders developed regional organizations that coordinated and promoted sporting activities and events on and between reserves and hosted provincial championships and multi-sport events. In doing so, they had successfully created a sport system by Indigenous people for Indigenous people—apart from the mainstream—which ran counter to underlying federal assumptions about funding for Indigenous sport.

Government officials had assumed the First Nations leaders preferred the mainstream sport system and would thus want to have their programs feed into it rather than developing a parallel Indigenous system. In other words, federal officials believed Indigenous people would naturally want to assimilate into the dominant (mainstream) sport system and were taken aback at the thought that Indigenous people had their own ideas about what Indigenous sport should look like. At one point, government leaders insisted that the First Nations leaders amalgamate their programs with those of the broader system funded by Fitness and Amateur Sport—and threatened to withdraw funding if they did not do so—but the First Nations leaders held firm.[39] By the late 1970s, when the government shifted its focus from encouraging participation to elite-level competitive development, Fitness and Amateur Sport began withdrawing its funding for the Native Sport and Recreation Program, arguing that the Indigenous sport programs would not produce elite-level athletes, when in fact, a close look at the list of Tom Longboat Awards recipients would have shown otherwise. By 1981, the funding had stopped altogether, and the activities that were fostered during the lifespan of the program ceased to exist because of lack of resource support.[40]

First Nations leaders responded by taking a different route to achieve their vision for sport. In the early 1980s, three leaders from Alberta—J. Wilton Little-child, Charles Wood, and John Fletcher—began developing the concept for the North American Indigenous Games (NAIG).[41] The purpose was to counteract discrimination within the Canadian sport system by providing an all-Indigenous space for athletes to develop and excel without having to put up with overt forms of discrimination, especially stereotyping and racism, or constantly having to battle institutionalized inequality, such as the lack of resource support for Indigenous visions for sport as demonstrated by the government's response to the Native Sport and Recreation Program. Indigenous leaders had learned that no matter what, their vision for sport would not be achieved by working within traditional government structures, even though they might at times connect to the opportunities it provided.[42]

With the demise of the Native Sport and Recreation Program, First Nations leaders throughout the country also became increasingly concerned about their youth, who had few positive avenues through which to channel their energies and to identify as Indigenous people. Indigenous leaders viewed the re-establishment of the Indigenous sport system as vital for youth development. In 1985, Littlechild wrote a letter to the Chiefs of Alberta, the regional political body representing First Nations interests in Alberta, requesting their support for the development of the NAIG:

> A non-Indian community has a structure and system to assist and support its youth's talent. From this experience, one cannot relate to the hardships of young Native athletes who show so much promise but never have the opportunity to fulfill their potential. Whether this is the fault of the Native communities or the selecting committees is not what we are trying to determine, but rather to develop a method whereby young native athletes' skills can be developed and create an awareness within the non-Indian community of the emergence of the native athlete.[43]

The NAIG, as a central component of the nascent Indigenous sport system, was thus a vehicle through which to address such concerns. In this way, the origins of the NAIG are rooted in clear social and political goals, not merely sporting outcomes.

Littlechild, Wood, and Fletcher began organizing the first NAIG in 1988. The event, to be hosted in Edmonton, Alberta, in the summer of 1990, would feature 17 sporting events in addition to a program of cultural activities that showcased the diversity of Indigenous cultures throughout Canada and the United States. Funding would soon become a major stumbling block. In 1989, the three Alberta sport leaders pitched the idea of the NAIG to leaders in the federal and provincial government in a proposal called "The Spirit—Strong, Brave, True." The title of the proposal would become the motto for the first NAIG, and it remains so today. For instance, at the 2017 NAIG in Toronto, Ontario, that motto was featured on one of side of the gold, silver, and bronze medals, while the host logo was featured on the other side.

Although federal and provincial government leaders had initially stated their commitment to financially support the first NAIG, there was little action on their part so that by the time the Games were scheduled to open, the organizers were desperate. How could they host a major sport and cultural festival if they could not even pay for the venues? On June 12, 1990, two weeks prior to the start of the Games, Littlechild, who was by then a member of Parliament, used his political position to enhance the profile of the NAIG in government in an attempt to secure funding. He spoke about the concept and the purpose the Games, including their mission: "To improve the quality of life for Indigenous peoples by supporting self-determined sports and cultural activities which encourage equal access to participation in the social and cultural fabric of the community they reside in and which respects Indigenous distinctiveness." In the end, the federal government did not financially support the first Games, forcing the organizing committee to explore other sources of funding. A last-minute financial boost from the City of Edmonton, as well as donations from several Indigenous groups, provided the organizing committee with the money it desperately needed to host the NAIG.[44]

When the Games opened on July 30, 1990, approximately 1,000 last-minute registrants overwhelmed the organizers, who had been prepared to serve the 1,500 athletes who had preregistered for the events. From an operations standpoint, it must have been chaotic trying to accommodate this kind of influx only hours before the events were to start. But from a policy standpoint, the influx signalled to the NAIG leaders that there was something special about the Games. People had come from near and far to participate in spite of the social and economic conditions they faced. In a sense, the NAIG were fulfilling their mission by the first Games and continues to do so; the mission statement that Littlechild brought to the federal government in June 1990 remains the guiding vision for the Games today.

The Struggle for Meaningful Inclusion

Government support for the NAIG remained a key issue for many years afterwards and this affected when and where the Games could be held, as well as how they were to be funded. Though originally planned on a two-year cycle, with Canada and the United States alternating as host countries, the Games have more often been hosted in Canada because of greater government support for sport and a centralized system that makes it easier to coordinate activities with government. Even with Canada being potentially a more financially stable place to host, the lack of federal support for the second NAIG, planned for Prince Albert, Saskatchewan, forced organizers to move the event from 1992 to 1993. When federal support was finally forthcoming, the Department of Indian Affairs and Northern Development (DIAND), through its medical services branch, contributed $200,000 CDN to help organize the 1993 event. By relegating federal responsibility for the NAIG to DIAND, and not Sport Canada (formerly Fitness and Amateur Sport), the government had signalled its perception that the NAIG did not fit the government's criteria for sport.[45]

Through the years the total number of athletes who competed at the Games, as well as the events held, has varied greatly depending on the host, with fewer athletes competing at the NAIG when they are hosted in Canada because of a more formal organizational structure. A number of key developments thus mark the NAIG's history from a struggling fringe event to a major multi-sport and cultural festival recognized and funded by the Canadian federal, provincial or territorial, and local governments. Some of these developments include the establishment of the NAIG Council in 1993. Its responsibility is to oversee the direction and management of the NAIG. The council consists of 26 mandated representatives, 13 from Canada and 13 from the United States (see table 4.1). Similar to other major multi-sport competitions, athletes at the NAIG represent their province, territory, or state, although some Indigenous peoples, like the Mohawks of Kahnawá:ke, Quebec, have competed at the NAIG as a distinct Indigenous nation.

With the establishment of the national ASC in 1995, the NAIG were led by a new generation of Indigenous sport leaders. Alwyn Morris, the ASC's founder and first president, was a gold and bronze medallist in canoe-kayak at the 1984 Olympic Games in Los Angeles, California, and three-time Tom Longboat Award recipient (1974 regional recipient for Quebec; 1972 and 1984 national recipient). Morris reached out to Rick Brant, a former elite Indigenous athlete who competed internationally in track and field and a fellow Tom Longboat Award recipient (1987 national recipient), to lead the organization as its executive director. Among the first items on the ASC's agenda was to secure ongoing federal financial support for the NAIG.

As the franchise holder for the NAIG, and the custodians of the Games when they are held in Canada, the ASC successfully helped secure government support for the Games. In 1999, the federal, provincial, and territorial ministers responsible for sport, physical activity, and recreation (FPT SPAR) agreed to work with the ASC in three priority areas, including the development of the NAIG. In 2003, the FPT SPAR ministers agreed to support the hosting component of the NAIG when they are held in Canada.[46] This meant there would be ongoing financial support for operational items, such as venues and equipment rental. Funding for team travel and preparation took longer to negotiate, but in 2009, the FPT SPAR ministers agreed to provide up to $1 million CDN for these costs whether the Games were held in Canada or the United States. While $1 million does not go very far when spread across 13 regions, and in light of the fact that many Indigenous people live in rural and remote areas, the agreement was nevertheless a success.[47] Clearly, work remains ongoing as the political landscape for Indigenous people keeps changing in Canada. For instance, in

Table 4.1   North American Indigenous Games (NAIG) Council, Regional Membership

Canada	United States
Region 1 Indigenous Sport, Physical Activity and Recreation (British Columbia)	**Region 1** Alaska, Hawaii, Washington
Region 2 Indigenous Sport Council (Alberta)	**Region 2** California, Idaho, Nevada, Oregon
Region 3 Federation of Sovereign Indigenous Nations (Saskatchewan), Métis Nation of Saskatchewan	**Region 3** Arizona, Colorado, New Mexico, Utah
Region 4 Manitoba Aboriginal Sports and Recreation Council	**Region 4** Montana, North Dakota, Wyoming
Region 5 Indigenous Sport and Wellness Ontario	**Region 5** Kansas, Nebraska, South Dakota
Region 6 First Nations of Quebec and Labrador Health and Social Services Commission; Eastern Door and the North	**Region 6** Illinois, Iowa, Missouri, Minnesota
Region 7 Aboriginal Sport and Recreation New Brunswick	**Region 7** Arkansas, Louisiana, Oklahoma, Texas
Region 8 Mi'kmaq Sport Council of Nova Scotia	**Region 8** Indiana, Michigan, Ohio, Wisconsin
Region 9 PEI Aboriginal Sport Circle (Prince Edward Island)	**Region 9** Connecticut, New Hampshire, Massachusetts, Maine, Vermont, Rhode Island
Region 10 Aboriginal Sport and Recreation Circle of Newfoundland and Labrador	**Region 10** New Jersey, New York, Pennsylvania,
Region 11 Yukon Aboriginal Sport Circle	**Region 11** Delaware, Maryland, Virginia, Washington DC, West Virginia
Region 12 Aboriginal Sport Circle of the Northwest Territories	**Region 12** Georgia, Florida, North Carolina, South Carolina
Region 13 Sport and Recreation, Government of Nunavut	**Region 13** Alabama, Kentucky, Mississippi, Tennessee

June 2016, the FPT SPAR deputy ministers expressed support for a new hosting model for the NAIG in Canada, such that the NAIG would be hosted in 2020 and every four years thereafter in Canada. The NAIG Council and ASC agreed to this new model in 2016.

PROMINENT PEOPLE: ALWYN MORRIS (1957-PRESENT)

Alwyn Morris, a Mohawk from Kahnawá:ke, Quebec, has dedicated his life to creating visibility and space for Indigenous athletes to thrive in Canada. As an athlete, he represented Canada at the international level in the sport of canoe-kayak and is most widely known for winning a gold and bronze medal at the 1984 Olympic Games in Los Angeles, where he became a worldwide figure after raising an eagle feather at the podium (see figure 4.3). This act of reverence in honour of his grandfather has become an iconic image representing pride in one's culture and identity. Since then, Alwyn has become one of the

Canada's Sports Hall of Fame - Pantheon des sports canadiens
SPORTSHALL.CA - PANTHEONSPORTS.CA
Object ID: 2006.801.1.1

Figure 4.3   Hugh Fisher, left, and his partner, Alwyn Morris, right.

most influential people in the Canadian sport system, founding the ASC. He has received numerous awards of distinction including the Queen's Golden Jubilee Medal in 2002 and the Order of Canada in 1985, and he was inducted as an Honoured Member in Canada's Sports Hall of Fame in 2000. He also founded the Alwyn Morris Educational and Athletic Foundation, which, for many years, supported sport and educational opportunities for Indigenous youth in Canada.

Conclusion

In June 2008, a Truth and Reconciliation Commission (TRC) was launched with the purpose of investigating the history of the Indian residential school system in Canada. More than 6,000 people, mostly former students, testified at gatherings held throughout the country and their stories formed the basis for the suite of reports that the TRC published in 2015, completing the organization's mandate.[48]

Altogether, the nine reports totaled more than 4,000 pages of text and images that told of how the Canadian state, in collaboration with religious institutions, attempted to eradicate Indigenous ways of life throughout the country, not only through the institution of schooling but through other social institutions as well, from health to justice to economics. In other words, the history of the Indian residential school system in Canada is best understood in the broader context that gave rise to it, the type of thinking and practices that sustained it, and the politics that eventually led to its dissolution. Therefore, context is crucial.

Even the fact that a TRC was triggered for Canada is important. With the launch of the TRC, "Canada became the first G8 nation and long-standing liberal democracy to initiate such a forum," placing a "self-proclaimed liberal democratic nation" in the same political category as "apartheid in South Africa, civil war in El Salvador, and military dictatorship in Chile."[49] By agreeing to engage in a TRC, Canada had thus conceded its attempt at Indigenous cultural genocide, placing itself alongside nations that the state had previously condemned for atrocities that had been committed elsewhere.

In light of its findings, the TRC, in its 527-page executive summary, left readers to address one important question: "Now that we know about residential schools and their legacies, what do we do about it?"[50] Canadians were thus challenged to think through the problems that led to the development and maintenance of a school system that was predicated on the erasure of Indigenous ways of life.

In countries with a colonial history such as Canada, sports have been used widely in the project of Indigenous assimilation. Colonial officials, including government officials, religious authorities, and leaders of amateur sport organizations, were not unaware of the power of sports to change lives. Nor were Indigenous people unaware of these efforts; they often resisted these colonizing attempts or adapted the activities to meet their own needs and aspirations—albeit always in limited ways because they did not control the rules and resources for sports. To return briefly to the start of the chapter, this is also why Indigenous sport histories do not align easily with empowerment ideologies so common today. Histories of Indigenous sport, and by extension Canadian sport, privilege settler ways of understanding and engaging in sports, and Indigenous people continue to struggle to find ways to engage in these activities.

DISCUSSION QUESTIONS

1. The word *colonization* is widely used in the scholarly literature, in government reports, in media, and in everyday life, but what does it mean?

2. Concepts are useful only if you know how to apply them. For instance, how do you know when something is being colonized? Provide some examples from sport.

3. How has sport been used as a tool for Indigenous colonization in Canada?

4. Consider how the Indigenous sport leaders valued (and continue to value) the Tom Longboat Awards and the North American Indigenous Games as vehicles for social and political development. How does this view align with or challenge your view of sport?

5. How can researchers do a better job of incorporating Indigenous histories into the written record of sport in Canada?

SUGGESTED READINGS

Forsyth, Janice. "The Indian Act and the (Re)Shaping of Aboriginal Sport Practices," *International Journal of Canadian Studies* 35 (2007), 95-111.

Miller, J.R. *Shingwauk's Vision: A History of Native Residential Schools.* Toronto: University of Toronto Press, 1996.

Paraschak, Vicky. "'Reasonable Amusements': Connecting the Strands of Physical Culture in Native Lives," *Sport History Review*, 29 (1998): 121-131.

Pettipas, Katherine. *Severing the Ties That Bind: Government Repression of Indigenous Religious Ceremonies on the Prairies.* Winnipeg: University of Manitoba Press, 1994.

Woolford, Andrew. *This Benevolent Experiment: Indigenous Boarding Schools, Genocide, and Redress in Canada and the United States.* Winnipeg: University of Manitoba Press, 2015.

CHAPTER 5

COLONIAL ENCOUNTERS, CONSERVATION, AND SPORT HUNTING IN BANFF NATIONAL PARK

Courtney W. Mason, PhD
Thompson Rivers University

LEARNING OBJECTIVES

In this chapter you will

- critically assess the early histories of national park development in Western Canada;
- identify the factors that positioned Indigenous subsistence practices of hunting, fishing, and gathering as intolerable, and eventually illegal, in the park's system;
- examine how conceptions of race and emerging ideas of conservation determined who had access to the park and the recreational opportunities they could engage in;
- understand how park policies were connected to larger colonial processes of cultural assimilation.

Banff National Park is Canada's first and most iconic protected area. It is a place that is celebrated nationally, and it forms a significant part of the Canadian identity. Internationally, promotional materials on the park have shaped tourists' perceptions of the nation for generations. Banff is a place that is protected for the enjoyment of all Canadians, and it also has a history as a recreation paradise. Skiers, hikers, mountaineers, and paddlers have been attracted to the Canadian Rocky Mountains for well over a century. Sport hunting was also an important recreational activity that brought thousands of tourists to the region throughout the first few decades of the 20th century.

Prior to these developments in Banff, the valley was a key gathering place for diverse groups of Indigenous peoples. For centuries, the Nakoda, and other groups of Indigenous communities, lived throughout the Banff–Bow Valley in what would become the western Canadian province of Alberta. For example, the Banff–Bow Valley and the Bow River, called Mînî Thnî Wapta (Cold Water River), have been the traditional spiritual centre of the Nakoda peoples since time immemorial.[1] As the giver of life, the valley provides traditional foods, medicinal plants, shelter, and animals to hunt, as well as sacred areas and vision quest sites for Nakoda peoples. The river forms the centre of Nakoda culture, economies, family, and ways of living off the land.[2] Beginning with the arrival of Europeans to the valley in the late 18th century, Indigenous peoples were forced to undergo a series of significant changes that would alter aspects of a well-established way of life that had persisted for millennia.[3]

The formation of Canada's first national park had significant consequences for local Indigenous communities.[4] Through the creation of the park, new ideas around the conservation of wildlife emerged. These ideas of conservation were central to the new parks system and the restrictions placed on Indigenous communities that repressed their cultures. As the park was redefined as a protected space, new regulations targeted Nakoda hunting and subsistence practices. Competing ideas of conservation and what constituted wilderness informed further government policies designed to assimilate the cultures of Nakoda peoples, which extended the impacts of the 1877 Treaty 7 agreement.[5] Because of the perceived threat of their hunting to local wildlife, Nakoda communities were displaced from their traditional territories when the park was formed, and for decades they were continually denied access to the region. During this period when Nakoda peoples encountered serious constraints to hunt, fish, and gather, sport hunting by Euro-Canadians and tourists alike was actively encouraged inside park boundaries because of the popularity of these recreational activities and their importance to bourgeoning tourism economies.

Despite these regulations, the Nakoda refused to accept some colonial policies and continued to access the park for cultural or spiritual purposes, as well as to hunt, fish, and gather. Nakoda leaders also sought out opportunities for their people to engage in Banff's developing tourism industries, and some community members found work as hunting, fishing, and mountaineering guides. Informed by primary evidence, including oral histories of the region, this chapter focuses on the formation of Banff National Park and the development of protected areas policies. We examine how these policies shaped regional recreational practices and the consequent impacts on local Indigenous communities. More specifically, we discuss the roles of Nakoda peoples in local tourism economies, why they were displaced from Banff, and how they eventually returned to sacred spaces inside park boundaries.

Histories of Indigenous Peoples in the Banff–Bow Valley

The Banff–Bow Valley includes the area between the headwaters of the Bow River at Bow Lake and the Kananaskis River, which is south of the current boundary of Banff National Park and at the western border of the Nakoda Reserve at Morley (see figure 5.1). Diverse groups of Indigenous peoples lived in

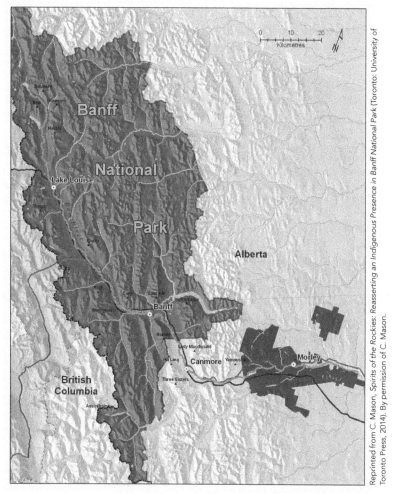

Reprinted from C. Mason, *Spirits of the Rockies: Reasserting an Indigenous Presence in Banff National Park* (Toronto: University of Toronto Press, 2014). By permission of C. Mason.

Figure 5.1 The upper section of the Banff–Bow Valley, with current boundaries of Banff National Park and the Nakoda Reserve at Morley.

and migrated through what is now considered the Banff–Bow Valley. Evidence collected from archaeological research indicates that Indigenous peoples used this landscape for millennia before any European presence. Archaeological studies reveal evidence of semi-permanent settlements dating as far back as 11,000 years.[6] The Nakoda (Stoney), Ktunaxa (Kootenay), Tsuu T'ina (Sarcee), Piikani (Peigan), Siksika (Blackfoot), Kainai (Blood), Secwépemc (Shuswap), and members of the Cree Nations lived, fished, hunted, gathered, and traded throughout the eastern slopes of the Canadian Rockies for many centuries before the arrival of the first Europeans.[7] Just before the turn of the 18th century, as a consequence of the massive fur-trading networks that were formed in Western Canada, members of other Indigenous groups, including the Iroquois, Nipissing, and Saulteaux, and the Métis from the Great Lakes, St. Lawrence River districts, and prairies, also began to live and work in the region. Although the valley has been of importance to diverse groups of Indigenous peoples, the region is of particular significance to the Nakoda peoples who inhabited the foothills and mountain ranges for several centuries and currently have reserve lands near both the northern and southern sections of the valley. Not only has this land been vital to Nakoda peoples for their subsistence land uses but also has been for their spiritual and cultural practices anchored in these landscapes.[8]

Oral accounts from members of Nakoda First Nations reinforce the idea that Nakoda peoples have been living in the valley for a significant period. Nakoda Elder Roland Rollinmud explains, "We have been living here on this very land . . . from the beginning of time."[9] Elder Lenny Poucette provided a bit more detail on their presence in the valley:

> While at times my people did not permanently reside in this area, as for centuries we followed the buffalo herds throughout the plains of North America . . . in years of drought or when we had troubles finding the herds we would rely on food sources closer to the mountains . . . you know like the bighorn, elk and goats.[10]

WORKING WITH PRIMARY SOURCES: ORAL HISTORY INTERVIEWS

Oral accounts complement archival evidence by introducing first-hand perspectives that in some cases are completely absent from documents and cannot be obtained through any archive. Unstructured oral history interviews give the researcher a broader knowledge base for an individual's life, rather than just the interviewee's specific perspective on a certain topic. Interviews were conducted with individuals who were identified by the communities as having extensive knowledge of regional history. My multiple interviews with Roland Rollinmud were transformative for this area of research. Roland is a respected Nakoda Elder, leader, and artist. His perspectives of the impacts on Nakoda communities of being displaced from the newly formed parklands were instrumental to my understandings of local Nakoda history.

Because the bison herds were severely threatened by the late 1870s, Nakoda peoples began to rely more heavily on mountain ecosystems for their main forms of subsistence. This partly explains why they adapted so well to mountain ecosystems after the bison no longer provided their principal source of food. Their transition to hunting and gathering in the mountains was successful because of their previous experiences of seasonal or periodic reliance on this region for subsistence. Compared with many of the Plains peoples who were forced to make drastic changes to their hunting practices after the collapse of the bison herds, as skilled hunters and gatherers Nakoda peoples adapted well to alternative resources.[11] They developed a hybrid lifestyle based on hunting bison in the plains as well as alpine and subalpine hunting, fishing, and gathering.

The Arrival of Europeans to Banff

The arrival of Europeans in the region through the fur trade in the late 18th century created new rivalries between Indigenous groups over control of fur markets. This facilitated a shift in balances of power between communities as conflict rapidly extended the territories of some groups while displacing others. As historian E.J. Hart notes, "the period of first white contact was one of jealousy, rivalry and sometimes open hostility at the mountains' foot."[12] This shift of power accounts for the successful transition of the Nakoda to the Banff–Bow Valley. Although the Cree encroaching from the north and the Piikani from the south had already encouraged the Ktunaxa to spend more time over the continental divide on the western slopes of the Rockies before the presence of Europeans, disputes sparked by the fur trade ensured more conflict in the area.[13] Also, a consequence of the European explorers and fur traders heading west, the smallpox epidemic ravaged the plains and eventually reached the mountains by the late 18th century. This affected all groups, but especially the Piikani, and they subsequently were not able to assert their presence in the region. These shifts of influence allowed the Nakoda to actively inhabit the Banff–Bow Valley and adjacent regions.[14]

In addition to these factors, the Nakoda also made alliances with neighbouring groups, including the Cree who occupied land north of the Banff–Bow Valley. Nakoda Elder Poucette's explanation of this process is related to his peoples' knowledge in producing medicines from plants and animals found in the mountains. At times Nakoda peoples shared some aspects of this knowledge with local groups and often made alliances through these processes.[15] Despite the European presence in the mountains that altered the well-established trade networks supporting extensive networks of Indigenous peoples, Nakoda communities continued to successfully live and work on the eastern slopes of the Rocky Mountains and in the Banff–Bow Valley by assuming numerous adaptive strategies. In the last quarter of the 19th century, however, Nakoda peoples began to face additional threats to their ways of life.

Indigenous Uses of the Hot Springs

Before expanding on the early history of the Banff Hot Springs Reserve, which emerged through the federal government's efforts to secure lands surrounding a series of hot springs near the current location of the Banff townsite, it is critical to recognize that for many centuries these unique geologic formations held significance to local Indigenous communities. Some early histories represent the late 19th-century discovery of the Cave and Basin mineral hot springs by railway workers in a manner that attempts to erase the Indigenous presence in the Banff–Bow Valley by failing to acknowledge their extensive use of the region. While recognizing the presence of Indigenous peoples in the Banff–Bow Valley, some historians have claimed it was only Europeans who understood the value of the hot springs. For example, popular historian and park employee Mabel B. Williams wrote: "It is probable that the Indians had known of the existence of the springs for years, but as usual they ascribed their peculiar behaviour, as they did everything they could not understand, to evil spirits, and regarded the spot as a place that was wise to avoid."[16] In discussing Williams' histories of the parks and her failure to acknowledge the previous and current presences of Indigenous groups, historian Alan MacEachern notes that she must have considered how her histories of presence or absence in the parks were incredibly convenient, as "erasing the native presence in the parks allowed her to start the parks' history with European exploration and the fur trade, better positioning the parks in the broader history of Canadian nation-building and so defining them more easily as part of our national birthright."[17]

To recognize the presence of Indigenous peoples in the region and respect their experiences, it is critical to consult local perspectives of their communities' historical uses of the hot springs.[18] In direct contradiction to what some Euro-Canadian authors contend, in addition to other Indigenous groups who at times have migrated through or lived in the Banff–Bow Valley, Nakoda peoples had significant cultural practices related to their multiple uses of the hot springs. In 1954, Nakoda Chief Tatanga Mani (Walking Buffalo), or George McLean, elaborated on the importance of the hot springs to local Nakoda peoples and how it was believed a great spirit lived in the waters:

> They would bathe in the springs because of the medicine in them. Then they would drop something in the water as a sacrifice, as a thank you to the spirits for the use of their water. . . . But since the white people came, the strength has gone out of the water. That mysterious power that comes from the spirits is there no more. Probably the white peoples do not pray to get well. In the old days, the Indians used to pray to the spirits to cure them of their sickness. Then they were healed by the mysterious strength of the waters.[19]

Other oral accounts suggest that the hot springs were sacred sites for Nakoda peoples. Elder Poucette indicated that, as a result of the unique microclimate produced by the warm waters, the lands surrounding the springs were vital locations for gathering herbal medicines.[20] Nakoda Elder Margaret Snow stated that her grandparents told her of the important cultural significance of the hot springs for their communities. Marriage and initiation ceremonies, which celebrated young men and women reaching adulthood, were held at sites near the Cave and Basin mineral hot springs.[21] Nakoda Elder Rollinmud also spoke of these sacred ceremonies:

> Yeah, the Cave and Basin was a place for baptisms that we would do. So the youth and the younger generations were blessed there. . . . Everybody was, but the young generations were blessed there to become an adult. . . . It was about getting as much knowledge for the journey of life and knowledge to understand the earth.[22]

Based on oral accounts, it is clear that the hot springs were important cultural sites for Nakoda communities. In addition to the significance of the area for its healing potential, medicines, and cultural ceremonies, the springs represented a key meeting location where Nakoda peoples, and sometimes other Indigenous groups, would gather at certain points throughout their seasonal migrations.[23] Nakoda perspectives of their histories provide understandings of why the creation of the park and the subsequent limitations on access to the region had implications that extended far beyond just constraining their hunting practices in the valley.

Euro-Canadian Claims and the Establishment of the Banff Hot Springs Reserve

Early Europeans in the region also visited the hot springs, including geologist James Hector in 1859, prospector Joe Healy in 1874, and the McDougall missionaries who established a mission site at Morley in 1875, but it was not until three railway workers reported a series of hot springs in the fall of 1883 that the federal government took notice.[24] Recognizing the potential of the springs and the surrounding landscape, Frank McCabe, William McCardell, and Tom McCardell immediately made efforts to secure ownership of the hot springs and proximal lands by developing them as a homestead and a mineral claim. In 1885, following a dispute between several parties that lasted over a year, the federal government settled the conflicting claims by creating a 26-square-kilometre (10 square mile) reserve surrounding the Cave and Basin mineral hot springs.[25] Direct parallels can be drawn between the foundation of national parks in the United States, as Spence reveals about the 1872 foundation of Yellowstone: "The creation of the first national park had less to do with ideas about undisturbed nature than a desire to keep the region's scenic wonders out of the hands of private interests."[26] Based on two earlier American examples, the Hot Springs Reservation in Arkansas (1832) and Yellowstone National Park (1872), the Banff Hot Springs Reserve was part of the Canadian government's first initiative to establish federal protected areas. Just two years later, on June 23, 1887, the area was expanded to 673 square kilometres (260 square miles), and Rocky Mountains Park, Canada's first national park, was formed. The expansion of the park would soon have detrimental consequences for local Nakoda communities.

The Pass System and Rocky Mountains Park

In 1885, the same year the Banff Hot Springs Reserve was created, the pass system was introduced throughout Canada to monitor and restrict the migrations of Indigenous peoples. This was a system whereby Indigenous peoples, mostly living on reserves, had to apply to a local government official (Indian agent), or in some cases a missionary, in order to receive a pass to leave the reserve. This required Indigenous peoples to seek permission to leave their reserve to hunt or for any other purpose. A pass was then either granted or denied based on the subjective decision of the local official. People were threatened with fines or even incarceration if they were found off the reserve without the proper documentation, and this had severe impacts on local hunting practices.

Initially, the pass system was not strictly policed in Morley, so many Nakoda groups ignored it and continued their seasonal hunting in the mountains. By 1889, restrictions were tightened through a number of methods and it became progressively more complicated for community members to leave the reserve for lengthy periods.[27] However, budget cuts that decreased the amount of government food rations, along with low production from reserve lands from either agricultural or ranching endeavours, gave Nakoda communities few options but to rely on hunting, fishing, and gathering. In the face of worsening conditions, decades after the signing of Treaty 7, some Nakoda peoples successfully continued their subsistence practices in the mountains. At times these practices took individuals and groups considerable distances away from the reserve.

The pass system and the requirement for Indigenous communities to remain on the reserve to collect their food rations allowed government agents and missionaries to pursue their assimilation strategies with a new level of intensity. Although severe cuts were made to the rations that were promised to communities in the treaty, there was a healthy budget committed to the promotion of the "civilizing" mission.[28] Missionaries had been performing services at the church and teaching classes at the school they built with community support since 1875, yet local participation in these institutions was not very high. By the late 1880s, with more Nakoda peoples forced to remain on reserve lands because of the strict pass system and their need for rations, the Indian agents eagerly encouraged local church and school attendance. By 1894, many community members were attending church services, and despite objections from Nakoda leaders, residential school attendance was made mandatory by the government.[29] Restricting the movements of Indigenous peoples, and the undermining and transforming of their cultures, was a critical strategy of colonialism.

In Nakoda communities, this was the beginning of a period where movements from their reserve were increasingly constrained. Although the pass system initially was not strongly imposed at the Nakoda Reserve at Morley, a significant factor motivating the enforcement of these restrictions in years to come was the formation of Rocky Mountains Park. The Rocky Mountains Park Act specified that the forceful exclusion and removal of trespassers who did

TRANSFORMATIVE MOMENTS: ROCKY MOUNTAINS PARK ACT, JUNE 23, 1887 (*STATUTES OF CANADA, 50-51 VICTORIA, CHAPTER 32*)

The Rocky Mountains Park Act specified that the forceful exclusion and removal of trespassers who did not adhere to the new park regulations were critical to the early development of the park. While the act also had important conservation principles to protect wildlife and preserve the region for the benefit of civil society, the majority of evidence suggests that even though the federal government did claim they were securing land to be used as a public park for the benefit of the people of Canada, they were initially motivated by natural resource and tourism development opportunities. As long as they did not impair the usefulness of the park for the purposes of public enjoyment and recreation, these developments were encouraged and at times facilitated by the government. In 1928, a survey of Rocky Mountains Park recommended that the Kananaskis and Spray Lakes watersheds be removed from the park and secured for the province of Alberta to develop hydroelectric power as well as coal and timber extraction facilities.

not adhere to the new park regulations were critical to the early development of the park.[30] Indigenous hunting became a source of conflict between park managers and local Nakoda communities.[31] At the time of the creation of the park, the majority of Nakoda peoples continued their subsistence land uses in the mountains, as they considered them their right affirmed by the Treaty 7 agreement. Nakoda Elder Lazarus Wesley explains their understandings of how the establishment of the park infringed on their rights to hunt in the mountains: "At the time [1877] nothing was ever mentioned about the cutting up of the land here and there into recreational areas and parks. The government didn't tell them it would eventually be doing this. It is because of these special areas that we can't go hunting."[32]

Lack of Consultation With Local Communities

The government did not consult with or inform Nakoda peoples about the formation of the reserve or the national park. This lack of consultation continued to bring Nakoda peoples into direct conflict with park policies and those who enforced them. The government, as well as individuals and organizations that held a vested interest, successfully repositioned the hot springs as a potential tourism site. These new, tourist-focused uses of the hot springs stood in direct opposition to the ways local Indigenous communities used them. As demonstrated by their extensive uses of the location for centuries before a European presence, different foundations of knowledge formed Nakoda understandings of the springs as sacred spaces. The contrasting conceptualizations of this site would constitute one of several conflicts between tourism producers and

Indigenous peoples that would justify further regulation of Nakoda hunting practices throughout the coming decades.

Nakoda Hunting as the New Target of Park Regulation

In 1886, the government's Department of the Interior sent a biologist, W.F. Whitcher, to report on the state of the mountain ecosystems. The Whitcher report, as it was known, directly implicated the hunting practices of local Nakoda peoples, as well as depredations by foxes and wolves, in the decline of large game mammals in the region. In addition, the report recommended the establishment of limited hunting seasons and the hiring of police officers and forest rangers to strictly enforce regulations with fines and penalties.[33] In his history of grassroots conservation movements in Western Canada, historian George Colpitts notes that as early as the late 18th century, Europeans blamed local Indigenous hunters for the lack of big game.[34] When Whitcher made his recommendations in 1886, he did not consider the rights of Nakoda communities that were solidified through the treaty agreement, suggesting that "exceptions of no kind whatever should be made in favour of Indians. Those who now invade that territory are stragglers and deserters from their own reserves, where they are well cared for in food and clothing at the public expense."[35]

The Whitcher report led to the first wildlife regulations in Canadian national parks. They did not, however, serve to maintain all mammal and fish populations. Instead, the regulations were designed to sustain the region as a sporting and recreational playground, rather than to preserve a healthy and intact ecosystem. By the early 1890s, both Canadian Pacific Railway (CPR) representatives, who were deeply invested in local tourism economies, and the federal government, recognized the value of creating a recreational paradise. In 1895, partly based on Whitcher's assessment, park superintendent George Stewart recommended in his first official report that Indigenous peoples be excluded permanently from the park because of the threat to wildlife. Motivated by the creation of Algonquin Provincial Park in Ontario (1893), Stewart also asked for an expansion of the park to protect wildlife, especially around the southern section of the park, next to the Nakoda Reserve.

With the completion of the railway between Calgary and Banff, the increasing number of sportsmen and -women attracted to Banff created further interest in the restriction of Indigenous hunting and fishing in the park. Indigenous subsistence practices were in direct opposition to the sports code of etiquette, which specified that big game was not to be eaten but used for sport and hunting trophies. The differing objectives for hunting often formed an entirely separate code for hunting practices.[36] Referring to the Western Canadian context, Tina Loo contends that "with the recreational use of wildlife established as normative, wise use and waste were defined in different terms, ones that marginalized those who hunted to eat rather than those who hunted for trophies."[37] Not surprisingly, this sporting ethic, which originated in urban elite Euro-Canadian understandings of landscapes, was quite foreign to Indigenous peoples. The sporting ethic, which was inherently linked with new ideas of conservation, aimed to conserve large mammals for sportsmen and -women. It was also this ethic that supported harsh and, at times, completely unfounded critiques of Nakoda hunting practices.

Indigenous hunting methods were regularly deemed wasteful by European standards. Based on cultural knowledges formed over millennia of experiences, Indigenous hunters often took large quantities of game when opportunities were presented. Many Indigenous peoples, especially the Plains peoples, believe that animals offer themselves at key moments to hunters. Based on intricate relationships formed over millennia between mammal species and the people who rely on them, there are strong spiritual components to hunting practices and the ethics that guide them for Nakoda peoples. In comparison, a differing sense of ethics directed the hunting methods of sport hunters. This made it easier for Euro-Canadians to portray Nakoda hunters as wasteful or detrimental to conservation policies.[38] While Indigenous peoples did contribute to the demise of animal species like the bison and the beaver through their participation in colonial mercantile systems,[39] many researchers convincingly assert that Indigenous knowledge systems had built-in methods to ensure the conservation of animal and plant species, even though they were not characterized as conservation from a European lens.[40]

Colonial Sport Hunting Organizations

Even though rights to fish and hunt had been guaranteed by treaties only a few years earlier, Indigenous peoples across the country were targets of condemnation by sport and game clubs as well as related authorities. By 1893, strong opposition was mounted against Indigenous hunting in the Rocky Mountains by gun and hunting clubs located throughout much of what would become the province of Alberta in 1905.[41] In 1893, the Calgary Rod and Gun Club identified the importance of enforcing the pass system to conserve local game populations for the future use of Euro-Canadian hunters.[42] The impacts of the railway, the increased numbers of sport hunters, mining and timber operations were often discounted as factors in the decreasing populations of large mammals. Despite these influences, Indigenous peoples became the main target of sport hunting clubs of the period. These organizations were powerful advocates that at the time outweighed any alternative voices in the region.[43] As a result of their influence, sport hunting organizations lobbied the federal government to increase hunting and fishing restrictions on local Indigenous peoples.

The importance of sportsmen and -women to the tourism economy in Banff, which was growing rapidly at the beginning of the 20th century, aligned them with major tourism producers, such as local entrepreneurs as well as the CPR.[44] This alliance entrenched the power of sport hunting organizations that had been established over several decades. This was clearly the case in the Banff–Bow Valley, as tourism entrepreneurs like Jim Brewster often complained about Nakoda peoples hunting in or near the park. In 1905, Brewster criticized the hunting practices of the Nakoda, claiming "there is no discrimination in their shooting. . . . Rams, ewes, and lambs all look alike to the Indian and if a whole herd is cornered up they are all exterminated."[45] He requested that the Nakoda bands be moved into the prairies away from the Rocky Mountains. The merit of Brewster's concerns does not warrant much consideration because he was deeply invested in protecting large game. These resources were imperative to his own hunting and outfitting businesses, which he marketed to affluent sport hunters and tourists for many decades.

Although produced two decades earlier, the Whitcher report is also part of the same stream of colonial policy and evidence during this period. The report not only condemned Nakoda hunting practices but also connected these practices to new ideas of conservation, situating Indigenous peoples as the central target of emerging conservation movements committed to preserving fish and mammal populations for the pleasure of sport hunters and the benefit of the tourism industry. In this case, biological science was taken up in ways that contributed to ideas of conservation that effectively excluded Indigenous peoples and their ways of knowing. The findings of the report, allegedly founded in the rigour of scientific inquiry, added to the support for the exclusion of Indigenous peoples from parklands and the repression and assimilation of their cultural practices. Although wildlife management was highly localized until the late 19th century, the state took an increasingly active role in the 20th century. Ecology and game management were powerful ideas that emerged out of the biological sciences and began to shape conservation practices and principles. However, there was no recognition of the central roles humans had played in the health of these ecosystems. For example, practices of prescribed burning or the roles of humans as apex predators were completely absent from these scientific reports. Conservation policy effectively marginalized local uses of wildlife, and in this sense it was part of the very colonization of Canada.

Unfortunately, this would not be the last time the rigours of scientific and ecological knowledge were used by the administration of parks and protected areas to exclude the presence of Indigenous peoples and their related subsistence practices.[46] In his research on conflicts that arose in the formation of reserves and parks in the southern portions of the Yukon Territory, David Neufeld indicates that by the 1920s animals were commodified as an economic resource in the region.[47] Big-game outfitting businesses were established and trapping permits were encouraged, but there was no acknowledgment of the subsistence reliance on hunting of many local Indigenous communities. As early as the 1940s, the number of conflicts between Indigenous subsistence practices and the tourism industry increased because big game needed to be protected for these developing businesses. While soldiers, construction workers, and prospectors were all depleting large mammal populations, the hunting practices of Indigenous communities were targeted by conservation regulations. The Canadian government did set aside large tracts of land in the southwestern portion of the territory for the protection of big game, but hunting was forbidden to preserve various species in anticipation that they would become tourist attractions. Consequently, Indigenous communities were displaced as the hunting practices that sustained them were made illegal.

Colonial Surveillance

Returning to the context of Banff, while no hunting was permitted in the park in 1890, it was not until a few years later that the North-West Mounted Police (NWMP) were notified of concerns the government and special interest groups had about Nakoda subsistence hunting practices (see figure 5.2).[48] Over the next few years, the movements of Nakoda peoples were more closely monitored. In 1893, the Indian agent was directed to inform the police if any individuals were missing from the reserve. Indian Affairs specified that Indian agents were to be very attentive to "the movements of their Indians," and the police were to investigate any anomalies.[49]

While it is clear that several groups did combine their efforts with the objective of limiting Nakoda hunting in the mountains, there were certainly individual exceptions to the strident opposing voices that were so audible during this period. There are examples of government officials, police, and missionaries who

Camp at Indian Grounds - John Simeon, Eli Rider, Eli Rider's mother, John Salter and Ben Kaquitts at Banff Indian Days Stoney First Nation, ca. 1910-1920, Byron Harmon/photographer, Whyte Museum of the Canadian Rockies, Byron Harmon fonds (V263/I/A/i/a/na-3254)[50]

Figure 5.2   Nakoda hunters at a campground near Banff townsite in 1910. Pictured are John Simeon, Eli Rider, Eli Rider's mother, John Salter, and Ben Kaquitts (from left).

openly defended Nakoda subsistence practices against the unjustified charges of stakeholder groups such as sport hunting organizations.[51] Of course, Nakoda peoples also greatly resented the manner in which their hunting practices were (re)imagined as unethical and illegal. One example of their objection to these processes is a 1907 letter to the federal government where Nakoda leaders express their resistance to the game laws and remind the government of its treaty commitments to protect their subsistence practices.[52]

Extension of Rocky Mountains Park

In 1902, the boundaries of the park were extended to cover 11,400 square kilometres (4,400 square miles). This massive expansion greatly affected Nakoda communities because their hunting grounds were almost entirely swallowed up by the extension of parklands. Nakoda Elder Rollinmud explains the impact this had on their communities: "It cut off all the circulation that was providing us of life . . . which is our game and berries. . . . Anything that's in the mountains is brought back and is preserved. When we lost access to the area this meant straying away from all of our roots and our physical and spiritual energy."[53]

In the park's annual report in 1903, Nakoda hunters were directly blamed for decreases in populations of large mammals. By 1909, under rising pressure from sport hunting organizations and stakeholders in the local tourism economy, the government introduced game wardens into the park. The government's keen interest in curbing Nakoda hunting in the region was exemplified by their selection of Howard E. Sibbald as the first park warden. In addition to being the Indian agent at Morley from 1901 to 1904, Sibbald was not an advocate for Nakoda hunting. His position on the issue was reflected in his annual report in 1903: "As long as they can hunt, you cannot civilize them. . . . With the exception of a few of the younger ones, they are no more civilized now than they were when I first knew them, and I blame hunting as the cause."[54] The selection of Sibbald as the first game warden was a clear indication that the government viewed Nakoda hunting as a problem to be solved. Moreover, Sibbald's appointment also reveals that the government intended to prohibit the subsistence land uses of Nakoda peoples to appease the interests of sport hunting organizations and, ultimately, the tourism industry. Finally, with the support of J.B. Harkin, the commissioner of Dominion Parks, in 1913 a game preserve was declared on the southern border of the park directly north of the Nakoda Reserve. The preserve was designed to protect big-game populations, including deer, bighorn sheep, and goats. This severely inhibited Nakoda subsistence practices in one of the last remaining locations for Nakoda hunters.[55]

Paradoxically, in 1912 the CPR actively began to promote the exceptional hunting and fishing opportunities in the park to international audiences. These opportunities became one of the region's largest draws for early tourists. Again, scientific-based studies and reports were used to document and provide support for ideas that subjugated Indigenous peoples and their ways of knowing. In this case, parks explicitly endorsed a conservation ethic that was deeply linked to knowledges produced by and through individuals who were invested in the tourism industry. These particular ways of understanding conservation later informed assimilation practices. The conservation ethic of the period was deeply connected to ideas that positioned Indigenous peoples as illegal trespassers and poachers on their own land. The conservation of large mammals to satisfy sport hunting organizations and tourism producers was a key objective of government policies designed to limit the hunting practices of Nakoda communities.

Ultimately, the expansion of the park and the enforcement of regulations greatly restricted access to the region for Indigenous peoples. Relying on the new ideas of conservation, tourism producers, government directors, and park officials excluded Nakoda peoples and other Indigenous groups from living in key protected areas on the continent and practising their subsistence land uses. Although it was in direct contradiction to the treaty agreement and it required several decades to implement, by the mid-1920s, the restrictions had ensured that few Nakoda community members relied on hunting, gathering, or fishing as their main forms of subsistence.[56] On May 30, 1930, there was a fundamental shift in the direction of Canada's national park system with the establishment of the National Parks Act. Along with changing the official name to Banff National Park, the act settled the disputes between provincial development aspirations and protection of lands in national parks. Despite these changes, no concessions were made for local Indigenous communities. A new conservation ethic emerged, and with it all hunting practices were officially made illegal inside park boundaries.[57]

TRANSFORMATIVE MOMENTS: NATIONAL PARKS ACT, MAY 30, 1930 (*STATUTES OF CANADA*, 20-21 GEORGE V, CHAPTER 33)

Along with changing the official name to Banff National Park, the act settled the disputes between provincial development aspirations and protection of lands in national parks. Especially in the Rockies, the shifting of park boundaries removed lands with industrial potential and left them in trust to the provinces. In Banff, this included Canmore, Exshaw, the Spray Lakes, and the Kananaskis Valley. The act altered the park's administration and fundamental premise in declaring that parks were to be left unimpaired for the enjoyment of future generations. Even though the legislation did permit leases for grazing and small-scale mining, as well as timber and water rights for the purposes of replenishing park and railway supplies, a conservation ethic emerged that ended industrial resource extraction and restricted tourists' consumption and recreation practices. Rather than change the orientation of tourism markets, the National Parks Act only reinforced the intentions of tourism entrepreneurs to promulgate the perception of the parks as a natural wilderness area.

PROMINENT PEOPLE: JAMES B. HARKIN (1875-1955)

James B. Harkin was a Canadian-born journalist and politician who is known as the father of the Canadian national parks system. Harkin was appointed as the first commissioner of the Dominion Parks Branch in 1911. He helped expand the national parks system beyond Banff to include Elk Island, Mount Revelstoke, Point Pelee, Kootenay, Wood Buffalo, Prince Albert, Riding Mountain, Georgian Bay Islands, and Cape Breton Highlands. While also holding some principles around ecosystem conservation, Harkin believed that parks should have an economic foundation and in this regard he supported tourism development throughout Canadian protected areas.

International Perspectives
of Conservation and Park Development

Conservation principles were also used to exclude Indigenous peoples in numerous national parks and protected areas throughout the United States from as early as the 1870s.[58] In the United States during this period, there were incredibly similar processes unfolding concerning Indigenous communities. As Spence meticulously details in his histories of the first U.S. national parks, the parks were created because "outdoor enthusiasts viewed wilderness as an uninhabited Eden that should be set aside for the benefit and pleasure of vacationing Americans."[59] As a consequence, the foundation of the first national parks necessarily entailed the removal of Indigenous peoples, precisely because their hunting practices did not align with Euro-American understandings of natural landscapes.

In 1872, the Yellowstone Park Act incorporated lands where several Indigenous groups were exercising their off-reservation treaty rights to hunt, fish, and gather. The removal of Indigenous peoples from Yellowstone National Park set a precedent for the creation of further conservation spaces in the United States with the same founding principles. In this respect, Yellowstone not only was the first example on the continent of the removal of communities to preserve nature, but it also provided a model for the displacement of Indigenous peoples from national parks in the decades to come. Parallels with the experiences of other Indigenous groups reveal a pattern of exclusion that was part of regional and national policies throughout the continent rather than an isolated occurrence in Yellowstone and the Banff–Bow Valley. Also similarly to the Nakoda experiences in Banff, park officials in the 1880s collaborated with the Indian Service, the military, and the federal judiciary to displace several groups of Indigenous peoples from Yellowstone.[60] During the 1920s, cooperative efforts were also made by park rangers, Montana state game wardens, and reservation officials to remove the Blackfeet from Glacier National Park and restrict hunting practices in the park and on their reservation.[61] These collaborations among Euro-American individuals, groups, and institutions effectively displaced Indigenous communities and, at the very least, marginalized their hunting practices.

To parallel what occurred internationally for Indigenous peoples, during this period colonial governments, particularly in Africa and Asia, were also pursuing similar policies concerning Indigenous peoples. Under the guise of conservation and wildlife management, Indigenous communities were displaced, access to lands were denied, and their hunting practices were either severely restricted or in some cases rebranded as illegal. In his analysis of conservation movements in Bengal, India, Sivaramakrishnan contends that "the colonial regime's policies for forest management, hunting regulation, and disciplining tribal people invented social categories and also filled them by means of criminalization, displacement, or paternalist isolation of specific groups."[62] There are a number of excellent international studies on the exclusion of Indigenous peoples from protected areas and parks.[63] In most cases, their exclusion was precipitated by conflicts between their hunting practices and the protection or management of wildlife. In an American context, Spence argues that the foundation of the first national parks occurred simultaneously with and was influenced by developments in 19th-century Indian policy, especially the creation of the reservation systems.[64] In other words, the production of conservation ideas supported the assimilatory objectives of the government by the ways nature, and the spaces designated to preserve it, was founded and exemplified in the first national parks. Consequently, it is crucial to link conservation processes to assimilation objectives that were concurrently pursued by governments and other collaborative members of the colonial bureaucracy. Across North America and in other colonial environments internationally, there were further rationales behind the intentions to limit the subsistence and cultural practices of Indigenous peoples.

Tourism and the Promotion of "Naturalness"

From the 1880s until the middle of the 20th century, the development of tourism economies in the Banff–Bow Valley initiated a dynamic period in the region's history. Local Indigenous peoples participated in the tourism industry and in various capacities contributed to the production of "naturalness," which was central to the marketing of Rocky Mountains Park and the Banff townsite. By selling certain images of the region while actively concealing others, tourism entrepreneurs promoted the Banff–Bow Valley as an international tourist destination. Nakoda community members influenced these tourism promotional campaigns through their involvement in the tourism industry.

Increasing significantly with the package travel business in the 1860s and the creation of the British travel firm Thomas Cook, Western elites toured mountain ranges like the European Alps and later more exotic destinations such as the Canadian Rockies. The touring of these environments emerged as these landscapes began to offer recreational experiences for elite tourists. Urban-elite conceptions of these environments also arrived with the affluent tourists and the flow of economic capital that facilitated the development of the tourism industry. Although established two decades after Thomas Cook, the CPR became one of the world's largest travel companies by the turn of the 20th century.

The 1887 formation of Rocky Mountains Park was the beginning of tourism infrastructure development in the Canadian Rocky Mountains. As a joint venture between the Canadian federal government and the CPR, the national park was the first of its kind in Canada and was originally established as a means of generating railway tourism with few conservation or preservation objectives considered. As was the case for much of Canada's early history, and especially in the development of the west, public and private interests were strongly linked in the formation and development of the park.[65] The construction of the national railway and the building of a new nation brought about severe financial challenges. Through the creation of the park, the federal government and private corporations sought to develop the tourism industry to recover some of the mounting costs of completing the east–west railway that linked central Canada to the emergent west.[66] As William Cornelius Van Horne, the president of the CPR, stated in 1888: "If we cannot export the scenery, we will import the tourists."[67] The park solidified a symbiotic relationship between the CPR and the federal government that would prosper throughout much of the 20th century. The park became a convenient way to establish a monopoly on transportation access to the region that effectively controlled development. The establishment of the national park designated governmental control of natural resource management and the leasing of property. Although this is a less glamorous account than some historians have put forward, few conservation principles shaped these decisions because the park was originally created to centralize control of the lands and restrict access to the region.[68]

Balancing Conservation, Recreation, and Tourism

While some researchers argue that early Canadian national park policies also had important conservation principles to protect wildlife and preserve the region for the benefit of civil society,[69] the majority of evidence suggests that even though the federal government did claim it was securing land to be "set apart as a public park and pleasure ground for the benefit, advantage and enjoyment of the people of Canada,"[70] it was initially motivated by natural resource and tourism development opportunities. During this early period in the Canadian west, it was local governments, recreational groups, and tourism entrepreneurs rather than conservationists that campaigned for the expansion of the national park system.[71] Legislation endorsed the growth of the tourism industry and permitted, under government direction, the development of mining sites, timber interests, and grazing lands, as long as they did not "impair the usefulness of the park for the purposes of public enjoyment and recreation."[72] Martin states:

"As critics of both the Canadian and American national parks systems have often noted, an avowed commitment to wilderness preservation by government administrators has not always prevented intensive development and environmental modifications in the national parks."[73] This was most certainly the case in the first few decades of park policy in both the United States and Canada.

In Rocky Mountains Park during the early 1880s, a small silver and copper mining town, referred to as Silver City, developed near Castle Mountain only 30 kilometres (19 miles) north of the Banff townsite. The formation of the park allowed the CPR and the government to shift the mining enterprise from a private operation into a public asset while also prohibiting the alcohol and gambling lifestyles of Silver City miners. There is little record of opposition to resource-extraction activities in the park during this period, and the federal policy of the Conservative government in the 1880s emphasized the desire to exploit natural resources in order to develop the national economy.[74] Parks leadership also reflected the government's development intentions. Commissioner Harkin, in his annual report, stated that "nothing attracts tourists like National Parks. National Parks provide the chief means of bringing to Canada a stream of tourists and a stream of tourist gold."[75] If one reviews early government policy and practice, it is clear that tourism and natural resource development were the primary rationale for the formation of the park. In addition, it is now apparent that Harkin used an economic argument, based on tourism development, in order to expand the national parks system after 1910.[76]

Banff as an Elite Wellness and Spa Destination

In terms of tourism, the Banff townsite began as a spa destination for elite guests of considerable financial standing. The luxurious facilities built by the CPR, like the Banff Springs Hotel, completed in 1888, were designed to meet the needs of its affluent clientele and were some of the continent's most opulent accommodations during the period. As Canada's first prime minister, Sir John A. Macdonald, stated during the development of the townsite, "the doubtful classes of people will probably not find an overly gracious welcome at Banff."[77] The Macdonald administration advocated developing the townsite in the style of an elite European resort community and leasing the land only to affluent individuals who could afford to erect buildings that would complement the local environment and reflect the government's vision of the townsite. The marketing of Banff also reflected the objective of attracting the urban elite of North America and Europe. Lynda Jessup's research recounts the processes that led to the CPR's hiring of members of Canada's famous Group of Seven artists to paint the Rocky Mountains and promote the region for tourism.[78] Her study reveals how the CPR endeavoured to "establish the value of the region, not in the eyes of the traveler as such, but in the eyes of the urban elite that, like the artist it patronized, possessed the cultural capital necessary for discriminating between different landscapes."[79] While the initial promotional campaigns of the park concentrated on the wealthy clientele that had the leisure time to undertake an extended sojourn and the capital to facilitate it, tourism producers soon expanded the tourism market.

Democratization of Tourism and the Expansion of Infrastructure

Access to the Banff townsite and the park was rapidly increasing with the 1914 creation of the Calgary–Banff coach road and the proliferation of the automobile. After the road was completed, the CPR monopoly on transportation access to the region ended and individual entrepreneurs began to expand the tourism market by providing cheaper accommodation and alternative forms of recreation. Although access to the region was opening up, this did not signify the end of the CPR's dominant influence in Banff because the company developed strategies to capitalize on new forms of automobile tourism.[80] It was not until the 1920s, when several accommodation options were developed for middle-class visitors and the road became more frequently used, that access to the park was granted to a larger portion of society. By 1930, 88 percent of the 188,000 tourists who arrived in Banff came by automobile.[81] The park as a playground for more than society's elite began with the rise of the automobile and the subsequent expansion of road and highway infrastructure that provided greater access to the region.[82]

With the democratization of tourism, local entrepreneurs began to shift marketing campaigns and subsequently changed the reputation of Banff. It was during this period that local tourism producers made efforts to convince the CPR that Banff did not have much of a future as a tourist destination if it continued to be marketed solely as an affluent spa or resort town similar to many elite European tourist locations throughout the Alps and the Pyrenees.[83] These businessmen felt that Banff should be sold as a place that could offer all tourists outdoor recreational experiences. Entrepreneurs made convincing arguments for the expansion of the tourism industry to reach new markets, and as a consequence, the region began to be promoted as a destination that could provide outdoor leisure opportunities to tourists from diverse socioeconomic backgrounds. Facilitated by transportation infrastructure and marketing campaigns, the attraction of middle-class tourists to Banff and the consequent expansion of accommodation and recreation opportunities to meet these visitors' needs led to a distinct shift in the orientation of the townsite. Although initially established as an elite tourist destination, with the introduction of the automobile, it was transformed into a place that also catered to middle-class tourists with an infrastructure that would accommodate the mass tourism of the coming decades.

Indigenous Participation in Early Tourism Economies as Hunting Guides

Nakoda communities contributed to changing perceptions of Banff as a tourist destination through their engagement in local tourism economies. While restrictions eventually reduced the number of Nakoda peoples who travelled inside the lands redefined as parks, there were individuals who formed unique relationships with entrepreneurs in the Banff region through the tourism industry. As a result of their extensive knowledge of the land and local ecosystems, Nakoda peoples often served as effective guides in the mountains. The history of Nakoda peoples as guides in the Rocky Mountains extends back to the first European explorers, who relied on Indigenous knowledge in their attempts to establish transportation and fur-trading routes.[84] CPR employees also drew from the knowledge of local Indigenous peoples in their early surveys of the Rockies to denote the best mountain passes for railway construction.[85] The labour of First Nations peoples was key to early Canadian capitalist expansion through industry. This was particularly the case in the western and northern parts of the country.[86]

With park restrictions increasing the difficulty for Nakoda peoples to continue their hunting practices, by the 1880s some community members began to pursue alternative types of employment in the tourism and development industries. The experiences of William Twin, a Nakoda man, are prime examples of the adaptability that many Indigenous peoples exhibited during this period. In the 1880s, the CPR employed Twin, who had previously worked for the Hudson's Bay Company, as a guide and labourer. In 1888, Twin began to work in the Banff townsite for the Brewster family, which was actively involved in the region's tourism industry. Although he was initially employed as a labourer in the family's dairy, in 1892 he began guiding trips throughout the park for the Brewster tourism ventures. Over the ensuing decades, Twin established long-lasting relationships with several members of the Brewster family.[87] He also worked with Tom Wilson, another notable tourism entrepreneur in the Banff–Bow Valley. After Edwin Hunter, a Nakoda man from Morley, took Wilson to Ho-run-num-nay (Lake of Little Fishes, later renamed Lake Louise) in 1882, Wilson began a small guiding operation based near the lake. Twin worked with Wilson guiding affluent tourists in the area throughout the 1880s and 1890s. In 1894, Twin and Tom Chiniquay, another Nakoda man from Morley, worked for the CPR maintaining trails around the CPR's chalet at the famed lake.[88] Because of their skill set and experience in the mountains, some Nakoda peoples were offered employment by local tourism producers and, in some cases, unique opportunities to travel. In 1895, Twin ventured to New York City, with the approval of the local Indian agent, to participate in the CPR's exhibit in the New York Sportsman Show. On the trip, Twin represented a real grizzly bear hunter and promoted CPR railway tourism in the Canadian Rockies.[89] The irony of this event was that, of course, Indigenous hunting in the park was illegal.

Clearly there are examples of how some Nakoda men were able to participate in these developing economies associated with the tourism industry, but in almost all cases, Euro-Canadian families owned these tourism productions and Nakoda men simply worked as labourers and guides in these profitable businesses. Even though personal relationships were established over the many years that Nakoda men, such as Twin, worked for the Brewster family, at least initially these relationships were formed because Twin and others possessed exceptional skill sets and knowledge that tourism entrepreneurs needed to facilitate their businesses. These relationships, although unique during this period, cannot be considered outside the historical contexts in which they occurred. Thus, while it is important not to devalue the meaningful relationships that developed over many decades between Nakoda peoples and local tourism entrepreneurs, we also need to interrogate how localized power dynamics and broader Indigenous–Euro-Canadian race relations informed this period of history.[90]

In addition to employment as labourers and guides, some Nakoda peoples also pursued their own opportunities to profit from the developing tourism economies as well as interact with tourists. Especially after the proliferation of the automobile, opportunities for Nakoda peoples to engage with tourists travelling from Calgary to the park greatly increased. Ralphine Locke, a Euro-Canadian woman whose family has lived in the Banff–Bow Valley for generations, recalls some of the ways that Nakoda peoples contributed to local tourism economies:

> Yes, a lot of the Stonies [Nakoda] had big horse businesses in those days and people would come out and go camping in the mountains with their horses and so they were employed through that as well as being guides and horsemen. So there was a lot of activity and exchange through tourism . . . and quite a few relationships formed.[91]

Along with renting their horses to local guides and outfitters, some Nakoda peoples initiated their own small-scale tourism operations that catered to the needs of transient tourists. Several Nakoda peoples participated in the early tourism economies, but for the most part, access to the Banff–Bow Valley was greatly restricted for Nakoda communities and many individuals had difficulty consistently securing adequate employment. Furthermore, most of these opportunities were restricted to younger men, who were flexible enough to leave the reserve to pursue alternative occupations. Although the tourism economies were growing at exponential rates in Banff and many entrepreneurs were subsequently prospering, during this same period Nakoda peoples at Morley were facing difficult socioeconomic conditions. Without their subsistence practices and access to their traditional territories that were enclosed inside park boundaries, many Nakoda peoples were struggling to adapt to an entirely new way of living.

PROMINENT PEOPLE: TATANGA MANI (WALKING BUFFALO), OR GEORGE MCLEAN (1871-1967)

Nakoda Chief Tatanga Mani (Walking Buffalo), or George McLean (see figure 5.3), was elected Chief of Nakoda First Nations in 1920 and was actively involved in local leadership until his death in 1967. As well as a strong and committed leader, Tatanga Mani was well known for his great sense of humour and his insistence on the acceptance of Indigenous peoples as an important part of Canadian society. He regularly played with aspects of his own identity and those of tourists or Banff residents. Often to the delight of large crowds, he was known to refer to Euro-Canadians as "White savages" when speaking in public.

Figure 5.3 Tatanga Mani (Walking Buffalo), or George McLean, Nakoda Nation.

Conclusion

When you drive on the Trans-Canada Highway to Banff National Park from Calgary, Alberta, you begin on the open spaces of the prairies, emerge in the foothills, and eventually arrive at Banff townsite, the heart of the Banff–Bow Valley. Walking down Banff Avenue, surrounded by towering peaks, it is easy to appreciate the aesthetic beauty of the location. However, it is difficult to imagine that these landscapes are also filled with complex histories of conflict, displacement, and cultural loss. The expensive tourist shops on Banff Avenue that welcome millions of tourists annually do not reflect these histories of conflict and their impacts on local Indigenous communities.

Many Canadians admire national parks for the ecosystems and wildlife they protect. Yet the cultural values they also preserve are not as readily acknowledged. As MacLaren contends, "parks and protected areas are often heralded for the species they protect, but are seldom examined for the ideologies or cultural values that they protect and project."[92] In all of the special protected areas across the country that Canadians and international tourists value, few landscapes can be imagined as untouched by human and Indigenous presences. As this chapter demonstrates, this includes the lands currently protected inside iconic national parks like Banff. In Canada, there are over 77 different types of protected area designations.[93] This diversity leads to serious complications over land use management decisions and the plethora of stakeholders invested in them. Only a small percentage of protected lands and waters (less than 3 percent) are governed by co-management structures where Indigenous and Crown governments partner to jointly share decision making.[94] While co-management arrangements of protected areas may not be a panacea for Indigenous communities, who are still healing from the cultural loss of being displaced from their traditional territories, it is a step in the right direction. Recognizing these uncomfortable pasts of colonial conflict is a critical component towards public education, owning these complex histories, and building the bridges or alliances that respect Indigenous cultures and histories.

DISCUSSION QUESTIONS

1. Why were the Nakoda and other Indigenous groups displaced from the lands that would become Banff National Park?
2. What kinds of impacts did the denial of access to their traditional territories have in Nakoda communities?
3. Why were Nakoda subsistence practices, such as hunting, fishing, and gathering, targeted by park officials and those invested in tourism and recreation activities in Banff?
4. How did some Nakoda community members resist these colonial regulations and policies?

SUGGESTED READINGS

Binnema, Theodore, and Melanie Niemi. "'Let the Line Be Drawn Now': Wilderness, Conservation, and the Exclusion of Aboriginal People from Banff National Park in Canada." *Environmental History* 11, no. 4 (2006): 724-750.

Hart, E.J. *The Selling of Canada: The CPR and the Beginning of Canadian Tourism*. Banff, AB: Altitude, 1983.

Hildebrandt, Walter, Dorothy First Rider, Sarah Carter, and Treaty 7 Elders and Tribal Councils. *The True Spirit and Original Intent of Treaty 7*. Montreal: McGill-Queen's University Press, 1996.

Smith, Keith. *Liberalism, Surveillance and Resistance: Indigenous Communities in Western Canada, 1877-1927*. Edmonton: Athabasca University Press, 2009.

Snow, John. *These Mountains Are Our Sacred Places: The Story of the Stoney Indians*. Toronto: Fifth House, 2005.

CHAPTER 6

THE IMPACT OF INDUSTRIALIZATION ON SPORT, RECREATION, AND THE ENVIRONMENT

Robert Kossuth, PhD
University of Lethbridge

David McMurray, MA
University of Lethbridge

LEARNING OBJECTIVES

In this chapter you will

- explore the relationship between the industrialization of Canadian society and changing attitudes towards physical recreation in natural environments;
- identify the key factors that led to the development of organized outdoor activities and play spaces for adults and children;
- assess how the perceived pressures of urban life led to the pursuit of controlled wilderness adventures such as fishing, hunting, downhill skiing, and mountain climbing;
- reflect on the role of class, gender, and race in the participation of Canadians in outdoor sport and recreation.

When entrepreneur and brewer John Molson began operation of Canada's first steam-powered ship, the *Accommodation*, between Montreal and Quebec City in 1809,[1] it was a bold gamble. Utilizing a Canadian-made six-horsepower engine, the 26-metre (85 foot) *Accommodation* made the 290-kilometre (180 mile) trip down the St. Lawrence to Quebec City in only three days.[2] However, its return trip against the current took the woefully underpowered vessel a week to complete and by 1811, the *Accommodation* had been relegated to the scrapyard after failing to produce an adequate return on investment.[3] Nevertheless, the advent of steam-powered transportation on the St. Lawrence highlighted an emerging new era of technological change, industrial production, and population distribution that would profoundly shape the development of sport and recreation in Canada. Though it would be many decades before steam-powered locomotives and ships became commonplace, the industrialization and urbanization of Canada in the late 19th and early 20th centuries was a disruptive force, particularly in relation to human interactions with the environment. As populations began to shift from rural and agrarian communities to urban-industrial centres, white middle- and upper-class Canadians grew increasingly nostalgic for a highly romanticized agrarian past. In particular, they looked to the natural environment as a way of offsetting the ill effects of urban-industrial life. By re-creating nature through urban public parks and safe swimming facilities, or through highly controlled adventures in the wilderness, as discussed in chapter 5, white Canadians sought to improve the health and protect the morality of those living in cities through accessible space and opportunities for rational recreation.

Industrialization and Urbanization in Canada

Industrialization began in Britain during the 18th century and subsequently spread to the United States and then to Canada. However, this was an uneven and unequally distributed process not only between countries but also between regions within countries. Economic historians Kris Inwood and Ian Keay observe that the path to industrial transformation in the United States, "differed from that of Britain, and Canada differed from that of the USA, despite sharing many institutional, economic, and geographic features."[4] In the case of Canada, the industrialization of society did not truly begin to occur until the mid-19th century, and perhaps more accurately, after Confederation in 1867—though as in the case of Molson's steamship, the *Accommodation*, some Canadians had the unique opportunity of seeing technological advances decades before they entered widespread use. In the realm of sport, industrialization developed in a similarly uneven manner; however, the impacts of industrial development were first and most keenly experienced in Canada's cities and towns.

As historian Alan Metcalfe notes, industrialization and urbanization are both processes and products, and "the relationship between urbanization and industrialization is so close that it is difficult, at times, to discern which was cause and which effect."[5] For Canadians living in 1871, only one in five resided in an "incorporated urban centre"; however, by 1911, this had increased to 45 percent of the population.[6] Indeed, with the settlement of the West came an economic "wheat boom" in the early 20th century that helped fuel this rapid transition from agrarian to urban-industrial society. Unfortunately, this meant that as cities sprung up on the prairies, or as cities such as Montreal, Toronto, and Hamilton sought to capitalize on new economic opportunities, the migration of workers from the countryside coupled with the arrival of immigrants from overseas placed an enormous strain on living conditions that municipal governments struggled to manage. For example, in 1915, the Commission of Conservation—established in 1909 by Prime Minister Wilfrid Laurier to "begin a science-led planning of resource use"[7]—wrote in its annual report that industrial smoke in Toronto and Hamilton

> disfigures buildings, impairs the health of the population, renders the whole city filthy, destroys any beauty with which it may naturally be endowed and tends, therefore, to make it a squalid and undesirable place of residence, and this, at a time when economic influences are forcing into our cities and ever increasing portion of our population. These conditions press especially on the poor who must reside in the cities and cannot escape from these evils by taking houses in the suburbs.[8]

Moreover, in assessing the state of Canadian cities in the early 20th century, Robert Craig Brown and Ramsay Cook observe, "In short, the Canadian city at the turn of the century was a place of violent contrasts, a home for the very rich and the very poor, for the rural immigrant from a neighbouring county or a far distant land and the native urbanite, for respectable church-goers and for prostitutes, a place of conspicuous expenditure and forced destitution."[9]

It was in the midst of this social disruption that white middle- and upper-class urban Canadians began to view nature as a cure for the ill effects of urban-industrial life and as a way to safeguard public morality through ordered and rational outdoor activities. It is also no coincidence that this highly romanticized and nostalgic perspective became prevalent during a time that "witnessed patterns of urbanization, industrialization, and technological sophistication through which humans attained ever more control over vast swaths of the northern North American environment."[10] Certainly, the mass production of goods coupled with mass communication, and technological innovations such as railways, allowed urban Canadians greater knowledge of, and access to, what were once remote wilderness locales. Though as Denis McKim highlights, the idea of wilderness during this time was a "malleable imaginative construct . . . which allowed it to be deployed for a wide variety of reasons and in an equally wide variety of contexts, ultimately enhancing its resonance."[11] Thus, many white middle- and upper-class urban Canadians held a paradoxical worldview of the environment—one that sought to both conquer nature through intellectual and technological progress and to be set free by it through either controlled forays into the wilderness or through re-creating it in the form of urban parks and playgrounds.[12]

Urban Parks and Playing Fields

The ability of Canadians living in a growing number of urban centres to easily escape the endemic social and industrial problems emerging in 19th-century cities was limited. Even wealthy city dwellers who enjoyed the privileges of living in large houses, and who had access to readily available transportation and time free from work, struggled to locate easily accessible places to play. To these practical ends, individuals, groups, and governing bodies in Canadian towns and cities began to wrestle with the challenges associated with meeting recreation needs, and this often contested process occurred largely through attempts to secure and set aside land for constructing parks and facilities for recreation and play.

Establishing Public Parks in Canadian Communities

One element of the broader processes of industrialization and urbanization in late 19th-century Canada was the issue of setting aside public land in towns and cities for parks. This undertaking represents one of the critical foundations for the provision of leisure and recreation opportunities for Canadians through to the present. Although several early social institutions such as private sports clubs[13] and local public houses or taverns[14] provided urban populations with opportunities to participate in leisure practices, equally important by the later 1800s was the creation of public municipal parks. How town and city governments developed policies concerning parks in the later decades of the 19th century provides insight into the ways these corporate bodies chose to address the need for public spaces for sport and leisure. Decisions in these matters were primarily local, yet towns and cities also had to operate within legal policies framed by provincial legislation. Additionally, the social importance of providing spaces for play shaped decisions concerning public recreation, including the broader parks movement in English-speaking North America, and existing ideas regarding the use of public land based within British common law.

In Britain, municipal parks existed as early as the 17th century. However, it was not until the early 19th century, during the period of rapid population increases in urban centres resulting from industrialization, that official recognition of the need for urban parks first arose. In 1833, the Select Committee on Public Walks presented a report to the British Parliament suggesting parks would improve the health of those living in cities and provide accessible space for rational recreation.[15] Following this, a succession of legislative acts passed in Britain to preserve existing public lands, or commons, and to ensure the creation of new parks in towns and cities. The first piece of legislation passed to meet these ends was the Enclosure Act of 1836. This law exempted common fields from enclosure, a process that began in the 1100s where wealthy members of the nobility over the centuries privatized previously communal lands. This legislation barred enclosure of any common land within 16 kilometres (10 miles) of London, England.[16] A second piece of legislation, the 1848 Public Health Act, stated that "Local Boards of Health are empowered to provide, maintain and improve land for municipal parks and to support and contribute towards such land provided by any person whomsoever."[17] Thus, by the middle of the 19th century, legislators in Britain had already started to address the need to provide open public lands for people in order to address their health and recreation needs. In concert with Britain, colonies in British North America also began to address similar issues regarding the provision and regulation of public lands for leisure and recreation.

The first land in the British North American colonies to be set aside specifically for the purpose of public recreation and leisure occurred in 1763 when the lieutenant-governor of Nova Scotia granted a 240-acre site to the citizens of Halifax.[18] Still in existence today, part of this historical land grant is locally known as the Halifax Common. In Ontario, the first evidence of agitation for public land to be set aside for leisure purposes occurred in 1826 when a group advocated for a "Public Walk" in Toronto.[19] A quarter century later, in 1851, Toronto City Council established the Committee on Public Walks and Gardens. Charged with the retention and development of garrison land leased to the city by the British military authorities, this committee determined ways to repurpose this property for citizens' pleasure and recreation. Shortly thereafter, an 1860 bylaw entrusted care of all the city's public walks, gardens, and parks to this committee, stipulating that garrison lands could not be used for games without city council's permission.[20] This early example of the regulation and use of public land exhibits the tight control municipal leaders believed necessary, particularly in terms of the appropriateness of the types of recreation activities taking place in these public spaces.

In Canadian communities, local recreation bureaucracies such as city park boards and volunteer playground committees acted as instruments of prevailing legislation and popular social reform and improvement movements, existing primarily to meet the needs of elite citizens. In turn, these men of wealth and privilege were more often than not primarily concerned with the financial implications involved in providing public recreation places and spaces. However, this explanation is probably overly simplistic and does not account for the agency of those residents who were genuinely guided by the belief that a city and its inhabitants could be socially improved through public recreation initiatives. Thus, the continued need to balance financial costs—primarily the expense of purchasing and improving the land—with the purported social benefits quickly led to conflict among the men who governed these communities. This ongoing conflict underscored much of the debate surrounding the early organization of public recreation in the City of London, Ontario. Ultimately, disagreement over how to secure and use public lands rested on two practical matters: (1) the amount to spend for purchasing land and (2) the acceptable forms of recreation practices allowed on this public land.

Parks and Playgrounds in London, Ontario

The formation of public parks in London, Ontario, during the late 1800s provides insight into the motivations and idiosyncrasies surrounding the idea of civic involvement in providing citizens with accessible spaces and facilities for recreation and leisure. Through the late 1860s and early 1870s, municipal politicians in London began to consider ways to secure land for an urban park. In May 1867, London alderman James Egan first moved to secure funds to provide for a public park in the city.[21] The following year, on May 4, 1868, Aldermen Egan and John Christie successfully brought forward a motion to form a special Park Committee that would provide a report to council on the practicality of securing grounds for a public park.[22] Obtaining suitable land for a permanent park proved to be a more difficult task than Alderman Egan had anticipated, and as a temporary measure in June of 1868, Middlesex County Council—the regional government authority—granted the City of London use of the grounds of the County Court House as a park. There were two stipulations placed on this arrangement: first that it be open only from 5:00 a.m. to 8:30 p.m., and second that the city plant ornamental trees on the grounds.[23] This early attempt to secure a park suggests timidity on the part of municipal politicians to undertake any project for public recreation requiring the expenditure of public money. In the end, this temporary arrangement with the county council did not prove sufficient for meeting Londoners' public recreation needs.

Following several attempts to purchase land in London for a park, Alderman Egan travelled to Ottawa to request title to a portion of the old military garrison grounds for use as a public park. The government offered the city 13 acres of this land, which eventually became Victoria Park in 1874.[24] Initially, this new park served a variety of uses, including as a site for football and cricket;[25] additionally, the owner of the London Tecumsehs Baseball Club petitioned to use part of the site for his team, a request that was ultimately rejected.[26] London's use of centrally located public lands for these purposes did not represent a unique circumstance in Canada. For example, in Lethbridge, Alberta, a piece of land known as the Square hosted sports including cricket, baseball, football, and lacrosse in the last decade of the 19th century.[27] The importance of a visible, central location for these activities demonstrates the prominence of sporting activities for white middle-class men who migrated to the West. In 1905, the influential Galt family donated this land to the City of Lethbridge. The city renamed it Galt Gardens in 1910 and operated it as a park—not a site for sports or games—in perpetuity.[28] This shift in use of this land as a site for sports and games into a public park mirrored a similar alteration for Victoria Park in London more than 30 years earlier.

In 1878, after much vacillating, the City of London reached a final decision concerning the use of Victoria Park. London City Council voted to employ Charles Henry Miller, the designer of the United States Centennial Exhibition at Philadelphia, Pennsylvania, in 1876 and at that time the head gardener at Fairmont Park in the same city, to landscape Victoria Park (see figure 6.1).[29] One prevailing reason for Victoria Park being turned from a site for sports and games into an ornamental landscaped space lay in its close proximity to the mansions of London's wealthy elites. These men, some of whom sat on city council, viewed the restyled park as a way to further insulate themselves from the less cultured elements in the city. Additionally, this decision served the financial interests of wealthy Londoners who understood the improvements to the park "had the effect of raising the value of the property in the neighborhood very considerably."[30] Although evidence does not explicitly suggest members of the city's lower classes were actively excluded from this space, the decision to design the park to reflect appropriate middle-class values almost certainly established for whom and how the park ought to be used. Thus, after four years of debate and conflict, the fate of Victoria Park had finally been decided, and London could boast a park to serve its citizens as a site of rational and moderate recreation well into the 20th century.

To avoid the complications that accompanied the creation and development of Victoria Park, in 1879 the city drafted and passed a bylaw to formally establish Queen's Park. This legislation established the conditions for managing this new park. The first clause of the bylaw clearly set out the purpose of the grounds: to exist as "a public Park for the recreation and amusement of the citizens of London."[31] Administered by city-appointed trustees, Queen's Park served as a site for fairs and exhibitions in the years prior to the creation of a permanent site, the Western Fair Association in 1887.[32] Before an estimated crowd of 6,000, the opening ceremonies for Queen's Park were followed by an athletics meet held on the new 200-yard track, along with a lacrosse match between the London Lacrosse Club and an Indigenous team.[33] Queen's Park existed to meet the needs of those Londoners interested in physical recreation who had lost the use of Victoria Park for these types of activities after 1878. The development of

Figure 6.1 A bird's eye view of Victoria Park in London in 1900.

the parks system in London was unique to the city and its citizens. However, the case of London also provides insight into broader concerns surrounding the provision of space for a variety of rational recreation and leisure practices. In the end, towns and cities throughout the country wrestled with these issues as parks began to dot Canada's urban landscapes.

Swimming in Hamilton Harbour

In addition to public parks, the most accessible locations for public recreation in towns and cities were local waterways and lakes. In many communities these bodies of water became sites for formalized swimming activities and facilities. For example, in London, Ontario, city council first explored the idea of a public swimming facility on the Thames River in 1880 to address complaints made to the police of people swimming and bathing in the river at indiscrete locations and times. This decision also coincided with several young men from the city, including one John Mason in June 1880,[34] being fined and even briefly jailed for swimming illegally.[35]

London is not the only city that had to deal with issues concerning the appropriate use of local waterways for swimming and bathing. A stark example of the changes brought about by urban and industrial growth in the late 19th century is found in the history of Hamilton Harbour. With the prosperity brought about by industrial growth in the latter decades of the 1800s, Burlington Bay (Hamilton Harbour after 1919) at Hamilton, on the western tip of Lake Ontario, became a site for discharging both residential and industrial waste. For years, the sewage transported by the city's system, including quantities of untreated human and industrial waste, went straight into the harbour. According to Nancy Bouchier and Ken Cruikshank, by 1890 the city's medical officer of health began to call attention to the higher level of water-borne disease in the mainly working-class North End of Hamilton.[36] One solution to address this concern was to extend the sewers to deposit waste farther into the bay, while another was to in-fill the heavily polluted inlets. These solutions were acceptable to local politicians who sought to limit public spending, yet some Hamilton residents continued to argue that the bay's dirty water threatened the healthful activity of recreational swimming.

Swimming, as opposed to bathing for hygiene purposes, became an increasingly respectable physical activity and sport participated in by appropriately dressed men in the 1860s and 1870s. This growing acceptance of swimming emerged from an expanding social and moral open-mindedness, along with a developing interest in competitions organized by a variety of private social clubs.[37] Enthusiasts promoted swimming as an appropriate response to the problems associated with city life—dirty air and the lack of physical activity among middle-class workers. Despite the attempts by the middle-class clubs and other groups to bring swimming under their morally acceptable sphere of influence, many Hamiltonians continued to swim for enjoyment or bathed in unsupervised areas, causing consternation among the city's leaders over both moral and safety concerns. Building public swimming areas in the harbour and controlling where and how swimming could take place was one potential solution to this problem. For example, a 1910 Hamilton bylaw required everyone except boys under 14 to cover themselves with a swimming suit from the neck to the knees.[38] The problem of regulating and controlling bathers and swimmers persisted through this period, as did continuing concerns over pollution in the bay, a situation that became progressively worse through the mid-20th century.

About the time of the First World War, Hamilton's city council was forced to address the problem of providing public swimming areas that were both morally safe and physically clean. Water quality continued to be a concern through the 1920s even as city leaders generally agreed that swimming possessed positive moral and physical value to their citizens. However, these same politicians found little common ground when it came to questions of swimmers' access to safe facilities and improving the quality and safety of the water. Swimming pools, some argued, ought to be a viable alternative to the polluted bay—petrochemical waste had become more prevalent, with swimmers often emerging from the water coated in oil. Yet there was little interest in allocating the funds necessary to build a sufficient number of in-ground pools for public use. By the mid-1940s, Hamilton's Medical Officer of Health determined that no locations on the bay existed where it remained safe for swimming.[39] Thus, the increasing levels of pollution largely ended the popular pastime of swimming in the harbour. Hamilton city leaders could no longer argue that people could swim in the bay instead of building swimming pools. Most affected by the deteriorating water quality were working-class children who had to deal with both the city's attempt to control their recreation and the continually declining quality of their favourite summer playground. As had been the case with early parks in London, providing swimming in Hamilton required city leaders to consider the physical and moral anxieties against the public expense, and normally it was this latter concern that won out in these debates.

Building Playgrounds for Children

A critical influence for an increasing interest in safe and rationally administered public park systems in Canadian towns and cities by the turn of the 20th century was the North American playground movement.[40] The playground movement grew out of the broader international and national social reform initiative that sought to provide children with a physically and morally safe environment for recreation, particularly during time away from formal schooling. Elsie McFarland identifies the role played by the National Council of Women of Canada (NCWC), its local councils, and its member organizations in organizing and administering the playground movement in Canada.[41] It was at the eighth annual meeting of the National Council of Women of Canada, held in London, Ontario, in 1901, that the issue of playgrounds came to the fore. At this meeting the NCWC passed the following resolution:

> Whereas the agitation for vacation schools and playgrounds where children may find organized recreation having become so widespread that it is now known as the playgrounds movement, and whereas the establishment of such vacation schools and playgrounds is acknowledged by educators and philanthropists to be desired in every community, and whereas the necessity for such schools and playgrounds to improve the condition of children in the cities of Canada is obvious, therefore, be it resolved that this National Council of Women of Canada declare themselves in favour of the establishment of vacation schools and playgrounds, and pledge themselves to do all in their power to promote their organization.[42]

This resolution represented a call for all local councils to petition school boards to allow use of playgrounds, under proper supervision, for recreation during the summer months. As a result, the NCWC established programs through their local councils to promote the concept of vacation schools and playgrounds throughout the country. These initiatives occurred in cities throughout the country, including Montreal, Halifax, Saint John, Toronto, Hamilton, Ottawa, Winnipeg, Vancouver, London, Port Arthur, Peterborough, Brantford, and Sault Ste. Marie, with the goal of establishing programs and facilities for children.[43] In chapter 10, Danielle Peers and Lisa Tink provide a critically informed examination of Canada's playground movement, disrupting and questioning the dominant middle-class discourse surrounding the seemingly innocuous provision of play spaces and programs at this time.

In London, the push to create playground space for the city's children emerged from a variety of locations. According to local historian Pat Morden, the Civic Improvement Society of London represented the first public group to call for public land to be set aside for children's play.[44] This group, along with the London Council of Women (LCW), actively sought sites for playgrounds in the city.[45] In a speech to London City Council in August 1904, Mayor Adam Beck provided some indication that these groups had been able to exert a degree of influence over local politicians. The mayor, in his address, called for the city to secure land for park purposes, in particular, grounds suitable for children's playgrounds. Mayor Beck argued the city's schools did not provide sufficient land for playground purposes because much of the land surrounding schools had been sold off in the past, leaving little room for playgrounds. Finally, the mayor pointed to the successes of public playgrounds for children in cities such as Buffalo, New York, and London, England, arguing that "truant officers, I believe, where play grounds exist, have little to do, for the playground instructors keep an eye on the children who ought to be at school."[46] Despite the mayor's positive stance in support of playgrounds, it was not until 1908 that a playground association formed in London to supervise playground, skating, and swimming programs.[47]

A year later, in 1909, Adam Beck, in his role as a member of the London Board of Water Commissioners, was instrumental in acquiring land to create Thames Park. This became the first new park created in the city since the dedication of Queen's Park in 1879.[48] Thames Park became one of the first public playgrounds for children in Canada.[49] Yet the playground association that operated in London from 1908 to 1912 received no operating funds from the city, and it was not until after the First World War that authorities directed public money to this end through the Public Utilities Commission, which administered all parks in the city. By 1926 the Playgrounds Department boasted of operating "fourteen playgrounds, and employ[ing] a staff of thirty-five supervisors and lifeguards."[50] Although London represents only one example of a city establishing public spaces for children to play, it is clear that the impetus for their actions arose from the broader social and political concerns regarding moral and physical safety of children living in what many perceived to be an increasingly hazardous urban environment.

At the same time that eastern Canadian cities such as London established public playgrounds, similar initiatives were occurring in larger western Canadian urban centres. Similar to the work of the LCW in London, volunteer service groups in other parts of the country also often had to fill the void in providing for children's play facilities. For example, the Gyro Club of Edmonton funded and opened its first playground in the city in 1922.[51] As a men's voluntary service association, the Gyro Club espoused a set of social reforming values. According to Paulina Cecilia Retamales and PearlAnn Reichwein, members sought "a place for men in the day-to-day lives of children . . . [where] ideals of modern citizenship and civic life were constructed and controlled through children's playgrounds, and, at the same time, promoted a distinctive Gyro culture of creative holistic outdoor play for children shared by the public."[52] Ultimately, these types of social reforming initiatives emerged from the broader concerns of white urban middle-class Canadians who believed that modern life, defined by sedentary work and an increasingly contaminated environment, had to be addressed through creating spaces and opportunities, particularly for children, to escape these threats. At the same time, these activities and programs needed to reproduce dominant middle-class values through the adoption and promotion of rational and acceptable activities. These initiatives, and the positive social and moral training that sport, games, and play provided, were not unique to towns and cities, and similar values existed in the sports of hunting and fishing, becoming vehicles for bringing Canadians closer to their wilderness heritage.

Hunting and Fishing: Escaping the Industrial Society

An excellent example of the tension between 19th- and early 20th-century industrialization and the environment lies within the traditional field sports of hunting and fishing. Although these activities were historically distinct from each other in practice and philosophy,[53] white middle- and upper-class men and women both used hunting and fishing as a way of escaping the pressures of an increasingly industrial society, with its crowded cities, polluted air, and taxing work schedule. In North America, by the end of the 19th century, the idea of spending time in nature or the wilderness had taken root, where the "over-civilized man [was urged] to escape the clangor of the wearisome city for green hills and tall forests."[54] Moreover, for white women, fishing in the wilderness offered a partial reprieve from the Victorian ideology of separate spheres that sought to keep them confined to a private domestic world, while for white males, the opportunity to venture into nature to hunt offered a chance to reclaim a sense of masculinity that was perceived to be eroding modern urban-industrial life.[55] Regardless of the sport, expression of these needs became a reality through the emergence of a lucrative tourism and service industry that

WORKING WITH PRIMARY SOURCES: A WOMAN'S VOICE IN THE WILDERNESS

In 1900, Mary Harvey Drummond in her article "A Woman's Trip to the Lauren-tides," published in the magazine *Rod and Gun in Canada*, provides a travel narrative that includes detailed accounts of fishing excursions. Reflecting on arriving at their destination after a day of travelling by train and wagon, she writes: "It was simply delightful to sit there quietly and be rowed over this beautiful sheet of water, calm as the proverbial mill pond, and made picturesque beyond description by the lofty mountains rising sheer out of its depth on our left."[56] After a day of rest, Drummond describes her eagerness to join one of the fishing parties: "The following morning found me the first arrival at the breakfast table, my light bamboo rod lying on the bench outside, and my fly book on the table beside me, just to let folks know I meant business. . . . Then a few whispered words of kindly advice from the manager, and I was off.[57] Reflecting on the day, she writes: "Ah, me! Shall I ever forget that experience of a tramp through the woods, or the wild excitement of playing my first speckled trout? 'Mademois-elle can fish better dan some of les messieurs;' my guide remarked, when at least a dozen fish lay in the bottom of the boat. No doubt he thought he had paid me a great compliment, but my womanly pride was up in arms. 'Some of les messieurs can't fish at all, can they?' I queried a trifle scornfully."[58] Writing about the demands of the day, Drummond notes, "The fatigue of the backwoods life is a very different thing to the weariness engendered by city toil." She goes on: "I was tired, it is true, but only enough to make rest a luxury, not a necessity, and my delight knew no bounds when it was announced that that same evening a 'caribou dance' would be held in the big Club room."[59]

Mary Harvey Drummond's account of her excursion provides insight into the classed and gendered experience of fishing in a wilderness setting in turn-of-the-century Canada. Drummond ends her article by encouraging women to take advantage of the benefits of venturing into the woods. She writes: "We women of to-day talk much if our rights, and while our tongues wag, we are letting slip by us the very things we clamour for. In the woods of Canada, equality with our brothers and husbands awaits us, and a share in the sports that give health to body and mind. But how many of us avail ourselves of such privileges? Too few indeed. The seaside resort with its second-rate bands, euchre parties, and boundless opportunities for the display of diamonds and dress, still reigns supreme favourite of the gentler sex, proving more strongly than anything else, that the day of emancipation has not yet dawned for women."[60]

was made possible through technological advances such as railways and steam-ships, and commercialized by an economy transitioning to industrial capitalism. As Courtney W. Mason highlights, these advances were underscored by a sporting ethic imbued with new ideas of conservation that were "committed to preserving fish and mammal populations for the pleasure of sport hunters and the benefit of the tourism industry" (see chapter 5) while excluding Indigenous peoples and practices. Thus, the growth of fishing and hunting among white middle- and upper-class urbanites was ultimately an extension of the colonial gaze that sought to control the landscape—and the peoples thought to be a part of it—through science and technology.

Women, Fishing, and Tourism

Fishing for recreation, or angling, dates back to the earliest days of European contact with Canada. For elite British women, fishing had been an acceptable recreation since the Renaissance through its association with the "virtues of gentleness, patience, contemplation, and Christian devotion."[61] As women travelled and immigrated to North America, "they brought a tradition of angling that was readily adopted and adapted" by white middle- and upper-class Canadian women.[62] In 19th-century Canada, socially visible fisherwomen included Lady Dufferin, the wife of Governor General the Earl of Dufferin; Princess Louise, whose husband, Lord Lorne, was also a Governor General; and author Susannah Moodie, whose *Diary of Susannah Moodie* (1838) and *Life in the Clearings* (1858) provided accounts of pioneer life in Upper Canada to eager audiences in Britain.[63]

These women, along with their contemporaries, modelled and detailed their passion for angling to family, friends, and ultimately, the public. Likewise, mass-produced Canadian newspapers and magazines such as *Rod and Gun in Canada* were quick to highlight the angling prowess of the female members of the British Royal Family. For example, in 1905, *Rod and Gun in Canada* observed that not only was the King a fly fisherman, but "Her Majesty the Queen does not allow him to surpass her skill in casting the fly. All their children follow the parental example in this respect and their eldest daughter, the Duchess of Fife, is said to excel any members of the Royal Family as a fisherwoman."[64] Thus, the acceptability for a woman to not only fish but also demonstrate skill and mastery came to exemplify middle- and upper-class Canadian women from the highest level of society. For women in the Canadian West (see figure 6.2), despite having "significantly different life experiences compared to urban women in Central Canada," adherence to the same set of middle class values was still expected.[65] That many western Canadian newspapers highlighted such stories and encouraged their readers to read the latest issues of *Rod and Gun in Canada* indicates it was not only eastern Canadian women who were inculcated by angling's respectable reputation.[66]

Fishing the Highwood River, southern Alberta 1910, NA-5060-3, Courtesy of Glenbow Library and Archives, Archives and Special Collections, University of Calgary

Figure 6.2   Highwood River excursion in 1907.

This relatively unquestioned respectability for angling allowed opportunities for middle- and upper-class white women to travel into nature and create a space for themselves as tourists. Indeed, as Canadian (and American) women ventured into the wilderness either alongside their husbands, brothers, and fathers or by themselves, they participated in a burgeoning tourism industry that, under the guise of conservation, sought to transform nature through the implementation of regulations and practices that Courtney W. Mason notes had little to do with preserving "a healthy and intact ecosystem" (see chapter 5) and everything to do with creating ideal spaces for recreational hunting and fishing. That the Canadian Pacific Railway (CPR) and other railroad companies actively promoted fishing as a tourist venture furthered the incursion of white urban anglers into rural and, at one time, remote locales. As Lynda Jessup notes, "The completion of the Intercolonial Railway through New Brunswick in 1876 made salmon rivers in the region easily accessible from both central Canada and the northeastern United States."[67]

Once in the wilderness, wealthy tourists found an ideal sporting playground where their angling adventures could be carefully and publicly documented within widely circulated travel narratives and outdoors magazines. For some women, it was a chance to vocalize the opportunities and agency offered to them through fishing, otherwise limited to them in urban society. As visitors who were passing through, these women had the luxury of "utilizing their preconceived images of gender, race and class in a flexible manner according to each new experience they encountered."[68] For example, Mary Harvey Drummond took offence when her skill as an angler was underestimated by her guide when he marveled that she was better at fishing than some men. She then used this incident to vocalize her agency and authority, calling for other women to realize that activities such as fishing, offered the chance to experience a level of equality that could only be talked about in a domestic, urban setting.

As the business of nature tourism grew, and as cities and towns began to expand and build larger residential and industrial zones—often altering neighbouring natural features such as rivers to the detriment of fish populations—the problem arose of what to do about depleting natural resources. Indeed, by the turn of the 20th century, the economic value of a western Canadian sport fishery had been clearly identified. North-West Mounted Police officer J.H. McIllree noted in his 1890 District of Calgary fishery report:

> The trout fishing is one of the chief attractions in this District, both to residents and visitors. In a new country every natural attraction should be made the most of to induce residents to remain in and visitors to visit and bring money into the country. I should recommend most strongly that stringent laws be passed regarding the preservation and capture of fish, especially on these points, a sufficient close time every year, fish to be caught only with a hook and line, standard size of fish to be caught, heavy penalties to be enforced for using fish traps, nets or illegal instruments, and regulations as to the sale of trout.[69]

The need to preserve fish stocks to ensure the continued influx of money from white middle- and upper-class anglers led to the emergence of numerous fish and game clubs that lobbied local, provincial, and federal governments for stricter conservation laws. These laws often brought groups of privileged anglers, be they resident or tourists, into conflict with less privileged locals who fished for subsistence or commercial purposes. This was particularly true for Indigenous peoples, who, as Mason notes, "were targets of condemnation by sport and game clubs as well as related authorities" who chose to overlook the more obvious impacts of railways, industries, and increasing numbers of sport hunters and anglers on the depletion of game (see chapter 5). Furthermore, lower-class white anglers could also be singled out for exclusion. For example, in the case of Hamilton, where 19th-century urban and industrial expansion destroyed fish-rearing marshes and polluted the waters of Lake Ontario, Nancy Bouchier and Ken Cruikshank note that "class-based definitions of proper recreation shaped conservation initiatives such as [John] Kerr's: fish and game would be protected if mid-Victorian ideas of cultivated and legitimate sporting behaviour were extended to fishing and hunting."[70] Thus, for the elite anglers of Hamilton, the creation of new laws and restrictions for subsistence and commercial fishers "testified to the power of elites to mould nature into their own image."[71] Moreover, in the West, the presence of fisherwomen on rivers and lakes may have further legitimized calls for state-sponsored conservation efforts as well as economic initiatives aimed at attracting tourists to the region. For, as Sheila McManus observes, many white women, "believed that they had a special awareness of that fragility and a special duty to help protect it because they were women."[72]

Tourism also allowed urban middle- and upper-middle-class white anglers access to Indigenous culture through the employment of male fishing guides. Viewed to be part of nature itself, white anglers perpetuated the "dominant perception that civilization and progress would soon alter both the landscape and Indigenous culture," and thus, there was urgency on behalf of white anglers to encounter Indigenous peoples before they "disappeared."[73] Since they were merely passing through the landscape, white anglers felt free to utilize their preconceived images of race and class as they saw fit. For example, "fisher-women would often comment on either the intelligence or 'civility' of their guides based on their ability to facilitate the desired adventure or because of the supposed 'purity' of the guide's blood lines."[74] Indeed, while the physical attributes of Indigenous male guides were often lauded, they were also viewed to be lacking "the self-restraint identified with hegemonic ideals of manliness," which resulted in what white fly fishers deemed to be "reckless environmental practices" such as spearfishing.[75] Therefore, tourism served to commodify Indigenous peoples, placing a value on them according to the degree to which they were able to meet the expectations of elite visitors who had paid for a true wilderness experience.[76]

Gentlemen Hunters and Indigenous Relationships to the Environment

While fishing provided white women a respectable reprieve from an urbanized and highly gendered life, sport hunting provided white middle- and upper-class men and boys the opportunity to demonstrate their masculinity during a time when many Canadians "believed too many urban boys led sedentary lives that provided little opportunity for differentiation between the sexes."[77] Hunting not only provided ideal training of men and boys for war but also connected males with a controllable wilderness experienced that hearkened a return to the "core cultural values" of manhood.[78] Moreover, as George Colpitts observes, as sport hunting grew in popularity among urbanites, many came to believe that participation in the ancient sport fostered personal rejuvenation through a distinct connection to nature.[79]

Central to the notions of sport in the natural environment for white men in colonial Canada was the British sporting idea of the sportsmen's code that "outlined appropriately aristocratic methods for big-game hunting . . . and distinguished the gentlemen hunters from their moral, racial, and class inferiors."[80] Actions distinguishing gentlemen sport hunters from those who hunted for subsistence included employing active hunting skills rather than baiting or luring prey, and using skill and technique when approaching the animal to determine if it was suitable to shoot and kill.[81] Therefore, this code not only defined these elite hunters' "whiteness, Britishness, and elitism . . . [but also] created socio-political space between the hunters and Aboriginal guides and colonist pothunters, whom they deemed morally inferior."[82] When combined with the new ideas of conservation described by Courtney W. Mason in chapter

5, the code allowed for, and justified, the need for elite hunters to claim ownership of the wilderness, so that it could be protected and ultimately civilized.

This appropriation of nature was most obvious through how elite hunters portrayed themselves and their interpretations of the wilderness for their urban peers. As Lynda Jessup states, "In Canada, as elsewhere, the removal of Native rights to the animal world through the introduction of policies and laws restricting hunting and fishing technologies went hand in hand with this aesthetic appropriation of the environment as landscape."[83] For example, as part of their widely distributed heroic hunting narratives, elite hunters often included illustrations or paintings of the wilderness through which they travelled. When used in combination with textual descriptions of nature such as *vast*, *rich*, and *fertile*, these highly contextualized images—often placing the elite hunter or fisherman in the foreground of a pastoral scene while obfuscating the facial features of Indigenous peoples—communicated a powerful message of an uninhabited, resource-rich landscape that was ready to support colonization.[84]

In contrast, in the case of Indigenous hunters, different understandings of hunting emerged from a culture that viewed both hunter and prey in a relationship linked to the perpetuation of a balanced and viable world. The many and varied Indigenous cultures who lived in Canada before contact with European colonists provide alternative understandings of hunting through the traditional knowledge passed down through oral tradition from generation to generation. One example of this is the "Swampy-Cree worldview, [where] hunters and animals were all part of an intricate interplay of reciprocal responsibilities, ensuring the survival of both humans and animals."[85] Traditionally, Swampy Cree hunters adhered to rules for hunting similar to gentlemen hunters such as not killing pregnant and young animals. However, because Indigenous peoples hunted for survival and not sport prior to contact, they did engage in practices viewed by gentleman hunters as unsporting, including mass hunts when conditions and animal populations allowed. Yet beyond practical considerations, the "Swampy-Cree understood that the world they were part of worked in perfect order, made by the Creator. Animals did not live in utter chaos but had certain rules and regulations to follow. Predatory animals, for instance, did not kill their prey randomly but only in order to nourish themselves and their offspring . . . and animal behaviour served as a guideline for humans"[86]

The close relationship between hunter and prey in Indigenous culture is evident among the Niitsitapi, or Blackfoot peoples of the southwestern Canadian prairies. According to Niitsitapi writer Mike Mountain Horse, animals "could feel, perceive, and reason as might a man, and that they possessed these qualities even after death."[87] Thus, when a Niitsitapi hunter killed an animal, they took great care not to offend its spirit, often offering a prayer or an apology. Therefore, Indigenous conceptions of nature and animals had a strong influence on how they hunted, though contact and the emergence of a trading economy with European settlers disrupted many of these traditional notions. Additionally, the laws and regulations enacted by Canadian authorities in various jurisdictions drew primarily on British concepts of hunting that negatively affected both Indigenous peoples and the environment. Despite this, Braden Te Hiwi cautions that this "should not be interpreted as the end of Indigenous hunting culture, or the weakening of Indigenous cultures." Rather, their ability to adapt highlights "Indigenous cultures are dynamic and living," with "connections between culture in the past, present, and future" (see chapter 3). Of course, urbanization and industrialization had an impact on hunting and fishing activities for all people, yet these and other outdoor pursuits remained important cultural markers and were viewed as antidotes for overcoming the problems of modern life.

Outdoor Recreation Into the 20th Century

The problems commonly attributed to urban and industrial life in Canada persisted through the 20th century, and, as was the case in the past, sport and recreation activities reemerged through the 1900s in new forms but remained connected to earlier notions that healthful outdoor activities could provide an antidote to the ills of modern living. Examples of these new activities included the popular Boy Scouts and Girl Guides, mountain climbing, skiing, and bicycling. This is certainly not a comprehensive list of all the outdoor pursuits that became popular pastimes, yet each of these examples provides a way to consider the social values attached to sporting practices that took place outside an urban setting, specifically notions of healthful living in an age defined by increasingly limited opportunities to escape the dangers of living and working in overcrowded and contaminated towns and cities.

Recreating Outside the Modern City: The Boy Scout and Girl Guide Movements

At the time when social reformers were actively addressing the need for safe and productive play opportunities in towns and cities, new organizations were developing to provide boys and girls with opportunities to escape to the Canadian wilderness. The most notable of these early 20th-century organizations was the Boy Scouts. In 1907, Robert Baden-Powell founded the Boy Scouts in Britain as a quasi-militaristic program focused on instilling positive social values such as patriotism, fellowship, and good citizenship.[88] In Canada the Boy Scouts caught on quickly. Several years later Baden-Powell also founded the Girl Guides based on similar but gender-appropriate social ideals.[89] These movements were clearly colonial in their influence, imparting British values throughout the empire, where Boy Scouts and Girl Guides in Canada established and promoted gendered identities as prescribed in their respective handbooks. For the Boy Scouts, the "hyper-masculine school ethic of 'playing the game,' a sporting metaphor for doing one's patriotic duty, remained a constant through every edition."[90] Similarly, "by 1912, the Girl Guides had created their own instructional literature titled *How Girls Can Help to Build Up the Empire*,"[91] a guide that sought to promote an appropriately feminine approach to loyalty and patriotism. However, after the First World War, Canadian Scouts reinterpreted their handbook, where author Gerald Brown introduced both the flora and fauna of Canada while asserting the nation's independence from Britain through redefining the idea of *empire*.[92] Beyond these ideological concerns, the Boy Scouts and Girl Guides also represented important institutions that brought young people out of the cities and into the wilderness, even if under strictly controlled circumstances.

Girl Guide and Boy Scout programs involved a wide variety of activities that sought to provide training in gendered vocations and avocations including, for example, "homekeeping" and "mothercraft" for girls[93] and military skills such as tracking, mapping, and first aid for boys.[94] Outdoor activities provided girls and boys similar experiences, where

> camping and woodcraft . . . occupied a central place in the mythology of Guiding and Scouting, [and] were the products of a particular set of circumstances in late nineteenth- and early twentieth-century North America and western Europe as middle-class adults, concerned about the physical and moral effects of urban life, sought beauty, authenticity, and restorative escape through anti-modernism and wilderness tourism.[95]

Camping, in particular, represented a principal activity of Boy Scouts throughout the British Empire, taking place on permanently acquired, rented, or borrowed land and under canvas tents. Both Boy Scouts and Girl Guides participated in comparable activities, "including cooking, cleaning, swimming, and telling stories around the camp fire."[96] Although Boy Scouts and Girl Guides participated in similar activities while camping, the social values that leaders sought to impart remained quite different. The opportunity for outdoor adventure and training awaited boys, while girls participated in "sensible pastimes that would teach them femininity and domestic skills while appealing to their 'natural' spiritual and maternal instincts."[97] Despite these differing goals, the universal goal for young people to spend time in the wilderness away from the ills of urban life offered a powerful and attractive influence to reinforce the expected social ideals that formed part of a productive and respectable childhood.

Mountaineering and Skiing as Wilderness Sports

Through the early 20th century, sport and leisure activities were increasingly organized and linked to notions of competitive achievement. This trend in sport remained consistent for a variety of outdoor pursuits including mountaineering, skiing, and bicycling. These sports emerged at a time when urban Canadians started to search out activities that would take them away from the city and into nature. Although many of the popular outdoor leisure activities were not established sports, there were people who actively sought to apply the ethos of sport and competitive physical activities through conquering nature, or providing the opportunity to test oneself against others in a wilderness setting outside the traditional sporting arena. The emergence of outdoor wilderness sport as an organized undertaking can be traced back to the latter 1800s when the transcontinental railway opened the western reaches of Canada and white middle-class sporting men and women sought to challenge themselves in the Selkirk and Rocky Mountains.

The history of mountaineering in Canada, specifically in the western mountain ranges of Alberta and British Columbia, is tied to a variety of influences including Canadians' interest in engaging in manly sports and a growing nationalism as projected by the Canadian government's policy of westward expansion via the CPR.[98] Drawing on the existing British and European traditions of alpinism, by the 1880s Canadian enthusiasts including Sir Sandford Fleming considered the need to form a Canadian alpine club. Little progress occurred in this quest until the turn of the 20th century, when a number of actors including the CPR, which sought to cultivate tourism in the region, surveyor Arthur Wheeler, and Winnipeg-based alpine enthusiast Elizabeth Parker initiated the project. Parker in 1905 argued that "it was both important and necessary to establish a Canadian alpine club because, in the absence of one, foreign mountaineers would conquer Canada's virgin peaks."[99] In March 1906, 27 delegates met in Winnipeg, including Wheeler and Parker, to form the Alpine Club of Canada (ACC). At these inaugural meetings, club officers were elected, a library was established (temporarily in Parker's home), arrangements were made for the first annual camp in British Columbia, and a journal was established—the *Canadian Alpine Journal*—to maintain a record of the club's ongoing activities.[100] Thus, in a relatively short period, this group started the process of making the mountains in the west Canada's mountains.

According to Zac Robinson, the golden age of mountaineering in Canada was from 1886 until 1925. The earlier date coincides with the opening of the western mountains through rail access in the form of the CPR, while the latter date is the year of the successful ascent of Mount Logan (Canada's highest peak at 5,959 metres [19,550 feet]) in the Yukon Territory.[101] During this period, mountain climbing enthusiasts relied on the skills of imported professional European mountain guides, while the ACC provided leadership for the sport of mountaineering. Increasingly, alpinism in Canada became a competitive undertaking for climbers who sought first ascents and to test themselves against the newly accessible mountains. Ultimately, the ACC assumed leadership of both the protection and conquering of the mountains, and although a third of the club's members were women by 1907, decisions as to who could attempt more difficult peaks were clearly based on gender, where women were relegated to attempt easier routes and ascents.[102] Thus, by 1925, when the ACC organized the attempt on Mount Logan, "the exhibition was a meticulously organized, large scale siege"[103] and, importantly, included members of the prominent alpine clubs from the United States and Britain. As a sport, mountaineering represented the ultimate in an organized contest against the natural world, an undertaking that involved manly courage and skillful preparation and execution. Indeed, the exploits of these climbers were embraced as part of the nationalist ethos of conquering—and to a lesser degree preserving—the highest peaks in the land and provided all Canadians with an example of how to appropriately interact with the nation's natural environment.

As the Golden Age of mountain climbing, marked by exploration and first ascents in Canada's western mountain ranges, was coming to an end, popular interest in mountain-based recreation and sport shifted to more stylized activities including skiing. Robinson notes the first skiers made their way to the eastern Rocky Mountains prior to the First World War, and in the decades after the war, the popularity of both back and front country skiing grew. One event that raised the popularity of both skiing and the tourism potential of the region was the Banff Winter Carnival, inaugurated in 1917, an event supported by the CPR. The festival held sporting events including skiing to entertain the 1,000-plus spectators; despite the existence of local athletes, the majority of competitors were drawn primarily from local Norwegian clubs, while Banff-based ski club members watched.[104] By the early 1920s, making turns down a slope, or "ski running," steadily grew in popularity at Mount Norquay. Adding to these developments, of course, was the introduction of new techniques and equipment, such as the stem turn, shorter skis, and climbing skins, advancements then common in Europe.[105] With these technological changes, along with money from American investors, skiing enthusiasts cleared trees to create the first runs, and by the end of the decade, downhill skiing had become part of the Banff winter sports landscape.

Downhill skiing became a popular and competitive sport for men and women with means throughout much of Canada by the 1930s. According to M. Ann Hall, by "1935, the Seigniory Club at Montebello [Quebec] instituted the first Dominion Championships for women."[106] Of course, the impetus for competitive skiing was closely tied to the sport's prominent place in the recently instituted 1924 Winter Olympics. The sport of skiing relied on facilities constructed in the hills and mountains outside of cities, providing the mid-20th-century bourgeois element of society a reason to travel and play in the Canadian hinterlands. This need to move and recreate outside the urban areas can be traced back to mid-19th-century Montreal and the snowshoeing trend that saw middle-class men dressed in their club attire tramping through the open lands immediately outside the city.[107] Thus, skiing represented an extension of earlier popular sport and recreation activity, providing a means to escape the urban environment. Indeed, in the brief Canadian summer months another sport, cycling, functioned in a similar manner, taking city dwellers into the country for both leisure and competition.

Bicycle Racing on Country Roads

The first bicycle to appear in Canada rolled through the streets of Montreal in 1874.[108] This arrival signalled the beginning of three decades of prominence for cycling in Canada (see figure 6.3). By the early 1880s, clubs such as the Montreal Bicycle Club provided young middle-class men the opportunity to demonstrate their manliness and social status. To these ends, members of these clubs organized "'outings' or rides into the country after the fashion of the Montreal Snowshoe Club tramps."[109] Although cycling was largely a men's sport, historian M. Ann Hall notes that women were always involved in the sport, riding large tricycles and the more accessible and popular safety bicycle in the late 1880s. Furthermore, outside the confines of these clubs and leisure riding, there were instances of highly competitive women racing on high-wheelers, most notable of whom was Canadian Louise Armaindo.[110] Yet in the male middle-class enclave of amateur bicycle clubs, long leisurely rides on bumpy country roads were accompanied by opportunities for the intense athletic competition of track and road racing. For example, in London, Ontario, the Forest City Bicycle Club's annual championship for the Irving Medal included a race held on a road course. This competition provided members the opportunity to test their rugged masculinity over an extended distance on rough country roads. In 1890, the final race for the Irving Medal began in the town of Lucan, Ontario, and finished in London's Victoria Park, a distance of roughly 29 kilometres (18 miles). Mr. W.G. Owens and Mr. S.F. Lawrason had accumulated the same number of points after a series of races, and a final tiebreaking duel was to be held over this country course. Yet when the final race started, Lawrason with-

Galt Museum & Archives

Figure 6.3 The Chinook Bicycle Club in 1897.

drew because of an injury sustained the week prior, and all Owens had to do was ride the course to claim the championship.[111] This type of race is suggestive of the broader interest particularly among young men to both test their skills against their peers and to engage in the challenges of cycling the rough lands outside their cities.

Similarly, in Western Canada in the late 1880s and early 1890s, cycling clubs and competitions in Calgary, Lethbridge, and Medicine Hat afforded middle-class men opportunities comparable to those available to their eastern counterparts. Yet on the recently settled prairies, interest in comparing the practicality of the bicycle against the horse became a point of interest with respect to which mode of transportation worked best on the open range. In April 1888, a poem republished in the *Lethbridge News*—likely from an American source—lampooned the chance meeting of a cowboy and cyclist on the prairies.

> The first we saw o' the hightoned tramp
>
> War' over thar at our Pacos camp;
>
> He war' comin' down the Santa Fe trail
>
> Astride of a wheel, with a crooked tail,
>
> A skinnin' a long, with a merry song,
>
> An' ringin' a little warnin' gong.
>
> He looked so outlandish, strange and queer
>
> That all of us grinned from ear to ear,
>
> An' every boy on the round-up swore
>
> He had never seen sich a hoss afore.[112]

The cowboy, in this fictional story, proposes a race over 10 miles, wagering his bronco against the cyclist's machine. By maintaining a steady pace the cyclist wins the race, and it is only at the end of the tale that the cowboy learns he has just lost to a man that has ridden his bicycle around the world.[113] Although a simple and humorous tale, the idea of riding on the wilds of the open range, or around the world, suggests the distinctly pastoral opportunities cycling could provide. It was not until the early 20th century that automobiles supplanted the bicycle, and despite this change in technology, drivers continued to demonstrate similar practices to their cycling predecessors by driving and racing through the countryside.

Conclusion

Today, Canadians continue to interact with the natural world in ways quite similar to people who lived in towns and cities in previous generations. As in the past, towns and cities continue to provide green space and parks to serve as a respite from urban life. Indeed, historically these sites, whether parks, playgrounds, or swimming facilities, were expected to provide children and adults access to safe and morally respectable leisure activities. At the same time, urban Canadians continue to search out recreation opportunities in the wilderness much the same way as hunters, anglers, and mountain climbers did more than a century ago. Again, these wilderness-based avocations provide a myriad of opportunities to inoculate Canadians against the ailments caused by living in large, often polluted urban centres. Therefore, the influence of industrialization and urbanization on the sport, leisure, and recreation lives of Canadians must be understood as being both formative and reactionary. First, new technologies and urban life changed how people worked and played. The telegraph, railways, roads, and the radio, for example, forever altered how people lived. Yet as these revolutions disrupted life, social reformers with romanticized notions of returning to a healthier past took actions to counter changes—often problems related to physical and moral safety—brought about by modern living. In the end, much of the appeal that continues to foster our interaction with the environment and the natural world remains tied to the past and the ongoing attempts to recapture the purity of our lost preindustrial heritage.

DISCUSSION QUESTIONS

1. Under what circumstances and for whom were the first municipal parks in Canada created?
2. Why was providing safe and accessible swimming facilities in the late 19th century controversial and often considered an unnecessary extravagance?
3. How did the ideological underpinnings of white Canadian hunters differ from Indigenous peoples' traditional reasons for hunting?
4. Why did middle-class Canadians around the turn of the 20th century look to the countryside or natural settings for their sporting experiences?

SUGGESTED READINGS

Adams, Carly. "Supervised Spaces to Play: Social Reform, Citizenship, and Femininity at Municipal Playgrounds in London Ontario, 1900-1942." *Ontario History* 103, no. 1 (2011): 60-81.

Bouchier, Nancy B., and Ken Cruikshank. *The People and the Bay: A Social and Environmental History of Hamilton Harbour.* Vancouver: UBC Press, 2016.

Gillespie, Greg. "The Empire's Eden: British Hunters, Travel Writing, and Imperialism in Nineteenth-Century Canada." In *The Culture of Hunting in Canada.* Edited by Jean L. Manore and Dale G. Miner. Vancouver: UBC Press, 2007.

Jessup, Lynda. "Landscapes of Sport, Landscapes of Exclusion: The 'Sportsman's Paradise' in Late-Nineteenth-Century Painting." *Journal of Canadian Studies* 40, no. 1, (2006): 71-124.

Reichwein, PearlAnn, *Climbers Paradise: Making Canada's Mountain Parks, 1906-1974.* Edmonton: University of Alberta Press, 2014.

CHAPTER 7

IDEOLOGICAL STRUGGLES AND THE EMERGENCE OF CRICKET, LACROSSE, AND BASEBALL

Craig Greenham, PhD
University of Windsor

LEARNING OBJECTIVES

In this chapter you will

- discover that the evolution of 19th-century Canadian sport owed much to ideological debates about the nature of sport and recreation;
- explore the influence of British and American ideals on the development of Canadian sport;
- learn about the efforts of key individuals and organizations in the promotion of their respective sports; and
- understand that organized sport in Canada in the mid-19th century was exclusionary in terms of gender, race, and class.

The alteration of Canada's sport landscape during the 19th century, from its onset to its conclusion, profoundly shaped the nature and direction of national sport. Canadian sportsmen[1] transitioned athletics from largely individual recreational pursuits and loosely created clubs with mostly social objectives to team sports with formalized league structures and an emphasis on victory. As the century progressed, modern sport emerged. Sport historian Michael Robidoux defines modern sport as organized events that were played inside certain confines and in agreement with uniform rules upheld by leagues and organizations. Over time, equipment became standardized and the happenings of a game became recorded and measured.[2] Ultimately, greater uniformity was achieved, which limited the localized methods of individual and community-based expressions of athletics.[3] *Modern*, however, implies more than changes in play; it also involves the political motivations responsible for these modifications. The political purposes behind the modernization of sport in Canada cannot be separated from the actual changes in the games themselves.

It is important, therefore, to take a step back and place sport development within the national context in which it existed. From Confederation to the outbreak of the First World War, Canada had seemingly limitless potential but very little direction. The young dominion had an abundance of land and natural resources, yet no consensus existed among the country's intellectuals, let alone its mass citizenry, in regard to Canada's plan for the future. What kind of country should Canada be? What international relationships needed to be fostered and which discouraged? To complicate matters, Canada's history, geography, regionalism,[4] and relative youth as a country added to the ideological tug-of-war to decide the course Canada should pursue. While the debate's public discourse was largely waged by Canadian literati and politicians, the competing directions for the country conflicted society as a whole and pitted advocates of imperialism, continentalism, and nationalism against each other. This ideological struggle shaped the development and organization of sport in Canada.

For many Canadians, the choice was clear. The ethnicity and history of the country as well as its institutions suggested that the majority cherished British traditions and desired close links with Britain.[5] Promoters of imperialism also believed Canada could attain important international status through active membership in the British Empire. Inherent in this philosophy was an anti-American bias, for its revolution and subsequent republicanism were seen as objectionable. The second voice in the ideological debate came from Canadians, including many Quebeckers, who felt that Canada should cut ties with the Empire and pursue its own path. These nationalists felt the obligation to the mother country was too burdensome and hindered national growth and independence. They argued that Britain and the United States, Canada's closest allies, did not always act in the country's best interest, and through more autonomy, a self-reliant Canada would emerge. The third group felt that nationalism was unrealistic, and imperialism was impractical. Continentalists argued that Canada was not powerful enough to stand on its own, as the nationalists believed, and that an alliance and membership within the Empire was not a viable option given the distance between the two entities, both in terms of space and mindset. As Canada grew to maturity, the ideals of British imperialism became more unnatural. Continentalism, in a lot of ways, was natural. Canada shared many things with her American cousins—similar geography, values, culture, language, religion, lifestyle, and economic interests. Continentalism was practical, if not as romantic as imperialism.

This chapter uses the evolution of team summer sports from the mid- to late 19th century to illustrate the impact these political beliefs and principles had on the emergence and control of Canadian sport. Each sport was closely linked to an ideology that had prominence in Canada during the era: cricket and imperialism; lacrosse and nationalism; baseball and continentalism. Through a comparative case study, you will be introduced to the factors that worked for and against the success of cricket, lacrosse, and baseball and the implications of their political affiliations. These respective ideological linkages uniquely flavoured the ascendance and decline of these sports. Cricket, lacrosse, and baseball's popularity in 19th-century Canada evolved differently, but each owed much to ideological influence.

Cricket and British Imperialism

Domestically, cricket reached its zenith in the 1850s and 1860s, at which time Canadian cricketers trailed only their British and Australian counterparts in the international hierarchy.[6] The sport was established in Canada during the first half of the 19th century, with cricket clubs being formed in Saint John (1828),[7] Toronto (1834), Kingston (1835), Halifax (1842), and Montreal (1845).[8] Clubs were also established in the West's major hubs in the second half of the century.[9] In the years that preceded Confederation in 1867, sport in British North America, at least for settlers, was dominated by British games. Immigrants, soldiers, and native-born subjects filled with the sport traditions of the motherland generally played games of British origin.[10] Cricket, the quintessential sport of imperialism, was the first summer sport to take hold in Canada.[11]

During Queen Victoria's reign (1837-1901), cricket was the game the British were encouraged to carry with them to foreign lands and to introduce to their Indigenous charges.[12] According to British sport historian Roger Hutchinson, "The Victorian British did not introduce cricket to their Empire solely because they enjoyed the game. They took it with them because they felt that they had a duty to do so. Just as it taught discipline and honour to their young officer cadets, so those qualities might rub off on to some of the subject peoples."[13] The effort to celebrate Anglo superiority and British imperialism became an obsession for many politicians, philosophers, and militarists. This attitude was particularly evident in the 1850s, a decade of various deliberate demonstrations that were intended to symbolize the achievements of Victorian Britain. Among the accomplishments in the colonies was the completion of the Victoria Bridge across the St. Lawrence River in 1859.

That same year marked the arrival of George Parr's British cricket club to play teams from Montreal and Hamilton and flex some imperial muscle.[14] Parr's club won these matches handily, and the success of these exhibitions began a parade across the Atlantic by teams within the British Empire to play Canadian clubs. These visits, particularly from British cricketers, injected the domestic version of the game with much enthusiasm. The tours were opportunities for locals to become invested in Canada and root for Canadian cricket. For Britain, these cricket tours were used as a test to gauge the growth of cricket in the colonies.[15] Visiting international clubs also reinforced upon Canadians that cricket was a prestigious game. Sport historian David Brown remarked, "The onset of foreign teams to Canada merely accentuated the elite and imperial dimensions of cricket and of those who patronised the game."[16]

Muscular Christianity

Anglophiles who sought to spread Victorian values[17] to all reaches of the globe took this effort very seriously. Central to this moral code was the tenet of muscular Christianity. This masculine ideal was not only achieved purely through moral endeavour but also through the attainment of physical strength and fitness acquired through rigorous exercise. The merits of muscular Christianity can be traced to the New Testament, but the phrase was coined by Charles Kingsley, and Thomas Hughes prominently promoted its virtues in British novels.[18] Kingsley and Hughes were not only writers but also social critics who staunchly supported British imperialism. In the mid-19th century, the duo was concerned that asceticism and effeminacy undermined the Anglican Church. Kingsley and Hughes wanted the church to exemplify more manly traits if it was to be a suitable vessel through which British imperialism was promoted. Physical fitness became as central to the model of the ideal man as moral qualities. Cricket was considered a manly activity and a pursuit able to improve a man's body "for the protection of the weak, and the advancement of all righteous causes."[19]

Hierarchical Society

According to Canadian sport historian Nancy Bouchier, from the time of cricket's introduction to Canadian society, the sport's culture symbolized what it meant to be gentlemen. For cricketers, the sport reinforced their allegiance with the ruling class of England as the townspeople imitated the social pursuits of Britain's landed aristocracy.[20] The locals carried this emulation to demonstrate their social superiority symbolically in what they felt to be a natural ranking.[21] It was those atop the hierarchy that supported cricket most earnestly, and it was established as the game for society's well heeled, in no small part because of a top-down promotion model. Early lieutenant-governors of Upper Canada, Sir John Colborne and Sir Francis Bond Head, publicly championed the sport prior to 1850. Sir Charles Stanley, fourth Viscount Monck, ordered the creation of a cricket pitch on the premises of the Governor General's residence at Rideau Hall.[22] The game was also ensconced within Canada's prestigious private schools, which used British public schools as their standard. Toronto's Upper Canada College, for example, officially adopted cricket in 1836 (see figure 7.1).[23] Schools such as these catered to students from middle- and upper-class English immigrant families and Canadian anglophiles who kept cricket within their own social confines.[24]

Cricket was not a game for the masses and was strictly the preserve of a rather small but powerful elite. Many cricket clubs were socially

City of Toronto Archives, Fonds 1568, Item 197.

Figure 7.1 Cricket match in 1908 at Upper Canada College, a private boys' school in Toronto.

exclusive. As Canada's population grew during the 19th century, more Canadian-born or Canadian-educated cricketers took leadership roles in the game's domestic development. These people were male, usually educated in an independent school, and from a select group of middle- and upper-class families that were either first- or second-generation immigrants from Britain. They settled in the young country's important metropolises like Toronto, Hamilton, Ottawa, and Montreal and were instilled with the merits of amateurism.

Those involved in Canadian cricket were in strict adherence to the Victorian values that dominated the social philosophy. Amateurism was regarded as the only way to develop gentlemen and for sport to remain pure from gambling and other unseemly vices that were associated with the professional sport model emanating from the United States. Among the most dogged defenders of amateurism, Canadian cricketers were strictly unpaid to keep the sport a virtuous endeavour.

Cricket's Downfall

Despite its prestigious standing in the British Empire, by the early 1860s Canadian cricket was in decline. Although advocates in Canada initially celebrated the sport's connection to the Empire, sport historian David Cooper has since argued this link eventually impeded the game's domestic growth.[25] Unlike in Australia where cricket enjoyed considerable success, Canadians never modified the game to fit their North American environment—cricket was merely copied and protected. Australian sport historian Richard Cashman suggests that two steps must occur for a sport to be successfully transplanted from one society to another. The first stage is adaptation, which occurs when the game is altered or changed to fit the society into which the game has been introduced. The second step is assimilation, which occurs when the game becomes part of society's dominant sporting culture. It is important to note that while the rules and regulations of the game affect a sport's popularity, it is not the games themselves that prosper or decline. Instead, Cashman reminds us that ultimately the players, spectators, administrators, and promoters are responsible for the fate of particular sports.[26]

Any success cricket had in the mid-19th century was due to continued British immigration and a few Canadian gentlemen living in urban areas. These cricketers did not want adaptation or assimilation but preferred that the game remain as British as possible, right down to afternoon tea.[27] Cricket was never Canadianized and adopted into domestic culture because society's elites never truly sought to bring the game to working-class Canadians. Conversely, the general Canadian public demonstrated no appetite to make cricket theirs. It is not only the "agents of proselytism" that influence the process of adaptation and assimilation, but also the recipients from the host society who might play, watch, and administer the game. Canada's largely rural population, of various ethnic backgrounds, had not the time, nor inclination, for a British upper-class game that consumed valuable daylight working hours.

Furthermore, cricket's elite status did not endear it to the nationalists and continentalists who favoured games with more appeal across the class divide. Bouchier wrote that cricket's "most visible organized form in elite enclaves, such as Canada's private school system, made it seem inaccessible—or maybe just distasteful—to many. The promotion of this model of the sport, by extension, would be at odds with the middle-class agenda. . . . They relegated cricket to a marginal role in community sporting life."[28]

Moving Away From British Sport

Some Canadian sportsmen wanted to create their own distinct sporting culture. Aside from Newfoundland,[29] Canada was Britain's oldest colony and a need for various forms of independence was expected.[30] The independent thinking of Canadian nationalism was not the only factor at work. Sport historian Keith Sandiford writes of the multicultural immigration pattern that had developed: "The Canadian culture which emerged from the melting pots was consequently much less Anglo-Saxon than it was destined to remain in places like Australia and New Zealand."[31] British sport was repelled relatively easily in Canada because of the French population's aversion to British institutions. Cricket was not widely played in Quebec outside of Montreal's English elite.[32]

The influence of American culture, which ignored cricket completely, had a profound impact on the way Canadian sportsmen viewed the game.[33] Americans rejected British political control and, in so doing, developed their own distinctive sporting identity. This effort enabled Canadians to tap into popular leisure pastimes of their powerful neighbour.[34]

Many Canadians, on some level, rejected British cultural imperialism and cricket's rigid devotion to the amateur philosophy. Canadian cricketers and administrators were more ardent on amateurism than even the British, the originators of the code. Cooper lamented that policy limited the infusion of top cricket talent into the domestic game and was a major factor in severely slowing cricket's development in Canada.[35] Additionally, the barnstorming international clubs that toured Canada and initially created excitement around the game soon had the opposite impact. The record of Canadian cricketers in these matches against foreign clubs yielded just 10 wins in 98 matches.[36] These defeats, usually by large margins, drew criticism from the Canadian public and press, and deflated any enthusiasm for Canadian cricket that was created by the pregame hype. Particularly against British clubs, whose goal was to demonstrate the superiority and national greatness of the motherland, Canadian cricket teams were frequently left with only "shock and shame."[37]

Lacrosse and Canadian Nationalism

Prior to the Great War, cricket clubs in major Canadian hubs came and went. Although they were started with the grandest of intentions, interest waned in these ventures and they became dormant. The *Woodstock Weekly Review* boldly proclaimed in 1871 that "this old English game will be played, and continue popular, long after the very names of many others of ephemeral renown have been forgotten,"[38] but the sporting alternatives to cricket proved more viable and surpassed the British game in popularity. Some devoted to sport believed that where cricket had failed in Canada, lacrosse could succeed—particularly given its entrenched domestic roots. Lacrosse was a game played for centuries by First Nations peoples, who knew it as baggataway or tewaa:rathon, and for whom there were many variations of the sport. It was renamed lacrosse[39] by early French players who were taught the game by their First Nations peers.

George Beers

Lacrosse was indigenous to Canada and differed from cricket, but these circumstances were not enough to ensure the sport's success. Promotion was necessary to take the game beyond a First Nations sport and to elevate it as the national alternative to cricket. Dentist, devout Canadian nationalist, and athletic promoter Dr. W. George Beers was its chief advocate. Some Canadian sport historians argue that Beers sought to create a Canadian national identity. In so doing, he tried to eliminate imperial influence over domestic sporting culture and constructed a national mythology in its place. Robidoux argued: "Beers turned to indigenous sports as a means of portraying the soul of a nation. What better place to look, he surmised, than Canada's First Peoples whose game of baggataway—filled with speed, violence, and skill—appeared to best embody the harsh and grueling existence of Canadian natives as well as the trials of early Canadian settlers in this new and untamed land."[40] Beers' promotion of lacrosse and his actions as an organizational force for the sport can be viewed through a lens beyond nation building. Historian Allan Downey asserted that lacrosse serves as a valuable case study because it demonstrates how "non-Indigenous people appropriated it as their own and used it to express their national identity even as it remained an integral part of Indigenous societies, cultures and epistemologies "[41] (see also chapter 3).

While it is undeniable that Beers was a nationalist and desired a strong national identity for Canada, a thorough scan of his writings on lacrosse softens the anti-imperial light in which he is often depicted. Like many of the self-proclaimed Canadian nationalists of the late 19th century, Beers believed that Canada's British ancestry and its links to the British Empire were valued possessions. Beers was a gifted synthesizer who skillfully embedded imperial links into the developing national identity. He demonstrated the connection among sports, war, and character development by using the British examples of the Duke of Wellington and Waterloo. He pointed to the British school of Eton and the relationship between healthy exercise and a Christian education. When he highlighted lacrosse's ability to summon the energies of young males and to instill courage, resolve, and manliness, Beers illustrated how these qualities were developed in British naval hero Admiral Horatio Nelson.[42] Because of Beers' affinity for the British Empire, he sought to incorporate some of its traditions in lacrosse—namely amateurism. When Beers' Montreal Lacrosse Club formed in 1856, Victorian values were applied. In September 1860, Beers, having finished his dental apprenticeship, wrote the pamphlet "The Game of Lacrosse," which outlined and standardized the rules of the game so it could be played with more ease between communities.

Canada's National Sport?

Beers, never one to miss an opportunity, took advantage of the patriotic enthusiasm generated by Confederation in 1867. Shortly following the birth of the country, he campaigned relentlessly to have lacrosse declared Canada's national sport. Beers proclaimed that the new government had made the title official, even though Parliament had yet to sit, let alone discuss the matter of national sport.[43] Beers actively sought out the press to publicize his claim that it was Canada's sport. In one of his propaganda pieces that appeared in the *Montreal Gazette* he remarked: "There is such unanimity of feeling with regard to the acceptance of Lacrosse as Our National Field Game, that not only should players use the present season to secure its permanency but lovers of sports who believe in the mental and moral as well as the physical utility of these exercises should support us in our efforts to spread and nationalize this fine field game of Lacrosse."[44] Perhaps Beers' announcement of lacrosse's status went uncontested because no one cared enough to oppose him—it was immaterial to a new nation with more pressing demands. Lacrosse historian Donald Fisher argued otherwise, however, and wrote that part of the reason Canadians adopted lacrosse as the national game without hesitation was because it was a unifying symbol for the emerging Canadian nationality, right along with the beaver.[45]

No matter its claim to fame and the myth that propelled it, lacrosse, with the help of Beers, gained some initial popularity. The National Lacrosse Association (NLA) was indicative of the groundswell of enthusiasm that Beers helped create. The NLA was formed in Kingston in September 1867 under Beers' leadership to standardize rules and govern lacrosse. Alan Metcalfe demonstrates that Beers' public relations campaign worked. In May 1867, before Beers falsified his national sport claim, there were eight lacrosse clubs in Canada, all located in or near Montreal. When Beers assembled delegates just four months later, 27 lacrosse clubs had joined the NLA. Although membership had limited geographical reach—only Ontario and Quebec teams joined in 1867—the NLA's beginning had promise. This potential was particularly true in Ontario. Toronto began 1867 without a club but by October it boasted 13 with 600 players.[46] What is equally important is that Beers' organizational efforts were an attempt to wrestle away control of the sport from its Indigenous inventors. Downey points out, however, that Indigenous peoples never ceded ownership of lacrosse despite Beers' attempts to craft an identity with an appropriated sport.[47]

The advocates of lacrosse were so determined to have the game branded as Canada's national sport that they expanded from their domestic achievements and toured foreign countries to play exhibitions for the purpose of demonstrating authentic Canadian culture. No doubt inspired by the touring international cricketers that showcased their proficiency in their sport on Canadian soil, lacrosse promoters sent Canadian clubs to Britain in 1876.[48] These lacrosse games on foreign soil represent a purposeful attempt to exhibit Canadian identity and independent athletic culture.[49]

The photograph of the St. Regis Lacrosse Club (see figure 7.2) was taken by William Notman, Canada's most famous early photographer. Part of the collection at the McCord Museum in Montreal, this photograph was taken in 1867, the year the NLA was formed, and represents happier times for the club. By 1880, St. Regis was removed from the NLA's successor, the National Amateur Lacrosse Association (NALA), as it tried to expunge those it associated with professionalism—which included First Nations teams.

Moral Character

While supporters saw lacrosse as a point of distinction and independence, the game made inroads because it appealed to those who wanted to create a strong and virtuous generation of young men. Bouchier's study found that boosters in Ingersoll and Woodstock in Ontario, believed their promotion of lacrosse kept youth off the streets and crime low.[50] In addition, lacrosse filled a need for Canadian boys and young men of this period that was not being satisfied in everyday life. The apprenticeship model that so many adolescent males traditionally relied on was passed over more frequently in favour of longer schooling. Bouchier wrote that boys were under female scrutiny and influence for a longer duration and that organized lacrosse exposed boys to respectable versions of masculinity. The vigorous game of lacrosse embodied the principles

Figure 7.2   The St. Regis Lacrosse Club in Montreal in 1867.

of muscular Christianity even better than cricket.[51] This notion was not lost on Beers, who wrote in his promotional work on lacrosse, "If our National game, while exercising the manly virtues, also trains the national and the moral, it will, undoubtedly, help to make us better men; and genuine 'pluck' will never go out of fashion in Canada."[52]

Amateurism Versus Professionalism

If lacrosse was king of Canadian sport, its reign was short-lived. Don Morrow and Kevin B. Wamsley argue that lacrosse's halcyon days lasted from 1867 to 1885.[53] Although it was promoted as the national game and attained much of its publicity because of its domestic roots, imperial and continental sporting ideals ultimately plagued lacrosse. Like cricket enthusiasts, lacrosse's promoters proudly declared their sport's strict adherence to amateurism. Those ideals, however, conflicted with powerful trends that emanated from the United States— where professionalization had changed the nature of sport and created space for players based on skill, regardless of their social class. The clash between the sanctity of British ideals and the allure of American-style competition and profit proved too much for the national game, and its popularity never truly recovered.

As competition intensified and violence increased, critics blamed the professionalization of lacrosse for the game's ills. Metcalfe wrote, "The 'lacrossists' of the 1870s and 1880s were convinced that they knew the most important single cause of the problems besetting lacrosse—professionalism."[54] The sport became increasingly vicious as clubs vied for championships during these decades and the emphasis on victory surpassed that of sportsmanship and social betterment. For its part, the press was generally critical of the increased competition in lacrosse that resulted from the trends towards professionalization. The *Woodstock Sentinel* published a strongly worded piece authored by members of the Woodstocks, a newly formed amateur lacrosse team: "We have no sympathy whatever with 'professional sport,' as it is now carried on in the interests of speculators and gamblers. . . . the result of a professional baseball match has no more interest for us than the result of a fight between two ownerless street curs."[55] When the title was on the line, the rough play intensified. The *Montreal Star* claimed that lacrosse's popularity waned because "the championship matches undoubtedly damaged the game."[56] Some teams decided not to participate in championship games because of the potential for injury to their players as well as to the reputation of lacrosse.

Expulsion of First Nations Clubs

Organized lacrosse was so beleaguered that the NLA was disbanded in 1880 and reformed as the NALA. The extra *A* in the reborn organization's name stood for *amateur* and its mandate was clear—combat the blight of professionalism. Among the NALA's first casualties were First Nations clubs like St. Regis and Caughnawaga. These clubs were already under-represented in the old NLA, barred from representation in the organization's executive level. In 1880, the First Nations clubs were designated as instruments of professionalization by virtue of their players' race and banished by the NALA.[57]

Physical intimidation in order to gain an advantage advanced worries that professionalism harmed the sport. Some matches showcased overt warfare and not athletic skill. Even the clubs with wholesome reputations became aggressive in their pursuit of victory. Metcalfe argued that involvement by devoted sportsmen of the amateur code in rough games was a clear indication the tide had turned against Victorian values.[58] Violence was more likely when First Nations or Catholic teams faced the Victorian Protestants. First Nations and Irish Catholics,[59] theorized Metcalfe, were more interested in winning than the exclusive Montreal and Toronto teams.[60] In all likelihood, racial and ethnic tensions were a factor in these highly contested matches, and perhaps it served as hollow justification for the NALA to rid itself of any First Nations membership.

The concern that lacrosse had changed from an activity that instilled values to a win-at-any-cost competition became widespread within the sport's Victorian-steeped organizational structure. Letters to newspaper editors and minutes from league meetings serve as evidence that many involved in the game felt player conduct was as important as victory. Sportsmanship was easily enforced during lacrosse's earlier years because most of the players were drawn from the same social group where consensus was readily maintained. A homogeneous group applied pressure to ensure adherence to the same sporting values. The social and ethnic concentration of lacrosse players became diluted in the 1880s as championships became the focal point. The 1888 championship of the NALA was riddled with accusations and counter-accusations regarding foul play, poor sportsmanship, the use of professionals, and bribery. Again, professionalism was singled out as the root of the problems.[61] With an increased emphasis on winning, competition extended beyond the upper and middle classes. Some of the more successful teams of the late 1880s were drawn from different social backgrounds. The Montreal Shamrocks, for instance, were largely composed of Irish Catholic working-class men.

Policing the Professionals

The Amateur Athletic Association of Canada (AAAC), formed in 1884, was dominated by parties in Montreal and Toronto who shared an interest in protecting amateurism in Canadian sport from the evils of professionalism that had infiltrated the lacrosse fields. The AAAC defined an amateur as an athlete who never competed for prize money, never made a bet on a sporting event, never played with or against a professional, or never taught, instructed, or coached athletics to make a living. In 1898 the organization changed its name to the Canadian Amateur Athletic Union (CAAU) to more closely resemble its American counterpart. No matter its name, the organization struggled in its effort to keep professionalism out of Canadian sport. In 1897 alone, it handled 47 cases of professionalism, mostly in lacrosse. The number of incidents showed no signs of slowing. The CAAU acted rigidly in these cases. Any contact with professionals or with money, regardless of the amount, provided sufficient grounds for the governing body to professionalize the individual athlete, his team, and even his opponents. Some influential lacrosse clubs felt this application of the rule was too strict, but the CAAU was unyielding. By 1904, most of the senior lacrosse clubs in Canada had been professionalized by CAAU decree.[62]

Despite the puritanical stance taken by rigid defenders of amateurism, the process common in the United States of creating clubs with victory in mind, as opposed to purely social betterment, leached into Canada by the late 1800s. As early as 1869, the Cincinnati Red Stockings demonstrated that a baseball player could make a decent living as an athlete. Although amateur authorities in Canada enacted restrictive rules to banish from sport those who earned any sum of money from playing, a foundation for commercialism was established. Rewards for gifted athletes often went beyond a cash payment. A player might also be given a good job or some other benefit in exchange for his athletic services. Ultimately the calibre of play was raised through the practice of financial compensation so that by 1900, *professional* meant not only a player who competed for money but also one who was highly skilled. The spectator, particularly the paying spectator, understandably opted to watch the best players compete.[63] Eventually with the rise of the commercial leagues, the influence of promotion managers, and the reach of radio, the idea came to be that if an athlete was sufficiently skilled, he would be rewarded with money. It followed that the more skilled he was, the more money he would receive. Canadian sport historian Frank Cosentino noted that the idea of compensation for skilled players was so prevalent and accepted that "in time, the reverse came to be accepted. If the athlete was not being paid he could not be very good, it was reasoned."[64]

A Problem Too Big

At the dawn of the new century, the CAAU tried to counteract this growing phenomenon through player suspensions, but these had no effect. In 1904, the Montreal Shamrocks, whose professional leanings were openly acknowledged, won the Minto Cup—awarded to Canada's top amateur team. Just two years later, the Montreal Amateur Athletic Association expressed its desire to use professional players on its hockey and lacrosse teams in order to compete against other pseudo-amateur teams. This conflict with the CAAU led to the formation of the Amateur Athletic Federation of Canada (AAFC) in early 1907, and its constitution permitted professionals to play against amateurs. In 1909, the AAFC could not sustain itself and came back into the same organization as the CAAU but renamed the Amateur Athletic Union of Canada (AAUC). The squabble over amateurism and professionalism continued over the next few years, with new organizations tasked with the creation of a solution, but any meaningful and lasting resolution remained elusive.

By 1914, it was clear that lacrosse had lost much of its prewar popularity. The increase in violence, however, had been only a symptom and not the cause of the sport's downfall. The internal dissension over professionalism proved to be a conflict from which lacrosse could not recover. The treatment of the issue by club and league officials was borderline farcical, and they never opposed professionalism with either conviction or a united front. As Fisher argued, there were too many lacrosse clubs that hypocritically championed amateurism as a public ideal while secretly paying players. Despite an admission charge to the games, clubs could never admit to athlete compensation. The hypocrisy became the proverbial millstone around the sport's neck. While lacrosse clubs struggled with their morals, Canadian sports fans' interest in America's national pastime devastated the growth of the proposed national game.[65]

Baseball and Continentalism

Although arguments have been made that the first game of baseball was played on Canadian soil, it can be agreed that the game's development and growth were a result of its place in American culture. The fact that Canadian sport enthusiasts embraced an openly professional American game and shunned the quasi-professional Indigenous game baffled some in the Canadian media. In May 1914, magazine writer Fred Jacob made a plea to Canadian sport fans to give lacrosse a second chance. He stated his bemusement over his fellow Canadians' choice to adopt a fully professional American game and reject the professional version of Canada's "national game."[66] Baseball's status in Canada highlighted the slow but steady growth of the cultural influence of the United States on its northern neighbour. Baseball had clearly dethroned lacrosse as the primary spring and summer sport in Canada, and its success solidified a cultural bond with the United States. The exchange of sporting culture, however, was only one-directional. As an export, lacrosse showed little potential. After Canadian tours abroad, a few clubs were established for a short period in Britain. Lacrosse proved to be an equally hard sell in the United States. It had a successful run in some colleges, particularly Johns Hopkins University in Baltimore, but was still considered a fringe sport—a Canadian game.

Metcalfe and other sport historians attribute lacrosse's downfall to its brutality and inner conflict with professionalism.[67] Baseball, on the other hand, was caught in no such conundrum. Its promoters did not aspire to satisfy a particular moral code that prized amateurism and derided professionalism. Instead, baseball's promoters tended to be more interested in profit, competition, and civic boosterism. People played baseball not only for the enjoyment but also for victory. The game championed aptitude over social standing. Accordingly, it was open to all classes and, to some degree, both men and women. While cricket took pride in its place within the British Empire and lacrosse's status symbol was being Canada's national game, the American sport of baseball appealed to the locally minded, and teams were seen as a representation of a city.

Negative Press

Before examining baseball's success in prewar Canada, it is important to note that the sport was met with hostility in certain circles, largely because of its ties to American culture. Baseball promoters in Canada seldom drew notice to the sport's privileged place within American society, but its detractors' criticism often mentioned the game's Americanism. As baseball's popularity surpassed that of cricket and lacrosse, those who saw baseball as an unwanted American intrusion and the voice of an unruly working-class culture questioned the game's respectability. Rowdiness, gambling, thrown games, and the consumption of alcohol by fans and sometimes by the players themselves were among their concerns.[68]

The Canadian media often led the charge against perceived American cultural intrusion. In the early 20th century, prominent newspapers like Toronto's *Mail and Empire* as well as the *Toronto Globe* were apprehensive about the American influence on Canadian culture. Some newspapers lamented that American culture promoted lower morals.[69] In all likelihood, media anxiety stemmed from its own industry's bleak economic outlook. American publications dwarfed those of Canada, and by 1912, imported American and British periodicals outsold domestic publications in Canada 10 to 1.[70] Nevertheless, some Canadian newspapers saw it as their duty to assail cultural infringement from the south—of which baseball, they believed, was a key element. The *Hamilton Spectator* warned about Canadian baseball's subservience to American leagues, and the *Hamilton Times* complained about the American-style professionalization of the Canadian game: "The question of the championship was a mere question of dollars and cents, and by this manner London has come to the fore. Baseball is meant to develop the muscle of the youth, and not the gambling speculation for roughs. Cricket has steered clear of this. Why shouldn't baseball?"[71]

Baseball's Prevalence in Politics

But for all the negative press and criticisms baseball received from certain Canadian newspapers, the momentum of its popularity seemed unstoppable to some. The *Victoria Times* remarked: "In sport, the continent is rapidly becoming 'Americanized.' It would appear to be useless to attempt to stem the tide, even if it were desirable to attempt such a thing."[72] While some newspapers bemoaned the game's prominent presence in Canada, others were key players in the dissemination of baseball's happenings. Samuel Moffett, American intellectual and journalist, wrote in *The Americanization of Canada* (1907): "The Canadian newspapers print fuller telegraphic accounts of the great baseball contests of the National, the American and the Eastern Leagues than they do of the proceedings of the British Parliament. The American baseball language, which would be entirely unintelligible to an English reader, is fully familiarized in the Canadian press."[73]

Baseball even had an impact on Canadian politics. The Ontario Legislature concluded the day's proceedings early in 1905 when the Eastern League season had its opening day; Ontario premier Sir James Whitney was on hand to throw out the first ball.[74] In St. Thomas, local politicians even more overtly supported America's national pastime. For the opening of the 1905 Western Ontario League (WOL) season, Mayor Thomas Meek issued an afternoon holiday proclamation for the city that was generally obeyed. In the afternoon a parade marched down the St. Thomas streets, led by a military band, trailed by the competing ball clubs on foot. The procession closed with the alderman and prominent citizens in automobiles and carriages. At the ballpark, the local judge delivered an address. To add to the spectacle, the mayor, attired in a catcher's uniform, crouched behind the plate as the county clerk took his spot in the batter's box. The alderman assumed the role of the umpire and the judge pitched the ball. Finally, the championship pennant was raised from the previous season and the two teams took the field to play the game.[75]

America's Athletic Gift

For their part, some Americans seemed glad that their sport had been successfully transplanted north of the border. In an attempt to demonstrate the existence of genuine American culture around the world, legendary baseball promoter, sporting goods tycoon, and nationalist Albert G. Spalding toured the New York Giants and Chicago White Sox across the western United States, Japan, China, Hong Kong, Manila, Australia, Egypt, Italy, France, and Britain from October

1913 to February 1914. A smaller, less successful tour was also made in 1924.[76] The American press portrayed the ballplayers as semi-religious figures. The famous *Time* magazine commented: "Instead of Bibles and hymn-books, these missionaries carry with them balls, bats, mits [*sic*]. Instead of love and light, these missionaries shed baseball fanaticism all over Europe."[77]

While baseball's global success was the ultimate goal for promoters and patriots, like Spalding, Americans had witnessed baseball's presence in Canada, and its rise to the top of the sporting world north of the border did not go unnoticed. Moffett wrote:

> In social life the convergence of the Republic and the Dominion is very marked. It is no trivial matter that baseball is becoming the national game of Canada instead of cricket. It has a very deep significance, as has the fact that the native game of lacrosse is not able to hold its own against the southern intruder. "It has not one player in Canada," regretfully observes the Toronto *Mail and Empire*, "where base-ball has a score. Thousands of people will quit work of an afternoon to applaud two contending gangs of salaried aliens at Diamond Park, while as many hundreds would not be induced to attend a lacrosse match."[78]

If Americans took delight in baseball's success in Canada, it might have been because they helped create it. On the diamond, Canadian baseball was influenced by trends initiated in the United States that filtered north to alter the domestic game. In the 1860s, the New York rules replaced Ontario rules and stripped the local game of its provincial identity in an effort to achieve uniformity in rules across the continent.[79] American civic boosterism took root in Ontario as small- and medium-sized cities looked for promotional opportunities. The brand of professionalization that Canadian teams employed was based on the American model that had fared well south of the border. Lastly, the importation of American players to compete on Canadian clubs improved the quality of play but decimated the local character of the game at higher levels of competition. These were all factors that profoundly affected baseball's development in Canada.

Rules and Variations

Until the mid-19th century, baseball was a game of many regional variations. There were three dominant styles of play, all named for the region that observed those particular rules—New York, New England, and Philadelphia. There were also lesser-known styles, including an Ontario brand of baseball. Of the three major American styles, the Ontario game most closely resembled the New England version, which allowed for 8 to 15 players per side, overhand pitching, no foul territory, and soaking (throwing the ball at the runner to get him out); it was played on a square field, not a diamond. While the Ontario game had some similarities to the New England game, it had differences, too. It was generally played with 11 players to a team, all of whom got to bat each inning, and used four bases, plus a home plate, not three. This local version of baseball remained very popular in the province until the end of the 1850s. American cultural influence was too strong to ignore, and the New York rules began to dominate Ontario play at the start of the 1860s. These rules were similar to those we see today—three outs, no soaking so that a harder ball could be used, three bases separated by 27 metres (90 ft) instead of four bases, and nine players to a side. These rules were considered better for players and spectators alike because they allowed for quick exchanges between offence and defence. The rules were codified and, once universally accepted, were not subject to the regional interpretation that prevented the game from growing on a larger scale. It was also at this time that teams expanded their competition base to include opposition from neighbouring towns, no longer relying solely on intersquad matches.

In 1859, teams from Hamilton and Toronto[80] played the first recorded game in Canada using the New York rules. Perhaps not surprisingly, given the standardization of play fostered by the New York rules, this game was also the first mention of a match in Canada between teams representing rival cities. The Hamilton Burlingtons' loss to the Buffalo Niagaras in 1860 in the first-ever international match sealed the fate of the regionally differentiated Canadian game. Of the game, Canadian baseball historian William Humber writes, "Buffalo had adopted the New York rules in 1857 and the pragmatic young merchants and businessmen of the Burlington club, which had been formed in 1855 with 50 members . . . willingly made the switch."[81] The transition was not without controversy, but once it was decided, it signalled the end for the Ontario game. Other clubs followed the Burlingtons' lead, largely urged by the Hamilton club to do so, to foster international play.[82] Ontario clubs acquiesced to the rule changes but there were some holdouts. In 1860, Woodstock and Ingersoll continued to play the Canadian version of 11-a-side baseball. Both towns were a short buggy ride from Beachville, Ontario, where baseball's Canadian roots are deepest. Perhaps their attachment to the Ontario version was tougher to give up since it had been played in the area for three decades.[83]

Standardized rules were an important step for the creation of organized baseball in Canada. They brought a level of consistency to the sport and allowed teams to play outside of their immediate area without fear that one club would have an unfair advantage over the other because of the version of rules being employed. Combined with train transportation, standardization of rules made intercommunity competition a reality, opening up new possibilities for players and clubs. By the end of the 1860s, community-based baseball teams were playing more games against neighbouring cities and towns than the intracommunity or intersquad games that had once dominated their schedules.[84] From this change grew the appeal of civic pride and town spirit.

Civic Pride

Particularly in Ontario, local businessmen and entrepreneurs noticed the trend in the United States and soon began to equate a successful city ball club with improved business prospects in the province. Not surprisingly, Hamilton was one of the first places in Ontario where baseball promotion became popular. It was a town that underwent boom–bust cycles like many American cities of similar size. Hamilton's population ballooned from 6,000 in 1846 to 16,000 a decade later, and civic boosters tried to assert Hamilton's identity as an ambitious city. The Great Western Railway gave Hamilton a temporary and slight economic edge over Toronto because it allowed Hamilton to serve as a hub for western Ontario. In 1854, the Hamilton Young Canadians (later renamed the Maple Leafs) became the first organized formal baseball club in Canada. A commercial depression brought on by overspeculation in the railway industry after 1857 and Toronto's invasion of the western hinterland, made possible by the completion of the Great Western Railway, permanently curtailed Hamilton's ability to control the economic prospects of the region. Nevertheless, it was among the first Ontario cities to use baseball as a civic booster.[85]

Although Hamilton was one of the first towns where entrepreneurs and city leaders recognized the successful trend in the United States of using baseball as a tool of community marketing, it certainly was not the last, nor the most effective. No local leader in Ontario understood civic promotion through baseball as well as Guelph's George Sleeman. Through the efforts of civic-minded entrepreneurs, rivalries were created, modelled on those formed in the United States. In 1861, the first real baseball rivalry was established between Hamilton and Woodstock. Their games attracted 800 fans or more.[86] Humber argues: "There was a certain irony to these initial sporting encounters. At the same time as they gave territorial significance to towns only a few generations old by breeding an 'us against them' mentality, on a more profound level they were the glue that created a regional and, in some cases, a national sense of unity."[87]

Travelling American clubs were also a big draw in Ontario. Fans showed up to the ballpark en masse to watch the locals compete against barnstorming Americans. The Boston Red Stockings came to Guelph in 1872 and 2,500 spectators attended. To put this number in perspective, that was more than one-third of Guelph's population at the time.[88] Attendance numbers grew through the decade, thanks largely to international contests along with the heated rivalry that developed between the Guelph Maple Leafs and London Tecumsehs. A game in London between the two clubs on May 24, 1876, drew between 6,000 and 9,000 fans, many of whom made the journey from Guelph.[89]

Civic boosterism and the playing of baseball for championship trophies and awards led clubs to pursue and retain the best players. This strategy was copied from the American style of professionalism[90] and led some critics to notice that baseball was losing its amateur status. They lamented that baseball had become more about professionalism and winning instead of gentlemanly amateurism and participation. These critics proved to be in the minority, however, as baseball flourished in Ontario under the professional model in the late 19th century.

American Imports

Baseball in Ontario resembled American professional leagues even more when some clubs imported American players. In 1873, Kingston, Guelph, and Ottawa recruited players from the United States.[91] Even though the Guelph Maple Leafs employed American players, albeit not as many as Kingston, the city newspa-

PROMINENT PEOPLE: GEORGE SLEEMAN (1841-1926)

In many ways, George Sleeman (see figure 7.3) was Mr. Guelph and perfectly represents the 19th-century civic booster who understood how sport had the ability to put a town on the map. A captain of local industry, he operated the Silver Creek Brewery and held two terms as Guelph's mayor. Sleeman was an avid sportsman, and no game was closer to his heart than baseball. His first involvement in the managerial side of baseball was his organization of a team composed of brewery employees, and that is where he implemented enterprising ways to field a competitive team by hiring new employees based on their baseball talents. Sleeman's love of competition and ability to attract good ballplayers in exchange for undemanding employment ushered in a new style of baseball

Figure 7.3 George Sleeman.

Courtesy of the Sleeman Family and the University of Guelph.

management in Ontario. His efforts with the Silver Creeks were observed by the city's top club, the Guelph Maple Leafs, and Sleeman was offered the job of club president. In his new role, Sleeman continued to find ways to improve his roster—this time by importing American players. This practice became normalized through the efforts of men like Sleeman as Canadian sport began to transition towards open professionalism. Sleeman was inducted into the Canadian Baseball Hall of Fame in 1999.

per lashed out at the Kingston club when it achieved an unexpected victory over the juggernaut Guelph club. The *Guelph Evening Mercury* editorialized: "Reports from Kingston say the reason the Maple Leafs sustained such a defeat at the hands of the Kingston club was because they had an American pitcher and catcher to face."[92] This charge by the *Guelph Evening Mercury* did not stop the importation of American professionals by provincial baseball clubs. In fact, nearly all of Kingston's starting nine were American, and despite the Guelph newspaper's rant, the importation created little public uproar at the time. There was a time when, with the exception of two players, London's team was made up of Americans.[93] In the final analysis, the majority of fans supported the system of hiring professionals to play in Canada, whether they hailed from north or south of the border, because it improved the quality of local play. More spectators attended this popular form of entertainment and this, in turn, encouraged entrepreneurs to hire even better players to improve their chances of winning.[94] It was a simple equation well understood by William Bryce. In 1876, Bryce wrote in the *Canadian Base Ball Guide*—the first substantial publication on baseball in Canada—that the importation of American players had improved the game and, as such, the gates were better.[95]

Baseball continued to be very popular through the end of the 19th century and early into the 20th century. The cities of London and Guelph had brief and successful stints in the International Association, a major league mainly composed of American clubs during the 1870s. Commercialization had made baseball the dominant sport in the province.[96] In the end, neither team could afford to compete with the richer clubs in the United States and folded. When the London Tecumsehs collapsed in 1878, baseball at the major-league level ceased to exist in Canada for more than nine decades, until the Montreal Expos began to play in the National League in 1969. At the minor-league level, however, Canada proved fertile ground in the early 20th century. Many cities, large and small, claimed a professional team in a minor-league circuit. The Toronto Maple Leafs and the Montreal Royals played in the International League—the highest circuit outside Major League Baseball.

Beyond Ontario

Baseball's prominence in the late 19th century and early 20th century was not isolated to one province. Indeed, the sport flourished throughout most of Canada[97] in ways that mirrored Ontario but with its own regional flavour. The Maritime region has a rich baseball history. In Saint John, New Brunswick, for example, baseball played a role in the city's religious rivalry. The city's Protestant club, the Saint Johns (formerly the Saint John Athletic Association and the Nationals), duelled with the Catholic club, the Shamrocks, in hotly contested games in the latter decades of the 19th century. Victory was paramount when those clubs met. The clubs imported players, often from the United States, to bolster their chances of success, and fans enthusiastically gambled on the outcomes.

In Western Canada, baseball's early development in British Columbia was influenced by its American neighbours to the south more than any promotional effort by the sport's enthusiasts in Central Canada. A four-team amateur league was formed in 1901 with clubs in Vancouver, Victoria, Nanaimo, and New Westminster as transportation improved and the appetite for intercommunity baseball grew. It folded after two short years when the Vancouver club engaged in methods inconsistent with an amateur club, offering indirect compensation to skilled players.[98] Clubs from Vancouver and Victoria opted to join a professional baseball circuit with teams from the American Pacific Northwest in 1905. Amateur baseball, if in name only, continued to operate in Vancouver throughout this era, including a team called the Asahi that drew its players from the Japanese-Canadian community (see chapter 14).[99]

The Prairies also quickly adopted baseball as a favourite summer pastime. Alberta and Saskatchewan joined Confederation as provinces in 1905, and within two years there was professional minor-league baseball in the region. The Western Canadian League (WCL) began in Alberta as a small circuit with only four teams—Edmonton Grays, Calgary Broncos, Medicine Hat Hatters, and Lethbridge Miners. The league went on hiatus in 1908 but reappeared in 1909 in an eight-team expanded format that included the two other Prairie provinces, adding the Moose Jaw Robin Hoods, Regina Bonepilers, Winnipeg Maroons, and Brandon Angels. Membership in the league remained in flux in the years that led up to the First World War and although logistics and travel plagued the league, belief in baseball as an important and potentially profitable civic institution remained.

Beyond Men

As mentioned earlier in the chapter, baseball offered more to 19th-century sport-minded women than either cricket or lacrosse, but as Canadian sport historian M. Ann Hall demonstrates, this involvement had limitations. Baseball entrepreneurs of this era courted women but only as spectators, not as athletes. The motivation to include more women in the crowds was rooted in the desire of promoters to bolster baseball's credibility, thus leading to greater profits for the entrepreneurs.[100] Women were sometimes admitted to ballparks free of charge, provided they were accompanied by a male escort, and they were seated in a special section to minimize their involvement with the undesirable element. Canadian sport historian Colin Howell added that strategies to recruit women spectators were only mildly successful. As baseball's popularity grew among working-class men, their habits of drinking, gambling, tobacco chewing (and thus, spitting), and using foul language made the ballpark an uncomfortable environment for middle-class women.[101]

Early women's baseball in Canada did have connections with the United States, particularly in the form of barnstorming women's teams from the south that wanted to tour parts of Canada in an attempt to make money. Howell chronicled the visit of the Blackstockings, who came to the Maritimes from Chicago in 1891 to much fanfare. A crowd of more than 3,000 watched them play some local men in Halifax, but the visiting Americans' sense of pageantry and grasp of the theatrical outweighed their baseball acumen and they were no match for the local men. Haligonians, from the press to the clergy, were left perturbed by what they witnessed. The players were critiqued as frauds and, in some cases, not even permitted to play.[102] Similar complaints were heard in Vancouver when the Boston Bloomer Girls visited in 1900. Local media complained that paying crowds were misled by the Bloomer Girls' collection of unskilled women ballplayers and men posing as women in drag. Despite the negative reception, the Boston Bloomer Girls pushed on with their tour and were met with disdain on the Canadian prairies. The opposition to the visiting Boston club had little to do with their ties to the United States and more to do with an objection to women playing baseball.[103] Despite the derision, barnstorming American teams are partially credited for providing inspiration for Canadian women to organize their own baseball teams in the early 20th century.[104]

Outside the realm of male team sports, Canadian sportswomen of the era also grappled with issues of control, but their struggle was less about the amateur versus professional debate and more about being able to govern their own athletic organizations and contests. According to Hall, golf was the first sport in which women attempted self-governance, resulting in the Ladies' Golf Association of Canada (LGAC) in 1900. The LGAC was based on its British counterpart, seven years its predecessor. Ultimately this fledgling organization died in infancy because, as golf historian James Barclay hypothesizes, the Royal Canadian Golf Association (RCGA) modified its constitution the next year to accommodate national tournaments for women and a separate ladies' branch, rendering the LGAC redundant.

Wikimedia Commons

Figure 7.4 Canadian golfers George S. Lyon, Mabel Thomson, and Florence Harvey in 1909.

Perhaps it should have surprised no one that the RCGA's intimations of female autonomy over their own affairs went largely unfulfilled. Hall credits Florence Harvey (see figure 7.4), a member of the Hamilton Golf Club, and her trip to England in 1912 to play in the British championship as the turning point. While in England, Harvey was exposed to the Ladies' Golf Union (LGU), which had a comprehensive organizational structure that boasted a uniform system of handicapping, annual championships, promotional mechanisms, and a legislative body. When the two best British golfers came to Canada the following year, Harvey ensured they had an opportunity to speak to the benefits of the LGU. The Canadian women golfers liked what they heard, and the Canadian Ladies' Golf Union (CLGU) was formed in 1913. Hall points to Harvey as likely the first women's sport executive in Canada and she proved up to the challenge, establishing three geographical divisions that were truly national in reach (9 clubs in the Maritimes; 24 in Quebec, Ontario, and the Prairies; 4 in the Pacific region), with membership dues that paid for the administration and awards. Only the outbreak of the First World War in 1914 slowed the progress, and the major tournaments were cancelled for the duration of the war. Despite the overseas turmoil, Harvey worked tirelessly to keep the CLGU intact, and the organization held fundraising tournaments to support the war effort. When Harvey went to Serbia in 1918 as a military ambulance driver, the CLGU disbanded. Its legacy, however, saw many women play more active roles in their home clubs, assuming more organizational responsibility.

Conclusion

Organized sport in Canada's early years mirrored the ideological struggle at the heart of Canadian political life. It is important to think about those historical realities when our present context for sport is considered. Are there ideological implications for Canadian sport today? Evidence suggests that sport in Canada remains continentally focused. Many Canadian sport fans follow the same sports leagues as their American neighbours. These leagues, with the exception of the National Football League and the Canadian Football League, are a blend of Canadian- and American-based teams, and their domestic popularity demonstrates that Canadians remain culturally aligned with Americans.

Continentalism is not the only ideology to resonate. Nationalist forces continue to use sport as indication of a distinct Canadian identity. While many Canadians struggle to define what makes them Canadian, loving hockey remains a fairly constant characteristic. No shortage of ink has been spilled making that connection. Books like Bruce Dowbiggin's *The Meaning of Puck: How Hockey Explains Modern Canada* (2008) and Summit Series hero Paul Henderson's offering (co-authored by Jim Prime), *How Hockey Explains Canada: The Sport That Defines a Country* (2011), represent two of the countless efforts to try to tell Canadians something about themselves through what they love—or are supposed to love by virtue of their birth certificate. Beyond hockey, Canadians have generally laid claim to winter sports, and the Canadian Olympic Committee adopted the #WeAreWinter hashtag in 2013 to engage with climate aspects of the national identity and to unite a country beyond our athletes who competed in the 2014 Winter Olympics in Sochi, Russia.

What of imperialism? Do Canadians ignore the traditional sports of imperial Britain? While no one will argue that cricket is Canada's most popular sport among athletes and spectators, it is clear that some interest in the sport remains. The source of cricket fandom does not stem from Canadians with British ancestry, however, but from those who moved to Canada from countries in Asia, Oceania, and the Caribbean that Britain had colonized.

The three ideologies that shaped the emergence of organized Canadian sport continue to manifest, but the athletes and builders are no longer a white middle-class male monolith who controlled Canadian sport in the 19th century. This privileged demographic played and shaped sport but largely kept it for themselves. Although this exclusivity should not be surprising—Canada's past is no stranger to inequity—it stunted the development of Canadian sport and women athletes' continued efforts to overcome the historical relegation of their sex. Great strides have been made in the push for parity, however, and signs of progress are promising. One can look to the Olympic roster for the 2018 Winter Olympics and see that 103 of the 225 athletes who represented Canada were women. At the 1908 Summer Olympics, all 91 athletes who competed for Canada were male. This example is one of many that demonstrate measurable advancements in the world of sport, and Canadian society should be heartened by those indicators. Still, progress has its limits and the hockey world was saddened and diminished when the Canadian Women's Hockey League (CWHL) folded in 2019 after a dozen years of operation. Some see the CWHL's collapse as proof that society is not ready for women's professional sports, while others consider its 12-year existence as proof of concept that will bolster the chances of new leagues arising from its ashes. Whatever the case, organized sport in contemporary Canada represents both continuity with and divergence from its 19th-century roots.

DISCUSSION QUESTIONS

1. What conclusions about mid-19th-century British imperialist sentiment can be drawn from the rejection of cricket by Canadian sportsmen?
2. What was the result of Victorian ideals (e.g., amateurism) on the "national" sport of lacrosse?
3. What parallels, if any, exist between the criticism lacrosse received for rough play and the modern discourse around violence in sport?
4. Canadians have long been critical of American ideals and values. With that noted, why did Canadians embrace the American cultural export of baseball and the system of professionalism it encouraged?

SUGGESTED READINGS

Bouchier, Nancy. *For the Love of the Game: Amateur Sport in Small-Town Ontario 1838-1895.* Montreal: McGill-Queen's University Press, 2003.

Cooper, David. "Canadians Declare 'It Isn't Cricket': A Century of Rejection of the Imperial Game." *Canadian Journal of History of Sport* 26, no. 1 (1999): 51-81.

Humber, William. *Diamonds of the North: A Concise History of Baseball in Canada.* Toronto: Oxford University Press, 1995.

Metcalfe, Alan. *Canada Learns to Play: The Emergence of Organized Sport, 1807-1914.* Toronto: McClelland & Stewart, 1987.

Morrow, Don. "The Powerhouse of Canadian Sport: The Montreal Amateur Athletic Association, Inception to 1909." *Journal of Sport History* 8, no. 3 (1981): 20-39.

CHAPTER 8

THE DEVELOPMENT AND ORGANIZATION OF PROFESSIONAL SPORT

Robert Kossuth, PhD
University of Lethbridge

LEARNING OBJECTIVES

In this chapter you will

- identify how 19th-century professional athletes in Canada competed in sport for money and prizes as a means of work and survival;
- understand the ways early professional team sports served the interests of a variety of groups and individuals including entrepreneurs and gamblers;
- recognize how men's professional sport came to dominate the Canadian sporting landscape by the middle of the 20th century; and
- understand why professional sport ultimately became the dominant model for sport at all levels in Canada.

Sport in Canada today is primarily a product of the professional sport model that emerged in the late 19th and early 20th centuries. Typically, this included privileging physical practices that were competitive, male dominated, and administered to generate income, or at least achieve cost neutrality. Essentially, sport changed from its very early incarnations in the 1800s as a variety of often locally meaningful activities to, by the middle of the 20th century, a common and universally understood way of playing. How did professional sport assume the mantle of leadership of sport in Canada? The answer to this question lies in a potent mix of influences shaping how Canadians experienced sport, particularly those who profited from their involvement and those who sought to advance physical competition as being more than just a business where sport defined the culture and ideologies of a strong and vibrant nation. In the end, the story of professional sport's domination in Canada is about more than just playing for instrumental gains; it also helps define the essential meanings and structure of sport in our society.

The Emergence of Early Professional Sport

Professional sport in Canada emerged during the 19th century at a time when sport shifted from preindustrial forms into practices that are recognizable today. In fact, the idea of professional sport did not exist in the way it does today. Those individuals with athletic ability who were able to profit from sport did just that, and this occurred in the absence of the defining and accepted structures of professional sport—leagues, teams, corporate sponsors, media recognition, and endorsements. As Craig Greenham demonstrates in his examinations of late-19th-century lacrosse and baseball in chapter 7, a clear distinction between professional and amateur sport began to emerge by the late 1870s. This occurred largely through the efforts of middle-class men and their class-based notions of appropriate conduct in the realm of games and play. Prior to this, people from all sections of Canadian society played, and for some this included the opportunity to compete for monetary rewards.

Professional Athletes in Early Canada

In Canadian towns, settlements, and rural regions, people participated in games and play in a variety of settings. Examples range from organized curling and the formation of the Montreal Curling Club in 1807[1] to less orderly activities taking place in local taverns like prizefighting and animal baiting. Where people gathered and lived they played. In his examination of the sports organized by the British garrison in Halifax between 1749 and 1906, Robert D. Day noted the military's prominence in organizing cricket, rowing, horse racing, and curling.[2] Throughout the colonies that became the Dominion of Canada in 1867, all manner of sports, games, and play flourished. Evidence of this can be found in local newspaper reports of sporting activities, where these events often occurred as part of celebrations linked to public holidays. One notable example is a baseball game described by Adam E. Ford played in Beachville, Ontario, in 1838, on the birthday of King George III, a militia muster day.[3] The game, played by local rules, reflected the unorganized reality of early sport without specialized facilities or equipment. Within this milieu of sporting activities, certain activities and events caught people's attention, and some athletes were able to turn this interest into an opportunity to earn an income. Numerous examples demonstrate how this took place; however, this chapter focuses on four individuals—Roderick McLennan (highland games), Edward "Ned" Hanlan (rowing), Louise Armaindo (cycling), and Api-kai-ees (distance running)—who provide insight into how early professional sport existed in 19th-century Canada. Specifically, these examples demonstrate the realities of early professional sport, largely an individual pursuit providing a precarious income, where the athletes were often at the mercy of the men who managed them or the entrepreneurs who staged the events.

Roderick McLennan, according to the *Dictionary of Canadian Biography*, was an "athlete, contractor, businessman, newspaper owner, militia officer, and politician."[4] Born in Charlottenburgh Township, Upper Canada, in 1848, McLennan, like his brothers, excelled in athletics and as a young man began to throw the hammer. While working as a railway construction contractor in the 1860s, he challenged and regularly defeated Scottish or Caledonian games competitors in Canada, the United States, and the Maritimes, usually for a cash prize. Early in his career, "at the queen's birthday celebrations in Cornwall in 1865, he defeated the one-handed Scottish-games champion, Thomas Jarmy of Guelph . . . winning $1000 in prize money."[5] By 1870, McLennan competed in and won the heavy-hammer contest in games held by the Toronto Caledonian Society in front of an estimated crowd of 12,000 to 15,000.[6] Although he likely did not consider himself to be a professional athlete, McLennan's throwing career is demonstrative of elite athletes from this period. First, he competed as an individual in competitions that were usually challenge events as part of tours or within irregular festivals. Second, sport represented only one part of his working life, where in this case, McLennan ended his throwing career in 1877 at the age of 35,[7] when he was already well on his way to becoming a successful businessman and politician. Although certainly an exceptional athlete, it is possible to consider McLennan as a man who both enjoyed his sporting accomplishments and the prize money he won, despite not necessarily defining himself as an athlete.

Rower Ned Hanlan differed from Roderick McLennan, yet his sporting career also echoed McLennan's in many respects. Unlike McLennan, who would be considered middle class, Hanlan, born in Toronto in 1855, arose from a less prosperous background as the second son of an Irish fisherman who also operated a hotel on Toronto Island.[8] Additionally, Hanlan viewed sport as his primary occupation, and according to Frank Cosentino, "much of Hanlan's success was due to a number of organizational and mechanical advantages that he enjoyed."[9]

Beyond having grown up rowing on the Lake Ontario waterfront, Hanlan's advantages as a competitive rower included having a group of committed financial backers (the Hanlan Club) and his mastery of a new technology—the sliding seat.[10] Success on the water quickly turned into financial rewards for the Hanlan Club. In 1876 Hanlan entered and won in a record time the Centennial Regatta in Philadelphia, Pennsylvania. By 1878, his popularity resulted in railroad companies offering him a reported $3,900 for drawing spectators to his rowing exhibitions held in southern Ontario.

The same year, Hanlan began a series of races against American amateur champion Charles Courtney, whom Hanlan defeated in their first race to win a purse of $10,000. This rivalry culminated in 1880 with a race held on the Potomac River in Washington before an estimated crowd of 100,000.[11] These races, all of which included organized gambling and controversy surrounding the performances of both oarsmen, can be understood to have been pure entertainment for profit. Hanlan, as the dominant rower in these contests, adjusted his performances to win by a small margin in order to keep the crowds engaged and the betting odds in his favour. In November 1880, Hanlan defeated English rower Edward Trickett on the Thames in London to claim the championship of the world.[12] Until his defeat by Australian champion William Beach in 1884,[13] Hanlan reigned supreme on the water, becoming a legend and arguably Canada's first sports star.

The year following his retirement from competitive rowing in 1897, Hanlan became an alderman in Toronto. In 1926, 18 years after his death, he received the honour of being commemorated with a bronze statue erected on the grounds of the Canadian National Exhibition.[14] Hanlan's success came at least in part from his unique entertainment-focused approach to rowing at a time when sport for public consumption remained limited to a select few activities, of which rowing was one.

Although the majority of athletes who managed to forge professional sport careers in the latter decades of the 19th century were men, some women also managed to earn a living in this manner. One example is Louise Armaindo, born Louise Brisbois in 1860, a French Canadian from Sainte-Anne-de-Bellevue near Montreal (see figure 8.1).[15] Armaindo, according to M. Ann Hall, "began her professional athletic career first as a strongwoman then as a trapeze artist before

Photographer John Wood (1883)

Figure 8.1 Louise Armaindo, high-wheel bicycle racer.

she became a pedestrienne."[16] As the popularity of competitive race walking (pedestrianism) began to decline in the early 1880s, Armaindo turned her athletic talents to the new craze of bicycling. On a 131-centimetre (51 inch) high-wheel bicycle, she engaged in a variety of contests including long-distance races of up to six days where competitors sought a percentage of the gate admissions as the prize.[17] On one occasion, in March of 1882, Armaindo completed 993.8 kilometres (617.5 miles) in 72 hours. The same year in Toronto she defeated male cycling champion T.W. Eck in a 16-kilometre (10 mile) race.[18] Eck, who also served as Armaindo's manager beginning as early as 1879, became a regular opponent, often to create spectator interest when required.[19] Because of the popularity of women's bicycle racing as a spectator sport, cyclists such as Armaindo were in demand; promoters sought Armaindo out to compete in their events. Armaindo's story provides clear evidence that some Canadian female athletes capitalized on their athletic prowess to publicly demonstrate their skills and earn a living. However, for those Canadians who were not male and European, earning a living as an athlete often left them open to mistreatment and exploitation, often by their own managers and promoters.

Siksika distance runner Api-kai-ees competed using the name Deerfoot in Calgary in the 1880s (see figure 8.2).[20] The moniker Deerfoot was likely borrowed from Api-kai-ees' more famous Seneca (United States) predecessor who ran competitively in the United States and Britain under that name in the 1850s and 1860s. After success as a distance runner on his reserve, in a manner similar to Ned Hanlan, a syndicate of backers from Calgary sought to profit from his abilities through arranging races against touring professional runners. In 1886, Deerfoot won the Dominion Day one-mile race in Calgary, and news of his prowess led to his backers arranging a race against British runner J.W. Stokes and Winnipeg racer George Irvine. Api-kai-ees won this race despite being hindered by a lap-counting controversy. It is unclear how much he earned while running for the gambling syndicate; however, the arrangement with this group was undoubtedly exploitative and Api-kai-ees left his promotion team in 1886.[21] This example of a talented Indigenous athlete provides stark evidence of a man who possessed athletic ability but because of racist circumstances

Deerfoot, Blackfoot runner, 1887, NA-250-3, Boorne and May, Calgary, Alberta, Courtesy of Glenbow Archives, Archives and Special Collections, University of Calgary

Figure 8.2 Api-kai-ees (Deerfoot), Blackfoot runner in 1887.

could not avoid the pitfalls of professional sport in a colonial context. This point becomes particularly apparent when considering how Api-kai-ees' running career ended. Caught stealing two blankets from a settler's home, he escaped custody and remained at large for two years before turning himself in and being sentenced to six weeks in prison. He never returned to competitive running after this incident and subsequently contracted tuberculosis during one of his many later imprisonments, eventually succumbing to the disease in 1897.[22]

Roderick McLennan, Ned Hanlan, Louise Armaindo, and Api-kai-ees are examples of the varied experiences of Canadian athletes who competed as professionals immediately following Confederation. For these individual athletes, sport represented only one part of their lives because physical competitions did not exist in the highly organized manner that became increasingly common by the early 20th century. Professional athletes in this early era worked in an unstable environment where competitions were irregular, gamblers and promoters posed a threat to their independence and livelihoods, and their careers remained generally precarious. Additionally, as discussed in chapter 7, these athletes and others of their time increasingly encountered the growing influence of middle-class amateurism, an ideological construct that sought to control sport and restrict who could participate.

Professional Team Sports in Early Canada

Individual competitor professional sports such as running, rowing, cycling, and prizefighting continued to be popular activities for spectators and attractive to athletes in the late 1800s. Yet it was the rise of team sports at this time that engaged both economic and social entrepreneurs to fully appreciate sport's value as a spectacle. As C.A. Tony Joyce argues, almost all sports in late-19th-century Toronto, including team sports, "promoted a new revenue-generating component of Toronto's economy,"[23] primarily serving the interests of men with social, political, and economic power. In Canada in the 1870s and 1880s, the sports of lacrosse and baseball set the stage for the emergence of regular and profitable sporting enterprises that eventually became the standard to which later professional sports and athletes were held.

Lacrosse became the first sport to gain broad regional popularity in post-Confederation Quebec and Ontario. Appropriated from Indigenous peoples by middle-class men in Montreal in the mid-1800s,[24] it quickly became the sport young Anglophone Canadians could hold up as an example of their unique Canadian identity. In chapter 7, Greenham provides a thorough examination of the connections between lacrosse and a developing Canadian nationalism, specifically the tensions in the 19th century between amateur and professional interests. It is important to note that as the sport's popularity grew after the formation of the National Lacrosse Association (NLA) in 1867, competitive lacrosse migrated from its middle-class roots to organizations with working-class roots, such as the Montreal Shamrocks Club. Additionally, because the Euro-Canadian version of lacrosse developed prior to the widespread acceptance of amateurism in the early 1880s, the sport inherently possessed an element of professionalism based on its competitive nature and focus on elite performers.

The Montreal Shamrocks were an Irish working-class lacrosse club formed in 1867. The club, led by middle-class professional men, drew its players from the Irish men who worked in the city's industrial sector. The team quickly became the strongest in Montreal, drawing the enmity of their chief rivals the Montreal Lacrosse Club.[25] Early games between the Montreal adversaries often became violent affairs, and the Shamrocks' singular focus on winning drew the ire of their opponents, whose understanding of sport developed from more cultured conceptions of the social value of games reflective of then current middle-class ideals. By the 1880s, concerns surrounding the professional approach adopted by the Shamrocks started to create divisions within the sport. As Alan Metcalfe notes, the essential differences between the Shamrocks and their amateur rivals from middle-class clubs was first their commitment to winning, and thus aggressive play, and their inclination to play for money.[26] Although the Shamrocks, in order to maintain amateur status, did not outright pay players, through the 1880s the club's ideology aligned much more closely with the ethos of professionalism. In many respects, the Shamrocks were more closely aligned with the early professional baseball teams that appeared in southern Ontario in the 1860s and 1870s. The most famous of these clubs was the Guelph Maple Leafs,[27] who, along with their contemporaries the London Tecumsehs Base Ball Club, illustrate how early professional baseball provided communities the opportunity to make their name, and local entrepreneurs the possibility of enhancing their personal fortunes and reputations.

The London Tecumsehs Base Ball Club, named after the local Tecumseh Hotel, formed in 1868 through the amalgamation of two existing clubs—the London and Forest City Base Ball Clubs. The constitution outlined the organization and operation of the club, including requirements for membership, the responsibilities of the administrators, and the goals of the club in terms of baseball participation. The second article of the constitution stated, "The object of this Club shall be to improve, foster and perpetuate the game of Base Ball and to advance the interests of its members."[28] This club persisted for several years into the early 1870s but eventually disbanded because of unstable leadership and a lack of competitive results.

In 1875, a reconstituted London Tecumsehs Base Ball Club formed; however, this reincarnation was a quasi-professional venture under the presidency of local oil promoter and businessman J.L. Englehart.[29] By the start of the 1876 season, Englehart set about constructing a team capable of competing against London's perennial rival the Guelph Maple Leafs. After securing land to build a stadium, Englehart signed several professional players from the United States in order to improve the team and generate ticket sales. The professional version of the Tecumsehs excelled during the 1877 season. The highlight of that year was a victory in the International Association Championship, an early professional league composed of Canadian and American teams.[30] However, the relationship between the professional Tecumsehs and the citizens of London began to sour during the 1878 season, a situation incited by ongoing accusations of gambling and game fixing levied against several of the players. Problems initially arose in early July when star pitcher Fred Goldsmith came under scrutiny for being involved with gamblers after suspiciously losing a game to a Syracuse team.[31] Despite the accusations, no conclusive proof surfaced to confirm whether or not Goldsmith had purposely lost the game, or whether he was in fact involved with gamblers. Nevertheless, the damage to the team's reputation was done. Over the remainder of the season the club faced declining revenues and mounting debts, primarily a result of the sharp drop-off in patronage at games. At the end of the 1878 season the team disbanded, and professional baseball did not return to London until the late 1880s.

The experiences of early professional baseball in London, Ontario, is an exemplar of the larger issues related to professional baseball and sport at this time. As historian Colin Howell contends, baseball was a "game that attracted promoters, entrepreneurs, and gamblers, those who recognized its potential as a marketable commodity, and whose interests diverged in many ways from those interested in moral rehabilitation through sport."[32] As Howell's observation suggests, baseball and other sports from this era were understood to serve a variety of purposes, including as a means for economic gain while simultaneously being viewed as potential sites for social disruption. These differing perspectives fell largely along class lines, with middle-class men attaching notions of social progress and appropriate masculinity to sport, while members of the working classes approached sport and play more pragmatically, viewing it as a source of respite or as a potential means for economic advancement. These distinctions formed, at least in part, the emerging conceptions of sport on one hand as an amateur pursuit, versus the belief that sport held opportunity for economic advancement as a business venture.

Early Professional Sport and the Warring Amateurs

Sport in Canada in the final decades of the 19th century began to change with the rising influence of middle-class professional men in the middle decades of the 1800s, resulting in political, economic, and social changes that led to greater self-government in the colonies and eventually Confederation in 1867. In addition to these broad influences, middle-class Euro-Canadian men applied their work skills and social values to sport, in much the same manner as their counterparts in Britain and its other colonies. The ethos of amateur sport (see chapter 7) defined these changes, emerging as a direct challenge to working-class sportsmen and women and those entrepreneurs who sought to profit from play.

The early decades of amateurism represented a relatively stable phenomenon punctuated by intermittent infighting between sporting groups located in Central Canada's major urban centres. In 1898, when the national amateur body became the Canadian Amateur Athletic Union (CAAU),[33] two decades of relative stability for amateur sports began to wane. By 1909, the Amateur Athletic Union of Canada (AAUC) replaced the CAAU after several years of conflict over how to define an amateur. This struggle arose between two groups, one from Montreal—led by the Montreal Amateur Athletic Association—and a broader national coalition led by amateur sportsmen from Toronto.[34] This conflict has been referred to as an athletic war, pitting the more moderate Montreal group, who argued that amateurs ought not lose their status if they played with or against a professional, and the more conservative Toronto-led body, who believed in the strict enforcement of amateur rules that precluded any mixing with professionals. From the conclusion of this conflict in 1909 to the dissolution of the AAUC in 1970, amateur hardliners fought a losing battle. Ultimately, as Alan Metcalfe argues, "it was the individual who made the decision whether to play as an 'amateur' or a 'professional.'"[35] Metcalfe ultimately asserts that, "from the outset [the very existence of amateurism was] based on a false premise; that the meaning of sport was related to the amateur-professional dichotomy."[36] Despite this clear logic, the dichotomy of amateur versus professional athlete persisted through most of the 20th century, creating a divide based less on economics and more about social status and class structures.

Therefore, by the early 1900s, the social and moral underpinnings of amateurism had already begun to unravel. Often supporters of amateurism pointed to whether a professional athlete could be a real man. For example, Tom Longboat, the famous Indigenous distance runner who won the 1907 Boston Marathon and competed for Canada at the 1908 Olympic Games in London, England, often had his manliness and patriotism called into question, particularly after he turned professional. According to Bruce Kidd, when Longboat struck out on his own, "he was no longer seen to be running unselfishly for Canada, but [selfishly] for personal gain."[37] At the same time, because his critics refused to recognize the increased level of competition he faced as a professional, Longboat's detractors continued to consistently question this perceived decline in the runner's abilities. As was the case with many athletes who turned their backs on amateur sport, Longboat's decision to seek financial gain from his athletic talent resisted popular notions of amateur purity where he and other professionals faced potential social costs, including the loss of opportunity to compete for their country in the Olympic Games. However, this and other social sanctions could not stem the tide of interest in professional sport, particularly for those who competed in work-based sports away from the gaze of urban middle-class sporting enthusiasts.

Rodeo Women and Men Playing at Their Work

Studies examining sport in Canada at the turn of the 20th century have traditionally focused on the country's larger urban centres, such as Montreal and Toronto. It was largely in this rarified setting that supporters of amateur and professional sport waged their battles, while those in the rest of the nation either followed or ignored the decrees of organizers and the national sporting bodies they represented. Largely, it was members of the working classes who derived little benefit from adhering to amateur rules. One example of a sporting tradition not defined by urban and class-based sporting ideologies was rodeo. Rodeo as a work-based competition emerged from challenges between ranch workers during their daily activities, starting in Mexico and the western United States and eventually moving to the western Canadian prairies with the establishment of the cattle industry in the early 1880s.[38] Popular folklore and stories about the North American west created widespread interest in the lives of ranchers and cowboys on the Canadian prairies, and the cattle ranching industry eventually capitalized on this attention with the creation of the country's most famous rodeo event of the early 20th century, the Calgary Stampede. These nascent rodeo competitions included both male and female competitors who often won cash prizes for their accomplishments. Two of these early rodeo professionals who plied their trade in Canada were Indigenous cowboy Tom Three Persons, who won the saddled bronco (saddle bronc) competition at the 1912 Calgary Stampede, and Fannie Sperry, an American from Montana who often competed north of the border and who also won bronco riding events at both Calgary in 1912 and the Winnipeg Stampede in 1913.

By the early decades of the 20th century, rodeo provided opportunities for both men and women to compete and earn money to supplement their income. For Fannie Sperry (see figure 8.3), born in 1887 in Mitchell, Montana, a childhood of riding horses led to her finding work as a performer as she reached adulthood. As Mary Lou LeCompte notes, "In 1905 Sperry was offered one hundred dollars a month plus expenses to become a relay race rider for W.R. Wilmont. For the next three years she and several others known as the 'Montana Girls' raced throughout the Midwest and in Canada."[39] In 1912, Sperry received an invitation from Calgary Stampede organizer Guy Weadick to compete in the bronco riding event for women. On the final day of the stampede, Sperry drew Red Wing and after a spectacular ride became the "Lady Bucking Horse Champion of the World," a title that earned her $1,000, a new saddle, and a belt buckle.[40] It is possible that Sperry represents an exceptional example; however, evidence of women's participation in early rodeo contests in Canada suggests this was not necessarily the case. As professional athletes, Sperry and other female rodeo athletes competed in Canadian events and received payment for their performances because they drew on the growing interest in western ranching culture that existed throughout the country. Similarly, Tom Three Persons, a member of the Kainai First Nation in southern Alberta, despite the ongoing racism he faced as a rodeo athlete, became, if only briefly, a Canadian sports hero.

Tom Three Persons, born on March 19, 1888, was raised on the Blood (Kainai) Reserve until being "enrolled" at St. Joseph's, a Catholic boarding school in May 1903. Following his release from residential school, he set about pursuing his vocation as a cowboy and neophyte rancher under the tutelage of his uncle Bobtail Chief. In 1907, Three Persons spent two months participating in

Figure 8.3 Fannie Sperry Steele at the Winnipeg Stampede in 1913.

the roundup of government and Indigenous cattle on the lands in and around his reserve.[41] It was not long before Three Persons, recognized by his peers for his riding ability, entered a broncobusting competition as part of the livestock events at the 1908 Lethbridge Fair, where he finished in second place, winning the approval of spectators and news correspondents alike.[42] When the call came from Guy Weadick, the promoter of the first Calgary Stampede in 1912, to secure the top competitors for the rodeo, Julius Hyde, the Indian agent for the Blood Reserve, specifically wrote Weadick to endorse Three Persons' entry in the two bucking horse contests.[43] The letter from Hyde to Weadick, written on behalf of Three Persons, stated that Three Persons had "made up his mind to enter" and asked "if the Stampede management provides the horses" because Three Persons would have difficulty finding one on the reserve.[44] The letter also indicated that Three Persons would have his entrance money submitted by August 1.[45] This rather innocuous correspondence is an example of the colonial regulation under which First Nations peoples lived. In this case, Tom Three Persons required permission—a pass—from the government-appointed Indian agent in order to legally leave his reserve to compete in the Stampede. This represents one of the many difficulties Indigenous athletes faced in Canada in the early 20th century.

Three Persons subsequently won the saddle bronc contest by overcoming the previously unridden horse Cyclone, winning $1,000, a saddle, and a championship buckle. He also expected to receive an additional $500 offered by stampede sponsor Patrick Burns for any "Canadian" who won at the "broncho [*sic*] buster championship."[46] Three Persons claimed he did not receive the $500 from Burns, and a dispute arose over this additional prize. It remains unclear whether he ever received the money, but the incident does highlight the difficulty competitive cowboys faced at times collecting their winnings.

The expectation was Three Persons would build on his Calgary victory by defending his title at the Winnipeg Stampede the following summer. However, a back injury sustained in an exhibition ride in Montana led to his not attending that event.[47] Three Persons' approach to rodeo competitions after his Calgary victory followed a pattern of remaining close to his home, where he continued competing in riding events in nearby communities, including Lethbridge and Gleichen in Alberta. Over the remainder of his rodeo career, Three Persons never approached replicating his greatest achievement of the 1912 Calgary Stampede championship. Yet over the ensuing three decades, he continued to garner broad acclaim for his skills as a bronco rider, calf roper, and rodeo promoter in southern Alberta.[48]

Rodeo competitions in Canada and the United States in the early 20th century were a popular spectator sport. After the First World War, promoters sought to bring rodeo as a facsimile of the authentic west to cities in the east, affording rodeo athletes an improved opportunity to make a living from their sport.[49] By the mid-1930s a cowboy could earn between $2,000 and $3,000 a year, a sum well above that earned by teachers and close to the earnings of a dentist at that time. Yet rodeo remained a dangerous activity, and in 1929, the Rodeo Association of America (RAA) formed to organize the sport and provide support for rodeo athletes. That same year, rodeo star Bonnie McCarroll died in a bronco riding

PROMINENT PEOPLE: TOM THREE PERSONS (1888-1949)

An Indigenous athlete (a member of the Kainai Nation) who won the 1912 Calgary Stampede saddle bronc championship, Tom Three Persons (see figure 8.4) managed to negotiate the racist and colonial barriers to become one of the most accomplished Canadian rodeo athletes of the early 20th century. Although he was successful, Three Persons chose to spend his life close to his home in southern Alberta and became a successful rancher, rodeo promoter, and racing horse owner in his later years.

Tom Three Persons, Blood cowboy, Fort Macleod, Alberta, 1912, NA-4600-3, Swenson, J. E., Fort Macleod, Alberta, Courtesy of Glenbow Archives, Archives and Special Collections, University of Calgary

Figure 8.4 **Tom Three Persons, Kainai Nation.**

accident, and the RAA increasingly began to remove events for women from stock (bull and horse riding) events. In 1936, Canadian and American cowboys, concerned about the autocratic administration of the RAA, went on strike and subsequently formed the Cowboys' Turtle Association to protect the interests of independent rodeo athletes.[50] Therefore, rodeo professionals in Canada, in conjunction with their American colleagues, represent one of the first sports to formalize relations between athletes and organizers, although the sport did so at the expense of female competitors, whose involvement became increasingly marginalized. Of course, contractual obligations between athletes and owners had been in existence for years; however, in the case of rodeo, the athletes were able to organize and protect their interests in a manner not obtainable for athletes in traditional professional organizations at this time, including the National Hockey League.

After the War Over Athletics

Increasingly, by the first decades of the 1900s, sport in Canada had fractured, with professional interests challenging the power of amateur sport organizers and administrators. The Montreal Shamrocks, a working-class Irish Catholic lacrosse team, represent one example of a high-profile team operating within the world of amateur sport prior to the turn of the century. As Colin Howell notes with respect to the challenge posed by those who did not adhere to the amateur ideal, "middle class commentators [were] fearful that the diffusion of sport across the social spectrum would lead to a breakdown in the social order."[51] Under these conditions, individual athletes, whether participating in team or individual sports, were often left to the mercy of amateur sport officials when it came to keeping or losing their status. Even in cases where the offence was unknowingly competing with or against a professional, athletes had little power to control their fate. For those who fought to maintain the purity of amateur sport, athletes who pretended to adhere to amateur rules, but who for practical purposes were being financially rewarded for their athletic prowess, were referred to as "shamateurs." Sport in Canada following the end of the athletic war in 1909 had diverged on two paths, amateurism and professionalism. In hockey, this separation becomes particularly evident when examining the histories of the two most influential organizing bodies for the sport at this time—the Ontario Hockey Association (OHA) and the National Hockey Association (NHA), the predecessor of the National Hockey League (NHL).

Formed in 1890, the OHA initially remained closely tied to Toronto where the organization set about creating the structures for organized hockey. By 1896 the OHA operated as an administrative body ruling on issues related to player eligibility and residency requirements, along with organizing championships at the senior, junior, and intermediate levels.[52] However, it was not until 1897 that the issue of player payment emerged when a team from Stratford, Ontario, complained about two of their players being offered $5 and $7, respectively, by a rival club. The OHA's response, according to Alan Metcalfe, "was immediate, and ruthless, . . . and . . . [i]t was moved and carried "nearly unanimously" that "when the status of an individual is questioned the burden of proving his innocence shall rest with the accused . . ." [who] was judged guilty until proven innocent."[53] This ability to determine who was an amateur proved to be the basis of the ongoing power possessed by the OHA to control amateur hockey in the province.

Over the ensuing three decades, the OHA continued to exert its influence over the eligibility of players in the leagues operating under its jurisdiction. At times, the powerful executive members ruled to refuse re-entry into the amateur ranks for players who had previously competed as professionals. In 1914, the OHA played a leadership role in the formation of the Canadian Amateur Hockey Association[54] (see chapter 9), and this affiliation effectively afforded the men who administered the OHA control over who could and could not play amateur hockey in Canada. Yet after the First World War, the composition of the OHA executive shifted away from staunch advocates of amateurism to a group of more pragmatic administrators. Also, with the rapid growth of new leagues representing a broader spectrum of society, by the mid-1920s the OHA had to relent somewhat in order to bring potential rivals—emerging industrial and commercial leagues—within their control under amateur rules.[55] In the end, it was the professional leagues in Canada and the United States that benefitted from the work of the OHA and similar organizations because in the 1920s, 40 percent of professional players made their way through the amateur leagues operated by the OHA.[56]

At the same time amateur hockey was flourishing in Canada, professional teams and leagues emerged from a growing public interest in watching the best players and teams and the economic potential entrepreneurs saw in the sport. However, professional hockey did not initially gain a foothold in the larger urban centres, where amateur hockey dominated at the elite senior male levels. It was in smaller, more remote communities with resource-based economies that entrepreneurs first challenged the dominance of the amateur game. The first professional hockey team formed in Houghton, Michigan, in 1903. A year later the International Hockey League (IHL) formed, made up of teams from Houghton, Calumet, and Sault Ste. Marie in Michigan and Sault Ste. Marie, Ontario.[57] Although the IHL survived only until 1907, it influenced existing Canadian hockey clubs to become openly professional or face losing their best players as well as the opportunity to attract fans and challenge for top hockey honours.[58] One of the first and most influential hockey leagues to form in the wake of this turn towards open professionalism was the NHA.[59]

In the final years of the first decade of the 1900s, professional hockey began to filter out of the smaller towns north of Canada's big cities. At this time, many of the elite amateur clubs covertly offered money to secure players and charged fans a fee to watch the games, while ostensibly operating as nonprofit entities.[60] For example, the Shamrock Hockey Club of Montreal, winners of the Stanley Cup in 1899 and 1900, represented the Irish Catholic community in the city. By this time, the team had already demonstrated the hallmarks of the emergent professional game. First, the Shamrocks often faced criticism for their poor sportsmanship and overly aggressive play, a consequence of the priority placed on winning. Second, their games attracted large audiences, upwards of 10,000 at the Montreal Arena, a clear indication of their interest in securing a large gate income.[61] Although still amateur, teams at the elite senior level like the Shamrocks were already adopting many of the values and structures that would become characteristic of later professional hockey organizations.

By 1907, a number of prominent teams including "the Montreal Wanderers, Montreal Shamrocks, and Ottawa Victorias simply declared themselves to be professional hockey clubs."[62] The NHA formed in 1909 under the leadership of mining and industrial magnate M.J. O'Brien. This new league was made up of professional teams, all of which O'Brien either owned or had an interest in, apart from the Montreal Wanderers.[63] That same season, O'Brien paid Cyclone Taylor $5,250 to play for his team, the Renfrew Creamery Kings.[64] Over the ensuing years, with O'Brien's economic backing, the NHA managed to increase its hold over the professional game in Central Canada. The imposition of a salary cap in 1910 and the emergence of rival leagues in other regions of Canada, such as the Patrick brothers–led Pacific Coast Hockey League, challenged but could not break the NHA's stranglehold over professional hockey.

Although the vast majority of hockey in Canada remained amateur, the elite male and professional form of the game began to exert its power, particularly with the support of commercial interests and ultimately the monies made available to the sport from investors in the United States. The NHL formed in 1917 as a way for NHA owners to disassociate from the owner of the Toronto franchise. It would be almost another decade before the first American-based teams entered the NHL with the sale of franchises to Boston in 1924 and Pittsburgh in 1925.[65] It was at this point that professional hockey began to consolidate and refine the commercial elements of the game in order to remain viable and profitable investments for the owners. Between 1920 and 1931, 8 of the 10 NHL franchises moved into newly constructed arenas, all with artificial ice, and average seating capacity rose from 7,166 to 13,195. Additionally, the NHL went from a 22-game schedule in 1917-18 to 44 games in 1926.[66] The growth of the league through the 1920s, referred to by some as the golden age of the NHL, suggested a bright future. Although the onset of the Great Depression caused the league to contract in the 1930s, the NHL remained the dominant professional hockey league in Canada and the United States, unchallenged until the World Hockey Association began play in 1972.

Fighting, Violence, Masculinity, and the Business of Sport

Competitive sport in 19th- and early 20th-century Canada was steeped in the masculine tradition of demonstrating physical prowess over opponents and, if necessary, the use of violent actions to secure victory. From the tavern culture of the colonial era where men tested themselves against their peers in feats of strength and physical combat, to the early sporting contests of middle-class athletes who were expected to demonstrate the same bravery and bodily sacrifice found on the field of battle, violent actions became integral elements of sporting culture. This propensity towards violence is evident when examining hockey, boxing, and wrestling, amusements that were more than willing to provide customers with an entertaining and often violent spectacle.

Professional hockey in Canada in the early decades of the 20th century embodied two essential traits, overt manliness and violent play. Although hockey was not the only male-dominated violent pastime to attract audiences and entrepreneurial investment at this time, the sport does provide important insight into the processes by which professional hockey in Canada became a cultural institution. As a product of amateur middle-class ideologies, early hockey was a place where young men could demonstrate appropriate masculinity, or manhood. As a way to transmit broader social conceptions of what made a man, hockey promoted the rougher masculinity believed important for cultivating a more passionate and martially prepared man, inoculating against the overly feminizing and civilizing influence of modern white-collar work.[67] Essentially, rough play and violence became central to hockey and other manly sports, and these activities were understood to be a reasonable and reputable way for men to demonstrate their physical prowess and test themselves against other men. In most respects, these same characteristics pervaded early professional hockey, where strong, tough, hard players who engaged at times in violent play were readily accepted and often rewarded. Media coverage of the games and the accompanying violence became a staple of the professional game through the 20th century.

Though many examples can be found of violent play in early hockey, one rivalry, at the point of hockey's shift to professional play in 1907, provides some insight into the strong links between masculinity, violence, and the growing popularity of elite men's hockey. The rivalry between the Ottawa Silver Seven and the Montreal Wanderers played out both on the ice and in the newspapers over the 1907 season. Violence has always been a central element of hockey culture. In one incident concerning these two teams, "assault charges were brought against three members of the Ottawa team, . . . [where] Charles 'Baldy' Spittal, Harry Smith, and Alfred Smith were involved in separate stick attacks on Montreal players."[68] That injuries could be severe and in rare cases fatal is unsurprising, yet evidence of how both the legal system in Canada and those in authority in the sport reacted to these issues has been historically consistent. Almost universally, acts of violence on the ice were—and in many respects continue to be—argued to exist as part of the game and rationalized as normal and accepted. As a result, punishments were generally lenient, and the male-dominated criminal justice system continued to tolerate on-ice violence, remaining reluctant to become involved in what was understood to be a concern of hockey and not "the real world."[69] Although often the most visible example, hockey was not the only sport where violent actions and even death were understood to be part of the game.

Boxing, like hockey, possessed a degree of social acceptance because it was understood to provide men with important physical training that protected them against effeminacy and poor health. Of course, boxing, a gentleman's sport, was not prizefighting, the vulgar form of organized combat banned in Canada by 1881.[70] As a result of middle-class moral concerns over prizefighting, by the early 1900s enterprising boxing promoters had adopted the Queensberry rules—requiring the use of boxing gloves and a limited number of timed rounds—to present a more acceptable spectacle while marketing their fights as exhibitions of manly and scientific pugilism. One such Canadian promoter was Tommy Burns, born Noah Brusso in 1881 in Hanover, Ontario, who was briefly the world's heavyweight champion before losing his title to the Black American boxing legend Jack Johnson.

Burns, although a very successful boxer in his own right, was in many respects better known for being an astute businessman who managed himself through much of his career and then directed other fighters following his retirement in 1909.[71] The business of boxing at this time relied heavily on securing the social sanction of those who upheld the laws while simultaneously projecting moral acceptability by attracting respectable citizens, including women, to attend the fights. This was the case in 1913 when Burns, who was living in Calgary, promoted a fight between heavyweight contenders Canadian Arthur Pelkey and American Luther McCarty, billed as the White Heavyweight Championship of the World. In the first round Pelkey struck McCarty and the latter died in the ring, yet it remained unclear whether Pelkey's blow actually caused McCarty's death. Pelkey, exonerated by a coroner's jury, was nevertheless arrested by the North-West Mounted Police and charged with manslaughter.[72] The ensuing trial, while focused on determining what led to McCarty's death, demonstrated "the attitudes and values that were widely shared among men of all social classes, and that violence in sport was seen as a legitimate masculinizing practice."[73] Predictably, Pelkey received a complete discharge, and charges against Burns for staging a prizefight quietly disappeared following Burns' relocation of his boxing business from the city. Ultimately, as in the case of hockey, professional sport relied on the commonly held beliefs concerning the social value of sport, particularly for men. This sanctioning of violence allowed businessmen to sell professional sport to their audiences, thus reinforcing both the values of sport as a site for advancing manliness along with its connections to the capitalist ethos.

Professional wrestling was a combat sport that shared strong links to boxing. Although wrestling in a variety of forms enjoyed popularity in communities throughout the country, it was after the First World War that the professional form of the sport began to gain increased popularity. By 1922 in Manitoba, wrestling fans had become acculturated to the rougher tactics of the new form of professional wrestling that had moved north out of the United States. Heavyweight grappler Jack Taylor arrived in Winnipeg in 1922 and quickly received local support based on being Canadian, even though he had wrestled in the United States for most of his career. His opponent on August 2, 1922, was Jatindra Gobar, who naturally wrestled in an Indian style and dressed as expected in a turban and coloured robes.[74] Although Taylor defeated his opponent, this match demonstrated the parochial nature of professional wrestling, where opponents became attractions rather than athletes because of their exotic ethnicity. Additionally, these new-style wrestlers were "highly marketable commodities . . . [similar to] figures such as baseball player Herman 'Babe' Ruth and pugilist Jack Dempsey [who] achieved unprecedented fame as a result of careful management and increased coverage granted to sports in newspapers."[75] Local Winnipeg wrestling promoter Emil Klank carefully built up Taylor as a Canadian boy (he was actually 35 years old) following his victory over Gobar, positioning Taylor to fight a variety of foreign menaces including Mouradoulah ("the Terrible Turk") and Polish rival Stanislaus Zbyszko. Vigorous promotion of the match between Taylor and Zbyszko successfully played on the fighters' nationality and ethnicity and resulted in a crowd of nearly 3,000 spectators attending the event.[76] Ultimately, the purpose of the fights was to sell tickets and fill the arenas, and the mix of rough violence, national pride, and fear of the exotic "other" served this purpose.

The examples of professional wrestling and boxing suggest a changing landscape for sport in Canada in the first decades of the new century. One of the important influences on early professional sport was strengthening ties to sporting culture in the United States. This was evident not only in individual sports but also in the NHL's increasing reliance on the economic power of large American cities and their potential for attracting new spectators for shaping the fortunes of the league (see chapter 9). Beyond the search for new and more lucrative markets, as in the case of professional wrestling, audiences increasingly expected an entertaining spectacle, and this included rougher and more violent contests. Yet this move towards spectacle and aggression had to effectively draw on and reconcile with existing legitimacy concerns surrounding sport generally—the valued goals of promoting appropriate masculinity, fair play, and, following the First World War, nationalist inclinations. In the end, the men who promoted sport for financial gain had to be able to demonstrate the legitimacy of their product while simultaneously providing the entertaining spectacle their customers expected.

The Business of Sport in Canada Before and After the Second World War

Like many businesses, professional sport in Canada during the 1930s suffered some setbacks due to the economic impact of the Great Depression. Three NHL teams folded—the Pittsburgh Pirates (briefly operating as the Philadelphia Quakers prior to folding), the Ottawa Senators (the St. Louis Eagles at time of folding), and the Montreal Maroons.[77] Yet professional sport did not disappear altogether, and Canadians' appetite persisted through this decade. In many ways, the spectacle of, and interest in, professional sport that had taken root the previous two decades continued to define for Canadians what a real sport looked like. Amateur sport continued to remain relevant, particularly with respect to the Olympic Games, yet participants in these sports were primarily representative of the more affluent segments of Canadian society. Sporting opportunities for women expanded during the 1920s, although female teams remained largely underfunded and women's sport was not generally viewed as fertile grounds for professional competition. Thus, hockey remained the primary professional team sport, along with baseball at the minor-league level. As in the past, some individual athletes competed for prize money in sports like boxing. In addition to these existing possibilities, sports such as Canadian football were moving towards open professionalism, providing athletes with additional opportunities to earn a salary through their sporting prowess.

The Rise of Professional Canadian Football

The ascendancy of professional sport in Canada by the middle of the 20th century is evident through the example of Canadian football. Like hockey, Canadian football (more commonly referred to as Canadian rugby before the Second World War) emerged from middle-class sporting institutions in the later 19th century. As with other sports promoted in clubs, schools, and universities, football promoted amateur ideals including the importance of physically demanding team sports for training young men. Canadian rugby football developed from its English rugby union roots through the decades before and after the turn of the 20th century. This process included the adoption of rules from American football—a line of scrimmage, snapping the ball back to the quarterback, and eventually the forward pass—while also maintaining the unique character of the Canadian game. Prior to competing for the Grey Cup beginning in 1909, Canadian rugby teams competed at the senior, intermediate, and junior levels in Quebec, Ontario, and the western provinces; in Central Canada some of the strongest teams represented colleges and universities.[78] On the west and east coasts, the dominance of rugby union continued through the early decades of the 20th century.[79]

As with other popular sports in the early 1900s, the elite amateur clubs led the way. Leagues and teams administered by the Canadian Rugby Union (CRU) ultimately played for the Dominion Championship. This national honour was dominated by university teams up to 1924, following which the top senior men's teams from Montreal, Toronto, Hamilton, and Ottawa—known as the Big Four—dominated these championships through the middle of the century. Although strong senior men's teams operated in Winnipeg, Regina, Calgary, and Edmonton, travel issues limited play between eastern and western teams over this period.[80] Starting in the 1930s, Canadian rugby became Canadian football. In 1931, the CRU adopted the forward pass, a tactic then popular in the American game. Canadian teams and coaches sought to capitalize on this innovation by recruiting strong American-trained quarterbacks. As a result, most competitive senior teams at this time paid their top American recruits for the games they played. This was not yet open professionalism; however, for teams to keep up with their opponents, they needed to recruit top talent from the United States. It was largely because of these changes that university teams such as Toronto and Queen's withdrew from senior competition (the top leagues that competed for the Grey Cup).[81] This shift initiated the move towards Canadian football becoming a professional sport in the years after the Second World War.

The Canadian Football League (CFL) came into being in 1958 when the Canadian Football Council withdrew from the CRU at a meeting held in Winnipeg.[82] Over the previous two decades, elite teams had been moving in the direction of greater professionalization. For example, the 1948 Grey Cup champion Calgary Stampeders, coached by American Les Lear, had stopped relying on younger players from small American colleges and had started to sign former American professional players.[83] In addition to Calgary's defeat of Ottawa, the 1948 Grey Cup became legendary for the large number of Calgary supporters who took the train to Toronto. These fans' antics have become the stuff of legend, including the unconfirmed folktale of a Calgary supporter riding his horse into the lobby of the Royal York Hotel.[84]

The popular interest in the Grey Cup and elite-level Canadian football continued to increase, and leading clubs including the Vancouver Lions, Toronto Argonauts, and Ottawa Rough Riders competed for top American talent, going so far as signing star National Football League (NFL) players.[85] Television also provided an avenue for promoting and further professionalizing the sport. Following the formation of the CFL in 1958, the league set about adopting a more business-like approach, including forging peaceful relations with the NFL, the

TRANSFORMATIVE MOMENTS: CANADIAN FOOTBALL LEAGUE

Officially formed in 1958, the CFL (see figure 8.5) represents a sport with British roots (rugby union) and a strong American influence, yet it is one of the few uniquely Canadian professional sports. Professional football in Canada can be understood as the product of a sport that needed to pay players in order to attract top talent from the United States. Although Canadian football has never reached

Figure 8.5   Early CFL football in Canada.

the stability and heights of popularity of hockey, it remains relevant to many Canadians because of its symbolic value, particularly the Grey Cup, which has been awarded to the top team since 1909.

league upon which the CFL sought to model itself. Over the ensuing decade, the CFL instituted new policies including increasing the gate receipt percentage for visiting teams, standardizing waiver costs for American and Canadian players, establishing a nationwide draft of Canadian college players, and even standardizing player dress and adopting American names for positions.[86] By the 1960s, the CFL had become a fully and openly professional league with negligible resistance from traditional amateur sport supporters. In most men's team sports, even those that were not professional, the structure of the organizations and the conduct of the players had become increasingly professionalized. This, in part, arose from the decreasing influence of amateur sporting bodies—with the possible exception of the Olympic Games—and the implicit support by the federal government to support elite international sport.

Government Sport Funding and the Decline of the Olympic Amateur Influence

In the years following the Second World War, elite team sports in Canada increasingly adopted the professional model, while at the same time the government of Canada began tentative forays into the promotion of sport and fitness for Canadians. In 1943, the federal government passed an act to establish a national council for the purpose of promoting physical fitness, known as the National Physical Fitness Act,[87] as an immediate action to address concerns over military recruits failing standard recruitment fitness tests. However, federal politicians had no real concept of the essential differences between fitness and sport, and over the process of enacting legislation to address fitness, much of the government's focus shifted to supporting elite athletics. For a variety of reasons the National Physical Fitness Act remained largely ineffective and was eventually repealed in 1954. Yet one outcome of the government's initial engagement with physical activity and fitness was a renewed debate concerning the question of the place of sport in Canadian society.

In 1961, new legislation passed in the form of Bill C-131, the Fitness and Amateur Sport Act.[88] This more pragmatic piece of legislation had the stated goals of addressing the problem of poor physical fitness among Canadians and providing support for groups involved in international sports competitions.[89] Despite having an annual budget of $5 million, the legislation lacked a clearly defined purpose with respect to the promotion of physical fitness, a task further complicated by jurisdictional disputes between various levels of government, specifically the provinces. Eventually, the easiest and most obvious route forward for the bureaucrats in charge of this program was to focus on "elite sport development—the training of world-class athletes . . . [realizing] that the sports-governing bodies staffed by dedicated volunteers were unable to deliver programs."[90] This recognition further supported nationalist goals of improving performances at international sporting events, the kind of visible achievements that could reflect positively on the government of the day. Ultimately, the model of professional sport with the goal of winning and providing a public spectacle made more sense to both politicians and many Canadians when it came to spending public money.

By the 1950s, the idea of amateur sport as an inferior brand of competition had taken hold. One example demonstrating this shift towards valuing professionalism is the career of figure skater Barbara Ann Scott (see figure 8.6). Winner of the gold medal at the 1948 Winter Olympics in St. Moritz, Switzerland, Scott become one of Canada's most popular athletes. Although technically an amateur athlete, Scott's skating career suggests an approach to training and competing that was, for practical purposes, professional. She began skating seriously at age six, passing through the various levels quickly with the help of professional coaching, even being tutored privately so as to be able to access the ice during the day.[91] As Scott's career progressed and her accomplishments accumulated, she received incredible public and media attention not only for her skating skill but also for the traits of being "ladylike, calm, tiny, dainty, . . . sweet and above all else feminine."[92] After winning the European and world championships in 1947, Scott became embroiled in a public scandal when her hometown of Ottawa gifted a new convertible automobile in appreciation of her successes. This gift put Scott's future of competing for Olympic glory the following year in jeopardy as the International Olympic Committee (IOC) viewed the gift as a contravention of their strict amateur rules.[93] Despite this allegation and others concerning possibly monetizing her celebrity, Scott managed to maintain her amateur status and win the gold in 1948. She promptly turned professional in 1949 and remained in the sport until her retirement in 1954.

To argue that Scott's amateur and professional careers represented distinctly separate experiences is not entirely accurate, and ultimately she played the IOC's game until such time as to be able to openly perform as a professional. In terms of her training and recognition as a popular culture icon, no discernable differences existed between 1947 and 1949. The line between amateur and professional athlete, if it had ever truly existed, had certainly been largely erased by this time. As with the case of the 1972 Summit Series between the amateur Soviet Union hockey team and the professional Team Canada, this distinction became increasingly meaningless by the second half of the 20th century.

Arguably, hockey is Canada's preeminent sport and has held this position for the better part of the past century. Although Canada supported only two NHL franchises—the Toronto Maple Leafs and Montreal Canadiens—in the Original Six era (prior to the first round of NHL expansion in 1967), the vast majority of professional players were Canadians who made their way to the NHL via league-sponsored Junior A teams providing

Canada's Sports Hall of Fame | Panthéon des sports canadiens
SPORTSHALL.CA | PANTHEONSPORTS.CA
Object ID: X981.725.1.7

Figure 8.6   Barbara Ann Scott, Canadian figure skater.

a steady supply of hockey talent.[94] Canada dominated amateur international hockey through the middle of the 20th century, until the rise of the Soviet Union's national team in the late 1950s, which similarly dominated the world championships and Olympic Games over the next four decades. Although Canadian hockey supporters consoled themselves by noting the best players in the world were Canadian NHL stars, hockey administrators and government officials recognized the need to reform top-level amateur hockey in order to compete with the Soviets.

A fourth-place finish by the Trail Smoke Eaters at the 1963 world championship in Stockholm, Sweden, led the Canadian Amateur Hockey Association to implement the vision of Father David Bauer to form a Canadian national team—as opposed to sending the Allan Cup champions—to represent the country in international competition.[95] This team, made up of the top amateur players in the country, represented a threat to the NHL through the loss of control over elite amateurs and control over amateur hockey in Canada. By 1968, the government of Pierre Elliott Trudeau commissioned a task force on sport that recommended the creation of Hockey Canada, made up of representatives from both professional and amateur hockey organizations, to address concerns regarding international hockey success. In 1969, Hockey Canada lobbied the International Ice Hockey Federation (IIHF) to allow professionals to play in international tournaments, and although some professionals were allowed to play in the 1970 world championship, the IIHF quickly backtracked to require teams to be fully amateur.[96] This set of circumstances, in part, set the stage for the Summit Series between Canada and the Soviet Union.

The Summit Series has become a legendary, even nation-defining event in Canadian history. Billed as the first opportunity for top Canadian professionals to challenge the Soviet Union team of supposedly amateur Red Army officers, many Canadians thought the series would be an easy victory. However, the series turned into a tense eight-game battle that the Canadians eventually won in the final game in Moscow. Much has been written about this event and its importance in defining Canada and the importance of hockey for representing the nation.[97] Yet for many Canadians this event also cemented the primacy of professional sport over the increasingly antiquated concept of amateurism. Why could athletes not demonstrate their national pride while also being paid for their involvement in sport? Bruce Kidd argues that "by the outbreak of the Second World War, the NHL had begun to impose a new unity of practice and discourse on the most popular sectors of Canadian sports."[98] Essentially, this argument recognizes that capitalist sport interests, represented most visibly by the NHL, effectively defined what exemplified legitimate sport and the ultimate meanings implied through sporting experiences. To extend Kidd's position, one can argue that by the latter 20th century the dominance and primacy of professional sport was complete, a circumstance evidenced by the almost universal endorsement by Canadians, including the federal government, for paid elite male performances. In this sense, all sport today now mirrors to some degree professional sport.

Conclusion

From the first appearance of sport in the colonies that would become Canada in 1867 to the middle of the 20th century, athletes, teams, and sport organizations sought to make a profit. This profit most often involved the payment of wages or the winning of prizes, and despite this extrinsic goal, sport continued to provide enjoyment and meaning. Because sporting practices represented important cultural activities, various groups sought to control how and who could participate. At times this took the form of businessmen who promoted and profited from organizing sporting contests. By the 1880s, middle-class men sought to control sport by excluding others by establishing amateur rules. However, by the early 20th century, professional teams and athletes began to define sport for all Canadians, who then began to adopt the characteristics of this most visible and accessible form of play. Eventually, whether a person was paying to, or being paid to, play became increasingly irrelevant, and ultimately for Canadians sport became a largely uniform experience, one that in most respects reproduces the elite male professional practices that receive the majority of our attention when written about in newspapers or online and broadcast on radio and television. In this sense, a way of participating in sport—the professional game—has become the way we understand and experience sport in Canada today.

DISCUSSION QUESTIONS

1. Why did some early professional athletes compete in sports such as running or rodeo despite being subjected to poor treatment by promoters and their own managers?
2. How did cheating and gambling in late-19th-century professional team sport create problems for both athletes and owners?
3. In what ways did professional hockey assume greater importance after 1910 and the end of the amateur wars over athletics?
4. How was violence in professional sports such as boxing, wrestling, and hockey attractive to spectators, and how did promoters employ this to their advantage?
5. Why did the Canadian government provide public funding to elite international sport through adopting the professional sport model by the second half of the 20th century?

SUGGESTED READINGS

Hatton, C. Nathan. *Thrashing Seasons: Sporting Culture in Manitoba and the Genesis of Prairie Wrestling*. Winnipeg: University of Manitoba Press, 2016.

Joyce, C.A. Tony. "Sport and the Cash Nexus in Nineteenth Century Toronto." *Sport History Review* 30, no. 2 (1999): 140-167.

Kidd, Bruce. *The Struggle for Canadian Sport*. Toronto: University of Toronto Press, 1996.

LeCompte, Mary Lou. "Cowgirls at the Crossroads: Women in Professional Rodeo, 1885-1922." *Canadian Journal of History of Sport* 20, no. 2 (1989): 27-48.

Wamsley, Kevin B., and David Whitson. "Celebrating Violent Masculinities: The Boxing Death of Luther McCarty." *Journal of Sport History* 25, no. 3 (1998): 419-431.

CHAPTER 9

HOCKEY, IDENTITY, AND NATIONHOOD

Carly Adams, PhD
University of Lethbridge

Russell Field, PhD
University of Manitoba

Michel Vigneault, PhD
Université du Québec à Montréal

LEARNING OBJECTIVES

In this chapter you will

- consider how hockey evolved from a variety of premodern pastimes and became codified as a modern sport;
- identify how some groups have exercised hegemony, while others have been excluded at different moments in time from fully participating in Canadian hockey;
- investigate what is meant by commercialization and how, in hockey, this altered the "national" character of the sport; and
- explore how hockey's history informs the current structure of the sport and contemporary issues in youth hockey.

On April 6, 2018, the Humboldt Broncos, a Junior A team of 18- to 20-year-old men, were travelling down a rural highway in Saskatchewan on their way to a playoff game when tragedy struck: The team bus collided with a semi-trailer truck. Fourteen people on board the bus were killed instantly, two more died subsequently, and many others were badly injured. The event had a tragic impact on the lives of family members, friends, surviving teammates, and residents of the rural community of Humboldt, Saskatchewan. The accident led to an outpouring of support from beyond the local community, resonating in Canada and around the world. Millions of people expressed their sympathy and support through social media, by donating to a GoFundMe account created to support the team or by participating in countless vigils, moments of silence, and jersey days in honour of the team. This tragedy and the reactions and events that followed provide another opportunity to think about sporting nationalisms (see chapter 7), an imagined Canadian identity, and the significance of sport, in particular hockey, in communities across Canada.

"The relevance of hockey to Canadian history," writes historian Andrew Holman, "rests in its ability to act periodically as a sort of social glue."[1] There are many moments in Canadian hockey history that serve as examples of sporting nationalism. Sidney Crosby's overtime goal during the Canada–United States men's final at the Olympic Games in Vancouver on February 28, 2010, is a significant example; 7 minutes and 40 seconds into overtime, Crosby scored the sudden-death goal that won the game and secured gold for the country. This triggered emotional, explosive celebrations of national pride across the country. What about the men's gold medal win at the 2002 Olympic Games in Salt Lake City, Utah? This was the first men's hockey gold medal at the Olympic Games since 1952. By the end of the game 12.6 million viewers had tuned in, making it the most watched television program in Canadian history at that time.[2]

We also need to consider why some events do not get defined as "national" moments despite considerable media and public attention. Both of the preceding examples come from men's hockey. Although the men's gold medal win in 2002 has become firmly rooted in the collective memories of Canadian hockey fans, the women's gold medal win that same year only four days earlier was not celebrated with the same intensity—as an expression of Canadian nationalism. As Mary Louise Adams suggests, the difference in the ways these two victories were celebrated "made clear the centrality of gender to national mythmaking."[3]

Hockey's Place in the Imagined Canadian Identity

Hockey holds a place in the national identity, and it is often a part of conversations about the history of the Canadian nation.[4] The game has been naturalized as part of Canadian culture and is referred to as one of "winter's expectations," "our common passion," and "the game of our lives."[5] In Canada, we live in an imagined hockey community, one in which, in the words of Benedict Anderson, "we will never know most of our fellow-members, meet them, or even hear of them, yet in the minds of each lives the image of their communion."[6] Certainly, the immediate outpouring of support in the aftermath of the Humboldt Broncos tragedy points to the strength of the imagined community among Canadian hockey supporters and participants.

Yet while hockey in Canada holds tremendous nostalgic power, it is also an area of considerable contestation, tension, and conflict. Some sport scholars encourage us to think critically about popular discourses that mythologize hockey and to question why and how it has been linked to Canadian identity. Richard Gruneau and David Whitson, for example, suggest that hockey's connection to Canadian identity "creates a kind of cultural amnesia about the social struggles and vested interests—between men and women; social classes, regions, races and ethnic groups—that have always been part of hockey's history."[7] Adams suggests we must consider "whose lives" get represented as part of the Canadian hockey identity: "If hockey is life in Canada, then life in Canada remains decidedly masculine and white."[8] Arguably, stories that contribute to the national discourse are primarily about professional hockey—a hockey space mostly taken up by white heterosexual men.

Few non-white players have played the game professionally in Canada. Since the mid-1950s non-white players, such as Fred Sasakamoose from Ahtahkakoop Cree Nation, Black Canadian Willie O'Ree, Inuk Jordin Tootoo, and Carey Price from Ulkatcho First Nation, for example, have graced the ice in professional men's hockey. In women's hockey, Jocelyn Larocque from the Métis Nation in Manitoba, Brigette Lacquette from Cote First Nation, and Black Canadians Angela James and Sarah Nurse have played with Team Canada. These players are often held up as exemplars of diversity within the game, but their symbolic value only highlights their marginalization. Their stories of struggle, racism, and discrimination point to the dominance of some bodies over others in Canadian hockey discourses and our collective imaginings about our national game.

As Shan Dhaliwal writes, we must question "who the 'we' is in Canadian hockey."[9] The relative absence of non-white and non-male-identified players, writes Holman, "has been a curious cultural statement about Canada, a country that publicly proclaims itself equitable, inclusive, and multicultural."[10] Similarly, despite the number of girls and women who have played informal and organized games in towns and cities across the country since the late 1800s, there is not a professional league for women's hockey paying a living wage in North America.[11] Although hockey holds a firm place in discussions about the Canadian nation, hockey as an expression of our national identity is complicated and fraught with tension, silences, and inequalities.

In this chapter, we examine why our assumptions about the present are often accepted without question and perpetuated over time.[12] Why has hockey been a part of the Canadian collective identity since Confederation in 1867? Why has men's professional hockey dominated discourses about the game in Canada? How and why are some groups more present in Canadian hockey while others have been excluded at different moments in time from fully participating? To understand why hockey is so firmly embedded in our national stories and the collective memories of so many Canadians, we need to consider how hockey developed in Canada. We begin this examination with a consideration of the origins of the game.

Origins of the Game

The debate on the origins of hockey—in particular, the location of the first game—has raged for many years. Many historians have attributed different dates and sites to the origins of the game: Deline, North West Territories, in 1826; Montreal in 1837; Windsor, Nova Scotia, in the 1840s; or Kingston, Ontario, in 1855.[13] On one hand, it is worth understanding the continued importance of such investigations. There are numerous references to premodern ball-and-stick games on ice, including those represented on 17th-century Dutch winter landscape paintings. Elements of what is now the codified sport of ice hockey existed in a variety of loosely organized regional pastimes. The continued presence of similar games such as bandy and hurling, as well as informal forms of hockey such as shinny, points to these varied origins. On the other hand, we need to ask whether the search for a mythical "first game" contributes to the narratives that celebrate hockey's place in an imagined Canadian identity. If there is little continuity between these premodern pastimes and modern hockey, what role do they play in helping us understand the contemporary sport?

Early Indigenous Ball-and-Stick Games

Although many Canadian communities claim to be the location for the first game of hockey, historical sources suggest that ball-and-stick games were being played on lands we now call Canada long before the arrival of settlers.[14] "The origin and evolution of ice hockey," writes historian Paul Bennett, "can be seen as another innovation assumed to be associated with settler colonialism."[15] Bennett argues that as historians debate the origins of hockey, they are missing an important piece, that these debates often perpetuate and support "the advance of settler-colonial society by obscuring, submerging, or erasing Indigenous presence on the land."[16] Like many sport historians, Bennett suggests that we need to discuss the origins of the game of hockey, like the evolution of all sports, as a "dynamic process of cultural exchange and transformation."[17]

The stories of the game that are now firmly embedded in the Canadian national imagination and folklore can be traced through Indigenous histories on these lands. While there is still much being revealed about Indigenous ball-and-stick games, one precursor is the Mi'kmaq field and ice game called oochamkunutk.[18] Material culture, such as sticks carved by Mi'kmaq carvers and dated to the mid-1600s, also provides evidence that ball-and-stick games have a long tradition in Mi'kmaq communities and that the origins of the game can be traced back much further than the 1800s. Indigenous histories challenge assumptions about the origins of the game of hockey and suggest it is very much "an amalgam of games and traditions"[19]

The Codification of Hockey in Montreal

Despite new evidence and emerging histories of ball-and-stick pastimes, some historians have declared that the modern sport of ice hockey was inaugurated on March 3, 1875, at the Victoria Skating Rink in Montreal, in a match between teams drawn from members of the Montreal Football Club and students from McGill University. In 2008, the International Ice Hockey Federation identified this game that took place on March 3, 1875, as the first game of organized hockey.

An announcement of the game in the *Montreal Gazette* encouraged spectators to come out to watch because "the players are reputed to be exceedingly expert at the game."[20] The postmatch report signalled that while the game offered new elements, the sport itself was not unknown. The *Montreal Gazette* compared the proceedings to a similar game from New England ("ice polo") and to lacrosse, with which readers were arguably familiar. The teams in Montreal that day played nine a side, used "a flat block of wood" rather than the ball used in the field game, and played three "games," each one ending when a goal was scored.[21]

This "first" game was played at a skating rink, which meant the hockey players had to compete with pleasure skaters. Although the *Montreal Gazette* noted that spectators were "well satisfied with the evening's entertainment," tempers flared between hockey players and skaters.[22] After 90 minutes of play, some skaters jumped onto the ice to complain that the hockey game had gone on too long. Some received sticks to the head for their trouble.[23]

Several features of this game are significant, beyond what took place on the ice. Montreal was central to the development of modern sport in Canada. It was from the emerging professional middle class that the impetus came to organize and codify premodern pastimes as sports to be practised and played in consistent ways and according to agreed-upon rules. Men like James Creighton—or George Beers in lacrosse (see chapters 3, 7, and 13) promoted their sports as consistent with the values of amateur masculinity. As Michael Robidoux noted, "advocating for institutionalized sport served as an important means of reproducing a Victorian social order in Canada, where young men learned to be honorable and genteel gentlemen."[24]

That the Montreal game included only men was unsurprising. Sport at this time was as much a place for men to socialize and hone their skills as it was for the public display of athletic prowess. But the fact that that evening's proceedings at the Victoria Skating Rink, with nine players on each side playing by rules that included no forward pass, looked vastly different from modern hockey is also a reminder that social practices are continually evolving.

WORKING WITH PRIMARY SOURCES: JAMES CREIGHTON AND "THE MONTREAL GAME"

James George Aylwin Creighton is a principal character in the first hockey game in March 1875. He is emblematic of the kinds of middle-class men who championed amateur sport in Canada in the late 19th century. Creighton was an engineer from Halifax who had studied at Dalhousie University before moving to Montreal in 1872. As a sportsman, he joined the Montreal Football Club (MFC) as well as the Victoria Skating Club, which owned the rink where the March 1875 hockey game was played.

Creighton introduced his colleagues at the MFC to ricket, a ball-and-stick game on ice that was played in Halifax and was similar to the New England game of ice polo. Using sticks made by Mi'kmaq carvers, which were familiar to Creighton, the Montrealers amended ricket to incorporate elements from lacrosse and rugby, which included adding a goaltender and banning forward passes.[25]

For some, Creighton is "the father of modern hockey." He wrote the "playing rules of the game of hockey," published in the *Montreal Gazette* on February 27, 1877. The rules were based on field hockey rules and are as follows:

1. The game shall be commenced and renewed by a Bully in the centre of the ground. Goals shall be changed after each game.

2. When a player hits the ball, any one of the same side who at such moment of hitting is nearer to the opponents' goal line is out of play, and may not touch the ball himself, or in any way whatever prevent any other player from doing so, until the ball has been played. A player must always be on his own side of the ball.

3. The ball may be stopped, but not carried or knocked on by any part of the body. No player shall raise his stick above his shoulder. Charging from behind, tripping, collaring, kicking or shinning shall not be allowed.

4. When the ball is hit behind the goal line by the attacking side, it shall be brought out straight 15 yards, and started again by a Bully; but, if hit behind by any one of the side whose goal line it is, a player of the opposite side shall hit it out from within one yard of the nearest corner, no player of the attacking side at that time shall be within 20 yards of the goal line, and the defenders, with the exception of the goal-keeper, must be behind their goal line.

5. When the ball goes off at the side, a player of the opposite side to that which hit it out shall roll it out from the point on the boundary line at which it went off at right angles with the boundary line, and it shall not be in play until it has touched the ice, and the player rolling it in shall not play it until it has been played by another player, every player being then behind the ball.

6. On the infringement of any of the above rules, the ball shall be brought back and a Bully shall take place.

7. All disputes shall be settled by the Umpires, or in the event of their disagreement, by the Referee.[26]

Organizing Amateur Hockey

Amateur hockey—which in the late 1870s and early 1880s was an almost exclusively white, male, middle-class pastime—remained centred around Montreal in the early years of the sport's development. Following the iconic 1875 game, new teams were created in Montreal and other parts of Quebec. In 1876, the Creighton group divided itself into two teams, the Metropolitans and the St. James. McGill University students, some of whom were part of the 1875 game, established their first team in January 1877.[27] The Victoria Skating Club introduced the Victoria Hockey Club in 1879, and other teams followed in Quebec City (1880) and Ottawa (1883).[28] Although these teams played challenge matches against one another—either for pleasure or competition—few lasted more than a season or two.

Following the popularity of winter carnival matches, club organizers sought more regular competition. In 1886, a new competition was created called the Dominion Challenge. Four Montreal teams (the Crystals, McGill, the Victorias, and the Montreal Hockey Club, which was formed in 1885) faced each other in a round-robin, while Quebec and Ottawa played a home-and-home series. In the final game, the Crystals faced Quebec. This contentious match illustrated the evolving nature of hockey's rules, as the sport's physicality intersected with amateur notions of gentlemanly competition: Quebec lost a player to injury while accusing the Crystals of rough play. When the Montreal club would not abide by an unwritten custom and remove one of their own players, the Quebec team left the ice. The championship was then awarded to the Crystals by the referee.

The growing interest in regular competition led to the formation of some early amateur hockey associations, which constituted an attempt by Montreal-based organizers to consolidate their hegemony over the sport. The Dominion Challenge teams, except Quebec, created the Amateur Hockey Association of Canada (AHAC). Instead of a regular schedule of games, the teams adopted a challenge system. The champion of the previous season played a challenger, and the winner played a new challenger the following week, and so on. The last match crowned the winner of the season. This worked until 1892, when the Montreal Amateur Athletic Association (MAAA, also known as the Montreal Hockey Club) won the final match, its only win of the season. The 1891 champion, Ottawa, had won its first nine challenge matches in 1892, only to lose the championship to the then-winless MAAA.

A revised format was introduced for 1893. A schedule of games was established, with each team playing the same number of matches and the champion being the team having the most victories at the end of the season. That year, the Governor General, Lord Stanley, donated a silver bowl to be awarded to the amateur men's hockey champions of the Dominion Hockey Challenge Cup. Contested in a challenge format, which was administered by the trophy's trustees, it was first awarded to the MAAA. What today is better known as the Stanley

Winter Carnivals, Early Men's Hockey in Montreal, and the Development of Women's Hockey in the West

Outdoor winter festivals have been popular in Canada since the late 1800s, with outdoor sports and activities such as snowshoe races, ice hockey games, skiing tours and contests, tobogganing, curling bonspiels, and skating exhibitions positioned as the main attractions.[30] The first Montreal Winter Carnival was organized in 1883 by snowshoe clubs and commercial enterprises such as local hotels who had an interest in promoting tourism.[31] Three clubs competed in hockey—the Victorias and McGill from Montreal and a team from Quebec City. The latter came with only seven players, so the Montreal teams had to drop two players each to ensure fair competition. This led to the seven-a-side teams that were common into the 20th century. Following McGill's victory, Ottawa (1884) and the newly formed Montreal Hockey Club (1885) would triumph at the next two Montreal carnivals.

In Banff, Alberta, by contrast, civic boosters exploited images of a rugged Canadian landscape and representations of Indigenous cultural practices to attract people in the winter months. Building on the long tradition of winter Carnivals in Ontario and Quebec, and with the support of the Canadian government, the first annual Banff Winter Carnival was held in 1917.

In their report of the first carnival, the *Crag and Canyon*, the local Banff newspaper, claimed that women's hockey was "one of the best money-getters" and included a description of a women's hockey match between the Calgary Regents and the Calgary Crescents: "The rink was crowded at the hockey match, which was well contested. The Regents won a hard fight [sic] contest with a score of 1-0. Close checking was one of the main features, many members of both teams receiving bad spills."[32] Carnival organizers built on this interest, inviting teams from across Alberta and British Columbia, such as the Vancouver Amazons (see figure 9.1), and soon promoted the women's hockey tournament as one of the highlights of the carnival.[33]

Vancouver Amazons vs Calgary Byngs [Women's hockey game, Mather's rink, Banff Winter Carnival]. Ca. 1930. Peter and Catharine Whyte fonds. V683 / II / A / 1 / PD - 3. Archives and Library, Whyte Museum of the Canadian Rockies.

Figure 9.1   The Vancouver Amazons at the Banff Winter Carnival in Banff, Alberta in 1921.

Cup was an explicit attempt by political elites, like Stanley, to foster Canadian nationalism through sport. As Jordan Goldstein notes: "Stanley believed it his responsibility to promote unity throughout the country. Sport provided an essential cultural activity that could accomplish this goal."[29]

At the local level, the organization of men's hockey—as in other sports—was constantly evolving, as competitive team sports grew increasingly popular in the late 19th century. In 1888, the AHAC added a junior league for younger men (usually between 16 and 20), and in 1892, the demand for playing time led to the creation of an intermediate league, between junior and senior (usually for 18 to 20 years old). Many of the high-profile clubs in central Canada (primarily in Montreal and Ottawa) entered teams in multiple levels. But this structure soon led to tension as successful intermediate teams often wanted promotion to the senior level, only to meet resistance. A struggle over the potential promotion of the Ottawa intermediate team resulted in the senior teams quitting the AHAC and forming a new league, the Canadian Amateur Hockey League (CAHL), for the 1899 season.

Elsewhere, by 1900, high school, church, and YMCA teams and leagues for younger players (10 to 16 years old) were organized in larger cities across Canada. It was not until the 1930s that provincial hockey organizations introduced what we now know as minor hockey.

Organizing Hockey for Girls and Women

The earliest accounts of women's hockey date to the early 1890s. Photographs and newspaper reports from this time suggest that games were played before the development of leagues and formal competitions.[34] By the turn of the century, university and community women's teams existed in dozens of towns and cities across Canada. There is evidence of teams from as far north as the Yukon, as far west as British Columbia, and as far east as the Maritimes. Universities such as Queen's University in Kingston, the University of Toronto, and McGill University in Montreal had women's teams by the 1900s, accessible to those women who had access to higher education. The First World War brought changes to all areas of women's lives, including sport and recreation.[35] Teams were popping up across Canada. The Ottawa Alerts, for example, were formed in 1915, drawing players from the Ottawa Ladies' College and the YWCA. The Alerts, whose roster included Eva Ault (see figure 9.2), played against teams from Montreal, Renfrew, Cornwall, and Pittsburgh. The Cornwall Victorias (previously named the Nationals) were led by star player Albertine Lapensée.[36]

By the 1920s, women were flooding into Canadian cities in search of employment. They were also turning to sport and recreation as a way to fill their spare time. This led to a grassroots movement to develop working-class women's sport clubs.[37] Formed in 1922, the Ladies Ontario Hockey Association (LOHA) was the first provincial governing body for women's hockey in Canada.[38] The association attempted to model itself on the Ontario Hockey Association (OHA), the provincial governing body for men's hockey, with a few changes that better

Figure 9.2 Eva Ault, member of the Ottawa Alerts women's hockey team. Following her retirement, Ault served as the vice-president of the Ladies Ontario Hockey Association in 1924 and 1925.

suited the women's game, such as increasing the number of substitutes for each game to four, allowing clubs that played on outdoor ice to join as members, and granting membership to commercially sponsored clubs.[39] While the creation of the LOHA was supported by the Toronto Hockey League and the OHA, the association was not recognized by the Canadian Amateur Hockey Association (CAHA). In 1923, in a majority vote, the CAHA officially denied the LOHA recognition as the provincial governing body for women's hockey. The president of the OHA, William Alexander Fry, describing the discussion at the CAHA, explained:

While participation of women and girls in many competitive sports, such as tennis, swimming, skating, and track and field events is growing, my belief that hockey, for various reasons, should be an exception, led me at the executive meeting of the C.A.H.A., held in Port Arthur, to vote with the majority not to give them [the LOHA] official recognition. In my opinion there is all the necessary scope for them in games where the personal contact element is not a factor."[40]

In the 1920s, despite the large numbers of women playing the sport across the country, as Fry's remarks suggest, there were widely held beliefs that hockey was too rough for women.[41] Despite this setback, the Women's Amateur Athletic Federation was created under the leadership of Alexandrine Gibb (see chapter

TRANSFORMATIVE MOMENTS: THE PRESTON RIVULETTES AND THE POLITICS OF REPRESENTATION

On December 22, 2017, at a ceremony in Cambridge, Ontario, the Canadian government recognized the Preston Rivulettes as historically significant.[44] In front of a crowd of over 150 dignitaries, family members, and hockey supporters, the team's achievements were praised and commemorated. From 1931 until 1940, the Preston Rivulettes (see figure 9.3) dominated Canadian women's hockey, claiming 10 Ontario championships and four national titles.[45] The Rivulettes played hard, aggressive, skillful hockey, and they are one of the most successful teams in Canadian hockey history.

Despite this success, however, the Preston Rivulettes and the players have not been inducted into the Hockey Hall of Fame (HHOF) in Toronto. Hilda Ranscombe, star player of the team throughout the 1930s, was inducted into Canada's Sports Hall of Fame in 2015, but her nomination for consideration in the HHOF has repeatedly been denied.

Courtesy of the City of Cambridge Archives Photograph Collection

Figure 9.3   Preston Rivulettes (c. 1934).

Many newspaper and secondary source accounts of the Rivulettes suggest the team has already been indicted to the HHOF. This misunderstanding can be traced back to a newspaper article from 1963. Under the headline "Rivulettes to Enter Hockey Hall of Fame," an article in the *Galt Evening Reporter* suggested that the HHOF contacted Hilda Ranscombe as they wanted to "recognize the team's outstanding achievements by placing the championship trophy and pictures within the hall's confines."[46] Although inclusion in the Hall's exhibits is an important recognition of the team's success, this was not equivalent to induction into the HHOF's list of honoured members.

Institutions such as halls of fame and museums contribute to discourses about how sport is remembered, and through induction ceremonies and exhibits, they signal which teams, athletes, and builders are worthy of being remembered.[47] This is especially true of hockey, which, as Gruneau and Whitson note, "has become one of this country's most significant collective representations—a story that Canadians tell themselves about what it means to be Canadian."[48] When halls of fame focus predominantly on the accomplishments of certain groups and elevate these bodies as the worthy recipients of public recognition, it obscures the involvement of others and erases some experiences from national collective memories.

The historic exclusion of women from hockey halls of fame, for example, diminishes women's contributions to the sport. Yet these circumstances have slowly begun to change. In 2010, American Cammi Granato and Canadian Angela James were the first two women inducted into the HHOF. Since then the Hall has inducted a handful of women as honoured members including Canadians Geraldine Heaney, Danielle Goyette, Jayna Hefford, and most recently, Hayley Wickenheiser. While these are steps in the right direction, the HHOF as the arbiter of hockey recognition could make a much more significant contribution to shifting national discourses of Canada's winter game.

12).[42] The LOHA also paved the way for other provincial governing bodies for women's hockey across the country and for the formation of the Dominion Women's Amateur Hockey Association (DWAHA) in the early 1930s. Throughout the 1930s, the DWAHA was the national governing body for women's hockey in Canada, with the primary focus of coordinating a national women's hockey series. The Preston Rivulettes dominated play in the LOHA in the '30s, but it was the Edmonton Rustlers who were crowned the first national champions in 1933.[43]

Men's Hockey Beyond the White Upper-Middle Class

Organized hockey was first played by Montreal's English, male upper-middle class. The game grew in part because of its popularity, as well as the pleasure taken from play. This process, however, was aided by the spread of amateur sport in general across Canada, and the power of middle-class ideologies of progress and personal achievement (see chapters 7 and 8). However, participation outside of Montreal's anglophone, white, male middle-class has to be viewed through the lens of colonialism. Nondominant groups might find a way to organize hockey teams, but access to the sport still meant abiding by the rules and bodily practices of the hegemonic group. In the late 19th century, as Robidoux notes, "regulated sport quickly became a vehicle for cultural imperialism."[49]

Despite some important class differences, the Montreal clubs of the AHAC were essentially exclusively anglophone: The MAAA were mostly English, the Victorias were Scottish, and the Shamrocks were Catholic Irish. It was not until the early 20th century that the city's Jewish and Italian communities produced hockey teams. However, some French-Canadian players participated in early hockey games at Montreal's Catholic colleges—primarily Sainte-Marie and Mont-Saint-Louis—in the mid-1890s, usually learning the game from their Irish-Canadian colleagues.[50] Although the French-Catholic clergy initially opposed the game on the grounds that it would weaken students' language and faith, they soon came to see the benefits of sport.[51] The first francophone player to win the Stanley Cup was Métis Antoine "Tony" Gingras of the Winnipeg Victorias in 1901 (see figure 9.4).[52] Fifteen years later, the Montreal Canadiens of the National Hockey Association in 1916 would be the first French-Canadian team to win the Stanley Cup, their first of 24 wins.

In the Maritimes, the appeal of hockey also extended beyond the white upper-middle class. In 1895, four leaders in the African Nova Scotian community in Halifax, including pastors and laypersons, founded the Coloured Hockey League of the Maritimes.[53] They too saw a benefit in sport, hoping to attract young men to Sunday services if a hockey game was to follow. The league started with only three teams, but by the turn of the century, the Dartmouth Jubilees had been joined by the Africville Seasides (see figure 9.5 and chapter 11), Truro Victorias, Charlottetown West End Rangers, Amherst Royals, and Hammond Plains Moss Backs, many of which also played baseball in the summer.

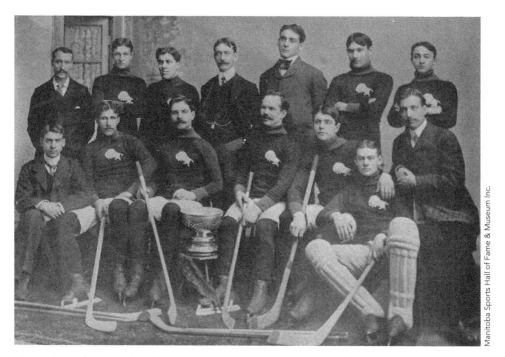

Figure 9.4   The 1901 Stanley Cup Champions, the Winnipeg Victorias.

Figure 9.5   The Africville Seasides hockey team.

Teams played at local rinks, but only after white teams had finished their seasons. Nevertheless, a 1902 match between the Seasides and the West End Rangers was played in front of 1,200 spectators. A dispute with local officials made it difficult to obtain ice time, and there are no media accounts of matches after 1911. The league was reformed with three teams in the 1920s—the Seasides, Victorias, and Halifax All-Stars. These and other teams managed to keep Black hockey alive in the Maritimes into the 1930s, but organized competition did not survive the years during the Depression and the Second World War.

Players on teams such as these paved the way for groundbreaking moments well into the 20th century. One of the first Indigenous players to reach the NHL, Fred Sasakamoose, and the first Black Canadian to play in the NHL, Willie O'Ree, both achieved these milestones in the 1950s (see chapter 11). Nevertheless, many accomplished players, like Black Canadian Herb Carnegie, were never given such an opportunity.

The Amateur Versus Professional Debate

In 1906, the Montreal Wanderers won the Stanley Cup and subsequently declared themselves a professional team. The Cup's trustees, however, were reluctant to accept the concept of professionalism. The debate over the amateur ideology that was central to the emergence of modern sport, the desire of some of the sport's top players to be paid for their labour, and the interest of hockey entrepreneurs to reap the profits of commercial spectacle occurred as Canadian sport more generally found itself embroiled in an "athletic war" (1906-1909; see chapter 8) .

Although the amateur game was still dominant, especially in media coverage, some amateur clubs found ways to hide professionals among their ranks. The Montreal Wanderers had competed in 1906 in the new Eastern Canada Amateur Hockey Association (ECAHA), which replaced the CAHL. For the 1907 season, the ECAHA required each team to declare which players were paid and which were not. This system lasted until 1909, when the ECAHA dropped *Amateur* from its name and the league's two amateur clubs left for a new fully amateur circuit, whose championship trophy, the Allan Cup, is still awarded to the Canadian senior amateur champion.

But the ECAHA was not hockey's first professional league. In 1904, the International Hockey League was created, with teams in Calumet, Houghton, and Sault Ste. Marie in Michigan; Pittsburgh, Pennsylvania; and Sault Ste. Marie, Ontario. All the players were Canadians and thus forbidden to play for pay in Canada at the time. Following the acceptance of professionalism in Canadian hockey in 1907, a number of new professional leagues were formed, including the Manitoba Professional Hockey League (1907-1909), the Ontario Professional Hockey League (1908-1911), and the Maritime Professional Hockey League (1912-1914).

In response to these developments, the CAHA was established in 1914 as the governing body to supervise amateur hockey in Canada, which remained predominantly male. Nevertheless, there were also women's professional leagues during this era such as the Eastern Ladies Hockey League (1915-1920), a Montreal-based league with four teams: the Westerns, Maisonneuves, North End Stanleys, and Telegraph.

On the west coast, the Pacific Coast Hockey Association (PCHA) was an influential enterprise. Founded in 1912 and run by the Patrick brothers (Lester and Frank), who would become prominent figures in the National Hockey League (NHL), the PCHA played in Canada's first arenas with artificial ice, experimented with the forward pass to make the game more offensive-minded and attractive to fans, and importantly for the commercialization of hockey, ran the league as a syndicate, with all teams owned by a single corporate entity.[54] PCHA champions contested the Stanley Cup starting in 1915, before amalgamating into a short-lived Western Hockey League (WHL) with the remaining teams of the Western Canada Hockey League.

Many of these professional leagues had teams contest the Stanley Cup in the 1910s and 1920s, but only teams from the PCHA and WHL managed to capture the trophy, competing against first the new eastern league, the National Hockey Association (NHA), and subsequently the NHL. Formed in 1910, the NHA merged with the rival Canadian Hockey Association two weeks into its inaugural season to become the major professional league in Eastern Canada. The two circuits' 10 combined teams emerged as a seven-team NHA. Of the two French-Canadian teams, only the NHA's Canadiens survived the merger. The team would become the Club de hockey Canadien when it was incorporated in 1916, and a year later it found itself a charter member in a renamed NHA, as the most prominent commercial hockey league in Canada got off to an inauspicious beginning.

The Commercialization of Hockey

On November 22, 1917, prospective club owners from three cities met to form what would become the most enduring commercial sports entity in Canadian history, the National Hockey League (NHL). Less a milestone than a coup, the meeting was essentially an attempt by owners of clubs in the National Hockey Association (NHA) to rid themselves of the fractious Eddie Livingstone, owner of the league's Toronto entry.[55] Despite this, the moment has come to be seen as the founding of a Canadian sport juggernaut.

The Hegemony of the NHL

Over the next two decades the pre-eminence of the NHL led to the consolidation of the hegemonic position of professional hockey over the amateur game. At the same time, the NHL emerged as the dominant commercial entity in North American hockey. Competitive professional leagues in Western Canada folded during the 1920s. By 1927, meanwhile, the Stanley Cup had become emblematic of the NHL's postseason playoff champion. There was no other North American league competing at the same level.

A number of factors account for the NHL's emerging hegemony in the inter-war years. Shifting understandings of professionalism—away from the term's previous unsavory associations and towards being a marker of excellence—contributed to the growing popularity of professional hockey at the expense of the amateur game (see chapter 8). The growing sport media, both radio and the press, influenced these shifting attitudes (as discussed later; see also chapter 12). Commercial sport also benefitted from the growing consumer economy of the 1920s, which encouraged using disposable income on entertainment such as tickets to hockey matches.

But the most significant factor in the NHL's assumption of a dominant posi-tion over commercial hockey was the influx of U.S. capital. The expansion of the league to the United States was spearheaded by entrepreneur Tom Duggan, who worked through the early 1920s to find suitable owners and facilities for hockey south of the border.[56] His greatest success came in Boston, which became the NHL's first U.S.-based franchise in 1924, and New York, where the Ameri-cans joined a year later with the Pittsburgh Pirates. A second New York team followed in 1926, along with teams in Chicago and Detroit.

The franchise fees paid by these new clubs lined the coffers of the NHL's existing franchises. This revenue not only secured the NHL's dominance over other commercial hockey leagues but also helped cement the ascendancy of the professional (men's) version of the sport. The waning influence of amateurism over hockey was signalled in 1936 when the Canadian Amateur Hockey Asso-ciation (CAHA) negotiated an agreement with the NHL that made the latter's rules standard in Canadian hockey and effectively established the ways in which amateur clubs would provide players to the pro ranks.[57]

Although the NHL today markets its early history as the era of the Original Six franchises, the league existed in a state of fluctuating commercial viability, with clubs folding and relocating for many years (1917-1942) leading up to the quarter century (1942-1967), when it consisted solely of the Boston Bruins, Chi-cago Black Hawks, Detroit Red Wings, Montreal Canadiens, New York Rangers, and Toronto Maple Leafs. The latter era saw the establishment of dominant teams in Montreal (led by Maurice Richard and Jean Beliveau, among others), Detroit (where Gordie Howe set NHL scoring records), and Toronto. However, operating with a half-dozen teams in the northeast limited playing opportuni-ties for many talented professionals stuck in the minor leagues.

It was the rapid growth of U.S. sport television in the 1960s that provided the impetus for change (as would also be the case in American football and basketball). The NHL dramatically doubled in 1967, with all six new teams based in the United States (in Los Angeles, Oakland, Philadelphia, Pittsburgh, Minneapolis, and St. Louis). Six more teams would be added before the mid-1970s, with all but one (Vancouver) in an American market.

Burgeoning U.S. television revenues for sport led not only to expansion among the major team sports but also to the creation of rival circuits looking to capitalize on these trends and capture untapped markets. The World Hockey Association (WHA) presented the most significant challenge to the NHL's hegemony in nearly half a century when it was announced in 1971. The league began with 12 teams in 1972. For the rest of the 1970s, the WHA would garner headlines by luring away some of the NHL's highest-profile talent, including established veterans such as Bobby Hull and Gordie Howe (who came out of retirement to play with his sons) and emerging stars like Bernie Parent and Derek Sanderson. Although it reached markets as yet unserved by the NHL, the WHA battled financial problems, spotty television ratings, poor attendance, and frequent franchise relocations.

The NHL reasserted its hegemony beginning in the 1990s. Having absorbed four WHA teams in 1979 (located in Edmonton, Winnipeg, Quebec City, and Hartford) as its rival ceased operation, the league began a new round of expansion in the 1990s. Focused primarily on significant markets in the U.S. Sun Belt, new teams were added in San Jose (1991), Ottawa and Tampa Bay (1992), Miami and Anaheim (1993), Nashville (1998), and Atlanta (1999). Franchise relocations during the period also emphasized major untapped U.S. television markets with teams in Quebec City, Winnipeg, Hartford, and Minneapolis moving to Denver, Phoenix, Raleigh, and Dallas, respectively.

Spectatorship

A number of developments accompanied the consolidation of the NHL's hegemony over Canadian hockey and the growing influence of the commercial model of sport in the interwar years. One of the most prominent was the construction of a generation of iconic hockey arenas, the Montreal Forum and Toronto's Maple Leaf Gardens among them. These places came to be identified with some of the game's most prominent players and dramatic moments, but first they ushered in an era of sport consumption as spectating became integral in Canadian sport.

Stadium construction was influenced both by the changing economics of commercial sport and the influx of American capital that fuelled the NHL's expansion in the 1920s. Although new arenas were built in Ottawa (1923: 7,500 seats) and Montreal (1924: 9,300 seats),[58] it was the construction of the new Madison Square Garden in New York City in 1925 that radically altered the economics of professional hockey. The arena reaped the benefits of being able to sell nearly twice as many tickets—with a capacity for hockey of over 18,000—as any other venue in the NHL. The increased revenues generated by such facilities allowed the league to pay higher salaries than their competitors, primarily in Western Canada, and expand to new markets. NHL teams found their way to cities in which new arenas were constructed: The Olympia opened in Detroit in 1927, the Bruins moved into the Boston Garden in 1928, and Chicago Stadium opened in 1929.[59]

These arenas held considerably more spectators than the buildings in Ottawa and Montreal that had been built only five or six years earlier. Canadian clubs in the NHL could not compete with their new American cousins (and before the end of the 1930s, teams in Hamilton, Ottawa, and Montreal would all cease operation or move to the United States). The new arenas could not only seat more patrons but also were frequently owned by the same interests that controlled the clubs, so that teams were not paying rent to an arena owner but were retaining all ticket revenues. This was the case in Toronto, where Maple Leaf Gardens opened in 1931, built largely in response to the financial changes that were occurring in the NHL. The Maple Leafs moved from leasing an 8,000-seat arena to owning their own venue, which had more than 50 percent greater capacity.[60]

The new generation of hockey arenas both reflected and affected the changing economics of commercial sport in the interwar years. They also changed the nature of spectating as a social practice. Prior to the new generation (1925-1931) of NHL arenas, most teams played in venues that, while they had seating, did not cater in any special way to spectators. Public skating times were still common. Newer facilities, such as Maple Leaf Gardens, were designed with the spectator in mind, including offering tiers of seating that reflected different ticket prices. Within such spaces, people watched games in the presence of other fans, as spectating became a social practice central to the nature of commercial sport by the interwar years.[61]

It would take more than half a century—and expansion—for the physical spaces of professional hockey to modernize. A new Madison Square Garden was built in 1968, and the clubs that joined the NHL in 1967 and thereafter introduced new facilities to the league. The Montreal Forum was renovated and expanded in 1948 and again in 1968, increasing its seating capacity to 16,000. Although the Red Wings moved from the Olympia to the new Joe Louis Arena in 1979, it was not until the mid-1990s that the nature of NHL spectating changed again. Many expansion (and relocated) teams in the U.S. Sun Belt played in newer venues, while in Canada, Vancouver opened a new arena in 1995, the Montreal Forum gave way to the Molson Centre in 1996, and the Maple Leafs left the Maple Leaf Gardens for the Air Canada Centre in 1999. By the early 21st century, commercial sport facilities were fully embedded within economies of consumption and entertainment. Teams operated their own digital television stations and, as was the case in Toronto and Winnipeg, invested in residential and commercial real estate ventures to develop the neighbourhoods in which their arenas were located.

Mass media

While Maple Leaf Gardens was still in the conceptual stages, radio broadcaster Foster Hewitt announced on the air that interested fans could order a prospectus to learn more about the new arena by sending 10 cents to the hockey club. Consequently, the Maple Leafs sold 91,000 such programs with drawings of the new arena during the 1930-31 season.[62] This anecdote points to the power of sport radio by the 1930s.

The media contributed to the growing commercial success of sport in the 1920s. Sportswriters celebrated athletes in a variety of sports, including, in the

American context, Babe Ruth in baseball, Bill Tilden in tennis, Red Grange in football, and Jack Dempsey in boxing. Howie Morenz was hockey's equivalent transcendent star. His popularity was forged not only by the press but also by a new medium: radio.

Hockey games were first broadcast on the radio in 1923, with the audience growing as the wireless set became a significant consumer good. The relationship between hockey and radio was firmly established in 1931, when as Maple Leaf Gardens was being built, Hewitt visited Eaton's College Street department store in Toronto, walking from one floor up to the next and peering into the store's atrium until he decided he was at the best height from which to call a hockey game on the radio. And, it was at this height, so the potentially apocryphal story goes, that Hewitt had the cage from which he broadcast games (the subsequently famed "gondola") installed in Maple Leaf Gardens (see chapter 12).

Hewitt's national weekly radio broadcasts of games from the Toronto arena, which eventually came to be called *Hockey Night in Canada*, were one of Canada's most iconic media properties. They made the Maple Leafs, in modern terms, a national brand and constructed Maple Leaf Gardens as the home of hockey in English Canada. Oral histories of the period highlight the significance of listening to hockey broadcasts to socializing during the Great Depression.[63] The growing prominence of radio had a lasting commercial impact on hockey, connecting *Hockey Night in Canada* to prominent sponsors, first General Motors and then Imperial Oil, whose Three Star gasoline at its Esso stations became the still-used branding for the selection of a game's top three stars on radio and television broadcasts. When the Canadian Broadcasting Corporation introduced television to Canada in 1952, *Hockey Night in Canada* was one of the network's flagship programs.

International Hockey

The debates over amateurism and professionalism (see chapters 7 and 8) that shaped the development of commercial hockey in Canada also influenced the emergence and development of international hockey. In the same year as the Canadian Amateur Hockey Association (CAHA) agreement with the National Hockey League (NHL), the fifth Olympic hockey tournament was contested at the 1936 winter games in Garmisch-Partenkirchen, Germany. The Canadian team finished second, losing the gold medal after a 2-1 loss to a Great Britain team that the CAHA claimed included players who were under CAHA suspension.[64] The controversy was a harbinger of how nationalism and at times problematic patriotism would come to shape international hockey.

Men's International Hockey

Men's ice hockey first appeared on the Olympic program at the 1920 Summer Olympics in Antwerp, Belgium, with the Canadian entry—the Winnipeg Falcons—capturing the gold medal. International hockey had been institutionalized a dozen years earlier with the formation of the Ligue International de Hockey sur Glace, now the International Ice Hockey Federation (IIHF), by the inaugural members: Belgium, Bohemia, France, Great Britain, and Switzerland. Following the silver medal in 1936, the Canadian entry at the 1948 Winter Olympics, the Royal Canadian Air Force (RCAF) Flyers, and the Edmonton Mercurys in 1952, returned Canada to the top of the Olympic podium. These successes, however, represented Canada's last Olympic men's hockey gold medals for half a century as international hockey—indeed virtually all of international sport—was shaped by the competing issues of nationalism and amateurism. This was exemplified most starkly by the entry of the Soviet Union into international sport, which had a significant impact on Canadian men's hockey.

Following the Russian Revolution in 1917, the new Soviet Union government withdrew from international sport. In 1948, the same year the RCAF Flyers were capturing Olympic gold, the Communist Party's Central Committee in Moscow passed a resolution supporting the promotion of the Soviet Union state through success in international sport.[65] This included participation in the Olympic Games and competing in ice hockey. The Soviet Union joined the Olympic movement in 1951 but did not compete in the Winter Olympics until 1956. The Soviets first participated at the world ice hockey championship in 1954, with a club of relatively unknown players. They finished the tournament undefeated, beating the amateur team from East York, Ontario, which represented Canada, 7-2 in the tournament's final game. That Canada's place in the international hockey order had been usurped was confirmed two years later at the 1956 Winter Olympics in Cortina d'Ampezzo, Italy, where the Kitchener-Waterloo Dutchmen settled for a bronze medal behind the Soviet Union and U.S. teams.

The emergence of the Soviet Union (as well as Czechoslovakia) as an international hockey power during this period took place in the context of the Cold War and the geopolitical tensions that existed between the communist East and capitalist West. Sport was frequently a metaphorical battleground in these tensions, which only magnified the failures of Canada's international hockey representatives. Three more Canadian clubs won the world championship before the end of the 1950s, but only one (the Trail Smoke Eaters in 1961) was victorious in the 31 world championships from 1960 to 1993. This lack of international success in a sport so closely linked to a sense of Canadian identity was broadcast into Canadian homes with the increasing popularity and ubiquity of television.

Hockey results were not the only motivating factor, but in the early 1960s the federal government of Prime Minister John Diefenbaker decided to introduce the most comprehensive state intervention into physical activity in Canadian history. The Fitness and Amateur Sport Act (1961) established an advisory council to distribute money to each province, which would fund amateur athletes, train coaches, and support research. Despite this initial intervention, there were virtually no standing national teams in any sport, with the notable exception of hockey. Father David Bauer's attempt at establishing a national men's hockey team yielded a bronze medal at the 1968 Olympic Games.

Despite this success, Canada withdrew from international hockey competition in 1970, asserting the growing belief that state-funded athletes in the Soviet Union and other communist countries were de facto professionals. Canada could only compete (and succeed) if it too was allowed to involve its best players (professionals competing in the NHL). Highlighting the ways in which debates over amateurism intersected with national interests, the government of Pierre Trudeau (elected in 1968) reinterpreted the Fitness and Amateur Sport Act to centralize the operation of amateur sport so that state funds could be directed towards the pursuit of success in elite competitions. In hockey, this meant that federal officials worked with the NHL, especially Alan Eagleson, the powerful head of the NHL Players' Association, to arrange eight exhibition games in September 1972 between the Soviet Union national team and a team of Canadian NHL players. Canadian players who had signed with the rival WHA—most prominently Bobby Hull of the Winnipeg Jets—were precluded from participating, reflecting how international sport was also increasingly becoming bound up in the commercial tensions of professional sport.

It was anticipated that the 1972 Summit Series would see Canadian NHLers dominate the Soviet Union team, who despite their international success were assumed by many to be no match for the best professionals Canada could offer. The first game took place at the Montreal Forum, with Prime Minister Trudeau dropping the puck for the ceremonial faceoff. The Canadians jumped out to an early 2-0 lead before the Soviets silenced the crowd by scoring seven of the next eight goals and cruising to an easy 7-3 victory. After losing the fifth game, Canada was in the position of needing to win the final three games to capture the series. Two straight one-goal wins by Canada led to a deciding eighth game, where Paul Henderson's dramatic series-winning goal with 34 seconds left became one of the most iconic moments in Canadian sporting history.

Estimates for the series' final game ranged from 7.5 to 12.5 million viewers (at a time when the country's population was approximately 21.8 million). With the commercial potential of international hockey thus affirmed, East–West hockey clashes became a fixture on the sport's calendar in the 1970s. The WHA held its own eight-game series in 1974, pitting its best Canadian players against the Soviet Union national team; club teams from the USSR began regular tours against NHL teams; and the NHL decided to forgo its 1979 all-star game in favour of a three-game Challenge Cup between its best and the Soviet Union national team.

The professionalization of international hockey continued throughout the 1970s, with the success of the Summit Series leading to the inaugural Canada Cup, organized by Eagleson and involving the best professional players from six nations. The tournament was repeated in 1981, 1984, 1987, and 1991. A similar format—labelled a World Cup—was held in 1996 and 2004. But it was the entry of NHL players into the Winter Olympics, beginning in Nagano in 1998, that firmly entrenched the NHL's hegemonic position and affirmed the commercial potential of international hockey—culminating in Crosby's dramatic overtime goal in Vancouver in 2010. That the NHL launched its own World Cup in 2016—including two teams created for the competition that did not represent national boundaries—before deciding to not allow its players to participate in the 2018 Winter Olympics, suggests the league may be seeking to retain as much of the financial and marketing benefits of international play as possible.

Women's International Hockey

The first known international women's hockey game took place between teams from Canada and the United States in 1916 at a tournament in Cleveland, Ohio.[66] Although Canadian women played against teams from the United States in the 1910s, national and international governing bodies did not sanction international competitions for women until the 1990s. Although men's hockey was first a part of the Olympic Games in 1920, women's hockey was not on the program until 1998. Julie Stevens suggests that two key events helped women's hockey gain an international profile in the 1980s: The Brampton Canadettes Dominion Ladies' Hockey Tournament in 1985 added an international division that attracted teams from Canada, the United States, the Netherlands, and Germany; and in 1987, Canadian women's hockey leaders staged a larger international women's hockey tournament that included teams from Canada, the United States, Sweden, Switzerland, Japan, and the Netherlands.[67] Although not sanctioned by the IIHF, the 1987 tournament forced the IIHF to look seriously at women's hockey as an international event.[68] The result was a European championship in 1989 and ultimately the first women's world hockey championship in 1990. The CAHA was asked to host the eight-team tournament in 1990 based on Canada's recognition as the world's most developed women's hockey nation.[69] This was also the first time women's hockey was extensively televised.[70]

By sanctioning the world hockey championship in 1990, the IIHF effectively positioned itself as the sole voice for women's hockey internationally; it had co-opted the women's game.[71] The IIHF set out the guidelines for women's international competition and forced women to play hockey under specific terms. For example, in the mid-1980s, Canada, the United States, and Japan had banned bodychecking in women's hockey, yet the IIHF insisted it be included in the world tournament in 1990. The IIHF was reinforcing the prevailing notion that "real" hockey included tough, physical, aggressive play.[72]

In the early 1990s, formal policy changes were occurring within the International Olympic Committee (IOC) with respect to women's sport. The 1991 IOC Charter states: "Any form of discrimination with regard to a country or a person on grounds of race, religion, politics, sex, or otherwise is incompatible with belonging to the Olympic movement."[73] For the first time, the word *sex* had been included in this statement. The timing was right for the IOC to concede to lobbying pressures for women's hockey to be included on the Olympic program.[74] On July 21, 1992, women's hockey was announced as a new Olympic sport.[75] Although organizers of the 1994 Winter Olympics in Lillehammer, Norway, refused to accept women's hockey on its program because of lack of facilities and funds, after negotiations and the promise of support by the IIHF, the Nagano Organizing Committee agreed to host the first official Olympic women's hockey competition in 1998 in Nagano, Japan.[76] When the United States won the women's hockey gold medal at the 1998 Olympic Games, it was more than "just" an Olympic victory—it represented victory in a long fight for recognition and inclusion in the highest levels of international hockey.

Youth Hockey and the Contemporary Landscape

By 2018, more than 620,000 Canadian children and youth were registered in minor hockey.[77] Historically, the development of minor hockey in Canada was part of a broader social and moral reform movement (see chapters 6 and 10). The growth of minor hockey across Canada is also inextricably intertwined with the commercialization of the game. Foster Hewitt and other broadcasters, as well as a generation of sportswriters, helped inculcate the persistent values of hockey among fans young and old, celebrating toughness, playing through pain, and often violence as hockey's ideal version of manliness (see chapter 8). Narratives such as these continue to resonate, ensuring that some of the most prominent debates in contemporary minor hockey have their roots in the history of the game.

Minor hockey

Despite having been established in 1914 as the governing body for all amateur hockey in Canada, it was not until the 1930s that the Canadian Amateur Hockey Association (CAHA) actively created age categories for boys and young men. In the early 1930s, the CAHA awarded grants to each of its active provincial branches with the explicit purpose of encouraging the "promotion of juvenile, bantam and, in some instances, intermediate hockey."[78] This initiative happened in the midst of a number of tensions including the pressures exerted by the amateur ideology of the time (see chapter 7) and the increasing commodification of hockey.

The protection of young players was central to conversations about the potential recruitment of young men by professional teams. For example, during the annual meetings of the CAHA, long-time member George Dudley spoke vehemently about ensuring that young men remain amateurs as long as possible. "The younger boys . . . need protection," he argued. "If a professional club offers [them] a few dollars, [they] may make this jump to [their] everlasting regret."[79] Dudley and his supporters tried unsuccessfully to push through a resolution that would preclude men under the age of 21 from trying out with professional teams.

Until the 1930s, the National Hockey League (NHL) and CAHA operated as separate entities, and players could play under the umbrella of only one organization. However, by the early 1920s, the NHL took an interest in boys' hockey, and "child buying" became a common practice of professional teams.[80] NHL teams identified promising prospective players and provided sponsorship in the form of a retainer or paying for schooling in exchange for their agreement to sign with the team if they joined professional hockey.[81] In 1938, the agreement the NHL had with the CAHA not to directly scout young boys dissolved, paving the way for the formal sponsorship agreements put in place in the coming decades.[82] By the 1940s the CAHA needed NHL sponsorship dollars to operate and some NHL teams needed junior players as men went off to war.

Gruneau and Whitson suggest it was not until the mid-1940s, following the Second World War, that the CAHA acknowledged its role as a feeder system for professional hockey.[83] In 1947, the NHL and several amateur governing bodies such as the CAHA, the IIHF, and the Amateur Ice Hockey Federation of the United States came to an agreement that gave the NHL control over elite hockey. Through the signing of the mandatory CAHA registration card, boys were bound for life to the NHL team that sponsored their local club. For example, boys in Fredericton were "Black Hawk Property" and boys in Winnipeg were "Boston Bruins Property."[84] Bruce Kidd and John Macfarlane suggest this partnership was a strategic move on behalf of the CAHA and its longevity because it made the governing body "an active partner in the development of a country-wide NHL farm system."[85] However, this move has also led to a win-at-all-cost mentality as young boys endeavour to play in the NHL, with only a small percentage of them actually achieving this goal.

Although girls and women have been playing hockey in Canada since the 1890s, it was not until the 1970s that opportunities to play organized minor hockey became increasingly available across the country.[86] When Abigail Hoffman joined the St. Catharines Teepees in the mid-1950s, she was the only girl among hundreds of boys in the league. It was well into the season before it was discovered that "Ab" was a nine-year-old girl. M. Ann Hall shares that Abigail's parents "went along with the deception so she could play, taking her to the arena fully dressed."[87] Stories like this speak to the tensions of the time and the challenges for young girls to play ice hockey without any organizational structures in place to support their development. In the 1970s, groups of women across the country came together to form club teams and advocate for opportunities for girls and women to play. In 1975, the Ontario Women's Hockey Association was established with the mandate of providing opportunities for women and girls of all abilities to play hockey provincially and a vision of equalling the Ontario Hockey Association (OHA) in strength and membership.[88] As Adams and Laurendeau suggest, "the relatively late emergence of institutionalized minor hockey for girls (as well as the continued marginalization of girls' hockey) tells us not only about gender and sexism in sport" but also about the cultural discourses and ideologies that exist in Canadian sport.[89]

Elite Youth Hockey and the Pay-for-Play Model

In 2013, Randy Turner of the *Winnipeg Free Press* penned a story titled "Parents who can afford it scramble to get kids into elite hockey programs."[90] The article told of a "revolution taking place in Canadian minor hockey," in which "teams are being spawned by the hundreds outside the long arm of Hockey Canada." These teams, Turner argues, "have become a beacon for parents with needs to fill and money to spend—whether they can afford it or not." Over the last 15 years, Canadian youth hockey has undergone two interrelated cultural shifts: Athletes are facing pressure to specialize in hockey both full time and at younger ages, if they hope to realize the promise of elite-level success; and private pay-for-play institutions have emerged to offer more of these opportunities.

Hockey Alberta, for example, suggests players are searching out elite opportunities such as sports academies, with players paying as much as $30,000 in tuition per year for the opportunity to attend. Minor hockey programs "are facing increasing pressure from private entrepreneurial entities, sport schools and sport academies, and these pressures impact players and families."[91] Moreover, there is evidence that enrolling children in pay-for-play programs that provide year-round hockey opportunities for young people is not producing the benefits promised by such programs.[92]

In 1972, Kidd and Macfarlane prophesized that the increasing specialization of youth sport and the pay-for-play model of youth hockey, which often come at the expense of playing for fun, could signal the "death of the game."[93] While this has not yet come to pass, we are seeing a privatized sports model whereby sports academies and other elite hockey opportunities are commonplace and in most cases a required stepping stone for professional hockey. Given the escalating costs associated with this model of sport, only certain families can afford to participate.[94]

Hockey's Darker Side

The numbers of girls and boys playing in the minor hockey system is decreasing across Canada. A 2013 survey of families in Nova Scotia and Ontario found that affordability was a factor in parents choosing not to enroll their children in organized minor hockey.[95] Significantly, this was only one of four factors that explained declining participation rates. The others were safety concerns, the time-consuming schedule, and a lack of fun (with the latter two highlighting issues raised by the critics of the year-round hockey academy model). Cost, though, has been identified as one of the factors precluding new Canadians from taking up hockey. Indeed, an important issue for hockey organizers has been making the sport relevant in the face of Canada's increasing ethnocultural diversity.[96] As noted earlier, hockey's history is considerably more diverse than many accounts suggest. Much work remains to be done to uncover stories of hockey that are more representative of those who are (and were) playing the game and to create a sport where opportunities to play hockey at a variety of levels are equally accessible to all.

Home Game: Rethinking Canada Through Indigenous Hockey

By Sam McKegney, Queen's University, Ontario, and Michael Auksi, University of Toronto

THE CONVERSATION

This article is republished from The Conversation under a Creative Commons license on May 22, 2019. The original article can be found here: https://theconversation.com/home-game-rethinking-canada-through-indigenous-hockey-115084

"Damn, we got it. We won one in their barn!"

To Cree hockey player Eugene Arcand (see figure 9.6), these words made little sense. You see, in the 11 years he had skated for two Saskatchewan Indian residential schools—as sweater number 14, residential school number 781—no settler teams had ever visited the dilapidated outdoor rinks at St. Michael's residential school in Duck Lake or the Qu'Appelle school in Lebret.[97] It wasn't until he was 23,

Figure 9.6   Eugene Arcand.

when Arcand became the only Indigenous player in the region's Intermediate AAA hockey league, that he learned from settler teammates that "home ice" is supposed to be "an advantage."

We—Mike Auksi (Anishinaabe/Estonian) and Sam McKegney (white settler of Irish/German descent)—are researchers with the Indigenous Hockey Research Network (IHRN).[98] We interviewed Arcand in Kingston, Ont., as part of our network's preliminary work to cultivate critical understandings of hockey's role in relations between Indigenous and non-Indigenous peoples in Canada.

Arcand, whose Cree/*nēhiẏaweēwin* name is aski kananumohwatah and whose treaty number is 380, knows what it's like to be denied the right to play in a "home barn" in his traditional territory Treaty 6.[99] He was a member of the Indian Residential Schools (IRC) Truth and Reconciliation survivor committee and has been honoured for his work in support of Indigenous sport in Saskatchewan and across the country.[100] As such, he understands hockey as a site of prejudice, but also as a site rife with potential for positive change.

"We Didn't Ever Get to Socialize"

Regimentation, discipline and control were at the core of residential school design, as a means of conditioning Indigenous children to shed their cultural values. Physical education was well suited to this enterprise, say Indigenous studies scholar Braden Te Hiwi of the University of British Columbia and sport historian and sociologist Janice Forsyth of Western University, also an IHRN researcher.[101] Exactly how sport curricula was used varied over time and territory, as well as along gender lines, during more than 100 years of residential schooling in Canada. Where they were present, sports like hockey were built into the institution's social engineering regime as what University of Ottawa health researcher Michael Robidoux calls a "disciplining device."[102]

Yet, the experiences of Indigenous players were not confined by institutional objectives or the goals of individual overseers. Forsyth and historian Evan Habkirk, also of Western University, argue that sports helped many students "make it through residential school" by being a forum in which they could develop "a sense of identity, accomplishment and pride," even in the context of trauma and abuse.[103] As Cree residential school survivor Philip Michel explained in a talk he gave at Opaskwayak Cree Nation:

> *"We were told we were no good in residential school. But in hockey, we were good. We were just as good as anybody. In many cases, we were better."*

Arcand recalled his teammates showcasing their skill against settler teams at tournaments. However, their experiences differed dramatically from those of the non-Indigenous kids:

> *"We'd put all our equipment on at the school and get on the bus and we'd go to whatever town . . . and we'd play sometimes three games in one day. After each game, we'd get back on the bus. . . . . We didn't ever get to socialize against our opponents."*

Years later, Arcand asked a former supervisor from the residential school, "Why would you make us wear our equipment all day like that? Other kids got to undress. Other kids got to run around the rink. And we didn't. We had to wear our same stinky equipment all day long." The supervisor replied, "So you wouldn't run away."

Project to Assimilate

In an 1887 memorandum to cabinet, John A. Macdonald, prime minister and minister of Indian Affairs, identified the "great aim" of the Indian Act legislation as being to assimilate the Indian people in all respects with the other inhabitants of the Dominion."[104] Contradictions, however, persisted at the heart of this legislation. When residential schools were at their peak, policies like The Pass System on the Prairies actively prevented Indigenous people from integrating into settler society.[105] While residential schooling was ostensibly about absorption, contemporary policies enacted barriers to inclusion by restricting mobility. In Arcand's team's segregation from the settler teams, we see a similar contradiction at play. Residential schools were intended to condition Indigenous youth to self-identify not as Indigenous but as Canadian—with hockey functioning as a marker of such identification. Yet the Indigenous players at the tournament were treated as second-class citizens, forbidden from fraternizing with the other players. The government's political goal

(continued)

Home Game: Rethinking Canada Through Indigenous Hockey *(continued)*

of eliminating Indigenous rights and identities was never accompanied by a similar commitment toward eliminating settler perceptions of Indigenous inferiority. Assimilation, in Canada, has never meant equality.

Calls to Action in Sport

Another factor complicating Indigenous experiences of hockey is the way the sport is romanticized in this country.[106] The IHRN's early research suggests that hockey is linked to the naturalization of settler entitlement.[107] Hockey belongs to Canadians because it belongs in the Canadian landscape, so the story goes. Thus, participation in the game allows settlers to imagine they belong here too—with adverse implications for Indigenous people. Arcand remembers the ferocious nature of anti-Indigenous racism in Saskatchewan hockey in the 1970s. So much so, he shares, that when his team's trainers packed up the sticks after a road game, they'd leave his out for safety.

"I had to use my stick to defend myself in those arenas."

Anti-Indigenous racism persists in Canadian hockey today. In the past year, the First Nation Elites Bantam AAA team faced taunts of "savages" from spectators, players and coaches at the Coupe Challenge tournament in Québec.[108] Five First Nations teams from Manitoba found themselves without a league to play in when the non-Indigenous teams against which they used to play formed a new league from which they were excluded.[109] Yet teams, coaches, players and fans are not without the artillery to make positive change. The Final Report of the TRC provides guidance via Calls to Action 87 to 90 on Sport and Reconciliation.[110] The report calls for government-sponsored athlete development, culturally relevant programming for coaches, trainers and officials, as well as anti-racism awareness training.

Arcand has worked much of his life to eliminate barriers to participation in sport for Indigenous, racialized and economically challenged athletes. To truly foster inclusion, he says, hockey associations need to confront racism and settler entitlement through disciplinary actions with sufficient teeth to create conditions of safety.

"Why are the people in power," he asks, "not stepping up to properly enforce excluding these people who deserve to be excluded from the sport?"

"We Still Need the Game"

Between 1975 and 1981, long before Colin Kaepernick's[111] and other football players' celebrated acts of protest, Arcand refused to stand for the Canadian national anthem. When told to do so during a playoff game, he responded, "Coach, you want me to stand up? I'm going to get up and you'll never see me again. Your choice. Make it right now." The coach never bothered him again. Years later, when the horrors of residential school were coming to light through the TRC, one of Arcand's settler teammates from those days embraced him at the International Ice Hockey Federation World U20 Hockey Tournament in Saskatchewan. He told Arcand, "Now we understand."

Arcand, a target of brutal assimilation policies and racist violence, says:

"Sports saved my life, hockey saved my life."

Provided Canadians reckon with hockey's relationship to settler colonialism and racism, Arcand insists, "We still need the game."

The persistent whiteness of mainstream Canadian hockey was on display in two incidents that captured national media attention in late 2019. First, long-time television commentator Don Cherry was fired for insensitive remarks about immigrants to Canada. Cherry, whose feature, "Coach's Corner," was a mainstay on *Hockey Night in Canada* telecasts for three decades, was known for remarks that perpetuated hypermasculine, nationalist, and xenophobic attitudes through hockey. Only weeks later, two NHL coaches came under fire for the emotionally abusive tactics they used to "motivate" their players. One was accused by a former player, Akim Aliu, of incorporating racist epithets into his taunts.

Beyond its content, such behaviours have become increasingly associated with unhealthy cultures of hazing within hockey. Hazing practices often involve emotional, physical, and sometimes sexual abuse and, according to journalist Laura Robinson, pervade a number of levels of elite hockey in Canada.[112] Such practices have been perpetuated because of the code of silence often associated with locker-room culture. At its worst, such silences have masked violence against young people. Two high-profile incidents—with the coach of the Swift Current Broncos junior team and among staff members at Maple Leaf Gardens—highlighted how the lure of access to hockey and the power to control this access can be used to harm.[113] The courage of survivors such as Sheldon Kennedy and Theo Fleury to tell their stories, however, is a reminder that it is possible to talk about reforming the sport without sacrificing the pleasure that many have taken in playing the game.[114]

Conclusion

Hockey's place in Canadian culture remains unquestioned and seemingly unimpeachable. Despite this, a growing awareness of social issues continues to shake the sport's foundations. As the third decade of the 21st century began, debates over the emotional, mental, and physical treatment of the players were part of the narrative surrounding the dismissal of the coaches of both Calgary's and Toronto's NHL teams, while women players across the country continued to advocate for playing opportunities that were accompanied by a living wage. Understanding the historical origins of hockey is one way to understand the significance of such issues.

The modern sport of hockey drew upon a variety of ball-and-stick pastimes on ice, many of them connected to Indigenous cultural practices. At a time when modern sports were emerging, hockey's popularity was tied first to narratives linking climate with national identity that sought to establish a uniquely Canadian sport; and second, the game was popular among the anglophone, white, middle-class men who saw sport as a way to embody the values of the amateur ethos. Hockey became a place to practise a respectable form of masculinity, where physicality (even violence) was contained by the rink. As amateur hockey lost ground to the men's professional game, such values were reified by a sport media whose financial fortunes were tied to celebrating the Canadian-ness and manliness of hockey.

Throughout this 150-year history, women as well as the men originally excluded by the rules of amateurism have struggled for both opportunities and recognition within hockey. The induction into the Hockey Hall of Fame of the NHL's first Black player, Willie O'Ree (in 2018), and perhaps women's hockey's most dominant star, Hayley Wickenheiser (in 2019), suggests that hockey's culture is slowly becoming more inclusive. But the implications of the historical origins of hockey will be more fully recognized when players such as Rivulettes star Hilda Ranscombe and Herb Carnegie of the Quebec Aces are similarly enshrined.

DISCUSSION QUESTIONS:

1. How did modern pastimes influence the earliest codified forms of modern hockey?
2. What factors account for the demise of the amateur ideology in hockey and the rise of the professional game in the early decades of the 20th century?
3. What role did commercialism and the growth of the media play in the popularization of particular forms of hockey in the interwar years?
4. Who have been the prominent players and teams in women's hockey? How do you account for the gap in the prominence of women's hockey between the 1930s and 1980s?
5. How does the history of hockey in Canada help you understand contemporary issues in the sport?

SUGGESTED READINGS

Ellison, Jenny and Jennifer Anderson, eds. *Hockey: Challenging Canada's Game/ Au-dela du sport national.* Ottawa: University of Ottawa Press/Canadian Museum of History, 2018.

Holman, Andrew, ed. *Canada's Game: Hockey and Identity.* Montreal and Quebec: McGill-Queen's University Press, 2009.

Blake, Jason and Andrew Holman, eds. *The Same But Different: Hockey in Quebec.* Montreal and Quebec: McGill-Queen's University Press, 2017.

Whitson, David and Richard S. Gruneau, eds. *Artificial Ice: Hockey, Culture, and Commerce.* Toronto: Garamond Press, 2006.

Wong, John Chi-Kit, ed. *Coast to Coast: Hockey in Canada to the Second World War.* Toronto: University of Toronto Press, 2009.

CHAPTER 10

REREADING HISTORIES OF INCLUSIVE RECREATION, PHYSICAL EDUCATION, AND SPORT

Danielle Peers, PhD
University of Alberta

Lisa Tink, MA
University of Alberta

LEARNING OBJECTIVES

In this chapter you will

- learn about the difference between dominant progressive histories and genealogy;
- re-examine recreation's historical values and explore how eugenic notions of white supremacy still exist in contemporary discourses and practices;
- question how inclusion in physical activity contexts can be used to exclude and marginalize people; and
- re-examine purely celebratory accounts of the Paralympic Movement and Paralympism's usefulness for supporting a more inclusive sport system.

Canada prides itself on being "a leading sport nation":[1] not because we win the most medals, but because—as the Government of Canada website tells us—we have a demonstrated history of sporting innovation and have developed a "sport system [that] allows Canadians from all segments of society to get involved in sport activities at all levels and in all forms of participation."[2]

It is not only Canadian sport that claims national excellence by virtue of its inclusivity and by drawing on its history of important sporting innovators. "A Framework for Recreation in Canada 2015: Pathways to Wellbeing" builds Canada's future recreation vision on the following historical narrative:

> Through much of the 20th century, public recreation was regarded as a "public good." The emphasis was on accessibility for all, outreach to disadvantaged groups and a belief in the universal benefits to the whole community, not just to users. . . . Leaders in recreation have continued to stress the need for equitable recreational experiences for all, with a call for the renewed importance of public recreation's historic mandate of addressing the inclusion of vulnerable populations.[3]

Claiming the early 20th century as a golden age for inclusion, this framework argues that we must look to our past to inspire more inclusive recreation futures. Sometimes this leveraging of heroic histories (and historical innovators) to promote particular ideas of future inclusion is more implicit. For example, Physical and Health Education (PHE) Canada's website hosts a page for the McKenzie award. The webpage reads:

> This award is PHE Canada's most prestigious award and is named after the distinguished Canadian physician, sculptor and physical educator, Dr. R. Tait McKenzie. The award epitomizes Dr. Tait McKenzie's professional ideals, his service to humanity, and his dedication to the advancement of knowledge and understanding of physical and health education, recreation and dance.[4]

The award page hangs under an extra-large web banner featuring a close-up of a young girl bearing the facial markers of Down syndrome. The word *inspire* sits in the left corner of the image, presumably pointing to Dr. McKenzie's famed leadership in including people with disabilities within physical education.

In these three examples, national organizations use claims about Canada's innovative and inclusive histories, often highlighting heroic Canadian innovators, to frame Canada's contemporary identities and practices and to spark and justify future actions and directions. This chapter complicates and critiques such framings of Canada's inclusive past, present, and future by returning to the very historical periods these texts most celebrate. To this end, we offer three case studies. The first centres on the early 20th-century playground movement, which is often acknowledged as a precursor to our modern inclusive recreation systems. Our second case study centres on inclusive physical education in the early to mid-20th century, around the time of Dr. McKenzie. Our third case study focuses on the mid-20th-century emergence of Paralympic sport: arguably, the most widely celebrated model of inclusive sport in Canada. We begin this chapter, however, with a brief discussion of Foucauldian genealogy: a method for doing historical research that de-centres the importance of individual actors and uses historical research to ask important questions of the present and to reimagine our futures otherwise.

Foucauldian Genealogy

Canadian histories are central to our ideas of what it means to be Canadian. Canadian values, institutions, and practices not only reinforce nationality as a project of the present but also are built upon particular memories of the past. These memories represent the dominant political histories, where "what happened" is presented to us as an objective actuality understood from the vantage point of the present.[5] When presented this way, these dominant histories confirm our belief that the present is an intentional product of progress and necessity. The past acts of "important people" (most of whom are white colonial settlers) are not only chronologically ordered and captured in text but also categorized as heroic, courageous, progressive, and causal. The end result is a linear narrative that credits particular men and women with the creation of a safe, inclusive nation built upon the founding principles of tolerance, multiculturalism, and social supports.

The Canadian histories that are produced within the dominant political terrain are, however, not value-free assessments of the past. Much of what we know about Canadian history has been mitigated by the revisionist gaze of those who experience enough privilege to be able to tell our national stories. These individuals, most of whom have been educated in the white Western world, often ignore (both intentionally and unintentionally) the acts of marginalized populations. In doing so, they not only maintain the integrity of our national narrative but also establish "a historical right to a specific territory and a territorial right to a particular history."[6] It is here, when the ignored, concealed, or forgotten pasts are excluded from our national memory, that counter-histories become imperative.

Unlike dominant histories, which use hegemonic discourses to represent "the voice of the nation," counter-histories articulate the perspectives of those who are systemically silenced and marginalized (e.g., Indigenous peoples, disabled people, women).[7] Paying attention to violent injustices experienced by these marginalized communities and to their important acts of resistance and resilience, counter-histories not only present alternative memories but also contest our dominant histories by denying their empirical and moral authority. For example, in chapter 4—Case Studies of Indigenous Sport—Janice Forsyth centres Indigenous historical perspectives on residential schools, the Tom Longboat Awards, and the North American Indigenous Games to challenge hegemonic ideologies about Western sport empowering Indigenous people. Thus, counter-histories and dominant histories exist in relation to one another. As the "official" constructions of the past are analyzed and contested by counter-histories, the dominant histories are potentially redefined. This forces us to question our dominant histories and demonstrates how the telling of history is an ongoing process in which different interpretations of the past engage with and struggle against one another.[8]

Understood this way, Canadian history can no longer be presented as a series of facts that have been objectively gathered and strung together. Instead, the telling of history becomes a complex interpretive process where questions about our past are asked and answered in an attempt to advance or refute a claim, to levy praise or assign blame, or to justify or condemn a state of affairs.[9] But what if, instead of asking questions about our past, we use this same historical curiosity to ask questions about our present? What if, instead of celebrating the important acts of certain historical figures, we analyze the everyday relations of power (e.g., policies, practices, institutional structures) and illustrate how the logics and actions of the past continue to animate the present? A wonderful example of this approach is Christine M. O'Bonsawin's contribution to this textbook (chapter 13), in which she analyzes complex webs of national and global colonial power in order to recontextualize not only Canada's colonial sport pasts but also the ways these continue to animate the present. Our chapter seeks to make a similar intervention: to analyze past relations of power in order to more critically question and change our present. Our historical curiosity of the present has taken the methodological form of Foucauldian genealogy.[10]

Put simply, Foucauldian genealogy is an investigation of the present through a detailed examination of the past.[11] Genealogical investigations begin by identifying a current problem—often a naturalized or seemingly benevolent story that activists are trying to challenge—and working backwards to highlight the conditions that have led to this problem's being understood in a particular way.[12] Therefore, like historians, genealogists uncover and analyze fragments of the past. What separates genealogists from some traditional historians, however, is their belief that there are no objective final truths about history, but rather nearly infinite, complex, and messy happenings that are selectively left in or out and then woven together to fit some kind of historical narrative, often a progress narrative.[13] Instead of believing our present is the unavoidable culmination of past heroes, villains, and important events, the genealogist suggests our present is the effect of an entangled web of everyday relations of power (e.g., policies, practices, institutional structures). These everyday relations of power are, however, not self-evident, natural, or normal. Instead, they are the effect of particular ways of thinking and acting at precise moments in history.[14] The genealogist's job is to analyze this entangled web of everyday relations of power and demonstrate how our historical ways of thinking and acting (particularly those violent ways we believe we have left behind us) continue to actively exist in and shape our present, often under guise of a more benevolent or even natural order of things. As will be demonstrated in the three case studies in this chapter, it is through this type of historical analysis that we can ask new questions of the present in order to create the possibility of imagining and enacting less violent and dominating futures.

Canada's Playground Movement

We begin the genealogical retelling of our national stories with the case of Canada's playground movement. The playground movement, so the dominant story goes, began in 1901 at the eighth annual meeting of the National Council of Women of Canada (NCWC) when Mabel Peters brought forward the following resolution:

> Whereas the agitation for vacation schools and playgrounds where children may find organized recreation having become so widespread that it is now known as the playground movement, and whereas the establishment of such vacation schools and playgrounds is acknowledged by educators and philanthropists to be desired in every community, and whereas the necessity for such schools and playgrounds to improve the condition of children in the cities of Canada is obvious, therefore be it resolved that this National Council of Women of Canada declare themselves in favour of the establishment of vacation schools and playgrounds and pledge themselves to do all in their power to promote their organization.[15]

The resolution was ostensibly drafted out of concern for children living in working-class and poor neighbourhoods. Suggesting the incidents of crime, disease, and drunkenness were higher for these children than their middle-class counterparts, playgrounds were viewed as a way to prevent and heal physical, social, and moral "disorders" and ensure the healthy development of Canadian children.[16] The members of the NCWC, committed to improving the condition of children in the cities of Canada, carried the resolution. The following year they named Peters the convener of a standing committee on playgrounds.[17] For the next 11 years, she became a zealous campaigner for supervised playgrounds at the local, national, and international levels.[18] Her annual reports to the NCWC describe in detail the ways she campaigned for supervised playgrounds, educated the public as to their value, and visited members of the American Playground Association in Chicago, Washington, and New York.[19] And while she became ill and died before realizing her dream of a National Canadian Playground Association, her activities between 1901 and 1914 are said to have influenced the work of local women's councils in over 15 cities.[20]

In addition to being described as "the Mother of the Canadian Playground Movement,"[21] Peters has been positioned as a "pioneer in the provision and promotion of recreation services."[22] By advocating for playing spaces in close proximity to every residence, she, along with other supporters of the playground movement, are credited with taking the first steps towards the extensive public recreation systems enjoyed today (see figure 10.1).[23] In a paper commissioned for Canada's 2011 National Recreation Summit, Tim Burton writes, "It was the efforts of the Playground Movement that evolved most naturally into municipal recreation and parks departments."[24] Thus, as evidenced by "A Framework for Recreation in Canada 2015," the importance of children's play remains a central component of contemporary recreation services:

City of Toronto Archives, Fonds 200, Series 372, Subseries 52, Item 51

Figure 10.1   The Elizabeth Street playground in Toronto in 1913.

While unstructured play is important for all ages, the evidence suggests it is particularly critical for children in today's society. Over the last few decades, children's lives have become increasingly structured and media oriented, reducing their time in active unstructured play. This shift has contributed to increasing levels of physical inactivity, sedentary behaviour and excess weight in children and youth. There is a particular concern for the missed opportunity of outdoor play, which has been shown to increase a child's capacity for creativity, problem-solving, and emotional and intellectual development.[25]

Rereading the History

As demonstrated by the historical narrative, it is easy for our contemporary recreation systems to be traced back to the progressive and courageous acts of Peters. By stringing together the archival fragments left by her, and about her, it is (too) simple to proclaim that "her legacy of playgrounds for children lives on in every Canadian city."[26] But what if, instead of focusing on the *acts* of Mabel Peters, we used the tools afforded by Foucauldian genealogy to examine the *ideas* she supported through the *arguments* she and her contemporaries were making? If we did this, it would become apparent that Mabel Peters, like other women in the early 20th century, embraced her civic duties in political and social life by supporting a number of seemingly unrelated reforms commingling under the progressive ideology of women's suffrage.

As Carol Bacchi writes, "The ideology of late-nineteenth and early twentieth-century reform in Canada, as expressed in the suffrage movement, was complex."[27] Canadian suffragists were not a homogenous group, nor did they focus only on the political rights of women. Suffragist campaigns also called for a number of reforms (ranging from moderate interventions to complete state welfare) in the areas of social security, education, and public health.[28] Despite the diversity of this suffragist network, however, there was a unifying theme across each of these reforms—a concern for the protection and advancement of "the Canadian race."[29] A common argument made by Canadian suffragists was that white women, because of their moral authority as caretakers and mothers, had both a responsibility and a natural desire to protect Canada's youngest nationals. In order for women to do this, however, they needed to be able to act as full citizens. Thus, the advancement of the nation was dependent on the advancement of white women.[30] As articulated by Katja Thieme, "Moral authority allowed suffragists a claim to politics—it was out of moral concern that they were interested in participating in politics, and it was through moral authority that they were qualified to do so."[31]

Given this connection between women's moral authority and suffrage, most suffragists saw themselves as reformers first and suffragists second.[32] It is therefore not surprising that in addition to being remembered as "the Mother of the Canadian Playground Movement,"[33] Peters is also remembered for her work "promoting women's suffrage."[34] Like many middle-class Anglo-Saxon women during the early 20th century, she appears to have believed the future of the Canadian race and women's participation in politics were inseparable.

Like the suffrage movement, the playground movement can therefore be understood as a logical extension of maternal responsibility. Converging around the notion of early childhood intervention, supporters of both movements argued that the future of the Canadian race depended on the proper development of Canada's youngest nationals. Peters clearly articulates this belief when she says, "All methods of reform that do not begin with childhood, strike only at the leaves and branches of evil, and fail to touch the root. Train the child correctly and the adult will not need reform."[35] Thus, her campaigns were largely based on the notion that when children (particularly those children who lived in overcrowded squalor) were provided with opportunities for "rational activity and healthy play,"[36] they could overcome "the evils of enforced idleness" (e.g., poor health, crime, drunkenness).[37]

Read within the confines of traditional history, Peter's desires to ensure the healthy development of children are seemingly benevolent. When read alongside the ideas of eugenics (a second movement fervently supported by Canadian suffragists), however, the morality of the playground movement becomes more complex.

Eugenics in Canada

The term *eugenics* describes both an area of study and a movement. As an area of study, eugenics combined racist research from numerous academic domains (e.g., biology, early genetics, demography, and anthropology) to study how particular human traits were inherited and how they could be increased or decreased within a population[38], thereby enabling "the self-direction of human evolution." As a movement, eugenics describes the policies and programs (e.g., immigration controls, population segregation, targeted sterilization, procreation incentives, and genocide) that aimed to diminish or eradicate the propagation of inheritable characteristics perceived to be detrimental to the improvement of the nation or race, while supporting and incentivizing the propagation of traits

TRANSFORMATIVE MOMENTS: RISE OF EUGENICS

Eugenics was a white supremacist, ableist social movement and research area, popularized in North America and Europe, that sought to improve the evolution of particular populations by supporting the propagation of purportedly superior European hereditary traits over all others. The dominant metaphor of the eugenics movement was horticulture, and in particular, the tree. In addition to the tree's being widely used as the logo for eugenics,[41] eugenicists used metaphors of trees and plants ubiquitously, speaking of family trees, genetic or hereditary roots, "degenerate offshoots," and the need for not only proper training but also frequent "pruning."[42] *Pruning* for eugenicists meant the removal of people deemed to have undesirable or backwards traits from the reproductive pool. This was achieved through lifelong institutionalization in sex-segregated facilities, immigration bans on non-Europeans, marriage bans, forced sterilization, and genocidal mass murders. Although involuntary sterilizations were made illegal in Canada in 1986, there is evidence that systemic, coerced, and covert sterilizations of Indigenous and disabled women in Canada have been performed as recently as 2017.[43] These active eugenic practices exist alongside more ubiquitous passive "newgenic" technologies like genetic screening, the removal of children from disabled parents, and laws that ban those with disabilities from immigrating to Canada.[44]

perceived to be more evolved.[39] Situated within theories of biological racism,[40] eugenic research and the larger movement are both built upon the idea that white, nondisabled, heterosexual, middle- to upper-class Western European men are the most evolved and thus physically, intellectually, and morally superior to other humans. This notion of white supremacy meant that eugenic interventions were designed to support the life and reproductive opportunities of white nationals while curtailing the life and reproductive opportunities of those we now think of as people of colour, people living in poverty, and people with disabilities, as well as Indigenous, queer, and trans people.

During the late 19th and early 20th centuries, many Canadian suffragists began to position women's enfranchisement in relation to the idea of eugenics.[45] The basic argument underpinning this position was that "the uplift of the race could not happen without the uplift of women."[46] Eugenic discourses of race betterment therefore converged significantly with feminist discourses of suffrage. This cross-pollination saw a number of feminists advocating for particular kinds of social engineering in order to ensure the production of "better" children. Nellie McClung's book *In Times Like These* is an example of how the discourses of these two movements converged:

> It does not seem to the thoughtful observer that we need more children nearly so much as we need better children. . . . it is a doubtful favour to the child to bring it into life under any circumstances, but to bring children into the world, suffering from the handicaps caused by ignorance, poverty, or criminality of the parents, is an appalling crime against the innocent and hopeless, and yet one about which practically nothing is said. Marriage, homemaking, and the rearing of children are left entirely to chance, and so it is no wonder that humanity produces so many specimens who, if they were silk stockings or boots, would be marked "seconds."[47]

This quote makes clear that children with disabilities, poor children, and children born to criminals were liabilities inhibiting the progress of the (white) Canadian race. Describing them as specimens who could be marked as seconds, McClung uses eugenics to belittle particular members of the population and to uphold others. This not only reflects her commitment to a nationwide crusade to purge Canadian society of its immoralities[48] but also highlights her demand for greater social supports for white women around marriage, childbirth, and child-rearing in order to reduce the number of "undesirables" born in Canada:[49] a demand that maps perfectly upon the rationalities of the playground movement.

The feminism of McClung, like that of many other suffragists, is often positioned as a response to domestic insecurities. Quick to capitalize on the moral panic associated with the "ills" of industrialization (e.g., immigration, health, poverty, and drunkenness), these eugenic feminists mobilized the belief that the quality of life of Canadian nationals (i.e., middle-class Anglo-Saxons) was dependent on the eradication of internal weaknesses (e.g., crime, poverty, drunkenness, disease, disability) and external threats (e.g., immigrants and Indigenous people). The result was a series of campaigns aimed at creating a whole host of social, mental, and racial hygiene programs and policies (e.g., welfare programs, immigration controls, institutionalization, procreation incentives, targeted sterilization) that attempted to secure the race and the nation from degeneration.[50]

Eugenics in the Playground Movement

Returning now to the playground movement, it is difficult to ignore its eugenic undertone. Like Nellie McClung, Mabel Peters was committed to purging Canadian society of its immoralities (e.g., crime, drunkenness, idleness). Positioning play as a way to normalize Canadian children, her campaigns emphasized the usefulness of playgrounds for social engineering. Touted as laboratories where the weaknesses and deficiencies of the current generation could be repaired and the makeup of future generations improved (under the watchful eye of white women), supporters of the playground movement campaigned with the promise of improvements in physical fitness, social behaviours, and morality.[51] Thus, play was positioned not only as an activity central to childhood development but also as a reform required to cure society of degeneracy.

In this context the playground movement, which previously seemed so benevolent, now bears an uncomfortable resemblance to deeply racist, colonialist, and ableist ideas of eugenics. Peters' suggestion that "all methods of reform that do not begin with childhood, strike only at the leaves and branches of evil, and fail to touch the root"[52] now seems strikingly similar to the eugenic tree metaphors and those presented by Luther Burbank (famed horticulturist and eugenicist) in his book *The Training of the Human Plant*:

> Now, to the extent that we leave children of the poor and these unfortunates, waifs and foundlings, to themselves and their evil surroundings, to that extent we breed peril for ourselves. . . . Begin training these outcasts, begin the cultivation of them, if you will, much as we cultivate plants, in order that their lives may be turned into right ways, in order that the integrity of the state may be maintained. Rightly cultivated, these children may be made a blessing to the race; trained in the wrong way, or neglected entirely, they will become a curse to the state.[53]

WORKING WITH PRIMARY SOURCES: REPORT UPON THE CARE OF THE FEEBLE-MINDED IN ONTARIO

All the signs of the times point to the fact that we have amongst us to-day an increasing number of individuals who are not up to the average standard of moral, mental, and physical vigour. Individuals who are not only utterly incapable of furthering human progress but are even incapable of subsisting by their own efforts; who must be helped by the Poor Law, by old age pensions, by State insurance or by private philanthropy. The presence of this class is beginning to be seriously felt. . . . I belive [sic] the real cause of the presence of this parasitic class is not external, but internal, that is due to a germinal impairment, and that no little of it springs from the manner in which the the [sic] hereditarily tainted, the feeble-minded, the insane, the epileptic, the habitual criminals and paupers, and other degenerate creatures are allowed to propagate without let or hinderance. The vigour of the nation is being gradually undermined, its character in the aggregate is falling to a lower plane, and its strength is being sapped at its very root by admixture with these degenerate stocks. If national progress is to take place we must go even further and do more to encourage the breeding of our best.[54]

This excerpt is from Dr. Helen MacMurchy's 1911 "Report Upon the Care of the Feeble-Minded in Ontario," commissioned by the Legislative Assembly of Ontario. In her annual 60-plus-page reports, MacMurchy often cites eugenic best practices from across North America and Europe, arguing for more intensive eugenic programs in Canada. Here, she quotes prominent eugenicist Dr. A.F. Tredgold at length. Note the tree and horticulture metaphors, as well as the palpable disdain for those the province purports to care for.

Our point in making this connection is not to argue that Peters was a eugenicist. Rather, the purpose of connecting the playground movement to eugenics is to demonstrate that if we de-centre the importance of individuals like Peters and instead trace the ideas and practices of specific historical moments, we can highlight particular aspects of our pasts that have been obscured by our dominant history. In the case of the playground movement, these pieces are the deeply racist, colonialist, and ableist logics of eugenics.

Turning Towards the Present

Having disrupted our dominant history of the playground movement in Canada, we now turn our historical curiosity and ask ourselves whether these racist, colonialist, and ableist ways of thinking and acting continue to shape our present. In other words, does white supremacy continue to inform the discourses and practices of contemporary recreation? One hint to a possible answer to this question comes from "A Framework for Recreation in Canada 2015," which explicitly states that there is "an urgent need for recreation to reaffirm historic values."[55] This statement, when read through a genealogical lens, highlights the importance of asking, which historic values?

Early advocates of recreation programming did not simply hold eugenic views; rather, eugenics was one of the driving forces behind imagining and implementing Canadian playgrounds. Therefore, to write off ideas of eugenics as simply ignorant beliefs of their time that should not detract from the celebration of recreation's other ideas and ideals is dangerous for a number of reasons. First, it ignores the degree to which the efforts that "evolved most naturally into municipal recreation and parks departments"[56] were deeply entwined with, and won through, dangerous racist, colonialist, and ableist ways of thinking and acting that had significant effects on the life chances of marginalized people. Second, claiming eugenics as the thinking of the time refuses to acknowledge that they chose eugenics when many of their contemporary activists and scholars were fighting against it on both scientific and moral grounds.[57] Third, by ignoring the role eugenics played in the development of Canada's municipal recreation system, we are refusing to acknowledge how these historical ways of thinking and acting continue to weave—in only slightly altered forms—throughout our contemporary recreation discourses and practices. Take, for example, a statement from "A Framework for Recreation in Canada 2015": "Recreation has the potential to address socio-demographic challenges and troubling issues."[58] What, or perhaps more dangerously, who, is being referred to as socio-demographic challenges, and what troubling issues are they constructed as producing?

To answer this question, we begin by noting that demography (the statistical study of populations) was one of the foundational sciences used by eugenic thinkers.[59] Indeed, Munich's Demographic Study Unit at the German Research Institute for Psychiatry was one of the world's foremost eugenics research hubs during the first half of the 20th century.[60] In the Canadian context, Claudia Malacrida demonstrates that throughout the 20th century, "demographic findings were combined with other scientific developments in biology and genetics in ways that attributed the problems of poverty, ill health and poor education to hereditary rather than social causes."[61] As Edmund Ramsden argues, this is true of social demography in particular.[62] Eugenicists have always constructed demographic shifts away from populations made up mostly of white European ancestry as a major challenge and threat. Indeed, the expected demographic changes, to which "A Framework for Recreation in Canada 2015" refers, include aging (mostly white) baby boomers; birth rates remaining highest in Indigenous and newcomer families; and increased immigration largely from non-European countries such as the Philippines, India, Syria, China, and Pakistan.[63] These shifts in demographics are, notably, not articulated as opportunities, or cause for multicultural celebration, but as "socio-demographic challenges" that are likely to cause "troubling issues."[64] These kinds of neo-eugenic sentiments bring us not to the question of how to reaffirm recreation's historic values, but rather of how to reimagine inclusive recreation outside of the ableist, colonial, white supremacist, and eugenic values from and through which it emerged.

Inclusive Physical Education

Our second case study concerns Canada's inclusive physical education movement. Like the playground movement, dominant histories of Canada's inclusive, and in particular disability-inclusive, physical education movement trace roots back to the ideas and actions of a heroic Canadian: doctor and physical educator Dr. R. Tait McKenzie.[65] Such histories paint McKenzie as a tireless advocate, not only for the inclusion of physical education in all of Canada's schools but also for the inclusion of "the physical activity needs of every individual regardless of ability."[66] Ted Wall, for example, traces the progress of physical education from military-style drills within the bourgeoning Canadian public school systems to more "health education, physical training and corrective exercises."[67] The history then takes us through how important acts of various others led to the increasing professionalization of physical education, including the establishment of national governing bodies, postsecondary training programs, and eventually, national fitness policies ensuring that every child in Canada would have access to the joys and health benefits of physical education as part of their grade school education.

Universal Public Education

Inclusive physical education occurred within the context of Canada's universal public education movement. Education is under provincial jurisdiction, and at different points between Confederation and the end of the Second World War, provinces began funding universal public education systems and making at least some years of primary education mandatory for all residents. Ontario and British Columbia passed Canada's first mandatory schooling acts in 1871 and

1873, respectively. Most provinces followed suit in the first decade of the 20th century, with the final provinces coming on board in the early 1940s.[68]

Although universal access to education is generally something that would be understood as positive, two critiques help contextualize this legislation and the dangers of inclusive physical education to follow. The first is the question of who was excluded from universal education; the second is a question of how education was used to better enable the exclusion of certain kinds of people from Canadian society more generally.

First, universal education was never really designed to be universal. Many of these early universal education laws applied only to children of certain ages, certain religions, certain familial nationalities, certain genders, or certain geographical areas.[69] Further, schools were segregated in such a way as to ensure there would never be universal access to the *same* education. Indeed, various laws ensured that certain children received their mandatory education in different buildings, with different curricula, using different pedagogical and disciplinary techniques, for different purposes, all leading to deeply different consequences for their quality of education, physical and emotional well-being, and overall life chances (including the opportunities to make a living, to live well, to give life, and even to stay alive).

A famous example of this is Canada's residential school system, a system outlined and critiqued in more detail by Janice Forsyth in chapter 4 of this textbook. Through this system, Indigenous children were forcibly separated from their families, cultures, and languages, as well as from the children of white settlers.[70] These youth, for the most part, were not just denied the same quality of education as their settler peers; they were educated in ways that undermined their connection to familial and cultural knowledges and, further, exposed to pedagogical techniques that amounted to physical, emotional, and sexual abuse. As a result of such abuses, neglect of health protocols, and a shocking indifference to human life, such mandatory schooling laws all but secured an early death for many of those whom they "educated." For example, the Chief Medical Officer of Indian Affairs, Peter Bryce, calculated that the annual death rate at such residential schools was, at the lowest, 24 percent.[71]

This was not, however, Canada's only segregated residential school system. Canadians also maintained numerous provincially run residential schools designed to house and educate or train both children and adults who were deemed "mentally defective," "feeble-minded," or "degenerates,"[72] people who would now largely be understood as having congenital disabilities (like cerebral palsy), developmental or intellectual disabilities (such as Down syndrome), mental illnesses (such as depression), medical conditions (such as epilepsy), and non-normative gender or sexual identities (such as gay and trans people), as well as those (mostly women) who were sexually promiscuous.[73] It is worth noting that the determinations of feeble-mindedness were deeply gendered and racialized, with women and Indigenous and racialized people being institutionalized far more often.

Those who were forced to live in such schools were treated more as inmates than students. They were forcibly kept in these institutions, often for the entirety of their lives, or at least until they had passed reproductive age.[74] They were separated from their families and communities, often with no visitation rights, and were offered almost no educational programming.[75] They were forced into manual labour in order to pay for running the schools.[76] Further, as Claudia Malacrida details throughout her book *A Special Hell: Institutional Life in Alberta's Eugenic Years*, they were abused, neglected, involuntarily and dangerously researched on, left to die at alarming rates, and, in some provinces, sterilized without their consent or knowledge.[77] All these things were done under the euphemism of schooling and with explicitly eugenic aims.

Even within the mainstream Canadian schools, mandatory public education played an important role in the eugenic movement and in the segregation and oppression of many. As Dr. Helen MacMurchy—prominent Canadian feminist, doctor, public health advocate, and eugenicist—proudly proclaimed, schools were an ideal "place of observation, a kind of 'Sorting House'" for Canada's youth.[78] That is, public schools centralized a community's youth, subjected them to standardized measurements and expert observation, and thus helped identify subnormal members of the community to be sent to schools for the feeble-minded. In other words, schools were a crucial part of the provincial and national war against racialized, sexualized, colonized, and pathologized populations; public schools offered an ideal tool for famed eugenicist Henry Goddard's vision: "to study them very seriously and very thoroughly . . . to hunt them out in every possible place and take care of them."[79]

Universal Physical Education

It is in this context of newly established "universal" schooling and the early 19th-century popularity of eugenics that physical education classes became mandated curriculum in schools across Canada, and North America more broadly. Although they largely began as a series of military drills used to prepare Canadian soldiers,[80] such classes increasingly incorporated discourses and techniques of social hygiene, as well as techniques for developmental assessment and observation developed by eugenicists. As Lynn Couturier argues: "The eugenics movement influenced the field of physical education and . . . physical educators participated in the mechanisms of [eugenic] expert discourse."[81] Physical education, which often incorporated sex and hygiene education, was widely understood "as a means to overcome race degeneration."[82]

Indeed, it was argued by many educators, doctors, and politicians that the physical fitness and mental fitness of the population were deeply linked to each other and to the racial fitness of the population as a whole, which had to be defended or improved at all costs.[83] *Fitness*, here, did not refer to one's cardiorespiratory or muscular capacities but rather to Francis Galton's eugenic reading of (his cousin) Charles Darwin's famous phrase "survival of the fittest."[84] It referred, briefly, to the degree to which one's body, capacities, desires, and heritage fit within the white supremacist notions of superior European evolution.[85] This notion of fitness can be read into the following impassioned plea for mandatory physical education classes in the 1914 *Nova Scotia Journal of Education*:

> Instruction in school hygiene . . . [including] the maintenance of a normal standard of efficiency in the physique, and therefore in the minds of the children [is] . . . a practical eugenics, which shall assist in the elimination of mental deficiency and preventable physical deformity.[86]

The distinction between mental deficiency and preventable physical deformity, in this quote, is crucial. In eugenic terms, *mental deficiency* referred to human characteristics that were understood as undesirable, racially degenerate, permanent or progressive hereditary traits, regardless of whether they were expressed as physical (e.g., progressive muscle weakness), sexual (e.g., perceived homosexuality or promiscuity), or mental (e.g., low IQ scores, depression).[87] In eugenic logic, physical, sexual, mental, and racial (un)fitness were inextricably linked. *Physical deformity* (sometimes termed *physical defects*), on the other hand, referred to acquired injuries or developmental delays (mostly of white boys and men of Northern European ancestry) that were the result of context rather than genetics.

R. Tait McKenzie: Hero of Inclusive Physical Education?

The distinction between mental deficiency and physical deformity is critical in the work of McKenzie. McKenzie is one of Canada's most celebrated and influential inclusive physical education advocates, a man who is widely considered the father of adapted physical activity.[88] McKenzie argued that the rise of urban living was making much of the Canadian population more sedentary, disrupting naturally developed patterns and threatening to leave "the permanent stamp of disease, deformity or neglect" on Canadian boys.[89] He believed that physical education could reverse these nonhereditary forms of disease and physical deformity. As such, he was a tireless advocate of mandatory physical education classes in schools, which would serve as prophylactic against the ills of urbanization. He was also a particular advocate for physical education programs to treat injured and deformed schoolchildren, and later injured war veterans, because of the curative powers of physical activity.

An added bonus of universal physical education, R. Tait McKenzie argued, was that the curative effects of physical activity on those with acquired impairments (i.e., physical deformities or defects) would help teachers to more easily differentiate those who could not be cured as having inherent, and thus inheritable, "mental dullness, backwardness, arrested development or feeble-mindedness."[90] Such degenerates, McKenzie insisted, were incapable of reaching a normal level of physical fitness. This made physical education classes the ideal educational "sorting house."[91] Although McKenzie is now celebrated as an early champion of inclusive physical education, he was explicit in his writings that those identified by physical education classes as racial degenerates should be housed in sex-segregated institutions, apart from the general population, for their entire reproductive lives so "that they may not have an opportunity to yield to the physical temptations to which they are so peculiarly susceptible, and so propagate their own kind."[92]

Despite physical educators like McKenzie arguing that physical education could never be curative or rehabilitative for "mental defectives," physical training was widely used in residential institutions in order to create more "self-supporting, if not self-controlling" inmates.[93] As one expert in the *Nova Scotia Medical Bulletin* boasted, through such physical training regimens, "feeble-mindedness may be converted from a liability to an asset":[94] a more easily controlled and confined incarcerated workforce.

Physical education was used in not dissimilar ways in residential institutions that targeted Indigenous youth. As Janice Forsyth describes in detail, Indian Affairs officials and residential school administrators used calisthenics, military drills, and the teaching of sports to instill discipline, respect for (white) authority, and the physical skills necessary for their working-class employment.[95] This physical education curriculum, Forsyth argues, also played two additional roles in colonization efforts. First, Euro-Canadian sports and games replaced banned traditional ceremonies, dances, and Indigenous sports, thereby further supporting assimilation of Indigenous youth. Second, sport competitions and militaristic drills were put on public display to demonstrate to settlers how successful the schools had become at controlling, Christianizing, and assimilating Indigenous communities. Forsyth argues: "This discourse revolved around notions of 'racial uplift.' Successful curricula would not only help Native students to rise above their 'race' and assume positions in the labour force, they might entice them to give up their Native status as well."[96]

Questioning Past and Present Universal Inclusion

In short, universal and inclusive physical education programs were not initially designed to be either universal or inclusive. Rather, in many cases, they were explicitly designed to support the success, well-being, and normalization of white able-bodied settler boys while furthering the segregation, assimilation, colonization, incarceration, sterilization, and systemic abuse of the nations' Others. What such genealogical analyses can teach us about inclusive physical education and physical activity in the present is to be extremely mindful of claims about both universality and inclusivity.

Such an analysis, for example, enables us to ask, who is *not* rendered imaginable as the Canadian "us" served by programs proudly touted as universal? For example, Canada prides itself on certain welfare principles, such as universal health care and education.[97] Yet Canada's own Human Rights Tribunal has ruled that "First Nations children and families living on reserve and in the Yukon are discriminated against in the provision of child and family services" by the federal government.[98] This discrimination includes funding for education and health care, which the Canadian government funds at a fraction of the rate of non-Indigenous Canadians.

Such genealogical critiques may also move us to ask, are the benefits and dangers of inclusive programs equally distributed across all the groups it purports to include? For example, consider how contemporary inclusive physical education programs have been shown to most often result in youth with disabilities sitting on the sidelines rather than participating,[99] and most LGBTQ youth being bullied, abused, and discriminated against to the point of drop out or even self-harm.[100]

Last, we might ask, when does inclusion in programs amount to a further opportunity for marginalized people to be increasingly observed, measured, and compared to standardized norms in ways that reify their difference and justify their systemic exclusion and oppression?[101] For example, adapted physical education textbooks continue to articulate that constant assessment (much of it standardized) of students with disabilities is the cornerstone of inclusive physical education.[102] One of the most widely used instruments for such assessment is the Movement Assessment Battery for Children, through which movement is assessed based on a child's degree of failure in relation to standardized age-related norms.[103] The tool claims to enable the educator or therapist to "identify delay or impairment in motor development; plan intervention programs; measure change as a result of intervention."[104] Of note, the interventions suggested often consist of the child's removal from the inclusive physical educational environment to perform repetitive, prescriptive exercises designed to normalize their bodies and capacities. In other words, inclusion in mainstream physical education classes for youth with disabilities often leads to greater surveillance, measurement, intervention, and segregation from their peers.

Paralympic Sport

Canada is one of the many countries that have signed on to the 2006 United Nations Convention on the Rights of Persons with Disabilities. In 2014, the Canadian government published its first periodic review of its compliance with the convention, in which it claims that it "strives to enhance opportunities for Canadians with disabilities to participate in and enjoy cultural life, recreation, leisure and sport."[105] This claim is backed up entirely through reference to Canada's disability sport programs, and in particular, its "Paralympic sport system,"[106] which is widely (self-)celebrated as a world leader that both models and sparks the meaningful inclusion of people with disabilities.[107]

These claims of Canadian leadership in parasport are well supported by the ubiquitous histories written about the Paralympic movement. The oft-told story is that sport for people with disabilities began in 1944 when Dr. Ludwig Guttmann of the Stoke Mandeville Hospital in England—"the father of the Paralympic movement"—purportedly invented the use of sport to rehabilitate veterans who had spinal cord injuries.[108] Guttmann soon began hosting international competitions for those with spinal cord injury at Stoke Mandeville, which eventually morphed into a roaming competition tied to the Olympic

Bettmann Archive/Getty Images

Figure 10.2 Canadian Paralympic basketball team in 1952: Tom Somerville, Syde Palmer, Vic Maggillivray, Bill Handley, and Bob Hughes, all of Montreal (from left to right).

quadrennial (see figure 10.2). Although these are virtually universally celebrated as the roots of parasport, there is also widespread celebration of the transition from these rehabilitation-minded roots to the modern Paralympic movement: one that purportedly focuses on sport rather than rehabilitation, that became closely aligned with the Olympic Games through the formation of the International Paralympic Committee, and that includes all people with disabilities, not just those with spinal cord injury.[109] Notably, Canada's Dr. Robert Steadward, the International Paralympic Committee's founding president, is often credited as the architect of this modernization.[110] Beyond his international role, Steadward is often credited for helping Canada become a country of Paralympic champions, and a country that champions sport for all people with disabilities.

Stories Our Histories Obscure

These discourses on Canadian inclusive sport supremacy, however, contradict the Government of Canada's own findings that only 1 percent of Canadians with disabilities are served by national sport programs, and only 3 percent are involved in organized sport of any kind.[111] We argue that the dominant history of the progressively inclusive Paralympic movement may represent our past in ways that make it difficult to contextualize today's broad nonparticipation and that make it harder to work for a future that engages with sport and recreation in more broadly meaningful ways.

Our first critique of this history is the centralizing of Paralympic sport, and of Ludwig Guttmann in particular, within disability sport histories (and presents). This, we argue, tends to perpetuate the centring of wheelchair users with spinal cord injury in our imaginations of disability. From the international symbol of accessibility (a wheelchair user drawn in white on a blue background), to the focus on ramps as a primary means of rendering a space accessible, the young, white, self-propelling wheelchair user with a traumatic spinal cord injury is centred in many of our discussions of disability sport and disability history more broadly. Yet less than 2.5 percent of Canadians with disabilities have spinal cord injuries,[112] and only a portion of these use self-propelled manual wheelchairs. In other words, this impairment group is drastically overrepresented in our histories, sports, images, and imaginaries.

The second problem is that privileging this history effaces other communities and histories. For example, archives show that deaf athletes had been organizing international sporting events for their own communities since 1888.[113] Schools for the blind were holding interscholastic competitions since at least 1909.[114] Injured war veterans were competing in, and at times creating and organizing, various sports in the United States, Canada, and Europe around the same time as Guttmann was said to "invent" disability sport.[115] Polio survivors were part of self-organizing national-level recreation clubs in South America by 1956.[116] Further, it would be deeply Eurocentric to assume that just because settlers never made a record of them, that there were no disability-inclusive sporting and recreation practices long before the 1940s in Indigenous communities.

Further, celebratory histories of early parasport as rehab make it difficult to think critically about the connection between parasport and eugenic histories. Spurred by writers like R. Tait McKenzie, many Western countries deepened their commitments to rehabilitation during the wars at the same time as promoting the institutionalization, sterilization, and even extermination of "degenerates" deemed incapable of rehabilitation.[117] Sweden and Canada, for example, both had some of the world's most extensive postinjury medical and welfare supports and also two of the world's longest running eugenic sterilization programs.[118] Wartime German governments not only developed the most extensive rehabilitation program in the world but also orchestrated the mass murders of 240,000 people with disabilities who were deemed unfit for rehabilitation.[119]

Although the Holocaust seems a far way off from parasport histories, it is worth noting that Guttmann was born and medically trained in Germany and was practising in England because he was Jewish and feared Nazi persecution.[120] Canada was not an innocent bystander in this history: Our government refused to take in Jewish refugees during the Second World War, even though House of Commons debates demonstrate full awareness that genocidal atrocities were taking place.[121] After the war, during the Nuremberg trials, North American and European governments refused to accept the mass eugenic murders of people with disabilities as part of the Holocaust, or to hold anyone accountable for them.[122]

Perhaps most disturbingly, although the Holocaust had decreased the popularity of the eugenic movement in the United States,[123] Canada's eugenic institutionalization and sterilization programs increased following the Second World War. These programs increased significantly during the 1950s and peaked in the 1960s; the final official eugenic sterilization programs ended only when courts forced their closure in the 1970s.[124] In other words, Canada's eugenic policies thrived long after the Nazi atrocities came to light, long after the scientific basis for such programs had been debunked in the 1930s,[125] and a long way into the national development of disability sport programs. The question is, which people with disabilities were being targeted for sport, and which were being targeted for sterilization?

Canadian Support for Disability Sport

The first archival evidence of parasport within Canada was inter-hospital sports competitions for war veterans.[126] Focusing largely on three of the four most commonly survivable injuries of the Second World War (spinal cord injury, amputation, and visual impairment), sport was framed as a valuable part of the rehabilitation program and "as part payment of a debt which the country owes the man who has been disabled in the long-drawn battle for the rights of civilization."[127] Notably, no such sporting opportunities awaited those who came home with the other most common impairment: post-traumatic conditions then called *shell shock*. Susceptibility to any form of mental distress, and the lack of capacity to quickly recover from it, was read by many Canadian doctors during both wars as evidence of "undetected feeble-mindedness" or "pre-existing mental weakness" and thus such veterans were seen as unworthy not only of sport but also of soldiers' pensions and other supports.[128]

Borrowing from Dr. R. Tait McKenzie, sport programs in Canada were created both as a means of rehabilitating white soldiers with physical defects (i.e., injuries) and as a means for proving these soldiers to be simply injured versions of the white Canadian racial stock: categorically different from racial degenerates.[129] It was argued that if the superior recovery of such soldiers through physical activity proved anything, it was that we need to support a future population that would be as strong and fit as these men were, particularly in light of how many such men had been killed in the wars.[130]

Similar eugenic arguments leveraging the racial fitness of injured and fallen soldiers were mobilized during and after the wars to support a host of programs designed to support the healthy development of Canadian children and adults, while curtailing the life and reproductive chances of others. This includes the most racially and disability-restrictive immigration and refugee policies in Canadian history—and in the Commonwealth at the time[131]—as well as a steep increase in government investments in the institutionalization and sterilization of those deemed mental or moral degenerates.[132] After the First World War, for example, such discourses were used to legitimize the creation of the Department of Health's national Division of Child Welfare, naming prominent eugenicist Dr. Helen MacMurchy as its first director in 1920.[133]

In 1943, this same department—now renamed the Department of National Health and Welfare—housed the National Council on Physical Fitness. This council was mandated to promote physical fitness in Canadians by supporting amateur sport, physical education, and importantly, "the amelioration of physical defects through physical exercise."[134] While promoting sport and physical fitness for those with physical defects, this same Department of National Health and Welfare sent thousands of Indigenous people and people with disabilities to be sterilized between the 1940s and the 1970s, even within jurisdictions where the practice was illegal.[135] In other words, disability sport was not a progressive set of policies that replaced the historical ignorance of eugenics. Disability sport shared the same time frame, the same discourses, and the very same governmental agency as eugenics.

Beyond the Physically Defective Soldier

Some soldiers who had enjoyed sport during their rehabilitation eventually returned home and decided to start local leagues in their hometowns. Supported by the new National Physical Fitness Act, these soldiers began recruiting—and even sharing government-paid wheelchairs with—Canadians who acquired similar impairments through work or through contracting polio.[136] As Ian Gregson outlines throughout his history, numerous people with disabilities and nondisabled folks started to organize local and regional leagues throughout Canada, to recruit and coach new athletes, and to invent new adapted sports.[137] For the most part, these sporting opportunities remained, for decades, the purview of injured white men from the same three original impairment groups.[138]

By the late 1960s and early 1970s, some scholars—including Canada's Frank Hayden—were arguing against the popularized assumption that people with congenital and intellectual impairments could not benefit from physical activity and sport.[139] Thus, while eugenic programs were still in practice in some Canadian provinces, local, national, and international sports organizations emerged for the very populations eugenics was designed to target. This included sport for those diagnosed with cerebral palsy, intellectual disabilities, and various other diagnoses that were grouped under the umbrella *les autres* (literal translation, *the others*). Many Paralympic stakeholders, including Ludwig Guttmann, fought vehemently against the inclusion of these athletes in the Paralympic Games. By the 1980s, partially because of pressure from the International Olympic Committee, athletes with cerebral palsy and *les autres* athletes were eventually allowed to compete.[140] Despite the massive growth of the Special Olympics over this period, however, athletes diagnosed with intellectual and developmental disabilities were not added to the Paralympics until 1996.[141]

Erosion of Newly Won Paralympic Opportunities

After only two Paralympic Games, there emerged rumours of some "cheaters," most notably from the Spanish basketball team, who had only "pretended" to have intellectual disabilities.[142] This offered sufficient leverage for many on the International Paralympic Committee (IPC) who were opposed to the inclusion of athletes with intellectual and developmental disabilities to ban them from the Games until 2012.[143] While this 12-year suspension of this entire class of athletes is constructed by the IPC as reasonable and necessary, to ensure fair classification and participation, it is worth noting that there are ongoing rampant claims of athletes with spinal cord injuries and visual impairments cheating by exaggerating or faking their impairments, or by taking performance-enhancing drugs.[144] Such rumours—some of them substantiated—have never led to similar motions to suspend an entire impairment class of athletes. Even individual Paralympians who have been caught using steroids have received only 4-year suspensions, showing the 12-year suspension of all athletes with intellectual disabilities to be about anything but fairness.[145]

Further, just at the moment when eugenically targeted athletes began gaining access to Paralympic sport systems, the IPC—under the presidency of Canada's

Robert Steadward—began reorienting the modern Paralympics from explicit rehabilitation models to those of competitive, and economically productive, spectator sport. The IPC's first move was to distance itself from events and athletes that—in the words of the IPC's chief medical officer at the time— "reduce the competitive or aesthetic impact of the Paralympic Games for the spectators."[146] That is, it began combining classification groups (e.g., making athletes with cerebral palsy compete against athletes with spinal cord injury, or making athletes with more significant impairments compete against those with

TRANSFORMATIVE MOMENTS: "NOTHING ABOUT US WITHOUT US!"

For most of the 20th century, the majority of disability organizations were *for* not *of* disabled people: That is, all the decision making was done by nondisabled people. Many such organizations refused to allow those they purported to serve to vote or to take on significant leadership roles.[152] Of note, Paralympic organizations were among these: Ludwig Guttmann refused to have athletes as decision makers in the movement; and for much of Robert Steadward's reign, the IPC's athlete council was refused even a single vote at the general assembly.[153]

It is not surprising, therefore, that the most common demand of disability rights movements across the globe has been "Nothing About Us Without Us!": That is, no decision should be made about disabled people's lives without their having a significant say.[154] Notably, deaf communities at the end of the 19th century were the first to create their own local and international advocacy and sporting organizations. Some early Canadian self-advocacy efforts included war veterans with visual impairments and spinal cord injuries collaborating with nondisabled allies to create the Canadian National Institute for the Blind in 1918 and the Canadian Paraplegic Association in 1945.[155] Canada was also one of the first countries to create a robust People First movement: a movement of those deemed to have intellectual disabilities that focused on self-advocacy and deinstitutionalization.[156]

Notably, Canada also played a major role in the activist coup attempted at the 1980 World Congress of Rehabilitation International in Winnipeg. Tired of not having a say, an international group of activists (led largely by Canadian and Swedish delegates with disabilities) proposed a motion resolving that people with disabilities should make up half of the voting delegates.[157] Two-thirds of the (mostly nondisabled) delegates voted down the motion, leading many of the disabled delegates to create their own organization *of* (not *for*) disabled people. Named Disabled Peoples' International (DPI), its charter focuses on self-representation, capacity building, and justice rather than pathology and charity. Its headquarters remain in Canada to this day.

It is worth noting that at the time of this chapter's writing, self-representation remains scarce in many disability organizations, including sport organizations. The IPC has nowhere near 50 percent disability representation at the general assembly. Many provincial and national disability sport organizations do not have a single employee or board member with a disability.

less significant impairments). Further, the IPC began cutting events performed by athletes whose bodies or capacities differed most from the able-bodied sporting aesthetic, or that were not well enough supported internationally to create large competitive playing fields.[147] The athletes most affected by these cuts were, by definition, the most marginalized: women, athletes with more significant impairments, athletes with congenital disabilities, and often a combination of all three.[148] In other words, the IPC used sporting and capitalist discourses to target precisely those who had been targeted by eugenics.

This cutting of the most marginalized classes of athletes from the Paralympic Games also led to the erosion of their grassroots programs at home.[149] This was made worse when Robert Steadward and other mostly nondisabled parasport leaders pushed for the integration of Canada's sport system. This meant defunding disability sport organizations (which ran both elite and grassroots programming) in favour of funding mainstream organizations (like Athletics Canada) to run parasport alongside its mainstream programs. Such changes led to athletes with disabilities having far less of a say in their own sporting cultures and also undermined the systems that advocated for both the most marginal athletes and grassroots disability sport in general.[150] Such decisions reaffirmed eugenic hierarchies of disability, creating a context in which athletes with spinal cord injuries, visual impairments, and low-level amputations come to be increasingly celebrated, sponsored, and supported as elite athletes in Canada and internationally, while those with congenital, developmental, and intellectual impairments come to be increasingly marginalized and excluded, both within and through sport.[151]

Continued Prioritizing and Marginalizing of Parasports

Just as dominant histories are used to celebrate Canada as a world leader in the modern Paralympic movement and in disability sport inclusion, we can use historical analyses to critique the ways the Paralympic movement has reproduced inequities that trace back to eugenic disability hierarchies. Through genealogical analysis we can mobilize history to question a sporting system that all but ensures that nondisabled people are making the most important decisions about disability sport.[158] We can use it to question why Canada's "inclusive" disability sport system prioritizes Paralympic sport and disproportionately serves athletes with relatively minimal impairments in one of three classification categories: spinal cord injury, amputation, or visual impairment (when these groups represent less than 15 percent of disabled people in Canada).[159]

Conclusion

In this chapter, we argue that stories about our past are important: They are used to naturalize present practices and to justify future plans that build on historical traditions. This is why the ubiquitous stories about Canadian heroes and progressive pasts can be so dangerous. Written most often by the people who have profited from systems of privilege and oppression, they tend to normalize, obscure, and thus reproduce social injustices and inequities. Alternative histories, like many of those in this textbook, challenge not only what we have said about our past but also importantly what these pasts (and how we have told them) say about us in the present as well.

Thus, we tried to demonstrate why it is important to tell different kinds of histories. Within each case study, we used the archives to tell stories that refuse to honour the perspectives of privilege, to centre the acts of heroic white saviours, and to construct a progress narrative. We told, instead, the story of dangerous eugenic practices and knowledges that have morphed but not disappeared. We traced how seemingly changing systems, like the modernization of parasport, continue to privilege the same bodies. We demonstrated how the movements orchestrated by the privileged to include often reinforce and justify marginalization and inequity rather than challenge and transform it. We also briefly touched on the importance of narrating moments of resistance and struggle.

In other words, in refusing to tell (and perpetually retell) celebratory, progressive histories, we gain the opportunity to tell multiple, more complex histories. Further, because progressive stories of our past help normalize presents and justify the same kinds of futures, genealogical questioning of our past can help us recontextualize and critique the injustices that we currently face as well as conceptualize and mobilize for more just futures.

DISCUSSION QUESTIONS

1. Why might it be useful to trace ideas through history instead of focusing on the acts of important people?
2. How do your local recreation programs and facilities continue to support notions of eugenics and white supremacy?
3. Explain how inclusive physical activity or physical education programs might not necessarily be in the best interests of disabled people.
4. How has thinking critically about parasport history changed the ways you might choose to run an inclusive sport program?

SUGGESTED READINGS

Couturier, Lynn. "The Influence of the Eugenics Movement on Physical Education in the United States." *Sport History Review* 36 (2005): 21-42.

Howe, P. David. *The Cultural Politics of the Paralympic Movement: Through an Anthropological Lense.* London: Routledge, 2008.

Malacrida, Claudia. *A Special Hell: Institutional Life in Alberta's Eugenic Years.* Toronto: University of Toronto Press, 2015.

Mobily, Kenneth. "Eugenics and the Playground Movement." *Annals of Leisure Research* 21, no. 2 (2018): 145-160.

Peers, Danielle. "Sport and Social Movements by/for Disability and Deaf Communities: Irreconcilable Histories?" In *Palgrave Handbook of Paralympic Studies.* Edited by Ian Brittain and Aaron Beacom. Basingstoke: Palgrave Macmillan, 2018, 71-97.

CHAPTER 11

BLACK CANADIAN SPORTING HISTORIES IN THE 19TH AND 20TH CENTURIES

Ornella Nzindukiyimana, PhD
St. Francis Xavier University

Kevin B. Wamsley, PhD
St. Francis Xavier University

LEARNING OBJECTIVES

In this chapter you will

- learn about the historical origins of the notion of the natural Black athlete;
- identify the effect of race and gender on the sporting practices of Black men and women in Canada;
- examine the sociocultural significance of Black athletes' success in different sports in the late 19th century;
- explore stories of Black Canadian athletes who distinguished themselves in sport throughout the 20th century before the First World War, during the interwar period, and after the Second World War; and
- investigate how Black Canadians' participation in sport in the last two centuries is a complex experience that entwined discrimination, acceptance, and empowerment.

In dominant narratives, sport is presented as a locus of enjoyment for all, whether spectators or participants. However, comprehensive historical analyses demonstrate that, in Canada and in the West at large, sport has stood on pillars of exclusivity and discrimination. Yet the white supremacist and masculinist foundations of sport opened up space for oppressed minority groups such as Black Canadians to challenge prejudiced norms and assumptions, as well as to redefine and attempt to emancipate themselves in an unequal society. As the 20th century progressed, sport became one of the few areas of public life in which Black men and women could compete with white athletes on a relatively level playing field—a rarity in a race-conscious society.[1]

Canadian racial minorities have had similar, but separate, experiences. Focusing on Black Canadians, this chapter offers an overview of the ways in which the concept of race constructed Black sport experiences, colouring the Canadian sporting landscape throughout the 19th and 20th centuries. Analyzing the role of anti-Black racism in sport in constructing a specific image of Canada offers a unique perspective within broader understandings of Canadianness.[2]

Perception and Interpretation of Black Bodies

In the British colonial context, people of colour and Indigenous peoples were considered as lesser and ostracized; notably, Indigenous peoples were declared inferior, a position that justified their subordination within Canadian institutions and the disregard for their land treaties (see chapters 3 and 13). In the 18th and 19th centuries, many Western societies encouraged "race-based understandings" of the behaviour of socially determined groups,[3] resulting in various racisms, including, but not limited to, anti-Semitism and anti-Indigenous, anti-Chinese, anti-Japanese, and anti-Black racism; these racisms had various origins, purposes, and consequences.[4] Anti-Black racism was only one form of racial discrimination exercised by colonial powers. The European conquest of Indigenous lands and the establishment of the Canadian state has largely obscured the histories of various groups that came to what is currently Canada, whether by choice (e.g., settlers), by circumstance (e.g., refugees), or by force (e.g., enslaved, 1628-1834).[5] Thus, Black peoples' history in Canadian sport serves as a lens to observe the consequences of one form of racism on social experiences, interactions, and life chances.

At the height of the transatlantic slave enterprise, the delineation of people into races based on their position legitimized distinction and separation. The centuries-long enslavement of Black African peoples had ramifications beyond the forced displacement of millions of people from African ports to the Caribbean and the Americas, including Canada.[6] Who was moving whom and what each looked like mattered in the widespread justification of Black Africans' bondage and subsequent subordination in the new lands.[7] Soon, enslavement became a "Black condition" when, beforehand, slavery was a systemic non-ethnic-specific means of extracting cheap labour.[8] Hierarchies thus established gave rise to daily and lifelong forms of discrimination (i.e., racism).[9]

Conceptualizing Black Africans as a separate "Negroid" category distanced their plight and fate from that of other groups, such as "Caucasians." Race was rendered scientifically credible because it was based on identifiable, albeit arbitrary, phenotypical features (i.e., genetically determined external physical characteristics) imagined as natural markers of biological and sociocultural differences.[10] Despite the physical features of a given race being too diverse to be so simply categorized,[11] these markers legitimized race, concealing the evidence of its social construction.

Hence, in the colonization and capitalism projects, white Europeans declared all aspects of their lives—dress, religion, behaviour, and so on—as superior to their imagined racial and class subordinates.[12] White privilege and entitlement became firmly embedded in law (who could have land, vote, and enjoy the benefits of citizenship), culture (through separation of tasks and public spaces), and the economy (through unequal access to resources and opportunities). Racial segregation was just another step towards cementing imagined differences and elevating whiteness. Given those circumstances, racial distinction became very difficult to refute, even long after slavery's abolition. Over centuries, Blackness became synonymous with incivility and mental or physical underdevelopment, an assessment that became embedded in North American institutions—including the justice system, education, and, eventually, sport.[13]

White Supremacy Ideology in Structural Barriers to Participation

Prevailing understandings of race had a profound effect on the interpretation of Black men's, and later Black women's, entrance into sport. In the mid- to late 19th century, sport became a manly enterprise for the British, emphasizing courage, leadership, toughness, and stoicism through artificial combat or manufactured conditions of adversity. However, the same attributes for ostensibly dangerous Black men were labelled careless, empty, obstinate, merely daring, and, in some cases, as proof of animalistic tendencies.[14] Therein lies the basis of racialization: viewing the Other in terms of their racial identity and, therefore, enabling the understanding of their behaviour, successes, and failures only through a racial (and often stereotypically prejudiced) lens. Racialization establishes given characteristics as positive when expressed by the "right" group and as negative when expressed by the "wrong" one.

Physical control and discipline were a mark of elevated intellectual capacity, until Black athletes displayed those traits.[15] Black athleticism was, and continues to be, devalued and exaggerated: In the 19th century, when few Black people had access to sport, they were considered too primitive for such a civilized activity; however, Black athletes' success in the early 20th century was conceptualized as empty-headed technique or proof of superhuman genetics (i.e., unfair animalistic advantage).[16] Racial discrimination in sport also prevailed because mingling in any space (neighbourhoods, recreation, and education) invoked fears of race mixing and racial impurity, both direct threats to whiteness. In other words, segregation prevented confrontations on the field of play that could challenge white power and authority, while also strategically preventing contact between white people and Black people.[17] Also, as discussed in chapter 7, the amateur rules, which excluded remunerated athletes, guaranteed a social position to middle- and upper-class men that was incontrovertibly more civilized.[18] The systemic ideology, in sport as in the rest of society, demanded white victory for its sustainability.[19]

Professional sport, governed by different rules, soon challenged the pristine amateur framework. In 1908, this came to a head when Black American Jack Johnson defeated white Canadian Tommy Burns for the world heavyweight boxing title, a key symbol of white masculine superiority over all other races and women. Burns' defeat dared suggest that, perhaps, white men were not physically superior. In response, there was an informal campaign across the Western world to find a white boxer to dethrone Johnson. The campaign, known as the search for a "great white hope," aimed to restore the status quo; it lasted seven years. As well, following Burns' defeat, new critics sought to discredit boxing

Racialization and the Natural Athlete

Pseudoscientific notions about racialized athletes perpetuate the idea that race is natural. Given the hypervisibility of Black athletes, "The world of sports has . . . become an image factory that disseminates and even intensifies our racial preoccupations."[23] The athletic gene associated with Blackness is a residual of the race science of the 19th century, as elusive as the single distinguishing attribute of said Blackness.[24] Importantly, the construct of Black natural athleticism was not meant to elevate Black athletes. Rather, as white people conceded athletic superiority to position whiteness as intellectually superior, Black athletic success and ability were conceptualized as effortless and illegitimate, cementing their inferiority.[25] The notion of the Black superathlete maintains the illusion of race.

Socio-historically speaking, it is because of the 19th and 20th centuries' intransigent colour lines and amateur rules (see chapter 7), which enforced inequities in access, that sport participation was divided along racial lines; it was not because certain races were more suited to certain sports. In fact, white athletes dominated sports prior to the ascension of Black athletes in a few mass spectator sports like boxing, track and field, football, and basketball. Over decades, potential white athletes, informed by "race science," avoided what culturally became Black sports.[26] White sports, like golf, swimming, and skiing, were historically exclusive by virtue of the cost of participation and access, and remain so. White athletes continued to dominate the greater majority of disciplines (from aquatic sports to winter and club sports), yet whiteness escapes the same scrutiny. It is never rationalized that white swimmers, skiers, and so on are unnaturally gifted.[27] Although socially constructed, race holds considerable power, and this power is wielded unequally.

as an animalistic activity that was not suitable for civilized gentlemen. In 1915, in Havana, Cuba, white American Jess Willard finally secured the title, and a colour line was firmly drawn. There were no Black challengers for the next 22 years, and this was not from a lack of contenders.[20]

By the time Willard came to the rescue, the damage was done: white men could no longer, as a matter of course, claim physical superiority.[21] As outlined in the athlete profiles presented in this chapter, other Black athletes (boxers or other), before or during Johnson's era, disproved the notion of Black frailty; Johnson simply cemented it. In response, the double standard when it comes to race in sport became plain: If non-white groups were not feeble, weak, and unfit for sport, as expected, then athletic prowess became further evidence of their racial difference. White Europeans' victories also had more value because white athletes were judged more trainable (i.e., in possession of more brains than brawn).[22] Thus, a white athlete's athletic aptitude came to symbolize industriousness, while the success of a Black athlete was deemed effortless.

Femininity, Blackness, and Sport

The notion of the superhuman Black athletic body also applied to women. The legacy of centuries of forced violent servitude promoted the idea of Black women as lesser than women from the dominant group in often contradictory ways: The Black woman's body was hypersexualized while also being denigrated and deemed undesirable. Black female athletes were expected to be, and not scolded for being, aggressive like men, which called into question their femininity.[28] This history complicated and complicates Black women's engagement in the so-called feminine sports, such as gymnastics and figure skating, because Black femininity does not fit the parameters of purity, grace, delicacy, and litheness set around hegemonic femininity.[29]

All women struggled to negotiate their place in sport, but white middle- and upper-class women broke through earlier, in the 1880s. In contrast, there is little evidence of Black Canadian female sport involvement before the 1930s, especially at the competitive and elite levels.[30] Black female athletes had to overcome entering a male-dominated domain as women while facing racial discrimination and prejudice as Black people and, as primarily working class, they scarcely had the time, money, or social standing to participate. Thus, the triple jeopardy of race, gender, and class delayed or prevented their participation in sport.[31]

Black Sportsmen in the 19th Century

As sport spread beyond exclusive white clubs in the late 1800s, a few Black Canadians stood out in boxing, baseball, rowing, and hockey. Black histories in those sports help us understand the meaning of race in Canadian sport, especially because success at this early stage set the foundation for emergence into the 20th century.

Boxers and Early Sport Integration

In the 19th century, few sportsmen could expect to be remunerated. But, through barnstorming, Black boxers accessed an income that could elevate them as "full men": When menial jobs were the only option, boxing allowed these men to acquit themselves of a sense of symbolic manhood (feeding their families) as well as literal manhood (physical prowess and athleticism).[32] Some even attained the most remarkable fame and fortune of their time. In the mid to late 1800s, this was the case for two of the most prominent Canadian boxers (Black or white): George "Old Chocolate" Godfrey[33] (1853-1901) and George "Little Chocolate" Dixon (1870-1908).

Canadian Heavyweight Champion George Godfrey

George Godfrey (see figure 11.1) was of a generation of men who sought sport employment to "assert their manly independence."[34] As a child, the native of the Bog district of Charlottetown, Prince Edward Island—a shanty area that was home to many of the province's Black residents—moved to Boston, Massachusetts, with his family in search of a better life. Rejecting menial work, a 23-year-old Godfrey pursued a fighting career as a heavyweight in 1880.[35] Prizefighters were especially imposing figures in the austere Victorian society, making Black prizefighters' breakthrough, at a time when Black athletes were being driven out of sports (horse racing and baseball began segregationist policies in the late 19th century), suggestive of a major shift.[36] The fighting game's individual format and the public's growing interest allowed Black boxers to prosper where they could not in other sports.[37] This was especially true in less prestigious lighter weights, because heavyweights did not thrive easily (as Jack Johnson later experienced).[38] But while a successful career meant significant socioeconomic advancement, boxing was not a sure bet; some athletes were forced to quit the sport because promoters could not arrange fights for them.[39] As with many boxers, Godfrey's rise to riches from nothing was quickly followed by a fall back to poverty.

During his career, Godfrey boldly and openly challenged white men (via newspapers), including the American self-proclaimed champion of the world, John L. Sullivan, and all other men in the country who could fight. Fighters like Sullivan, however, avoided Godfrey; for good measure, Sullivan often proclaimed that "he did not fight 'niggers'."[40] Well before Jack Johnson entered the ring in 1908, fights between Black and white fighters—especially in the heavyweight category—symbolized battles for race supremacy. Fight-

Figure 11.1 **George Godfrey, Canadian** heavyweight champion.

Wikimedia Commons

ing a boxer of Godfrey's calibre was inadvisable for white boxers,[41] despite the belief that Black boxers were inferior. Consequently, in the 1890s, as Black prizefighters rose to prominence, anthropologists advanced pseudoscientific ideas about Black physicality and superhuman abilities. This included claims of Black peoples' thicker and higher-density bones, which, presumably, rendered them invincible.[42] This at once explained Black boxers' prowess and rationalized discrimination.

World Champion George Dixon

Not long after Godfrey, George Dixon emerged as a force within the sport. Dixon is perhaps the most famous athlete from the all-Black segregated community of Africville (settled along the Halifax Harbour in the mid-1800s), although during his career, white Maritimers also held him in high esteem.[43] At 16, Dixon's first professional fight occurred in Halifax in the paperweight (now flyweight) division—hence the "Little" in the nickname "Little Chocolate."[44] Soon after, he moved to Boston to launch a remarkable and successful career as a world-class fighter.[45] At his peak, Dixon was one of the wealthiest Black men in the United States.[46]

With a majority of boxing fans being white, he stood little chance of fair officiating and, in fact, he fought in the middle of the ring to avoid the grasp of aggressive fans.[47] White fighters also chose to avoid him, which did not deter him in the least; not long after his debut, he started winning consistently.[48] In 1890, at age 20, he won the official world bantamweight title, becoming the first Black world champion in any sport and the first Canadian world titleholder.[49] The fight took place in England, where the colour bar was less rigid at the time.[50] Two years later, he became the featherweight champion, the first person to win a second world title in a different weight class, and the first universally recognized champion in that category.[51] That year, Dixon beat a white challenger in New Orleans so soundly that there was an attempt to ban interracial matches across the United States.[52] Several Black fans also attended the match,[53] prompting a newspaper writer to reassure readers that the beating from Dixon had just been a mistake. The writer asserted, however, that there was a great risk in letting Black people believe this was an indication of racial equality.[54] The colour line may have been less rigid than it was with the "heavies," but the threat of a Black champion was ever present.

Baseball Barnstormers

Jackie Robinson was the first Black major-leaguer of the 20th century, but he was not the first to break the colour bar of the sport's highest league. Fellow American Fleetwood Walker was, in fact, the first and last identifiably Black major leaguer in the 19th century.[55] Robinson's debut on the Brooklyn Dodgers' Montreal farm team in 1946, a season before his famous Dodgers start, was not the first stab at integration in Canada either: Across Canada, a handful of 19th-century baseball teams used Black players, including Moose Jaw, territorial

PROMINENT PEOPLE: LARRY GAINS (1900-1983)

During the 22 years it took for another Black man to hold the world title after Jack Johnson, Black heavyweights were gradually eroding other colour lines in the sport, and some progressive changes were occurring. The Canadian amateur boxing championship banned mixed-race bouts in 1913, but Black athletes continued fighting at the provincial level in the 1910s. Ontario's Larry Gains (see figure 11.2) was crowned national professional heavyweight champion in 1927 and went on to defeat a white South African to win the British Empire heavyweight boxing title in 1931. Gains was the first Black man able to challenge for the Empire title, and newspaper accounts suggest that the public and the press were supportive of his bid for the world championship. But the politics being

Canada's Sports Hall of Fame - Pantheon des sports canadiens
SPORTSHALL.CA - PANTHEONSPORTS.CA
Object ID: X981.827.4.16

Figure 11.2   Larry Gains.

what they were, Gains was not given the chance. He was, nonetheless, one of many in the post-Johnson hiatus who imposed themselves despite discrimination. Canadian champions like British-born Lennox Lewis later followed in Gains' and his contemporaries' footsteps. Lewis won a gold medal for Canada at the 1988 Olympic Games and multiple world titles in the 1990s and early 2000s, beating the likes of Mike Tyson, Evander Holyfield, and Vitali Klitschko.

champions of 1895, and the Woodstock Bains, an 1898 amateur team.[56] Rather, at century's close, North American Black baseball players were gradually pushed out as white teams refused to face Black teams or teams with Black players on their rosters. Fleetwood Walker quit under threat of a violent mob.

White Canadians did not immediately adopt a rigid stance against Black athletes, but they were quick to comply with outsourced white American players who refused to participate in interracial baseball.[57] For instance, in 1881, American players on the Guelph Maple Leafs outrightly rejected New York native Bud Fowler when he signed with the team. One part-time player even led a team revolt, prompting the *Guelph Herald* to defend Fowler. Despite the support, Guelph released Fowler soon after.[58] The Ontario team's willingness to sign a Black player was not, as Fowler's quick release and Canadian informal segregation demonstrated, evidence of lack of prejudice in society. Some reporters' descriptions of Black players reflected this as well: In 1887, a Black community leader in Hamilton demanded an apology from the local newspaper after the Newark Little Giants' all-Black battery that defeated Hamilton's team were called "coons" in the match's report.[59]

It appears that white Americans exported segregationist views into a fickle Canadian sporting landscape that otherwise may have been prepared to grant Black athletes some opportunities.[60] Thus, segregation was enforced on principle.[61] The American influence did not play out just on the diamond, nor just in the 1800s: George Giles (a player in the 1920s and 1930s) remembered that Canada "used to be sweet" for travelling American negro league players, until an increasing number of American tourists started requesting the kind of segregation they were used to; for example, a favourite Winnipeg hotel rejected his team's request for accommodations.[62] Skill was not enough to shield these athletes from racist hostility;[63] antagonistic white fans, opponents, teammates, and administrators held power and authority, so the latter's policy became to avoid "coloured players" in senior leagues.[64]

During the early years of the 20th century, Black players played on all-Black teams amongst each other and only sometimes against white teams.[65] Others joined the negro leagues,[66] since Canadian all-Black teams could form but could not sustain all-Black leagues; population size, dispersion, and financial means were substantial barriers. Further, many Black athletes playing baseball in Canada were from American barnstorming teams.[67] Black Canadian teams that were able to form were a novelty that attracted enthusiastic white fans, and they survived as best as they could within the constraints imposed on them. Teams often barnstormed together, as was the case for the Fredericton Celestials and the Halifax Victorias in the 1890s.[68] Barnstorming was ongoing in the mid-20th century.

Rowing Champion "Black Bob"

Rowing was a very popular sport in Canada at the turn of the 20th century. Regattas drew great crowds that boarded steamboats to follow the action more closely.[69] Unlike some contemporary amateur pedestrian (fast walking) and horse racing events in Quebec and Ontario, rowing races did not draft explicit anti-Black rules.[70] This did not mean that Black contestants were welcome. It was with some resistance that Robert "Bob" Berry, a fisherman, made a name for himself in competitive rowing in the Toronto region.[71] Berry's introduction at the 1863 Toronto Bay Championship Rowing Regatta, organized by an exclusive Newark horse racing social club, did not sit well with fellow competitors who discovered on race day that he was Black. They refused to race if Berry did.[72] Nearly 30 years before, the club had stipulated that "no black man will be allowed to compete under any pretext whatsoever."[73]

Berry nevertheless continued to race and later became a crowd favourite, described as "[Toronto's] own ebony champion," competing both in Canadian and American regattas.[74] Nicknamed "Black Bob,"[75] by the time he raced at the 1868 Toronto Rowing Club, his racial identity was no longer a secret.[76] Organizers expected him to be bested, yet he acquitted himself so well that one opponent challenged him to race again twice. Berry won both races.[77] Perhaps the challenger had not followed Berry's career up until that point: Two years before, at the 1866 Toronto Rowing Club Regatta, he was already a reputed rower.[78]

Not being bound by discriminatory amateur rules may explain Berry's access and success, since the 1866 regatta was a prize-winning event, as were his races in the 1870s.[79] This is notable, because in some sports, competing for money, or even against people who had, was a disqualifiable offense; "social sportsmen" of the upper classes wrote amateur rules to prevent occupational athletes whose jobs, like Berry's fishing, were perceived to provide technical or physical advantages. Edward "Ned" Hanlan, the white Torontonian world champion rower in the 1880s, also had a fishing background. As in Berry's case, amateurism did not hinder Hanlan, who went on to become one of Canada's first great sport heroes.[80]

Coloured Hockey League of the Maritimes

In the 1890s, Black hockey players were such a rarity that, as such things go, there developed pseudoscientific explanations for their absence. One popular theory suggested that Black people had weak ankles.[81] The Coloured Hockey League (CHL) of the Maritimes quickly dispelled that myth in the late 19th and early 20th centuries. Black players rose to prominence and were praised by both Black and white communities, a fact that is commonly forgotten.[82] Indeed, the segregated league, which did not compete for a trophy,[83] attracted wide audiences for a few years at the turn of the 20th century.[84]

Because the sport developed as particularly middle class, with great emphasis on amateurism, its colour line was considerably rigid.[85] While there was no law against interracial hockey, mixed teams and competition were not encouraged. Black teams made the most of subpar equipment and minimal access to public indoor rinks: "Only when the quality of the ice surface at indoor rinks deteriorated, usually in late-February or early March, did blacks play indoors and whites consider their own hockey season over."[86] Segregation in the sport thus reflected and reproduced society's racial tensions, although racism did not necessarily dictate the play and experiences of the CHL's players.[87] Further, Black players' minority status and the lack of self-produced media mean that the lens through which historians rediscover them is distorted by contemporary white observers' prejudiced views.[88] In blatantly racist newspaper reports, white journalists attacked many aspects of the play, derided players' looks (laughing at supposedly indistinguishable players), denigrated players' speech in quotations (e.g., "Dey knowed we du dem. We had de bes' of dem and dey stopped"), and employed colourful commentary framed by racist tropes (e.g., "fading away like a watermelon before a southern darkey").[89]

Like white leagues, the CHL simply reflected community rivalries and, until the Second World War, aggressive play was common.[90] However, Black hockey play was often considered unorganized, too ludicrous and aggressive, and more like carnival display than skilled sport. In fact, extravagant demonstrations from players were understood within their community as "poking fun" at the game's aggression and engaged the audience to join in. Black men and women were particularly animated in the stands, which astounded and impressed white reporters.[91]

For a period of roughly five years, between 1899 and 1904,[92] interest in Black hockey games grew in white Maritime communities. White people attended, officiated, and, in some cases, financed the CHL; the once burlesque nature of Black hockey was viewed as a good exhibition of the sport, and reporters encouraged white spectators to attend games.[93] Spectators were attracted to the league's fast

TRANSFORMATIVE MOMENTS: WHAT'S IN A MASCOT?

In exhibition games, some all-Black teams resorted to stereotypical behaviour to amuse an often-majority white audience. American Negro baseball leagues especially played up this trope, with teams like the Miami Ethiopian Clowns and the Zulu Cannibal Giants and corresponding antics and costumes. Some teams even travelled with actual clowns.[99] In the 1930s, the aforementioned two teams

photo file via The Windsor Star

Figure 11.3 Windsor–Walkerville OHA team (1901-1902).

toured the Maritimes using "African savage" imagery to drive up ticket sales. But under the getups, skits, and nicknames were quite talented players and championship-winning teams.[100] The Coloured Hockey League in the Maritimes had also used this strategy in the late 1890s, before and after the brief period of mainstream popularity they enjoyed in the 1900s. The players' use of exaggerated moves to attract crowds was considered "playful" yet "clownish" by white spectators and reporters, often further Othering Black people.[101] As sport became more and more segregated in the early 20th century, Black men were conditionally included on white teams in subordinate and denigrating roles, such as mascots.[102] The mascot position was usually reserved for children or animals. Figure 11.3 depicts the 1901 to 1902 Ontario Hockey Association Windsor–Walkerville team, in which Jud White, guitar in hand, was the mascot.

and exciting style of play, and some claimed that Black hockey teams attracted more white spectators than white leagues.[94] Certainly, the CHL had gained a measure of respectability by 1904 and operated at the level of white leagues.[95]

Since the CHL retained amateur status, white and bourgeois interest may have been due to the rise in professionalism in hockey. Indeed, displaying Victorian values through sport helped Black players escape some harsh racist treatment.[96] This translated to less derogatory press reports for teams that embraced the "bourgeois sporting ideal."[97] Some Black hockey teams even named themselves after British monarchs or used British-themed names (e.g., the Jubilees and the Victorias). In the fight for justice and full citizenship, Black peoples' strongest argument was that they were also British.[98]

Black Sport in the 20th Century

The specter of racial inequality endured during the better part of the 20th century. But in the last three decades of the century, significant improvements meant that race and anti-Black racism did not always define athletes' experiences. However, Black athletes retained a complex relationship with the public and the press. Gender was also a factor; it was not until the 1930s that Black Canadian female athletes started rising to prominence.

Significant diversification of the playing field occurred in the aftermath of the Second World War. A wave of integration spread, spearheaded by Jackie Robinson's love affair with Montreal on his way to the major leagues, finally reaching the last great "whitestream" sport: hockey. This section details the Black athlete's experience as framed by the world wars.

Before the First World War

Early in the 20th century, mainstream opportunities became available in track and field (amateur) and in boxing (amateur and professional). Opportunities in track and field particularly expanded with the increasing international significance of the Olympic Games (inaugurated in 1896) and the British Empire Games (inaugurated in 1930, precursor to the Commonwealth Games).

Breaking Into Track and Field

Not much has been written about Black track and field athletes before the 1910s, but a colour line on the Canadian Olympic team prior to 1912 suggests they were present. Aboriginal athletes had already been part of official Canadian Olympic teams,[103] but on the eve of the track and field trials for the 1912 Olympic Games in Stockholm, Sweden, it was announced that, for the first time, three Black athletes would be trying out.[104] Two of the candidates were from the Ottawa YMCA track team, including its captain, but only the third qualified: John Armstrong "Army" Howard (1888-1937) from Winnipeg.[105]

Howard's selection is noteworthy because of Canada's sociopolitical stance at the time. A recent Black U.S. immigrant, he was the type of person the Immigration Act of 1910 (focused on the construction of a white European nation) sought to ban.[106] In fact, a Canadian Olympic victory was expected to make a great impression with white Europeans, the "right kind" of immigrants. Towards that goal, Howard and his teammates were expected to perform well at the Games to impress Scandinavia. Such use of athletes of colour to further white supremacist nations' growth was not uncommon throughout the century,[107] when athletes fulfilled duties to nations (e.g., winning medals and joining the military) that considered them second-class citizens.

Support for Howard was lukewarm, although, as a champion in his events (100-metre and 200-metre sprints), there was little doubt that he could medal. However, his performance fell short and he did not make the final in his events. As was typical at the time, condescension permeated press reports about Howard: He was consistently designated as "dusky" or "coloured," and one caricature depicted him with stereotypical "Black Sambo" exaggerated features. Pseudoscientific racial notions also coloured perceptions of Howard's ongoing conflict with the coach: For instance, similar to assessments about Indigenous athlete Tom Longboat at the previous Games, it was posited that low intellectual capacity made him untrainable.[108] Moreover, Jack Johnson's victory over Tommy Burns only four years earlier influenced the white coach's treatment of Howard: The coach later admitted that he punched Howard after a disagreement and that he had punctuated this action by a warning that he (the coach) was "one White man that a nigger can't lick."[109] Howard's hometown of Winnipeg, however, was behind him, even explicitly lamenting biased Canadian administrators.[110]

Struggles in Early 20th-Century Boxing

As evidenced by the threat uttered by Army Howard's coach, Johnson's time as champion (1908-1916) reverberated beyond the boxing ring. The heavyweight champion's impact on other boxers of the time, however, was even more pronounced. This was the case for one of Johnson's most prominent challengers: Sam Langford (1886-1956). Born in Weymouth Falls, Nova Scotia, Langford left for Massachusetts as a 13 year old.[111] He discovered boxing in Cambridge and won his first fight in 1901. Like his predecessors, Langford was subject to a racialized nickname ("the Boston Tar Baby") but, unlike them, he was also impressively known as "the Boston Terror," "the Weymouth Wizard," and "the Boston Bone Crusher."

As he gained a solid reputation as a lightweight, so many boxers avoided him that he began facing heavier opponents. In 1906, two years before Johnson won the world title, a 30 pounds lighter Langford fought him and lost. Johnson never faced him again and effectively avoided him, seemingly, for fear of losing.[112] Early 1920s light heavyweight champion Georges Carpentier also refused the Boston Terror a fight. Langford was confined to the segregated World Colored Heavyweight Championship.

During his career, Langford earned upwards of $200,000, an especially impressive amount because he was paid far less than white boxers (even less talented ones) and had to fight several times per month.[113] Even after losing an eye in a 1917 fight, he continued to fight successfully and remained a threat. White boxer Jack Dempsey, who later became a world champion (1919-1926), avoided fighting Langford even with that handicap, purportedly because Dempsey's manager was looking for easy fights.[114] For many boxers, avoiding the Boston Bone Crusher had as much to do with protecting their reputations as it did preserving the illusions of race. At the end of 200 recorded career fights in 1938, he followed the path of many boxers, losing the fortune he had amassed. He died blind and broke at age 69 in Harlem, New York.[115] To this day, Sam Langford remains one of the best boxers never to win, or even challenge for, a world championship. Nonetheless, he fostered pride in his native Nova Scotia.[116]

Interwar Period

Discussed here are the flourishing opportunities of the interwar period. As Black women appeared in the sport arena, more Black men left their mark in track and field and baseball's rigid segregation was gradually eroded.

Black Women on the Track

During the interwar period, Black Canadian women began to rise to prominence in elite sport, especially in track and field. The significance of this was twofold: First, few sports were as accessible to women of colour and of lower socioeconomic classes; second, track and field was considered a masculine sport unfit for feminine women, legitimizing the success and tolerance of "mannish" Black women in the sport. As such, stereotypical notions of Black femininity made it more acceptable for Black women to be in track and field than it was for white women.[117]

In the late 1930s, Barbara Howard (see figure 11.4) from Vancouver was running national record times at age 17. She qualified to represent Canada at the 1938 British Empire Games, becoming the first Black woman to represent Canada in international sport competition.[118] The Games were in Sydney, Australia, where Howard was also among the first women and first Black women to participate in the event since their inception in 1930.[119] She stood out so much that, according to a Toronto sports columnist, Australians were fascinated with the young "dusky" sprinter, an observation made in a manner that suggested Canadians were well used to such a sight.[120]

As viewed through the lens of Black female athletes' experiences, sport created opportunities to rise above socioeconomic and authoritarian barriers to challenge the colour line. It has,

City of Vancouver Archives; photographer Matthews, James Skitt, Major

Figure 11.4   Barbara Howard, Canadian track athlete from Vancouver.

for instance, been surmised that Black women in this period ran and jumped to attain social heights they could not otherwise reach.[121] For the best amateur track and field athletes in the United States, sport often provided a path to post-secondary studies. Howard was able to travel and reach new horizons thanks to sport,[122] as did Jean Lowe, a 1940s champion sprinter from Ontario, who left to attend the Tuskegee Institute in Alabama as a student-athlete.[123] Howard's participation at the British Empire Games marked the beginning of Canadian Black women's participation in a sport they would later dominate, especially from the 1960s onwards, when Black women's successes shone brightly, sometimes more than any other cultural contribution.[124]

Track and field grew to be even more integrated in the years after the Second World War. In the 1930s and 1940s, several other Black athletes, men and women, were celebrated on the tops of podiums as well as in newspapers, including Phil Edwards (British Guiana and Montreal), Ray Lewis (Hamilton), Sammy Richardson (Toronto), and Rosella Thorne (Montreal). These athletes excelled in their respective eras and were some of the most visible Black Canadians of their time. Following in Army Howard's footsteps after the First World War were Phil Edwards and Ray Lewis. Edwards won five Olympic medals while competing for Canada,[125] and Lewis was the first Black Canadian Olympic medallist.[126] and Thorne is one of the first (if not the first) Black female Olympians (Helsinki, 1952). The press media was not as condescending in their coverage as in earlier years, although being qualified by their Blackness was common; reports typically included labels such as "negro," "negress," "dusky," or "coloured" but did not explicitly denigrate athletes' speech or looks. However, their success sustained the notion of the rise of the natural Black athlete established around the era of Jack Johnson and cemented in the 1930s by American Jesse Owens' outstanding performance at the 1936 Olympic Games in Berlin, Germany.

Baseball Breaks the Colour Line

Because of the rigid colour line in turn-of-the-century baseball, several skilled Canadian players opted to play in the Negro leagues instead.[127] One such player was Ollie Johnson, from Oakville, Ontario, who played for the Cuban Giants in 1916 before returning to Canada to join the military for the First World War.[128] One of his contemporaries, Wellington, British Columbia–born Jimmy Claxton, was an exceptional case. Claxton, a left-handed pitcher for the Oakland Pierce Giants (a Black team), "accidentally" integrated professional baseball and played a few innings for the Oakland Oaks (Pacific Coast League) in 1916. The Oaks were under the impression that he was an Aboriginal player, which was partly true, since Claxton was of mixed heritage.[129] The team released him upon learning his full racial identity, but Claxton still became the first Black player to be featured on a baseball card.

As some players left Canada to play south of the border, several Black teams were travelling north for barnstorming, "looking for new markets."[130] As discussed earlier in the chapter, in the 1920s and 1930s, barnstorming allowed players (Black and white) to become visible and Black teams to sometimes play against semi-professional or professional white teams.[131] In the 1930s, several notable teams across Canada counted numerous American players. The Montreal Black Panthers, who played in 1936 and 1937, for instance, were mostly American southerners.[132] Barnstorming was not a sustainable means of income, but it provided a modest supplement and covered travelling costs.[133] Important to note is that travelling inflicted not just financial costs; Black players were routinely denied entry to hotels and restaurants.

A standout team during that period was the Chatham Coloured All-Stars, who formed in the small Ontario community in 1933. The All-Stars won the Ontario Baseball Association championship in their inaugural season (the first Black team to do so) and developed a loyal following in Chatham, particularly in the area's Black community.[134] Family and friends gathered on game days to support their team, and although players faced racial slurs at games and bigotry in the press,[135] their supporters staunchly defended them.[136] One could still find all-Black teams in the 1950s, although the breaking of the colour bar in the major leagues and the erosion and dispersion of Black communities led to their steady decline.

Baseball's integration began slowly in the 1930s. In 1935, the Quebec Provincial League featured Alfred Wilson, pitcher and outfielder, the first professional player to be integrated in Canada.[137] The Canadian senior baseball champions of 1944, the London Majors, also counted pitcher and former Chatham All-Star Earl "Flat" Chase.[138] So when Jackie Robinson joined the Montreal Royals, he was not the only Black player on Canadian-based minor-league teams; five others were signed to the minors that year, including standout Canadian hockey player Vincent "Manny" McIntyre.[139] Out of the five, two quickly joined Robinson in Major League Baseball after his 1948 debut precipitated a wave of integration in the league—the last team to integrate was the Boston Red Sox, in 1986.

After the Second World War

As professional hockey carried discrimination into the 1950s, challenging racism in sport became less about outright segregation and more about lingering prejudices. This was especially evident in Black athletes' relationship to the media room. The Black athlete, a controversial figure since the turn of the century, found escaping entrenched white supremacist ideas challenging.

Hockey Integration

Hockey's colour line was the last high-level colour line erased in professional sport.[141] As a homogeneously white masculine space, hockey made the entry of people of colour difficult. Even white women have struggled to carve themselves a space into the national sport. Athletes such as Herb Carnegie, Ossie Carnegie (Herb's brother), and Manny McIntyre of the Quebec Senior League—who formed the first all-Black line in professional hockey—were popular talents in the 1930s, but they never set foot on National Hockey League (NHL) ice.[142] It

WORKING WITH PRIMARY SOURCES:
ANDY LYTLE BASEBALL EDITORIAL

Below is an impassioned editorial from 1942 written by Andy Lytle, a white sports editor at the Toronto Star. About the colour line in organized baseball and hockey, it illustrates the attitudes some had towards the treatment of Black athletes, here referred to as "coloured" or "Negro" athletes:

> *The rule against inclusion of the colored athlete in baseball is an unwritten one. But it is rigorous, nevertheless, as every ball follower in the country, from bat boy to league president and from the bleacher fan to stuffed shirt in a plush-lined box knows as well as a Moslem zealot knows the Koran.*
>
> *In numerous Canadian cities there are colored athletes who make track teams, are given regular berths in [Canadian Hockey Association] teams, [and] play without too much question of race prejudice on amateur ball clubs. But a Negro with the speed of [American sprinter] Eddie Tolan, the grace of [Canadian middle-distance runner] Phil Edwards and the hitting power of [American heavyweight boxer] Joe Louis could not, because of organized baseball's unwritten rule, one that [baseball commissioner Kenesaw] Landis tries to obscure by legal subterfuge, catch a place on Toronto's International league club.*
>
> *Surely, if a man is good enough to be given citizenship, if he is considered sound enough politically to fight for his country, he is good enough to play for it. In that respect, because we come up against the great American prejudice—one that isn't admitted—Canada occupies a slightly less hypocritical position than her great neighbor country, the alleged 'arsenal of democracy.'*
>
> *There is nothing in the rules or constitution of the National Hockey league against Negroes playing for it—but let any of them try to crash one of those gilded gates and if he gets a contract I'll eat your oldest hat in front of The Star building at high noon and take a jigger of nitrate of silver as a chaser.*
>
> *If the white race is, as alleged, superior to the African, I'll be hanged if we can prove it by examination of sporting and athletic records.*[140]

Lytle's words suggested that Canadian society was not fair to athletes who competed for Canada. His exposé (and use of stereotyping language) also conveyed that absence of official discriminatory policies in the manner of Jim Crow laws did not mean absence of discrimination.

was not until the next generation that Willie O'Ree (born in 1935, in New Brunswick) broke into the NHL with the Boston Bruins (1958). However, O'Ree did not usher in an era of integration like Jackie Robinson did with baseball; it was 16 years (1974), before another player, Ontario's Mike Marson (born in 1955), entered the League, via the Washington Capitals.

Throughout hockey's history, a tacit standardization of white hockey players developed despite the long record of non-white people playing hockey. Even today, young Black players face racial slurs and bigotry on the ice. Hockey was not just anti-Black, although Black athletes were the last major racialized group to integrate the NHL: in 1948, Larry Kwong (1923-2018) became the first Asian-Canadian NHL player, and Fred Sasakamoose (1933-), an Ahtahkakoop Cree, was the first Indigenous player in 1953. Hockey's intolerance festered despite the presence of talented Black athletes within the sport's system. The barring of Black people from hockey, the epitome of Canadian sociocultural spaces, was symbolic of prevailing anti-Blackness within the nation. It reflected, for instance, the 1936 case of a man who was refused service at a Montreal Forum bar for being Black, a decision upheld by the Supreme Court.[143] A decade later, Viola Desmond was famously jailed for sitting in the wrong section of a New Glasgow movie theatre in Nova Scotia. Likewise, in 1950s Vancouver, Valerie Jerome and her brother, Harry, both future Olympians, were pelted with rocks by classmates.[144] Until 1982, when Canada implemented a human rights charter (30 years after Ontario became the first province to adopt antidiscrimination laws), such cases were common across the nation.

Author Andreas Krebs also argues that hockey reproduces white male colonialism, merging identities of sport with nation.[145] As discussed in chapter 9, the link between hockey and Canada after Confederation was fortified with the donation of the Stanley Cup by Governor General Lord Stanley at the end of the 19th century. Hockey was one of the sports eventually used to shape national identity, focusing disparate and dispersed populations together around a common cultural identity unique to Canada.[146] The conception of hockey as white was, thus, effortless, because Canada's position as exclusively white had great support among nation builders. This added to the masculine hegemony within the sport in its early days, and it fixed and normalized the idea of white male hockey players while marginalizing Indigenous, Black, Asian, and all women players. Consequently, pioneering women athletes of colour faced several barriers. Angela James, the highly dominant Team Canada player of the early 1990s, climbed multiple steep hills as a Black and female player to reach success. James also faced the ubiquitous sexual identity barrier in sport on her way to becoming the second Black person and first openly gay player inducted into the Hockey Hall of Fame.[147]

Navigating the Press Room

The experiences of two Black sprinters in the last decades of the 20th century—Harry Jerome and Ben Johnson—illustrate the precarious position of athletes of colour in late 20th-century Canada. Jerome often had to contend with an inflammatory Canadian press that continuously depicted him as an aloof, unruly, undisciplined, and arrogant athlete.[148] This resembled what the press had done to his grandfather, Army Howard, decades earlier.[149] Ben Johnson, for his part, faced ambiguous coverage as he slowly rose through the ranks to become one of the world's biggest stars leading into the 1988 Olympic Games. As a champion, he was promoted from "Jamaican-Canadian" athlete to "Canadian," only to be swiftly demoted to "Jamaican-Canadian" soon after his fall from grace due to his infamous doping scandal. The hyphenation was an effort to distance white Canada from Black Jamaica.[150] An upsurge of first- and second-generation Black (typically Caribbean) immigrant athletes in the 1980s[151] emphasized the tension between Blackness and Canadianness, as perceived misbehaviours prompted such "they are not us" media representations.[152] Blackness, especially when tied to immigration, is often evinced from the Canadian concept of nation, especially when it is inconvenient.[153]

A contentious figure, the Black athlete had long walked on a tightrope, but the upsurge in immigrants in the 1960s and 1970s came with specific expectations, within the press, of athlete behaviour. In the 1990s and early 2000s, immigrants and children of immigrants like sprinters Donovan Bailey and Bruny Surin, hurdler Perdita Felicien, and wrestler Daniel Igali made their mark in Canadian sport. Among them, Igali received particularly high media support following his 2000 Olympic gold medal celebration in which he enthusiastically kissed the Canadian flag and raved about his adopted country.[154] Loyalty, deference, and gratefulness to the nation remained mandatory for Black athletes at the dawn of the 21st century.

Public challenges to Canada's benevolence have traditionally not been well received by Canadians. Refusal to recognize anti-Black racism and Blackness within Canada has long persisted as a national trait, particularly since Canadians often relativize to "worse" U.S. racial relations. In the mid-20th century, when Black football players spoke out against the racism they encountered, widespread denial followed.[155] Because several American footballers had chosen to play in Canada to escape dire racial relations in the United States, the perception prevailed that Canada had little to no cause for concern. Decades later, shortly after capturing Olympic gold in the 100-metre sprint in 1996, Donovan Bailey similarly faced fairly strong backlash when he was quoted in the *Toronto Globe and Mail* as saying Canada was "as racist as the United States."[156] He later alleged that he was misquoted—clarifying to say that Canada was "not" as racist as the United States—but the controversy remained. By his career's end in the early 2000s, Bailey was still skeptical of Canada's support for him as a Black man.[157]

Conclusion

Historically, Black people were excluded from the playing fields of Canada. As citizens, they were portrayed as mentally, morally, and physically unfit for Canadian society, its values, and cold climate.[158] These discriminatory attitudes became embedded within sociocultural institutions, dividing and segregating society along a colour line. The web of notions and beliefs about race then justified the exclusion of Black people from sport. Once Black athletes disproved the idea that they were unfit for sport, new notions of natural athletic advantages emerged to perpetuate racial hierarchies. For Black women, gender was an additional layer to the challenges of accessing sport. Yet this did not preclude the use of sport as an escape from harsh treatment and fostering pride to marginalized communities.[159] Eventually, colour bars in Canadian sport were lifted, although Black athletes continue to face various challenges into the 21st century. Despite their many accomplishments, Black athletes experience sport differently and are framed differently by the media.

DISCUSSION QUESTIONS

1. Why were Black people historically excluded from Canadian sport?
2. How did white people rationalize it when Black men defeated white men in sporting events?
3. Why did Black women face extra barriers in their quest to participate in sport?
4. What characterized Black histories in sport before the First World War, during the interwar period, and after the Second World War?
5. Which Black athletes' histories illustrate discrimination? Acceptance? Empowerment?

SUGGESTED READINGS

Jerome, Valerie, and Stuart Parker. "The Conservative Vision of the Amateur Ideal and Its Paradoxical Whitening Power: The Story of Valerie Jerome in 1950s and 1960s Canadian Track and Field." *Sport in Society* 13, no. 1 (2010): 12-19.

Joseph, Janelle, Simon Darnell, and Yuka Nakamura. *Race and Sport in Canada: Intersecting Inequalities.* Toronto: Canadian Scholars' Press, 2012.

Longley, Neil, Todd Crosset, and Steve Jefferson. "The Migration of African-Americans to the Canadian Football League during the 1950s: An Escape from Racism?" *International Journal of the History of Sport* 25, no. 10 (2008): 1374-1397.

Nzindukiyimana, Ornella, and Kevin B. Wamsley. "Lowering the Bar: Larry Gains's Heavyweight Battle for a Title Shot, 1927-1932." *Sport History Review* 47, no. 2 (2016): 125-145.

Walker, Barrington. "Finding Jim Crow in Canada, 1789-1967." In *A History of Human Rights in Canada: Essential Issues.* Edited by Janet Miron. Toronto: Canadian Scholars' Press, 2009.

CHAPTER 12

THE SPORTS–MEDIA COMPLEX AND CANADIAN CULTURE

Stacy L. Lorenz, PhD
University of Alberta, Augustana Campus

Jay Scherer, PhD
University of Alberta

LEARNING OBJECTIVES

In this chapter you will

- reflect on how the interests of sport organizations, media producers, and advertisers have been historically connected in a mutually beneficial relationship;

- identify the most important factors that contributed to the growth of sports coverage in Canadian daily newspapers during the 19th and early 20th centuries;

- examine how radio coverage of sport developed in Canada during the 1920s and 1930s;

- assess how different Canadian television networks and cable channels utilized sports broadcasts from the 1950s to the 1980s; and

- explore how media coverage of sport socially constructs cultural narratives that shape our understandings of gender, race, ethnicity, and local and national identities.

Daily newspapers first developed in Canada during the late 19th and early 20th centuries. As these new mass circulation newspapers focused more and more of their content on sport, they played a crucial role in creating local and national audiences for sport in Canada.[1] The rise of radio in the 1920s and 1930s and the growth of television in the 1950s and 1960s extended and accelerated this process, as sport quickly became an important component of both radio and television programming. Coverage of local clubs and events encouraged fan interest and helped build a sense of community identity and civic pride around a city's sports teams. Meanwhile, increased media coverage of major sporting events occurring outside the city, in other parts of Canada, and around the world brought people together in a much wider community of interest centred on sport. By the early 20th century, this new universe of mediated sport occupied a prominent position in a developing Canadian national popular culture. No matter where fans and spectators lived, they could follow, discuss, and pay attention to the same group of athletes, teams, leagues, and events.[2] By constructing audiences for high-level amateur and professional sport, newspapers, radio, and television transformed major-league sports into national institutions and entangled sport within local and global "circuits of promotion" linking media, marketing, and merchandising.[3] As a result, it is impossible to understand the development of sport since the late 19th century— and the nature of sport in today's society and culture—without considering the historical connections between sport, various components of the mass media, and commercial advertising.

This chapter examines the growth of the key public and private institutions that constitute the sports–media complex in Canada, beginning with the rise of the daily press and the telegraph in the second half of the 19th century and continuing through the development of radio, television, and new forms of social media in the 20th and 21st centuries. By sports–media complex, we mean the symbiotic relationship between sport organizations, media, and commercial sponsors and advertising. This relationship has, historically, been one of mutual interdependence and prosperity, with each of the allied interest groups receiving rewards and benefits as a result of their linkages with each other.[4] Sport organizations have, for example, received substantial amounts of revenue from the sale of media rights and have benefited from local, national, and international exposure. Meanwhile, various media, both public and private, gained substantial advantages from popular sports content: Sports programming attracted large audiences that could be sold as a commodity to advertisers, thus generating considerable advertising revenue. Sporting events were also relatively inexpensive to cover and, later, to produce as radio and television content, in some cases enabling the Canadian networks to meet Canadian content requirements. Finally, commercial sponsors gained prestige and publicity from being associated with a particular sport or event, and advertisers achieved increased product sales by marketing consumer goods. In particular, sporting events created sizable audiences in a demographic group that was especially attractive to advertisers: males between 18 and 49 years of age.

In what follows, we assess the main factors that contributed to the expansion of the mass media in Canada during this time, while accounting for the prominence of sports coverage—in particular men's professional sport—within each new element of the popular media. This chapter therefore explores the patterns of continuity and change in the sports–media complex in the context of the overall development of the media in Canadian society and culture. Why did sports coverage become so prominent in daily newspapers and in early Canadian radio and television? How were later changes in media coverage of sport related to other changes in the media industries? Why did certain sports receive greater amounts of media coverage than others? What historical narratives and cultural identities were emphasized in coverage of various sports? These are the kinds of questions addressed in this chapter.

Emergence of the Daily Press

Early newspapers in British North America were directed at the small, literate elite of business and professional men in each colony, and most papers were tied directly to one of the major political parties. These party journals were generally published once or twice a week. However, between 1840 and 1900, the Canadian newspaper industry was revolutionized by the emergence of the urban daily press.[5] The first successful daily newspapers in Canada were a pair of party-affiliated papers—the conservative *Montreal Gazette* and the liberal *Montreal Herald*—that switched over to daily publication in the early 1840s. By the end of the 1850s, the leading Ontario papers and the most prominent anglophone journals in Montreal were all dailies. By the mid-1870s, publishers in Atlantic Canada, francophone Quebec, and Manitoba had followed suit. As a result, Rowell's *American Newspaper Directory* of 1873 indicated 48 daily newspapers operating throughout Canada. In 1900, there were 121 dailies in the country, and by 1913, this total had climbed to 138. Meanwhile, the total circulation of the daily editions of newspapers in Canada climbed from 113,000 in 1876 to 575,000 in 1900.[6]

A number of factors contributed to the development of the mass press in Canada during the second half of the 19th century.[7] First, improvements in printing technology and paper manufacturing enabled publishers to produce greater numbers of newspapers, more quickly and efficiently. At the same time, accelerating industrial expansion allowed newspapers to generate greater advertising revenue as manufacturers and retailers attempted to sell more consumer goods to wider groups of people beyond the cultured class. In addition, the mass press benefitted significantly from the expanding markets that emerged from a fast-growing, increasingly urbanized population with greater levels of discretionary income and "free" time thanks to an increasingly distinct delineation between work and leisure (see chapter 6). The continued development of the country's largest cities—particularly Toronto and Montreal—and the rise of new urban centres across the country—especially in Western Canada—helped sustain the growth of the daily press in the late 19th and early 20th centuries.[8] Finally, widespread public education and rising literacy rates considerably broadened the potential market for daily newspapers.[9]

The most important change in the Canadian newspaper industry between 1890 and 1920 was the transformation of the Canadian press into a corporate and commercialized institution. Although newspapers still functioned as political advocates, more entrepreneurial-minded publishers now believed "the prime purpose of newspapers was to make money by attracting more readers and thus more advertisers."[10] An influential new group of more independent "people's journals" led the way in this pursuit of profit through the sale of mass audiences. The most successful practitioners of this first wave of people's journalism in central Canada were the *Star* (1869) and *La Presse* (1884) of Montreal; the *Telegram* (1876), the *World* (1880), the *News* (1881), and the *Star* (1892) of Toronto; the *Ottawa Journal* (1885); and the *Hamilton Herald* (1889).[11] These new dailies appealed not only to businessmen, professionals, and party supporters but also to clerks, working-class men, and women and children from across the social spectrum. Most important, the people's press placed a much higher priority on bringing readers news and information rather than opinion. Publishers devoted more space to sensational subjects like war, crime, disaster, and scandal while emphasizing human interest stories, leisure, and local events. The people's journals also added an assortment of special features aimed at specific groups of readers. These features included humour, gossip, and advice columns; crime stories and serialized novels; women's sections and children's pages; and comic strips and sports coverage. This distinct shift towards news, entertainment, and popular culture produced a substantial increase in press coverage of sports.

The close connection between newspapers, sports teams, and local identity was a crucial contributor to the prominence of sport in the print media. As promoters of their city, newspapers were important instruments of civic boosterism—the effort on the part of local politicians and business leaders to encourage economic and population growth by developing a dynamic image for their town or city in comparison with its competitors (see chapter 7).[12] By the 1900s, while newspapers assumed the role of civic builder, sports teams were emerging as symbolic representatives of their communities. As a result, it is not surprising that media coverage of sport embodied aspects of boosterism, civic identity, and community pride. At first, teams were made up almost exclusively of local athletes, but civic and business leaders soon began to import professional players—and give them jobs and money—in order to ensure success on the field or ice.[13] These developments, in particular the emergence of an open labour market of travelling players, gradually diminished the organic connection between teams and their communities. Soon, it simply did not matter whether players were local "products," just as long as they won and put the community on the map.

The symbiotic relationship between newspapers, civic elites, and sporting entrepreneurs helped drive the emergence and growth of professional team sports in the late 19th and early 20th centuries. Through daily sports coverage, "metropolitan papers developed serial-type narratives around the fortunes of their home teams, beginning with pre-season signings and prognostications, and continuing through the successes and disappointments of a sporting season."[14] Because of its serialized nature, this continuous local sports coverage was extremely effective in mobilizing civic identifications around a city's sports teams. In addition, when newspapers started paying more attention to sport, they became valuable publicity agents for local clubs and athletes. Across Canada, media coverage of sport flourished within the cauldron of intercommunity rivalry. "Teams were to be supported," as Whitson has noted, "both as civic institutions and local businesses, and the language in which fan loyalty was solicited mixed the promotional jingles of business with the rhetoric of community pride in a frank and unapologetic way."[15]

Another significant development in sports journalism during the late 19th and early 20th centuries was the increasingly national and international scope of sports coverage. With the advent of the telegraph and national and international wire services, the daily press could supply readers with immediate sports results from other parts of Canada, the United States, and the world. Newspapers quickly "became some of the biggest customers of the telegraph companies, and the . . . information in their pages became both fuller and timelier."[16] Wire services like the Associated Press and Canadian Press enabled people in all parts of North America to share a common base of information, drawing them into a broad-based community of fans and followers of sport beyond locally representative teams and individual athletes.[17] Thus began a gradual process of delocalization, where sports fans were increasingly encouraged to embrace mediated elective affinities as consumers of national and continental sporting events, teams, and celebrity athletes.

Indeed, events perceived to be of national or international significance attracted considerable media attention by the late 19th century, and coverage of nationally important leagues, teams, and events accelerated after the First World War.[18] For example, media coverage of the 1892 heavyweight championship boxing match between John L. Sullivan and James J. Corbett, held in New Orleans, Louisiana, was extensive, with newspapers across Canada carrying several columns of writing about the fight and its aftermath.[19] Likewise, baseball's World Series was described as "Canada's greatest 'national' sporting event" in the 1920s, as newspapers throughout the country provided detailed reports on the games themselves, the players involved, and other happenings surrounding the series.[20] Prior to the 1929 World Series, for instance, the *Manitoba Free Press* assured its readers that "arrangements have been completed for a thorough coverage of the series in the *Free Press*, by the best sportswriters of the United Press and the Associated Press. Not a detail will be missed."[21] In helping to establish civic followings and communities of interest for various teams and athletes, the media thus played a monumental role in the making of major-league sport, in the establishment of the major leagues as national institutions across Canada, and in the creation of fan and consumer identities.

TRANSFORMATIVE MOMENTS: TELEGRAPH RECONSTRUCTIONS

By the early 1900s, sport was becoming an entertainment commodity that attracted significant numbers of spectators. One of the frequently overlooked aspects of sports spectatorship and the development of the sports media is the way people gathered to experience distant games and events "live" through telegraph reconstructions. As the first element of the electronic media to have an impact on sport, the telegraph not only carried sports news to wide numbers of fans but also enabled interested followers of sport to enjoy major events as they were occurring elsewhere. The telegraph opened up the possibility of a completely new experience of sport when someone had the idea of bringing telegraphers right to the boxing ring, ballpark, or hockey arena in order to create simultaneous coverage of important matches.[22] The telegraph operator sat with a sportswriter or other knowledgeable fan and sent reports of the action to newspaper offices, hotels, or theatres, where "decoded game accounts were either read aloud to assembled fans, or transcripts were posted on bulletin boards."[23] More elaborate reconstructions developed later for baseball, in particular, as large crowds watched games charted on illuminated model diamonds while an announcer with a megaphone described the action from the telegraph wire.[24]

The 1896 Stanley Cup challenges between the Winnipeg Victorias and the Montreal Victorias were likely the first two games in which the technology of telegraphy was applied to the sport of hockey in such a way that large crowds in distant cities could experience matches as they were being played.[25] For example, in February 1896, hundreds of hockey fans met at three of Winnipeg's most prominent hotels to listen to telegraph reports sent from Montreal over Canadian Pacific Railway wires as the prairie club became the first team from Western Canada to capture the Stanley Cup.[26] In December 1896, the *Montreal Star* emphasized how its telegraph arrangements would create a strong sense of immediacy and participation among local fans who could not attend the Stanley Cup in Winnipeg: "Every incident of the game will be sent in as it occurs over the *Star*'s special wire to the *Star*'s operator in the booth in the Victoria Rink [in Montreal], and will be posted without loss of time on the bulletin boards so that the people here will be told of what has happened almost as soon as the people in Winnipeg see it happen."[27]

The Sports Pages

The emergence of sports reporting in Canadian dailies, the development of the profession of sports journalism, and the introduction of entire sections of the paper devoted to sports coverage were linked closely to the growing significance of commercial advertising in the newspaper business. These changes were driven by the emergence of a new form of commercial advertising in general, one that sought to stimulate demand and the desire to consume rather than simply provide information about a product and its cost. By 1900, as these new strategies took hold, advertising revenue made up 65 to 70 percent of the total income of Canadian newspapers.[28] Publishers increasingly looked upon their newspapers "not so much as products to be sold to readers, but more as vehicles that organized audiences into clearly identifiable target groups that could be sold to advertisers; the audiences themselves became the 'products' generated by the media industry."[29] Although owners of mass circulation dailies introduced many new features aimed at women and children, especially in their weekend editions, they recognized that male wage earners and businessmen constituted the core market for daily newspapers. Along with reports on politics, business, and labour, sports coverage was an effective means of consistently and reliably reaching this audience. In addition, as Richard Gruneau and David Whitson point out, the sports pages were

> proving to be good not only for building circulation, but also for opening up connections to new sources of advertising revenues from businesses interested in speaking primarily to male consumers. These businesses included beer, alcohol, and tobacco-product producers in addition to sporting goods companies, sports promoters, rail and tram companies, and hotel operators.[30]

Publishers didn't just sell newspapers to readers; they also sold readers to advertisers. Sports coverage—and the establishment of a distinctive sports page—helped them achieve their goals in both of these areas.

The popularity of the people's journals spurred changes in the traditional party press. Copying the industry's most successful innovations, these transformed "quality" papers also sought a bigger audience by expanding their news coverage and their use of special features, including sports reporting.[31] Competition "had forced newspapers to find readers among all classes of the community," and, as a result, the daily paper "was fast becoming a standardized product."[32] By the early 20th century, most Canadian newspapers grouped sports news together on a distinctive sports page, including such widely read papers as the *Montreal Star*, the *Montreal Gazette*, *La Presse* of Montreal, the *Toronto Globe*, the *Toronto World*, the *Manitoba Free Press*, and the *Winnipeg Tribune*. Newspapers that had not yet established a separate sports page—such as the *Halifax Herald*, the *Saint John Sun*, the *Vancouver World*, and the *Victoria Colonist*—usually published a special column or two of sports information each day. By 1910, newer dailies in Saskatchewan and Alberta, such as the *Regina Leader*, the *Saskatoon Phoenix*, the *Calgary Herald*, and the *Edmonton Bulletin*, also set aside a specific page for sports coverage. In their Saturday editions, some papers included a more comprehensive sports section that ranged from two to eight pages and was filled with stories, photos, and illustrations.[33] By the 1920s, this sports section was a standard element of the daily newspaper, bringing readers across Canada detailed summaries, statistics, pictures, opinions, and analysis.

By reporting on recent happenings, commenting on current issues, and advising people about future events, urban dailies—and the sports journalists who worked there—became highly effective sport promoters and helped cultivate paying customers. When American baseball writers formed a national association in 1887, they noted that "the game has found in the reporters its best ally and most powerful supporter."[34] In some cases, members of the press played a more direct part in the promotion and organization of teams and leagues. For example, two of the most prominent figures in Canadian amateur hockey around the turn of the century were newspaper owners: John Ross Robertson, publisher of the *Toronto Telegram* and president of the Ontario Hockey Association from 1899 to 1905, and P.D. Ross, publisher of the *Ottawa Evening Journal* and a Stanley Cup trustee. Similarly, W.A. Hewitt, sports editor at the *Toronto Star*, served as the influential secretary of the OHA for many years, while Frank Calder, sports editor at the *Montreal Herald*, became the first president of the National Hockey League (NHL) in 1917.[35] Lou Marsh worked in various capacities for the *Toronto Star* between 1893 and 1936, including stints as a reporter, editor, and, in particular, a widely read and respected sports columnist. Meanwhile, Marsh also coached champion sprinter Bobby Kerr and marathon runner Tom Longboat, refereed boxing matches, and became involved in sailing, motorboat racing, and horse racing. Most notably, Marsh officiated Olympic hockey games in 1924 and 1932 and worked as an NHL referee for more than a decade, while continuing to write about the players he policed and the games he supervised.[36]

By the late 1920s, female sports journalists were also extensively involved in the coverage, promotion, and administration of women's sport. Alexandrine Gibb became a popular sports columnist for the *Toronto Star* in 1928 after effectively leading several local, provincial, and national sport organizations and managing a number of international athletic teams.[37] In 1928, Gibb was also named manager of the extraordinarily successful Canadian women's Olympic track and field team in Amsterdam, Netherlands, and elected president of the Women's Amateur Athletic Federation of Canada. Her column, "No Man's Land of Sport: News and Views of Feminine Activities," appeared six days a week in the *Star*'s sports pages until 1940, often alongside sports editor Marsh's column, "With Pick and Shovel."[38] As a result, Gibb had a powerful platform for distributing news, information, advice, and commentary on women's sport.

Newspaper columns focusing on women's sport popped up all over the country in the 1920s and 1930s, contributing significantly to the growth of women's sport in the interwar period and "ensuring regular and sympathetic coverage of happenings and debates."[41] Gibb was one of a number of women sportswriters who used their high-profile positions in the media, their athletic experiences, and their roles in various sport organizations to publicize and develop sport for women and to boost readership for newspapers. Phyllis Griffiths wrote her column, "The Girl and the Game," for the *Toronto Telegram* from 1928 to 1942, and Myrtle Cook's column, "In the Women's Sportlight," appeared in the *Montreal Star* for more than 40 years, beginning in 1929.[42] Fanny "Bobbie" Rosenfeld began writing her column in the *Toronto Globe and Mail*, "Feminine Sports Reel," in 1937, and it continued until 1958.[43] In Western Canada, Patricia

PROMINENT PEOPLE: ALEXANDRINE GIBB (1891-1958)

A successful athlete, organizer, and journalist, Alexandrine Gibb (see figure 12.1) wrote a column covering women's sport as part of the *Toronto Star's* sports section from 1928 to 1940. As an administrator, Gibb's guiding principle was to establish "girls' sport run by girls": In M. Ann Hall's words, "She was determined that women should run their own sports, that girls should be coached by women, and although men were encouraged as advisors, they must stay in the background."[39] Still, while Gibb's views of athletic opportunities and power for women were progressive in many ways—especially in her "focus on ensuring girls and women equal access to sport and recreation opportunities long available to boys and men"—her ideas about "femininity and athleticism fitted the prevailing attitudes of the time." Hall notes, "She was forever reminding readers about the beauty of Canadian women athletes with comments like she is a 'looker' or a 'fair-haired beauty', and at the same time, she was caustically critical of 'mannish women athletes' especially when the Canadian 'dainty girl runners' had to compete against them."[40] Nearly a century later, many of the tensions evident in Gibb's newspaper writings continue to frame our conversations about contemporary female athletes.

City of Toronto Archives, Fonds 1257, Series 1057, Item 3059

Figure 12.1 Alexandrine Gibb.

Page Hollingsworth wrote "Feminine Flashes" for the *Edmonton Journal* (1935-1940), Lillian "Jimmy" Coo wrote "Cherchez la Femme" for the *Winnipeg Free Press* (1937-1942, 1946-1947), and Ann Stott (1939-1941) and Ruth Wilson (1943-1945) wrote "Femmes in Sport" (later "Femmes and Foibles in Sport") for the *Vancouver Sun*.[44] However, following the Second World War, these prominent media voices supporting women's sport had largely disappeared as the reach and visibility of men's professional sport—and the value of postwar male audiences in the television era—continued to expand.[45]

The Radio Era

During the 1920s and 1930s, radio began to contribute significantly to the development of sports audiences in North America, radically altering their experiences by bringing live transmissions of sporting events into homes across the country.[46] Canada's first radio transmitter licence was issued in 1919, and over the next two decades radio expanded rapidly across the dominion.[47] In 1923, there were 9,954 receiving licences in Canada. By 1929, Canadians owned 297,398 receiving licences, and 85 broadcast stations were operating in the country. Similarly, the production of radios rose from 48,000 in 1925 to 150,000 in 1929. In 1931, approximately one-third of Canadian households owned a radio. By 1940, 75 percent of Canadian homes possessed a radio receiver of some kind.[48] These radio sets were tuned in to programs that originated in a variety of locations, ranging from a broadcaster just down the street to a station hundreds of miles away.

Canadian broadcasters faced strong competition from programming that originated in the United States in this period, particularly in the 1920s. First, Canadian stations were low powered compared with American stations, which could often beam their programming across the continent. In addition, the lack of agreement between the two countries on the allocation of radio wavelengths meant Canadian stations were often overwhelmed by powerful foreign stations on or near the same channels—a matter of tremendous concern for cultural nationalists who decried the increasing incursion of U.S. popular culture. As a result, many Canadians—particularly in rural areas—received Canadian signals with great difficulty or not at all. While "every radio receiver in Canada could pick up an American station, only three in five Canadian radios could receive a Canadian station."[49] According to one journalist, "Nine-tenths of the radio fans in the Dominion hear three or four times as many United States stations as Canadian."[50] Even in cities, most Canadians seem to have listened to American broadcasts, especially in the evenings; a notable exception to this pattern was, of course, in Quebec and other francophone communities, where French-language programming was dominant.

In the early years of radio, the bulk of the sports broadcasting received by Canadians therefore came from U.S. stations. Radio's commercial potential was first demonstrated in 1921 when the Jack Dempsey–Georges Carpentier heavyweight championship fight was broadcast to audiences across North America. Like their counterparts in the print media, radio manufacturers and broadcasters soon turned to sports programming to stimulate sales of radio sets. And when station owners began to recognize the potential profitability of radio advertising, they began using sport to build audiences to sell to advertisers, thus extending the reach of advertising and further normalizing consumerism. By the late 1920s, "U.S. radio was well established as an advertiser-driven commercial system with a major proportion of programming devoted to sports and light entertainment."[51] The importance of the national marketing possibilities offered by radio sports was by now undeniable:

> The early successes of professional sports broadcasts in attracting listeners far from their "home" cities also attracted the attention of major manufacturers of mass consumer products. Companies like GM, Gillette, and Imperial Oil were looking, in the interwar years, for effective ways of advertising to national audiences, and their initiatives in sponsoring networked broadcasts of professional sports

contributed in no small way to establishing the status of the "major leagues" as national institutions, as well as themselves as national brand names.[52]

Early radio coverage of sport focused mainly on the biggest national and continental events, rather than on local, regularly scheduled contests, and on capturing a largely male audience commodity that could be sold to advertisers. In fact, "many owners of professional sports teams were initially suspicious of radio, believing that people would simply stay home and listen to games rather than attend games live."[53] Nevertheless, major happenings like the World Series, championship boxing matches, and the Rose Bowl quickly became staples of radio programming. Broadcasts of World Series games, for example, attracted millions of North American listeners by the mid-1920s.[54] Boxing broadcasts also proved to be extremely popular. In 1927, the more than 104,000 people who attended the second Jack Dempsey–Gene Tunney match at Chicago's Soldier Field were joined at ringside by the approximately 50 million radio listeners tuning in to a 73-station radio network assembled by NBC.[55] In 1938, as many as two-thirds of Americans—and likely a similar proportion of people in Canada—heard Joe Louis knock out Germany's Max Schmeling in the first round. "Probably no other event in radio history . . . enjoyed such a large audience," writes Benjamin G. Rader.[56]

By the 1930s, sports programming was carried regularly by Canadian radio stations as well, and these broadcasts quickly became central to the rhythm of the lives of Canadian sports fans. Although privately owned stations continued to exist, the Radio Broadcasting Act of 1932 created a government-owned Canadian Radio Broadcasting Commission (CRBC) to regulate radio broadcasting and provide radio service to all Canadians. However, the commission did not have sufficient funding to fulfill this mandate. In 1936, the CRBC was reorganized into the Canadian Broadcasting Corporation (CBC). Although a completely government-owned broadcasting system never came into being, the CBC achieved considerable success in assembling a Canada-wide network of CBC-operated stations and privately owned affiliates.[57] The CBC network also provided extensive coverage of major national and international sporting events, as indicated by the following summary of sports broadcasts in the CBC's *Annual Report* for 1937-38:

> The CBC was able to make available to its listeners throughout Canada most of the principal sporting events of the period, in Canada, the United States, and England. These included running commentaries on the Ryder Cup Matches (BBC), American Yacht Races (NBC), the principal rugby games, including the Big Four Championship game, the Farr-Braddock Fight (special CBC commentary), the NHL Hockey Games (Imperial Oil Company), the Strickland-Delaney Fight (BBC), the Dominion Ski Championships, the Governor General's Curling Match, the World Baseball Series (NBC), the Davis Cup Matches (BBC), the Bisley Shoot (BBC), the Canadian Tennis Tournament, the Dominion Lacrosse Finals, the International Dog Sled Derby from Quebec City, [and] the Grand National Steeplechase (BBC).[58]

Although Canadians were avid followers of baseball and boxing, in particular, these sports could not match the remarkable popularity that hockey broadcasts had achieved in Canada by the end of the 1930s. Regular Canadian radio coverage of hockey started in 1923 with broadcasts of local amateur games on CFCA, the *Toronto Star*'s radio station. In 1931, Toronto Maple Leafs owner Conn Smythe, MacLaren Advertising, and General Motors worked out a deal that paved the way for regular Saturday night broadcasts of Maple Leafs games. In January 1933, coast-to-coast hockey broadcasts began in Canada when General Motors put together a loose network of 20 stations across the country to carry its Saturday night NHL broadcasts. As a result, "NHL hockey became one of the first radio programs to address a national Canadian audience."[59]

To solidify this national radio audience, General Motors bought the broadcast rights for the Montreal Canadiens and the Montreal Maroons in the summer of 1933. The acquisition of rights to the games of the NHL's three Canadian-based clubs "set the stage for truly national hockey broadcasts, with Montreal games broadcast in English and French in Quebec and Toronto games aired across the rest of the country."[60] In 1934, these General Motors broadcasts were reaching more than a million Canadians. By the end of the 1930s, *Hockey Night in Canada*—now sponsored by Imperial Oil and carried on the CBC network—had a national audience of two million listeners. Foster Hewitt's broadcasts from Maple Leaf Gardens in Toronto turned millions of Canadians into followers of NHL hockey—and, especially, into fans of the Maple Leafs (see figure 12.2).[61] Don Twaits, a former advertising manager with Imperial Oil, summarized the impact of these radio broadcasts in a 1984 interview:

Archives of Ontario, reference code C 5-1-0-110-2

Figure 12.2 Sports broadcaster Foster Hewitt in his office in 1944.

For years *Hockey Night in Canada* was really the only "national" broadcasting in Canada. . . . It was one of the few network shows that carried right across Canada and into the far reaches of the North. It was a unique sports broadcasting program. Nothing ever like it in North America, in those terms—no other kind of audience. After that it was not unusual for surveys to tell you they had 65 per cent of everybody in the country listening to NHL playoffs.[62]

In 1934, for example, an estimated 72 percent of the approximately one million radio sets in Canada tuned into the MacLaren hockey network's coverage of the Stanley Cup semifinals.[63] These nationwide hockey broadcasts, which were available for any Canadian with a radio set, were milestone events in the development of a Canadian national popular culture. "Never had so many Canadians in all corners of the country regularly engaged in the same cultural experience at the same time."[64]

Content and Cultural Narratives: Sports Media Texts

Much of this chapter approaches the sports media from an institutional perspective by describing and analyzing the media structures—mainly newspapers, radio, and television—through which Canadians have experienced sport culture. Another approach to understanding media is to examine the content—in other words, the media texts and cultural narratives—that readers, listeners, and viewers have engaged through these institutions.[65] In particular, we focus here on how the media has shaped perceptions of gender, race, ethnicity, and local and national identities. We also examine these media texts in relation to larger cultural discourses and social relations. In this way, we introduce the ideas and methods utilized in historical studies of sports media narratives in order to understand the cultural meanings constructed by and through the sports media.

A helpful approach to the study of sports media texts is offered by Michael Oriard in his studies of American football since the late 19th century.[66] Oriard explores the multiple cultural narratives created by football reporting, commentary, stories, illustrations, photographs, films, and other media representations of the game. His research reveals there was no "single monolithic interpretation of the game but multiple narratives to which readers could respond."[67] Football coverage—like sports reporting in general—was characterized by a variety of competing and conflicting media discourses related to gender, race, class, and ethnic and community identities. As a result, media coverage of football offered fans and spectators a variety of meanings and interpretive possibilities. For example, Oriard highlights the dramatically different messages about youth football presented by the media.[68] The cover of the September 1936 issue of *Good Housekeeping* magazine featured a romantic, sentimentalized image of a cute, curious young boy putting on what appeared to be his big brother's football shoes. Inside the magazine, however, a chilling article titled "Death on the Football Field" described what could happen if the reader's son—someone like the kid on the cover—was "brutally hit" and severely injured after catching a ball: "If the accident happens in a little town, he will be rushed in some bouncing, honking automobile to a hospital cot, there to die in a little while in a haven ill-equipped to combat such unique visits of death."[69] These contrasting portrayals of football within the same issue of a popular periodical illustrate the potential for the media to present a variety of cultural and ideological narratives to consumers.

Sport historians and sociologists have often used textual analysis of sports coverage to shed light on the cultural meanings of sport over time. Such studies of sports media texts have provided important insight into questions of social identity and difference in Canadian sport history. For instance, an examination of sports reporting provides a valuable perspective on perceptions of female athletes in different time periods. Carly Adams shows how women's hockey teams challenged prevailing notions of femininity and athleticism in the 1920s and 1930s by playing a fast, tough, and exciting brand of hockey that attracted significant numbers of spectators.[70] Women's hockey was "one of the best money-getters" at the Banff Winter Carnival between 1917 and 1939, and carnival organizers responded by "endorsing women's hockey in carnival brochures, inviting teams to compete during the carnival, and positioning the women's hockey tournament as a marquee event."[71] Banff's *Crag and Canyon* newspaper described a "well contested" women's hockey match on a "crowded" rink at the town's first winter festival as "a hard fight": "Close checking was one of the main features, many members of both teams receiving bad spills."[72]

However, when "women hockey players pushed the boundaries of acceptable femininity" in this way, "they often faced reprimand and rebuke for playing hockey aggressively and competitively."[73] For example, a *Calgary Herald* reporter criticized the Calgary Regents team after a violent game in 1922: "Regents resorted to rough play on more than one occasion. The ladies must remember that although the hockey dished up by them in the past has been appreciated the fans will not tolerate any rough stuff, and besides it will not get them anywhere, except the cooler."[74] Narratives of skilled, popular, and physical female hockey players therefore existed in tension with admonishments to avoid, in the words of a *Toronto Star* writer, "anything which savours of rough and unladylike play."[75]

Different meanings and standards for male and female athletes are also evident in media coverage of Olympic sport in this period. During the 1920s, women's growing presence in international sporting competitions gave them a role in manufacturing national identities as "icons of liberty," but these new athletic heroines were also used by newspapers and magazines for their "sex appeal" and promoted as "objects of desire."[76] For example, Mark Dyreson shows that in photographs published during the 1920 Olympic Games, American female swimmers and divers "appeared in alluring poses in their swim-suits under headlines that celebrated their physical appeal, such as 'A Bevy of Fair American Mermaids.'"[77] The athletic appearance of male Olympians contrasted with the contrived postures of female athletes, as in a series of 1922 photographs depicting swimmers Johnny Weissmuller and Ethelda Bleibtrey:

Weissmuller appears in an action pose, ready to leap into the pool, above the caption "The Fastest Swimmer in the World". Bleibtrey's snapshot appears right next to Weissmuller's, her hand on one of her hips, her breasts prominently displayed in silhouette, smiling beguilingly at the camera, above the caption "A Modern Mermaid With No Rival".[78]

Similarly, newspapers covered Canadian athletes like high jumper Ethel Catherwood—the 1928 Olympic champion and world record holder—in a style normally reserved for movie starlets, merging nationalism, celebrity, and sexuality. Catherwood's nickname—"the Saskatoon Lily"—emphasized her "statuesque beauty" over her athletic ability, and writers often highlighted her popularity with photographers and her potential as a Hollywood actress. For instance, a *Toronto Star* article published during the 1928 Summer Olympics featured Lillian Gibbell, a "famous beauty specialist in Hollywood," analyzing Catherwood's and sprinter Myrtle Cook's attractiveness and complexion, and assessing their chances of making it onto the silver screen.[79] At the same time, however, Catherwood's gold medal (and world record) in the high jump and, on the same day, the Canadian track team's first-place finish (and world record) in the women's 4 × 100-metre relay put the country's female Olympians on the front page of the sports section in Canadian newspapers as a result of their athletic accomplishments.[80]

Nevertheless, despite the increased attention paid to female athletes in the interwar period, male professional teams and players—as well as a number of elite male amateur athletes—continued to dominate coverage of the sporting world. During the 1920s and 1930s, the North American mass press was manufacturing national and international male sports heroes like never before. As journalists paid more attention "to individual players, their skills, styles, and personalities," and wrote about the best players "in a mythic style of language that spoke to popular desires for larger-than-life events and personalities," they focused on star athletes like Babe Ruth, Christy Mathewson, Jack Dempsey, Joe Louis, Red Grange, Bobby Jones, Bill Tilden, and Jesse Owens.[81] This exclusion and marginalization of high-level women athletes in favour of male sports "superstars" continues across many different media platforms today.

Media coverage of sport included implicit and, at times, more overt narratives of race, as well. For example, one way that mainly white audiences encountered Black baseball players prior to the integration of professional baseball after the Second World War was through "barnstorming" tours in which "coloured" teams travelled throughout Canada and the United States and played games against local clubs (see chapter 11).[82] Colin Howell writes that these "barnstorming black teams found themselves caught in the contradictions of a predominately white market-place," and, as a result, "they often had to cultivate an image of 'otherness' that played upon white racial theories about the different characteristics of the races." To attract fans, touring Black baseball teams frequently engaged in "clowning and buffoonery" that "appealed to the worst racial stereotypes." At the same time, however, these highly skilled athletes displayed "the smooth and slick style that black players brought to the game."[83]

Sportswriters often commented on the "ludicrous" and comical incidents that occurred during such tours, echoing an 1896 *Sporting News* article that described Black players as "full of original humor, and the best entertainer[s] imaginable."[84] For instance, a team known as the Zulu Cannibal Giants toured the Maritimes in 1936, winning the vast majority of their games and drawing large crowds while "pushing all of the stereotypes associated with African tribal life to the limit": "Dressed in regulation pants and baseball shoes, the Cannibal Giants were stripped to the waist, wore fuzzy head-dresses, and painted their chests and faces 'in the best cinematic presentation of a cannibal.'"[85] Media representations of Black baseball therefore expressed discourses of racial difference and marginalization alongside admiring accounts of athletic accomplishment.

Other media reports, meanwhile, constructed narratives of Indigenous engagement with sport against the historical backdrop of genocide by the Government of Canada and churches against Indigenous peoples. Andrew Holman's study of the 1927 to 1928 hockey barnstorming tour carried out by 18 members of the Cree and Ojibway First Nations based in northern Ontario offers a unique historical view of sport and race relations.[86] Holman begins with a photograph of two teams of Indigenous players "dressed in ice hockey gear, buckskin jerseys, and feathered headdresses," gathered in front of a charter bus below a sign advertising the "Cree & Ojibway Indian Hockey Tour" (see figure 12.3).[87] The tour reached 22 towns and cities in Ontario and the northeastern United States, with the group sometimes dividing into two teams and facing off for what was billed as the "Indian Hockey Championship of Canada," and at other times challenging a local aggregation of white settler players.[88]

Figure 12.3   Cree and Ojibway hockey teams in Queen's Park in Toronto on January 11, 1928.

The Cree and Ojibway teams were commonly framed by media for an audience of settler Canadian readers within widely held racial stereotypes that drew upon Wild West imagery, "replete with references to raiding parties, scalping, and Native 'savagery.'"[89] For example, looking ahead to the tour's arrival, the *Windsor Star* reported, "From the pine-clad . . . shores of old lake Temagami, a feather-crested tribe of Cree redskins will sweep into the Border Cities Monday night to do battle with the Windsor Chicks hockey brigade on the local Arena's ice surface. The Indians from the north are touring the Dominion and expect to collect a few scalps on their Windsor stop."[90] Similarly, the *Orillia Packet and Times* wrote, "With hockey sticks instead of war clubs, and skates in place of moccasins, and puck in lieu of arrows, the touring Indian tribe of Ojibways [sic] put the Orillia junior O.H.A. team to the rout, with a total of three scalps to one."[91]

Holman identifies three specific narratives created by local sportswriters to explain the meanings and significance of the Cree–Ojibway barnstorming tour: hockey "as an authentically indigenous game" that originated in northern Native culture; the tour as "a clever exercise in modern enterprise" designed to benefit First Nations players in their summer employment as hunting and fishing guides by selling northern tourism to white audiences; and the sporting spectacle as "a subversive self-parody, a drama of racial mockery and power inversion" in which Indigenous athletes had "a laugh at their paying customers' expense."[92] First, Holman explores the complex ways in which Indigenous players were praised by sportswriters as the ancient inventors of hockey and admired for their individual skill and determination, while, at the same time, being criticized for retaining a "primitive" approach to the sport that lacked both scientific teamwork and the strategic use of violence.[93] Second, Holman shows that the tour's organizers, Willie and Joe Friday, were experienced wilderness guides and successful promoters who used the hockey excursion as a means of developing and renewing connections with wealthy white "sportsmen in southern Ontario and the United States, who continued to bring their families and their wallets to northeastern Ontario when summer came."[94] Finally, Holman suggests the Fridays and other tour participants subtly used racial imagery and expectations for their own purposes by "playing Indian," thereby poking fun at prevailing ideas of race and at "those who could not see them as they really were, namely, modern capitalists with a sense of humor and a flair for the dramatic."[95] He concludes that the Cree and Ojibway hockey tour became "a prompt for a larger discourse about identity: who Natives had become in the popular mind of the 1920s cast alongside (and against) who they wished to be."[96]

Sports media texts also offer insight into unequal ethnic relations in Canada. Most notably, they demonstrate the French–English divide that has characterized Canadian society and culture. A vivid illustration of tensions between French Canadians and English Canadians can be seen in newspaper coverage of the Richard Riot in Montreal in March 1955.[97] Following a violent altercation with members of the Boston Bruins, Montreal Canadiens superstar Maurice "Rocket" Richard was suspended by NHL president Clarence Campbell for the remainder of the 1955 regular season and playoffs. Richard was widely viewed as a representative symbol of French-Canadian identity, and he had previously called Campbell out as a "dictateur" who was biased against francophone players.[98] When Campbell attended the next Canadiens game at the Montreal Forum, fans greeted him with insults and a barrage of tomatoes thrown from higher in the stands. After a tear gas bomb exploded inside the building, the arena was evacuated and a riot began on the streets outside. Suzanne Laberge's examination of press responses to Richard's suspension shows a clear French–English split in perceptions of Campbell's decision: "Anglophone newspapers emphasized Richard's unacceptable violence on the ice and Campbell's necessary firmness, while the French-language newspapers unanimously denounced Campbell's unwarranted severity and the ethnic discrimination it represented."[99] Similarly, while articles and opinion pieces in English newspapers praised Campbell's courage in appearing at the Forum and denounced the "hotheads" and "hooligans" who started the riot, the francophone press blamed Campbell for blatantly provoking and challenging French-Canadian fans. For example, a writer in *Dimanche-Matin* stated, "Mr. Campbell is nothing but a windbag and a demagogue who is not afraid to risk the lives of hundreds of people to satisfy his personal pride."[100]

As noted earlier, with its power to express community aspirations, sport has acted as a vehicle for the dramatization of interurban rivalries in Canada since the late 19th century. As a result, the relationship between sport and community identity is another rich area of possibility for the textual analysis of sports coverage. Owners and editors of urban dailies eagerly promoted their cities and advertised them to the outside world as prosperous, modern places to attract greater numbers of settlers and greater amounts of capital. At the same time, competitive sporting events provided opportunities to uphold civic pride and advance community prestige. As early as the 1850s, narratives of civic boosterism were evident in newspaper coverage of sport.[101] "A grand curling match is to be fought to-day between the crack players of Toronto and Hamilton," reported the *Toronto Globe* in 1855. After giving a list of the Toronto curlers, the writer added that "if they don't lick the 'ambitious little city,' they need never again show their faces in Toronto!"[102] Two days later, the *Globe* posted a follow-up:

> The great trial of strength between the Curlers of Toronto and Hamilton came duly off on Saturday on Burlington Bay. The day was delightful, the ice good, and the contest keen. The Torontonians won the day—so they may come home. . . . We are glad to see they did the thing generously; it would not have looked well in a great city like Toronto to beat severely a rising little place.[103]

Similarly, the Maritime rivalry between the cities of Saint John and Halifax was reflected in the sports pages through coverage of professional baseball in the late 1880s:

> Whenever it could, the Saint John press contrasted the bustling exuberance of the New Brunswick centre to that of somnolent Halifax. A dispatch from the

Saint John Telegraph, carried in the Halifax newspapers on 31 July 1888, described games between the Nationals of Saint John and the Atlantas of Halifax as a "very easy contract" and suggested that if Halifax remained uncompetitive, the Nats would have to go south of the border to find better competition. "The Atlantas play good ball in the quiet town of Halifax," the *Telegraph* concluded, "but when they come to a great city like Saint John, the noise and bustle and excitement seem to unnerve them."[104]

Finally, shared media experiences of distant games and events connected Canadians in new ways by inviting fan and consumer identifications across local, regional, and national boundaries. The telegraph, wire services, and radio—along with railways, automobiles, telephones, mass-market periodicals, department stores, and national advertising campaigns—changed earlier conceptions of time and distance. As a result, people increasingly imagined themselves as belonging to larger and larger communities.[105] These developments helped create an emerging Canadian popular culture by the 1920s—a national popular culture that embraced a wide range of American entertainment products, including professional sport. During the interwar period, American movies, magazines, and radio programs found large audiences in Canada, at least outside of Quebec. For instance, Major League Baseball's teams, players, and major events originated almost entirely in the United States. As one writer pointed out in *The Canadian Forum* in 1927, when Canadian children "bowed down to Babe Ruth," they demonstrated that Canada had been conquered by the "American Empire."[106]

Professional hockey, on the other hand, was cherished as something uniquely Canadian—despite the fact that the expansion of the NHL into the profitable American market in 1925 began the league's transformation into a U.S.-dominated business.[107] Bruce Kidd also observes that by focusing exclusively on the NHL—particularly the Toronto Maple Leafs—*Hockey Night in Canada* radio broadcasts marginalized other versions of hockey in Canada, including top-flight community-based men's amateur and semi-professional hockey, women's teams, and hockey in other regions outside the Montreal–Toronto corridor.[108] Nevertheless, despite promoting the "metropolitan monoculture" of NHL hockey, CBC's *Hockey Night in Canada* "gave many people their strongest sense of pan-Canadian identity." Kidd adds, "The trials and achievements of the favourite players, the impassioned dramas of the annual Stanley Cup playoffs, and the richly textured symbolisms of the great rivalries provide many of us with an endless source of cultural narratives to ponder and share."[109] Knowing something about teams from various cities, having opinions on how the season would turn out, understanding the progress of a prominent NHL player's career—all of these had become widely recognized elements of Canadian popular culture by the 1920s and 1930s. Newspapers and radio therefore contributed to the development of a shared North American sporting culture while, at the same time, helping to create national cultural meanings for sport in Canada.

Game Change: Television

"Television didn't create sports madness," writes Paul Rutherford. "That it inherited from the press and radio. But just about any sport, even something so slow-moving as baseball, was more enjoyable with pictures."[110] His trolling of baseball aside, Rutherford makes an important point here about the continuities in how newspapers, radio, and television have been connected to sport over the past century or so—and how televised sport transformed this relationship in certain ways. Since the development of large-scale manufacturing, national brand names, and local and national markets for a wide variety of consumer products in the late 19th and early 20th centuries, the mass media has been the main vehicle through which these consumer goods, as well as a growing number of new services, have been marketed to the public.[111] The popularity of sports coverage in the print media and early radio "demonstrated the potential of sport to attract large and predictable audiences for advertisers."[112] And while the nature of this relationship has changed over the years, the power of newspapers, radio, and television to construct audiences around sport is even more apparent today.

If television was initially an emergent medium in the postwar years, it soon became dominant, further transforming the experiences of sports fans who could now watch telecasts of live sporting events in their living rooms, first in black and white and then in colour, further accelerating a process of delocalization and the creation of national, continental, and, eventually, global fan communities that had commenced decades earlier. J.M. Bumsted describes the incredible growth of early Canadian television as follows:

> Canada's first two television stations were opened in September 1952; there were 146,000 television receivers in Canada at the time. By December of 1954 there were nine stations and 1,200,000 sets; in June of 1955 twenty-six stations and 1,400,000 sets were in operation, and by December of 1957 there were forty-four stations and nearly 3 million sets. The rate of set expansion was almost twice that of the United States, and the market for new sets had been saturated within five years.[113]

Television extended patterns established by radio. First, the policy of public control and operation in the Canadian broadcast industry continued into the age of television. The federal government initially granted licensing power for television to the CBC's board of governors and gave the CBC a mandate—and a monopoly—to establish a national television network in both official languages, using a combination of CBC-owned and privately operated stations. Second, Canadian television viewers—like Canadian radio listeners—showed a clear preference for American shows, especially in prime time, although the viewing patterns of francophone viewers remained remarkably different. Most Canadian homes received American television stations, and Canadian broadcasters (both the CBC network and, later, the independent second channels in each city) carried a great deal of U.S. entertainment programming. To boost ratings and increase advertising revenues, Canadian stations imported popular American programs, particularly variety shows, domestic dramas, crime shows, comedies, and westerns. For instance, according to 1960 ratings surveys, "nearly 80 per cent of total Toronto viewing was of American programming"; even "in Edmonton, which received only Canadian stations, 66 per cent of total viewing time was spent watching American programs."[114]

Third, Canadian television followed radio by giving considerable attention to amateur and professional sports programming on the CBC network, including its French-language network, with the intention of capturing large—and primarily male—audiences that could be sold to advertisers. Indeed, by the end of the 1950s, a national network of 8 CBC stations and 41 privately owned affiliates was in place, and live sports content could be broadcast across Canada. In 1953, 11 percent of the CBC television schedule was devoted to a wide variety of sports such as hockey, football, boxing, wrestling, and baseball.[115] However, it was men's professional sport, especially the annual Grey Cup game and the Stanley Cup playoffs, that lured some of the country's biggest TV audiences, helping the CBC attract the advertising dollars of corporate sponsors. CBC/Radio-Canada and the NHL first launched a radio and television simulcast of Saturday night hockey games during the 1952 to 1953 season. As Rutherford points out, the focus was on the Canadian NHL teams: "one week the Montreal game would go coast-to-coast, the next week Toronto's, the other game shown on a local or regional basis." No local blackout was imposed when the home team was playing. However, "the telecast of games began after roughly a third of the action had passed by, this to ensure that ticket-holders got something more than was available on the tube."[116] By the early 1960s, *Hockey Night in Canada* (or *La Soirée du hockey*) consistently came out on top in the weekly ratings, drawing as many as 3.5 million viewers on the CBC network (English) and 2 million viewers on Radio-Canada (French).[117] "Not only was hockey consistently more popular than any other made-in-Canada show; it was also the one offering that could on occasion beat out the American imports in English Canada," writes Rutherford.[118]

The CBC's monopoly, however, came to an abrupt ending in 1961 with the establishment of the country's first private national network: CTV. Sport was instrumental to the creation of CTV. Businessman John Bassett, the owner of the Toronto Argonauts football club, had been awarded the private television licence for the Toronto market by the Board of Broadcast Governors (BBG), which had been established in 1958 as the governing body of Canadian broadcasters and was the predecessor of the Canadian Radio-television and Telecommunications Commission (CRTC), formed in 1968 as the Canadian Radio and Television Commission. To both the dismay and surprise of the CBC, Bassett had purchased the 1961 and 1962 rights to broadcast eastern CFL games, as well as the first right of refusal for the Grey Cup, all while lacking a genuinely national network to distribute the content. Shortly after, however, he would join Spencer Caldwell, one of Bassett's rivals for the Toronto television licence, who had been awarded the right to form a national network, to distribute the football games and secure advertising revenue. This arrangement ultimately prompted seven other newly licensed private stations to join the national private network, which received final approval to operate in 1961. Without this popular sports content, "CTV might never have emerged as a network."[119]

Importantly, CBC now had to compete with CTV for sports broadcast rights— a development that escalated the cost to secure those rights—and the two networks expanded their coverage of sport dramatically to deliver significant audiences for advertisers. Indeed, during years of growth and prosperity in the postwar period, "sport officials grew increasingly aware of how television could enhance the popularity of their activity and television executives became more appreciative of how sport could help them attract larger audiences and advertising dollars."[120] Sports broadcasts, in particular, captured a middle- and upper-class male audience commodity (between 18 and 49 years of age) that CTV and CBC could then sell to advertisers for significant sums of money. As Rutherford notes, "Sports were undeniably a 'male' genre: that was the only brand of programming in which the typical adult audience contained more men than women." Varda Burstyn adds, "Throughout the postwar period, sport has given the networks an unfragmented, high-income male audience that could be sold to advertisers for enormous sums."[121] As a result, it is not surprising that the major sponsors of televised sport in Canada have been oil companies, automobile manufacturers, tobacco companies, and breweries. NHL hockey in the 1960s, for example, was supported by Imperial Oil, Ford of Canada, and Molson Brewery.[122] And during the brewery war of the late 1970s and 1980s, "Carling O'Keefe, Labatt, and Molson tried to buy whatever sports properties were available and at almost any price just to ensure that a rival brewery did not get them."[123] Many of these patterns, of course, continue to this day.

Facing similar economic pressures to secure advertising revenue, both CBC and CTV increased their coverage of sports in three ways throughout the 1960s and 1970s to further capture the male audience commodity as well as a broader demographic of weekend television audiences. First, they bought programs from American networks, including National Football League (NFL) telecasts. CTV, meanwhile, began to show broadcasts of *Wide World of Sports*, exposing Canadians to a variety of sports coverage: water skiing, softball, horse shows, car racing, wrestling, golf, soccer, and tennis. The private network also introduced a range of new programming and sports-related commentary, including the *Sports Hot Seat*, which brought together "an opinionated panel of questioners and a strong guest from the sporting world to respond to a controversial, topical issue . . . [to] stimulate interest among viewers."[124] Second, both networks broadcast more games in sports they already covered extensively—notably NHL hockey and Canadian football. And, finally, they branched out into other sporting events such as curling, figure skating, golf, swimming, skiing, bowling, and international hockey events like the 1972 Summit Series between Canada and the Soviet Union. Although the range of sports that Canadians were exposed to on CTV and the CBC expanded, the vast majority of the coverage remained devoted to showcasing men's professional sport and to capturing a male audience commodity.

The competition between CTV and the CBC for the most popular sports rights that could capture truly national audiences was not only fierce but also complementary to a degree. CTV, for example, began to air NHL hockey on Wednesday nights and provided coverage of a succession of Winter Olympics, beginning with the 1964 Olympic Games in Innsbruck, Austria. CBC and Radio-Canada, meanwhile, continued to televise the Summer Olympics, while the weekly Saturday night broadcast of *Hockey Night in Canada* (or *La Soirée du hockey*) remained the most valuable and popular programs for the public broadcaster. In Rutherford's words,

> The arrival of independent TV only improved the situation for sports fans. CTV secured the rights to Big Four Football telecasts, and began to offer evening games during the late summer and early fall; then the CBC began to carry NFL Sunday football in retaliation. The CBC had made viewing of hockey on Saturday night a winter ritual, and CTV and the independent French-Canadian Channel 10 in Montreal responded with Wednesday-night hockey. Wrestling disappeared from Radio-Canada's evening schedule but re-emerged on Channel 10's. Note that sports survived in primetime in Canada, while in the United States, once boxing disappeared from the schedules, regular coverage of the sports world was generally confined to Saturday and Sunday afternoons.

"No matter what other sport might be on the air, though," Rutherford adds, "the most important offering remained NHL hockey."[125]

Although the CBC was able to provide over-the-air sport telecasts for all Canadians in both official languages on a national network, the more limited reach of the CTV network complicated these matters and raised important questions about whether citizens ought to have live access to sporting events of national significance as a right of cultural citizenship. These questions first emerged in 1960 when CTV had purchased the rights to the 1962 Grey Cup, even though only 60 percent of Canadians were able to receive CTV's signal. The CBC and CTV subsequently entered into negotiations to provide national distribution of the game, although the public broadcaster was initially unwilling to open its airwaves to a competitor and refused to air the commercials of CTV's sponsors.

The BBG eventually intervened in the dispute and ordered the CBC to carry CTV's feed, complete with commercials—a controversial ruling that would have permitted CTV to extend its audience using CBC affiliates. Indeed, for the CBC, the BBG was essentially acting as an instrument of private television in its aspiration to promote cross-programming between the two networks, and there were suspicions that the owners of CTV were intent on "either borrowing, seducing or kidnapping the key stations" of the public network "in the pursuit of more profit."[126] In response to the BBG's directive, the CBC refused to carry CTV's feed and secured an opinion from the Department of Justice to support its position. Despite these developments, though, a resolution was reached only days prior to the Grey Cup when the CBC agreed to provide sponsors with five courtesy announcements during the game and arranged to sell airtime to those sponsors before and immediately after the broadcast.

Certainly, one of the key issues in this era was whether regulatory agencies—first the BBG and eventually the CRTC—had the political authority to intervene in these types of disputes, and whether a policy was needed to protect the viewing rights of Canadian citizens to have access to telecasts of sporting events in both official languages. Still, although the BBG considered implementing regulations that prohibited "any broadcaster from entering into an exclusive contract to carry certain sporting events of outstanding national interest," no further political action was undertaken.[127] This development escalated the cost of sports broadcasting rights and limited the ability of regulatory agencies to intervene in similar disputes that would arise in the future, as they did at the 1976 Canada Cup, 1988 Winter Olympics in Calgary, and 2010 Winter Olympics in Vancouver.[128]

Sport Specialty Channels and the Digital Era

The entrance of cable television further complicated these matters and radically transformed the national broadcasting landscape throughout the 1960s and 1970s and into the 1980s. Even greater amounts of U.S. content could now reach Canadian audiences on U.S. signals and through subscription cable systems—developments that placed additional economic and political pressure on both CTV and CBC to retain popular content and, hence, audiences. Live sporting events—especially ones that counted as Canadian content—were extraordinarily valuable in this context, and both CTV and CBC escalated their competition for sports broadcasting rights.

One of the most significant developments in the history of the Canadian sports–media complex occurred in 1984, when Canada's first 24-hour cable specialty sports channel was launched. The Sports Network (TSN), which was owned by Labatt Brewing Company, was founded to market the Labatt brand; it was intended to be a cross-promotional tool for the brewery to market its baseball team, the Toronto Blue Jays, to an audience of predominantly men.[129] The network's licence application described the "typical TSN viewer" as "the dedicated sports fan who has an appetite for more television sports programming than is available on conventional television"—clearly, the traditional male sports audience. Despite claiming to be eager to experiment with innovative and progressive programming that would reach "men and women of all age groups," TSN soon settled into a familiar approach to content and style that gave the network "a distinctly 'high tech' and *masculine* image and appeal."[130] Between 1985 and 1991, women's sports events made up less than 3.1 percent of total network broadcast hours on TSN—a number consistent with the dismally low coverage of female athletes in the broadcast media worldwide over the past few decades.[131]

The establishment of TSN, and the all-sport French-language service Réseau des sports (RDS) in 1989, radically restructured the Canadian sports–media complex. Unlike CBC and CTV—networks that carried a diverse range of television shows at specific times (e.g., the news)—TSN was solely dedicated to sports coverage and could air entire tournaments, sporting events, and play-off series without disrupting a pre-existing television schedule. The CBC, for example, regularly faced criticism from across the country over the disruption of its regularly scheduled prime-time shows during the lengthy NHL playoffs. These developments provided TSN with a considerable advantage over the national networks in the competition for sports rights, while growing numbers of sports enjoyed even greater coverage and publicity thanks to the emergence of new sports talk shows and highlight shows like TSN's *SportsCentre*. Still, the sports–media complex was becoming increasingly privatized; sports fans now had to pay additional costs (e.g., cable fees, cable boxes) to access popular sports content that was once provided over the air for all Canadians.

In the late 20th and early 21st centuries, sports coverage has proliferated, albeit in uneven ways, and sports audiences have only fragmented further as a result of digitalization. For instance, in a multichannel and international television industry, sports programming is now crucial not only to the traditional television networks but also to an increasing number of regional and specialty sports channels, including Sportsnet, which was launched by CTV in 1998 and fully acquired by Rogers Communications in 2001. At the same time, vertical integration in the media and entertainment industries has reshaped their relationship to sport, as the owners of regional cable or satellite television networks and other "infotainment" and communications conglomerates increasingly assume ownership of professional sports franchises. According to Whitson, these "mergers of distribution with content" mark "the incorporation of sports into a global 'promotional culture' . . . in which different products in a large media empire are used to promote each other."[132] But the bulk of the content distributed on these circuits of promotion remains overwhelmingly North American men's professional sport and an increasing number of global sporting products (e.g., the English Premier League and the UEFA Champions League).

A perfect example of this trend is Rogers: As the owner of the Toronto Blue Jays and the various media platforms of Sportsnet—including television, radio, and the sportsnet.ca website—the company could utilize its presence in sport to market its communications technology and subscription services. In addition, Rogers paid $5.2 billion for exclusive NHL Canadian television rights from 2014 to 2026 and bought the naming rights for the baseball stadium in Toronto (Rogers Centre) and hockey buildings in Vancouver (Rogers Arena) and Edmonton (Rogers Place). Finally, in 2011, Rogers teamed up with its main rival, Bell Canada Enterprises (BCE)—owners of Bell Canada and Bell Media (including CTV and TSN/RDS, which BCE acquired in 2000)—to purchase Maple Leaf Sports and Entertainment. This gave the combination of BCE/CTV/TSN and Rogers/Sportsnet ownership of the Toronto Maple Leafs and the Toronto Raptors of the National Basketball Association (NBA), as well as Scotiabank Arena (formerly Air Canada Centre), the home arena of the Leafs and Raptors.

In the new era of cross-ownership, cross-marketing, corporate synergies, and global consumerism, the lines between men's professional sport, media, merchandising, and advertising are becoming more blurred than ever before. Still, the focus for companies like Rogers remains securing a largely male audience commodity and capturing subscribers for various telecommunication products and services. All these developments, of course, help explain the resilience of an ongoing historical trend: the paucity of coverage of women's sport, amateur sport, and parasport, despite the availability of an unprecedented number of digital sports channels and distribution networks, as well as the expansion of various sporting opportunities for many groups—and markets—across Canada who were once excluded from participating in various sports.[133]

Conclusion

Our experience of modern sport occurs mainly through the sports media. While thousands of fans gather in stadiums and arenas to watch sporting events live, millions of people engage a mediated world of sport by reading newspapers and websites, watching television, listening to radio broadcasts, playing fantasy sports and video games, following fan blogs, and interacting through social media. In this chapter, we explore the historical development of the sports–media complex in Canada since the 19th century. In so doing, we emphasize the patterns of continuity and change associated with the emergence of various forms of media (e.g., newspapers, the telegraph, radio, and television, both analog and digital) that have set powerful limits and pressures on the types of sports that Canadians have traditionally been exposed to, and continue to consume in today's digital era, albeit on far more interactive and privatized distribution outlets (i.e., smartphones) and social media platforms like Twitter and Facebook.

Much of the content (including advertising) that Canadians consume has remained remarkably consistent over the years, especially the historical emphasis on men's professional sport. Michael Messner argues that "there is still a center to the cultural and structural gender regime of sport," and it can be found "by 'following the money' to the most highly celebrated, rewarded, and institutionalized bodily practices that are defined largely by physical power, aggression, and violence."[134] Despite the addition of female anchors and sportscasters from a wider range of racial and ethnic backgrounds on national sports highlight shows, broadcast journalists are still constrained by dominant expectations of femininity and sometimes seen as intruders on traditional white, male television space. Similarly, although some television networks have tried to reach a more diverse set of markets in an increasingly multicultural Canada, such as the CBC's *Hockey Night in Canada: Punjabi Edition*, these efforts remain almost solely dependent on the promotion of men's professional sport. In addition, comments and discussion on blogs and social media often reproduce the persistent structures of inequality, sexism, racism, and homophobia that have always been expressed through sports media narratives.

In many ways, then, new forms of social media extend historical patterns of consumption, gathering fans and followers of sport into communities of interest and making it possible to share media experiences of sport across different locations. Websites, video games, Twitter feeds, Facebook pages, and Instagram posts—whether they originate with media companies, individual journalists, teams, advertisers, fans, or, increasingly, athletes themselves—still generate interest and revenues as part of the circuits of promotion that have constituted the sports–media complex since the 19th century. On the other hand, though, today's social media platforms offer new ways to interact directly with other fans, players, teams, and media producers, as well as the possibility of generating content outside of the control of mainstream media. Some sports blogs, for example, offer more critical possibilities for social change and represent much-needed challenges to traditional ways of thinking and the uncritical "cheerleading" that has characterized much sports coverage in the past. The contemporary sports media world of digital TV, Twitter, and Instagram has many unique elements that distinguish it from the past, but, in its excitement, immediacy, and complex cultural meanings, it would not be entirely unrecognizable to the 19th-century sports fan reading the daily newspaper and following telegraph reconstructions.

DISCUSSION QUESTIONS

1. Why did newspaper publishers increase their coverage of sport in the late 19th century?
2. What are the main similarities in how sport was incorporated into radio and television programming?
3. Why has media coverage of sport emphasized men's professional sport so consistently over time?
4. How do media portrayals of women athletes, Black athletes, and Indigenous athletes in the past compare with coverage of these groups today?
5. How do contemporary forms of social media extend—or disrupt—the patterns of the past in terms of media experiences of sport?

SUGGESTED READINGS

Gruneau, Richard, and David Whitson. "Media, Audiences, and the NHL Monopoly." Chapter 4 in *Hockey Night in Canada: Sport, Identities, and Cultural Politics*, 79-106. Toronto: Garamond Press, 1993.

Hall, M. Ann. "Competing Images." Chapter 5 in *The Girl and the Game: A History of Women's Sport in Canada*, 2nd ed., 165-211. Toronto: University of Toronto Press, 2016.

Lorenz, Stacy L. "'Our Victorias Victorious': Media, Rivalry, and the 1896 Winnipeg-Montreal Stanley Cup Hockey Challenges." *International Journal of the History of Sport* 32, no. 17 (2015): 1987-2011.

Musto, Michela, Cheryl Cooky, and Michael A. Messner. "'From Fizzle to Sizzle!': Televised Sports News and the Production of Gender-Bland Sexism." *Gender & Society* 31, no. 5 (2017): 573-596.

Scherer, Jay. "The End of CBC Sports?" In *How Canadians Communicate V: Sports*. Edited by David Taras and Christopher Waddell, 55-77. Edmonton: Athabasca University Press, 2016.

CHAPTER 13

THE ASSERTION OF CANADA'S COLONIAL SELF IN NATIONAL AND INTERNATIONAL SPORT

Christine M. O'Bonsawin, PhD
University of Victoria

LEARNING OBJECTIVES

In this chapter you will

- learn about the oppressive practices of Canada as a colonial power and the role of sport as an instrument of Canadian imperialism;
- consider the rise of Canadian sport and the nation's burgeoning presence on the international sport stage during a period of exceeding colonial oppression;
- contrast Canada's outward acceptance of human rights standards to its enduring colonial domesticity, discovering how such ideological incompatibilities were exposed on the international sport state; and
- examine a period of assumed decolonization in Canada and consider the disingenuous ways Canada utilized the international sport model to circumvent legal processes concerning Indigenous rights.

In the literature of this country is the search for an essential
Canadian self. This is an arc created by our common voices and
vision, born with each new dreamer added to this space. Born of the
realization that humans hold a thread of hope, thin, stubborn and
resilient. Watered by poets, story-tellers and old writers, this hope
is held by all those who refuse to peer like cowardly voyeurs at the
world from behind the fence posts of a colonial fort.

Lee Maracle[1]

Canadian sport history, as a part of the literature of this country, has, too, been in the search for an essential Canadian self. As an area of scholarly focus, Canadian sport history received its impetus in the late 1960s and evolved in the succeeding decades, as methodological approaches in the field shifted from descriptive narrative to descriptive thematic, eventually moving into theoretical realms of political, social, and cultural history.[2] Alan Metcalfe's *Canada Learns to Play: The Emergence of Organized Sport, 1807-1914* remains a pivotal scholarly work in the historiography of Canadian sport.[3] It sought to break new ground using social history and scientific method, ultimately asserting that a critical analysis of sport history is central to understanding Canadian social history and thus Canadian culture.[4] This book focused on the development of organized sport in Canada during the 19th and early 20th centuries with the intent "to provide a clear outline of the emergence of organized sport within the context of 'basic social parameters,' namely the changing patterns of population distribution, industrialization, ethnicity, and the domination of the anglophone urban middle class."[5] Metcalfe reasoned that these shifting circumstances provided an edifice whereby Canadians could construct their national identity while simultaneously creating sport, and thus articulating a sport ideology founded on emergent nationalist tenets.[6] Canadian sport and nationalism have remained securely bound throughout the years, and the narratives presented in Canadian sport history generally corroborate this outward alliance.

Canada Learns to Play was admittedly limited in scope, however, as it largely excluded the experiences of women, Indigenous peoples, workers, and others from its analysis.[7] Over the last three decades, sport historians have productively engaged in social, cultural, and political history, ultimately lessening "the gap between what research exists and what should exist."[8] With respect to Indigenous peoples, sport historians have begun to examine the experiences of such peoples in Canadian sport history, focusing mostly on topics of imperialism, colonial oppression, resistance, and activism, and in more recent historical accounts, on matters of reconciliation and resurgence.[9] As such, Canadian sport history has indeed made positive strides forward, and in the process, we have learned a great deal about the experiences of Indigenous peoples in sport and thus about the "relationship between sport and society."[10] For example, using a case study approach, chapter 4 of this book considers questions from the point of view of history and colonization in Canada to understand how such processes allowed the dominant and powerful groups to build and secure their preferred vision for sport, which inevitably shaped how Indigenous peoples participate and think about organized sport in Canada.

In many regards, this chapter is less about sport and more about colonialism, as it situates colonialism as *the* most basic social parameter in the historical discourse of Canada.[11] Metcalfe determined, in 1987, that an immense gap remained between social and sport historians. In all probability, he notes:

> Social historians will find [*Canada Learns to Play*] wanting because too little attention is paid to sport's relationship to social variables, while sport historians will find it wanting because too little attention is paid to sport itself. My focus leads to a particular approach, one that emphasizes certain factors, briefly mentions others, and excludes others completely. More than anything this book is about Canada.[12]

More than anything this chapter, too, is about Canada; it seeks to uncover the essential Canadian self by shifting the point of intervention. Rather than concentrate on the experiences of Indigenous peoples in Canadian sport history and Canada's organized sport structure, this chapter positions sport as a form of social organization that was (and remains) firmly rooted within the apparatus of the colonial power.[13] A re-examination of Canadian sport history reveals that the productivity of Canadian colonialism was avowed repeatedly within the national sporting practices and evidenced through Canada's involvement in international sport. Accordingly, the political, legal, social, and economic processes of colonialism propelled the formation and rise of the Canadian state, the emergence of a nationalistic ideology, and ultimately the establishment of a domestic sport order premised on xenophobic principles.

This chapter divides Canadian sport history into four periodic discussion areas, distinguishing between periods of incremental and substantive change. The first discussion area considers imperialism, oppressive practices of the colonial power, and the role of sport as an instrument of Canadian imperialism in the late 19th and early 20th centuries (1876-1914). Second, the chapter contextualizes the rise of Canadian sport and the nation's burgeoning presence on the international sport stage within the context of Canadian colonialism, thereby juxtaposing a triumphant era in national sport to an exceedingly oppressive and violent period in Canada's colonial past (1915-1944). The third discussion area contrasts Canada's outward acceptance of international principles concerning human rights and antiracism standards to its enduring domestic colonial domesticity, highlighting how such ideological incompatibilities began to expose themselves on the international sport stage (1945-1976). Finally, the chapter considers the disingenuous ways in which settler Canada utilized the international sport model, specifically the Olympic Games, as a means to circumvent legal processes concerning Indigenous rights during a period of supposed decolonization in Canada (1977-2010). Dismantling the posts of the colonial fort begins with the admission that colonialism is the basic social parameter in which to understand the context of Canadian sport history, thereby revealing that in our search for an essential national self, our sporting accounts will inevitably expose Canada's colonial self.

Imperialism, Colonialism, and the Instrument of Sport (1876-1914)

This first discussion area begins in the year 1876, which is not owing to the fact that in this year lacrosse promoter and patriot George Beers escorted a Kanien'kehá:ka (Mohawk) team (see figure 13.1) to Britain to promote Canada's emerging national identity. Rather, 1876 is the point of departure because this is when Canada enacted one of the most oppressive racial policies in global history, namely the Indian Act. The act quickly became the predominant mechanism of control in colonial Canada; however, colonial administration did not begin with the official passage of the act (after all, as discussed later, Kanien'kehá:ka players were actively resisting Canadian colonialism by 1876). The formal adoption of the Indian Act simply meant the government was prepared, at this time, to merge its disordered administrative policies into one comprehensive statute and entrench its colonial objectives within Canadian law.[14] As Mi'kmaq scholar Pamela Palmater explains, "It is no secret that the underlying objective of Canadian Indian policy has been to get rid of Indigenous peoples through whatever means necessary, with a view to securing permanent access to Indigenous lands and resources for the settler population."[15] The colonial laws and policies adopted by the successive waves of European colonial powers in the pre-Confederation era, and ultimately entrenched within the Indian Act of 1876, were not born of wilful neglect, nor are they naïve policies gone wrong. On the

William Notman / Musée McCord

Figure 13.1 The Kanien'kehá:ka team travelled to Britain with George Beers in 1876, where they played lacrosse matches against their white gentleman amateur counterparts and performed for British audiences.

contrary, they are atrocious and purposeful attempts by the colonial power to culturally eradicate and physically remove Indigenous peoples from their lands, through whatever means necessary.[16]

The Sporting Apparatus of the Colonial Power

It is well documented that in 1876, George Beers organized a lacrosse tour involving two teams from Canada—a squad made up of white gentleman amateurs as well as a team of Kanien'kehá:ka (Mohawk) players—who travelled to Britain to compete in matches against one another with the express purpose of promoting a distinct Canadian representation to British spectators.[17] In the various accounts, we learn that Beers capitalized on the exotic spectacle of Indigenous dress and tradition, adorning Kanien'kehá:ka players in red and white jerseys and knickers, blue caps, beadwork, feathers, and jewelry, which was in stark contrast to the conservative uniforms of the white gentleman amateurs. The construction of such images was perhaps more important than the outcome of the sporting competitions, because the engendered messages were meant to articulate notions of Canadian imperialism and nationalism mainly to British observers. Canada's participation in economic, military, and sport exchanges in the late 19th and early 20th centuries was undoubtedly linked to Canadian patriotism, nation building, and a desire to establish a closer union with the British Empire, ultimately affording the young dominion influence over imperial policy and perhaps establishing Canada as an auxiliary kingdom within the Empire.[18] In acknowledging such linkages in Canadian history, and thus within our sporting histories, it must also be recognized that Canadian imperialism embodies an abhorrent urge on the part of the colonizer (Canada and its colonial predecessors) to dominate, exploit, and violate the seemingly underdeveloped areas and peoples of these lands.

In *Lacrosse: A History of the Game*, Donald M. Fisher observes that during the 1876 lacrosse tour some British audience members recognized the caricatured and self-lampooning behaviours of the Kanien'kehá:ka players who willingly participated in these exhibitions, routinely showcasing the supposed exotic and primitive qualities of North American Indians. As Fisher notes, through these lacrosse tours, promoters sought to create a distinct Canadian identity, allow spectators to see symbolic representations of Britain's imperial conquests, and in the process, cement the cultural ties between Britain and Canada.[19] The Kanien'kehá:ka players were not only outstanding athletes but also exceptional performers. They understood that if they cooperated with the requests of lacrosse promoters, they could secure income, fame, and travel opportunities, ultimately circumventing colonial policy.[20] Nonetheless, despite the exceptional showmanship of these players, they were not always successful in convincing their audiences of the authenticity of their performances. For example, during the 1876 lacrosse tour, a writer for the *Newcastle Daily Journal* noted, "At home [the Kanien'kehá:ka players] are staunch Conservatives, devout Roman Catholics, sit on Windsor chairs, and are more addicted to smoking bird's eye tobacco than to brandishing tomahawks."[21] Some audience members saw their performances as deceptive and fraudulent, leading some historians to interpret the historical record in such a way as to concede that these players indeed possessed a form of agency. Further, sport historians have correctly identified specific acts of resistance within these performances, on occasion even classifying these actions as colonial resistance. What Canadian sport history does not thoroughly cross-examine, however, are reasons for their resistance.

The *Newcastle Daily Journal* excerpt exposes more about the lived experiences of the Kanien'kehá:ka players than merely the fraudulent nature of their performances and the agency they possessed in deceiving foreign audiences. The previously quoted passage further suggests that by 1876 Indigenous peoples in the young dominion were becoming devout Roman Catholics who sat on Windsor chairs and were addicted to smoking tobacco. In other words, in the immediate post-Confederation era, Indigenous peoples in Canada were enduring religious conversion, coerced to conform to the behaviours of the colonizers, and beleaguered by alcoholism and addition. As such, this episode in Canadian sport history provides a point of entry whereby sport historians may begin to uncover the essential colonial Canadian self by shifting the point of intervention. We start not by isolating the past sporting encounters of these Kanien'kehá:ka players as historical subjects in our sporting past, and generally referencing the colonial circumstances they endured, but instead we begin by recognizing their sporting experiences as firmly rooted within the apparatus of the colonial power. As Homi Bhabha reasons, "To understand the productivity of the colonial power it is crucial to construct its regime of 'truth', not to subject its representations to a normalizing judgement."[22] Accordingly, we must name the basis of oppression, as experienced by these Kanien'kehá:ka players (and other Indigenous athletes throughout Canadian history), recognizing colonialism to have originated in a specific ideological space and sustained through the governmentality of the colonial power (i.e., Canada and its imperial and colonial predecessors), which ensured its colonial productivity.

Genocidal Practice and the Productivity of the Colonial Power

We now understand the various processes used to ensure the physical or cultural eradication of Indigenous to be forms of genocide. The Truth and Reconciliation Commission of Canada considered the relationships between Indigenous and settler peoples, in historical and contemporary times, and proposed three categories of genocide in its 2015 final report: "Physical genocide is the mass killing of the members of a targeted group, and biological genocide is the destruction of the group's reproductive capacity. Cultural genocide is the destruction of those structures and practices that allow the group to continue as a group."[23]

Throughout the 18th and 19th centuries, colonial governments used several strategies to ensure the permanent removal of Indigenous peoples from their lands. The first rendition of the Indian Act carried forward the disorganized rules and principles of early Indian policy, many of which were premised on genocidal practice and may be categorized as forms of physical genocide. On three occasions in the mid-1700s, for example, British colonial governments in Nova Scotia issued bounties for the scalps of Mi'kmaq men, women, and children.[24] With rising tensions throughout Mi'kma'ki (Mi'kmaq territory), for example, the British issued the second scalping proclamation in 1749 in response to Mi'kmaq opposition to increased British governing authority throughout their territories.[25] It was Governor Edward Cornwallis who issued this proclamation, "promis[ing] a reward of ten Guineas for every Indian Micmac taken or killed, to be paid upon producing such Savage taken or his scalp."[26] As Mi'kmaq historian Paul Daniel explains, the number of Mi'kmaqs killed during the 1744, 1749, and 1756 bloodsheds is undetermined; however, some records mention scalps delivered by the bagful. Daniel clarifies further that the number of Mi'kmaq deaths is unknown likely because the government documented the expenditures as miscellaneous or destroyed the records altogether after realizing the extent of its role in carrying out such atrocities.[27]

Another method of physical genocide used by various colonial administrations was a process that has commonly come to be known as smallpox-induced genocide. As the American Medical Association reasons, smallpox was first used as a biological weapon in North America during the French and Indian War (1754-1763) when blankets infected with the epidemic were purposefully distributed by British forces to Indigenous peoples, reducing the populations of some Indigenous Nations by over 50 percent.[28] In more recent historical accounts, historians have begun to uncover evidence that at various points throughout the 19th century, smallpox-induced genocide was practised sporadically throughout the western regions, including the Plains, Tsilhqot'in, Nuxalk, and Coast Salish territories, reducing some of these Indigenous populations by upwards of 70 percent.[29] In his monograph, titled *Clearing the Plains: Disease, Politics of Starvation, and the Loss of Aboriginal Life*, James Daschuk further dispels the myth that the history of Canada is one of peace and negotiation, revealing how infectious diseases and state-sponsored starvation combined to create a lethal and relentless catastrophe throughout the Plains regions.[30]

By the mid-19th century, it was clear that in spite of state-sponsored efforts, the physical eradication of Indigenous peoples was not occurring quickly enough to accommodate the imminent settlement of Europeans on Indigenous territories. Consequently, legislation was designed to ensure the permanent elimination of Indigenous people, if not in physical body than in law.[31] The legal eradication of Indigenous peoples began in the pre-Confederation period following the passage of various legislation, introducing the first definition for an "Indian person" in 1850 as well as a policy of enfranchisement in 1857.[32] Following Confederation, these laws became exceedingly gendered as the rubrics were further demarcated, denying recognition as Indian persons to Indigenous women who married non-Indigenous men. Children of such women too were denied recognition.[33] As previously mentioned, the colonial administration of Indigenous peoples did not begin with the official passage of the 1876 Indian Act; instead, its enactment meant the government sought to consolidate pre-

Confederation Indian policy into one comprehensive act, thereby embedding its colonial objectives within the laws of the newly formed nation.

The Indian Act established three primary mechanisms of control, which served to direct virtually every aspect of Indigenous livelihood. First, reserves were held in trust for the use and benefit of Indigenous peoples. Second, bands were established to manage the reserves through an imposed chief and council governing system. Third, expressly gendered definitions resolved who was (and was not) legally entitled to Indian status, who belonged to their respective bands, and who had the right to live on reserve.[34] This last mechanism of control was perhaps the most dangerous because it sought to eradicate Indigenous peoples, not through violence per se, but rather through the legislative process. Nonetheless, we must not mistake the passage of the Indian Act as suggesting the government had abandoned its inherently violent colonial practices. Conversely, the enactment of a comprehensive Indian policy meant the government had a principal instrument of control, and if Indigenous peoples did not physically disappear at a speedy enough pace, it could introduce violent and genocidal strategies within this all-encompassing framework, at any point. In 1894, the government amended the Indian Act, making it mandatory that Indigenous children under the age of 16 attend day, industrial, or residential schools where countless children were abused emotionally, spiritually, physically, and sexually, and thousands died while attending or trying to escape these horrific institutions.[35]

Sport as a Basis of Oppression and Mechanism of Control

Famous Onondaga runner Tom Charles Longboat (Cogwagee) attended one of these institutions; his life undoubtedly changed forever (see chapter 4). The historical record is only now beginning to shed light on early life experiences of one of the most famous athletes of the early 20th century, who, in 1899, was forcefully removed from his home at the age of 12 and sent to the Mohawk Institute Residential School. At the Mohawk Institute Residential School Longboat was starved, forbidden from speaking his language, required to read, write, and speak in English, and forced to worship a deity he did not understand.[36] There is very little information in the records concerning Longboat's experiences in the Indian residential school; however, in a conversation with his son later in his life, Longboat revealed that after he had achieved fame, becoming the most celebrated athlete in Canada at the time, he was invited back to the Mohawk Institute Residential School to speak about his sporting success. He refused. "If I was ever to go back, I would just tell them how I was abused. If I had it my way, I wouldn't even send my dog to that place."[37] Longboat experienced cruelty and adversity in the early years of his life, as did so many Indigenous children throughout Canada, and he is by no means the only Indigenous athlete whose experiences were defined by the colonial process outlined in the Indian Act. Through the vital work of the Truth and Reconciliation Commission, for example, we are learning a great deal more about the experiences of Indigenous children and youth, including in sport, during their years of detention in Indian residential schools in the latter part of the 19th and early 20th centuries (and beyond).[38]

Canadian sport history has exhaustively detailed the imperial and nationalistic objectives of the aforementioned lacrosse tours. More recent historical accounts have begun to position these tours within the framework of colonialism, identifying episodes of colonial resistance. In naming the basis of oppression, we call to attention the oppressive rubrics of the Indian Act that circumscribed the experiences of Indigenous peoples in Canadian society and thus sport.

The Indian Act was frequently amended between 1884 and 1914, preventing Indigenous peoples from engaging in cultural practices central to the governing, political, legal, and economic practices of Indigenous societies. This prohibition further restricted Indigenous peoples from performing in shows, exhibitions, performances, stampedes, or pageants in aboriginal costume, specifically where there was payment to Indigenous performers or where the wounding or mutilation of a dead or living body of any human or animal formed a part or was featured.[39] In 1884, for example, the Indian Act was amended to prohibit Indigenous peoples from engaging in cultural ceremonies, including the Potlatch and Sundance (commonly referred to as the Potlatch ban).[40] One year later, in 1885, the pass system was adopted informally through a series of correspondence between senior bureaucrats within the Department of Indian Affairs. Because many Indigenous nations had signed treaties with the Crown, the government was not legally permitted to enforce this initiative in law because the treaties guaranteed the unrestricted movement of Indigenous peoples. Senior bureaucrats nevertheless found means to implement an informal system of restricted movement, requiring Indigenous peoples to obtain the permission of an Indian agent or the North-West Mounted Police, and obtain a pass, if they wished to travel between reserves, to the United States, and beyond.[41] Furthermore, the pass system reinforced the anti-Potlatch ban.

These mechanisms of control are indeed central to our understanding of Canadian sport history. Although Indigenous peoples achieved remarkable sporting success throughout this period, such as Longboat and the Kanien'kehá:ka team (presumably from Six Nations of the Grand River[42]) that won a bronze medal at the 1904 Olympic Games in St. Louis, Missouri, their participation in such sporting events was not without complication, nor was it apolitical. Whereas Indigenous peoples were a desired (albeit caricatured) form of spectacle and exoticism in the early years of the dominion for purposes of nation building, by the turn of the century, it appeared as though Indigenous peoples were not disappearing at a speedy enough pace, and so the government implanted more oppressive and violent policies within its all-encompassing colonial framework. From a government standpoint, it was no longer politically acceptable, or desirable, to have Indigenous peoples travelling abroad promoting a distinct national identity premised on exotic spectacles and traditional Indian dress. From an Indigenous standpoint, however, many still wished to secure income, fame, and travel opportunities as afforded by the lacrosse tours of the period. As such, the participation and experiences of Indigenous peoples in international sporting events, such as the 1904 Olympic Games, were entirely dependent on how they might comply, circumvent, or perhaps oppose the shifting colonial policies of the late 19th and early 20th centuries.

Violence, Oppression, and the Rise of Canadian Sport (1915-1944)

Why is historical context concerning violence and oppression during this period in Canada's history critical to our understandings of Canadian sport history? First, it provides an appropriate explanation for the noticeable absence of Indigenous people in Canadian sport history discourse between the years 1915 and 1944. Supplied with this historical context, we may better understand this absence and recognize that during this period Indigenous peoples were confined mainly to the reserves and Indian residential schools. Participating in mainstream sport was in all likelihood not a possibility (or a priority) for the majority of Indigenous peoples, many of whom were struggling to survive the everyday oppressive and violent circumstances of their lives.[43] This is not to say that Indigenous peoples did not participate in sport at this time; it simply means that historians are only now beginning to uncover the colonial spaces—notably residential schools and reserves—and accessing rich oral history to learn more about Indigenous histories and experiences in sport (see chapters 3 and 4).

Second, this historical context is critical to our understandings of Canadian sport history because it infuses unfamiliar content and perspectives into the discourse. It locates colonialism as the most basic social parameter in the historical discourse and allows us to position sport as a form of social organization firmly rooted within the apparatus of the colonial power. Re-examining episodes in Canadian sport history reveals that the productivity of Canadian colonialism was avowed repeatedly not only within national sporting practices but also through Canada's engagement in international sport. Although Indigenous peoples remain mostly absent from Canadian sport history records, and their opportunities in international sport were limited, the 1920s and 1930s represent a period of significant growth in Canadian sport. Notably, in the period immediately following the Great War, the Olympic Games had emerged as the pre-eminent international global sport festival. The Olympic Games provided new opportunities to define nationhood and for countries to demonstrate their physical excellence and a supposed national superiority over other nations.[44]

A Legislated Policy of Violence and Oppression

In 1920, the Indian Act was amended to make attendance at day, industrial, and residential schools mandatory for Indigenous children between the ages of 7 and 15.[45] Although rules concerning compulsory Indian residential school attendance appeared first in 1884 (and this section of the act was amended periodically, including 1894 and 1908), the 1920 amendment is significant because it was ushered in and championed by then deputy superintendent of Indian Affairs, Duncan Campbell Scott. Upon introducing the bill, Scott infamously stated: "I want to get rid of the Indian problem. . . . Our objective is to continue until there is not a single Indian in Canada that has not been absorbed into the body politic and there is no Indian question, and no Indian Department, that is the whole object of this Bill."[46] The impetus for the residential school system was in place by the time Scott rose to the position of superintendent; however, his supervision over colonial administration during his tenure (1913-1932) represents the most radical and repressive in the history of the department. Scott attacked the "Indian problem" with a vengeance, instituting drastic amendments that have had devastating effects.[47]

The peak of the residential school era was 1931. In this year there were 80 residential schools in operation, compared with 18 industrial and 37 residential schools at the turn of the century. We are only now beginning to understand the full extent of the abuse, maltreatment, and neglect experienced by innocent children who were torn from their families and communities and detained in these horrific institutions, some never to return home. As pointed out in the 2015 final report of the Truth and Reconciliation Commission, as an exceedingly important part of the government's Indian policy, the residential school system was premised on genocidal practice. The report explains that residential schools were a form of cultural genocide because they sought to destroy the political and social institutions of the targeted group, seize lands by relocating people, prohibit language, persecute spirituality, and prevent the transmission of cultural values from one generation to the next.[48]

Admitting this policy and these schools to have been genocidal in philosophy and practice is a necessary first step. The next step is to recognize other forms of genocide practised within these spaces. Physical genocide is considered to be the mass killing of members of a targeted group. The death of approximately 6,000 innocent children most certainly constitutes a form of physical genocide. Many of these children died in the schools from disease or abuse, shortly after being sent home because of illness, or through efforts to escape these horrific institutions.[49] Furthermore, the government's wilful neglect of the tuberculosis crisis constitutes another form of physical genocide. As revealed by Dr. Peter Bryce in 1922, the government knowingly spread the tuberculosis disease, first, by purposely exposing healthy Indigenous children to those infected with the virus, and second, by sending diseased children home to their families on the reserves.[50] As demonstrated through this very brief overview of colonial policy, aimed to ensure the physical and cultural eradication of Indigenous peoples, this excessively oppressive and violent period marks perhaps the darkest era in Canadian history.

Unaffected by the Darkness: The Golden Age of Canadian Sport

Throughout the 1920s and 1930s, Canadian athletes achieved much success in international sport, particularly at the Olympic Games. By this time Canada had proven a dominant force in men's international hockey, capturing gold medals at the 1920 Olympic Games (Antwerp) and the Winter Olympics in 1924 (Chamonix) and 1928 Winter Olympics (St. Moritz). Although Canadian women also achieved sporting success in international sport throughout this period, this should not be misconstrued to mean they were participating on equal terms with Canadian men. Despite the marginalization of Canadian women in society, many women achieved remarkable success in sport at this time. In 1928, for example, a group of Canadian women, commonly referred to as "the Matchless Six," triumphed in the track and field events at the 1928 Olympic Games in Amsterdam, Netherlands. The Edmonton Commercial Graduates basketball team dominated regional, national, and international basketball from 1915 to 1940, defeating the majority of men's and women's teams they faced.[51] In fact, on three occasions, the Edmonton Grads were invited to the Olympic Games, including the 1924 and 1928 Olympic Games in Paris, France, and Amsterdam, respectively, and the contentious 1936 Olympic Games in Berlin, Germany. The Edmonton Grads' involvement in the 1936 Olympic Games deserves further attention because it marks a noteworthy achievement for the advancement of women in sport in Canada. The Canadian Olympic Committee formally recognized the Grads as part of the Canadian contingent in Berlin, permitting them to wear the official Olympic blazers and sit in the competitors' section in the stadium, even though women's basketball was not an official medal event at these Games. Nonetheless, despite uneasiness over increasing Nazi militarism and anti-Semitism, and perhaps owing to their marginalization in Canadian sport, as M. Ann Hall suggests, there is no evidence that the Grads questioned their participation in these controversial Olympic Games. As Hall reasons, "Although we will never know for certain, it is unlikely there was any discussion among the Grads about cancelling their third European journey, this time in conjunction with the Summer Olympics in Berlin."[52]

Although there was minimal support in Canada for a boycott of the 1936 Olympic Games, a modest anti-Olympic campaign began to form within a growing anti-fascist movement. The Communist Party of Canada managed the Olympic boycott movement and was supported by outside organizations such as the Workers' Sports Association and its triweekly Toronto newspaper, *The Worker*, which regularly reported on Nazi atrocities to a generally unsympathetic Canadian readership. Editorials in *The Worker* in 1935, for example, suggested that "sport and the Olympic Games cannot be carried out in isolation from the society that hosts them. . . . true sportsmanship requires peace and respect for human rights, neither of which exist in Nazi Germany."[53]

The established sport community and press in Canada were generally resistant to the anti-Olympic campaign. For example, the Canadian Olympic Committee allayed concerns for athlete safety by suggesting it had received assurances from German officials that Canadian athletes would not experience discrimination. The Canadian press, on the other hand, affirmed oversimplifications, promulgating that politics, propaganda, and hatred have no place in sport. Andy Lytle of the *Toronto Daily Star* noted: "There is essentially an age of propaganda. It has penetrated into Canadian sports before this. Always it does harm rather than serve any useful purpose."[54] At the peak of Nazi militarism and anti-Semitism, such oversimplifications pervaded sporting practices.

The peak of the residential school era was 1931. In 1932-33, the Indian Act was, once more, amended, and further restrictions were placed on Indian festivals, dances, and ceremonies. In 1936, the pass system remained in effect. There is no evidence to suggest any Indigenous athletes competed in Berlin, which perhaps comes as no surprise. Although it does not appear that Indigenous athletes competed in these Olympic Games, a contingent of white Canadians went to Berlin to compete in the international dance competition—in Indian dress. The prohibition of Indian festivals, dances, and ceremonies may have prevented Indigenous peoples from capitalizing on their identities, but this did not preclude white Canadians from appropriating representations of such peoples for individual and nationalistic gain. Olympic organizers extended an invitation to the Canadian Olympic Committee requesting that it send a dance contingent to compete in the Internationale Tanzwettspiele, a dance competition that was part of the cultural program of the Olympic Games. The invitation requested that dance groups arrive in Berlin with "ballet dances, dances for the concert stage, historical and national dance."[55]

In the competition, the Canadian contingent performed five pieces, including an Indigenous legend titled *Mala* and an Inuit legend titled *Mon-Ka-Ta*. For these pieces, "Indian maidens" adorned Hollywood-contrived headbands with a single vertical feather. The "warriors" were dressed identically in pan-Indian costumes, including Plains Indians–styled war bonnets and painted quill breastpieces (see figure 13.2). Following a performance in Toronto, and before their departure for Berlin, a writer for the *Toronto Star* noted, "The Olympic judges will not know whether these aboriginals are Micmacs from Nova Scotia or Swampies from Athabasca, but they will be excited by the dazzling costumes."[56] The Canadian performance was well received in Berlin, particularly the *Mala* and *Mon-Ka-Ta* pieces; nonetheless, it is important not to lose sight of the fact that the performances were scripted in highly problematic ways and contained deeply possessive messages. As Indigenous peoples were surviving colonial oppression and violence in Canada, imprisoned on the reserves and within the residential schools, settler Canadians travelled to Nazi Germany, freely entered into another political space of unimaginable tyranny, and ultimately mirrored their own caricatured representations of an oppressed peoples from their homelands who, too, were experiencing violence and persecution.

Human Rights, Global Sport, and the Colonial Rule of Law in Canada (1945-1976)

The global community was in a period of significant transition following the Second World War, principally because the world was more fully coming to understand the extent of the monstrosities carried out in Nazi Germany. The

Figure 13.2   "Indian maidens" perform *Mon-Ka-Ta.*

United Nations (UN) was founded formally on October 24, 1945, when the UN Charter was ratified by its five permanent members (China, France, the Soviet Union, the United Kingdom, and the United States) and the majority of other signatories.[57] In the aftermath of two cataclysmic global wars, world leaders sought to establish a framework for international peace and security between sovereign nations; however, the global community was also in search of a mechanism to protect and preserve the human rights and fundamental freedoms of all persons throughout the world. A universal human rights consciousness was emerging at this time, as many across the globe sought to ensure that never again would individuals be unjustly discriminated based on race, sex, language, or religion, and hence denied life, freedom, food, shelter, and nationality. Accordingly, the UN Charter established standards for protecting citizens from abuses by their respective governments, ensuring that nations were accountable for the treatment of all persons living within their borders. In these years of transformative global change, Canada was, for the first time, vulnerable to regular international inspection, thus obliging the nation-state to reappraise its treatment of Indigenous peoples and thus its more than century-old Indian policy.

International Declarations and Conventions: Canada's Outward Response

On December 10, 1948, three years after the creation of the UN and the ratification of this international intergovernmental organization, the UN adopted its Universal Declaration of Human Rights, recognizing the "barbarous acts which have outraged the conscience of mankind, and the advent of a world in which human beings shall enjoy freedom of speech and belief."[58] It was a global response to previously highlighted atrocities carried out in Nazi Germany during the Second World War. The majority of UN member states readily endorsed the Universal Declaration of Human Rights. Although Canadian legal scholar John Humphrey played a principal role in drafting the Universal Declaration of Human Rights, Canada remained in an adversarial position in the draft and early ratification stages. In fact, during the draft vote, Canada broke ranks with the majority of member nations and abstained (as did South Africa and Soviet bloc nations). The international community was surprised by Canada's isolating and hostile attitude, and that it had taken a position so clearly out of step with its traditional allies. When member nations came before the UN General Assembly three days later, Canada made an about-face, voting in favour of the Universal Declaration of Human Rights.[59]

Of important note is Canada's seeming cooperation in the sanctioning of the United Nation's Convention on the Prevention and Punishment of the Crime of Genocide, ratified on December 9, 1948, one day prior to the endorsement of the Universal Declaration of Human Rights. Article 2 of the Genocide Convention defines *genocide* as follows:

> Any of the following acts committed with intent to destroy, in whole or in part, a national, ethnical, racial or religious group, as such: (a) Killing members of the group; (b) Causing serious bodily or mental harm to members of the group; (c) Deliberately inflicting on the group conditions of life calculated to bring about its physical destruction in whole or in part; (d) Imposing measures intended to prevent births within the group; (e) Forcibly transferring children of the group to another group.[60]

Canada was in many ways a repressive society; its human rights record compared unfavourably with many of its allied nations and the majority of UN member states.[61] The endorsement of this version of the Genocide Convention by Canada and other member states was because the final declaration had been revised significantly from earlier drafts, which had acknowledged cultural genocide within the broad definition of genocide. Many ratifying states, including Canada, were concerned that if the final document accepted cultural genocide as a form of genocide, then they were potentially in breach of the declaration they had yet to sign. The five methods of cultural genocide rejected by these states cited forcible transfer of children, forced exile of individuals of a targeted group, prohibition of national languages, and destruction of historical, religious, and linguistic documents and monuments. The definition accepted and ratified in the final Genocide Convention describes genocide to be acts of physical genocide. Canada did not believe itself to be in contravention of such acts of physical genocide.[62]

As Canada implemented its redefined colonial procedures, discussed later, the world's attention remained fixed on other regions and jurisdictions of the world, notably South Africa. After the National Party's election into power in 1948, South Africa immediately began to implement racial separateness through apartheid legislation.[63] International pressure promptly mounted as the UN and its member states started to place embargos and trade restrictions on South Africa. The international sport community, too, responded relatively quickly as many traditionally conservative sport leaders, such as the president of the International Olympic Committee (IOC), Avery Brundage, eventually conceded that racism indeed permeates sport. As Malcolm MacLean explains, "The boycott campaign was one of the principal tools that the anti-apartheid movement had in its toolkit to dismantle the White South African government's systemic racial classification and oppression."[64] The campaign aimed at South Africa's disqualification from the Olympic Games was, perhaps, the most efficient of all the tools in the toolkit. President Brundage argued initially to keep the apartheid nation within the Olympic fold. He believed the South African problem impossible to separate from the political question, which he thought to be of no concern to the IOC. Brundage felt the South African National Olympic Committee should not be held responsible for the broader policies of its government.[65] His IOC colleagues perceived the situation in South Africa much differently, however, and voted to withdraw South Africa's invitations to the 1964 Summer and Winter Olympics in Tokyo, Japan, and Innsbruck, Austria, respectively.[66] Four years later, the IOC withdrew South Africa's invitation to compete in the 1968 Summer and Winter Olympics in Mexico City, Mexico, and Grenoble, France, respectively. In 1970, the IOC voted to expel South Africa from the Olympic movement.

The question of South Africa's participation in international sport culminated on the eve of Canada's hosting its first Olympic Games, partly Canada's own doing. Although South Africa had been formally ejected from the Olympic Games in 1970, its expulsion did not force countries with strong sporting ties to the apartheid nation, such as New Zealand, to break its associations.[67] A few months before the opening of the 1976 Olympic Games in Montreal, the New Zealand All-Blacks national rugby team participated in a tour of South Africa, drawing considerable scrutiny from anti-apartheid organizations within the realm of international sport. Notably, the Supreme Council for Sport in Africa (SCSA) called on the IOC and Government of Canada to ban New Zealand from the 1976 Olympic Games in Montreal. Whereas the IOC claimed the request was outside its jurisdiction because rugby was not an Olympic sport, Canada claimed the matter needed to be resolved by the parties directly involved, including the IOC, SCSA, and New Zealand. Canada's position in the lead-up to the Olympic Games in Montreal was consistent with its general approach to the South African question: Although it championed the anti-apartheid cause in principle, it followed through in highly ambiguous ways.[68] For example, Canada was criticized by the SCSA a few months earlier for sending a team to the world softball championships in New Zealand, even though the SCSA had called for a worldwide boycott of the event because of South Africa's participation. In returning to the Montreal question, the decision made by the IOC and Canada, in the end, was to do absolutely nothing. New Zealand, a Commonwealth nation and United Nations member in good standing, was permitted to participate in the Olympic Games, forcing the hand of numerous national Olympic committees. On the eve of the opening of these Olympic Games, roughly 30 nations elected to withdraw their teams from Montreal.

International Declarations and Conventions: Canada's Inward Response

Canada was in a precarious position. On the one hand, it was the host nation of the 1976 Olympic Games. Moreover, it was a signatory to the Universal Declaration of Human Rights (1948) and the Convention on the Prevention and Punishment of the Crime of Genocide (1948), and by this time, it had cooperatively endorsed the United Nations International Convention on the Elimination of All Forms of Racial Discrimination, ratified in December 1965 and entered into force in January 1969. The Racial Discrimination Convention defines *racial discrimination* as follows:

> Any distinction, exclusion, restriction or preference based on race, colour, descent, or national or ethnic origin which has the purpose or effect of nullifying or impairing the recognition, enjoyment or exercise, on an equal footing, of human rights and fundamental freedoms in the political, economic, social, cultural or any other field of public life.[69]

The anti-apartheid cause was certainly aided by the political actions of the UN, particularly through its Universal Declaration of Human Rights and the Racial Discrimination Convention,[70] which seeks to end racial discrimination through such measures as the condemnation of apartheid, the prohibition of propaganda and hate speech and hate crime, and the promotion of racial tolerance between racial, ethnic, and national groups.[71] Nonetheless, it is argued that it was ultimately through the social institution of sport that the word *apartheid* was brought to the front pages of newspapers throughout the world.[72] It was due, in large part, to the departure of athletes from approximately 30 countries because the IOC and the host nation, Canada, failed to take concrete measures to support mounting efforts to boycott the apartheid state and thereby South Africa from the world. On the other hand, Canada's precarious position was perhaps due in large part to its ongoing policy of racial segregation.

In 1951, following a review process, the Indian Act was revised. Although many of the oppressive laws contained therein, such as the Potlatch ban and mandatory attendance at Indian residential schools (this is not to say that the residential schools closed as a result, however), were dropped prior to the major revision of the Indian Act, the 1951 rewrite was mostly an exercise in legislative housekeeping.[73] Through its rewrite of the Indian Act, the government managed to introduce new procedures that would eliminate Indigenous peoples, specifically through the establishment of a central Indian registry as well as its transition procedures concerning Indigenous child welfare. First, it established a central Indian registry to be managed in Ottawa. Through this revision, however, the government failed to revise its century-old patriarchal method in determining Indian status, which continued to place Indigenous women in vulnerable and dangerous positions. Second, amendments to the Indian Act provided mechanisms for transferring services to the provinces, where no federal services existed. The transfer of child welfare to the provinces led to the apprehension of over 20,000 Indigenous children between the late 1950s and early 1980s. This dark period in Canadian history has come to be known as "the Sixties Scoop," an ensuing period of child abduction whereby Indigenous children were seized from their families and communities and sent to white foster homes, where many were neglected and abused.[74]

In the decades that followed the Second World War, the Indian Act remained racially discriminatory, genocidal in practice, and an infringement on the human rights of Indigenous peoples throughout Canada. Although the Indian Act was revised significantly in 1951, the government maintained its colonial rule in Canada, notably through preserving the Indian reserve system, the Indian residential school policy, and its mid-18th-century patrilocal parameters in determining Indian status. There are many parallels and comparisons to be made between Canada and South Africa. Through their unique colonial processes, both countries adopted policies of racial control and land policy to segregate the national population on the bases of race and ethnicity, ultimately denying the oppressed peoples access to land and resources.[75] In drawing this comparison, it does not mean that direct links exist between racial and land policies in Canada and South Africa. These claims are mostly conflated, elusive, and lacking in historical foundation. There were stark differences between the two systems of racial segregation, to be sure, and there is minimal evidence to suggest that South African officials travelled to Canada at any point throughout the 20th century to observe the advancements of its Indian policy and reserve system. Rather, in drawing these comparisons, we gain a fuller appreciation of the complex and nuanced nature of colonialism, which has "historical rootedness in larger imperial forms of interaction with local populations that were adapted in different ways in the two countries."[76] Accordingly, we may acknowledge these seemingly comparable colonial processes as being informed by a broader set of imperial values; however, we must see each form of oppression on its own terms.

In 1976, Canada endured as a colonial state, and Indigenous peoples remained oppressed through such measures as the Indian Act, the reserve system, residential schools, and child welfare policies. As evidenced by the expulsion of South Africa from the Olympic movement a decade prior, the global sports platform was, and remains, a powerful tool for drawing international attention to matters of human rights and fundamental freedoms. Canada was in a precarious position as it prepared and eventually hosted the 1976 Olympic Games in Montreal. Outwardly, Canadian political leaders toed the line, supporting international endeavours aimed at protecting the human rights and fundamental freedoms of citizens across the globe and ensuring that nation-states were accountable for the treatment of all persons living within their borders and that all persons were protected from abuses by governments. Inwardly, the nation continued to enforce policies of racial segregation and oppression aimed at Indigenous peoples. Innocent children continued to be abducted from their families and detained within residential schools and white foster homes; hundreds of thousands of people remained confined to the reserves; and Indigenous women were experiencing violent and abusive living situations as a result of the more than century-old patriarchal Indian policy.

Settler Canada, Decolonization, and the Olympic Games (1977-2010)

As the famous philosopher and revolutionary writer Frantz Fanon noted, over half a century ago, "Decolonization, as we know, is a historical process: that is to say it cannot be understood, it cannot become intelligible nor clear to itself except in the exact measure that we can discern the movements which give it historical form and content."[77] There is no prescribed process for decolonization. In settler colonial states, such as Canada, the form of colonialism exercised is unique from that of other types of colonialism.[78] Settlers arrived with the express purpose of making their new home on territories already occupied by Indigenous peoples, thereby asserting settler sovereignty over the land, water, air, subterranean earth, and peoples in the new domain they claimed for themselves. Settlers needed to disrupt, destroy, and remove Indigenous peoples from the lands to assert control in their new home, which they accomplished through physical force, law, legislation, and the reconceptualization of human relationships to the land. Lands were transformed from *places* of epistemological, ontological, and cosmological importance into *spaces* of capitalist interest, to be managed, controlled, and ultimately exploited. As it exists in Canada, settler colonialism is not temporally contained; instead, it is reasserted every day. The decolonization of settler colonial states such as Canada, as argued by Eve Tuck and K. Wayne Yang, cannot "easily be grafted into pre-existing discourses/frameworks, even if they are critical, even if they are anti-racist, even if they are justice frameworks. The easy absorption, adoption, and transposing of decolonization is yet another form of settler appropriation."[79]

Indigenous-Settler Relations: A Changing Canadian Legal and Political Landscape

According to Cherokee scholar Jeff Corntassel, "The decolonization process operates at multiple levels and necessitates moving from an awareness of being in struggle."[80] Indigenous peoples have, for many years, been astutely aware of such struggles. As early as the 18th century, for example, Kanien'kehá:ka leaders and delegations began travelling far distances to petition external diplomatic entities, such as the British monarch, requesting that their Indigenous rights be supported. The Kanien'kehá:ka went to places such as London, Geneva, and New York, as well as many others, on multiple occasions throughout the 19th and 20th centuries, requesting the support of entities such as the British Privy Council, League of Nations, and United Nations.[81] Further, the Nisga'a began contesting the Colony of British Columbia's illegal distribution of their lands in the Nass Valley in the 1880s, eventually petitioning their case to the British Privy Council in 1913.[82] The Government of Canada responded in 1927 with an amendment to the Indian Act, making it illegal for Indigenous peoples to hire legal counsel to pursue land claims.[83] In the 1950s, once the prohibition on legal counsel was repealed, the Nisga'a immediately moved their land claim forward, suing the Province of British Columbia in 1967. In 1973, the Supreme Court of Canada ruled in favour of the Nisga'a in the landmark *Calder v British Columbia* decision where, for the first time, Aboriginal title (the inherent Indigenous right to land or a territory) was acknowledged and entrenched in Canadian law.[84] As a direct result of *Calder v British Columbia*, the government was forced to establish an internal branch to respond to two forms of land claim concerns. The specific claims process was designed to address grievances and government failures to uphold the terms and conditions of the historical treaties (1700-1923). The comprehensive claims process (commonly referred to as modern treaties) was intended to address those territories in Canada where treaties had not been negotiated, and Aboriginal title had not been extinguished previously by treaty.[85]

In the 1970s, following such court proceedings and widespread Indigenous activism throughout North America, the government began to engage in the process of decolonization, albeit through a packaged approach to state decolonization using pre-existing justice frameworks. The question of whether to entrench the rights of Indigenous peoples within the repatriated Constitution was discussed and contested throughout the country during the 1970s and early 1980s. Although the government failed to engage Indigenous peoples meaningfully throughout the consultation process, First Nations, Métis, and Inuit peoples remained politically engaged, as they had historically, ensuring their legal rights were not ignored or disavowed at this critical juncture. Indigenous peoples saw the importance of political coordination, organizing delegations to travel great distances once again to petition national and international diplomatic entities.

In 1981, for example, Secwépemc leader George Manuel chartered two trains from Vancouver to Ottawa, in what famously came to be known as the Constitution Express, carrying approximately 1,000 people to Ottawa to publicly denounce the government's dismissal of Indigenous rights in the constitutional reform process. Following demonstrations in the nation's capital, delegations continued to the United Nations in New York as well as to European countries, including the Netherlands, Germany, France, Belgium, and England, to propagate information about Canada's ill treatment of Indigenous peoples and its unwillingness to consult with such peoples throughout the reform process.[86] The government eventually responded to mounting pressures, deciding—at the

11th hour and behind closed doors—to entrench constitutional protections for the *sui generis* rights owed to Indigenous peoples. Section 35(1) of the Constitution states, "The existing aboriginal and treaty rights of aboriginal peoples of Canada are hereby recognized and affirmed."[87] Unfortunately, Section 35 was decidedly ambiguous because the Constitution failed to demarcate what existing aboriginal rights were protected and how they might be defined. Nonetheless, the recognition of Indigenous rights within Canada's supreme law was a vital first step because it provided Indigenous peoples with a robust legal mechanism moving forward.

Exploiting the Olympic Medium to Contest State-Based Oppression

The 1980s proved a turbulent time for many Indigenous peoples throughout Canada. Although new political and legal mechanisms were available for contesting state-based oppression, Indigenous peoples continued to endure colonial abuse and significant discrimination within state-based apparatuses. In search of solutions to their domestic struggles, Indigenous peoples continued to petition international organizations and political entities, seeking support for their legal and human rights. Canada was scheduled to host its second Olympic Games in 1988. With the world's attention drawn to Canada in the years leading to the 1988 Winter Olympics in Calgary, a relatively small Cree Nation from northern Alberta led by Chief Bernard Ominayak decided to exploit the Olympic medium, ultimately drawing international attention to their sufferings and legal problems in the colonial state. To briefly explain, treaty negotiators missed the Lubicon Lake Cree Nation in both treaty commissions in the summers of 1899 and 1900. As early as the 1930s the Lubicon Cree began to petition the federal government formally, requesting their rightful inclusion in Treaty 8. For over 50 years their appeals were denied. The Lubicon and their supporters used opportunities presented in the planning and hosting phases of the 1988 Olympic Games in Calgary to protest in national and international spheres.

The torch relay, for example, was met with strong protest throughout Canada because the Lubicon and their supporters effectively publicized the co-sponsorship of the event by Petro-Canada and the federal government, both of which were illegally invading non-surrendered Lubicon territories. The Lubicon exerted most of their efforts on the international campaign, however, appealing for an international boycott of the Glenbow Museum's exhibition *The Spirit Sings*, sponsored by the federal government and Shell Canada (also actively invading Lubicon territories). The exhibition was to include hundreds of Indigenous artifacts that the Glenbow was to borrow from international lending museums. The truth was, however, that most of these objects—some of which were so spiritually sacred they were not intended to be on public display—had been stolen from their rightful owners years before. As per the lending agreements, all artifacts were to be returned to the lending museums at the exhibition's close. The Lubicon launched an aggressive letter-writing campaign requesting that international museums not contribute stolen objects to the Glenbow. In the end, the exhibition opened in the absence of contributions from 23 of the 110 international museums contacted by the Glenbow. The Lubicon received support from numerous national organizations, including the Assembly of First Nations, Indian Association of Alberta, Métis Association of Alberta, and Grand Council of the Crees. Moreover, international organizations expressed their support, including the World Council of Indigenous Peoples, the National Congress of American Indians, the World Council of Churches, and the European Parliament. By the late 20th century, the Olympic Games proved an effective instrument whereby Indigenous peoples could express grievances against colonial oppression in Canada and ultimately seek the support of domestic and foreign bodies.

Hosting the Olympic Games on Unceded Indigenous Territories

The topic of decolonization was front and centre by the time the Olympic Games returned to Canada in 2010. The nation had reached a state of crisis in the 1990s as violent confrontations between Indigenous peoples and Canadian security forces (e.g., police and military) unfolded at Oka (1990), Ipperwash (1995), and Gustafsen Lake (1995). Further, the atrocities of the nation's past came to the forefront of national politics at this time as prominent Indigenous leaders spoke openly, sharing stories of forced abduction, horrific abuse, and unimaginable neglect at the hands of the state in church-operated Indian residential schools. Following the standoff in Oka, Quebec, the government responded in 1991 with the establishment of the Royal Commission on Aboriginal Peoples (RCAP), tasked with investigating the tumultuous relationship between Aboriginal peoples and the Canadian government and Canadian society.[88] The RCAP's final report eventually led (albeit delayed) to the launch of a reconciliation process in Canada, which included government apologies, compensation packages for survivors and former students of Indian residential schools, and a formal process to document the history and impacts of the abusive school system. Further, as proposed in the RCAP final report, the only way to sincerely respond to the recommendations was for the Government of Canada to overhaul the existing treaty process completely.

The province of British Columbia recognized by the early 1990s that the comprehensive claims process was drastically flawed and that a made-in-B.C. treaty process needed to be established to attend to the unfinished business of treaty-making throughout the province. The solution came in the form of an independent body responsible for facilitating treaty negotiations between First Nations and the governments of Canada and British Columbia. The British Columbia Treaty Commission (BCTC) opened for business in 1993, and within its first decade of operation this process, too, proved to be defunct, as the BCTC had failed to ratify a single treaty. The first treaty to be finalized and implemented through the BCTC was, in fact, the 2009 Tsawwassen First Nation Final Agreement, less than one year before the Olympic Games in Vancouver.[89] The hosting of the Olympic Games placed Tsawwassen First Nation in a favourable negotiating position because it controlled two main seaports within the Lower Mainland, including the Tsawwassen Ferry Terminal and the Roberts Bank Port Facility, both situated on Tsawwassen lands. Because of their substantial investments in the 2010 Olympic Games, the provincial and federal governments were not willing to risk the possibility that—in the absence of a final agreement—the Olympic Games would be further disrupted by Indigenous protest, activism, or violence.

The organizing and hosting of these Olympic Games on the unceded territories of the Tsleil-Waututh, Musqueam, Lil'wat, and Squamish Nations, formally the Four Host First Nation, induced considerable protest and activism (see figure 13.3), once again leading to violent confrontations between Canadian security forces and Indigenous peoples. The fact remained that Canada had, rather unwisely, chosen to host these Olympic Games on the territories of Indigenous peoples who had not previously ceded their lands to the Canadian state through treaty or other legal means. As early as 2001, two years before the Olympic Games were awarded to Vancouver, the No Games 2010 coalition expressed criticism of the bid corporation's desire to host the Olympic Games on stolen Indigenous lands. Following the selection of Vancouver in July 2003, anti-Olympic activism quickly reordered under the Olympic Resistance Network with the No Olympics on Stolen Native Land slogan. The Olympic Resistance Network called attention to the fact that British Columbia

> remains largely unceded and non-surrendered Indigenous territories. According to Canadian law, BC has neither the legal nor moral right to exist, let alone claim land and govern over Native peoples. Despite this, and a fraudulent treaty process now underway, the government continues to sell, lease, and 'develop' Native land for the benefit of corporation, including mining, logging, oil [and] gas, and ski resorts. Meanwhile, Indigenous peoples suffer the highest rates of poverty, underemployment, police violence, disease, suicides, etc.[90]

Figure 13.3 Anti-Olympic protestors march through the streets of Vancouver prior to the opening ceremonies of the 2010 Olympic Games.

Although the campaign drew attention to various domestic claims, the fundamental injustices inflicted on Indigenous peoples in these territories (and elsewhere in Canada) were global in scope. It was a familiar narrative of colonial oppression, dispossession, and disempowerment, which is analogous with those settler colonial states throughout the globe that continue to deny the political, legal, and human rights of Indigenous peoples well into the 21st century.

In February 2007, Pacheedaht (Nuu-chah-nulth) Elder Harriet Nahanee (Tseybayoti) passed away following her incarceration in a provincial jail. The 71-year-old great-grandmother, not well at the time, was sentenced to two weeks in a provincial court after her participation in blockading construction upgrades to the Sea-to-Sky Highway over ecologically sensitive wetlands at Eagleridge Bluffs in preparation for the 2010 Olympic Games. During the judicial proceedings, Elder Nahanee held on firmly to a copy of the Royal Proclamation of 1763, which establishes the legal framework for treaty-making in Canada. In protecting the ecologically sensitive wetlands, Elder Nahanee was carrying out her sacred duty as a hereditary leader and Elder to defend the land, nonhuman relations, and future generations; in holding the Royal Proclamation during judicial proceedings, she was asserting the legal rights owed to her and other Indigenous peoples throughout Canada. Nahanee was found guilty of criminal contempt of court and sentenced to the Surrey Pretrial Services Centre, a male-dominated correctional facility notorious for its overcrowded conditions and frigid temperatures, a "noted hell-hole for women in poor health."[91] The Pacheedaht Elder died in St. Paul's Hospital two weeks later; doctors cited pneumonia and complications as the cause of death.

The untimely death of Elder Nahanee was undoubtedly symptomatic of the enduring colonial oppression of Indigenous peoples in Canada, and the nation's disinclination to move decolonization efforts forward. At a time of consider-

WORKING WITH PRIMARY SOURCES: UNIVERSAL DECLARATION ON THE RIGHTS OF INDIGENOUS PEOPLES

The United Nations Declaration on the Rights of Indigenous Peoples was ratified by the United Nations General Assembly in 2007. It is a nonbinding legal instrument that establishes a universal framework of minimum standards for the survival, dignity, well-being, and rights of Indigenous peoples throughout the world. In 2007, Canada was one of four nations to vote against the Declaration, along with Australia, New Zealand, and the United States. Canada was the last country to ratify the Declaration in 2015.

able uncertainty throughout the province of British Columbia, and Canada, the arrival of the Olympic Games seemed to expedite the possibility of government and corporate encroachments on non-surrendered Indigenous lands and thus served as an ingenious opportunity for government and industry to circumvent the legal process.

On September 13, 2007, the United Nations Declaration on the Rights of Indigenous Peoples (UNDRIP) was adopted in the General Assembly by a majority of 144 states in favour, 4 against, and 14 abstentions.[92] The UNDRIP is a nonbinding legal instrument; however, it establishes

> a universal framework of minimum standards for the survival, dignity, well-being and rights of the world's indigenous peoples. The Declaration addresses both individual and collective rights; cultural rights and identity; rights to education, health, employment, language, and others. It outlaws discrimination against indigenous peoples and promotes their full and effective participation in all matters that concern them. It also ensures their right to remain distinct and to pursue their own priorities in economic, social and cultural development. The Declaration explicitly encourages harmonious and cooperative relations between States and indigenous peoples.[93]

Canada was one of four countries to vote against the UNDRIP, along with Australia, New Zealand, and the United States, citing "significant concerns" in the wording of Article 26, which corroborates that "Indigenous peoples have the right to the lands, territories and resources which they have traditionally owned, occupied or otherwise used or acquired."[94] In November 2010, nine months after the close of the Olympic Games in Vancouver, Canada issued a statement of support.[95] It formally shifted its position from oppositional to "a supporter in principle," confirming Canada as the only nation that refused to accept the UNDRIP as a binding foundational framework for practical implementation. Further, through its formal statement, Canada declared itself to be a "strong voice for the protection of human rights" at the international level and avowed that Canada "continues to make exemplary progress" in building positive relationships with Indigenous peoples, based on good faith, partnership, and mutual respect. Curiously, the statement concludes by acknowledging the 2010 Olympic Games to be "a defining moment for Canada. The Games instilled a tremendous sense of pride in being Canadian and highlighted to the world the extent to which Aboriginal peoples and their cultures contribute to Canada's uniqueness as a nation. The unprecedented involvement of the Four Host First Nations and Aboriginal peoples from across the nation set a benchmark for how we can work together to achieve great success."[96] In the end, Canada successfully hosted the 2010 Olympic Games in Vancouver on the territories of the Tsleil-Waututh, Musqueam, Lil'wat, and Squamish peoples, lands that had yet (and have yet) to be negotiated through treaty and thus transferred legally to the Canadian state.

TRANSFORMATIVE MOMENTS: PROTEST AT EAGLERIDGE BLUFFS

In May 2006, Pacheedaht (Nuu-chah-nulth) Elder Harriet Nahanee and environmental activist Betty Shiver Krawczyk were arrested for protesting the expansion of the Sea-to-Sky Highway over ecologically sensitive wetlands at Eagleridge Bluffs, in preparation for the 2010 Olympic and Paralympic Games in Vancouver. Immediately before her arrest, Elder Nahanee asserted the rights owed to her as an Indigenous person and held onto a copy of the Royal Proclamation of 1763. The Royal Proclamation acknowledges Aboriginal title to the land and outlines the Crown's duty to negotiate treaties with Indigenous peoples, which it had failed to do throughout most of British Columbia. Protestors were opposing the decision to construct an additional 2.4-kilometre (1.5 mile) stretch of roadway through ecologically sensitive wetlands when sustainable alternatives were available. The government opted to build the additional stretch of highway because it was economically advantageous and beneficial to development plans in the Whistler, Pemberton, and Caribou regions. All of these regions, including Eagleridge Bluffs, remain unceded Indigenous territories.

In protesting the Olympics-supported highway expansion, Elder Nahanee was asserting the legal rights of Indigenous peoples as well as following through on her cultural obligations as a hereditary leader to protect the land, nonhuman relations, and the future generations. Elder Nahanee was not well at the time of her incarceration and was detained in the Surrey Pretrial Services Center, a male-dominated correctional facility known for its frigid temperatures. Shortly after her release, she was hospitalized at St. Paul's, where she passed away of complications from pneumonia. Although the death of Elder Nahanee was untimely, it was not in vain, as she has become an important symbol for the justice of Indigenous peoples, inspiring the next generation to defend the land, environment, and Indigenous rights, and thereby standing up against powerful interests, such as government, industry, and influential international organizations such as the Olympic movement.

Conclusion

In *Canada Learns to Play: The Emergence of Organized Sport, 1807-1914*, Alan Metcalfe suggested, in 1987, that an immense gap remained between social and sport historians. Metcalfe reasoned that social and sport historians would find his monograph lacking for various reasons; however, he recognized that his approach underscored certain factors, briefly mentioned others, and excluded others entirely. This chapter interrogates one of the basic social parameters in the historical discourse of Canadian sport that Metcalfe admittedly neglected, namely colonialism. More than anything, this chapter, too, is about Canada. It is about settler colonial Canada and the political, legal, social, and economic processes of colonialism that propelled the formation and rise of the Canadian state, the emergence of a nationalistic ideology, and, ultimately, the establishment of a domestic sport order premised on xenophobic principles. This chapter seeks to uncover the essential Canadian self by shifting the point of intervention. Rather than concentrate on the experiences of Indigenous peoples in Canadian sport history per se, this chapter positions sport as a form of social organization that was (and remains) firmly rooted within the apparatus of the colonial power.

The first area of discussion considers imperial forces, colonialism in the new dominion, and sport as a colonial instrument between the years 1876 and 1914, calling specific attention to the oppressive rubrics of the Indian Act, which circumscribed the experiences of Indigenous peoples in Canadian society and thus sport. Second, this chapter underscores the unmistakable absence of Indigenous peoples in national sport between the years 1915 and 1944, a period of noteworthy growth in Canadian sport, and further re-examines events in Canadian sport history, such as the 1936 Olympic Games in Berlin, where the productivity of Canadian colonialism was avowed in national and international sporting spaces. The third area of discussion considers the precarious position Canada found itself in between the years 1945 and 1976, as Canada continued to enforce a policy of racial segregation in a period marked by transformative global shifts towards human rights protections for all peoples around the world.

Finally, this chapter highlights settler Canada's absorption, adoption, and transposition of decolonization as a form of settler appropriation, and further considers the disingenuous ways in which government and industry capitalized on the arrival of the Olympic Games on unceded Indigenous territories. Instead of supporting decolonization efforts in Canada, the planning of the Olympic Games on non-treaty lands further facilitated opportunities for government and industry to circumvent legal processes and thus disregard legal rights owed to Indigenous peoples. A re-examination of Canadian sport history reveals and confirms that the productivity of Canadian colonialism was avowed repeatedly within the national sporting practices and evidenced by Canada's participation and engagement in international sport. The hope is that this re-examination of Canada's sporting past assists in revealing and thus confirming Canada's essential colonial self, and in the process, supports our efforts to move beyond the fences of our colonial fort.

DISCUSSION QUESTIONS

1. What were some of the oppressive practices in Canada in the late 19th and early 20th centuries, and how was sport used to sustain imperial objectives in Canada?

2. What restrictions were made to the Indian Act in the 1920s and 1930s, and how did this influence the rise of sport in Canada?

3. How were international human rights standards antithetical to Canada's enduring colonial domesticity after the Second World War? Provide a sporting example that best reveals these ideological incompatibilities.

4. How did the political and corporate elite in Canada use the Olympic Games to circumvent legal processes concerning the rights of Indigenous peoples?

SUGGESTED READINGS

Downey, Allan. *The Creator's Game: Lacrosse, Identity, and Indigenous Nationhood*. Vancouver: UBC Press, 2018.

Forsyth, Janice, and Audrey Giles, eds. *Aboriginal Peoples and Sport in Canada: Historical Foundations and Contemporary Issues*. Vancouver: UBC Press, 2013.

Manuel, Arthur, and Ron M. Derrickson. *Unsettling Canada: A National Wake-Up Call*. Toronto: Between the Lines, 2015.

Palmater, Pamela. "Genocide, Indian Policy, and Legislated Elimination of Indians in Canada." *Aboriginal Policy Studies* 3, no. 2 (2014): 27-54.

Tuck, Eve, and K. Wayne Yang. "Decolonization Is Not a Metaphor," *Decolonization: Indigeneity, Education, and Society* 1, no. 1 (2012): 1-40.

CHAPTER 14

AT HOME AND ABROAD: CANADA'S ENGAGEMENT WITH INTERNATIONAL SPORT AND RECREATION

Russell Field, PhD
University of Manitoba

LEARNING OBJECTIVES

In this chapter you will

- learn about sport-for-good and understand how such a vision for sport was reflected in the overseas work of organizations like the YMCA;
- explore the ways in which middle-class advocates used sport and recreation to encourage immigrant acculturation to Canadian society;
- compare the ways in which the women's and workers' sport movements offered alternative visions when contrasted with mainstream international sport;
- examine the motivations behind federal government financial support of fitness and amateur sport programs; and
- learn how Canadian organizations—both those funded by the federal government and NGOs—have been involved in sport-based programs designed to encourage international development.

On August 12, 1978, the crowd in the recently built Commonwealth Stadium watched as the third Commonwealth Games hosted in Canada ended. As athletes from across the Commonwealth paraded around the track during the closing ceremonies, some members of the Canadian team hoisted Iona Campagnolo onto their shoulders (see figure 14.1). Campagnolo was the federal Minister of Amateur Sport, a symbol of the government-funded sport system that had contributed to their athletic careers. It was a telling moment. The Canadian sport system was being not only honoured but also the significance of international sport was on display.

Over the course of the 20th century, Canadians became enmeshed in global movements that celebrated long-standing values associated with sport and encouraged debates about how the Canadian state should involve itself in the promotion of sport and recreation. Modern sport began by touting the benefits it offered—admittedly to a relatively exclusive group of middle- and upper-class anglophone white men (see chapter 7). These men promoted amateur sport as a healthy and manly pursuit in an increasingly urban, industrial world. Participation in their newly organized clubs with their increasingly codified practices was thought to deliver benefits that went beyond enhanced biophysical health. Sport would offer moral uplift, making leaders out of men, who in turn would become better citizens.

Graham Bezant/Toronto Star via Getty Images

Figure 14.1 Canadian athletes hoist sports minister Iona Campagnolo on their shoulders during closing ceremonies of the Commonwealth Games in Edmonton in 1978.

Adhering to the precepts of the amateur code, these men believed in what Simon C. Darnell, Russell Field, and Bruce Kidd have recently termed *sport-for-good*. Standing apart from the pursuit of "sport for sport's sake," sport-for-good "was not a belief that was married to sport, it was *inherent* to sport and the motivation to codify and formalized games culture in the first place."[1] The significance of sport-for-good, in this chapter, is that it was one of the foundational values of international sport and remains a guiding principle for a number of sporting interventions in Canada and around the world.

This chapter explores Canadian involvement in international sport. Emphasis is placed equally on both high-performance, elite sport and grassroots initiatives intended to deliver the presumed social and moral benefits of participation. As the chapter proceeds chronologically, the narrative shifts back and forth between the international context and the domestic sporting scene, because the latter influenced and was influenced by international developments. The chapter concludes with a discussion of the pursuit of international development through sport.

Canada's Early Involvement in International Sport: Exporting the Ideology of Amateurism

As was outlined in chapter 7, organized, modern Canadian sport has its roots in the efforts of a group of initially Montreal-based middle- and upper-class anglophone white men. Enabled by the conditions of industrial capitalism, they created amateur sport clubs in Canada, modelled on institutions elsewhere that had been similarly inspired by the games ethic developed in British public schools (what in Canada are boys' private schools). These developments were motivated not only by a desire to spend the newly emerging notion of leisure time on recreational pursuits but also by a strong belief in the character-building quality of sport. These were pursuits with a purpose, or what historians have come to call "rational recreation."[2]

The nascent modern Olympic movement owes its origins to the same values. Baron Pierre de Coubertin, the minor French aristocrat who spearheaded the creation of the International Olympic Committee in Paris in 1894—with the first modern Olympic Games taking place in Athens, Greece, two years later—believed in the potential of moral uplift through sport. In particular, Coubertin was "greatly impressed by what he viewed in the way of sport and physical education in England's so-called 'public schools.'"[3]

In Canada, by the end of the 20th century's first decade, amateur sport was overseen primarily by the Toronto-based Amateur Athletic Union of Canada (AAUC). AAUC leaders sought to expand amateur sport across the country, widely extending its perceived benefits and focusing initially, as Bruce Kidd argues, on "the process of playing sports, not the score or the spectacle."[4] The AAUC was also responsible for Canada's entries to the increasingly prominent quadrennial Olympic Games.

By the end of the 1920s, Canadian amateur sport leaders had shifted their focus to high-performance events like the Olympic Games—with athletic excellence symbolizing the moral superiority of amateur ideals. The men who ran amateur sport believed in their cause. They included people such as Norton Crow, who was a volunteer leader in the Canadian amateur movement in the early 1900s. He rose to the position of secretary with the AAUC, which strictly protected the rules of amateurism within Canada, and in 1924 proposed the idea for a competition between nations of the British Empire (an idea that would eventually become the Commonwealth Games). When Crow stepped down as AAUC secretary in 1924, he was replaced by Arthur S. Lamb, an instructor at the McGill School of Physical Education, who would go on to serve a term as AAUC president and was also chef de mission of the Canadian team at the 1928 Olympic Games in Amsterdam, Netherlands. Neither supported the entry of women into competitive athletics (discussed later). They were representative of the amateur sportsmen who were, at least in the Canadian case, as Kidd notes, a "satisfied alumni. All of them had been athletes themselves and had benefitted from the experience. Most of them still spent many weekends officiating at games and meets. First and foremost, they believed in sports *for themselves and their class.*"[5]

As a consequence, amateur sport leaders were committed to spreading the values of sport, often beyond the boundaries of the nation. There is no shortage of examples of sport accompanying the international expansion of other institutions—both colonial and missionary—in the last decades of the 19th century and into the 20th century. In Britain, many graduates of the public school system—schooled in sport's moral benefits—joined the foreign service as diplomats and civil servants or entered missionary work, contributing to the spread and maintenance of the Empire. They took their attitudes about sport with them. For example, Theodore Leighton Pennell, a medical missionary in the frontier where India now meets Afghanistan, introduced soccer to his charges and was celebrated in his obituary for his belief (typical of the racialized, colonial notions of the time) that "the proper use of athletics has served to strengthen moral backbone, which is often conspicuously weak, and has been an important auxiliary to Christian teaching."[6]

The YMCA and the Exporting of Sport-for-Good

If British amateur sport enthusiasts found opportunities to expound on the benefits of physical activity in the British Empire's outposts, some of their Canadian counterparts also shared these values beyond Canada's borders. Similarly, sport in the service of Christian proselytizing was an important element of their efforts—most prominently through the international arm of the Young Men's Christian Association (YMCA). Founded in England in 1844, before spreading to Canada, the United States, and elsewhere throughout the world, the YMCA's initial programming rejected sport and play before coming to see value in military drill (organized marching) and calisthenics. This commitment to moral uplift through physical activity has been labelled "muscular Christianity." It was largely under the guidance of Luther Halsey Gulick that sport and physical activity were added to the curriculum of the International Young Men's Christian Association Training School, better known as Springfield College (for its location in Springfield, Massachusetts) in 1887.

It was at Springfield College that Canadian James Naismith invented basketball in 1891. The school was a training ground for the physical educators who would use sport in the service of the YMCA's Christian mission work around the globe. Naismith had been McGill University's first full-time athletics instructor, before deciding that his interest in both sport and theology could best be put to use for the YMCA at Springfield College. Three decades later, Arthur S. Lamb started the first university physical education department at McGill, but while Naismith was still at the Montreal school, McGill would graduate another early Canadian physical educator, R. Tait McKenzie. McKenzie would become famous for both his sculptures of athletic bodies and his advocacy of physical activity as a rehabilitative practice during and after the First World War.

The efforts of Canadian YMCA physical educators in the early 20th century were organized out of a single continental office based in the United States: the International Committee of the YMCA of North America. Committed to engaging local communities through sport as part of their mission—and very much focused on the Caribbean and the Pacific (often in concert with U.S. foreign policy interests at the time)—the YMCA physical educators introduced and institutionalized a number of Western sports in East Asia and elsewhere by the 1920s. Basketball and volleyball became global sports thanks to the YMCA. In Brazil, for example, YMCA educators introduced basketball in 1896, with volleyball beginning not long after. YMCA international programs built the first indoor swimming pool in Japan (1917), created the first college physical fitness program based on Western ideals in China (1917), and started regular athletics competitions in both the Philippines and China.[7]

The introduction—or imposition—of Western sports and physical activity practices, along with the ideological values attached to them, followed a similar pattern internationally as did domestic interventions in Canada, the United States, and the UK. Participation in physical activity initially focused on creating healthy, productive bodies in support of what Stefan Hübner has called "the YMCA's ideas of the civilizing effects of sports and their values on a clean and healthy form of recreation."[8] Indeed, after a generation of YMCA interventions in his country, one Filipino sport leader reflected in 1936 that early sport programs in the Philippines had been "developed not so much to produce 'record-breaking athletes' as to produce virile, healthy, and physically efficient citizens."[9]

The "Civilizing" Impact of Sport

Such efforts soon included the pursuit of competition and sporting excellence. One example of this was the Far Eastern Championship Games (FECG), a multi-sport event held frequently (often every two years) between 1913 and 1934. The event was founded by YMCA physical directors active in the region, in particular Elwood S. Brown. Based in the Philippines, Brown founded a local amateur association—the Philippines Amateur Athletic Association—so that "the YMCA gained de facto control more or less of all physical education programs and amateur sports championships in the Philippines and was able to shape them according to its 'civilizing' aims."[10]

The vision of Brown and his like-minded colleagues soon broadened. The initial FECG was held in the Philippines and included athletes from China, Japan, and the host country. The notion of a multi-sport event that brought together athletes from the countries in which YMCA physical directors were working was originally intended to demonstrate the rightness of their vision for sport,

WORKING WITH PRIMARY SOURCES: J.H. CROCKER AND PHYSICAL EDUCATION IN CHINA

Born in 1870 in St. Stephen, New Brunswick, J.H. Crocker earned a master's degree at Springfield College before embarking on a career with the YMCA both in Canada and overseas. He was posted to the YMCA in Shanghai in 1911 and, in 1915, managed the Chinese team at the Far Eastern Championship Games. He retired from the YMCA in 1930 and spent the next 18 years as physical education director at the University of Western Ontario.

In his 1917 report on the activities of the YMCA in China, Crocker outlines the spread of Western leadership in physical education throughout the country:

> *Many of China's Associations have done splendid extension work among the schools and colleges, promoting physical education-planting seed in virgin soil among China's children, who do not know how to play. For centuries only the literary side of education has been valued and cultivated by the leaders of the people, with the result that China's men are fearfully lacking in imagination, and most of them lacking in initiative.*[12]

Noting that the efforts by the Chinese government to modernize the country are a great opportunity for the YMCA, Crocker writes:

> *Since the Revolution in 1911 China has been realizing that she was lacking in the qualities necessary to make her like other nations, and she has been turning her face westward in the hope of finding the remedy. This has been the Association's great opportunity in the physical as well as in all other departments, and we have tried to bring her that type of physical training related to the development of the whole man. Our Far Eastern Athletic Association, with its International Games every two years, has given not only the athletes, but many thousands of the people the opportunity to see the result of such training in the more advanced countries of Japan and the Philippine Islands. China is keenly alive to this result in other lands, and now in addition to the Young Men's Christian Associations, many of the government institutions are active in promoting physical education.*[13]

not to groom high-performance athletes. Brown was steadfast in his belief that "play and recreation affect citizenship in the sense of developing those qualities that are desirable in a good citizen of any country."[11] He was joined in this mission by Canadian J.H. Crocker, among others. From his posting as the YMCA's physical director in Shanghai, Crocker was instrumental in winning the support of local authorities to take a team of Chinese athletes to the inaugural FECG.

While there had been a shift from participation to achievement through sport, the emphasis on rational recreation remained. The focus of the early FECG was often team sports, such as volleyball, and other forms of mass participation. As Andrew Morris notes, "These games were put on by white men for the edification, masculinization, and Westernization of their weak Oriental pupils."[14] This belief that sport inculcated in Western values could improve the lives of others around the world, on terms set by Western countries, would inform many of the international sport initiatives of the rest of the 20th century.

Acculturation at Home: Sport and the Immigrant Experience

Similar sentiments—both about the need to civilize Others and the benefits of sport and physical activity in such circumstances—were applied back home as well. At the same time that J.H. Crocker was organizing sport programs at a YMCA in China, his colleagues in Canada were doing the same. The intended recipients of such efforts were often the immigrants migrating to Canada by the thousands, remaking the country's cities and quite literally changing the face of the nation.

The belief in healthy, rational recreation, which motivated organizations like the YMCA to take up sport in the late 19th century, also prompted sporting interventions in immigrant communities in the early 20th century. Yet many immigrants arrived in Canada with their own sporting practices. Sometimes these promoted ethnocultural identity and solidarity, but the overwhelming feature of sport and recreation among immigrant communities—regardless of whether it was imposed from outside or organized within—was the degree to which the belief in sport as a morally uplifting practice dominated.

From 1896 to 1914, Canada experienced an unprecedented increase in immigration. This briefly continued into the 1920s after the First World War. In the first decade of the 20th century, immigrants accounted for 39 percent of the increase in population, with a high of more than 400,000 entering the country in 1913. Newcomers to Canada changed not only the size of the country but also its racial composition as well.

The majority of early immigrants arrived from Britain and the United States, perpetuating the Anglo-Saxon whiteness of the country. But in the 1920s, for example, nearly 240,000 immigrants arrived from Central and Eastern Europe (predominantly), Italy and Southern Europe, and East Asia, with small contingents from elsewhere in Asia, Africa, the Caribbean, and Latin America. These visibly different Canadians were often expected to settle and farm agricultural land on the prairies (from which the state had worked to dispossess Indigenous peoples). But many also found their way to Canada's growing cities and contributed to the country's increasing urbanization. Many non-British immigrants migrated to ethnic enclaves in larger cities like Montreal, Toronto, Winnipeg, and Vancouver. These communities within cities offered a sense of the familiar to some. But they were also often neighbourhoods of urban poverty. It was this combination of people new to Canada living in unhealthy conditions that attracted social reformers, some of whom came armed with sport and physical activity interventions.

Practicing Sport-for-Good in Canada

A variety of institutions turned to sport, physical activity, and organized play as a means to help assimilate immigrants to Canada. On the new playgrounds of the early 20th century (see chapter 10), along with schoolyards and playing fields, "immigrants encountered the agencies and officials who would try to assimilate and control them."[15] Baseball (or softball for girls) and basketball were popular sports at institutions such as the YMCA and Young Women's Christian Association (YWCA), while the uplifting benefits of outdoor recreation in the natural world were pursued by organizations such as the Boy Scouts, Girl Guides, and Canadian Girls in Training. Although the targets may often have been young immigrant children, contemporary gender norms also held fast.

These interventions were motivated by the firmly held belief that "British and Canadian games could serve as agents of cultural socialization."[16] In Winnipeg, for example, D.S. Woods, the first dean of education of the University of Manitoba, contended in 1913 that play and recreation "leads to the heart of the foreign child as readily [as to that of] the British born."[17] These notions were put into practice in local schools. W.J. Sisler, principal of Winnipeg's Strathcona School, argued in his tellingly titled memoir, *Peaceful Invasion*, that a soccer program at his school "was a potent factor in creating good-will among children of many racial groups and differing religious beliefs."[18]

In these settings, often well-meaning physical educators and coaches would "emphasize athletics as a ladder of social and economic mobility."[19] Such promises foreshadowed the rhetoric of many of the sport-for-development programs that would emerge more than half a century later, which would tout the power of sport to positively affect people's lives. But in an earlier era, the success of Fanny (Bobbie) Rosenfeld, for example, Olympic medallist and multi-sport star, and also the daughter of Russian Jewish immigrants to Barrie, Ontario, not only indicated the rise of women's sport in the 1920s but also buttressed the claims of sport's assimilationist power.

Such beliefs flourished, in part, because of stereotypes concerning immigrant attitudes towards sport and recreation. K.W. Sokolyk has contended that first-generation Ukrainian Canadians at this time "viewed sports if not as an unnecessary luxury at least as a wasteful activity."[20] More broadly, Robert Harney argues that organized sports were perceived as "a threat to group solidarity, a process of deprivation, which meant the loss of ethnoculture, parental control, [and] esteem between generations," based primarily on the "assumption that newcomers generally wished to maintain old-world ways and ethnic group coherence."[21] In the face of such presumed opposition, assimilation advocates turned to sport as a vehicle of acculturation as well as moral and social uplift.

However, Harney also notes that immigrants were not "potential fossils, living in colonies of an old country, maintaining cultural baggage which changed little."[22] Despite dominant attitudes, individual immigrants and communities— although people of multiple origins and ethnicities cannot be characterized with a single narrative—sought out sport and recreation opportunities. Many were active agents in their own acculturation rather than passive recipients of the assimilation efforts of Anglo-Canada.

Sport in Japanese-Canadian and Ukrainian-Canadian Communities

Many participants in ethnocultural-based practices shared the values of rational recreation, often wholeheartedly adopting the values of sport as an instrument of moral uplift and personal betterment. Consider examples from two Canadian cities—Vancouver and Winnipeg—where immigrant communities were willing participants in the rhetoric of sport-for-good, while also viewing sport as a tool for maintaining ethnocultural community solidarity.

Formed in 1914, the Asahi baseball club was for nearly three decades one of the focal points of the Japanese community in Vancouver (see figure 14.2). British Columbia was the centre of Japanese-Canadian settlement (the 1941 Census indicated that 95 percent of all Japanese immigrants resided in the province). Playing out of the Powell Street Grounds in Vancouver's Little Tokyo, the Asahi were a point of pride for a community that was denied the right to vote and endured persistent racism. Including both Canadian-born Japanese and first-generation Japanese Canadians, the Asahi won city championships in 1926, 1930, and 1933, along with a variety of regional titles. The team continued to compete until the internment of Japanese Canadians in 1942, although baseball would also be played in the labour camps and ghost towns to which the community was forcibly relocated. As Shannon Jette argues, "The Asahi were able to symbolically resist or challenge the hegemony of the white community and foster a sense of pride and self-respect within their own."[23] At the same time, the team's success "symbolized Japanese-Canadians' successful integration into Canadian society."[24]

The experience of Ukrainian Canadians on the prairies during the same early decades of the 20th century presents an even more nuanced picture of the diverse narratives surrounding immigrant sport participation. As many as 170,000 Ukrainians immigrated to Canada between 1891 and 1941, partly in response to Canadian government incentives to develop agriculture on the prairies. Besides settling in rural areas, Ukrainian migrants also made their way to Winnipeg, forming a community in the city's north end. These immigrants

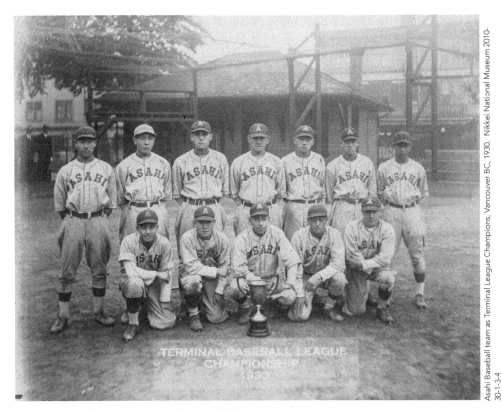

Figure 14.2   The Vancouver Asahi baseball team.

were offered sport opportunities that masked assimilation efforts. Participation in a United Church sport program, for example, came with the expectation that Ukrainian youth would "agree to attend the Church's Sunday Bible school."[25]

Despite such pressures, a number of Ukrainian-led sport groups emerged to serve community needs, often reproducing Anglo institutions. A local Winnipeg dentist, Manoly Mihaychuk, organized an annual sport day for the community, where activities included softball and track-and-field events, and which was held intentionally on Dominion Day (July 1). Other recreational opportunities were offered by the Ukrainian Boy Scouts and the Sporting "Stich" Association of Canada, which was founded in the 1920s and featured military-style drill.[26] Although such opportunities were meant to foster "a patriotic responsibility to Canada and the British Empire" while promoting Ukrainian nationalism and often advocating for a sovereign Ukrainian state, there were fears of "the potential for prejudice and discrimination" and "that Ukrainian youth in a non-Ukrainian sports environment would inevitably be alienated from the Ukrainian community."[27]

The Canadian Ukrainian Athletic Club (CUAC) was formed in Winnipeg in 1925 in response to such concerns. President V.K. Koman argued in 1928 that "to ensure that our youth want to be part of our organizations we must foster all aspects of sport."[28] As a result, the CUAC participated in local leagues in sports such as baseball, softball, hockey, soccer, and basketball. Much like the Asahi in Vancouver, CUAC teams—which were eventually opened to non-Ukrainians—became a fixture in Winnipeg city leagues. The CUAC's senior girls' softball team won 22 Manitoba championships, including 17 consecutive titles from 1957 to 1973, and captured the national championship in 1965.

Interwar Resistance Movements in International Sport

There were other opportunities for Ukrainian Canadians in Winnipeg interested in participating in sport and physical activity. One organization that offered a variety of recreations (sporting and otherwise) was the Ukrainian Labour-Farmer Temple Association. Although its name reflected the urban and rural nature of Ukrainian settlement on the Canadian prairies, its activities—which included sports teams and gymnastics troupes—were decidedly ideological. Sport in the Ukrainian Labour-Farmer Temple Association fell under the umbrella of the Workers' Sports Association of Canada (WSAC). The WSAC was established by the Young Communist League of Canada and was a domestic example of larger international movements that sought to infuse the politics of socialism and communism into the organization and practice of sport.

The two decades between the world wars offered competing visions that challenged the male, middle-class world of amateur sport. Working-class men and women and middle-class sportswomen fought for competitive opportunities in this period, although in very different ways and with different aims. Nevertheless, as much as these international movements challenged the established order of sport, they had at their core the belief that broadening access to sport would enhance the lives of participants, often in emancipatory ways. While Canada was rarely at the forefront of either the women's or workers' sport movements, Canadian athletes were certainly affected by their activism.

Workers' Sport

Ukrainians were not the only ethnocultural group whose members were active in workers' sport in Canada. Finnish and Ukrainian immigrants were the two largest communities among the WSAC membership. Both had carried traditions of labour activism with them to Canada. Many Finns settled in the mining and lumber towns of northern Ontario and British Columbia, and the more left-leaning sport enthusiasts among them were "the best organized and athletically gifted members" of the WSAC.[29] They organized clubs, such as Yritys (Endeavor), to practise sports such as Nordic skiing, track and field, gymnastics, and wrestling. One club held regular cross-country ski races from Beaver Lake (near Sudbury) to South Porcupine (near Timmins) in Northern Ontario.

Other sports were popular among the WSAC clubs, whose activities, Kidd argues, "were periodically associated with political struggle, but the focus was unquestioningly on sport."[30] Soccer teams were formed in a number of Canadian cities in the mid-1920s, including the Hammer and Sickle Club in Winnipeg. Basketball, a centrepiece of YMCA-inspired interventions, was also popular among the WSAC clubs, including a Hamilton team that competed during the 1933 to 1934 season. And, while not affiliated with the WSAC, the gymnasium at the One Big Union hall in Winnipeg was a popular home for boxing and wrestling in the city during the 1920s and early 1930s.[31]

Yet, as Kidd notes, "the staple of most clubs was gymnastics."[32] This was largely because "the great majority" of WSAC members "were Eastern European immigrants for whom it was a familiar and favourite form of activity."[33] Another reason for the popularity of gymnastics was the activity's performative nature. Tumbling, floor exercises, and the popular multi-person pyramids would all be performed in front of an audience to demonstrate the importance of working-class solidarity. During the 1930s, the gymnastics troupe of the Winnipeg WSAC toured throughout Manitoba, Northwestern Ontario, and North Dakota performing for working-class audiences.

Despite such activities, the membership of the WSAC was never substantial, peaking at about 5,000 members in 1933. Formed in 1928 by the Young Communist League of Canada, members were not required to be communist to participate in sport. Nevertheless, and irrespective of the organization's small size, the WSAC had ties to a much larger international movement. Red Sport International (RSI) was the sporting arm of the international communist movement. Based in Moscow, Russia, the RSI hosted Olympic-style multi-sport events (Spartakiads) every four years beginning in 1928 and claimed to have four million members worldwide.

The RSI had emerged as the result of an ideological split between socialists and communists, which affected another international left-wing sport movement. Socialist Workers' Sport International (SWSI; also called Lucerne Sport International after the Swiss city where it was founded) was officially formed in 1920 and grew to two million members between the world wars. Through the 1920s and 1930s, SWSI hosted Workers' Olympics, usually every six years. The 1931 Summer Workers' Olympics in Vienna attracted 76,245 worker-athletes from 23 countries. Kidd calls it "perhaps the most successful athletic festival ever held."[34]

Although a minority vision (in Canada) of how sport could be practised, workers' sport offered a critique of mainstream capitalist sport. It was open to all regardless of ability. The Workers' Olympics eschewed national symbols in favour of building class consciousness across geopolitical boundaries. Workers' sport gatherings often emphasized peace building, and the movement actively opposed the rise of fascist regimes in Europe in the interwar years. Finally, significantly greater numbers of women participated in the Workers' Olympics than in the International Olympic Committee's (IOC's) Games.

The 1936 Olympic Games were scheduled for Berlin, Germany. The violent persecution of Jews, labour leaders, and others by Hitler's Nazi Party led to widespread calls for nations to boycott the event. The rise of fascism led to a reuniting of communists and socialists in a popular front that extended to sport. The RSI and SWSI set aside political differences to be part of a People's Olympiad, scheduled to take place in Barcelona, Spain, in July 1936—two weeks before Hitler's Olympic Games. Although the opening ceremonies took place on July 19, the events, scheduled to begin on July 22, never got under way. The People's Olympiad were cancelled following a coup led by General Francisco Franco against the popular front government, which would escalate into the four-year-long Spanish Civil War.

It has been estimated that six thousand athletes from 23 countries would have participated in the People's Olympiad. Five Canadians travelled to the event—boxers Sammy Luftspring and Norman Yack, sprinters Tom Ritchie and Bill Christie, and high jumper Eva Dawes—along with boxing manager Harry Sniderman. The boxers were Jewish and reflected both the Canadian Jewish Congress's involvement in organizing the Canadian contingent as well as the widespread Jewish-Canadian opposition to Hitler's Germany's hosting of the Olympic Games. (Luftspring was one of Canada's best amateur boxers and would go on to win the Canadian welterweight championship as a professional.)

Dawes' (see figure 14.3) participation, however, was indicative of WSAC support of the People's Olympiad. The bronze medallist in the high jump at the 1932 Olympic Games in Los Angeles, California, she had participated in a WSAC-sponsored trip to the Soviet Union in 1935, which may have reflected her support of working-class politics or her disenchantment with amateur sport in Canada (there is some debate on this issue).[35] Nevertheless, among the Canadians who hoped to compete in Barcelona, "Dawes was by far the more experienced and travelled athlete."[36]

Women's Sport

Dawes' athletic career was not just an example of the influence of the workers' sport movement in the interwar years. Her success also reflected the increasing opportunities for women in competitive sport, both in

Figure 14.3   Eva Dawes, Canadian high jumper.

Canada's Sports Hall of Fame - Pantheon des sports canadiens
SPORTSHALL.CA - PANTHEONSPORTS.CA
Objet ID: 2008.44.7452

Canada and internationally. She was a member of the Toronto Ladies Athletic Club, which was at the forefront of a watershed era, having been founded in 1921 by Alexandrine Gibb and Mabel Ray, two of the leaders of women's sport in Canada. Such women were inspired by international developments that were opening up competitive opportunities for female athletes. A national women's track and field championship was first held in France in 1917. This led to a national organization, which by 1919 was under the leadership of Alice Milliat. One of Milliat's earliest efforts was to petition the IOC to include track and field competitions for women at the upcoming 1920 Olympic Games in Antwerp, Belgium. The IOC's refusal led Milliat and her French colleagues to host their own international meet in Monaco in March 1921, which attracted athletes from France, England, Italy, Norway, and Sweden.

The success of this competition and the attention it garnered emboldened women sport leaders. Later that year, in October 1921, representatives from Austria, Czechoslovakia, England, France, Germany, Spain, the United States, and the Scandinavian countries met in Paris to form the Fédération sportive féminine internationale (FSFI). Milliat was acclaimed as the organization's president the following year at the second FSFI congress. This congress was concurrent with the first FSFI-hosted Women's Olympic Games, held in Paris. While the FSFI continued to lobby the IOC to include women, the federation's leadership affirmed its commitment to continue to host the quadrennial Women's Olympic Games. At the time, the FSFI boasted 38 member countries from five continents, making it as sizable an organization as the International Amateur Athletic Federation (IAAF), the international governing body of (at the time, men's) track and field.

No Canadians competed at the first Women's Olympic Games in 1922, but in 1924, Canada gained membership in the FSFI. This was a year before the AAUC approved a women's branch in Canada, which led to the creation of the Women's Amateur Athletic Federation (WAAF), officially formed in 1926. This was the same year the second Women's Olympic Games were held in Gothenburg, Sweden—although no Canadians competed in the 12 events on the program.

It was FSFI efforts, in particular lobbying by Milliat, that resulted in the IOC's including five track and field events for women at the 1928 Olympic Games in Amsterdam, at the IAAF's urging. However, Florence Carpentier and Jean-Pierre Lefèvre argue that this was motivated by a desire on the part of male sport leaders to gain control over women's sport and to control the use of the word *Olympic* by entities other than the IOC.[37] In all, 277 women competed in Amsterdam, more than three times the number that had attended the second Women's Olympic Games in Gothenburg, Sweden, two years earlier. However, female sport leaders were far from satisfied. Milliat had demanded 12 events in Amsterdam, as found on the Women's Game program ("If women's participation is so limited, it will not serve the cause of making women's athletics better known") and insisted that the FSFI be recognized by the IOC on the same level as its member federations ("Women's athletics has proved itself and does not want to serve as an experiment for the Olympic Committee").[38] She was thwarted on both fronts. In the face of this defeat, and believing in the independence of the women's sport movement, the English women's team boycotted the Olympic Games in Amsterdam.

Nevertheless, 21 nations sent female athletes to compete in five events in Amsterdam. The Canadian contingent was chaperoned by sport administrator Alexandrine Gibb, the *Toronto Daily Star*'s women's sports columnist. The

Figure 14.4   The Matchless Six Canadian track and field team in 1928. The team members were Bobbie Rosenfeld, Jean Thompson, Florence Bell, Myrtle Cook, Ethel Smith, and Ethel Catherwood.

six-person team comprised runners Florence Bell, Myrtle Cook, Bobbie Rosenfeld, Ethel Smith, and Jean Thompson and high jumper Ethel Catherwood. The sextet was so successful that the media dubbed the women "the Matchless Six" (see figure 14.4). They won silver and bronze medals in the 100 metres, won bronze in the high jump, set a record time in winning the gold medal in the relay, and won the unofficial points championship. The growing recognition of women's sport in Canada was reflected not only in this success but also by the 200,000 people who greeted the Matchless Six at Toronto's Union Station upon their return to Canada.

Women's participation in the IOC Games continued, and the FSFI moved forward with the Women's World Games (no longer called "Olympics") in 1930 (Prague) and 1934 (London). As was the case with the workers' sport movement, the FSFI's momentum stalled during this decade and it ceased operation in 1936, ironically while the Olympic Games in Berlin were under way, the same event that the Barcelona People's Olympiad had unsuccessfully sought to undermine.

Dawes' athletic career was symbolic of this shifting ideological landscape. Two years after winning her 1932 Olympic bronze medal and two years before preparing to defy Canadian amateur sport officials by competing in the People's Olympiad in 1936, Dawes travelled to England. She placed fourth in the high jump at the 1934 Women's World Games. That event took place immediately after the second British Empire Games, at which Dawes also competed (winning a silver medal). That what would become known as the Commonwealth Games flourished while both the women's and workers' sport movements floundered speaks to the enduring power of amateur sport in the decades following the Second World War.

PROMINENT PEOPLE: FANNY "BOBBIE" ROSENFELD (1903-1969)

Fanny "Bobbie" Rosenfeld (see figure 14.5) was one of the greatest Canadian athletes of all time. Known as "Bobbie" because of her bob haircut, Rosenfeld was born in Russia in 1904 to Jewish parents. The family immigrated to Canada in 1905 and settled in Barrie, Ontario, 100 kilometres (60 miles) north of Toronto.

Rosenfeld's participation was emblematic of women's sport involve-

Canada's Sports Hall of Fame - Pantheon des sports canadiens
SPORTSHALL.CA - PANTHEONSPORTS.CA
Object ID: X981.712.1.8

Figure 14.5 Fanny "Bobbie" Rosenfeld.

ment during this era. She moved to Toronto with her family in 1922 and took a job at the Patterson Candy Co., where she played for the company softball team and competed for Patterson's athletic club. She won local tennis championships and also played for local amateur hockey and basketball teams. Rosenfeld excelled in a wide variety of sports and was comparable to other multi-sport stars of the era (such as Lionel Conacher in men's sport). James "Hud" Stewart of the 1932 Canadian Olympic team called Rosenfeld "the greatest hockey player, male or female, of the period."[39]

But it was as a member of the Matchless Six in 1928 that she achieved international success. Yet only a year later, Rosenfeld was diagnosed with severe arthritis; she was forced to retire from competition for good in 1933. She coached the Canadian women's track and field team at the 1934 British Empire Games before joining the *Globe and Mail* in 1937 as author of the Sports Reel column for 20 years. In 1950, Rosenfeld was named Canada's female athlete of the first half of the 20th century, and the Canadian Press award for Canada's female athlete of the year is named for her.

When Dawes went to Spain for the 1936 People's Olympiad, she told the communist newspaper, the *Daily Clarion*, she was "glad to compete in an Olympics where the true meaning of sport will exist."[40] While ideologically opposed to the capitalist sport of the bourgeois IOC Olympics, workers' sport in its own ways touted the moral values of amateur sport. Both the international examples discussed in this section resisted the dominant male, amateur approach to sport, yet both also affirmed that central to these oppositional movements was the belief that participation in sport created opportunities for human betterment.

International Success, Domestic Priority

The British Empire Games were started by Canadian amateur sport leaders and were first held in Hamilton in 1930. Their origin points to the influence that amateur values held over international sport into the 1930s and beyond. The failure of efforts to organize a boycott of the 1936 Olympic Games in Berlin and the slow but increasing inclusion of women within the Olympic program were indications of the continued strength of the middle-class, amateur vision of sport—in response to the alternative visions and resistance movements discussed in the previous section. At the same time, there were attempts to geographically broaden the reach of international sport. Canada was particularly active in the British Empire Games and also involved, although primarily as a host nation, in the Pan American Games.

Canada has hosted the now Commonwealth Games four times (Hamilton 1930, Vancouver 1954, Edmonton 1978, Victoria 1994) and the Pan American Games three times (Winnipeg 1967 and 1999, Toronto 2015). Throughout the middle decades of the 20th century, the motivations behind Canada's involvement in international sport reflected a number of themes: debates over how international sporting success reflected on the nation and how this nation defined itself in and through sport; the shifting role of the federal government in supporting Canadians in international sport and promoting general physical fitness; and the desire of amateur sport leaders to respond to the increasing popularity of commercial sport leagues (e.g., hockey, baseball) domestically. In this period, as Charlotte Macdonald observes, "physical exercise and sporting success were central to the way in which Canadians became modern and imagined themselves as a nation."[41]

The role the federal government should play in such efforts has been a matter of some contention for a century. As early as 1918, the AAUC proposed a national sport and recreation program to be funded by the federal government. Amateur sport leaders argued that a network of playgrounds and sport facilities complete with well-resourced programming, as well as enhanced physical education in schools, would improve the health of the nation after four years of war and as a global influenza epidemic was spreading. AAUC advocacy failed to realize this nationwide program. Two decades later, an attempt by Liberal Party backbench MP Hugh Plaxton—a one-time member of the University of Toronto men's hockey team—to create a federal ministry of sport, which would tend to the "national interests implicit in top sporting events," was also unsuccessful.[42]

Efforts to engage the federal government in supporting sport and fitness in the years between the world wars bore little fruit (provincial governments and municipalities were much more active in this regard). Yet amateur sport leaders were not wholly unsuccessful in advancing their vision of sport in this period. AAUC secretary Crow proposed an all–British Empire games at the AAUC's 1924 annual meeting. Such an event would provide a platform for demonstrating Canadian independence and athletic prowess, while at the same time reflecting the loyalty to the British Empire that was characteristic of the country's amateur sport leaders.

Crow's vision would be realized by Bobby Robinson, manager of Canada's 1928 men's Olympic track and field team and sports editor at the *Hamilton Spectator*. He convinced civic leaders to fund the inaugural British Empire Games in Hamilton in 1930. Approximately 400 athletes from 11 countries participated in six individual events (bowls, boxing, rowing, swimming and diving, track and field, and wrestling), although women were allowed to compete only in swimming. The opening ceremonies in Hamilton's newly built stadium was watched by 20,000—including the British Empire Games' honorary president, Governor General Viscount Willingdon.

In 1954, Vancouver hosted the renamed British Empire and Commonwealth Games. Over 660 athletes represented 24 countries, in an event best remembered for the "miracle mile" race, in which England's Roger Bannister and Australia's John Landy battled to break the four-minute mark in the mile. The British Empire and Commonwealth Games were the first to be broadcast in Canada on the new and increasingly popular television sets as sport became a visible front on which the ideological battles between the capitalist West and communist East, characteristic of what was known as the Cold War, were contested. It was in this same post-Second World War decade that the ambitions of regional sport leaders resulted in the first Pan American Games, held in 1951 in Buenos Aires, Argentina.

Yet the Canadian federal government's first significant involvement in the promotion of sport and physical activity occurred a decade earlier with the 1943 National Physical Fitness Act (see chapter 8). Introduced during the Second World War, this legislation was primarily motivated by concerns over the fitness of men available for military service. The act was repealed in 1954—the end of the war and the general prosperity of the 1950s "brought calls for less rather than more government," Macdonald argues, ending efforts "to make sport and physical exercise a national and public responsibility."[43]

These efforts would be resumed by the end of the decade, however. The new focus would highlight the "distinction between local recreation in peacetime and national fitness in wartime."[44] Accounts of international sport in the 1950s highlight the novelty of television's ability to bring sporting results into the homes of the nation, with the significance of wins and losses heightened by the geopolitical tensions of the Cold War.[45] In Canada, these narratives were most often framed around hockey (see chapter 9).

Amateur regulations prohibited the country's most prominent professional players from competing in the Olympics and world championships. At the same time, the Soviet Union had made a political decision to fund sport programs as a way to promote the strength of their nation. One of the sports emphasized by Soviet Union sport leaders was hockey. In a few short years, Canada's international dominance of the sport—even without its best players—had vanished. Canada would win the Olympic gold medal in 1952, but not again for half a century, and by 1954 was being soundly defeated by Soviet Union teams at the world championships.

Although television brought these failures into people's homes, its popularity was also a symbol of increasingly sedentary behaviour in a rapidly suburbanizing society. The nation's fitness levels as well as Canada's overall lack of success in international sport, despite being a financially well-off country, were themes taken up by HRH Prince Philip in a much-publicized address to the Canadian Medical Association in 1959.[46] The speech, a result of the lobbying of sport leaders such as Canadian Olympic Association president James Worrall and civil servants such as Doris Plewes, has been recognized by some historians as a catalyst for the changes in government policy that were to come.

The Diefenbaker Vision and the Fitness and Amateur Sport Act

It was within this context that John Diefenbaker became prime minister in 1957. He had, as Kidd notes, a "personal belief that successful athletic teams enhanced a nation's image abroad and strengthened capitalist voices in the Cold War."[47] The prime minister attributed these attitudes to his attendance at the 1936 Olympic Games in Berlin, which for all the controversy it generated was used by the German government, through the organization of events and the grand facilities constructed, as an opportunity to communicate to the world that Germany was a modern society recovered from the First World War. Diefenbaker recalled: "I vowed to myself that if I ever had the chance I would do the same things for Canadian athletes and the Canadian people, albeit under democratic auspices."[48]

The result of this commitment was the Fitness and Amateur Sport Act (FAS), passed in 1961. It established a fund of $5 million to support amateur sport and promote fitness. A national advisory council was created, the volunteer-led associations that administered amateur sport in Canada received financial support to train coaches and assist athletes, and agreements were negotiated with individual provinces to use funds to promote physical fitness among the population. Research into high-performance sport, which contributed to the development of kinesiology as an academic discipline, was also ramped up in the 1960s thanks to the FAS.

Despite Diefenbaker's lofty ambitions, the implementation of the FAS met with mixed success. Donald Macintosh, Tom Bedecki, and C.E.S. Franks attribute these failings to a lack of both time and funds provided to the advisory council, as well as to tensions between the federal government and the provinces. They and others have characterized the 1960s as indicative of a "kitchen table" era in Canadian sport, where national sport governing bodies were "still operating out of the kitchens of volunteer executive members."[49] Athletes travelling to Olympic Games or other major competitions had to self-finance, while coaches and other officials were unpaid volunteers.

Diefenbaker's hope of buttressing Canada's international reputation was not realized in sporting success. The six medals won by Canada at the 1956 Olympic Games in Melbourne, Australia, before the introduction of the FAS were nearly matched by the four won at the 1964 Olympic Games in Tokyo, Japan, and five at the 1968 Olympic Games in Mexico City, Mexico, in the years after the FAS.

The Trudeau Vision and the Making of the Canadian Sport System

Changing Canada's Olympic fortunes was only part of the rationale behind the Pierre Trudeau government's reinterpreting the FAS following its election in 1968. Trudeau argued that sport should be supported by the federal government because the success of Canadian athletes internationally was "important for the images Canadians have of themselves."[50] Kidd argues: "Whereas Diefenbaker was concerned with the ideological impact of national teams abroad, an acute crisis of federal legitimacy led Trudeau to focus on their image at home."[51]

Creating symbols of national identity was important because of contemporary challenges to the unity of the Canadian state. Most prominent among these was the rising nationalist, and at time separatist, movement in Quebec, which reached a violent apogee during the FLQ crisis and Trudeau's subsequent invoking of the War Measures Act in October 1970. There was also discontent with the federal government in Western Canada, challenges to Canadian sovereignty in the north, and increasingly visible (to settler Canadians) Indigenous rights activism.

In response, Trudeau pursued policies that supported pan-Canadian unity. One of these was promoting Canadian involvement in international sport. "For these goals," Kidd argues, "the high-performance sports project, which recruited athletes from every national and regional group for teams that would march behind a single Canadian flag, compete in identical red-and-white uniforms and glorify teamwork and discipline, was ideal."[52] A year before Trudeau's victory in the 1968 federal election, Winnipeg had hosted the Pan American Games, promoted as part of Canada's centennial celebrations in 1967. The event was run by 12 staff people and a sizable cadre of volunteers, indicative of "the middle-class volunteerism that characterized the administration of Canadian high-performance sport in the 1960s."[53]

Trudeau's vision for sport necessitated a reconsideration of this approach. The responsibility for this fell first to a three-person Task Force on Sport for Canadians. Their report was crafted into a white paper (a proposal for policy change) by Minister of Health and Welfare John Munro. It was titled "A Proposed Sports Policy for Canadians" and, when implemented, radically reshaped the federal government's involvement in sport by reimagining the FAS. Two new administrative agencies were created: Sport Canada and Hockey Canada.

The individual sport governing bodies (except hockey) were to be funded through Sport Canada and professionally managed out of a central administrative office, the National Sport and Recreation Centre, located just outside of Ottawa. This emerging Canadian sport system also included coaching development programs (what is now the National Coaching Certification Program), centralized training camps for national teams, national and provincial training centres, support for overseas camps and tours, and financial assistance for athletes through the newly created Athlete Assistance Program.

The Trudeau vision for sport was realized in a number of international events hosted in the 1970s. Hockey Canada was part of organizing the eight-game

Summit Series between Canadian NHL players and the Soviet Union's national team—the climax to the geopolitical tensions that had started in the 1950s. Trudeau dropped the puck at the ceremonial opening faceoff. Four years later, Canada hosted the world's best athletes at the 1976 Olympic Games in Montreal.

Although Canada became the first Olympic host nation to fail to win a gold medal, the additional funding for athletes put towards these Games (a program called Game Plan) was part of a federal government commitment to athlete development. This also included the Canada Games for youth athletes, the Arctic Winter Games for athletes in the Canadian North, and an Indigenous sport system, which was intended to develop high-performance athletes among Canada's Indigenous Peoples (see chapter 4). To be sure, such programs had ideological motives, including demonstrating Canada's sovereignty over its northern borders and limiting expressions of Indigenous culture (while offering assimilative programs instead). But they also foreshadowed subsequent decisions to connect federal funds for athlete development to occasions of

TRANSFORMATIVE MOMENTS: PARTICIPACTION

ParticipAction was an outcome of the reimagining of the Fitness and Amateur Sport Act under the government of Pierre Trudeau. The program was a social marketing agency that while arm's length from the federal government was funded primarily by Health Canada as well as private sponsorships. It created television, radio, print, and billboard ads "to increase public awareness of the need for daily physical activity and healthy lifestyle choices."[54] These messages reached homes, businesses, and schools through some of the era's most iconic advertising. A high-profile early TV campaign unfavorably compared the fitness of the average 30-year-old Canadian male to that of a 60-year-old Swede, while in the late-1980s, televised fitness tips (*Body Break*) made the segments' hosts, Joanne McLeod and Hal Johnson, national celebrities.

Despite its resonance as an aspect of Canadian popular culture, historians have critiqued ParticipAction. The Cold War tensions of the 1950s that led the Diefenbaker government to introduce the Fitness and Amateur Sport Act manifested themselves through a concern over the general fitness level of Canadians. The creation of ParticipAction in 1971 has been explained as a response to these issues, in the context of the Cold War. As Victoria Lamb Drover argues, ParticipAction "seemed an elegant solution to the created crisis in national health that was crippling Canada's contribution to the Cold War 'sports' race."[55]

Furthermore, ParticipAction has been viewed as a particularly neoliberal response to concerns over national fitness. The program provided messaging and suggested solutions but essentially positioned health and physical fitness as an individual responsibility, one that the government could be seen to be supporting through Health Canada's funding of ParticipAction, but which did not require an investment in grassroots programs or facilities. The agency lasted 30 years, until 2001, with a new ParticipAction being revived in 2007 under a modified mandate.[56]

hosting major Games, including the Best Ever program introduced for the 1988 Olympic Games in Calgary and Own the Podium for the 2010 Olympic Games in Vancouver.

The Diefenbaker vision for sport included some consideration of mass participation and national physical fitness. The Trudeau era's reimagining of the FAS, however, was decidedly focused on high-performance sport. The creation of ParticipAction—an agency that offered education programs and created public service advertisements encouraging individual Canadians to realize the benefits of physical fitness—was the primary contributor to grassroots fitness in this era.

Canadian sport policy emerged out of a desire by the federal government to use sport to promote particular visions of Canada. The athletic high-water mark for the Canadian sport system that the Trudeau government envisioned came in 1978 at the Commonwealth Games. Although the Game Plan athlete development funding had not produced a gold medal at the 1976 Olympic Games in Montreal, it had aided the training of a young generation of Canadian high-performance athletes.

Two years later, many of these athletes competed at the 1978 Commonwealth Games in Edmonton. Led by pentathlete Diane Jones Konihowski, the Canadian team finished atop the medals for the only time in the history of the British Empire/Commonwealth Games. Both the hosting of the event itself, in the new Commonwealth Stadium, and the success of Canadian athletes were taken as evidence of the strength of the more professional and bureaucratic approach to sport development.

Exporting Sport's Benefits: International Sport and Development in a Neoliberal Order

While the 1978 Commonwealth Games were a high point of federal government investment in sport, this was not Canada's only involvement with the Commonwealth over matters of sport in this period. The Commonwealth organization and the Commonwealth Games are administered separately. It was the former that sought to navigate a significant diplomatic and human rights tension that had played itself out through sport. Initiated formally in 1948 by the newly elected government of the National Party, apartheid was an official policy of racial segregation that divided South African society. The population was divided into distinct groups by race, creating a hierarchy within the country, with white South Africans retaining political power and privilege. In sporting terms, different racial groupings had their own sporting organizations and for the most part competed separately, but only white South Africans were selected to represent the country internationally. It was not until the 1960s that international sport governing bodies began to challenge these racist policies.

As a result, the inclusion of South Africa in international sport competitions, including the Commonwealth Games, was increasingly challenged. South Africa was barred from the 1964 Olympic Games in Tokyo and had its initial invitation for the 1968 Olympic Games in Mexico City rescinded after the IOC gave in to international pressure. Nevertheless, the country still had sporting contact with some nations (e.g., Australia, Great Britain, New Zealand) in non-Olympic sports (e.g., cricket, rugby). Some African nations boycotted the 1976 Olympic Games in Montreal over the participation of New Zealand, in protest over that nation's decision to engage in sporting competition with South Africa.

A similar boycott was threatened for the 1978 Commonwealth Games in Edmonton. The heads of government of the Commonwealth countries, including Pierre Trudeau, met at the Scottish resort of Gleneagles in 1977 to avert a boycott. The Gleneagles Agreement explicitly positioned the Commonwealth as opposed to racism, while member states agreed to end all sporting contact with South Africa. The episode not only highlighted the highly political nature of international sport but also revealed that a regional organization like the Commonwealth could be a vehicle through which to assert ideological values in sport.

It was subsequently under the auspices of the Commonwealth that the Canadian government took a leadership role in delivering programs that today are labelled sport-for-development. But before the Commonwealth became active in sport-for-development, and before Canadian government agencies actively engaged in supporting such programs, volunteer service organizations took the lead in connecting sport to development opportunities. These organizations emerged in a variety of countries in the late 1950s and early 1960s. In the West, they included most prominently the Peace Corps in the United States and Voluntary Service Overseas in Great Britain and Canadian University Service Overseas (CUSO) in Canada.

These organizations offered community development and education programs to the world's poorest peoples in the liberal democratic spirit of the age, which was most prominently embodied by the enthusiasm of young people for U.S. president John F. Kennedy, who introduced the idea of the Peace Corps during his election campaign in 1960. Gordon Cressy was one of the early wave of Canadian youth volunteers sent by CUSO to the Caribbean in the 1960s. He was assigned to work with the YMCA in Trinidad. While there he took it upon himself to create swimming opportunities for local youth, who found it unsafe to swim off the island's coast. Cressy organized the financial and human resources necessary to renovate a pool that had been abandoned by the U.S. military. This became Trinidad's first public swimming pool—a development project realized by a Canadian volunteer who had not travelled to the island to create aquatics infrastructure.

Similarly, most of the programs that made use of sport to achieve their community development or other objectives did so in ad hoc ways. By 1970, the Peace Corps in the United States had created a Sports Corps of coaches (who were working in 25 countries by 1972), but in most other cases few of these types of interventions were explicitly designed around sport programs. Instead many aid workers found that sport was a useful conduit to other goals. Moreover, the programs offered by organizations that touted their progressive values were often as ideological (and sometimes overtly anti-communist) as other programs that were more directly connected to Cold War politics.

In the same way, modern sport-for-development projects are not apolitical. In Canada, CUSO received federal support for its interventions in the 1960s, which extended well beyond sport. But it was not until the early 1990s that the Canadian government committed itself to support overseas aid work connected to sport. The earliest versions of these interventions were sport development rather than what later came to be known as sport-for-development. Some were initiatives sponsored by the Commonwealth.

Canadian leaders felt that taking a leadership role in sport development (and later sport-for-development) programs within the Commonwealth would enhance Canada's image internationally. Their successful lobbying of the Commonwealth heads of government resulted in the Commonwealth Sport Development Program (CSDP), which began in the 1990s. The CSDP was developed and operated by the Commonwealth Games Association of Canada (now known as Commonwealth Games Canada) and supported overseas by the Canadian International Development Agency (CIDA) and domestically by Sport Canada. CSDP officials oversaw Commonwealth sport development efforts in the Caribbean, South Asia, and southern Africa.

Despite the best intentions of planners in Canada and other developed nations, such programs were often planned in Western meeting rooms with not enough consideration of local needs and the resources available on the ground. One

What Is Development?

In many ways, sport-for-development is a modern manifestation of sport-for-good (discussed at the beginning of this chapter). Yet as political scientist David Black observes, what is meant by *development* is "inherently contentious and contested."[57] In general, though, international development projects most often focus on improving economic and social conditions in underserved regions of the world, which are typically southern and non-white (today often referred to as the Global South). They are most often organized and delivered by institutions based in the more affluent regions of the world, which are typically northern and white (the Global North).

Modern international development has been traced to the late 1940s, and since this time, development projects have utilized sport in a variety of ways. Sport development—or, as it was often termed from the 1950s to 1970s, sport aid—focused on providing infrastructure (facilities, equipment) and training (of both athletes and coaches) in underdeveloped regions around the world. Sport-for-development programs, by contrast, would in the late 1990s and early 2000s shift the emphasis beyond developing sports skills to try to achieve social and economic goals through sport programs.

The emerging field of sport-for-development was predicated on the logic that the benefits of involvement in sport extended well beyond motor skills and cardiorespiratory fitness. Today, sport-for-development programs "organize and mobilize sport and physical activity in order to contribute to gender empowerment, health promotion, economic development, and peace and conflict resolution, among other goals."[58]

pair of Canadian sport development officers were sent to support Zimbabwe's efforts to host the 1995 All-Africa Games. Once they were more familiar with local needs and partners, they played a part in designing an aerobics program for pregnant women that was offered in more than 120 clinics around Harare, the capital of Zimbabwe. The program was intended to use physical activity to improve birth outcomes and offer HIV and AIDS education. This example demonstrates the shift from sport development to sport-for-development.[59]

This change was motivated by more than just local needs. In 2000, the United Nations adopted the Millennium Development Goals (MDGs), which were signed by more than 190 countries and intended to, among other things, point the way to eradicating global poverty, improving education rates, and reducing the spread of HIV and AIDS, malaria, and other diseases. International development programs that focused on sport shifted their emphasis to meet these new challenges (and benefit from the funding available for them).

These priorities emerged at a time when many Western economic systems, including Canada's, were increasingly influenced by neoliberal thinking. Although a complex concept, neoliberalism shifted the focus of governments away from directly operating many social programs, including international development, and instead turning to private entities to take up this work and provide these services. In Canada, for example, federal government support of sport-for-development decreased in the 2010s as both CIDA and Sport Canada withdrew their funding of such programs.

This programming gap was filled by non-governmental organizations (NGOs) working in sport-for-development. The MDGs remained significant to these Western agencies committed to doing work in what was most often called the developing world or the Global South. Canadian expertise was exemplified by one of the most prominent sport-for-development NGOs, the Toronto-based Right to Play.

Led by Norwegian Olympic-champion speed skater Johann Olav Koss, Right to Play emerged out of an earlier organization known as Olympic Aid. Olympic Aid had initially existed to raise funds for international aid projects, but beginning in the early 2000s, Right to Play created sport-for-development projects to be delivered in the field. Right to Play, for example, partnered with the United Nations High Commissioner for Refugees to offer sport programs at refugee camps in Angola and Côte d'Ivoire, which were intended to serve refugees from the Congo and Liberia.

Programs spread throughout sub-Saharan Africa and to other regions in need, delivered by volunteer coaches (often from Canada and other Western nations). Right to Play's most public faces were its athlete ambassadors, high-profile professional and Olympic athletes who appear with the iconic Right to Play red soccer ball in promotional photographs. The photo ops of athletes making comparatively brief appearances in refugee camps or impoverished communities before moving on garnered Right to Play scorn in some quarters, resulting in the suggestion that some sport-for-development programs offered more style than substance.[60] Indeed, many sport-for-development initiatives—not just those that are Canadian led—have struggled to demonstrate how their sport programming tangibly alters people's economic and social circumstances. Regardless, the inability of modern sport-for-development to address the economic and social ills of the Global South has not dampened the belief in sport's utility.

Conclusion

Sport-for-good persists as a powerful narrative for both international high-performance sport and grassroots interventions. The earliest amateur advocates believed in the potential for sport to morally and socially uplift its participants. These values informed interventions by organizations such as the YMCA both at home and abroad. Even ideological challenges to amateurism's male, middle-class roots accepted the basic tenets of sport-for-good.

Canadian participation in international sport was informed by competing visions of how sport could be used to define national identity. Subsequent involvement on the international stage has connected aid and development projects to the rhetoric of sport-for-good. These values resonated (and continue to resonate) with contemporary efforts in sport-for-development.

DISCUSSION QUESTIONS

1. What are the central beliefs about sport (i.e., sport-for-good) that have informed efforts to promote participation internationally?

2. How did middle-class advocates in Canada believe that sport and physical activity would contribute to the acculturation of immigrants in the first half of the 20th century?

3. In what ways did the women's and workers' sport movement of the 1920s and 1930s offer alternatives to mainstream international sport? How were they similar to and different from one another?

4. Why did the Canadian federal government choose to become directly involved in the funding of international sport in the 1960s? How did the government's priorities change over time?

5. Outline the differences between sport development and sport-for-development. How are the values of sport-for-good reflected in international development programs?

SUGGESTED READINGS

Darnell, Simon C., Russell Field, and Bruce Kidd. *The History and Politics of Sport-for-Development: Activists, Ideologues and Reformers.* London: Palgrave Macmillan, 2019.

Field, Russell. "Sport and the Canadian Immigrant: Physical Expressions of Cultural Identity Within a Dominant Culture, 1896-1945." In *Race and Sport in Canada: Intersecting Inequalities.* Edited by Janelle Joseph, Simon Darnell, and Yuka Nakamura. Toronto: Canadian Scholars' Press, 2012.

Hall, M. Ann, and Bruce Kidd. "History and Individual Memory: The Story of Eva Dawes." *Sport History Review* 48, no. 2 (2016): 126-143.

Kidd, Bruce. "'We Must Maintain a Balance Between Propaganda and Serious Athletics'—the Workers' Sport Movement in Canada, 1924-1936." *Sport in Society* 16, no. 4 (2014): 565-577.

Macdonald, Charlotte. "Fitness for War and a Changed World: National Fitness in Canada." In *Strong, Beautiful and Modern: National Fitness in Britain, New Zealand, Australia and Canada, 1935-1960.* Vancouver: UBC Press, 2011.

CHAPTER 15

REFLECTION ON THE FIELD: SPORTS HISTORIES, TIMELINES, AND DE-CENTRING SETTLER COLONIAL PERSPECTIVES

Braden Te Hiwi, PhD
University of British Columbia

Carly Adams, PhD
University of Lethbridge

LEARNING OBJECTIVES

In this chapter you will

- consider how an individual's sport experiences are entwined with social and political events, drawing on the case of Waneek Horn-Miller;
- discuss the assumptions we make about time and the functions of timelines;
- understand that universal knowledge claims limit Indigenous peoples' histories and realities;
- discuss what it means to "de-centre settler perspectives" in the field of sport history; and
- consider the implications of the COVID-19 pandemic on histories of sport and recreation.

In 2019, Waneek Horn-Miller (Kanien'kehá:ka [Mohawk] from Kahnawá:ke territory) was bestowed the Order of Sport and inducted into Canada's Sports Hall of Fame (see figure 15.1). This is the highest honour in Canadian sport. Achieving induction and the Order of Sport goes beyond one's athletic accomplishments and successes. To be considered, a nominee must also "demonstrate exemplary values and/or personal characteristics" and make a "defining contribution to his/her sport and/or Canadian society."[1] Horn-Miller is a remarkable athlete and activist and her story connects the past, the present, and the future. As a high-performance athlete, she won over 20 medals at the North American Indigenous Games and was co-captain of the Canadian women's water polo team at the 2000 Olympic Games in Sydney, Australia—the first Kanien'kehá:ka woman to compete at an Olympic Games. In 2015, the Canadian Association for the Advancement of Women and Sport[2] declared her one of the most influential women in sport.

Horn-Miller first competed in the North American Indigenous Games in Edmonton in 1990 (see chapter 4). She became known in the press that same year as a 14 year old, but not for her athletic accomplishments in Edmonton. She was at the centre of a violent confrontation between Kanien'kehá:ka land defenders and the Canadian military. The Kanien'kehá:ka were attempting to stop land developers, intent on extending a private golf course, from encroaching on their ancestral burial grounds at Oka, north of Montreal. As Horn-Miller

Steve Russell/Toronto Star/Getty Images

Figure 15.1 Waneek Horn-Miller, Kanien'kehá:ka athlete and activist.

tried to leave the scene with her four-year-old sister she was stabbed in the chest, a centimetre from her heart, by a soldier's bayonet.

Following the event, physical activity and sport and her drive to compete at the Olympic Games helped Horn-Miller heal from the physical and emotional wounds she endured. Her tenacity and courage continued throughout her athletic career as she dedicated herself to using her position and profile as an elite athlete to speak out against injustice. In 2003, she was cut from the Canadian water polo team after blowing the whistle on abuse taking place within the coaching of Water Polo Canada. Her dismissal from the water polo team is tied up in complicated histories of discrimination and racism. This is one of many cases that illustrate the fallacy that sports and politics do not mix. Horn-Miller's advocacy, and the resistance to her whistle-blowing, highlight an argument made by many authors in this book—sport is *always* political.

The authors in this book have reinforced, in myriad ways, that sport and recreation practices shape and are shaped by broader social, cultural, political, and economic issues. They have encouraged you to ask questions and to challenge taken-for-granted assumptions in and about sport and recreation as you learn about enduring issues of inequality, discrimination, and colonial power and the ways these forces have been resisted and challenged. The intent of this book is not to tell a definitive or comprehensive history but to discuss research methods, share new perspectives, and contemplate new directions for understanding sporting pasts and how histories connect to presents and futures. Through the stories they tell and the histories they share, the authors challenge dominant narratives of sport and recreation practices in Canada to highlight some of the 'silences' in our historical processes.

Danielle Peers and Lisa Tink in chapter 10, for example, employ a historical method that de-centres the importance of individual actors in order to ask questions of the present and reimagine futures. They share counter-histories of Canada's playground movement, inclusive physical education, and Paralympic sport to articulate new perspectives, thus de-centring dominant histories. Similarly, in chapter 11 Ornella Nzindukiyimana and Kevin B. Wamsley centre the experiences of Black athletes to examine anti-Black racism in the development of sport and recreation. In chapter 3, Braden Te Hiwi uses imagery of the spiral and looping shape of the fern frond (see figure 3.1) as he shares an approach to history that weaves together the past, present, and future in his exploration of the changing contexts of Indigenous peoples' cultures and physical activities.

In this final chapter of the book, with Horn-Miller's story as our starting place and the histories shared by the contributing authors to guide us, we think about the multiplicities of sport and recreation histories as we contemplate the interconnectedness of pasts, presents, and futures. In the next section we go back to some of the concepts presented in chapter 3 to critique and consider the implications of Western-centric ways of thinking about the concept of time. We discuss alternative ways for thinking about timelines and representation. We then consider ways we might move forward as we work to de-centre settler perspectives in the field of sport history. In these final pages of the book, we encourage you to reflect on everything you have learned about the histories of sport and recreation in the country we call Canada and to use timelines as a way to engage in a critical reflection on the work done in our field.

Thinking Critically About Timelines

Timelines are not simply a collection of facts put on a time scale; they tell a story and shape how we think about the world in ways that are not neutral, objective, or natural. Like all stories, timelines not only have potential but should also be approached with caution. A timeline is included at the beginning of this book as a way of marking and highlighting specific moments and events in the histories of Canadian sport and recreation. More important, though, the timeline also sets the stage for the discussion that follows as we challenge assumptions about colonial orientations to time. We encourage you to think about timelines (including the one in this book) within the discipline of sport history, as an entry point to broader critiques of time, research, and colonialism.[3]

In the past, Canadians supported state efforts to delegitimize, silence, and terminate Indigenous peoples' communities, political autonomy, cultural practices, and knowledge, through mechanisms like the Indian Act.[4] However, government policies from the 19th and 20th centuries that banned Indigenous institutions, such as the Sundance on the Canadian plains,[5] and suppressed Indigenous language and cultural practices in residential schools[6] are now widely condemned by Canadians. In recent decades historians, and the Canadian public, have begun to de-centre settler perspectives of history to make visible the deeply troubling logic that Indigenous cultures were thought to be inferior to those of Western societies and to highlight that the rights and autonomy of Indigenous peoples were unjustly suppressed and curtailed for the state to impose its nation-building agenda.

Something as seemingly innocuous and mundane as a historical timeline has some of the same implications as the previously mentioned policies—specifically, the deeply troubling logic that Indigenous peoples' knowledges and cultures are inferior and irrelevant to history. Critical reflection upon how Indigenous peoples are represented in Canadian history is important now more than ever, as historians have been increasingly inclusive of Indigenous peoples, histories, and ways of knowing in consideration of the country's sporting past. This book is a case in point. We are not suggesting that Western orientations to time or the production of timelines is inherently bad or wrong; our point is that de-centring settler perspectives and employing critical methodologies will capture important limitations of the field of sport history. Understanding our own limitations as historians is an indicator of a strong and vibrant field of study. The process of decolonization is multifaceted and complex, and it works towards changing the material realities of Indigenous peoples (such as the restitution of Indigenous rights, settling Indigenous title to land, and the revitalization of Indigenous institutions); one aspect of decolonization includes non-Indigenous peoples' de-centring settler perspectives, which is the focus of our argument here.[7]

Time Shapes Our Thinking and Our Experiences

We often make assumptions about time as we think about and interpret the world around us. When sets of ideas are assumed, or taken for granted, we often do not consciously think about them, and by extension they are seldom, or never, challenged or critiqued. But being aware of your own ideas, assumptions, and perspectives is a hallmark of critical thinking. The assumptions we make can become so powerful that thinking about them can seem odd. When one writes or speaks (in English) about time in Canada, the common reference point is a Western conceptualization of time. It would be strange to hear Canadians say, "What is the Western orientation to the past? Or what is the time in a Western framework of thinking?" Most Canadians would simply ask, "What is the time?" This is the way we commonly reference time in our daily lives. Not so obvious to many is recognizing there may be other ways of thinking about and experiencing time. In this section, we introduce the need for awareness and reflective thinking about a Western conceptualization of time as a starting place. In particular, we consider the central assumptions about time that are the foundation for how we (are educated to) think about histories and their relationship to presents and futures.

A central feature of a Western approach to time is that it has a significant (although by no means exclusive) emphasis on linear orientation. This means time is often thought about as operating in a straight line, much like a timeline. McKay and Walmsley describe a Western orientation to time with the metaphor of a river.[8] Think of yourself, in a canoe, travelling down a river (see figure 15.2). Behind you are the waters you have travelled down, which is your past. The river you can see in front of you is the future. In the present, you paddle and occupy a particular space on that river that divides the past and the future. Although you will inevitably travel farther downriver, you will do so in a *new* present because you can never actually arrive in the future. The current in the river represents an immutable and unseen force, just like time, propelling you down the river from the past to the future; that force does not stop or slow down, nor can it be reversed. Two important points are worth noting: First, this orientation to time has a focus on the present experience of your location on the river, and second, it has a preoccupation with the future, because we have necessarily left the past behind us and instead we head towards the future indefinitely.

In Canada, and in many societies throughout the world, the linear framework of time takes the form of time of day and dates, which include the hour and minutes of the day, the day of the week, the month of the year, and a series of years that follow one after the other. This system of dates is known as the Gregorian calendar, in which we have 12 months and 365 days in a year, with the exception of leap years. Within such a calendar we can identify specific times and dates throughout history. For example, the 11th hour of the 11th day of the

Human Kinetics/Mark Anderman/The Wild Studio

Figure 15.2 **The river is a metaphor for a Western orientation to time.**

11th month is honoured as Remembrance Day, which is the specific time and date in the year 1918 that signify the end of the First World War. We can also measure time with scientific accuracy (e.g., the times of the 100-metre dash at the Olympic Games can be measured to 1/100th of a second). So deep and profound is our use of time that it is difficult for many Canadians to think about time outside of this system, and therefore years, hours, and dates are perceived as objective, neutral, and natural ways to understand time.

But what about communities that use different calendars? The Maya peoples, made up of multiple Indigenous nations in Central America, are well known for their calendar that, for instance, includes cycles such as the *Haab'* cycle (or one rotation of the earth around the sun) and the *Tzolk'in* cycle (of 290 days, which is the expected length of a woman carrying a baby to birth).[9] Other Indigenous communities use cycles of the moon to understand time and do not count and mark each year with a specific number and date. Do these experiences and practices of time count as legitimate ways to live in and experience the world? If so, how could the field of sport history account for these understandings of time and human experiences? If sport historians are to take the full range of human and environmental history seriously, we need to be aware of how assumptions about time influence the knowledge the field produces.

Reflecting On and Critiquing Timelines

The timeline on pages v-x contains a series of important events, peoples, organizations, and institutions from this book. As mentioned earlier, this timeline has two main functions. First, as the general function of timelines, it captures key historical events in chronological order, using dates to create a snapshot of a history as it develops over time. Like this book, the timeline does not represent a definitive history. Although the timeline attempts to broaden who and what count in Canadian histories, and the stories we tell about Canadian sport and recreation, by including moments, events, and people who are not always part of our mainstream understanding of sport in Canada, it is imperfect and incomplete. It is a starting point for thinking about sport and recreation practices of the past. Second, and this is a little different from most uses of timelines, we encourage critical and reflective thinking about timelines in Canada and within the field of sport history. We encourage you to go back to the timeline as you read this section of the chapter.

A starting place for critical thinking is to recognize the political effects of the historian's choices in creating a timeline. On the one hand, although the particular events or institutions and the specific dates can be verified as facts, the historian's selection of that particular event is not objective, and thus timelines should not be considered a simple fact. In the case of this book, decisions were made about what to include and what not to include on the timeline. Who and what get to count is a complex decision. The placing of events in a timeline is itself a choice, and this choice comes with assumptions about representing time. It is important to recognize that a standard timeline tells a narrative that shapes our knowledge of events into a rigidly ordered sequence; for instance, this includes an understanding that we are perpetually moving away from events of the past, as the river metaphor suggests. Indigenous experiences of time, which are explained in more detail elsewhere, are not necessarily locked into such a rigid and singular basis of time.[10]

Linear timelines are always political—sport *is* political, on the field or in a timeline. The linear timeline presented at the beginning of this book begins in 1763 with the creation of the Halifax Common. This is by no means intended to signify the beginning of Canadian sport history but rather is an early example of physical activity development in what came to be the country of Canada. Why would the 18th century be a good place to start a story about physical activity in North America? Could that story have started at an earlier date, or a later date, or without a date at all? What effects do the time frame of a story have on what is learned from the story? Many Canadian history books, sport specific or otherwise, begin telling the story during the period of colonization. What makes history from colonization onward not only a common approach to writing such histories but also the logical assumption? Is the assumption that history before colonization is of secondary importance, or worse, irrelevant in the telling of local history? In chapter 13, Christine M. O'Bonsawin offers a full discussion and critique of the centrality of colonialism in Canadian sport.

When writing, reading, thinking, or teaching about Canadian histories, very particular storylines and time scales are often taken for granted. The history of physical activities on the lands now known as Canada long predate colonial arrival, yet history often begins only after European colonization. Or at least, an overwhelming emphasis is placed on histories after European settlers arrived and the Canadian state began to be shaped. Take a moment to reflect; why is this?

You may find that history textbooks include a chapter on precontact physical activity (i.e., the activities of Indigenous peoples prior to *contact* with European colonialists), and you may find general Canadian history books do the same. Take, for instance, *Sport in Canada: A History* by Don Morrow and Kevin B. Wamsley, which includes the chapter "Games and Contests in Early Canada."[11] This type of chapter is important because it acknowledges and includes non-European precontact histories, recognizing a long period of human existence prior to European settlers, and asserts Indigenous peoples' existence and cultures. This attention on Indigenous peoples in Canadian sport history is important because it places Indigenous peoples in a grand narrative about Canadian sport; their long history was not invisible, nor are Indigenous peoples only to be understood as victims of colonization. In such a framing of Canadian history, however, time prior to European settlers on these lands is collected and framed as one period of time—that is, the period of precontact and early-contact physical activity. Why is this? And what implications might this have for understanding the history of North America?[12] Was this period created and understood as a means to structure historical insight into the periods of time, cultures, stories, experiences, worldviews, peoples, lands, and events of the many Indigenous nations spread across the continent? No. Instead it exists based on its differentiation from *European settler lives*; thus, the invention (it had to be created, it did not just exist naturally) of precontact as a way of thinking and understanding the world, even though it focuses exclusively on non-European lives, is part of a way of thinking that re-centres the colonial perspective.

Histories of precontact or early contact, often in the form of a section of a chapter, or perhaps a chapter or two towards the beginning of a grand narrative of Canada, frame the historical context and backdrop for the eventual development of the Canadian state. (Indeed, this book also places the majority of its Indigenous-focused chapters early in the telling of its story.) Thus, despite the presence of precontact history, the development of the state continues as the logical, seldom questioned, and rarely challenged time scale for producing history. It should be of no surprise that Canadian-centric stories rely on Canadian-centric time frames; but remember, thinking about our assumptions requires reflection about the obvious. When Indigenous histories are used in this way, even if they are inclusive within Canadian sport history, they are positioned as relevant because they operate in ways that leave untouched the colonial storyline that foretells the demise of Indigenous nations. The time frame that underlies this timeline can be dangerous in that it suggests the "inevitability" and "superiority" of colonial state progress and existence. Timelines are not an innocuous list of historical dates.

But how can histories exist outside of the logic of Canadian state development? We work within the field of *Canadian* sport history, after all. Chapter 3 includes a brief discussion of Allan Downey's (Dakelh) book *The Creator's Game*, which is a history of Haudenosaunee (a confederacy of Indigenous nations that border some of the Great Lakes) lacrosse, which begins with a creation history. Thus, for Downey and the Haudenosaunee participants in his study, the beginning of lacrosse stretches right back to the beginning of time; that is not your ordinary sport history time frame! Some Indigenous authors use time in a way that exists outside of the logic of Western understandings. Can you imagine a sport history relating back to, say, the Big Bang explanation of the origin of our universe? Indigenous peoples have histories and ways of living in time that operate outside of time scales of Western intellectual traditions and of Canadian state development. In what ways do historical timelines, linear time, and the Gregorian calendar complement Indigenous perspectives and realities on history, and in what ways do they present colonial obstacles to Indigenous peoples' historical and contemporary realities? A detailed analysis of time and the colonization of time in sport history is beyond this chapter, but de-centring the settler lens in timelines provides an entry point into these discussions.

Moving Beyond Universalism: One Step Towards De-centring Settler Perspectives in the Field

Indigenizing academic institutions will involve Indigenous peoples bringing their histories, perspectives, and knowledges to bear. It could mean writing about Indigenous peoples in textbooks, researching stories of Indigenous rights and resistance to colonialism, Indigenous historians bringing their own theories and methodologies to producing histories, and much more. A special issue in the *Journal of Sport History*, led by Murray G. Phillips, Russell Field, Christine M. O'Bonsawin (Abenaki), and Janice Forsyth (Cree), provides examples of this type of work and is a great place to start if you are interested in learning more.[13] Despite such positive developments for Indigenous history, efforts to Indigenize without decolonial transformation can fall short; that is, without a critical awareness of how the field of sport history operates and its effects, the growth of Indigenous scholarship can work to privilege, rather than challenge, colonial logic.[14] In this brief section, we encourage all sport historians and students of sport history to critically reflect on the colonial effects of our field as we work to de-centre settler perspectives. Such reflection needs to respect Indigenous leadership and guidance, but it is crucial to understand that it needs to be undertaken by non-Indigenous peoples who work and learn within our field. The passive acceptance (enthusiastic or tolerant) of including Indigenous research into a sport history class, or of support for more Indigenous histories, without an active process of reflection and transformation of oneself, individually and as a field, is not enough.

Researchers in the field of sport history have not yet engaged in a serious critique of colonialism in their epistemological position, on what historical knowledge is and therefore how we go about doing history. We need to move away from promoting universal knowledge, a single fundamental truth that is applicable for all people at all times. As explained in chapter 1 of this book, "the intent within the chapters of this book is not to tell *the* history of sport and recreation in Canada, a definitive or comprehensive history, but to discuss ongoing research, perspectives, silences, and new directions for understanding our sporting past." This is the work of reflecting on our assumptions, opening space for a plural rather than a singular way of knowing the world. Malcolm Maclean makes this point in his study of Indigenization and decolonization in the field of sport history (particularly in reference to the epistemological claims of the field), when he says that

> the decolonial objective of pluriversality requires that modernity's universalist claims to Truth are deprived of their legitimacy, and that there is a parity or equity between the voices that provide the texts of that pluriversal knowledge. This parity/equity is essential to build communities of understanding.[15]

Indigenous peoples have their own ways of knowing and experiencing the world, and therefore a single truth cannot represent it all; multiple, or pluriversal, ways of knowing the world are legitimate and necessary. Our field must undergo a critical transformation towards more thoroughly and deeply articulating (and questioning) its particular knowledge claims. What shape might a more radical transformation take?

Towards the beginning of this chapter we suggest that a traditional historical timeline can promote the deeply troubling logic that Indigenous peoples' approaches to history and time are inferior and irrelevant; we would now like to return to this with a lens on universalism. To many Canadians, the Gregorian calendar and the scientific measurement of time, capturing and categorizing exact dates and times with incredible specificity, are natural and unbiased (i.e., neutral and apolitical) ways to think about time. To many Canadians, the time frame of the nation-state's development, consequently at the expense of Indigenous nationhood, is the logical and obvious way to think about timelines. To many Canadians, the analogy of the river, in which we are oriented towards the future and moving away from the past, expresses something undeniably and objectively real about our lives. How could someone deny that the confederation of the Canadian nation took place in 1867, that there are seven days in a week, that we live in the present and always head away from the past and towards the future? These points are irrefutable—or is there more to the story? These examples express universal claims about the world that people often (implicitly) believe are a logical, natural, neutral, objective, and apolitical way of knowing. If the use of timelines that assume Indigenous sovereignty is of the past and has made way for the development of Canada, how can this be viewed as objective, neutral, or apolitical? How does an unchallenged belief in the time analogy of the river dismiss other ways for engaging in time, such as a cyclical and spiralling basis for time discussed in chapter 3?

Let's go back to Waneek Horn-Miller's ongoing activism as she speaks out against injustice and colonial abuse. In 2020, she followed the events unfolding as Indigenous land defenders from the Wet'suwet'en territory in northern British Columbia continued to fight against the construction of the Coastal GasLink pipeline project through their unceded lands. An advocate for Indigenous rights, Horn-Miller warned against the use of force to remove the rail blockades that had been set up across Canada in solidarity with the Wet'suwet'en hereditary chiefs. She, and many other commentators, reminds us that the events unfolding on Wet'suwet'en lands are not idiosyncratic. In other words, this conflict is simply the latest in a long line of conflicts that have arisen when Indigenous peoples and communities have insisted on their sovereignty, often by resisting "resource extraction" (or "development") projects on their lands.[16] In other words, Horn-Miller challenges readers to think about the histories shaping the events taking place in northern British Columbia. In particular, she recalls the moment in Oka in 1990: "That reminder of just the hate that bubbled to the surface, this anger . . . we were being called terrorists when we weren't bringing terror to anybody," she said. "We weren't exerting any kind of aggression towards anybody else. The terror was being brought to us."[17] Speaking in Ottawa on February 24, 2020, at a rally for Wet'suwet'en, Horn-Miller reflected on the importance of continuing to speak about past events and placing current events in historical context:

> In the last few weeks with Wet'suwet'en and the rail blockades we are actually seeing real negotiation. Not a lot of Canadians have understood that up until now we have been fighting from such an uneven position, an uneven playing field. If it doesn't affect the average Canadian, a lot of them don't care. Who cares if they don't have clean water, who cares if these types of things are happening. But what's also scary at the same time is that we have the possibility of great violence . . . we're on the edge of that. . . . It would be a horrible horrible thing not just for Indigenous people but for all people in this country for something like that to happen again. . . . It is going to take every single Canadian to actually ask themselves these questions—what does it mean to be Canadian and to really understand what they are fighting for in Wet'suwet'en and what's going on."[18]

When speaking publicly about her experiences, she reminds people about Indigenous histories and urges us "to never let that die, to never ever let that memory be shoved under the carpet."[19] When Horn-Miller speaks out, she does not move away from events of the past, leaving that part of the river behind her. Instead she embraces the past, returning to it again and again, as well as connecting to the future of Indigenous title again and again, in her present reality of Wet'suwet'en (and Indigenous peoples broadly) assertion of title and sovereignty.

TRANSFORMATIVE MOMENTS: THE PANDEMIC OF 2020

As this book goes to press, we are in the throes of the global COVID-19 pandemic. The world is changing quickly, sometimes daily, as the virus sweeps from nation to nation. Sports leagues have been cancelled at all levels across Canada and around the world—children's leagues and activities, community leagues, university leagues, and professional leagues. Stadiums and arenas have been closed indefinitely. The 2020 Olympic Games in Tokyo, Japan, have been postponed and the Arctic Winter Games and all other national and world championships have been cancelled. It is a global sports shutdown unlike any we have seen before. To put it in perspective, during the First and Second World Wars there were mass disruptions to sport—the Olympic Games were cancelled, and some leagues were forced to fold as countries shifted their attention to wartime concerns. But the COVID-19 pandemic is unprecedented—during the Second World War, sport continued, albeit in different forms and sometimes with different people competing. In Canada during wartime, sport was used as entertainment, to build community morale, as a support network for many people during a time of uncertainty, to raise funds for war-related causes, and for the well-being of citizens and military personnel.

The response and impacts of the COVID-19 pandemic are different and unparalleled. Governments around the world are implementing drastic sanctions such as limiting the numbers of people who can congregate in one place; insisting on physical distancing practices; closing schools, libraries, recreation facilities, parks, and playgrounds; and in some cases, imposing complete national lockdowns. In light of this, the futures of global systems and institutions, including sport, are being questioned. For years now, for example, some people have been questioning the viability and purpose of mass sporting events such as the Olympic Games—given the social, economic, and environmental impacts of planning and hosting these events, should they, in fact, continue to take place?

The pandemic may also have serious and long-lasting consequences for certain groups of people—women, children, trans people, people of colour, and many more. While global events such as the Second World War in many ways created new opportunities and opened doors for different groups of people to participate more actively in the public sphere, including sport, the pandemic is disrupting essential services, leading to potential increases in gender-based and race-based violence as resources shift to bolstering the national health care system.

While all of this is happening, daily exercise is being championed as a means to continued mental and physical health during these uncertain times, as a way to reduce stress, depression, and anxiety and to just keep moving during a moment when our lives are being constrained. Many instructors, trainers, and coaches are moving their services online, offering classes through their websites or social media platforms.

In this book, we have placed the COVID-19 pandemic as the last insertion on the timeline. What would happen if we thought about it as the first entry on a timeline or as an arc of a fern frond? Undoubtedly, the pandemic is a significant marker in sport histories and Canadian histories more broadly. As the global pandemic exposes limitations in social, economic, and cultural practices, we must consider this moment within our understandings of pasts, presents, and futures. How did we get to this moment? How and why did governments and governing bodies for sport and recreation respond in the ways they did? How and why did athletes react in certain ways? How has this moment changed the way we think about sport historically and in the present, and how are we able to imagine different sporting futures?

Horn-Miller posed the question "What does it mean to be Canadian and to really understand what they are fighting for in Wet'suwet'en?" How we come to think and act about Wet'suwet'en sovereignty and stewardship ought to include learning about Indigenous perspectives; thinking about time provides a gateway into such thinking. Are Wet'suwet'en assertions of title understood as a hearkening to an irremediable, no longer existent, barbaric past in the rear-view mirror of the modern Canadian state? We don't think so. Within a rigidly linear logic, the histories of Wet'suwet'en title since time immemorial, their historic attempts to assert their title over time, and the recent events of land defenders would be separated by vast time scales, disconnected by various periods of history and law, and would evolve away from the precolonial sovereign past and towards the present of state control. A different way of understanding time would position Indigenous assertions of title operating cyclically, in the present as much as the past, as much as the future; such an understanding is at odds with the rigid linear framework of the river metaphor. But what, you might ask, does this have to do with the field of sport history?[20]

If historians within the field provide universal truth, they are supporting the colonial logic of Indigenous inferiority of knowledge and experience. A field that obscures the possibility of other ways of knowing inhibits non-Indigenous peoples in understanding Indigenous peoples' assertion of sovereignty. De-centring settler perspectives thus requires that we (who read, learn, think, teach, and research in the field) do the work of understanding the knowledge claims of the field. This does not preclude us valuing a Western orientation of history, nor does it suggest Indigenous peoples do not want to connect to and learn from the field of sport history, but that de-centring of the field involves critical reflection of its perspective and the effects that has on the world around us; while we argue here this is specifically important for Indigenous peoples and Indigenous scholarship, it is surely an effort towards rigour worthy of engagement, in and of itself.

Writing More Complex Histories

Waneek Horn-Miller's ongoing activism reinforces how sport experiences are entwined with social and political events in ways that operate outside a Western framework of time that distances us from the past. Her activism brings together sport, Indigenous rights and governance, and Canadian colonial abuses of power to make visible the connections between pasts and presents. Her story and activism emphasize that although Canadian state leaders have expressed a commitment to implementing the 94 calls to action from the final report of the Truth and Reconciliation Commission, we have a long way to go before we can speak to reconciliation in a meaningful way (see chapters 3, 4, and 13).

As we "do" and "make" history we need to continue to be aware of the ways we (re)produce and privilege certain histories and ways of knowing. From digital technologies[21] to physical archives to the stories told and retold, we must think about how the field of sport history can continue to build upon its strengths, but also that it must grow and evolve. As we think about the future of Canadian sport histories, we encourage you to think back to Sarah Barnes and Mary Louise Adams' discussion in chapter 2 about the methodological and theoretical choices and approaches historians make when conducting their research. We must continue to consider and question the acts of power inherent in our research questions and practices. While we celebrate the changes and growth in Canadian sport and recreation over time, we must also heed the advice of Jaime Schultz and "cheer with reserve."[22] We must remember that the histories of sport and recreation get told and remembered in particular ways. Each of these moments, experiences, and events is complicated and must be situated within the negotiations, power relations, and systemic practices of that era. With this in mind, we must endeavour to research and write new histories, more complex histories, from different perspectives and points of view as a means to strengthen the knowledge produced by the field. We must continue, or in some cases, begin, to grapple with questions, issues, and the problems of the practices of settler colonialism as we work to de-centre settler perspectives in the field of sport history.

DISCUSSION QUESTIONS

1. Considering all the histories and arguments presented throughout this book, reflect on why sport and recreation histories matter. Has your answer changed since this question was first posed in chapter 1?

2. How do Canadian sport and recreation histories privilege Western ways of knowing?

3. Would you engage in de-centring settler perspectives in your own thinking? Why or why not? And if so, how would you do that?

4. Create a sport history timeline for the community where you grew up. Then consider the following: Why did you include these events and people? How did you make decisions about what to include and what not to include? What stories does the timeline tell about your community? What stories are missing?

5. How has the COVD-19 pandemic opened the door to re-imagining sporting futures?

SUGGESTED READINGS

Fabian, Johannes. *Time and Other: How Anthropology Makes Its Object.* New York: Columbia University Press, 2014.

Phillips, Murray G., Russell Field, Christine O'Bonsawin, and Janice Forsyth. "Indigenous Resurgence, Regeneration, and Decolonization Through Sport History." Special issue. *Journal of Sport History* 46, no. 2 (2019): 143-324.

Simpson, Leanne, and Kiera Ladner. *This Is an Honour Song: Twenty Years Since the Blockades.* Winnipeg: APR Books, 2010.

Stirling, Jennifer J., Murray G. Phillips, and Mary G. MacDonald. "Doing Sport History in the Digital Present." *Journal of Sport History* 44, no. 2 (2017): 135-145.

REFERENCES

Chapter 1

1. For more on the Alberta Japanese Canadian Bonspiel, see Carly Adams and Darren J. Aoki, "'Hey, Why Don't We Have a Bonspiel?'" *International Journal of the History of Sport* (forthcoming).

2. For more on the internment of Japanese Canadians, see Ken Adachi, *The Enemy That Never Was: A History of the Japanese Canadians* (Toronto: McClelland & Stewart, 1976); Ann Sunahara, *The Politics of Racism: The Uprooting of Japanese Canadians During the Second World War* (Toronto: James Lorimer, 1981).

3. Adams and Aoki "Why Don't We Have a Bonspiel," forthcoming.

4. E.H. Carr, *What Is History?* (New York: Random House, 1961), 35.

5. Don Morrow and Kevin B. Wamsley, *Sport in Canada: A History*, 4th ed. (Toronto: Oxford University Press, 2017), 2-3.

6. Thomas King, *The Truth About Stories* (Toronto: House of Anansi Press, 2003), 9-10.

7. The term "indigenous Canadian" employed here is now one that many critical scholars would trouble along two lines. First, as Daniel Heath Justice asserts, capitalizing "Indigenous" is important "as it affirms a distinctive political status of peoplehood, rather than describing an exploitable commodity..." See Daniel Heath Justice, *Why Indigenous Literatures Matter* (Waterloo: Wilfred Laurier University Press, 2018), 6. Second, the phrase "Indigenous Canadian" draws the ire of many critical observers, who suggest that Indigenous peoples in the lands claimed by Canada were granted citizenship as part of an assimilation project. From this perspective, "Indigenous communities, peoples, and nations... consider themselves distinct from other sectors of the societies now prevailing in those territories, or parts of them" (Martínez Cobo, 1986, as cited in Göcke, 2013, p. 18).

8. Gerald McMaster and Lee-Ann Martin, "Introduction," in *INDIGENA: Contemporary Native Perspectives*, eds. Gerald McMaster and Lee-Ann Martin (Toronto/Quebec: Douglas & McIntyre and the Canadian Museum of Civilization, 1992), 15.

9. Jim Logan, in *INDIGENA: Contemporary Native Perspectives*, eds. Gerald McMaster and Lee-Ann Martin (Toronto/Quebec: Douglas & McIntyre and the Canadian Museum of Civilization, 1992), 142.

10. Logan, *INDIGENA*, 142.

11. Logan, *INDIGENA*, 144.

12. See Carly Adams, "Editorial," *Sport History Review* 47, no. 1 (2016): 1-2.

13. Avery Gordon, *Ghostly Matters: Haunting and the Sociological Imagination* (Minneapolis: University of Minnesota Press, 2008).

14. Gerda Lerner, *Why Histories Matter: Life and Thought* (New York: Oxford University Press, 1997), 199.

Chapter 2

1. David Giddens, "The 15 Biggest Moments in Canadian Sports History," CBC Sports, June 29, 2017, www.cbc.ca/sportslongform/entry/the-15-biggest-moments-in-canadian-sports-history.

2. Giddens, "15 Biggest Moments."

3. Michel-Rolph Trouillot, *Silencing the Past: Power and the Production of History* (Boston: Viking Press, 2006), 9-10.

4. Trouillot, *Silencing the Past*, 9-10.

5. Ed Waring, "Table Tennis Growing to Large-Scale Sport," *Globe and Mail*, December 25, 1946, 17.

6. Suzanne Morton, "Colour, Colonialism, and the McGill Redmen," YouTube, last modified on November 15, 2018, www.youtube.com/watch?v=qfReCSFu5Xg.

7. John Chidley-Hill, "McGill University Students to Vote on Changing Team Nickname, " *Globe and Mail*, November 8, 2018, www.theglobeandmail.com/sports/article-mcgill-university-students-to-vote-on-changing-team-nickname.

8. Russell Field, "How We Think About Hockey, and Ourselves": Television, the 1972 Summit Series, and the Construction of a Pan-Canadian identity," *Canadian Issues/Thèmes canadiens* (2012): 40-45.

9. Field, "How We Think," 40.

10. Michael A. Robidoux, "Imagining a Canadian Identity Through Sport: A Historical Interpretation of Lacrosse and Hockey," *Journal of American Folklore* 115, no. 456 (2002): 209-225.

11. Parissa Safai, "A Critical Analysis of the Development of Sport Medicine in Canada, 1955-80," *International Review for the Sociology of Sport* 42, no. 3 (2007): 323.

12. "About the Collection," Library and Archives Canada, accessed November 26, 2018, www.bac-lac.gc.ca/eng/about-us/about-collection/Pages/about.aspx.

13. Safai, "Development of Sport Medicine," 323.

14. M. Ann Hall, *The Grads Are Playing Tonight! The Story of the Edmonton Commercial Graduates Basketball Club* (Edmonton: University of Alberta Press, 2011), 321.

15. Hall, *The Grads Are Playing*, 321.

16. "Browse Exhibits," The ArQuives, accessed December 11, 2018, https://digitalexhibitions.arquives.ca/exhibits.

17. Fiona Skillen, "Sports History: Reflections on My Journey So Far," *International Journal of the History of Sport* 34, nos. 5-6 (2017): 438.

18. Skillen, "Sports History," 438.

19. Gary Osmond and Murray G. Phillips, *Sport History in the Digital Era* (Champaign: University of Illinois Press, 2015), 15.

20. Osmond and Phillips, *Sport History*, 15.

21. Janice Forsyth, "Bodies of Meaning: Sports and Games at Canadian Residential Schools," in *Aboriginal Peoples and Sport in Canada: Historical Foundations and Contemporary Issues*, ed. Janice Forsyth and Audrey Giles (Vancouver: UBC Press, 2013), 35-45.

22. Christine O'Bonsawin, "From Black Power to Indigenous Activism: The Olympic Movement and the Marginalization of Oppressed Peoples (1968-2012)," *Journal of Sport History* 42, no. 2 (2015): 200-219.

23. Allan Downey, *The Creator's Game: Lacrosse, Identity, and Indigenous Nationhood* (Vancouver: UBC Press, 2018).

24. Katrina Srigley and Lorraine Sutherland, "Decolonizing, Indigenizing, and Learning Biskaaybiiyang in the Field: Our Oral History Journey," *The Oral History Review* 45, no. 1 (2018): 25.

25. Katrina Srigley, *The Nipissing Warriors*, directed and produced by Katrina Srigley (North Bay, ON: Regan Pictures, 2017), www.nipissingu.ca/warriors.

26. Srigley and Sutherland, "Decolonizing, Indigenizing, and Learning," 25.

27. Carly Adams, "(Writing Myself Into) Betty White's Stories: (De)constructing Narratives of/through Feminist Sport History Research," *Journal of Sport History* 39, no. 3 (2012): 406.

28. Joan Sangster, "Telling Our Stories: Feminist Debates and the Use of Oral History," *Women's History Review* 3, no. 1 (1994): 5-28

29. Sangster, "Telling Our Stories," 14.

30. Sangster, "Telling Our Stories," 11.

31. Katrina Srigley, "Oral History: The Stories Our Grandmothers Tell Us and More," in *Canadian History: Post-Confederation*, ed. John Douglas Belshaw (Winnipeg: Campus Manitoba, 2016), 866-869.

32. Sangster, "Telling Our Stories," 14.

33. Srigley, "Oral History," 866.

34. HuffPost, accessed January 25, 2018, www.huffpost.com.

35. The Allrounder, accessed January 25, 2018, http://theallrounder.co.uk.

36. *Hockey in Society*, accessed January 25, 2019, https://hockeyinsociety.com.

37. *Engaging Sport*, the Society Pages, accessed January 25, 2019, https://thesocietypages.org/engagingsports.

38. Morton, "Colour, Colonialism."

39. Hazel Meyer, "Muscle Panic," accessed December 11, 2018, https://hazelmeyer.com/Muscle-Panic-2015.

40. Eve Kornfeld, "The Power of Empathy: A Feminist, Multicultural Approach to Historical Pedagogy," *The History Teacher* 26, no. 1 (1992): 28-29.

41. Richard Wagamese, *Indian Horse* (Vancouver: Douglas & McIntyre, 2012).

42. "Richard Wagamese on His Novel Indian Horse," CBC Digital Archives, accessed December 10, 2018, www.cbc.ca/archives/author-richard-wagamese-on-his-novel-indian-horse-1.4673401.

43. Ornella Nzindukiyimana, "John 'Army' Howard, Canada's First Black Olympian: A Nation-Building Paradox," *International Journal of the History of Sport* 34, no. 11 (2017): 1140-1160.

44. Robert Pitter, "Racialization and Hockey in Canada: From Personal Troubles to a Canadian Challenge," in *Artificial Ice: Hockey, Culture, and Commerce*, ed. David Whitson and Richard S. Gruneau, Peterborough, ON: Broadview Press (2006): 128.

45. Pitter, "Racialization and Hockey," 128.

46. Jason Laurendeau and Carly Adams, "'Jumping Like a Girl': Discursive Silences, Exclusionary Practices and the Controversy Over Women's Ski Jumping," *Sport in Society* 13, no. 3 (2010): 431-447.

Chapter 3

1. Te Ahukaramū Charles Royal, "Māori Creation Traditions," *Te Ara: The Encyclopedia of New Zealand*, accessed August 3, 2018, www.TeAra.govt.nz/en/maori-creation-traditions/print.

2. Victoria Paraschak, "Native Sport History: Pitfalls and Promise," *Canadian Journal of History of Sport* 20, no. 1 (1989): 62-64.

3. Paraschak, "Native Sport History," 57; more recently Forsyth and Giles discuss the small but important Indigenous sport literature: Janice Forsyth and Audrey R. Giles, *Aboriginal Peoples and Sport in Canada: Historical Foundations and Contemporary Issues* (Vancouver: UBC Press, 2013), 3-5.

4. Paraschak, "Native Sport History," 63.

5. Chris Andersen, *Métis: Race, Recognition, and the Struggle for Indigenous Peoplehood* (Vancouver: UBC Press, 2014), 24.

6. Chelsea Vowel, *Indigenous Writes: A Guide to First Nations, Métis, and Inuit Issues in Canada* (Winnipeg: Portage & Main Press, 2016); Gregory Younging, *Elements of Indigenous Style: A Guide for Writing By and About Indigenous Peoples* (Edmonton: Brush Education, 2018).

7. Grant Jarvie, *Sport, Culture and Society: An Introduction*, 2nd ed. (Florence, KY: Taylor & Francis Group, 2011), 8.

8. Paraschak, "Native Sport History," 121-122.

9. Michael K. Heine, *Dene Games: A Culture and Resource Manual*, vol. 1 (Yellowknife, NT: Sport North Federation, 1999), 1-3 to 1-7.

10. Heine, *Dene Games*, 1-8 to 1-12.

11. Angela Cavender Wilson, "Power of the Spoken Word: Native Oral Traditions in American Indian History," in *Rethinking American Indian History*, ed. Donald Fixico (Albuquerque: University of New Mexico Press, 1997), 111.

12. Wilson, "Power of the Spoken Word," 111.

13. Morris Mott, "Games and Contests of the First 'Manitobans,'" in *Sports in Canada: Historical Readings*, ed. Morris Mott (Toronto: Copp Clark Pitman, 1989), 19.

14. Stewart Culin, *Games of the North American Indians: Games of Chance*, vol. 2 (Lincoln: University of Nebraska Press, 1992), 74, 102, 166-117, 155-158.

15. Bruce Miller, *Our Original Games: A Look at Aboriginal Sport in Canada* (Owen Sound, ON: Ningwakwe Learning Press, 2002), 12-13; See also Culin, *Games of the North American Indians*. Culin provides the most comprehensive historical detail from archival sources on this topic.

16. Mott, "First 'Manitobans,'" 19.

17. Culin, *Games of the North American Indians*; Miller, *Our Original Games*; Mott, "First 'Manitobans,'" 18-27; Heine, *Dene Games*.

18. Michael Heine, Ruth Carol, and Harvey Scott, *Traditional Dene Games: Games the Dene Elders Remember From the Old Days* (Yellowknife, NT: MACA GWNT, n.d.), 8.

19. Heine, Carol, and Scott, *Traditional Dene Games*, 12-13.

20. Michael K. Heine, *Dene Games: A Culture and Resource Manual*, vol. 1 (Yellowknife, NT: Sport North Federation, 1999), 1-26.

21. Culin, *Games of the North American Indians*, 399.

22. Culin, *Games of the North American Indians*, 405.

23. Heine, Carol, and Scott, *Traditional Dene Games*, 38-39.

24. Heine, Carol, and Scott, *Traditional Dene Games*, 38-39.

25. Paraschak, "Native Sport History," 61.

26. Allan Downey, *The Creator's Game: Lacrosse, Identity, and Indigenous Nationhood* (Vancouver: UBC Press, 2018), 6-7; Donald M. Fisher, *Lacrosse: A History of the Game* (Baltimore: Johns Hopkins University Press, 2002), 12-13.

27. Thomas Vennum, *American Indian Lacrosse: Little Brother of War* (Baltimore: Johns Hopkins University Press, 2007), 35; Culin, *Games of the North American Indians*, 589; Fisher, *Lacrosse: A History of the Game*, 17-18.

28. Heine, *Dene Games*, 1-49 to 1-50.

29. Vennum, *American Indian Lacrosse*, 29.

30. John Hayward, *The Natural and Aboriginal History of Tennessee* (Nashville: George Wilson, 1823), 285.

31. Downey, *The Creator's Game*.

32. Downey, *The Creator's Game*, 3-11.

33. Downey, *The Creator's Game*, 6-7.

34. Downey, *The Creator's Game*, 37.

35. Downey, *The Creator's Game*, 37.

36. The broader hunting example here is borrowed from Younging, *Elements of Indigenous Style*, 19.

37. Younging, *Elements of Indigenous Style*, 18-19.

38. Michael Heine, "'The Sunday Flag Is Up!' Western Arctic Aboriginal Cultures and the Sports of the Fur Traders," *Journal of Sport History* 41, no. 2 (2014): 317.

39. Heine, "'The Sunday Flag,'" 317.

40. Heine, "'The Sunday Flag,'" 318.

41. Sarah Quick, "The Social Poetics of the Red River Jig in Alberta and Beyond: Meaningful Heritage and Emerging Performance," *Ethnologies* 30, no. 1 (2008): 77-101.

42. Heine, "'The Sunday Flag,'" 320.

43. Heine, "'The Sunday Flag,'" 322.

44. Heine, "'The Sunday Flag,'" 322.

45. The strength-based approach is explored in detail by Victoria Paraschak and Kristi Thompson, "Finding Strength(s): Insights on Aboriginal Physical Cultural Practices in Canada," *Sport in Society* 17, no. 8 (2014): 1046-1060.

46. Downey, *The Creator's Game*, 43.

47. Downey, *The Creator's Game*, 44-49.

48. Downey, *The Creator's Game*, 43.

49. Paraschak, "Native Sport History," 57-68; Victoria Paraschak, "'Reasonable Amusements': Connecting the Strands of Physical Culture in Native Lives," *Sport History Review* 29, no. 1 (1998): 121-131; Braden Te Hiwi and Janice Forsyth, "'A Rink at This School Is Almost as Essential as a Classroom': Hockey and Discipline at Pelican Lake Indian Residential School, 1945–1951," *Canadian Journal of History* 52, no. 1 (2017): 80-108; Forsyth and Giles, *Aboriginal Peoples and Sport in Canada*.

50. Paraschak, "Native Sport History," 122-124; Janice Forsyth, "The Indian Act and the (Re)Shaping of Canadian Aboriginal Sport Practices," *International Journal of Canadian Studies/Revue internationale d'études canadiennes*, no. 35 (2007): 99.

51. Library and Archives Canada, Record Group 10, vol. 3826, file 60, 511-4A, Scott to Graham, October 4, 1921.

52. Allan Downey, "Playing the Creator's Game on God's Day: The Controversy of Sunday Lacrosse Games in Haudenosaunee Communities, 1916-24," *Journal of Canadian Studies* 49, no. 3 (2015): 118.

53. Downey, "Playing the Creator's Game on God's Day," 116, 121.

54. Downey, "Playing the Creator's Game on God's Day," 134.

55. See Paraschak, "'Reasonable Amusements,'" 126-128, for an extended discussion of this period of cultural revitalization through Indigenous nation building.

56. Vicky Paraschak, "Sport Festivals and Race Relations in the Northwest Territories of Canada," in *Sport, Racism, and Ethnicity*, ed. Grant Jarvie (London: Farmer Press, 1991), 76-77.

57. Vicky Paraschak, "The Heterotransplantation of Organized Sport: A Northwest Territories Case Study," in *Proceedings, 5th Canadian Symposium on the History of Sport and Physical Education* (Toronto: University of Toronto Press, 1982), 424-430; Paraschak, "Sport Festivals and Race Relations," 76-79.

58. Paraschak, "Sport Festivals and Race Relations," 80.

59. Paraschak, "Sport Festivals and Race Relations," 78.

60. For more detailed information on these games see, Michael Heine, "Performance Indicators: Aboriginal Games at the Arctic Winter Games," in *Aboriginal Peoples and Sport in Canada: Historical Foundations and Contemporary Issues*, ed. Janice Forsyth and Audrey Giles (Vancouver: UBC Press, 2013), 169-172.

61. See Heine, "Performance Indicators," 172-176, for more detailed information on these games.

62. Heine, "Performance Indicators," 177-178.

63. Heine, "Performance Indicators," 177-178.

64. Heine, *Dene Games*.

65. Paraschak, "'Reasonable Amusements,'" 121-123; Mary Jane McCallum, "This Last Frontier: Isolation and Aboriginal Health," *Canadian Bulletin of Medical History* 22, no. 1 (2005): 107-108; Braden Te Hiwi, "'Unlike Their Playmates of Civilization, the Indian Children's Recreation Must Be Cultivated and Developed': The Administration of Physical Education at Pelican Lake Indian Residential School, 1926-1944," *Historical Studies in Education/Revue d'histoire de l'éducation* 29, no. 1 (2017): 104-105, 109.

66. Michael Dubnewick, Tristan Hopper, John C. Spence, and Tara-Leigh F. McHugh, "'There Is a Cultural Pride Through Our Games': Enhancing the Sport Experiences of Indigenous Youth in Canada Through Participation in Traditional Games," *Journal of Sport and Social Issues* (2018): 213-216.

67. Audrey Giles, "Women's and Girls' Participation in Dene Games in the Northwest Territories," in *Aboriginal Peoples and Sport in Canada: Historical Foundations and Contemporary Issues*, ed. Janice Forsyth and Audrey Giles (Vancouver: UBC Press, 2012), 145; Robert Schinke, Duke Peltier, and Hope Yungblut, "Canadian Elite Aboriginal Athletes, Their Challenges, and the Adaptation Process," in *Aboriginal Peoples and Sport in Canada: Historical Foundations and Contemporary Issues*, ed. Janice Forsyth and Audrey Giles (Vancouver: UBC Press, 2013), 124-142; Lynn Lavallée and Lucie Lévesque, "Two-Eyed Seeing: Physical Activity, Sport, and Recreation Promotion in Indigenous Communities," in *Aboriginal Peoples and Sport in Canada: Historical Foundations and Contemporary Issues*, ed. Janice Forsyth and Audrey Giles (Vancouver: UBC Press, 2013), 206-228; Joanie Halas, Heather McRae, and Amy Carpenter, "The Quality

and Cultural Relevance of Physical Education for Aboriginal Youth Challenges and Opportunities," in *Aboriginal Peoples and Sport in Canada: Historical Foundations and Contemporary Issues*, ed. Janice Forsyth and Audrey Giles (Vancouver: UBC Press, 2013), 182; Braden Te Hiwi, "'What Is the Spirit of This Gathering?' Indigenous Sport Policy-Makers and Self-Determination in Canada," *International Indigenous Policy Journal* 5, no. 4 (2014): 6.

Chapter 4

1. For an assessment of empowerment discourses, see Jay Coakley and Peter Donnelly, *Sports in Society: Issues and Controversies*, 2nd Canadian ed. (Toronto: McGraw-Hill Ryerson, 2009), 243-244.

2. Coakley and Donnelly, *Sports in Society*, 12.

3. Government of Canada, "Aboriginal Peoples in Canada: Key Results from the 2016 Census." The Daily, Statistics Canada, October 25, 2017, accessed June 9, 2020, https://www150.statcan.gc.ca/n1/daily-quotidien/171025/dq171025a-eng.htm.

4. An excellent foundation for understanding sport as a social practice can be found in chapter 1 of Coakley and Donnelly, *Sports in Society*, 1-24. Indigenous examples tied to sport can be found throughout Don Morrow and Kevin Wamsley, *Sport in Canada: A History*, 4th ed. (Don Mills, ON: Oxford University Press, 2017).

5. Although Indigenous people have gained more control over their lives, many of the problematic aspects remain embedded in state-led structures and legal frameworks that prioritize and privilege dominant interests. In 2018, the Department of Indian Affairs was separated into two entities, Indigenous Services Canada and Crown–Indigenous Relations. The Indian Act remains largely unchanged since it last underwent major revisions in 1951. www.thecanadianencyclopedia.ca/en/article/aboriginal-affairs-and-northern-development-canada.

6. Donald M. Fisher, *Lacrosse: A History of the Game* (Baltimore: Johns Hopkins University Press, 2002), 310-314; Allan Downey, *The Creator's Game: Lacrosse, Identity, and Indigenous Nationhood* (Vancouver: UBC Press, 2018).

7. Vicky Paraschak, "'Reasonable Amusements': Connecting the Strands of Physical Culture in Native Lives," *Sport History Review* 29, no. 1 (1998): 1-21.

8. Katherine Pettipas, *Severing the Ties That Bind: Government Repression of Indigenous Religious Ceremonies on the Prairies* (Winnipeg: University of Manitoba Press, 1994), 135.

9. Brian Titley, *The Indian Commissioners: Agents of the State and Indian Policy in Canada's Prairie West*, 1873-1932 (Edmonton: University of Alberta Press, 2009), 103.

10. Truth and Reconciliation Commission of Canada, *Honouring the Truth, Reconciling for the Future: Summary of the Final Report for the Truth and Reconciliation Commission* (Winnipeg: Truth and Reconciliation Commission, 2015), 1, 3, 55, 70, 133, 183, 288.

11. Truth and Reconciliation Commission of Canada, *Summary of the Final Report*, 3. See also Janice Forsyth, "Bodies of Meaning: Sports and Games at Canadian Residential Schools," in *Aboriginal Peoples and Sport in Canada: Historical Foundations and Contemporary Issues*, ed. Janice Forsyth and Audrey Giles (Vancouver: UBC Press, 2013), 19.

12. Quote from the Indian and Eskimo Residential School Commission of the MSCC cited in Braden Te Hiwi, "Physical Culture as Citizenship Education at Pelican Lake Indian Residential School, 1926-1970," (PhD diss., University of Western Ontario, 2015), 71.

13. Royal Commission on Aboriginal Peoples, *Looking Forward, Looking Back: Report of the Royal Commission on Aboriginal Peoples*, vol. 1 (Ottawa: Minister of Supply and Services Canada, 1996), 340-341.

14. Downey, *The Creator's Game*, 98-99.

15. J.R. Miller, *Shingwauk's Vision: A History of Native Residential Schools* (Toronto: University of Toronto Press, 2000), 271-272.

16. Victor Satzewich, "Indian Agents and the 'Indian Problem' in Canada in 1946: Reconsidering the Theory of Coercive Tutelage," *Canadian Journal of Native Studies* 17, no. 2 (1997): 229.

17. Satzewich, "Indian Agents and the 'Indian Problem,'" 245.

18. Satzewich, "Indian Agents and the 'Indian Problem,'" 246.

19. Truth and Reconciliation Commission of Canada, *Canada's Residential Schools: The History, Part 2, 1939-2000, The Final Report of the Truth and Reconciliation Commission,* vol. 1 (Winnipeg: Truth and Reconciliation Commission, 2015), 18.

20. Truth and Reconciliation Commission of Canada, *Canada's Residential Schools*, 51.

21. Janice Forsyth and Michael Heine, "'A Higher Degree of Social Organization': Jan Eisenhardt and Canadian Aboriginal Sport Policy in the 1950s," *Journal of Sport History* 35, no. 2 (2008): 406-407.

22. Forsyth and Heine, "'A Higher Degree of Social Organization,'" 407-408.

23. Quote from Jan Eisenhardt cited in Janice Forsyth, "Make the Indian Understand His Place: Politics and the Establishment of the Tom Longboat Awards at Indian Affairs and the Amateur Athletic Union of Canada," *Sport in History* 35, no. 2 (2015): 253.

24. Forsyth, "Make the Indian Understand His Place," 259-260.

25. Quote from Jan Eisenhardt cited in Janice Forsyth, "The Power to Define: A History of the Tom Longboat Awards, 1951-2001," (PhD diss., University of Western Ontario, 2005), 93.

26. Jack Granatstein, "Tom Longboat," *Maclean's* 111, no. 26 (1998): 49-50.

27. Forsyth, "The Power to Define," 98-99.

28. A general description of the award's structure from 1951 to 1972, and the real and symbolic implications that flowed from its structure, can be found in Forsyth, "Make the Indian Understand His Place," 260. An extensive description can be found in Forsyth, "The Power to Define," 91-104.

29. Quote from Philip Phelan cited in Forsyth, "The Power to Define," 93.

30. Forsyth, "The Power to Define," 100.

31. Vicky Paraschak, "An Examination of Sport for Aboriginal Females on the Six Nations Reserve, Ontario from 1968 to 1980," in *Women of the First Nations: Power, Wisdom, and Strength,* ed. Christine Miller and Patricia Chuchryk (Winnipeg: University of Manitoba Press, 1996), 85-86; Vicky Paraschak, "Invisible But Not Absent: Aboriginal Women in Sport and Recreation," *Canadian Women's Studies* 15 (1995): 71-72; Vicky Paraschak, "Organized Sport for Native Females on the Six Nations Reserve, Ontario from 1968-1980: A Comparison of Dominant and Emergent Sport Systems," *Canadian Journal of History of Sport* 21 (1990): 76.

32. Thirteen women were named regional recipients between 1951 and 1974.

33. Phyllis Bomberry won the national award in 1968. Paraschak, "Organized Sport for Native Females," 76; Paraschak, "An Examination of Sport," 85-86. Also see M. Ann Hall, *The Girl and the Game: A History of Women's Sport in Canada*, 2nd ed. (North York: University of Toronto Press, 2016), 240-241, 243, 287. The second edition of *The Girl and the Game* is substantially different from the first, offering a highly nuanced and integrated history of women's experiences, including those of Indigenous women, such as Phyllis Bomberry.

34. Forsyth, "The Power to Define," 114-144.

35. Forsyth, "The Power to Define," 145-168. For a full list of the Tom Longboat Award winners please see https://en.wikipedia.org/wiki/Tom_Longboat_Awards.

36. Forsyth, "The Power to Define," 122-123.

37. Morrow and Wamsley, *Sport in Canada*, 227-229.

38. Vicky Paraschak, "The Native Sport and Recreation Program 1972-1981: Patterns of Resistance, Patterns of Reproduction," *Canadian Journal of History of Sport* 26, no. 2 (1995): 1-18; Vicky Paraschak, "Variations in Race Relations: Sporting Events for Native Peoples in Canada," *Sociology of Sport Journal* 14, no. 1 (1997): 1-21.

39. Paraschak, "The Native Sport and Recreation Program," 12-13.

40. Paraschak, "The Native Sport and Recreation Program," 12.

41. Janice Forsyth and Kevin B. Wamsley, "'Native to Native … We'll Recapture Our Spirits': The World Indigenous Nations Games and North American Indigenous Games as Cultural Resistance," *The International Journal of the History of Sport* 23, no. 2 (2006): 303.

42. Vicky Paraschak, "Aboriginal Peoples and the Construction of Canadian Sport Policy," in *Aboriginal Peoples and Sport in Canada: Historical Foundations and Contemporary Issues*, ed. Janice Forsyth and Audrey Giles (Vancouver: UBC Press, 2013), 103-108.

43. Forsyth and Wamsley, "Native to Native," 304.

44. Forsyth and Wamsley, "Native to Native," 306.

45. "Let the Games Begin," A6.

46. Janice Forsyth and Vicky Paraschak, "The Double Helix: Aboriginal People and Sport Policy in Canada," in *Sport Policy in Canada*, ed. Lucie Thibault and Jean Harvey (Ottawa: University of Ottawa Press, 2013), 281.

47. Forsyth and Paraschak, "The Double Helix," 282.

48. Two of the nine reports produced by the TRC were published in 2016: "Canada's Residential Schools: The Legacy" and "Canada's Residential Schools: Missing Children and Unmarked Burials."

49. Naomi Angel and Pauline Wakeham, "Witnessing in Camera: Photographic Reflections on Truth and Reconciliation," in *Arts of Engagement: Taking Aesthetic Action In and Beyond the Truth and Reconciliation Commission of Canada*, ed. Dylan Robinson and Keavy Martin (Waterloo, ON: Wilfred Laurier University Press), 94.

50. Truth and Reconciliation Commission of Canada, *Summary of the Final Report* (Winnipeg: Truth and Reconciliation Commission, 2015), vi. A good starting point for academics considering this question is Thomas Peace, "Truth and Reconciliation While Teaching Canadian History?," History Matters, November 23, 2015, accessed August 21, 2018, http://activehistory.ca/2015/11/truth-and-reconciliation-while-teaching-canadian-history/.

Chapter 5

1. The individuals from Nakoda First Nations (NFN) communities who participated in this research refer to themselves, and are referred to, by several appellations. Nakoda First Nations is the contemporary appellation that many individuals use in formal references. The word *Nakoda* means "the people." The name *Nakoda peoples* has mostly replaced the older reference to *Stoney peoples*, although Stoney is still widely used by many individuals in informal settings and exclusively by some Elders.

2. Roland Rollinmud, personal interview, November 1, 2008.

3. The Nakoda camped at the foot of Cascade Mountain, Mînî hrpa (waterfalls), which served as a place of worship and a gathering place for meetings, for healing, and for sweat lodges, as well as provided access to the sacred waters of the hot springs for spiritual cleansing. After the Banff Hot Springs Reserve was established in 1885, each summer the Nakoda people would visit the area as a special retreat. This is where they would celebrate their culture and renew their special relationship with Mother Earth. Roland Rollinmud, personal communication, April 14, 2014.

4. Currently in Canada, *Indigenous* has become a more useful term to refer to First Nations, Métis, and Inuit peoples. Throughout this chapter I have chosen the term *Indigenous* when describing general Canadian contexts. As Alfred recognizes, the term *Indigenous* represents an experience that is shaped by a politicized colonial past and present. However, it is critical to invoke an individual nation's own self-appellation whenever possible and I do this throughout, referring to Nakoda peoples. Attention to such terminological specificity prevents a homogenization of distinct cultures and recognizes the heterogeneity and diversity of Indigenous languages and cultural groups in Canada. Taiaiake Alfred, *Wasáse: Indigenous Pathways of Action and Freedom* (Toronto: University of Toronto Press, 2005).

5. Treaty 7 was an agreement between the Canadian federal government and several First Nations of the southern portion of the province of Alberta. The agreement was signed at Blackfoot Crossing of the Bow River on September 22, 1877. Not all representative Chiefs were present at the signing, but members of the Nakoda (Stoney), the Tsuu T'ina (Sarcee), and the Blackfoot Confederacy were in attendance. Treaty 7 is one of 11 numbered treaties signed between 1871 and 1921. The treaty established the reserve system, annual provisions, and the protection of First Nations rights to continue their subsistence practices. Walter Hildebrandt, Dorothy First Rider, Sarah Carter, and Treaty 7 Elders and Tribal Councils, *The True Spirit and Original Intent of Treaty 7* (Montreal: McGill-Queen's University Press, 1996).

6. Daryl W. Fedje, James M. White, Michael C. Wilson, Earle Nelson, John S. Vogel, and John R. Southon, "Vermilion Lakes Site: Adaptations and Environments in the Canadian Rockies During the Latest Pleistocene and Early Holocene," *American Antiquity* 60, no. 1 (1995): 81-108; Gwyn E. Langemann, "Zooarchaeological Research in Support of a Reintroduction of Bison to Banff National Park, Canada," in *The Future From the Past: Archaezoology in Wildlife Conservation and Heritage Management*, ed. Roel C.G.M. Lauwerier and Ina Plug (Oxford, UK: Oxbow Books, 2004); Gwyn E. Langemann, "Archeology in the Rocky Mountain National Parks: Uncovering an 11,000 Year-Long Story," in *A Century of Parks Canada, 1911-1921*, ed. Claire Elizabeth Campbell (Calgary: University of Calgary Press, 2011).

7. Adolf Hungry Wolf and Beverly Hungry Wolf, *Indian Tribes of the Northern Rockies* (Skookumchuck, BC: Good Medicine Books, 1989).

8. The Nakoda peoples were members of the Sioux Nation and Assiniboine groups who lived primarily throughout the plains of North America. Many centuries ago, Nakoda peoples split from the larger Sioux Nation and began to migrate towards the plains in the southern sections of what are now considered the Canadian provinces of Saskatchewan and Alberta. Nakoda peoples began to live closer to the foothills and mountain ranges of the eastern slopes of the Canadian Rockies as they broke into three bands as they moved west. The Chiniki, Jacob (later Wesley), and Bearspaw bands all preferred to occupy the foothills and mountain ranges. Jon Whyte, *Indians in the Rockies* (Banff, AB: Altitude, 1985); Hugh Dempsey, *Indians in the Rocky Mountain Parks* (Calgary: Fifth House, 1998).

9. Rollinmud interview, 2008. Among Nakoda peoples, *Elder* is a respected title given only to some members of the community. *Elder* is not necessarily a gender or age category. Elders are considered educators about cultural practices and life in general. Because of their unique experiences and knowledge base, their values and wisdom make them highly regarded as decision makers.

10. Lenny Poucette, personal interview, October 9, 2009.

11. John Snow, *These Mountains Are Our Sacred Places: The Story of the Stoney Indians* (Toronto: Fifth House, 2005).

12. E.J. Hart, *The Places of Bows: Exploring the Heritage of the Banff–Bow Valley* (Banff, AB: EJH Literary Enterprises, 1999), 15.

13. Hart, *The Places of Bows*, 15.

14. Whyte, *Indians in the Rockies*.

15. Poucette interview, October 9, 2009.

16. Mabel B. Williams, *The Heart of the Rockies* (Hamilton, ON: Larson, 1922), 11.

17. Alan MacEachern, "M.B. Williams and the Early Years of Parks Canada," in *A Century of Parks Canada, 1911–1921*, ed. Claire Elizabeth Campbell (Calgary: University of Calgary Press, 2011), 42.

18. Since the 1960s, the majority of historians have acknowledged the long history of Indigenous peoples in the region. When discussing the first Europeans to locate the hot springs, historians often utilize the stylistic device of putting the word *discovery* into quotation marks. While this does underscore the arrogant and absurd notion that diverse groups of Indigenous peoples who had lived in the Banff–Bow Valley for millennia had not located the hot springs, this strategy does little to develop the histories of Indigenous uses of the hot springs.

19. Ella Elizabeth Clark, *Indian Legends of Canada* (Toronto: McClelland & Stewart, 1960), 95-96.

20. Poucette interview, 2009.

21. Margaret Snow, personal interview, November 14, 2008.

22. Rollinmud interview, 2008.

23. Rollinmud interview, 2008.

24. Hart, *The Places of Bows*.

25. James Gordon Nelson, "Man and Landscape Change in Banff National Park: A National Park Problem in Perspective," in *Canadian Parks in Perspective*, ed. J.G. Nelson (Montreal: Harvest House, 1970).

26. Mark David Spence, *Dispossessing the Wilderness: Indian Removal and the Making of National Parks* (New York: Oxford University Press, 1999), 55.

27. Snow, *These Mountains*.

28. Snow, *These Mountains*.

29. Residential schools have a long history in Canada. Missionaries began some schools for Indigenous children in the late 17th century. The school networks were expanded significantly under the 1876 Indian Act. Funding and facilities were mainly provided by the federal government, but teachers came from several religious denominations. Children were forcibly removed from their homes from ages 6 to 15 for up to 10 months a year. The health conditions in schools were deplorable and there were high rates of disease and mortality, and at times horrendous levels of physical and sexual abuse. In 1948, mandatory attendance was abolished. J.R. Miller, *Shingwauk's Vision: A History of Native Residential Schools* (Toronto: University of Toronto Press, 1996); Desiree Streit

and Courtney W. Mason, "Traversing the Terrain of Land-Based Education and Health for First Nations Youth: Connecting Theory to Practical Program Development," in *A Land Not Forgotten: Indigenous Food Security and Land-Based Practices of Northern Ontario*, ed. Michael A. Robidoux and Courtney W. Mason (Winnipeg: University of Manitoba Press, 2017), 85-123.

30. Rocky Mountains Park Act, S.C. (1887), ch. 32, 50-51.

31. Whyte, *Indians in the Rockies.*

32. Hildebrandt et al., *The True Spirit*, 90.

33. Janet Foster, *Working for Wildlife: The Beginning of Preservation in Canada* (Toronto: University of Toronto Press, 1978).

34. George Colpitts, *Game in the Garden: A Human History of Wildlife in Western Canada to 1940* (Vancouver: UBC Press, 2002).

35. Theodore Binnema and Melanie Niemi, "'Let the Line Be Drawn Now': Wilderness, Conservation, and the Exclusion of Aboriginal People From Banff National Park in Canada," *Environmental History* 11, no. 4 (2006): 729.

36. Nancy Bouchier and Ken Cruikshank, "'Sportsmen and Pothunters': Environment, Conservation, and Class in the Fisheries of Hamilton Harbour," *Sport History Review* 28, no. 1 (1997): 1-18.

37. Tina Loo, *States of Nature: Conserving Canada's Wildlife in the Twentieth Century* (Vancouver: UBC Press, 2006), 45.

38. Colpitts, *Game in the Garden.*

39. Shepard Krech, *The Ecological Indian: Myth and History* (New York: Norton, 1999).

40. Les W. Field, *Abalone Tales: Collaborative Explorations of Sovereignty and Identity in Native California* (Durham, NC: Duke University Press, 2008); Ranginui Walker, *Ka Whawhai Tonu Matou: Struggle Without End* (Auckland, NZ: Penguin Books, 1990).

41. Loo, *States of Nature.*

42. Keith Smith, *Liberalism, Surveillance and Resistance: Indigenous Communities in Western Canada, 1877-1927* (Edmonton: Athabasca University Press, 2009).

43. Hugh Dempsey, *Indian Tribes of Alberta* (Calgary: Glenbow Museum Institute, 1997).

44. The CPR was formed in 1881 with the intention of building a railway that would unite central Canada to British Columbia and the Pacific coast, a task they completed in 1885. From the 1880s until the beginning of the Second World War, the CPR diversified into tourism ventures, including hotel and infrastructure construction, in addition to numerous other profitable businesses. See Marc H. Choko and David L. Jones. *Posters of the Canadian Pacific* (Toronto: Firefly Books, 2004).

45. Loo, *States of Nature*, 44.

46. Throughout the 20th century in Canada, because of conflicts with newly created conservation principles, Indigenous peoples have been effectively displaced by the foundation of a number of parks and protected areas. Even during the postwar period, the complex links between scientific discourse and state objectives were entangled as the Canadian Wildlife Service and "its scientists were more than willing to frame their scientific studies and management programs in terms of the administrative priorities of their bureaucratic masters" (John Sandlos, *Hunters at the Margin: Native People and Wildlife Conservation in the Northwest Territories* (Vancouver: UBC Press, 2007), 241. This continued to ensure that Indigenous communities were displaced and their subsistence practices marginalized throughout Canada.

47. David Neufeld, "Kluane National Park Reserve, 1923-1974: Modernity and Pluralism," in *A Century of Parks Canada, 1911-1921*, ed. Claire Elizabeth Campbell (Calgary: University of Calgary Press, 2011), 235-272.

48. Snow, *These Mountains.*

49. Snow, *These Mountains,* 82.

50. Archival analysis of photographs was critical to this project and an important source of historical knowledge. This photograph from the Whyte Museum of the Canadian Rockies is significant because it demonstrates that Nakoda peoples were gathering very near to Banff townsite at a hunting camp. This was a period when Nakoda hunting was officially illegal in the park, but as revealed in the image, the Nakoda were utilizing opportunities to access the park to pursue their cultural and subsistence practices.

51. Binnema and Niemi, "'Let the Line Be Drawn Now.'"

52. Snow, *These Mountains.*

53. Rollinmud interview, 2008.

54. Howard Sibbald, "Indian Agent's Annual Report," interview by Frank Pedley, *Annual Report of the Department of Indian Affairs,* no. 192 (December 23, 1903). This is a standard reference to a government document. [CA: I deleted personal connection. I think this is the confusion. Often we write this if the document was retrieved through a personal connection instead of from an archive. If it is confusing, it can be deleted.]

55. Foster, *Working for Wildlife.*

56. Snow, *These Mountains.*

57. National Parks Act, S.C. (1930), ch. 33, 20-21.

58. Spence, *Dispossessing the Wilderness.* Robert H. Keller and Michael F. Turek, *American Indians and National Parks* (Tucson: University of Arizona Press, 1999); Philip Burnham, *Indian Country, God's Country: Native Americans and the National Parks* (Washington, DC: Island Press, 2000); Karl Jacoby, *Crimes Against Nature: Squatters, Poachers, Thieves and the Hidden History of American Conservation* (Berkeley: University of California, 2001); Julie Cruikshank, *Do Glaciers Listen? Local Knowledge, Colonial Encounters, and Social Imagination* (Vancouver: UBC Press, 2005).

59. Spence, *Dispossessing the Wilderness,* 4.

60. Spence, *Dispossessing the Wilderness,* 4.

61. Burnham, *Indian Country, God's Country.*

62. Karthik L. Sivaramakrishnan, "Postcolonialism," in *A Companion to the Anthropology of Politics,* ed. David Nugent and John Vincent (Oxford, UK: Blackwell, 2004), 370.

63. Mahesh Rangarajan, *Fencing the Forest: Conservation and Ecological Change in India's Central Provinces, 1860-1914* (Delhi: Oxford University Press, 1996); Dawn Chatty and Markus Colchester, *Conservation and Mobile Indigenous Peoples: Displacement, Forced Settlement, and Sustainable Development* (Oxford, UK: Berghahn Books, 2002); Roderick P. Neumann, *Imposing Wilderness: Struggles Over Livelihood and Nature Preservation in Africa* (Berkeley: University of California Press, 1998).

64. Spence, *Dispossessing the Wilderness.*

65. Robert C. Scace, "Banff Townsite: An Historical and Geographical View of Urban Development in a Canadian National Park," in *Canadian Parks in Perspective,* ed. J.G. Nelson (Montreal: Harvest House, 1970), 187-208.

66. Although the railway was completed at Craigellachie, British Columbia, on November 7, 1885, it did not become officially operational until June of 1886. The completion of the railway fulfilled the 1871 commitment of the Canadian federal government to connect British Columbia to central Canada. The promise of a transcontinental railway was a significant factor in securing the western province in Canadian Confederation. John I. Nicol, "The National Parks Movement in Canada," in *Canadian Parks in Perspective,* ed. J.G. Nelson (Montreal: Harvest House, 1970).

67. Hart, *The Places of Bows*, 114.

68. Promoting mountain landscapes and the use of the railway to wealthy tourists was also a primary motivation behind the creation of iconic national parks in the United States such as Yellowstone, but especially Mount Rainier. Shadowing tourism development in or around parks and protected spaces in the United States, the formation of national parks in Canada was deeply shaped by American examples and experiences. Not only did public policy in the United States influence how Canadian processes unfolded, but the decisions that motivated Canadian leadership from the political and community side often mirrored what was occurring in the United States. Chris J. Magoc, *Yellowstone: The Creation and Selling of an American Landscape: 1870-1903* (Albuquerque: University of New Mexico Press, 1999); Theodore Catton, *National Park, City Playground: Mt. Rainer and the Twentieth Century* (Seattle: University of Washington Press, 2006); David Louter, *Windshield Wilderness: Cars, Roads and Nature in Washington's National Parks* (Seattle: University of Washington Press, 2006); Jacoby, *Crimes Against Nature*; Foster, *Working for Wildlife*; Ian S. MacLaren, "Rejuvenating Wilderness: The Challenge of Reintegrating Aboriginal Peoples Into the 'Playground' of Jasper National Park," in *A Century of Parks Canada, 1911-1921*, ed. Claire Elizabeth Campbell (Calgary: University of Calgary Press, 2011), 333-370.

69. Harvey Locke, "Civil Society and Protected Areas: A Lesson From the Canadian Experience," *George Wright Forum* 26, no. 2 (2009): 101-128.

70. Rocky Mountains Park Act, ch. 32, 50-51.

71. John Sandlos, *Hunters at the Margin: Native People and Wildlife Conservation in the Northwest Territories* (Vancouver: UBC Press, 2007).

72. Rocky Mountains Park Act, ch. 32, 50-51.

73. Brad Martin, "Negotiating a Partnership of Interests: Inuvialuit Land Claims and the Establishment of Northern Yukon (Ivvavik) National Park," in *A Century of Parks Canada, 1911-1921*, ed. Claire Elizabeth Campbell (Calgary: University of Calgary Press, 2011), 274.

74. Kevin McNamee, "From Wild Places to Endangered Spaces: A History of Canada's National Parks," in *Parks and Protected Areas in Canada*, ed. Philip Dearden and Rick Rollins (Oxford: University of Oxford Press, 1993), 15-44.

75. Sid Marty, *A Grand and Fabulous Notion: The First Century of Canada's National Parks* (Toronto: NC Press, 1984), 98; For an excellent resource on J.B. Harkin and his role in the development of the Rocky Mountain national parks, see E.J. Hart, *J.B. Harkin: Father of Canada's National Parks* (Edmonton: University of Alberta Press, 2009).

76. MacEachern argues that Mabel Williams played a key role in convincing commissioner Harkin of the value of tourism in parks. It was her idea to market tourism as an incentive to create national parks, and she delivered the important financial documents to encourage Harkin's agenda to expand the national park system. Part of the evidence that supported this economic argument was William's creative calculation suggesting that wheat fields were worth $4.91 an acre while scenery was valued at $13.88. Her calculation was even quoted at length in the U.S. Congress discussion about creating a national park service in 1916. For more see MacEachern, "M.B. Williams," 33.

77. Robert Craig Brown, "The Doctrine of Usefulness: Natural Resources and the National Park Policy in Canada, 1887-1914" in *Canadian Parks in Perspective*, ed. J.G. Nelson (Montreal: Harvest House, 1970), 46.

78. Lynda Jessup, "The Group of Seven and the Tourist Landscape in Western Canada, or the More Things Change . . .," *Journal of Canadian Studies* 37, no. 1 (2002): 144-179.

79. Jessup, "The Group of Seven," 150.

80. Leslie Bella, *Parks for Profit* (Montreal: Harvest House, 1987).

81. E.J. Hart, *The Battle for Banff: Exploring the Heritage of the Banff–Bow Valley, Part II* (Banff, AB: EJH Literary Enterprises, 2003).

82. Kathryn Manry, *West on One: The Stories Behind the Scenery* (Kelowna, BC: Sandhill Book Marketing, 2010).

83. E.J. Hart, *The Selling of Canada: The CPR and the Beginning of Canadian Tourism* (Banff, AB: Altitude, 1983).

84. Colpitts, *Game in the Garden.*

85. E.J. Hart, *Diamond Hitch: The Pioneer Guides and Outfitters of Banff and Jasper* (Banff, AB: Summerthought, 1979).

86. Taiaiake Alfred, "Colonialism and State Dependency," *Journal of Aboriginal Health* 5 (2009): 42-60.

87. Tolly Bradford, "A Useful Institution: Williams Twin, 'Indianness,' and Banff National Park, c. 1860-1940," *Native Studies Review* 16, no. 2 (2005): 77-98.

88. Manry, *West on One.*

89. Whyte, *Indians in the Rockies.*

90. In the United States, there are also examples of Indigenous peoples contributing to local tourism economies in national parks. From the mid-19th century, Yosemite Indians found labour work in the developing tourism industries associated with the national park. They supplied tourists with wild game and fish as well as performing a variety of tasks related to the development of the park infrastructure. Spence, *Dispossessing the Wilderness.*

91. Ralphine Locke, personal interview, July 18, 2009.

92. MacLaren, "Rejuvenating Wilderness."

93. Environment and Climate Change Canada, *Canadian Protected Areas Status Report 2012-2015* (Gatineau, QC: Parks Canada, 2016).

94. Indigenous Circle of Experts (ICE), *We Rise Together: Achieving Pathway to Canada Target 1 Through the Creation of Indigenous Protected and Conserved Areas in the Spirit and Practice of Reconciliation* (Gatineau, QC: Parks Canada, 2018).

Chapter 6

1. John Dickinson and Brian Young, *A Short History of Quebec*, 4th ed. (Montreal: McGill-Queen's University Press, 2008), 120.

2. Frank Mackey, *Steamboat Connections: Montreal to Upper Canada, 1816-1843* (Montreal: McGill-Queens University Press, 2000), 3, 11.

3. Mackey, *Steamboat Connections*, 11.

4. Kris Inwood and Ian Keay, "Diverse Paths to Industrial Development: Evidence From Late-Nineteenth-Century Canada," *European Review of Economic History* 16 (2012): 330.

5. Alan Metcalfe, *Canada Learns to Play: The Emergence of Organized Sport, 1807-1914* (Toronto: McClelland & Stewart, 1987), 49.

6. Inwood and Keay, "Diverse Paths to Industrial Development," 312.

7. George Colpitts, *Game in the Garden: A Human History of Wildlife in Western Canada to 1940* (Vancouver: UBC Press, 2002), 129.

8. Commission of Conservation, *Annual Report, 1915* (Ottawa, 1915), 63. Quoted in Robert Craig Brown and Ramsay Cook, *Canada 1896-1921: A Nation Transformed* (Toronto: McClelland & Stewart, reprint 1991), 99.

9. Brown and Cook, *Canada 1896-1921*, 101.

10. Denis McKim, "God's Garden: Nature, Order, and the Presbyterian Conception of the British North American 'Wilderness,'" *Journal of Canadian Studies* 51, no. 2 (2017): 400.

11. McKim, "God's Garden," 402-403.

12. David McMurray, "'The Charm of Being Loose and Free': Nineteenth Century Fisherwomen in the North American Wilderness," *International Journal of the History of Sport* 30, no. 8 (2013): 2.

13. Metcalfe, *Canada Learns to Play*, 20.

14. See Kevin Wamsley and Robert Kossuth, "Fighting It Out in Nineteenth-Century Upper Canada/Canada West: Masculinities and Physical Challenges in the Tavern," *Journal of Sport History* 27, no. 3 (2000): 405-430.

15. Hazel Conway, *People Parks: The Design and Development of Victorian Parks in Britain* (Cambridge: Cambridge University Press, 1991), 4.

16. Conway, *People Parks*, 224.

17. Conway, *People Parks*, 225.

18. Elsie McFarland, *The Development of Public Recreation in Canada* (Ottawa: Canadian Parks/Recreation Association, 1970), 7.

19. J.R. Wright, *Urban Parks in Ontario Part 1: Origins to 1860* (Ottawa: Province of Ontario, Ministry of Tourism and Recreation, 1983), 60.

20. Wright, *Urban Parks in Ontario*, 8.

21. Proceedings of London City Council, 20 and 27 May 1867, J.J. Talman Regional Collection, D.B. Weldon Library, Western University.

22. Proceedings of London City Council, 4 May 1868.

23. Proceedings of London City Council, 29 June 1868; *History of the County of Middlesex, Canada* (Toronto and London: Goodspeed, 1889), 238.

24. Pat Morden, *Putting Down Roots: A History of London's Parks and River* (St. Catharines, ON: Stonehouse, 1988), 8.

25. Robert S. Kossuth, "Spaces and Places to Play: The Formation of a Municipal Parks System in London Ontario, 1867-1914," *Ontario History* 97, no. 2 (2005): 171.

26. Proceedings of London City Council, 25 September 1876. The request to use Victoria Park was passed to the Park Committee, who turned down the Tecumsehs' request at the 9 October 1876, meeting of council.

27. "Athletics," *Lethbridge News*, March 20, 1891.

28. Alex Johnston, Summary of City of Lethbridge Council Minutes, 1901-1982, Alex Johnston Collection, 7 November 1910, 130, Galt Museum and Archives.

29. Proceedings of London City Council, 11 March 1878 (see regarding Miller's ongoing involvement in landscape architecture in late-19th-century Ontario); Pleasance Crawford, "Of Grounds Tastefully Laid Out: The Landscaping of Public Buildings in 19th Century Ontario," *Society for the Study of Architecture in Canada Bulletin* 11, no. 3 (1986): 6-7.

30. *History of the County of Middlesex*, 237; Kossuth, "Spaces and Places to Play," 172.

31. *By-law for Establishing a Public Park, to Be Called Queen's Park*, By-Laws of the Corporation of the City of London, 1879, 217-218, J.J. Talman Regional Collection, D.B.

Weldon Library, Western University.

32. *History of the County of Middlesex*, 204-206.

33. *London Free Press*, May 27, 1879.

34. *London Advertiser*, June 28, 1880.

35. Robert S. Kossuth, "Dangerous Waters: Victorian Decorum, Swimmer Safety, and the Establishment of Public Bathing Facilities in London (Canada)," *International Journal of the History of Sport* 22, no. 5 (2005): 803.

36. Ken Cruikshank and Nancy B. Bouchier, "*Dirty Spaces*: Environment, the State, and Recreational Swimming in Hamilton Harbour, 1870-1946," *Sport History Review* 29, no. 1, (1998): 63.

37. Cruikshank and Bouchier, "*Dirty Spaces*, 64-65.

38. Cruikshank and Bouchier, "*Dirty Spaces*, 66-67.

39. Cruikshank and Bouchier, "*Dirty Spaces*, 67-72.

40. Benjamin G. Rader, *American Sports: From the Age of Folk Games to the Age of Televised Sport*, 5th ed. (Upper Saddle River, NJ: Prentice Hall, 2004): 113-114.

41. McFarland, *Development of Public Recreation*, 19. According to McFarland, the National Council of Women was formed in 1893 in part because of the encouragement of Lady Aberdeen, who had been elected the president of the World Council of Women the previous year in Washington, D.C.

42. McFarland, *Development of Public Recreation*, 19. Referred from the National Council of Women of Canada, *Report of the Eighth Annual Meeting and Conference*, 1901 (Ottawa: Taylor and Clark, 1901), 152.

43. McFarland, *Development of Public Recreation*, 21-34.

44. Morden, *Putting Down Roots*, 49.

45. Mrs. James McNiven, "London Local Council of Women," *Local Council of Women, London, 1893-1914* (London: Talbot, 1937), 11. This brief history of the local council of women lists "providing of Recreation Parks and Children's Playgrounds" among the organization's primary accomplishments.

46. Proceedings of London City Council, 15 August 1904.

47. Morden, *Putting Down Roots*, 34.

48. Robert Duff, "London Parks and Recreation 1871-1973: A History of the Recreation Department," unpublished manuscript (Public Utilities Commission of London, June 1973), 88, J.J. Talman Regional Collection, D.B. Weldon Library, Western University, 6. This land, on the south side of the Thames River at Ridout Street, was purchased to augment the city's water supply.

49. Morden, *Putting Down Roots*, 49.

50. Carly Adams, "Supervised Spaces to Play: Social Reform, Citizenship, and Femininity at Municipal Playgrounds in London Ontario, 1900-1942," *Ontario History* 103, no. 1 (2011): 66-67.

51. Paulina Cecilia Retamales and PearlAnn Reichwein, "'A Healthy and Contented Band': The Gyro Club and Playgrounds in Edmonton Urban Reform, 1921-1944," *Sport History Review* 45, no. 2 (2014): 97-98.

52. Retamales and Reichwein, "'A Healthy and Contented Band,'" 96.

53. David McMurray, "'A Recreation Which Many Ladies Delight In'": Establishing a Tradition of Fisherwomen in Britain and North America Prior to the Mid-Nineteenth Century," *Sport History Review* 43, no. 2 (2012): 129.

54. Phoebe Kropp, "Wilderness Wives and Dishwashing Husbands: Comfort and the Domestic Arts of Camping in America, 1880-1910," *Journal of Social History* 43, no. 1 (2009): 8.

55. R. Blake Brown, "'Every Boy Ought to Learn to Shoot and to Obey Orders': Guns, Boys, and the Law in English Canada From the Late Nineteenth Century to the Great War," *Canadian Historical Review* 93, no. 2 (2012): 198 and 202.

56. Mary Harvey Drummond, "A Woman's Trip to the Laurentides," *Rod and Gun in Canada*, 2, no. 7 (1900): 388.

57. Drummond, "A Woman's Trip," 389.

58. Drummond, "A Woman's Trip," 389.

59. Drummond, "A Woman's Trip," 389.

60. Drummond, "A Woman's Trip," 389.

61. McMurray, "A Tradition of Fisherwomen," 129.

62. McMurray, "A Tradition of Fisherwomen," 143.

63. See McMurray, "'The Charm of Being Loose and Free,'" 853-870; McMurray, "Rivaling the Gentleman in the Gentle Art: The Authority of the Victorian Woman Angler," *Sport History Review* 39, no. 2 (2008): 99-126.

64. "Our Medicine Bag," *Rod and Gun in Canada* 6, no. 11 (1905): 627.

65. Nadine I. Kozak, "Advice Ideals and Rural Prairie Realities: National and Prairie Scientific Motherhood Advice, 1920-29," in *Unsettled Pasts: Reconceiving the West Through Women's History*, ed. Lesley Erickson, Sarah Carter, Patricia Roome, and Char Smith (Calgary: University of Calgary Press, 2005), 180.

66. See "The Princess Royal and Daughters," *Saturday News*, June 24, 1911; "Lady de Bathe and Her Hobbies," *Taber Free Press*, April 8, 1909; "Local and General," *Coleman Bulletin*, September 6, 1918, 5; "Of Local and General Interest," *Blairmore Enterprise*, August 4, 1916, 8.

67. Lynda Jessup, "Landscapes of Sport, Landscapes of Exclusion: The 'Sportsman's Paradise' in Late-Nineteenth-Century Painting," *Journal of Canadian Studies* 40, no. 1, (2006): 88. Jessup is paraphrasing a point made by Peter Thomas. She further notes that the Intercolonial "tempered" the concept of wilderness, thus opening it up to the presence of women.

68. McMurray, "The Charm of Being Loose and Free," 15.

69. J.H. McIllree and M.H. White Fraser, "Fishing in Southern Alberta," *Alberta History* 31 (1983): 37.

70. Nancy Bouchier and Ken Cruikshank, *The People and the Bay: A Social and Environmental History of Hamilton Harbour* (Vancouver: UBC Press, 2016), 37.

71. Bouchier and Cruikshank, *The People and the Bay*, 37.

72. Sheila McManus, *Choices and Chances: A History of Women in the U.S. West* (Wheeling, IL: Harlan Davidson, 2011), 177. McManus is talking about White American women, but it can be argued that the same values can be applied to White women in Canada. See also Karen Wonders, "A Sportsmen's Eden Part 2: A Wilderness Besieged," *The Beaver* 79, no. 6 (1999): 30-37.

73. McMurray, "The Charm of Being Loose and Free," 14.

74. McMurray, "The Charm of Being Loose and Free," 15.

75. Jessup, "Landscapes of Sport," 105.

76. Jessup, "Landscapes of Sport," 105.

77. Brown, "'Every Boy Ought to Learn,'" 202.

78. Brown, "'Every Boy Ought to Learn,'" 201-202.

79. Colpitts, *Game in the Garden*, 63.

80. Greg Gillespie, "The Empire's Eden: British Hunters, Travel Writing, and Imperialism in Nineteenth-Century Canada," in *The Culture of Hunting in Canada*, ed. Jean L. Manore and Dale G. Miner (Vancouver: UBC Press, 2007), 44.

81. Gillespie, "The Empire's Eden," 44.

82. Gillespie, "The Empire's Eden," 54.

83. Jessup, "Landscapes of Sport," 73.

84. Greg Gillespie, "'I Was Well Pleased With Our Sport Among the Buffalo': Big-Game Hunters, Travel Writing, and Cultural Imperialism in the British North American West, 1847-72," *Canadian Historical Review* 83, no. 4 (2002): 583; Jessup, "Landscapes of Sport," 100. Jessup discusses this subject in the context of angling.

85. Louis Bird and Roland Bohr, "Views of a Swampy-Cree Elder on the Spiritual Relationship Between Hunters and Animals," in *The Culture of Hunting in Canada*, ed. Jean L. Manore and Dale G. Miner (Vancouver: UBC Press, 2007), 90.

86. Bird and Bohr, "Views of a Swampy-Cree Elder," 91.

87. Mike Mountain Horse, *My People, the Bloods*, ed. by Hugh A. Dempsey (Calgary: Glenbow Museum and Blood Indian Council, 1989), 27.

88. Scott Johnston, "Boy Scouts and the British World: Autonomy Within an Imperial Institution, 1908-1936," *Canadian Journal of History/Annales canadiennes d'histoire* 51, no. 1 (2016): 34.

89. Kristine Alexander, *Guiding Modern Girls: Girlhood, Empire, and Internationalism in the 1920s and 1930s* (Vancouver: UBC Press, 2017), 4.

90. Johnston, "Boy Scouts and the British World," 40.

91. Johnston, "Boy Scouts and the British World," 40.

92. Johnston, "Boy Scouts and the British World," 42.

93. Alexander, *Guiding Modern Girls*, 46.

94. Boy Scouts: Youth Organization, *Encyclopedia Britannica*, accessed July 11, 2018, www.britannica.com/topic/Boy-Scouts.

95. Alexander, *Guiding Modern Girls*, 109.

96. Alexander, *Guiding Modern Girls*, 110.

97. Alexander, *Guiding Modern Girls*, 122.

98. Raymond Huel, "The Creation of the Alpine Club of Canada: An Early Manifestation of Canadian Nationalism," *Prairie Forum* 15, no. 1 (1990): 26.

99. Huel, "Creation of the Alpine Club," 28.

100. PearlAnn Reichwein, *Climbers Paradise: Making Canada's Mountain Parks, 1906-1974* (Edmonton: University of Alberta Press, 2014), 25-26.

101. Zac Robinson, "The Golden Years of Canadian Mountaineering: Asserted Ethics, Form, and Style, 1886-1925," *Sport History Review* 35, no. 1 (2004): 1-5.

102. Robinson, "Golden Years of Canadian Mountaineering," 8.

103. Robinson, "Golden Years of Canadian Mountaineering," 13.

104. Zac Robinson, "Off the Beaten Path? Ski Mountaineering and the Weight of Tradition in the Canadian Rockies, 1909-1940," *International Journal of the History of Sport* 24, no. 10 (2007): 1327.

105. Robinson, "Off the Beaten Path?," 1328.

106. M. Ann Hall, *The Girl and the Game: A History of Women's Sports in Canada*, 2nd ed. (Toronto: University of Toronto Press, 2016), 183.

107. Don Morrow, "The Knights of the Snowshoe: A Study of the Evolution of Sport in Nineteenth Century Montreal," *Journal of Sport History* 15, no. 1 (1988): 9.

108. Don Morrow, "Montreal: The Cradle of Organized Sport," in *A Concise History of Sport in Canada*, ed. Don Morrow and Mary Keyes (Toronto: Oxford University Press, 1989), 15.

109. Morrow, "Montreal," 15.

110. M. Ann Hall, *Muscle on Wheels: Louise Armaindo and the High Wheel Racers of Nineteenth-Century America* (Montreal: McGill-Queen's University Press, 2018), 13, 99-117.

111. Robert S. Kossuth and Kevin B. Wamsley, "Cycles of Manhood: Peddling Respectability in Ontario's Forest City," *Sport History Review* 34, no. 2 (2003): 174-175.

112. *Lethbridge News*, April 26, 1888, 1. This poem was written by Captain Jack Crawford (1847-1917), who also gained fame as a member of Buffalo Bill's Wild West Show. The date of the poem's first publication could not be verified.

113. Robert S. Kossuth and Kevin B. Wamsley, "Cycling on the Range: Men and Their Machines on the Canadian Prairie Frontier," in *Cycle History 16*, Proceedings of the 16th International Cycling History Conference, Davis, California, September 2005.

Chapter 7

1. Canadian sportswomen were not afforded an equal role in the development of Canadian sport in the 19th century. As an example, that typifies the chauvinistic sentiment females endured in Canadian sport at this time, *The Week* published on June 5, 1884, that 19th-century Canadian sportswomen preferred the straightforward game of lacrosse because cricket was too intricate for them to comprehend.

2. M.A. Robidoux, "Imagining a Canadian Identity Through Sport: A Historical Interpretation of Lacrosse and Hockey," *Journal of American Folklore* 115 (2002): 211.

3. Richard Gruneau, "Modernization or Hegemony: Two Views on Sport and Social Development," in *Not Just a Game*, ed. Hart Cantelon and Jean Harvey (Ottawa: University of Ottawa Press, 1988), 13.

4. It must be recognized that Canada was, and remains today, a country of regional interests, and this factionalism played a role in the three-way debate. It should also be understood that a consensus on the definition of Canadian identity was not reached within demographic groups that outwardly appeared homogeneous. For example, not all British immigrants pursued an imperialist agenda for Canada, just as not all Quebeckers wanted to sever ties with the British monarchy.

5. The *Canada Year Book* from 1914 (p. 60) reported that from the 1911 census, the Canadian population was 7,206,643, of whom 3,896,985 considered themselves of British origin. More specifically, 1,823,150 listed English; 1,050,384 stated Irish; 997,880 claimed to be Scottish; 24,848 were Welsh; and 723 said "other," which might suggest Isle of Man. This report is not entirely accurate because 75,681 reported to be Jewish and 16,877 were listed as Black, and these were enumerated separately even though some of these people would consider themselves British as well. Any Black citizens from Jamaica, for example, were likely listed only by their race and not from the island, which was a British colony.

6. Alan Metcalfe, *Canada Learns to Play: The Emergence of Organized Sport, 1807-1914* (Toronto: McClelland & Stewart, 1987), 18.

7. David Cooper, "Canadians Declare 'It Isn't Cricket': A Century of Rejection of the Imperial Game," *Canadian Journal of History of Sport* 26, no. 1 (1999): 69.

8. David Brown, "Canadian Imperialism and Sporting Exchanges: The Nineteenth Century Cultural Experience of Cricket and Lacrosse," *Canadian Journal of History of Sport* 28, no. 1 (1987): 56.

9. Cooper, "'It Isn't Cricket,'" 69.

10. Alan Bairner, *Sport, Nationalism, and Globalization: European and North American Perspectives* (Albany: State University of New York Press, 2001), 116.

11. Eric Midwinter, *Fair Game: Myth and Reality in Sport* (London: Allen and Unwin, 1986), 67.

12. Roger Hutchinson, *Empire Games: The British Invention of Twentieth-Century Sport* (Edinburgh: Mainstream, 1996), 160.

13. Hutchinson, *Empire Games*, 161.

14. Cooper, "'It Isn't Cricket,'" 53.

15. Cooper, "'It Isn't Cricket,'" 56.

16. Brown, "Canadian Imperialism and Sporting Exchanges," 56.

17. During the latter half of the 19th century, Victorian values were an influential moral code that all respectable people in the Empire were expected to uphold. The concept of "character" was an obsession for most Victorians. Great emphasis was placed on industriousness, morality, and gentility because these qualities were regarded as major cogs in the creation of "men of character."

18. Kingsley's *Two Years Ago* was published in 1856, and Hughes' *Tom Brown's School Days* first appeared in print in 1857 and the sequel *Tom Brown at Oxford* debuted in 1861.

19. Thomas Hughes, *Tom Brown at Oxford* (New York: Macmillan, 1932), 99.

20. While many historians focus on cricket's appeal to the Canadian elite, research shows that the sport became somewhat socially diverse in Atlantic Canada, particularly in the 20th century. Readers interested in learning more about the broadening appeal of cricket should consult John Reid and Robert G. Reid, "Diffusion and Discursive Stabilization: Sports Historiography and Contrasting Fortunes of Cricket and Ice Hockey in Canada's Maritime Provinces, 1869-1914," *Journal of Sport History* 41, no. 1 (1999): 87-113.

21. Nancy Bouchier, *For the Love of the Game: Amateur Sport in Small-Town Ontario 1838-1895* (Montreal: McGill-Queen's University Press, 2003), 89-90.

22. Subsequent Governors General openly endorsed sport as well. The Stanley Cup, Grey Cup, and Minto Cup were trophies awarded to top clubs in hockey, football, and lacrosse, respectively. Further information can be found in Gerald Redmond's "Imperial Vice-Regal Patronage: The Governors-General of Canada and Sport in the Dominions, 1867-1909," *International Journal of the History of Sport* 6, no. 2 (1989): 193-217.

23. Allen Guttmann, *Games and Empires: Modern Sports and Cultural Imperialism* (New York: Columbia University Press, 1994), 21.

24. Cooper, "'It Isn't Cricket,'" 61.

25. Cooper, "'It Isn't Cricket,'" 52.

26. Richard Cashman, "Cricket and Colonialism: Colonial Hegemony and Indigenous Subversion," in *Pleasure, Profit, Proselytism: British Culture and Sport at Home and Abroad, 1700-1914*, ed. J.A. Mangan (London: Frank Cass, 1988), 258-272.

27. Cooper, "'It Isn't Cricket,'" 70.

28. Bouchier, *For the Love of the Game*, 99.

29. Before Newfoundland joined Confederation in 1949, it had dominion status, which meant it was a self-governing state within the British Empire.

30. Derek Birley, *The Willow Wand: Some Cricket Myths Explored* (London: Queen Anne Press, 1979), 67.

31. Keith Sandiford, *Cricket and the Victorians* (Aldershot, UK: Scolar Press, 1994), 148.

32. Cooper, "'It Isn't Cricket,'" 75.

33. Cooper, "'It Isn't Cricket,'" 75.

34. Bairner, *Sport, Nationalism, and Globalization*, 117.

35. Cooper, "'It Isn't Cricket,'" 62.

36. From 1830 to 1920, Canadian cricketers were 10-72-16 against international competition and the first win did not come until 1886 with a Hamilton victory over a visiting club from the West Indies.

37. Brown, "Canadian Imperialism and Sporting Exchanges," 56.

38. *Woodstock Weekly Review*, March 28, 1871.

39. For a more detailed explanation of the name change, refer to Don Morrow and Kevin Wamsley, *Sport in Canada: A History* (Don Mills, ON: Oxford University Press, 2005), 90.

40. Robidoux, "Imagining a Canadian Identity," 212.

41. Allan Downey, *The Creator's Game: Lacrosse, Identity, and Indigenous Nationhood*. (Vancouver: UBC Press, 2018), 23.

42. W. George Beers, *Lacrosse: The National Game of Canada* (Montreal: Dawson Brothers, 1869), 44, 49-50.

43. Many Canadians accepted as fact this fabrication, which remained part of Canada's national folklore until disproved in the 1960s. For more information, consult Kevin Jones and George Vellathottam, "The Myth of Canada's National Sport," *CAPHER* (1974): 33-36. In 1994, an act of Parliament made the myth official as lacrosse and hockey were declared Canada's national sports. This declaration can be found on the Canadian Heritage site, "National Sports of Canada Act," www.pch.gc.ca/pgm/sc/legsltn/n-16-eng.cfm.

44. *Montreal Gazette*, June 29, 1867.

45. Donald Fisher, *Lacrosse: A History of the Game* (Baltimore: Johns Hopkins University Press, 2002), 26.

46. Metcalfe, *Canada Learns to Play*, 182-183.

47. Downey, *The Creator's Game*, 50.

48. A comprehensive account of the 1876 and 1883 lacrosse tours is provided by Kevin Wamsley, "Nineteenth Century Sport Tours, State Formation, and Canadian Foreign Policy. *Sporting Traditions* 13, no. 2 (1997): 73-89.

49. Brown, "Canadian Imperialism and Sporting Exchanges," 56.

50. Crime and street safety were not an issue in Ingersoll and Woodstock, but stories and rumours came from larger centres that foretold of restless young boys creating trouble for the police.

51. Bouchier, *For the Love of the Game*, 118.

52. Beers, *Lacrosse: The National Game of Canada*, xv-xvi.

53. Morrow and Wamsley, *Sport in Canada*, 104.

54. Alan Metcalfe, "Sport and Athletics: A Case Study of Lacrosse in Canada, 1840-1889," *Journal of Sport History* 3, no. 1 (1976): 7.

55. *Woodstock Sentinel*, April 18, 1884.

56. *Montreal Star*, May 21, 1872.

57. Metcalfe, *Canada Learns to Play*, 186.

58. Metcalfe, *Canada Learns to Play*, 11.

59. For more information on the Irish Catholics and lacrosse, see Dennis Ryan, *Irish Catholic Sport, Identity and Integration in Toronto, 1858-1920,* (unpublished MA thesis, The University of Western Ontario, 2000). Ryan contends that sport was essential in the formation and maintenance of a distinct Irish Catholic identity, but it also furthered integration. Their participation in sports, like lacrosse, reflected a shift in identity from Irish nationalism to Catholic Canadian.

60. Metcalfe, "Sport and Athletics," 12.

61. Metcalfe, "Sport and Athletics," 8.

62. Metcalfe, *Canada Learns to Play*, 111.

63. Frank Cosentino noted that hockey fans were among the first to eagerly accept professional players into commercial leagues such as the National Hockey Association of 1909. Their acceptance was probably eased by the decision of the trustees of the Stanley Cup to allow for no restrictions as to who was eligible to compete for the Cup, professionals or amateurs. The objective was to discover the best team.

64. Frank Cosentino, "A History of the Concept of Professionalism in Canadian Sport," *Canadian Journal of History of Sport and Physical Education* 20, no. 2 (1975): 79-80.

65. Fisher, *Lacrosse: A History of the Game*, 51.

66. Fisher, *Lacrosse: A History of the Game*, 52.

67. Metcalfe, *Canada Learns to Play*, 210.

68. Colin Howell, *Blood, Sweat and Cheers: Sport and the Making of Modern Canada* (Toronto: University of Toronto Press, 2001), 42.

69. J.L. Granatstein, *Yankee Go Home?: Canadians and Anti-Americanism* (Toronto: HarperCollins, 1996), 76.

70. Reginald C. Stuart, *Dispersed Relations: Americans and Canadians in Upper North America* (Baltimore: Johns Hopkins University Press, 2007), 30.

71. William Humber, *Diamonds of the North: A Concise History of Baseball in Canada* (Toronto: Oxford University Press, 1995) 32.

72. *Victoria Times*, May 13, 1905.

73. Samuel Moffett, *The Americanization of Canada* (Toronto: University of Toronto Press, 1972), 109-110.

74. *Mail and Empire*, May 6, 1905.

75. *St. Thomas Times*, June 1, 1905.

76. A detailed account of this tour can be found in James Elfer's *The Tour to End All Tours: The Story of Major League Baseball's 1913-1914 World Tour* (Lincoln: University of Nebraska Press, 2003).

77. *Time*, September 22, 1924.

78. Moffett, *The Americanization of Canada*, 109.

79. For more information on the standardization of baseball rules in Canada, consult the third chapter of Humber's *Diamonds of the North*.

80. Masters wrote in the conclusion of *The Rise of Toronto, 1850-1890* that Toronto differed from Montreal in this era because it was linked not only to London, like Montreal, but also to New York. This connection allowed Toronto to claim it was not only the most British city in Canada but also the most American. This latter distinction no doubt played a role in its early adoption of baseball.

81. Humber, *Diamonds of the North*, 25.

82. Humber, *Diamonds of the North*, 25.

83. Humber, *Diamonds of the North*, 24-25.

84. Morrow and Wamsley, *Sport in Canada*, 106.

85. Humber, *Diamonds of the North*, 23.

86. Humber, *Diamonds of the North*, 25.

87. Humber, *Diamonds of the North*, 26.

88. *Guelph Evening Mercury*, August 24, 1872.

89. *London Advertiser*, May 25, 1876, estimated the crowd at 6,000 while the *Guelph Daily Mercury*'s estimate for the same game came in at 9,000.

90. Robert Knight Barney, "Whose National Pastime?: Baseball in Canadian Popular Culture," in *The Beaver Bites Back?: American Popular Culture in Canada*, ed. David Flaherty and Frank Manning (Montreal: McGill-Queen's University Press, 1993), 156.

91. Spencer Lang, *Experimenting With Professional Baseball: An Examination of the Guelph Maple Leafs and the London Tecumsehs in Canadian Baseball's First Professional Era, 1872-1878* (unpublished MA thesis, The University of Western Ontario, 2003), 59.

92. *Guelph Evening Mercury*, July 23, 1873.

93. Humber, *Diamonds of the North*, 5.

94. Humber, *Diamonds of the North*, 6.

95. William Bryce, *Canadian Base Ball Guide 1876* (London, ON: William Bryce, 1876), 9-11.

96. Humber, *Diamonds of the North*, 34.

97. Baseball was played in Quebec in the 19th century but with less fervour than in other parts of Canada. It was quickly established as an urban game, particularly in Ontario, and Quebec remained largely rural throughout the 19th century. Even in its urban heart, Montreal, sport enthusiasts demonstrated a preference for lacrosse over baseball. The province's summer sport preferences tilted in baseball's favour in the 20th century, but the fact remains that Quebec was slower to adopt the American game.

98. Humber, *Diamonds of the North*, 93-98.

99. For more on the Asahi baseball team, see Shannon Jette, "Little/Big Ball: The Vancouver Asahi Baseball Story," *Sport History Review* 38, no. 1 (2007): 1-16.

100. M. Ann Hall, *The Girl and the Game: A History of Women's Sport in Canada*, 2nd ed. (Toronto: University of Toronto Press, 2016), 59.

101. Colin Howell, *Northern Sandlots: A Social History of Maritime Baseball* (Toronto: University of Toronto Press, 1995), 76.

102. Howell goes into great detail about this tour and dedicated a chapter in *Northern Sandlots* to its exploration. Readers who would like to learn more should consult chapter 5, pages 74-96.

103. Lewis Stubbs, *Shoestring Glory: A Prairie History of Semi-Pro Ball* (Winnipeg: Turnstone Press, 1997), 108-109.

104. Howell, *Northern Sandlots*, 93.

Chapter 8

1. Alan Metcalfe, *Canada Learns to Play: The Emergence of Organized Sport, 1807-1914* (Toronto: McClelland & Stewart, 1987), 20.

2. Robert D. Day, "The British Garrison at Halifax: Its Contribution to the Development of Sport in the Community," in *Sports in Canada: Historical Readings*, ed. Morris Mott (Mississauga, ON: Copp Clark Pittman, 1989), 18-27.

3. Nancy B. Bouchier and Robert Knight Barney, "A Critical Examination of a Source on Early Ontario Baseball: The Reminiscence of Adam E. Ford," *Journal of Sport History* 15, no. 1 (1988): 80.

4. Roderick McLennan, *Dictionary of Canadian Biography*, vol. XIII (1901-1910), accessed June 4, 2018, www.biographi.ca/en/bio/mclennan_roderick_13E.html.

5. McLennan, *Dictionary of Canadian Biography*.

6. Greg Gillespie, "Roderick McLennan, Professionalism, and the Emergence of the Athlete in Caledonian Games," *Sport History Review* 31, no. 1 (2000): 53.

7. Gillespie, "Roderick McLennan," 43. McLennan retired from the hammer throw after accidentally killing 13-year-old Ellen Kavanaugh when competing in a Caledonian Society games in Cornwall, Ontario.

8. Edward (Ned) Hanlan, *Dictionary of Canadian Biography*, vol. XIII (1901-1910), accessed June 5, 2018, www.biographi.ca/en/bio/hanlan_edward_13E.html.

9. Frank Cosentino, "Ned Hanlan—Canada's Premier Oarsman: A Case Study in 19th Century Professionalism," *Canadian Journal of History of Sport and Physical Education* 5, no. 2 (1975): 8.

10. Cosentino, "Ned Hanlan," 8.

11. Don Morrow, "Of Leadership and Excellence: Rubenstein, Hanlan, and Cyr," in *A Concise History of Sport in Canada*, ed. Don Morrow and Mary Keyes (Toronto: Oxford University Press, 1989), 38.

12. Morrow, "Of Leadership and Excellence," 38.

13. Morrow, "Of Leadership and Excellence," 39.

14. Cosentino, "Ned Hanlan," 16.

15. M. Ann Hall, *The Girl and the Game: A History of Women's Sports in Canada*, 2nd ed. (Toronto: University of Toronto Press, 2016), 21.

16. Hall, *The Girl and the Game*, 21.

17. Hall, *The Girl and the Game*, 21-22. For a detailed examination of the move by women such as Armaindo from pedestrianism to high-wheel cycling, see M. Ann Hall, *Muscle on Wheels: Louise Armaindo and the High-Wheel Racers of Nineteenth Century America* (Montreal: McGill-Queen's Press, 2018), 37-73.

18. Roberta J. Park, "Contesting the Norm: Women and Professional Sports in Late Nineteenth-Century America," *International Journal of the History of Sport* 29, no. 5 (2012): 740.

19. Hall, *Muscle on Wheels*, 68-75.

20. Api-kai-ees, *Dictionary of Canadian Biography*, vol. XII (1891-1900), accessed June 5, 2018, www.biographi.ca/en/bio/api_kai_ees_12E.html.

21. Api-kai-ees (Deerfoot), Alberta Sports Hall of Fame and Museum, Honoured Members, accessed June 5, 2018, http://ashfm.ca/hall-of-fame-honoured-members/browse/achievement-award/deerfoot.

22. Api-kai-ees, *Dictionary of Canadian Biography*.

23. C.A. Tony Joyce, "Sport and the Cash Nexus in Nineteenth Century Toronto," *Sport History Review* 30, no. 2 (1999): 165.

24. Gillian Poulter, "Snowshoeing and Lacrosse: Canada's Nineteenth Century 'National Games,'" *Sport, Culture, Society* 6, nos. 2/3 (2003): 304-313.

25. Metcalfe, *Canada Learns to Play*, 196-197

26. Metcalfe, *Canada Learns to Play*, 202.

27. Don Morrow and Kevin B. Wamsley, *Sport in Canada: A History*, 3rd ed. (Don Mills, ON: Oxford University Press, 2013), 96-98.

28. *Tecumseh Base Ball Club of London Minute Book*, 22 June 1868-1 May 1872, J.J. Talman Regional Collection, D.B. Weldon Library, Western University.

29. L.N. Bronson, "Three Tecumsehs made all-star baseball team in 1972," *London Free Press*, June 17, 1972. According to Bronson, the drive to move the city's primary representative team from an amateur side to a professional one lay in the need to compete against and defeat teams like the Guelph Maple Leafs side owned by brewer George Sleeman.

30. L.N. Bronson, "Old Time Baseball," (unpublished paper delivered to London-Middlesex Historical Society, February 15, 1972), 37-39, J.J. Talman Regional Collection, D.B. Weldon Library, Western University. The London Tecumsehs Base Ball Club won the Canadian Association Championship in 1876 and the International Association Championship in 1877.

31. Bronson, "Old Time Baseball," 39. See also "Base Ball Notes," *London Free* Press, July 10, 1878, and "Out-Door Sports,"*London Advertiser*, July 11, 1878.

32. Colin D. Howell, *Northern Sandlots: A Social History of Maritime Baseball* (Toronto: University of Toronto Press, 1995), 6.

33. Alan Metcalfe, "The Meaning of Amateurism: A Case Study of Canadian Sport, 1884-1970," *Canadian Journal of History of Sport* 26, no. 2 (1995): 33.

34. Metcalfe, *Canada Learns to Play*, 114-115.

35. Metcalfe, "The Meaning of Amateurism," 46.

36. Metcalfe, "The Meaning of Amateurism," 33.

37. Bruce Kidd, "In Defence of Tom Longboat," *Sport in Society* 16, no. 4 (2013): 523.

38. Robert Kossuth, "Men on the Closing Range: Early Rodeo Competition in the Southern Northwest Territories/Alberta," *Sporting Traditions* 24, nos. 1-2 (2007): 24-25, 31-32.

39. Mary Lou LeCompte, "Cowgirls at the Crossroads: Women in Professional Rodeo, 1885-1922," *Canadian Journal of History of Sport* 20, no. 2 (1989): 33.

40. LeCompte, "Cowgirls at the Crossroads," 33.

41. Hugh A. Dempsey, *Tom Three Persons: Legend of an Indian Cowboy* (Saskatoon: Purich, 1997), 18-20.

42. "Live Stock at the Lethbridge Fair," *Lethbridge Weekly Herald*, August 19, 1908, 3.

43. Dempsey, *Tom Three Persons*, 36.

44. Letter from Blood Indian agent on behalf of Tom Three Persons to Guy Weadick, July 26, 1912, Glenbow Museum and Archives, Department of Indian Affairs, Blood Indian Agency fonds, M-1788-207.

45. Letter from Blood Indian agent, July 26, 1912.

46. Letter from Blood Indian Agent on behalf of Tom Three Persons to Guy Weadick, November 19, 1912, Glenbow Museum and Archives, Department of Indian Affairs, Blood Indian Agency fonds, M-1788-207.

47. Letter from Macleod Indian agent to Glen Campbell, Chief Inspector of Indian Agencies, August 4, 1913, Glenbow Museum and Archives, Department of Indian Affairs, Blood Agency fonds, M-1788-201.

48. Dempsey, *Tom Three Persons*, 88-89.

49. LeCompte, "Cowgirls at the Crossroads," 40-41.

50. "Rodeo," Alberta Sports History Library, Alberta Sports Hall of Fame, accessed July 11, 2018, https://ashfm.ca/absportslibrary/rodeo/introduction.

51. Colin D. Howell, *Blood, Sweat, and Cheers: Sport and the Making of Modern Canada* (Toronto: University of Toronto Press, 2001), 38.

52. Alan Metcalfe, "Power: A Case Study of the Ontario Hockey Association, 1890-1936," *Journal of Sport History* 19, no. 1 (1992): 6.

53. Metcalfe, "Power," 7.

54. Metcalfe, "Power," 10.

55. Metcalfe, "Power," 17.

56. Metcalfe, "Power," 19.

57. Daniel Mason, "The International Hockey League and the Professionalization of Ice Hockey, 1904-1907," *Journal of Sport History* 25, no. 1 (1998): 4.

58. Andrew C. Holman, "Playing in the Neutral Zone: Meanings and Uses of Ice Hockey in the Canada-U.S. Borderlands, *American Review of Canadian Studies* 34, no. 1 (2004): 37.

59. Holman, "Playing in the Neutral Zone," 38.

60. Richard Gruneau and David Whitson, *Hockey Night in Canada: Sport Identities and Cultural Politics* (Toronto: Garamond Press, 1993), 86.

61. John Matthew Barlow, "'Scientific Aggression': Irishness, Manliness, Class, and Commercialization in the Shamrock Hockey Club of Montreal, 1894-1901," in *Coast to Coast: Hockey in Canada to the Second World War*, ed. John Chi-Kit Wong (Toronto: University of Toronto Press, 2009), 35-85.

62. Gruneau and Whitson, *Hockey Night in Canada*, 87.

63. Gruneau and Whitson, *Hockey Night in Canada*, 87-88.

64. Bruce Kidd, *The Struggle for Canadian Sport* (Toronto: University of Toronto Press, 1996), 193.

65. Kidd, *The Struggle for Canadian Sport*, 92-93.

66. Howard Shubert, *Architecture on Ice: A History of the Hockey Arena* (Montreal: McGill-Queen's Press, 2016), 85.

67. Stacy L. Lorenz, "Hockey, Violence, and Masculinity: Newspaper Coverage of the Ottawa 'Butchers', 1903-1906," *International Journal of the History of Sport* 32, no. 17 (2015): 2047.

68. Stacy L. Lorenz and Geraint B. Osborne, "'Talk About Strenuous Hockey': Violence, Manhood, and the 1907 Ottawa Silver Seven-Montreal Wanderers Rivalry," *Journal of Canadian Studies* 40, no. 1 (2006): 126.

69. Lorenz and Osborne, "'Talk About Strenuous Hockey,'" 150.

70. Kevin B. Wamsley and David Whitson, "Celebrating Violent Masculinities: The Boxing Death of Luther McCarty," *Journal of Sport History* 25, no. 3 (1998): 420.

71. Don Morrow and Terry Jackson, "Boxing's Interregnum: How Good Was Tommy Burns, World Heavyweight Boxing Champion, 1906-1908," *Canadian Journal of History of Sport* 24, no. 2 (1993): 40.

72. Wamsley and Whitson, "Celebrating Violent Masculinities," 424.

73. Wamsley and Whitson, "Celebrating Violent Masculinities," 428.

74. C. Nathan Hatton, *Thrashing Seasons: Sporting Culture in Manitoba and the Genesis of Prairie Wrestling* (Winnipeg: University of Manitoba Press, 2016), 171.

75. Hatton, *Thrashing Seasons*, 172.

76. Hatton, *Thrashing Seasons*, 174-175.

77. Kidd, *The Struggle for Canadian Sport*, 200-201.

78. Robert A. Stebbins, *Canadian Football: The View From the Helmet* (London, ON: Centre for Humanistic Studies, University of Western Ontario, 1987), 5.

79. Robert Kossuth, "Transition and Assimilation: English Rugby and Canadian Football in Nova Scotia, 1930-1955," *Football Studies* 2, no. 2 (1999): 19-21; Howell, *Blood, Sweat, and Cheers*, 48.

80. Stebbins, *Canadian Football*, 5.

81. Stebbins, *Canadian Football*, 9.

82. Charles Kupfer, "Crabs in the Grey Cup: Baltimore's Canadian Football Sojourn, 1994-95," *International Journal of the History of Sport* 24, no. 1 (2007): 51.

83. Frank Cosentino, "Football," in *A Concise History of Sport in Canada*, ed. Don Morrow and Mary Keyes (Toronto: Oxford University Press, 1989), 157.

84. Dylan Slade, "Calgary Horse in Royal York Hotel During 1948 Grey Cup: Fact or Fiction?" *Calgary Herald*, November 28, 2015, accessed July 11, 2018, http://calgary-herald.com/sports/football/cfl/slade-calgary-horse-in-royal-york-hotel-during-1948-grey-cup-fact-or-fiction.

85. Cosentino, "Football," 157.

86. Cosentino, "Football," 158.

87. Canada, 7 George IV, ch. 29, An Act to Establish a National Council for the Purpose of Promoting Physical Fitness, July 24, 1943.

88. Mary Keyes, "Government Involvement in Fitness and Amateur Sport," in *A Concise History of Sport in Canada*, eds. Don Morrow and Mary Keyes (Toronto: Oxford University Press, 1989), 325.

89. "Government Involvement," 328.

90. "Government Involvement," 330.

91. Don Morrow, "Sweetheart Sport: Barbara Ann Scott and the Post World War II Image of the Female Athlete in Canada," *Canadian Journal of History of Sport* 18, no. 1 (1987): 37.

92. Morrow, "Sweetheart Sport," 40.

93. Stephen R. Wenn, "Give Me the Keys Please: Avery Brundage, Canadian Journalists, and the Barbara Ann Scott Phaeton Affair," *Journal of Sport History* 18, no. 2 (1991): 241-247.

94. Paul Conlin, "The Cold War and Canadian Nationalism on Ice: Federal Government Involvement in International Hockey During the 1960s," *Canadian Journal of History of Sport* 25, no. 2 (1994): 56.

95. Conlin, "The Cold War and Canadian Nationalism," 58-59.

96. Conlin, "The Cold War and Canadian Nationalism," 64-66.

97. See, for example, Ken Dryden and Mark Mulvoy, *Face-Off at the Summit* (Boston: Little Brown, 1973); Scott Morrison, *The Days Canada Stood Still: Canada vs USSR 1972* (Toronto: McGraw-Hill Ryerson, 1989); and Brian Kennedy, *Coming Down the Mountain: Rethinking the 1972 Summit Series* (Hamilton, ON: Wolsak and Wynn, 2014).

98. Bruce Kidd, *The Struggle for Canadian Sport*, 263.

Chapter 9

1. Andrew Holman, "A Flag of Tendons: Hockey and Canadian History," in *Hockey: Challenging Canada's Game/Au-dela du sport national*, ed. Jenny Ellison and Jennifer Anderson (Ottawa: University of Ottawa Press/Canadian Museum of History, 2018), 35.

2. See James Deacon, "How Sweet It Is!" *Maclean's*, March 11, 2002, 21.

3. Mary Louise Adams, "The Game of Whose Lives? Gender, Race, and Entitlement in Canada's 'National' Game," in *Artificial Ice: Hockey, Culture and Commerce*, ed. David Whitson and Richard S. Gruneau (Peterborough: Broadview Press, 2006), 72.

4. For more on the historical significance of hockey in Canada, see Michael A. Robidoux, "Imagining a Canadian Identity Through Sport: A Historical Interpretation of Lacrosse and Hockey," *Journal of American Folklore* 115, no. 456 (2002): 209-225.

5. See Ken Dryden and Roy MacGregor, *Home Game: Hockey Life in Canada* (Toronto: McClelland & Stewart, 1989); Peter Gzowski, *The Game of Our Lives* (Markham: Paperjacks, 1983); Richard Gruneau and David Whitson, *Hockey Night in Canada: Sport, Identities and Cultural Politics* (Toronto: Garamond, 1992).

6. Benedict Anderson, *Imagined Communities: Reflections on the Origin and Spread of Nationalism* (New York: Verso, 1991/1983), 6.

7. Gruneau and Whitson, *Hockey Night in Canada*, 132.

8. Adams, "The Game of Whose Lives?," 71.

9. Shan Dhaliwal, "We Are Hockey—An Inclusive Re-telling of Canadian Hockey History," accessed December 16, 2019, https://hockeyinsociety.com/2019/07/16/guest-post-we-are-hockey-an-inclusive-re-telling-of-canadian-hockey-history.

10. Holman, "A Flag of Tendons," 38.

11. In 2007, a senior women's hockey league, the Canadian Women's Hockey League, was created. It was only in the last two years of league operations that players were paid a nominal stipend of $2,000 to $10,000 CAD. The team folded in July 2019. Apart from the Canadian national team, this was the highest level of women's hockey in Canada. For more on the folding of the league, see www.cbc.ca/sports/hockey/cwhl-ceasing-operations-unsustainable-finance-1.5078834. Some Canadian women also play in the National Women's Hockey League (NWHL) created in 2015. In 2020, the NWHL added a franchise in Toronto. See https://www.cbssports.com/nhl/news/nwhl-expands-into-canada-with-new-toronto-franchise.

12. Patricia Vertinsky, Shannon Jette, and Annette Hofmann, "Gender Justice and Gender Politics at the Local, National and International Level Over the Challenge of Women's Ski Jumping," *Olympika* 18 (2009): 27.

13. Carl Giden, Patrick Houda, and Jean-Patrice Martel, *On the Origin of Hockey* (Stockholm and Chambly: Hockey Origin Publishing, 2014), 260; "'First Hockey Game in History', in 1837, Described by Local Man," *Montreal Gazette*, February 14, 1941, 18; Garth Vaughan, *The Puck Starts Here* (Fredericton: Goose Lane Editions, 1996); *Origins of Hockey in Canada*, report submitted to the Canadian Amateur Hockey Association Annual Meeting, April 1942.

14. See, for example, Michael Heine, *Dene Games: A Culture and Resource Manual* (Yellowknife: Sport North Federation, 1999).

15. Paul W. Bennet, "Re-Imagining the Creation: Popular Mythology, the Mi'kmaq, and the Origins of Canadian Hockey," in *Hockey: Challenging Canada's Game*, 45.

16. Bennett, "Re-Imagining the Creation," 45.

17. Bennett, "Re-Imagining the Creation," 45. For more detailed discussions about the importance of examining the history of sport and recreation through a more comprehensive lens that considers economic, political, cultural, and social factors and experiences, see M. Ann Hall, *The Girl and the Game: A History of Women's Sport in Canada*, 2nd ed. (Toronto: University of Toronto Press, 2016); Colin Howell, *Blood Sweat and Cheers: Sport and the Making of Modern Canada* (Toronto: University of Toronto Press, 2001); Bruce Kidd, *The Struggle for Canadian Sport* (Toronto: University of Toronto Press, 1996); Alan Metcalfe, *Canada Learns to Play: The Emergence of Organized Sport, 1807-1914* (Toronto: McClelland & Stewart, 1987).

18. Bennett, "Re-Imagining the Creation," 51. See also Garth Vaughan, *Ice Hockey: The Origins of Canada's Great Winter Game* (Fredericton: Goose Lane Editions, 1996); Bruce Dowbiggin, *The Stick: A History, a Celebration, an Elegy* (Toronto: Macfarlane Walter & Ross, 2001).

19. Holman, "A Flag of Tendons," 26.

20. "Victoria Rink," *Montreal Gazette*, March 3, 1875, 3.

21. "Hockey," *Montreal Gazette*, March 4, 1875, 3.

22. "Hockey," *Montreal Gazette*, March 4, 1875, 3.

23. "The Victoria Rink," *Montreal Evening Star*, March 4, 1875, 3.

24. Robidoux, "Imagining a Canadian Identity Through Sport," 212.

25. On the influence of the Mi'kmaq and Halifax, see Bennett, "Re-Imagining the Creation," 45-59.

26. "Hockey on Ice," *Montreal Gazette*, February 27, 1877, 4.

27. Earl Zukerman, "This Week in History: McGill Hockey Team Turns 141 Years Old on Jan. 31," *The Official Site of McGill Athletics & Recreation*, accessed December 16, 2019, www.mcgillathletics.ca/news/2012/1/30/104242.aspx.

28. Arthur Farrell, *Hockey: Canada's Royal Winter Game* (Montreal: C.R. Corneil Print, 1899). For a list of teams in Montreal from 1885 to 1917, see the Annexe D, équipes et ligues de Montréal, 1885-1917, in Michel Vigneault, *La naissance d'un sport organisé au Canada : le hockey à Montréal, 1875-1917* (unpublished PhD diss., Université Laval, 2001), 368-479; Marc Durand, *La Coupe à Québec : les Bulldogs et la naissance du hockey* (Québec: Éditions Sylvain Harvey, 2012), 8; Paul Kitchen, *Win, Tie or Wrangle: the Inside Story of the Old Ottawa Senators* (Ottawa: Penumbra Press, 2008).

29. Jordan Goldstein, "Building a Canadian National Identity Within the State and Through Ice Hockey: A Political Analysis of the Donation of the Stanley Cup, 1888-1893" (PhD diss., Western University, 2015), 232.

30. See, for example, Carly Adams, "Troubling Bodies: 'The Canadian Girl,' the Ice Rink and the Banff Winter Carnival," *Journal of Canadian Studies* 48, no. 3 (2014), 200-220; Don Morrow, "Frozen Festivals: Ceremony and the Carnaval in the Montreal Winter Carnivals, 1883-1889," *Sport History Review* 27 (1996): 173-190.

31. Morrow, "Frozen Festivals," 173-190.

32. "Ladies Hockey Tournament at Banff Carnival," *Calgary Herald*, January 31, 1918, 10.

33. Adams, "Troubling Bodies," 200-220.

34. Hall, *The Girl and the Game*, 57.

35. See M. Ann Hall, "A History of Women's Sport in Canada Prior to World War I" (unpublished master's thesis, University of Alberta, 1968).

36. Canada's Leading Winter Sport: Women's Hockey All the Rage," *Cornwall Standard Freeholder*, February 10, 1916.

37. Hall, "A History of Women's Sport in Canada," 43.

38. For more on the history of the LOHA, see Carly Adams, "Organizing Hockey for Women: The Ladies Ontario Hockey Association and the Fight for Legitimacy, 1922-1940, in *Coast to Coast: Hockey in Canada to the Second World War*, ed. John Chi-Kit Wong (Toronto: University of Toronto Press, 2009), 132-159.

39. For more information on the OHA, see Scott Young, *100 Years of Dropping the Puck: A History of the OHA* (Toronto: McClelland & Stewart, 1989) and Alan Metcalfe, "Power: A Case Study of the Ontario Hockey Association, 1890-1936," *Journal of Sport History*, 19 (1992): 5-25.

40. Minutes of the OHA annual meeting, December 1, 1923, 2. OHA Papers, Library and Archives Canada, M2308.

41. See Hall, *The Girl and the Game*, 94; Adams, "Troubling Bodies," 200-220.

42. For more information about the WAAF, see Kidd, *The Struggle for Canadian Sport*, 113-119, and Hall, *The Girl and the Game*, 45-54.

43. Karen L. Wall, *Game Plan: A Social History of Sport in Alberta* (Edmonton: University of Alberta Press, 2012), 112.

44. See Jeff Hicks, "Preston Rivulettes Honoured for Their Historic Hockey Exploits." *The Record*, Waterloo (Ontario), accessed July 18, 2019, www.therecord.com/news-story/8022463-preston-rivulettes-honoured-for-their-historic-hockey-exploits.

45. For a more detailed analysis of the Preston Rivulettes, see Carly Adams, "Queens of the Ice Lanes": The Preston Rivulettes and Women's Hockey in Canada, 1931–1940." *Sport History Review* 39, no. 1 (2008): 1-29.

46. "Rivulettes to Enter Hockey Hall of Fame," *Galt Evening Reporter*, June 8, 1963, 14.

47. Bruce Kidd, "Missing: Women From Sports Halls of Fame," *Action CAAWS/ACAFS*, Winter (1995), 4; Carly Adams and Kevin B. Wamsley. "Moments of Silence in Shallow Halls of Greatness: The Hockey Hall of Fame and the Politics of Representation," in *Putting It on Ice: Women's Hockey-Gender Issues on and off the Ice*, ed. Colin. D. Howell (Halifax: Gorsebrook Research Institute, 2005), 13-17.

48. Gruneau and Whitson, *Hockey Night in Canada*, 13.

49. Robidoux, "Imagining a Canadian Identity Through Sport," 211.

50. Michel Vigneault, "Montreal's Francophone Hockey Beginnings, 1895-1910," in *The Same but Different: Hockey in Québec*, ed. Jason Blake and Andrew C. Holman (Montreal: McGill–Queen's University Press, 2017), p. 38.

51. Donald Guay, *La conquête du sport* (Montréal : Lanctôt Editeur, 1997), 244.

52. Gingras played for the Victorias when they won the Stanley Cup in 1901 and 1902. Two other Métis players, brothers Roderick and Magnus Flett, were on the 1901 and 1902 Winnipeg Victorias teams with Gingras. See Lawrence J. Barkwell, "Antoine 'Tony' Blanc Gingras (b. 1875)," Louis Riel Institute, 2010, accessed January 23, 2020, www.metismuseum.ca/media/document.php/11983.Tony%20Gingras%20hockey.pdf.

53. George Fosty and Darril Fosty, "Coloured Hockey League," *The Canadian Encyclopedia*, accessed January 7, 2020, www.thecanadianencyclopedia.ca/en/article/coloured-hockey-league; see also George Fosty and Darril Fosty, *Black Ice: The Lost History of the Colored Hockey League of the Maritimes, 1895-1925* (Halifax: Nimbus Publishing, 2008).

54. Kidd, *The Struggle for Canadian Sport*, 194-195.

55. Kidd, *The Struggle for Canadian Sport*, 184-195.

56. John Chi-Kit Wong, *Lords of the Rinks: The Emergence of the National Hockey League, 1875-1936* (Toronto: University of Toronto Press, 2005), 82.

57. Wong, *Lords of the Rinks*, 143.

58. The Forum was originally built for the Montreal Maroons. The Canadiens played initially at the Mount Royal Arena and moved to the Forum in 1926.

59. Kidd, *The Struggle for Canadian Sport*, 199.

60. Russell Field, "Passive Participation: The Selling of Spectacle and the Construction of Maple Leaf Gardens," *Sport History Review* 33, no. 1 (2002): 35-50.

61. Russell Field, "A Night at the Garden(s): A History of Professional Ice Hockey Spectatorship in the 1920s and 1930s" (unpublished PhD diss., University of Toronto, 2008).

62. Michael McKinley, *Hockey Night in Canada: 60 Seasons* (Toronto: CBC, 2012), 13.

63. Barry Broadfoot, *Ten Lost Years, 1929-1939* (Toronto: Doubleday Canada, 1973).

64. Wong, *Lords of the Rinks*, 147.

65. James Riordan, *Sport in Soviet Society: Development of Sport and Physical Education in Russia and the USSR* (Cambridge: Cambridge University Press, 1977), 165.

66. Joanna Avery and Julie Stevens, *Too Many Men on the Ice: Women's Hockey in North America* (Victoria: Polestar Books, 1997), 63.

67. Julie Stevens, "Thirty Years of "Going Global": Women's International Hockey, Cultural Diplomacy, and the Pursuit of Excellence," in *Hockey: Challenging Canada's Game*, 147-164.

68. Elizabeth Etue and Megan K. Williams, *On the Edge: Women Making Hockey History* (Toronto: Second Story Press, 1996), 269.

69. See *Globe and Mail*, March 24, 1990, A18.

70. See "Women's Hockey Breaks Through at the World Level," *Globe and Mail*, March 17, 1990, A15.

71. Carly Adams, "Body Check: Women's Olympic Ice Hockey and the Politics of Incorporation," in *Cultural Relations Old and New: The Transitory Olympic Ethos*, Seventh International Symposium for Olympic Research (London, ON: International Centre for Olympic Studies, 2004), 146.

72. Etue and Williams, *On the Edge*, 272.

73. *Olympic Charter* (Lausanne: International Olympic Committee, 1991), 9.

74. Etue and Williams, *On the Edge*, 272.

75. Wolf Lyberg, ed. "IOC Executive Committee Minutes, Meeting #186, Barcelona, 1992" (London, ON: International Centre for Olympic Studies), 91; for media coverage of the announcement, see also *Globe and Mail*, July 22, 1992, C6, and *New York Times*, July 22, 1992, 14.

76. Wolf Lyberg, ed. "IOC Executive Committee Minutes, Meeting #188, Lausanne, 1992" (London, ON: International Centre for Olympic Studies), 122.

77. Hockey Canada Annual Report, June 2017-June 2018 https://cdn.agilitycms.com/hockey-canada/Corporate/About/Downloads/2017-18-hockey-canada-annual-report-e.pdf, accessed January 23, 2020.

78. Minutes of the Eighteenth Annual Meeting, Canadian Amateur Hockey Association, 1935, http://heritage.canadiana.ca/view/oocihm.lac_reel_c4852/17?r=0&s=1, accessed January 23, 2020. See also "C.A.H.A Will Create Trust Fund of $35,000," *Globe and Mail*, April 18, 1938, 19.

79. Minutes of the Eighteenth Annual Meeting, CAHA.

80. See Bruce Kidd and John Macfarlane, *Death of Hockey* (Toronto: New Press, 1974), 52.

81. Kidd and Macfarlane, *Death of Hockey*, 54.

82. Kidd and Macfarlane, *Death of Hockey*, 55.

83. See Gruneau and Whitson, *Hockey Night in Canada*, 170.

84. Kidd and Macfarlane, *Death of Hockey*, 56.

85. Kidd and Macfarlane, *Death of Hockey*, 55.

86. See Carly Adams and Julie Stevens, "Change and Grassroots Movement: Re-Conceptualizing Women's Hockey Governance in Canada," *International Journal of Sport Management and Marketing* 2, no. 4 (2007): 353.

87. Hall, *The Girl and the Game*, 196.

88. Adams and Stevens, "Change and Grassroots Movement," 352.

89. Carly Adams and Jason Laurendeau, "Here They Come! Look Them Over!": Youth, Citizenship, and the Emergence of Minor Hockey in Canada," in *Hockey: Challenging Canada's Game*, 113.

90. Randy Turner, "Parents who can afford it scramble to get kids into elite hockey programs," *Winnipeg Free Press*, February 2, 2013, accessed January 23, 2020, https://www.winnipegfreepress.com/special/randy-turner/spring-fever-189487451.html.

91. Greg Nesom, "Alberta Female Hockey Review," Hockey Alberta, February 14, 2014, accessed January 11, 2020, www.hockeyalberta.ca/uploads/source/1324_-_Alberta_Female_Hockey_Review.pdf.

92. Brent Poplawski, "The Early Specialization in Hockey of Professional NHL Players from Winnipeg" (unpublished master's thesis, University of Manitoba, 2017).

93. Kidd and MacFarlane, Death of Hockey, 55.

94. For more on sport in a pay-for-play society, see Richard Gruneau, "Goodbye, Gordie Howe: Sport Participation and Class Inequality in the 'Pay for Play' Society," in *How Canadians Communicate V: Sports*, ed. D. Taras and C. Waddell (Edmonton: Athabasca University Press, 2016), 223-246.

95. Dan Ralph, "Canadian Families Shunning Hockey, Survey Finds," *Globe and Mail*, August 1, 2013, www.theglobeandmail.com/sports/hockey/bauer-survey-results-stun-former-nhl-great-messier/article13567822.

96. Lindsey Craig, "Where Are the Minorities? New Canadians and Visible Minorities Are Staying Away From Canada's Game," CBC News, January 9, 2009, www.cbc.ca/sports/hockey/where-are-the-minorities-1.835849.

97. See Shauna Niessen, *Shattering the Silence: The Hidden History of Indian Residential Schools in Saskatchewan* (Regina: Faculty of Education, University of Regina, 2017), accessed January 7, 2020, www2.uregina.ca/education/saskindianresidentialschools.

98. For more on the Indigenous Hockey Research Network (IHRN), see https://www.indigenoushockeycanada.com, accessed June 10, 2020.

99. For more information, see "Treaty 6," *The Canadian Encyclopedia*, accessed January 7, 2020, www.thecanadianencyclopedia.ca/en/article/treaty-6.

100. See "Meet the Members of the Indian Residential School Survival Committee (IRSSC), accessed January 7, 2020, www.trc.ca/about-us/meet-the-survivor-committee.html.

101. See Braden Te Hiwi and Janice Forsyth, "'A Rink at This School Is Almost as Essential as a Classroom': Hockey and Discipline at Pelican Lake Indian Residential School, 1945-1951, *Canadian Journal of History* 51, no. 1 (2017): 80-108.

102. Michael A. Robidoux, *Stickhandling Through the Margins: First Nations Hockey in Canada* (Toronto: University of Toronto Press, 2012), 13.

103. Evan J. Habkirk and Janice Forsyth, "Truth, Reconciliation, and the Politics of the Body in Indian Residential School History," *Active History*. http://activehistory.

ca/papers/truth-reconciliation-and-the-politics-of-the-body-in-indian-residential-school-history, accessed June 10, 2020.

104. See Malcolm Montgomery, *The Six Nations Indians and the MacDonald Franchise* (Toronto: Ontario Historical Society, 1965).

105. See Rob Nestor, "Pass System in Canada," *The Canadian Encyclopedia*, October 3, 2018, accessed January 6, 2020, www.thecanadianencyclopedia.ca/en/article/pass-system-in-Canada.

106. See, for example, "Exploring Hockey's Roots in Indigenous Communities," CBC Radio, March 28, 2019.

107. See Sam McKegney and Trevor J. Phillips, "Decolonizing the Hockey Novel: Ambivalence and Apotheosis in Richard Wagamese's *Indian Horse*," in *Writing the Body in Motion: A Critical Anthology on Canadian Sport Literature*, ed. Angie Abdou and Jamie Dopp (Edmonton: Athabasca University Press, 2018), 167-184.

108. See Susan Bell, Betsy Longchap, and Corinne Smith, "First Nations Hockey Team Subjected to Racist Taunts, Slurs at Quebec City Tournament," CBC News, May 31, 2018.

109. See Sarah Petz, "First Nations Argue New Hockey League Is 'Blatant Racism,' Segregates Indigenous, Non-Indigenous Teams," CBC News, December 19, 2018.

110. *Truth and Reconciliation Commission of Canada: Calls to Action*, 2015, Winnipeg, MB.

111. Scott McKenzie and Sameer H. Shah, "What Colin Kaepernick Can Teach Us About Citizenship," *The Conversation*, January 31, 2018.

112. Laura Robinson, *Crossing the Line: Violence and Sexual Assault in Canada's National Sport* (Toronto: McClelland & Stewart, 1998).

113. See Cindy Vine and Paul Challen, *Gardens of Shame: The Tragedy of Martin Kruze and the Sexual Abuse at Maple Leaf Gardens* (Vancouver: Greystone Books, 2002).

114. Theo Fleury With Kirstie McLellan Day, *Playing With Fire* (Chicago: Triumph Books, 2011); Sheldon Kennedy With James Grainger, *Why I Didn't Say Anything: The Sheldon Kennedy Story* (London, ON: Insomniac Press, 2011).

Chapter 10

1. "Sport in Canada," Government of Canada, accessed June 27, 2018, www.canada.ca/en/canadian-heritage/services/sport-canada.html.

2. "Sport in Canada."

3. Interprovincial Sport and Recreation Council and Canadian Parks and Recreation Association, "A Framework for Recreation in Canada 2015: Pathways to Wellbeing" (Ottawa: Canadian Recreation and Parks Association, 2015), 18.

4. "R. Tait McKenzie Award," Physical and Health Education Canada, accessed June 27, 2018, https://phecanada.ca/inspire/r-tait-mckenzie-award.

5. Ana Maria Alonso, "The Effects of Truth: Re-Presentations of the Past and the Imagining of Community," *Journal of Historical Sociology* 1, no. 1 (1988): 33-57; Michel Foucault, "Nietzsche, Genealogy, and History" in *The Essential Foucault: Selections From Essential Works of Foucault, 1954-1984*, ed. Paul Rabinow and Nikolas Rose (New York: New Press, 2003), 351-369.

6. Alonso, "The Effects of Truth," 41.

7. Alonso, "The Effects of Truth," 33-57.

8. Alonso, "The Effects of Truth," 33-57.

9. James C. Scott, *Weapons of the Weak* (New Haven: Yale University Press, 1985), 178.

10. Michel Foucault, *Discipline and Punish: The Birth of the Prison*, trans. Alan Sheridan (New York: Vintage Books, 1977), 23-31; Michel Foucault, *The History of Sexuality: Volume 1*, trans. Robert Hurley (New York: Vintage Books, 1978), 92-102; Foucault, "Nietzsche, Genealogy, and History," 351-369.

11. Foucault, *Discipline and Punish*, 23-31; Foucault, *The History of Sexuality*, 92-102; Foucault, "Nietzsche, Genealogy, and History," 351-369.

12. Hubert L. Dreyfus and Paul Rabinow, *Michel Foucault: Beyond Structuralism and Hermeneutics*, 2nd ed. (Chicago: University of Chicago Press, 1982), 168-204; Daphne Meadmore, Caroline Hatcher, and Erica McWilliam, "Getting Tense About Genealogy," *International Journal of Qualitative Studies in Education* 13, no. 5 (2000): 463-476.

13. Foucault, *The History of Sexuality*, 92-102; Foucault, "Nietzsche, Genealogy, and History," 351-369.

14. Foucault, *Discipline and Punish*, 23-31; Foucault, *The History of Sexuality*, 92-102; Foucault, "Nietzsche, Genealogy, and History," 351-369.

15. National Council of Women of Canada, *Yearbook*, 1901, 152.

16. Elsie Marie McFarland, *The Development of Public Recreation in Canada* (Ottawa: Canadian Parks and Recreation Association, 1970), 18-46.

17. National Council of Women of Canada, *Yearbook*, 1902, 184.

18. Susan Markham, "Leisure and the National Council of Women of Canada," (paper presented at the International Conference on Women and Leisure, May 1995), 1-8; McFarland, *Development of Public Recreation*, 18-46.

19. National Council of Women of Canada, *Yearbook*, 1907, 96-97; National Council of Women of Canada, *Yearbook*, 1908, 39; National Council of Women of Canada, *Yearbook*, 1913, 44-45.

20. McFarland, *Development of Public Recreation*, 18-46.

21. Markham, "Leisure," 4.

22. Markham, "Leisure," 8.

23. McFarland, *Development of Public Recreation*, 18-46.

24. Tim Burton, "Policy Imperatives for Recreation, Sport and Physical Activity: Re-examining Foundations," (paper prepared for the 2011 National Recreation Summit, October 2011), 8.

25. Interprovincial Sport and Recreation Council and Canadian Parks and Recreation Association, "A Framework for Recreation," 20.

26. Markham, "Leisure," 7.

27. Carol Bacchi, *Liberation Deferred? The Ideas of the English-Canadian Suffragists 1877-1918* (Toronto: University of Toronto Press, 1983), 104.

28. Bacchi, *Liberation Deferred?*, 104; Cecily Devereux, "Woman Suffrage, Eugenics, and Eugenic Feminism in Canada," Women Suffrage and Beyond: Confronting the Democratic Deficit, October 1, 2013, http://womensuffrage.org/?p=22106.

29. Bacchi, *Liberation Deferred?*, 104; Cecily Devereux, *Growing a Race: Nellie L. McClung and the Fiction of Eugenic Feminism* (Montreal: McGill-Queen's University Press, 1997), 17-50.

30. Devereux, *Growing a Race*, 17-50; Katja Thieme, "Language and Social Change: The Canadian Movement for Women's Suffrage, 1880-1918" (PhD diss., University of British Columbia, 2007).

31. Thieme, "Language and Social Change," 191.

32. Devereux, *Growing a Race*, 17-50; Thieme, "Language and Social Change," 18-72.

33. Markham, "Leisure," 4.

34. Markham, "Leisure," 6.

35. National Council of Women of Canada, *Yearbook*, 1901, 155.

36. National Council of Women of Canada, *Yearbook*, 1901, 154.

37. National Council of Women of Canada, *Yearbook*, 1901, 152.

38. Sharon L. Snyder and David T. Mitchell, *Cultural Locations of Disability* (Chicago: University of Chicago Press, 2006).

39. Angus McLaren, "The Creation of a Haven for 'Human Thoroughbreds': The Sterilization of the Feeble-Minded and the Mentally Ill in British Columbia," *Canadian Historical Review* 67, no. 2 (June 1986): 127-150.

40. Ladelle McWhorter, *Bodies and Pleasures: Foucault and the Politics of Sexual Normalization* (Bloomington: Indiana University Press, 1999), 63-140.

41. Eugenics Tree Logo, Eugenics Archive, DNA Learning Centre, accessed June 25, 2018, www.dnalc.org/view/10229-Eugenics-tree-logo.html.

42. Gerald O'Brian, *Framing the Moron: The Social Construction of Feeble-Mindedness in the American Eugenic Era* (Manchester, UK: Manchester University Press, 2015), 137.

43. "What Is Newgenics," Eugenics to Newgenics, accessed March 22, 2019, https://eugenicsnewgenics.com/2014/05/14654/what-is-newgenics?/; Kyle Kurkup, "Indigenous Women Coerced Into Sterilizations Across Canada: Senator," CBC, accessed November 12, 2018, www.cbc.ca/news/politics/sterilizations-indigenous-1.4902303.

44. "What Is Newgenics"; "A Hundred Years of Immigration to Canada, 1900-1991," Canadian Council for Refugees, last modified May 2000, http://ccrweb.ca/en/hundred-years-immigration-canada-1900-1999.

45. Bacchi, *Liberation Deferred?*, 104-116; Devereux, *Growing a Race*, 17-74.

46. Cecily Devereux, "Woman Suffrage, Eugenics and Eugenic Feminism in Canada," *Women Suffrage and Beyond: Confronting the Democratic Deficit*, October 1, 2013, http://womensuffrage.org?p=22106.

47. Nellie McClung, *In Times Like These* (Toronto: McLeod and Allen, 1915), 88.

48. Veronica Strong-Boag, introduction to Nellie McClung, *In Times Like These* (Toronto: University of Toronto Press, 1972), vii-xxii.

49. McClung, *In Times Like These* (Toronto: McLeod and Allen, 1915), 81-94.

50. Danielle Peers, "From Eugenics to Paralympics: Inspirational Disability, Physical Fitness, and the White Canadian Nation" (PhD diss., University of Alberta, 2015), 120-127, doi: https://doi.org/10.7939/R3377623P.

51. McFarland, *Development of Public Recreation*, 18-46.

52. National Council of Women of Canada, *Yearbook*, 1901, 155.

53. Luther Burbank, *The Training of the Human Plant* (New York: Century Company, 1907), 46-47.

54. Helen MacMurchy, "Report Upon the Care of the Feeble-Minded in Ontario, 1906-1911" (legislative report, Toronto, 1912), 50.

55. Interprovincial Sport and Recreation Council and Canadian Parks and Recreation Association, "A Framework for Recreation in Canada 2015: Pathways to Wellbeing" (Ottawa: Canadian Recreation and Parks Association, 2015), 7.

56. Burton, "Policy Imperatives," 8.

57. McLaren, "The Creation of a Haven," 127-150.

58. Interprovincial Sport and Recreation Council and Canadian Parks and Recreation Association, "A Framework for Recreation in Canada 2015," 7.

59. Claudia Malacrida, *A Special Hell: Institutional Life in Alberta's Eugenic Years* (Toronto: University of Toronto Press, 2015), 23; Frank W. Stahnisch, "The Early Eugenics Movement and Emerging Professional Psychiatry: Conceptual Transfers and Personal Relationships Between Germany and North America, 1880s to 1930s," *Canadian Bulletin of Medical History* 31, no. 2 (2009): 17-40.

60. Stahnisch, "The Early Eugenics Movement," 17-40.

61. Malacrida, *A Special Hell*, 24.

62. Edmund Ramsden, "Social Demography and Eugenics in the Interwar United States," *Population and Development Review* 29, no. 4 (2004): 547.

63. "Section 3: Analysis of the Results of the Long-Term Projections," Statistics Canada, accessed June 27, 2018, www150.statcan.gc.ca/n1/pub/91-520-x/2010001/part-partie3-eng.htm; "Canada: Immigrants by Source Country—2016," *The Canadian Magazine of Immigration*, accessed June 27, 2018, http://canadaimmigrants.com/canada-immigrants-by-source-country-2016/; "Section 3," Statistics Canada; "Aboriginal Peoples in Canada: Key Results from the 2016 Census, Statistics Canada, accessed June 27, 2018, www150.statcan.gc.ca/n1/daily-quotidien/171025/dq171025a-eng.htm.

64. Interprovincial Sport and Recreation Council and Canadian Parks and Recreation Association, "A Framework for Recreation in Canada 2015," 7.

65. "R. Tait McKenzie Award," Physical and Health Education Canada; A.E. (Ted) Wall, "The History of Adapted Physical Activity in Canada," in *Adapted Physical Activity*, ed. Robert D. Steadward, Garry D. Wheeler, and E. Jane Watkinson (Edmonton: University of Alberta Press, 2003), 27-44.

66. "History of Adapted Physical Activity," quizlet, accessed June 27, 2018, https://quizlet.com/186193211/history-of-adapted-physical-activity-flash-cards.

67. Wall, "History of Adapted Physical Activity," 29.

68. McLaren, "The Creation of a Haven," 127-150; Philip Oreopoulos, *Canadian Compulsory School Laws and Their Impact on Educational Attainment and Future Earnings* (Ottawa: Minister of Industry, 2005), www.worldcat.org/title/canadian-compulsory-school-laws-and-their-impact-oneducational-attainment-and-future-earnings/oclc/64503062.

69. Angus McLaren, *Our Own Master Race: Eugenics in Canada, 1885-1945* (Toronto: McClelland & Stewart, 1990), 91-94; Oreopoulos, *Canadian Compulsory School Laws*.

70. Janice Forsyth, "Bodies of Meaning: Sports and Games at Canadian Residential Schools," in *Aboriginal Peoples and Sport in Canada: Historical Foundations and Contemporary Issues*, ed. Janice Forsyth and Audrey Giles (Vancouver: UBC Press, 2013), 15-34.

71. Peter Bryce, *Report on the Indian Schools of Manitoba and the North-West Territories*, government report (Ottawa, 1907), 18, http://peel.library.ualberta.ca/bibliography/3024.html.

72. MacMurchy, "Report Upon the Care of the Feeble-Minded," 5.

73. Malacrida, *A Special Hell*, 3-27; Deborah Park and John Radford, "From the Case Files: Reconstructing a History of Involuntary Sterilization," *Disability & Society 13* (1998): 317-342.

74. MacMurchy, "Report Upon the Care of the Feeble-Minded," 17

75. Malacrida, *A Special Hell*, 15-17.

76. Samuel Prince, "Mental Hygiene: A General Survey," *Nova Scotia Medical Bulletin* 7 (1934): 322.

77. Malacrida, *A Special Hell*, 93-120.

78. MacMurchy, "Report Upon the Care of the Feeble-Minded," 7.

79. Henry Goddard (1916, 9) in Snyder and Mitchell, *Cultural Locations of Disability*, 117.

80. Wall, "History of Adapted Physical Activity," 29.

81. Lynn Couturier, "The Influence of the Eugenics Movement on Physical Education in the United States," *Sport History Review* 36 (2005): 32.

82. Couturier, "Influence of the Eugenics Movement," 32.

83. Couturier, "Influence of the Eugenics Movement," 32.

84. Mark Moss, *Manliness and Militarism: Educating Young Boys in Ontario for War* (New York: Oxford University Press, 2011), 50.

85. Peers, "From Eugenics to Paralympics," 131.

86. Smith Walker, "The Wealth of Nations: Education in Relation to Public Health," *Nova Scotia Journal of Education* 8, no. 1 (1914): 37.

87. Peers, "From Eugenics to Paralympics," 129-131

88. Wall, "History of Adapted Physical Activity," 28-29.

89. R. Tait McKenzie, "The Place of Physical Training in a School System" *Montreal Medical Journal* (1900), 7, www.archive.org/details/cihm_51075.

90. R. Tait McKenzie, *Exercise in Education and Medicine* (Philadelphia: Saunders, 1909), 210.

91. MacMurchy, "Report Upon the Care of the Feeble-Minded," 7.

92. McKenzie, "The Place of Physical Training," 213.

93. McKenzie, "The Place of Physical Training," 213.

94. Prince, "Mental Hygiene," 322.

95. Forsyth, "Bodies of Meaning," 15-34.

96. Forsyth, "Bodies of Meaning," 25.

97. Bruce Cheadle, "Universal Healthcare Much Loved Among Canadians, Monarchy Less Important: Poll," *Globe and Mail* (November 25, 2012), www.theglobeandmail. com/news/national/universal-health-care-much-loved-among-canadians-monarchy-less-important-poll/article5640454.

98. First Nations Child and Family Caring Society of Canada et al. v. Attorney General of Canada, T1340/7008, Canadian Human Rights Tribunal, 473.

99. Donna Goodwin, "The Voices of Students With Disabilities: Are They Informing Inclusive Physical Education Practice?," in *Disability and Youth Sport*, ed. Hayley Fitzgerald (New York: Routledge, 2009), 53-74.

100. Caroline Symons, Grant O'Sullivan, Erika Borkoles, Mark B. Andersen, and Remco C.J. Polman, "The Impact of Homophobic Bullying During Sport and Physical Education Participation on Same-Sex-Attracted and Gender-Diverse Young Australians' Depression and Anxiety Levels: The Equal Play Study" (research report, Melbourne, Australia, 2014), 11-17, www.beyondblue.org.au/docs/default-source/research-project-files/bw0255.pdf?sfvrsn=2.

101. Tanya Titchkosky, *The Question of Access: Disability, Space, Meaning* (Toronto: University of Toronto Press, 2011), 39.

102. Michael A. Horvat, Martin E. Block, and L.J.R Kelly, *Developmental and Adapted Physical Activity Assessment*, rev. ed (Champaign, IL: Human Kinetics, 2007), ix.

103. "Movement Assessment Battery for Children—Second Edition," Pearson, accessed June 29, 2018, www.pearsonclinical.com/therapy/products/100000433/movement-assessment-battery-for-children-second-edition-movement-abc-2.html#tab-details.

104. "Movement Assessment Battery for Children—Second Edition," product detail.

105. "Convention on the Rights of Persons With Disabilities: First Report of Canada," government report (Ottawa, 2014), 15. http://publications.gc.ca/collections/collection_2014/pc-ch/CH37-4-19-2013-eng.pdf.

106. "Convention on the Rights of Persons With Disabilities."

107. Robert Steadward and Cynthia Peterson, *Paralympics: Where Heroes Come* (Edmonton: One Shot Holdings, 1997).

108. Steve Bailey, *Athlete First: A History of the Paralympic Movement* (Chichester, West Sussex, UK: Wiley, 2008), 21.

109. Steadward and Peterson, *Paralympics*, 41.

110. Bailey, *Athlete First*, 261.

111. "Policy on Sport for Persons With a Disability," federal policy (Ottawa, 2006), sec. 3.4, http://canada.pch.gc.ca/eng/1414513635858/1414513676681.

112. Vanessa K. Noonan, Matthew Fingas, Angela Farry, David Baxter, Anoushka Singh, Michael G. Fehlings, and Marcel Dvorak, "Incidence and Prevalence of Spinal Cord Injury in Canada: A National Perspective," *Neuroepidemiology* 38, no. 4 (2012): 219-226; "A Profile of Persons With Disabilities Among Canadians Aged 15 Years or Older, 2012," Statistics Canada, accessed June 27, 2018, www150.statcan.gc.ca/n1/pub/89-654-x/89-654-x2015001-eng.htm.

113. David Legg, Claudia Emes, David Stewart, and Robert Steadward, "Historical Overview of the Paralympics, Special Olympics, and Deaflympics. *Palaestra* 20, no. 1 (2004): 30.

114. Bailey, *Athlete First*, 14.

115. Ian Gregson, *Irresistible Force: Disability Sport in Canada* (Victoria, BC: Polstar, 1999), 108.

116. Diane Driedger, *The Last Civil Rights Movement: Disabled People's International* (New York: St. Martin's Press, 1989), 18.

117. Snyder and Mitchell, *Cultural Locations of Disability*, 121-123.

118. Maria Bjorkman and Sven Widmalm, "Selling Eugenics: The Case of Sweden," *Notes and Records of Royal Society Journal of the History of Science* (August 18, 2010), 395. doi:10.1098/rsnr.2010.0009; McLaren, *Our Own Master Race*, 167-171.

119. Snyder and Mitchell, *Cultural Locations of Disability*, 121-123.

120. Bailey, *Athlete First*, 15.

121. "A Hundred Years of Immigration to Canada."

122. Snyder and Mitchell, *Cultural Locations of Disability*, 21-23.

123. Ladelle McWhorter, *Racism and Sexual Oppression in Anglo-America: A Genealogy* (Bloomington: Indiana University Press, 2009), 231-237.

124. Chinmaya Mishra, "The Involvement of Psychiatry and Psychiatrists in the Eugenics Program of Alberta," *Proceedings of the 20th Anniversary History of Medicine Days Conference 2011* (Newcastle, UK: Cambridge Scholars Publishing, 2011), 145-146.

125. McWhorter, *Racism and Sexual Oppression*, 245.

126. Gregson, *Irresistible Force*, 108.

127. "Fulfill the Promise, Pay the Debt, Re-establish the Man," government pamphlet (Department of Soldier's Civil Reestablishment, 1919), https://archive.org/details/informationbookl00cana.

128. Pensions, Soldier's Insurance and Re-establishment Committee, evidence and proceedings (Ottawa, 1922).

129. Peers, "From Eugenics to Paralympics," 130.

130. Canadian National Committee for Mental Hygiene, "Reconstruction and the National Committee for Mental Hygiene" (Toronto: Rous & Mann, 1919).

131. Charles Fraser, *Control of Aliens in the British Commonwealth of Nations* (London: Hogarth Press, 1940); "A Hundred Years of Immigration to Canada," n.p..

132. Mishra, "The Involvement of Psychiatry and Psychiatrists," 137-145.

133. "Helen MacMurchy: Pioneering Interest in Mental Hygiene and Child Welfare," *Canadian Public Health Journal* 28 (1937), accessed June 30, 2018, http://resources. cpha.ca/CPHA/ThisIsPublicHealth/profiles/item.php?l=E&i=1369.

134. National Physical Fitness Act, 1943, R.S.C., ch. 190 (1952), 4032.

135. Karen Stote, "The Coercive Sterilization of Aboriginal Women in Canada," *American Indian Culture and Research Journal* 36, no. 3 (2012): 125, 129-130.

136. Mary Tremblay, "Going Back to Civvy Street: A Historical Account of the Impact of the Everest and Jennings Wheelchair for Canadian Second World War Veterans With Spinal Cord Injury." *Disability and Society* 11, no. 2: 149-169.

137. Gregson, *Irresistible Force*, 70.

138. Bailey, *Athlete First*, 38.

139. Legg, Emes, Stewart, and Steadward, "Historical Overview of the Paralympics," 32.

140. Bailey, *Athlete First*, 38.

141. Steadward and Peterson, *Paralympics*, 38.

142. Bailey, *Athlete First*, 223.

143. "IPC Decides on Participation of Athletes With Intellectual Disability," *International Paralympic Committee*, last modified November 21, 2009, www.paralympic.org/press-release/ipc-decides-participation-athletes-intellectual-disability.

144. Bailey, *Athlete First*, 81, 125.; P. David Howe, *The Cultural Politics of the Paralympic Movement: Through an Anthropological Lens* (London: Routledge, 2008), 71.

145. Bailey, *Athlete First*, 218.

146. Bailey, *Athlete First*, 106.

147. Danielle Peers, "Patients, Athletes, Freaks: Paralympism and the Reproduction of Disability," *Journal of Sport and Social Issues* 36, no. 3 (2012): 295-316.

148. Howe, *Cultural Politics*, 76.

149. Howe, *Cultural Politics*, 76-78.

150. P. David Howe and Carwyn Jones, "Classification of Disabled Athletes: (Dis)Empowering the Paralympic Practice Community," *Sociology of Sport Journal* 23 (2006), 29-46; similar findings have been noted in Australia, France, and Norway. See, for example, Marit Sorenson and Nina Kahrs, "Integration of Disability Sport in the Norwegian Sport Organizations," *Adapted Physical Activity Quarterly* 23 (2006): 184-202.

151. Carla Silva and P. David Howe, "The (In)validity of *Supercrip* Representation of Paralympian Athletes," *Journal of Sport & Social Issues* 36 (2012): 174-194.

152. Driedger, *The Last Civil Rights Movement*, 36-40.

153. Bailey, *Athlete First*, 147.

154. James Charlton, *Nothing About Us Without Us* (Berkeley: University of California Press, 2000), 16-17.

155. Tremblay, "Going Back to Civvy Street," 156; Driedger, *The Last Civil Rights Movement*, 9-11.

156. Driedger, *The Last Civil Rights Movement*, 10.

157. Driedger, *The Last Civil Rights Movement*, 18-22.

158. Danielle Peers, "Sport and Social Movements by/for Disability and Deaf Communities: Irreconcilable Histories?" in *Palgrave Handbook of Paralympic Studies*, ed. Ian Brittain and Aaron Beacom (Basingstoke, UK: Palgrave Macmillan, 2018), 71-97.

159. "New Data on Disability in Canada, 2017," Statistics Canada, accessed June 26, 2019, www150.statcan.gc.ca/n1/pub/11-627-m/11-627-m2018035-eng.htm.

Chapter 11

1. Joseph Mensah, *Black Canadians: History, Experiences, Social Conditions*, 2nd ed. (Halifax: Fernwood, 2010), 185.

2. Janelle Joseph, Simon Darnell, and Yuka Nakamura, *Race and Sport in Canada: Intersecting Inequalities* (Toronto: Canadian Scholars' Press, 2012), 3.

3. Victoria Paraschak and Susan Tirone, "Ethnicity and Race in Canadian Sport," in *Social Dimensions of Canadian Sport and Physical Activity*, ed. Jane Crossman and Jay Scherer (Toronto: Pearson, 2015), 99.

4. Timothy J. Stanley, "Why I Killed Canadian History: Conditions for an Anti-racist History in Canada," *Social History/Histoire sociale* 33, no. 65 (2000): 94.

5. Stanley, "Why I Killed Canadian History," 83.

6. Christopher Michael Spence, *The Skin I'm In: Racism, Sport and Education* (Halifax: Fernwood, 1999), 17.

7. Anton L. Allahar, "When Black First Became Worth Less," *International Journal of Comparative Sociology* 34, nos. 1/2 (1993): 40, 48, 52.

8. Spence, *The Skin I'm In*, 17.

9. Paraschak and Tirone, "Ethnicity and Race," 99.

10. Ta-Nehisi Coates, *Between the World and Me* (New York: Spiegel & Grau, 2015), 7.

11. Genetic studies demonstrate that, among themselves, racial groups are more diverse than they are similar to each other. Within what we consider Black, white, or Asian, there are various skin shades, eye colours, hair textures, skin tones, and so on. John M. Hoberman, *Darwin's Athletes: How Sport Has Damaged Black America and Preserved the Myth of Race* (Boston: Houghton Mifflin, 1997), 191.

12. In the 18th and 19th centuries, people who were initially tied to a specific European heritage (e.g., English, French, Dutch, or German) became a unified group who shared not only the characteristic of paler skin but also economic, political, and social power. Hoberman, *Darwin's Athletes*, 100.

13. See Christopher Michael Spence, *The Skin I'm In: Racism, Sport and Education* (Halifax: Fernwood, 1999) and Barrington Walker, "Finding Jim Crow in Canada, 1789-1967," in *A history of Human Rights in Canada: Essential Issues*, ed. Janet Miron (Toronto: Canadian Scholars' Press, 2009).

14. Hoberman, *Darwin's Athletes*, 101.

15. Hoberman, *Darwin's Athletes*, 100.

16. Ben Carrington, "'Race,' Representation and the Sporting Body," (paper submitted to the CUCR's Occasional Paper Series, 2002), 33-36.

17. Hoberman, *Darwin's Athletes*, 108-109.

18. Hoberman, *Darwin's Athletes*, 99, 101.

19. Hoberman, *Darwin's Athletes*, 108-109.

20. See, for example, Ornella Nzindukiyimana and Kevin B. Wamsley, "Lowering the Bar: Larry Gains's Heavyweight Battle for a Title Shot, 1927-1932," *Sport History Review* 47, no. 2 (2016): 125-145.

21. Don Morrow and Kevin B. Wamsley, *Sport in Canada: A History*, 3rd ed. (Don Mills, ON: Oxford University Press, 2013), 115.

22. Hoberman, *Darwin's Athletes*, 106.

23. Hoberman, *Darwin's Athletes*, xiii.

24. See Mensah, *Black Canadians*, 199, 202-203, 207.

25. John Hoberman, "Racial Athletic Aptitude and New Medical Genetics: 'Black Dominance' and the Future of Race Relations," in *Sport, Race, and Ethnicity: Narratives of Difference and Diversity*, ed. Daryl Adair (Morgantown, WV: Fitness Information Technology, 2011), 156.

26. Hoberman, *Darwin's Athletes*, 134.

27. Mensah, *Black Canadians*, 199.

28. Jennifer H. Lansbury, *A Spectacular Leap: Black Women Athletes in Twentieth-Century America* (Fayetteville: University of Arkansas Press, 2014), 24.

29. Yevonne R. Smith, "Women of Color in Society and Sport," *Quest* 44, no. 2 (1992): 233.

30. See M. Ann Hall, *The Girl and the Game: A History of Women's Sport in Canada*, 2nd ed. (Toronto: University of Toronto Press, 2016).

31. See Patricia Vertinsky and Gwendolyn Captain, "More Myth Than History: American Culture and Representations of the Black Female's Athletic Ability," *Journal of Sport History* 25, no. 3 (1998): 532-561.

32. Louis Moore, *I Fight for a Living: Boxing and the Battle for Black Manhood, 1880-1915* (Urbana: University of Illinois, 2017), 11-12.

33. Not to be confused with American boxer George "the Leiperville Shadow" Godfrey (1897-1947)—born Feab S. Williams—who renamed himself after the Canadian.

34. Moore, *I Fight for a Living*, 2.

35. Moore, *I Fight for a Living*, 1.

36. Dan Streible, "A History of the Boxing Film, 1894-1915: Social Control and Social Reform in the Progressive Era," *Film History* 3, no. 3 (1989): 242; Jerome Zuckerman, Alan Stull, and Marvin H. Eyler, "The Black Athlete in Post-Bellum 19th Century," *Physical Educator* 29, no. 3 (1972): 142-146.

37. Moore, *I Fight for a Living*, 2.

38. Streible, "A History of the Boxing Film," 242.

39. His accomplishments, including becoming the first Canadian champion boxer (by holding the coloured heavyweight title, a segregated title for Black athletes, in 1884) and entering more than a hundred fights, remain remarkable. He retired in 1895 but continued to fight in exhibition fights, returning to his home province once. Welford H. Jackson, "The Negro in Boxing," *Negro History Bulletin* 15, no. 3 (1951): 53; Jim Hornby, "Godfrey, George," in *Dictionary of Canadian Biography*, vol. 13, University of Toronto/Université Laval, 2003, accessed May 10, 2018, www.biographi.ca/en/bio/godfrey_george_13E.html.

40. "Mack's Melange," *New Orleans Picayune*, January 5, 1902, as cited in Moore, *I Fight for a Living*, 94. See also Zuckerman, Stull, and Eyler, "The Black Athlete," 14.

41. Streible, "A History of the Boxing Film," 242.

42. According to Hoberman, in 1856, brain anatomist and anthropologist Louis Pierre Gratiolet wrote that "the skull of the white man is a temple divine but that of the brutish races is merely a helmet constructed to ward off heavy blows." Hoberman, *Darwin's Athletes*, 188-189.

43. Coverage of Dixon in some Canadian media demonstrated a rather welcoming stance to the Black boxer. This is a departure from analysis (e.g., Brian Lennox) suggesting that Dixon's acceptance by Maritimers was diminished by prejudice. Sheldon Gillis, "Putting It on Ice: A Social History of Hockey in the Maritimes, 1880-1914," (master's thesis, Saint Mary's University, 1994), 5; Brian Douglas Lennox, "Black Nova Scotia Boxers: A History of Champions" (master's thesis, Dalhousie University, 1990), 9-12.

44. At the start of his career, he weighed a mere 39 kilograms (87 pounds) and stood 161 centimetres (5 foot 3 and 1/2 inches). Naturally, Dixon's nickname was linked to Godfrey's ("Old Chocolate"). "George Dixon, 1870-1908," Nova Scotia Museum, accessed May 11, 2018, https://museum.novascotia.ca/collections-research/vanguard/gallery/objects/george-dixon-1870-1908; Lennox, "Black Nova Scotia Boxers," 9.

45. The term *world class* is used loosely here; world title bouts largely opposed only athletes from North America and Great Britain.

46. Jason A. Winders, "'Fought the Good Fight, Finished My Course': George Dixon Amid the Rising Tide of Jim Crow America," (PhD diss., Western University, 2016), 234.

47. Lennox, "Black Nova Scotia Boxers," 9.

48. Lennox, "Black Nova Scotia Boxers," 9.

49. "Official" because his 1889 world paperweight title went unrecognized. Lennox, "Black Nova Scotia Boxers," 10.

50. Lennox, "Black Nova Scotia Boxers," 10.

51. F. Daniel Somrack, *Boxing in San Francisco* (San Francisco: Arcadia, 2004), 41.

52. Protestors only managed to ban mixed fights in New Orleans, where Dixon never competed again. Lennox, "Black Nova Scotia Boxers," 11.

53. Black fans were seated separately. David K. Wiggins, ed., *African Americans in Sports*, vol. 1/2 (New York: Routledge, 2015), 85.

54. Gerald R. Gems, "The Politics of Boxing: Resistance, Religion, and Working Class Assimilation," *International Sports Journal* 8, no. 1 (2004): 90.

55. William Humber, *Cheering for the Home Team: The Story of Baseball in Canada* (Erin, ON: Boston Mills Press, 1983), 105; Zuckerman, Stull, and Eyler, "The Black Athlete," 144-145.

56. Humber, *Cheering for the Home Team*, 71, 108.

57. Humber, *Cheering for the Home Team*, 105-107.

58. Fowler may have been the first professional Black baseball player. Humber, *Cheering for the Home Team*, 106.

59. Humber, *Cheering for the Home Team*, 105.

60. Humber, *Cheering for the Home Team*, 106.

61. Humber, *Cheering for the Home Team*, 107.

62. John Holway, *Black Diamonds: Life in the Negro Leagues From the Men Who Lived it* (Westport, CT: Meckler Books, 1989), 64.

63. Morrow and Wamsley, *Sport in Canada*, 101.

64. Humber, *Cheering for the Home Team*, 106.

65. Morrow and Wamsley, *Sport in Canada*, 100.

66. Zuckerman, Stull, and Eyler, "The Black Athlete," 144-145.

67. Holway, *Black Diamonds*, 64, 95-96.

68. Humber, *Cheering for the Home Team*, 107.

69. Tony C.A. Joyce, "Sport and the Cash Nexus in Nineteenth Century Toronto," *Sport History Review* 30, no. 2 (1999): 154.

70. Morrow and Wamsley, *Sport in Canada*, 63; Paraschak and Tirone, "Ethnicity and Race," 101.

71. "Buffalo Regatta: Full Details of the Races," *Globe and Mail*, July 8, 1872, 4.

72. Morrow and Wamsley, *Sport in Canada*, 63.

73. Frank Cosentino, "A History of the Concept of Professionalism in Canadian Sport," (PhD diss., University of Alberta, 1973), 28-29.

74. "Buffalo Regatta," *Globe*, 4; "The Regatta: A Gala Day on the Bay," *Globe*, August 24, 1866, 2.

75. "Buffalo Regatta ," *Globe*, 4; Morrow and Wamsley, *Sport in Canada*, 63.

76. Morrow and Wamsley, *Sport in Canada*, 63.

77. Morrow and Wamsley, *Sport in Canada*, 63.

78. "The Regatta," *Globe*, 2.

79. In 1866, his crew were competing for $30. In 1872, in Buffalo, New York, he competed in a solo timed race for a $100 prize. Incidents in this race led judges to order a rematch, although it is unclear whether it took place. "The Regatta," *Globe*, 2; "Buffalo Regatta," *Globe*, 4.

80. Steven J. Jackson and Pam Ponic, "Pride and Prejudice: Reflecting on Sport Heroes, National Identity, and Crisis in Canada," *Culture, Sport, Society* 4, no. 2 (2001): 44; Morrow and Wamsley, *Sport in Canada*, 113-119.

81. Written accounts date back to the mid-1890s (i.e., organized participation). Like others, Black people likely engaged in pond hockey before that. Gillis, "Putting It on Ice," 72.

82. Gillis, "Putting It on Ice," 72-73.

83. Michael McKinley, *Hockey: A People's History* (Toronto: McClelland & Stewart, 2009), 26.

84. Gillis, "Putting It on Ice," 38.

85. Gillis, "Putting It on Ice," 80.

86. Gillis, "Putting It on Ice," 81-82.

87. Gillis, "Putting It on Ice," 7.

88. Gillis, "Putting It on Ice," 75.

89. Gillis, "Putting It on Ice," 75; McKinley, *Hockey: A People's History*, 26.

90. Gillis, "Putting It on Ice," 75.

91. Gillis, "Putting It on Ice," 76, 78-79.

92. There was a lack of competition among senior clubs—arguably the best competition to be had—in Halifax. So between 1899 and 1904, Black teams surprisingly filled that gap and "forced Maritimers into a reevaluation of their racist heritage." Gillis, "Putting It on Ice," 61.

93. Gillis, "Putting It on Ice," 82-83.

94. McKinley, *Hockey: A People's History*, 26.

95. Gillis, "Putting It on Ice," 85.

96. Gillis, "Putting It on Ice," 86-87.

97. The Halifax Eurekas, for instance, had a similar structure to white teams: They had a clubhouse and switched to baseball in the summer. Gillis, "Putting It on Ice," 87.

98. Gillis, "Putting It on Ice," 90.

99. Colin D. Howell, "The 'Others': Race, Ethnicity, and Community Baseball," in *Northern Sandlots: A Social History of Maritime Baseball* (Toronto: University of Toronto Press, 1995), 174.

100. Howell, "The 'Others.'" 176.

101. Gillis, "Putting It on Ice," 79; Howell, "The 'Others,'" 173-174.

102. Humber, *Cheering for the Home Team*, 107.

103. Prior to the 1908 Games, Canadian teams were not vetted by a national body and were instead composed of individuals who could finance their way to competition. In 1908, Tom Longboat, a Six Nations Reserve (Brampton, Ontario) marathon runner, was favoured to medal, but he came up short and faced racist criticism. See Bruce Kidd, "In Defence of Tom Longboat," *Sport in Society* 16, no. 4, 515-532; Ornella Nzindukiyimana, "John 'Army' Howard, Canada's First Black Olympian: A Nation-Building Paradox," *International Journal of the History of Sport* 34, no. 11 (2017): 2.

104. "Athletics: Canada May Send Two Colored Olympic Athletes," *Globe*, May 24, 1912, 15.

105. "Athletics," *Globe*, 15.

106. Nzindukiyimana, "John 'Army' Howard," 3-7.

107. Nzindukiyimana, "John 'Army' Howard," 13.

108. Nzindukiyimana, "John 'Army' Howard," 11.

109. He added, still from his own account, that he cautioned Howard that Johnson's current reign did not mean that Howard could beat anyone up himself. Walter Knox, "1912," *Notes for an Autobiography*, 2, Orillia Public Library.

110. Nzindukiyimana, "John 'Army' Howard," 11.

111. Lennox, "Black Nova Scotia Boxers," 15.

112. As champion, Johnson himself traced a colour line and avoided boxers of colour. Lennox, "Black Nova Scotia Boxers," 16.

113. Lennox, "Black Nova Scotia Boxers," 19.

114. Lennox, "Black Nova Scotia Boxers," 19.

115. For a biography of the man and boxer, see Clay Moyle, *Sam Langford: Boxing's Greatest Uncrowned Champion* (Seattle: Bennett & Hastings, 2012).

116. Greggory MacIntosh Ross, "Beyond 'The Abysmal Brute': A Social History of Boxing in Interwar Nova Scotia," (master's thesis, Saint Mary's University, 2008), 79.

117. Vertinsky and Captain, "More Myth Than History," 532-561.

118. Hall, *The Girl and the Game*, 133.

119. The 1938 Games were the third instalment, and the second at which women participated.

120. Bobbie Rosenfeld, "Feminine Sport Reel," *Globe*, February 19, 1938, 18.

121. Michael D. Davis, *Black American Women in Olympic Track and Field* (Jefferson, NC: McFarland, 1992): xviii.

122. Tabitha Marshall, "Barbara Howard," *The Canadian Encyclopedia*, accessed January 23, 2018, www.thecanadianencyclopedia.ca/en/article/barbara-howard/; Barbara Howard [video], 2015.5.6, Canada's Sports Hall of Fame Archives, https://cshof.pastperfectonline.com/archive/2572549B-E65F-468F-99AD-621486962610.

123. "A. Eugenia Lowe Butler: Class of 1950," Tuskegee University Athletic Hall of Fame, 1985.

124. Hall adds that "beginning with pioneer athletes of colour [like Barbara Howard and Rosella Thorne], to the highly successful track athletes whose parents immigrated to Canada in the 1980s and finally to the many fine high performance athletes of today in a great variety of sports, their accomplishments and contributions have been outstanding and out of proportion to their numbers in the general population." Hall, *The Girl and the Game*, 214.

125. Edwards still holds the Canadian individual Summer Olympics record. Ulf Lagerstroem, "Mr 800: Phil Edwards (Brit. Guiana/Canada)," *Journal of Olympic History* 19, no. 1 (2011): 37-39.

126. See John Cooper, *Rapid Ray: The Story of Ray Lewis* (Toronto: Tundra Books, 2002), 6, 7, chapters 3 and 5.

127. William Humber, *A Sporting Chance Achievements of African-Canadian Athletes* (Toronto: Natural Heritage Books, 2004): 46-48.

128. Humber, *A Sporting Chance*, 47.

129. After the Oaks, Claxton continued as an "itinerant moundsman" for teams across the United States. Gary Ashwill, "From the White Sox to the Union Giants: The Unusual Baseball Résumé of Bill Cadreau, a.k.a. "Chief Chouneau,'" *Black Ball* 5, no. 2 (2012): 15; Tom Hawthorn, "Jimmy Claxton," Society for American Baseball Research, accessed May 25, 2018, https://sabr.org/bioproj/person/43c05f0c.

130. Humber, *A Sporting Chance*, 49.

131. Howell, "The 'Others,'" 178-179; Lauren A. Miceli, "The 1934 Chatham Colored All-Stars: Barnstorming to Championships," *Great Lakes Journal of Undergraduate History* 4, no. 1 (2016): 8-16.

132. Morrow and Wamsley, *Sport in Canada*, 101.

133. Howell, "The 'Others,'" 180; Miceli, "1934 Chatham Coloured All-Stars," 10.

134. Miceli, "1934 Chatham Colored All-Stars," 14-15.

135. Miceli, "1934 Chatham Colored All-Stars," 12-13.

136. They played until the Second World War. Blake Harding and Pat Harding, "Breaking the Colour Barrier: An Oral History of the Chatham Coloured All-Stars," interview by Miriam Wright, May 25, 2016, in Chatham, Ontario, transcript, University of Windsor and the Chatham Sports Hall of Fame, Ontario, available online at http://cdigs.uwindsor.ca/BreakingColourBarrier/items/show/716.

137. Morrow and Wamsley, *Sport in Canada*, 101.

138. Chase had also been a part of the champion Chatham Coloured All-Stars. Humber, *Cheering for the Home Team*, 49; James Stewart Reaney, "My London: Star of Chatham Coloured All-Stars an Early Ground-Breaker," *Free Press* (London, ON), April 10, 2013, accessed May 30, 2018, http://lfpress.com/2013/04/10/my-london-star-of-chatham-coloured-all-stars-an-early-ground-breaker/wcm/4e3ad16b-28aa-f7e5-f4aa-9c9e9e3f14f7.

139. Two of the players were on the Royals roster with Robinson. Two others, American Roy Campanella and Don Newcombe, joined the Majors after Robinson. Howell, *Northern Sandlots*, 182; Jules Tygiel, *Baseball's Great Experiment: Jackie Robinson and His Legacy* (New York: Oxford University Press, 1983), 126-127.

140. Andy Lytle, "Speaking on Sports," *Toronto Star*, July 21, 1942, 12.

141. To a considerable extent, Asian-Canadian players are not yet a significant presence in the sport, despite Larry Kwong's playing in the NHL a decade before Willie O'Ree.

142. Humber, *A Sporting Chance*, 105-108.

143. Eric M. Adams, "Errors of Fact and Law: Race, Space, and Hockey in Christie v York," *University of Toronto Law Journal* 62, no. 4 (2012): 484-485, 487-488, 491, 494.

144. Valerie Jerome and Stuart Parker, "The Conservative Vision of the Amateur Ideal and Its Paradoxical Whitening Power: The Story of Valerie Jerome in 1950s and 1960s Canadian Track and Field," *Sport in Society* 13, no. 1 (2010): 12-13, 18.

145. See Andreas Krebs, "Hockey and the Reproduction of Colonialism in Canada," in *Race and Sport in Canada: Intersecting Inequalities*, ed. Janelle Joseph, Simon Darnell, and Yuka Nakamura (Toronto: Canadian Scholars' Press, 2012), 81-106.

146. Jordan Goldstein, "Building Canadian National Identity Within the State and Through Ice Hockey: A Political Analysis of the Donation of the Stanley Cup, 1888-1893," (PhD diss., University of Western Ontario, 2015), 114, 300.

147. See Tom Bartsiokas and Corey Long, *Angela James: The First Superstar of Women's Hockey* (Toronto: Women's Press Literary, 2012); J.D.M. Stewart, "Angela James," *The Canadian Encyclopedia*, accessed June 5, 2018, www.thecanadianencyclopedia.ca/en/article/angela-james/; see also Laura Robinson, *Black Tights: Women, Sport and Sexuality* (Toronto: HarperCollins, 2002), 70-72.

148. Jerome and Parker, "The Conservative Vision," 13.

149. Jerome and Parker, "The Conservative Vision," 13.

150. Jackson and Ponic, "Pride and Prejudice," 54.

151. Alongside Johnson in the 1980s, there was Angella Issajenko, also from Jamaica.

152. Gamal Abdel-Shehid, *Who da Man? Black Masculinities and Sporting Cultures* (Toronto: Canadian Scholars' Press, 2005), 38.

153. Janelle Joseph, "Culture, Community, Consciousness: The Caribbean Sporting Diaspora," *International Review for the Sociology of Sport* 46, no. 6 (2012): 6.

154. Abdel-Shehid, *Who da Man?*, 4, 92.

155. John Valentine and Simon C. Darnell, "Football and 'Tolerance': Black Football Players in 20th Century Canada," in *Race and Sport in Canada: Intersecting Inequalities*, ed. Janelle Joseph, Simon Darnell, and Yuka Nakamura (Toronto: Canadian Scholars' Press, 2012), 59.

156. Steven J. Jackson, "Exorcizing the Ghost: Donovan Bailey, Ben Johnson and the Politics of Canadian Identity," *Media, Culture & Society* 26, no. 1 (2004): 132-135.

157. Jackson, "Exorcizing the Ghost," 133, 137.

158. Agnes Calliste, "Race, Gender and Canadian Immigration Policy: Blacks From the Caribbean, 1900-1932," *Journal of Canadian Studies/Revue d'études canadiennes* 28, no. 4 (1993): 133.

159. Howell, "The 'Others,'" 195.

Chapter 12

1. These ideas are explored more thoroughly in Stacy L. Lorenz, "'A Lively Interest on the Prairies': Western Canada, the Mass Media, and a 'World of Sport,' 1870-1939," *Journal of Sport History* 27, no. 2 (2000): 195-227; Stacy L. Lorenz, "'In the Field of Sport at Home and Abroad': Sports Coverage in Canadian Daily Newspapers, 1850-1914," *Sport History Review* 34, no. 2 (2003): 133-167.

2. See Joshua Meyrowitz, *No Sense of Place: The Impact of Electronic Media on Social Behavior* (New York: Oxford University Press, 1985), especially 35-38, 115-118, 332-335; David Whitson and Donald Macintosh, "Becoming a World-Class City: Hallmark Events and Sport Franchises in the Growth Strategies of Western Canadian Cities," *Sociology of Sport Journal* 10, no. 3 (1993): 224-225.

3. David Whitson, "Circuits of Promotion: Media, Marketing and the Globalization of Sport," in *MediaSport*, ed. Lawrence A. Wenner (London: Routledge, 1998), 57-72.

4. Susan Marie Nattrass, "Sport and Television in Canada: 1952 to 1982" (PhD diss., University of Alberta, 1988); Sut Jhally, "The Spectacle of Accumulation: Material and Cultural Factors in the Evolution of the Sports/Media Complex," *Critical Sociology* 12 (1984): 41-57.

5. See Paul Rutherford, *The Making of the Canadian Media* (Toronto: McGraw-Hill Ryerson, 1978); Paul Rutherford, *A Victorian Authority: The Daily Press in Late Nineteenth-Century Canada* (Toronto: University of Toronto Press, 1982); Mary Vipond, *The Mass Media in Canada* (Toronto: James Lorimer, 1989); Minko Sotiron, *From Politics to Profit: The Commercialization of Canadian Daily Newspapers, 1890-1920* (Montreal: McGill–Queen's University Press, 1997).

6. Lorenz, "A Lively Interest on the Prairies," 198; Lorenz, "In the Field of Sport," 135-136; Rutherford, *The Making of the Canadian Media*, 9; Rutherford, *A Victorian Authority*, 67, 75.

7. This paragraph is drawn from Lorenz, "In the Field of Sport," 136. See also Rutherford, *A Victorian Authority*, 9-35, 40-42.

8. In 1871, only 19.6 percent of Canada's people lived in cities or towns, but by 1911 this number had climbed to 45.4 percent. See F.H. Leacy, ed., *Historical Statistics of Canada*, 2nd ed. (Ottawa: Canadian Government Publishing Centre and Statistics Canada, 1983), Series A67-69.

9. The literacy rate in Canada rose from about 70 percent in 1850 to approximately 90 percent in 1900, and to about 95 percent in 1921. See Vipond, *The Mass Media in Canada*, 8; Rutherford, *A Victorian Authority*, 26-33.

10. Sotiron, *From Politics to Profit*, 10.

11. Lorenz, "In the Field of Sport," 138-139. See also P.F.W. Rutherford, "The People's Press: The Emergence of the New Journalism in Canada, 1869-99," *Canadian Historical Review* 56, no. 2 (1975): 169-191; Rutherford, *The Making of the Canadian Media*, 49.

12. Carl Betke, "Sports Promotion in the Western Canadian City: The Example of Early Edmonton," *Urban History Review* 12, no. 2 (1983): 48; Sotiron, *From Politics to Profit*, 65; Lorenz, "In the Field of Sport," 148-152.

13. Dave Whitson, "Hockey and Canadian Popular Culture: The Making and Remaking of Identities," in *Method and Methodology in Sport and Cultural History*, ed. K.B. Wamsley (Dubuque: Times Mirror Higher Education Group, 1995), 190-192; Richard Gruneau and David Whitson, *Hockey Night in Canada: Sport, Identities, and Cultural Politics* (Toronto: Garamond Press, 1993), 67-72, 210-213.

14. Whitson, "Hockey and Canadian Popular Culture," 194. See also Whitson, "Circuits of Promotion," 61-62.

15. Whitson, "Hockey and Canadian Popular Culture," 192.

16. Vipond, *The Mass Media in Canada*, 5.

17. Lorenz, "A Lively Interest on the Prairies," 200-201; W.H. Kesterton, *A History of Journalism in Canada* (Toronto: McClelland & Stewart, 1967), 158-161; Rutherford, *The Making of the Canadian Media*, 54-55.

18. Gruneau and Whitson, *Hockey Night in Canada*, 95-96.

19. Lorenz, "In the Field of Sport," 152-155; Lorenz, "A Lively Interest on the Prairies," 202-205.

20. John Herd Thompson and Allen Seager, *Canada 1922-1939: Decades of Discord* (Toronto: McClelland & Stewart, 1985), 187; Stacy L. Lorenz, "'Bowing Down to Babe Ruth': Major League Baseball and Canadian Popular Culture, 1920-1929," *Canadian Journal of History of Sport* 23, no. 1 (1995): 28.

21. *Manitoba Free Press*, October 7, 1929, 1; Lorenz, "A Lively Interest on the Prairies," 210.

22. Lorenz, "A Lively Interest on the Prairies," 201-203.

23. Gruneau and Whitson, *Hockey Night in Canada*, 84.

24. Lorenz, "A Lively Interest on the Prairies," 211-212; Lorenz, "Bowing Down to Babe Ruth," 29-30.

25. Stacy L. Lorenz, "'Our Victorias Victorious': Media, Rivalry, and the 1896 Winnipeg-Montreal Stanley Cup Hockey Challenges," *International Journal of the History of Sport* 32, no. 17 (2015): 1987-2011.

26. *Manitoba Free Press*, February 15, 1896, 1.

27. *Montreal Star*, December 30, 1896, 8.

28. Sotiron, *From Politics to Profit*, 57-62; Rutherford, *A Victorian Authority*, 97-104; Lorenz, "In the Field of Sport," 137.

29. William Leiss, Stephen Kline, and Sut Jhally, *Social Communication in Advertising: Persons, Products, and Images of Well-Being* (Toronto: Methuen, 1986), 77.

30. Gruneau and Whitson, *Hockey Night in Canada*, 83.

31. Lorenz, "In the Field of Sport," 139-140.

32. Rutherford, *A Victorian Authority*, 77; Rutherford, *The Making of the Canadian Media*, 53.

33. Lorenz, "In the Field of Sport," 144-145.

34. Robert W. McChesney, "Media Made Sport: A History of Sports Coverage in the United States," in *Media, Sports, and Society*, ed. Lawrence A. Wenner (Newbury Park, CA: Sage, 1989), 54.

35. Gruneau and Whitson, *Hockey Night in Canada*, 86; Bruce Kidd, *The Struggle for Canadian Sport* (Toronto: University of Toronto Press, 1996), 262-263.

36. Don Morrow, "Lou Marsh: The Pick and Shovel of Canadian Sporting Journalism," *Canadian Journal of History of Sport* 14, no. 1 (1983): 21-33; Don Morrow and Kevin B. Wamsley, *Sport in Canada: A History*, 4th ed. (Don Mills, ON: Oxford University Press, 2017), 140-147.

37. M. Ann Hall, "Alexandrine Gibb: In 'No Man's Land Of Sport,'" *International Journal of the History of Sport* 18, no. 1 (2001): 149-172. See also M. Ann Hall, *The Girl and the Game: A History of Women's Sport in Canada*, 2nd ed. (Toronto: University of Toronto Press, 2016).

38. Hall, "Alexandrine Gibb," 156.

39. Hall, "Alexandrine Gibb," 154. See also Kidd, *The Struggle for Canadian Sport*, 109, 111-112.

40. Hall, "Alexandrine Gibb," 159. See also Christina Burr and Carol A. Reader, "Fanny 'Bobbie' Rosenfeld: A 'Modern Woman' of Sport and Journalism in Twentieth-Century Canada," *Sport History Review* 44, no. 2 (2013): 130-134.

41. Kidd, *The Struggle for Canadian Sport*, 97.

42. Hall, "Alexandrine Gibb," 157; Morrow and Wamsley, *Sport in Canada*, 152-160.

43. Burr and Reader, "A 'Modern Woman,'" 120-143.

44. Hall, "Alexandrine Gibb," 157.

45. Hall, *The Girl and the Game*, 322.

46. The following discussion of radio and sport is based on Lorenz, "A Lively Interest on the Prairies," 206-209.

47. On the early development of radio in Canada, see Mary Vipond, *Listening In: The First Decade of Canadian Broadcasting, 1922-1932* (Montreal: McGill–Queen's University Press, 1992); Michael Nolan, "An Infant Industry: Canadian Private Radio, 1919-36," *Canadian Historical Review* 70, 4 (1989): 496-518; Bill McNeil and Morris Wolfe, *The Birth of Radio in Canada: Signing On* (Toronto: Doubleday, 1982).

48. Robert Bothwell, Ian Drummond, and John English, *Canada, 1900-1945* (Toronto: University of Toronto Press, 1987), 284; Rutherford, *The Making of the Canadian Media*, 80; Vipond, *The Mass Media in Canada*, 39; Bruce Kidd, *The Struggle for Canadian Sport* (Toronto: University of Toronto Press, 1996), 223.

49. Donald G. Wetherell and Irene Kmet, *Useful Pleasures: The Shaping of Leisure in Alberta 1896-1945* (Regina: Alberta Culture and Multiculturalism/Canadian Plains Research Center, 1990), 290.

50. Thompson and Seager, *Canada 1922-1939*, 181-182.

51. Gruneau and Whitson, *Hockey Night in Canada*, 95-96.

52. Whitson, "Circuits of Promotion," 61.

53. Gruneau and Whitson, *Hockey Night in Canada*, 97.

54. Lorenz, "Bowing Down to Babe Ruth," 30-31.

55. Elliott J. Gorn and Warren Goldstein, *A Brief History of American Sports* (New York: Hill and Wang, 1993), 195.

56. Benjamin G. Rader, *In Its Own Image: How Television Has Transformed Sports* (New York: Free Press, 1984), 24-25.

57. Vipond, *The Mass Media in Canada*, 41-43.

58. *Annual Report of the Canadian Broadcasting Corporation for the Fiscal Year Ended March 31, 1938* (Ottawa: The King's Printer, 1938), 11.

59. Gruneau and Whitson, *Hockey Night in Canada*, 100. See also Scott Young, *The Boys of Saturday Night: Inside Hockey Night in Canada* (Toronto: Macmillan, 1990), 38-63.

60. Gruneau and Whitson, *Hockey Night in Canada*, 100-101.

61. Kidd, *The Struggle for Canadian Sport*, 222-223, 254-259.

62. Nattrass, "Sport and Television," 30.

63. Kidd, *The Struggle for Canadian Sport*, 223.

64. Gruneau and Whitson, *Hockey Night in Canada*, 101.

65. For examples of different approaches to the study of media, see Lawrence A. Wenner, ed., *MediaSport* (London: Routledge, 1998).

66. Michael Oriard, *Reading Football: How the Popular Press Created an American Spectacle* (Chapel Hill: University of North Carolina Press, 1993); Michael Oriard, *King Football: Sport and Spectacle in the Golden Age of Radio and Newsreels, Movies and Magazines, the Weekly and the Daily Press* (Chapel Hill: University of North Carolina Press, 2001).

67. Oriard, *Reading Football*, 115.

68. Oriard, *King Football*, 171-175.

69. Oriard, *King Football*, 173, 175.

70. Carly Adams, "'Queens of the Ice Lanes': The Preston Rivulettes and Women's Hockey in Canada, 1931-1940," *Sport History Review* 39, no. 1 (2008): 1-29; Carly Adams, "Organizing Hockey for Women: The Ladies Ontario Hockey Association and the Fight for Legitimacy, 1922-1940," in *Coast to Coast: Hockey in Canada to the Second World War*, ed. John Chi-Kit Wong (Toronto: University of Toronto Press, 2009), 132-159; Carly Adams, "Troubling Bodies: 'The Canadian Girl,' the Ice Rink, and the Banff Winter Carnival," *Journal of Canadian Studies* 48, no. 3 (2014): 200-220.

71. Adams, "Troubling Bodies," 201.

72. Adams, "Troubling Bodies," 201.

73. Adams, "Troubling Bodies," 204.

74. Adams, "Troubling Bodies," 211.

75. Adams, "Troubling Bodies," 211. See also Adams, "Organizing Hockey for Women," 147-152.

76. Mark Dyreson, "Icons of Liberty or Objects of Desire? American Women Olympians and the Politics of Consumption," *Journal of Contemporary History* 38, no. 3 (2003): 435-460.

77. Dyreson, "Icons of Liberty or Objects of Desire," 443.

78. Dyreson, "Icons of Liberty or Objects of Desire," 443. See also David B. Welky, "Viking Girls, Mermaids, and Little Brown Men: U.S. Journalism and the 1932 Olympics," *Journal of Sport History* 24, no. 1 (1997): 33-35.

79. *Toronto Star*, August 7, 1928, 7. See also Welky, "Viking Girls," 28-31.

80. *Calgary Herald*, August 6, 1928, 1, 6; August 7, 1928, 6; *Manitoba Free Press*, August 6, 1928, 14; August 8, 1928, 6; *Edmonton Journal*, August 7, 1928, 1, 10; Lorenz, "In the Field of Sport," 205.

81. Gruneau and Whitson, *Hockey Night in Canada*, 85. See also Gorn and Goldstein, *A Brief History of American Sports*, 188-197.

82. Colin D. Howell, *Northern Sandlots: A Social History of Maritime Baseball* (Toronto: University of Toronto Press, 1995), especially 171-184.

83. Howell, *Northern Sandlots*, 173.

84. Howell, *Northern Sandlots*, 174.

85. Howell, *Northern Sandlots*, 176.

86. Andrew C. Holman, "Telling Stories About Indigeneity and Canadian Sport: The Spectacular Cree and Ojibway Indian Hockey Barnstorming Tour of North America, 1928," *Sport History Review* 43, no. 2 (2012): 178-205.

87. Holman, "Telling Stories," 178.

88. Holman, "Telling Stories," 178, 181.

89. Holman, "Telling Stories," 188. See also Oriard, *Reading Football*, 237-238; Oriard, *King Football*, 285-291. Such stereotypes still underlie contemporary representations of Indigenous people, practices, and symbols associated with sporting mascots. See Laurel R. Davis, "The Problems With Native American Mascots," *Multicultural Education* 9, no. 4 (2002): 11-14.

90. Holman, "Telling Stories," 188.

91. Holman, "Telling Stories," 188-189.

92. Holman, "Telling Stories," 181.

93. Holman, "Telling Stories," 190-192.

94. Holman, "Telling Stories," 194.

95. Holman, "Telling Stories," 197.

96. Holman, "Telling Stories," 198.

97. Howard Ramos and Kevin Gosine, "'The Rocket': Newspaper Coverage of the Death of a Quebec Cultural Icon, A Canadian Hockey Player," *Journal of Canadian Studies* 36, no. 4 (2001): 9-31; Jean Harvey, "Whose Sweater Is This? The Changing Meanings of Hockey in Quebec," in *Artificial Ice: Hockey, Culture, and Commerce*, ed. David Whitson and Richard Gruneau (Peterborough, ON: Broadview Press and Garamond Press, 2006), 29-52; Suzanne Laberge, "The Richard/Campbell Affair: Hockey as the Catalyst for Quebec Francophone Affirmation," in *The Montreal Canadiens: Rethinking a Legend*, ed. Nicolas Moreau and Audrey Laurin-Lamothe, trans. Howard Scott (Toronto: University of Toronto Press, 2015), 9-24.

98. Laberge, "The Richard/Campbell Affair," 12.

99. Laberge, "The Richard/Campbell Affair," 15.

100. Laberge, "The Richard/Campbell Affair," 17-19.

101. Lorenz, "In the Field of Sport," 148-152.

102. *Toronto Globe*, January 20, 1855, 2; Lorenz, "In the Field of Sport," 150.

103. *Toronto Globe*, January 22, 1855, 2.

104. Howell, *Northern Sandlots*, 61.

105. Benedict Anderson, *Imagined Communities: Reflections on the Origin and Spread of Nationalism* (London: Verso, 1983); Stephen Kern, *The Culture of Time and Space 1880-1918* (Cambridge: Harvard University Press, 1983); Lorenz, "A Lively Interest on the Prairies," 196-197.

106. Robert Ayre, "The American Empire," *The Canadian Forum* 7, no. 76 (1927), 105; Lorenz, "A Lively Interest on the Prairies," 213-214.

107. Gruneau and Whitson, *Hockey Night in Canada*, 86-103; Kidd, *The Struggle for Canadian Sport*, 184-231, 267; Thompson and Seager, *Canada 1922-1939*, 187-190.

108. Kidd, *The Struggle for Canadian Sport*, 226-229, 254-270.

109. Kidd, *The Struggle for Canadian Sport*, 258, 259, 227.

110. Paul Rutherford, *When Television Was Young: Primetime Canada 1952-1967* (Toronto: University of Toronto Press, 1990), 240.

111. Rutherford, *The Making of the Canadian Media*, 61-62.

112. Whitson, "Circuits of Promotion," 59.

113. J.M. Bumsted, "Canada and American Culture in the 1950s," in *Interpreting Canada's Past*, vol. 2 (Toronto: Oxford University Press, 1986), 405.

114. Bumsted, "Canada and American Culture," 405-406.

115. Nattrass, "Sport and Television in Canada," 38.

116. Rutherford, *When Television Was Young*, 242.

117. Rutherford, *When Television Was Young*, 245-46.

118. Rutherford, *When Television Was Young*, 227-228.

119. Michael Nolan, *CTV: The Network That Means Business* (Edmonton: University of Alberta Press, 2001), 27.

120. Nattrass, "Sport and Television in Canada," 77.

121. Rutherford, *When Television Was Young*, 461; Varda Burstyn, *The Rites of Men: Manhood, Politics, and the Culture of Sport* (Toronto: University of Toronto Press, 1999), 115.

122. Rutherford, *When Television Was Young*, 323.

123. Nattrass, "Sport and Television in Canada," 226.

124. Nolan, *CTV*, 145.

125. Rutherford, *When Television Was Young*, 242.

126. Rutherford, *When Television Was Young*, 113.

127. Andrew Stewart and William H.N. Hull, *Canadian Television Policy and the Board of Broadcast Governors, 1958-1968* (Edmonton: University of Alberta Press, 1994), 109.

128. Jay Scherer, Jean Harvey, and Marcela Hofman-Mourão, "Power Plays and Olympic Divisions: Bilingualism and the Politics of Canadian Viewing Rights at the 2010 Winter Olympic Games," *Media, Culture & Society* 38, no. 6 (2016): 864-880.

129. Robert Sparks, "'Delivering the Male': Sports, Canadian Television, and the Making of TSN," *Canadian Journal of Communication* 17 (1992): 319-342.

130. Sparks, "Delivering the Male," 334.

131. Sparks, "Delivering the Male," 335; Hall, *The Girl and the Game*, 321.

132. Whitson, "Circuits of Promotion," 67, 59.

133. See Nicole Neverson, "Build It and the Women Will Come? WTSN and the Advent of Canadian Digital Television," *Canadian Journal of Communication* 35, no. 1 (2010): 27-48; Cheryl Cooky, Michael A. Messner, and Michela Musto, "'It's Dude Time!': A Quarter Century of Excluding Women's Sports in Televised News and Highlight Shows," *Communication & Sport* 3, no. 3 (2015): 261-287; Michela Musto, Cheryl Cooky, and Michael A. Messner, "'From Fizzle to Sizzle!': Televised Sports News and the Production of Gender-Bland Sexism," *Gender & Society* 31, no. 5 (2017): 573-596.

134. Michael A. Messner, *Taking the Field: Women, Men, and Sports* (Minneapolis and London: University of Minnesota Press, 2002), xviii.

Chapter 13

1. Lee Maracle, "The Post-Colonial Imagination," in *Unhomely States: Theorizing English-Canadian Postcolonialism*, ed. Cynthia Sugars (Peterborough, ON: Broadview Press, 2004), 206.

2. Don Morrow, "Canadian Sport History: A Critical Essay, *Journal of Sport History* 10, no. 1 (1983): 67-79.

3. Alan Metcalfe, *Canada Learns to Play: The Emergence of Organized Sport, 1807-1914* (Toronto: McClelland & Stewart, 1987).

4. See Morrow, "Canadian Sport History," 74; Nancy B. Bouchier, "Canadian Sport History," *Acadiensis* 28, no. 1 (1998): 98-103.

5. Metcalfe, *Canada Learns to Play*, 14.

6. Metcalfe, *Canada Learns to Play*, 10-11.

7. Bouchier, "Canadian Sport History, 98.

8. Metcalfe, *Canada Learns to Play*, 14.

9. A number of scholarly monographs, edited collections, and independent works that focus on Indigenous experiences in Canadian sport history have been produced since the mid-1980s. See Bruce Kidd, "In Defence of Tom Longboat," *Canadian Journal of Sport History* 14, no. 1 (1983): 34-63; Victoria Paraschak, "Native Sport History: Pitfalls to Promise," *Canadian Journal of Sport History* 20, no. 1 (1989): 57-68; Michael K. Heine and Kevin Wamsley, "'Kickfest at Dawson City': Native Peoples and the Sports of the Klondike Gold Rush," *Sport History Review* 27, no. 1 (1996): 72-86; Christine O'Bonsawin, "Failed TEST: Aboriginal Sport Policy and the Olympian Firth Sisters,"

(master's thesis, University of Western Ontario, 2002); Janice Forsyth, "The Power to Define: A History of the Tom Longboat Awards, 1951-2001," (PhD diss., University of Western Ontario, 2005); Christine O'Bonsawin, "Spectacles, Policy, and Social Memory: Images of Canadian Indians at World's Fairs and Olympic Games," (PhD diss., University of Western Ontario, 2007); Janice Forsyth and Audrey Giles, eds., *Aboriginal Peoples and Sport in Canada: Historical Foundations and Contemporary Issues* (Vancouver: UBC Press, 2013); Allan Downey, *The Creator's Game: Lacrosse, Identity, and Indigenous Nationhood* (Vancouver: UBC Press, 2018), to name a few.

10. Metcalfe, *Canada Learns to Play*, 14.

11. In considering imperialism and colonialism, these terms are often used interchangeably to discuss the exploitation and subjection of seemingly underdeveloped lands and peoples. I understand these concepts to have separate and distinct meanings. Therefore, for this chapter, imperialism is characterized by the practices, theories, and attitudes of a dominant metropolitan centre ruling a distant territory. In the context of Canada, colonialism is the consequence of imperialism, characterized by the attempted physical eradication of Indigenous peoples, expropriation of Indigenous lands, and permanent occupation by the settlers.

12. Metcalfe, *Canada Learns to Play*, 10.

13. Homi K. Bhabha, *The Location of Culture* (New York: Routledge, 1994).

14. The Indian Act generally consolidated existing Indian policy, notably the Gradual Civilization Act, 1857, and the Gradual Enfranchisement Act, 1869.

15. Pamela Palmater, "Genocide, Indian Policy, and Legislated Elimination of Indians in Canada," *Aboriginal Policy Studies* 3, no. 2 (2014), 30.

16. Palmater, "Genocide, Indian Policy and Legislated Elimination," 30.

17. David Brown, "Canadian Imperialism and Sporting Exchanges: The Nineteenth-Century Cultural Experience of Cricket and Lacrosse," *Canadian Journal of History of Sport* 18, no. 1 (May 1987): 55-66; Don Morrow, "The Institutionalization of Sport: A Case Study of Canadian Lacrosse, 1844-1914," *International Journal for the History of Sport* 9, no. 2 (1992): 235-251; Kevin B. Wamsley, "Nineteenth Century Sports Tours, State Formation, and Canadian Foreign Policy," *Sporting Traditions* 13, no. 2 (1997): 73-89; Donald M. Fisher, *Lacrosse: A History of the Game* (Baltimore: Johns Hopkins University Press, 2002), 30-32; Gillian Poulter, "Snowshoeing and Lacrosse: Canada's Nineteenth Century 'National Game,'" *Culture, Sport, Society* 6, nos. 2/3 (2003): 293-320; and Downey, *The Creator's Game*, 62-69.

18. Carl Berger, *The Sense of Power: Studies in the Ideas of Canadian Imperialism, 1867-1914* (Toronto: University of Toronto Press, 1970), 3-4.

19. Fisher, *Lacrosse: A History of the Game*, 30-31.

20. See David Blanchard, "Entertainment, Dance and Northern Mohawk Showmanship," *American Indian Quarterly* 7, no. 1 (1983): 2-26 and Christine M. O'Bonsawin, "Humour, Irony, and Indigenous Peoples: A Re-Reading of the Historical Record of the 1904 St. Louis Olympic Championship," *Sport History Review* 48, no. 2 (2017): 168-185.

21. Clipping from the *Newcastle Daily Journal* in *Montreal Amateur Athletic Association (MAAA) Scrapbook*, 15: 176, as cited in Don Morrow, "The Canadian Image Abroad: The Great Lacrosse Tours of 1876 and 1833," in *Proceedings of the Fifth Canadian Symposium on History of Sport and Physical Education* (Toronto: University of Toronto, 1982), 16.

22. Homi K. Bhabha, "The Other Question . . .," *Screen* 24, no. 6 (1983), 19.

23. "What Have We Learned: Principles of Truth and Reconciliation," Truth and Reconciliation Commission of Canada (2015), 5.

24. Paul N. Daniel, *We Were Not the Savages: A Mi'kmaq Perspective on the Collision Between European and Native American Civilizations* (Halifax: Fernwood, 2000), 109.

25. Mi'kma'ki is the territory of the Mi'kmaq people.

26. Scalping Proclamation, Edward Cornwallis, 1749, CO 217/9/118 (F100), microfilm at the Public Archives of Nova Scotia (PANS), as cited in Daniel, *We Were Not the Savages*, 110.

27. Daniel, *We Were Not the* Savages, 116.

28. American Medical Association, "Smallpox as a Biological Weapon: Medical and Public Health Management," *Journal of the American Medical Association* 281 (1999): 2127-2137.

29. Norbert Finzsch, "'[. . .] Extirpate or Remove That Vermine': Genocide, Biological Warfare, and Settler Imperialism in the Eighteenth and Early Nineteenth Century," *Journal of Genocide Research* 10, no. 2 (2008): 215-232; Tom Swanky, *The True Story of Canada's "War" of Extermination Plus the Tsilhqot'in and Other First Nations Resistance* (Surrey: Dragon Heart Enterprises, 2012); Tom Swanky, *The Smallpox War in Nuxalk Territory* (Surrey: Dragon Heart Enterprises, 2016).

30. James Daschuk, *Clearing the Plains: Disease, Politics of Starvation, and the Loss of Aboriginal Life* (Regina: University of Regina Press, 2013), 99-127.

31. Palmater, "Genocide, Indian Policy and Legislated Elimination," 32.

32. In 1850, the legislatures for Upper and Lower Canada passed parallel acts for the "protection" of Indians within their respective territories throughout the Province of Canada. The term *Indian* was defined in An Act for the Better Protection of Lands and Property of the Indians in Lower Canada to include "any person deemed to be Indian by birth or blood; any person reputed to belong to a particular band or body of Indians; and any person who married an Indian or was adopted by Indians." The 1857 Act to Encourage the Gradual Civilization of the Indian tribes in the Province sought to assimilate Indigenous peoples by allowing those Indians who were debt free, educated, and "of good moral character" to apply for a land grant, thereby encouraging concepts of private property and wealth accumulation, through a process of assimilation. See An Act for the Better Protection of Lands and Property of the Indians in Lower Canada, S.C. 1850, and An Act to Encourage the Gradual Civilization of Indian Tribes in this Province, and to Amend the Laws Relating to Indians, S.C. 1857.

33. "Provided always that any Indian woman marrying any other than an Indian, shall cease to be an Indian within the meaning of this Act, nor shall the children issue of such marriage be considered as Indians within the meaning of this Act; Provided also, that any Indian woman marrying an Indian of any other tribe, band or body shall cease to be a member of the tribe, band or body to which she formerly belonged, and become a member of the tribe, band or body of which her husband is a member, and the children, issue of this marriage, shall belong to their father's tribe only." See An Act for the Gradual Enfranchisement of Indians, the Better Management of Indian Affairs, and to Extend the Provisions of the Act, 31st Victoria, S.C. 1869, ch. 6.

34. "The term Indian means: First. Any male person of Indian blood reputed to belong to a particular band; Second. Any child of such a person; Thirdly. Any woman who is or was married to such a person." See An Act to Amend and Consolidate the Laws Respecting Indians, S.C. 1876, ch. 3.

35. "The Governor in Council may make regulation, which shall have the force of law, for the committal by justices or Indian agents of children of Indian blood under the age of sixteen years, to such industrial school or boarding school, there to be kept, cared for and educated for a period beyond the time at which such children shall reach the age of eighteen years." See An Act to Amend and Consolidate the Laws Respecting

Indians, S.C. 1894, ch. 138(2) and "Canada's Residential Schools: The History, Part 1 Origins to 1939: Final Report of the Truth and Reconciliation Commission of Canada Volume 1," Truth and Reconciliation Commission of Canada (2015).

36. David Davis, *Showdown at Shepherd's Bush: The 1908 Olympic Marathon and the Three Runners Who Launched a Sporting Craze* (New York: Thomas Dunne Books, 2012), 28-29.

37. Davis, *Showdown at Shepherd's Bush*, 29.

38. "Canada's Residential Schools," Truth and Reconciliation Commission of Canada.

39. The section of the Indian Act prohibiting Indian festivals, dances, and ceremonies was introduced in 1884 and amended in 1886, 1895, 1906, 1914, 1918, 1926-1927, 1927, and 1932-1933.

40. "Every Indian or other person who engages in or assists in celebrating the Indian festival known as the 'Potlatch' or in the Indian dance known as the 'Tamanawas' is guilty of a misdemeanor, and shall be liable to imprisonment." See An Act Further to Amend the Indian Act, 1880, S.C. 1894, ch. 27(3).

41. Alex Williams, *The Pass System: Life Under Segregation in Canada*, DVD, directed by Alex Williams (Toronto: VTape, 2016).

42. O'Bonsawin, "Humour, Irony, and Indigenous Peoples," 168-184.

43. For example, in the first comprehensive anthology on Indigenous sport in Canada, *Aboriginal Peoples and Sport in Canada: Historical Foundations and Contemporary Issues*, nominal attention is paid to the years 1915 to 1944. In the second edition of *The Girl and the Game: A History of Women's Sport in Canada*, M. Ann Hall sheds important light on many Indigenous women who achieved noteworthy success in sport, highlighting the accomplishments of athletes such as Phyllis "Yogi" Bomberry, Martha Benjamin, Roseanne Allen, and Sharon and Shirley Firth. In drawing attention to these glaring omissions, it should not be interpreted as criticisms of these seminal works, but rather testaments to the fact that we know very little about the participation of Indigenous peoples in sport, at this time, for reasons stated in the text. See Janice Forsyth and Audrey Giles, eds., *Aboriginal Peoples and Sport in Canada: Historical Foundations and Contemporary Issues* (Vancouver: UBC Press, 2013) and M. Ann Hall, *The Girl and the Game: A History of Women's Sport in Canada*, 2nd ed. (Toronto: University of Toronto Press, 2016).

44. Kevin Wamsley and Don Morrow, *Sport in Canada: A History* (Don Mills, ON: Oxford University Press, 2005), 229-231.

45. An Act to Amend the Indian Act, S.C. 1880, ch. 9.

46. National Archives of Canada, Record Group 10, vol. 6810, file 470-2-3, vol, 7, 55 (L-3) and 63 (N-3).

47. Brian Titley, *A Narrow Vision: Duncan Campbell Scott and the Administration of Indian Affairs* (Vancouver: UBC Press, 1986), 201-204.

48. "What We Have Learned: Principles of Truth and Reconciliation," Truth and Reconciliation of Canada Final Report, 2015.

49. The Truth and Reconciliation Commission confirmed 3,200 on the Register of Confirmed Deaths of Named Residential School Students and the Register of Confirmed Deaths of Unnamed Residential School Students; however, they recognize that this figure is inconclusive, notably because the government stopped recording the deaths of children because of the alarming death rates within schools. See "Canada's Residential Schools: Missing Children and Unmarked Burials: The Final Report of the Truth and Reconciliation Commission, Volume 4," Truth and Reconciliation Commission of Canada, 2015.

50. Peter H. Bryce, *The Story of a National Crime: An Appeal for Justice to the Indians of Canada—The Wards of the Nation; Our Allies in the Revolutionary War; Our Brothers-in-Arms-in-the-Great War* (Ottawa: James Hope and Sons, 1922), 5-6.

51. M. Ann Hall, *The Grads Are Playing Tonight! The Story of the Edmonton Commercial Graduates Basketball Club* (Edmonton: University of Alberta Press, 2011).

52. See Hall, *The Grads Are Playing Tonight!* 76.

53. As paraphrased from editorials in Bruce Kidd, "Canadian Opposition to the 1936 Olympics in Germany," *Canadian Journal of the History of Sport and Physical Education* 9, no. 2 (1978): 22.

54. Andy Lytle, *Toronto Daily Star*, November 8, 1935, in Kidd, "Canadian Opposition to the 1936 Olympics." 429.

55. James Pope, Artistic Dances Competition, in "Canada at the Eleventh Olympiad 1936 in Germany," *Official Report of the Canadian Olympic Committee 1933-1936*, ed. W.A. Fry (Dunnsville: Boris Volkoff Collection), n.p..

56. Augustine Bridle, "Volkoff School Gives Olympic Entry Show: Finale of Dance Fantasias Is Indian Legend to Feature Canada—15 Going to Berlin," *Toronto Star*, May 28, 1936.

57. Canada officially signed the UN Declaration on November 9, 1945. See *Charter of the United Nations*, United Nations, October 24, 1945, accessed April 10, 2019, https://treaties.un.org/doc/Publication/CTC/uncharter.pdf.

58. Universal Declaration of Human Rights, United Nations, December 10, 1948.

59. William A. Schabas, "Canada and the Adoption of the Universal Declaration of Human Rights," *McGill Law Journal* 43, no. 2 (1998): 403-441.

60. United Nations Convention on the Prevention and Punishment of the Crime of Genocide, United Nations, December 9, 1948.

61. Schabas, "Canada and the Adoption." 410.

62. David B. MacDonald and Graham Hudson, "The Genocide Question in Indian Residential Schools," *Canadian Journal of Political Science* 45, no. 2 (2012): 427-449.

63. Principal legislation includes the Prohibition of Mixed Marriages (1949), Population Registration Act (1950), the Group Areas Act (1950), the Immortality Act (1950), the Reservation and Separate Amenities Act (1953), the Bantu Education Act (1953), and various Pass Laws Acts (1952 and thereafter). See Malcolm MacLean, "Revisiting (and Revising?) Sports Boycotts: From Rugby Against South Africa to Soccer in Israel," *International Journal of the History of Sport* 31, no. 15 (2014): 1832-1851.

64. MacLean, "Revisiting (and Revising?) Sports Boycotts," 1833.

65. Jules Boykoff, *Power Games: A Political History of the Olympics* (London: Verso, 2016), 97-102.

66. "South Africa Banned From Olympics," BBC News, August 18, 1964, accessed September 14, 2018, http://news.bbc.co.uk/onthisday/hi/dates/stories/august/18/newsid_3547000/3547872.stm.

67. Bruce Kidd, "The Campaign Against Sport in South Africa," *International Journal* 43, no. 4 (1988): 643-664.

68. Linda Freeman, *The Ambiguous Champion: Canada and South Africa in the Trudeau and Mulroney Years* (Toronto: University of Toronto Press, 1997), 3-6.

69. United Nations Convention on the Elimination of All Forms of Racial Discrimination, United Nations, December 21, 1965 (entry into force January 4, 1969), 2.

70. Bruce Kidd and Peter Donnelly, "Human Rights in Sports," *International Review for the Sociology of Sport* 35, no. 2 (2000): 131-148.

71. United Nations Convention on the Elimination of All Forms of Racial Discrimination.

72. Andy Rigg, "Montreal Olympics: African Boycott of the 1976 Games 'Changed the World,'" *Montreal Gazette*, July 19, 2016, accessed September 14, 2018, https://montrealgazette.com/sports/montreal-olympics-african-boycott-of-1976-games-changed-the-world.

73. Canada, Royal Commission on Aboriginal Peoples, *Report of the Royal Commission on Aboriginal Peoples: Volume 1 – Looking Forward, Looking Back* (Ottawa: The Commission, 1996), 285-289.

74. Sarah Wright Cardinal, "Beyond the Sixties Scoop: Reclaiming Indigenous Identity, Reconnection to Place, and Reframing Understandings of Being Indigenous," (PhD dissertation, University of Victoria, 2017), 1.

75. Maria-Carolina Cambre, "Terminologies of Control: Tracing the Canadian-South African Connection in a Word: *Politikon* 34, no. 1 (April 2017): 19-34.

76. Simonne Horwitz, "'Apartheid in a Parka'? Roots and Longevity of the Canada-South Africa Comparison," *Journal of South African and American Studies* 17, no. 4 (2016): 467.

77. Frantz Fanon, *The Wretched of the Earth* (New York: Grove Press, 1963), 9.

78. According to Eve Tuck and K. Wayne Yang, *external colonialism* "denotes the expropriation of fragment of Indigenous worlds, animals, plants and human beings, extracting them in order to transport them to—and build wealth, the privilege, or feed the appetites of—the colonizers, who get marked as the first world." Conversely, *internal colonialism* is "the biopolitical geopolitical management of people, land, flora and fauna within the 'domestic' borders of the imperial nation." See Eve Tuck and K. Wayne Yang, "Decolonization Is Not a Metaphor," *Decolonization: Indigeneity, Education, and Society* 1, no. 1 (2012): 4.

79. Tuck and Yang, "Decolonization Is Not a Metaphor," 3.

80. Jeff Corntassel, "Re-envisioning Resurgence: Indigenous Pathways to Resurgence and Sustainable Self-Determination," *Decolonization: Indigeneity, Education, and Society* 1, no. 1 (2012): 89.

81. Coll Thrush, *Indigenous London: Native Travelers at the Heart of Empire* (New Haven: Yale University Press, 2016), 173-204.

82. Hamar Foster, Heather Raven, and Jeremy Webber, eds., *Let Right Be Done: Aboriginal Title, the Calder Case, and the Future of Indigenous Rights* (Vancouver: UBC Press, 2007), 241-245.

83. Indian Act, R.S.C. 1927, s. 141.

84. "Aboriginal title refers to the right to exclusive use and occupation of land, which is the rough equivalent of full ownership, although the courts have also made clear that Aboriginal title is *sui generis*—that is, not directly comparable to any other interest in the law." See Foster, Raven, and Webber, *Let Right Be Done*, 19.

85. Peter J. Usher, Frank J. Tough, and Robert M. Galois, "Reclaiming the Land: Aboriginal Title, Treaty Rights and Land Claims in Canada," *Applied Geography* 12 (1992): 109-132.

86. Arthur Manuel and Ron M. Derrickson, *Unsettling Canada: A National Wake-Up Call* (Toronto: Between the Lines, 2015), 65-75.

87. Constitution Act, 1982, Schedule B to the Canada Act 1982 (UK), 1982, ch. 11.

88. Royal Commission on Aboriginal Peoples. *Report of the Royal Commission on Aboriginal Peoples* (Ottawa, 1996).

89. Tsawwassen First Nation Final Agreement (2009), accessed September 16, 2018, www.bctreaty.ca/sites/default/files/Tsawwassen_final_initial_1.pdf.

90. "Why We Resist 2010," No Olympics on Stolen Native Lands: Resist the 2010 Corporate Circus, accessed May 8, 2008, www.no2010.com.

91. Rafe Mair, "Harriet Nahanee Did Not Die in Vain," *The Tyee*, March 5, 2007, accessed June 4, 2014, http://thetyee.ca/Views/2007/03/05/Eagleridge.

92. United Nations General Assembly, United Nations Declaration on the Rights of Indigenous Peoples, 61st session, October 2, 2007.

93. United Nations General Assembly, United Nations Declaration on the Rights of Indigenous Peoples, 6.

94. United Nations General Assembly, United Nations Declaration on the Rights of Indigenous Peoples, 19.

95. "Statement of Support on the United Nations Declaration on the Rights of Indigenous Peoples, Indigenous Affairs and Northern Development, November 12, 2010, accessed May 9, 2018, www.aadnc-aandc.gc.ca/eng/1309374239861/1309374546142.

96. "Statement of Support," Indigenous Affairs and Northern Development.

Chapter 14

1. Simon C. Darnell, Russell Field, and Bruce Kidd, *The History and Politics of Sport-for-Development: Activists, Ideologues and Reformers* (London: Palgrave Macmillan, 2019), 10, emphasis original.

2. Bruce Kidd, *The Struggle for Canadian Sport* (Toronto: University of Toronto Press, 1996), 28. As Kidd notes: "Along with others from the middle and working classes who established voluntary associations to promote public libraries, gardening clubs, and popular science lectures in the interests of purposeful leisure or 'rational recreation,' the middle-class amateurs hoped that sports would encourage good citizenship, social harmony, and nationalism."

3. Robert K. Barney, "The Olympic Games in Modern Times," in *Onward to the Olympics: Historical Perspectives on the Olympic Games*, ed. Gerald P. Schaus and Stephen R. Wenn (Waterloo, ON: Wilfrid Laurier University Press, 2007), 223.

4. Kidd, *The Struggle for Canadian Sport*, 46.

5. Kidd, *The Struggle for Canadian Sport*, 49.

6. "Obituary: Theodore Leighton Pennell," *British Medical Journal* 1: 761, cited in J.A. Mangan, "Soccer as Moral Training: Missionary Intentions and Imperial Legacies," *Soccer & Society* 2, no. 2: 43.

7. See Darnell, Field, and Kidd, *History and Politics of Sport-for-Development*, chapter 3, Institutionalizing and Internationalizing Sport-for-Good.

8. Stefan Hübner, "Muscular Christianity and the Western Civilizing Mission: Elwood S. Brown, the YMCA, and the Idea of the Far Eastern Championship Games," *Diplomatic History* 39, no. 3: 538.

9. Jorge B. Vargas, "Athletic Progress in the Philippines," in *Encyclopedia of the Philippines*, vol. 10, ed. Zoilo M. Galang (Manila: Philippines Education Co., 1936), 388.

10. Stefan Huebner, *Pan-Asian Sports and the Emergence of Modern Asia, 1913–1974* (Singapore: NUS Press, 2016), 24.

11. Cited in Huebner, *Pan-Asian Sports*, 24.

12. J.H. Crocker, *1917 Annual Report*, Young Men's Christian Association, China, 46. The full report can be found here: https://umedia.lib.umn.edu/item/p16022coll358:9156.

13. Crocker, *1917 Annual Report*.

14. Andrew D. Morris, *Marrow of the Nation: A History of Sport and Physical Culture in Republican China* (Berkeley: University of California Press, 2004), 22.

15. Robert Harney and Harold Troper, *Immigrants: A Portrait of the Urban Experience, 1890-1930* (Toronto: Van Nostrand Reinhold, 1975), v-vi.

16. Paul Axelrod, *The Promise of Schooling: Education in Canada* (Toronto: University of Toronto Press, 1997), 117.

17. Cited in Axelrod, *The Promise of Schooling*, 117.

18. Cited in Royden Loewen and Gerald Friesen, *Immigrants in Prairie Cities: Ethnic Diversity in Twentieth-Century Canada* (Toronto: University of Toronto Press 2009), 45.

19. Robert Harney, "Homo Ludens and Ethnicity," *Polyphony* 7, no. 1: 1.

20. K.W. Sokolyk, "The Role of Ukrainian Sports Teams, Clubs, and Leagues, 1924-52," *Journal of Ukrainian Studies* 16: 133.

21. Harney, "Homo Ludens and Ethnicity," 2.

22. Robert F. Harney, "Ethnicity and Neighbourhoods," in *Gathering Place: Peoples and Neighbourhoods of Toronto*, ed. Robert F. Harney (Toronto: Multicultural History Society of Ontario, 1985), 8.

23. Shannon Jette, "Little/Big Ball: The Vancouver Asahi Baseball Story," *Sport History Review* 37, no, 1: 6.

24. Jette, "Little/Big Ball," 7.

25. Sokolyk, "The Role of Ukrainian Sports Teams," 136.

26. Sokolyk, 134, notes that "Stich" was "a Ukrainian nationalistic organization whose ultimate goal was an independent Ukraine."

27. Sokolyk, "The Role of Ukrainian Sports Teams," 134, 136.

28. Cited in Sokolyk, "The Role of Ukrainian Sports Teams," 136.

29. Bruce Kidd, "'We Must Maintain a Balance Between Propaganda and Serious Athletics'—the Workers' Sport Movement in Canada, 1924-1936," *Sport in Society* 16, no. 4: 568.

30. Kidd, "'We Must Maintain a Balance,'" 569.

31. C. Nathan Hatton, *Thrashing Seasons: Sporting Culture in Manitoba and the Genesis of Prairie Wrestling* (Winnipeg: University of Manitoba Press, 2016), 207-14.

32. Kidd, "'We Must Maintain a Balance,'" 567.

33. Kidd, "'We Must Maintain a Balance,'" 567.

34. Kidd, *The Struggle for Canadian Sport*, 154.

35. See M. Ann Hall and Bruce Kidd, "History and Individual Memory: The Story of Eva Dawes," *Sport History Review* 48, no. 2: 126-143.

36. Hall and Kidd, "History and Individual Memory," 136.

37. Florence Carpentier and Jean-Pierre Lefèvre, "The Modern Olympic Movement, Women's Sport and the Social Order During the Inter-war Period," *International Journal of the History of Sport* 23, no. 7 (2006): 1112-1127.

38. Minutes of the fourth FSFI Congress, 1926, cited in Carpentier and Lefèvre, "The Modern Olympic Movement," 1120.

39. Kidd, *The Struggle for Canadian Sport*, 95.

40. *Daily Clarion*, July 4, 1936, 1, cited in Richard Menkis and Harold Troper, *More Than Just Games: Canada and the 1936 Olympics* (Toronto: University of Toronto Press), 163.

41. Charlotte Macdonald, *Strong, Beautiful and Modern: National Fitness in Britain, New Zealand, Australia and Canada, 1935-1960* (Vancouver: UBC Press, 2011), 127.

42. Macdonald, *Strong, Beautiful and Modern*, 132.

43. Macdonald, *Strong, Beautiful and Modern*, 144.

44. Macdonald, *Strong, Beautiful and Modern*, 147.

45. Donald Macintosh, Tom Bedecki, and C.E.S. Franks, *Sport and Politics in Canada: Federal Government Involvement Since 1961* (Montreal: McGill-Queen's University Press, 1987), 12.

46. Macdonald, *Strong, Beautiful and Modern*, 149; Macintosh, Bedecki, and Franks, *Sport and Politics in Canada*, 11.

47. Bruce Kidd, "The Philosophy of Excellence: Olympic Performers, Class Power and the Canadian State," *Sport in Society* 16, no. 4 (2013): 376.

48. Cited in Russell Field and Bruce Kidd, "Canada and the Pan-American Games," *International Journal of the History of Sport* 33, nos. 1/2 (2016): 221.

49. Macintosh, Bedecki, and Franks, *Sport and Politics in Canada*, 89. See also Lisa M. Kikulis, Trevor Slack, and C.R. Hinings, "Sector-Specific Patterns of Organization Design Change," *Journal of Management Studies* 32, no. 1 (1995): 77-78.

50. Cited in Kidd, "The Philosophy of Excellence," 377.

51. Kidd, "The Philosophy of Excellence," 377.

52. Kidd, "The Philosophy of Excellence," 377.

53. Field and Kidd, "Canada and the Pan-American Games," 224.

54. Victoria Lamb Drover, "ParticipAction, Healthism, and the Crafting of a Social Memory (1971-1999), *Journal of the Canadian Historical Association* 25, no. 1 (2014): 278.

55. Drover, "ParticipAction," 282.

56. Guy Faulkner, Lira Yun, Mark S. Tremblay, and John C. Spence, "Exploring the Impact of the 'New' ParticipAction: Overview and Introduction of the Special Issue," *Health Promotion and Chronic Disease Prevention in Canada: Research, Policy and Practice* 38, no, 4 (2018): 153-161.

57. David R. Black, "The Ambiguities of Development: Implications for 'Development Through Sport,'" *Sport in Society* 13, no. 1 (2010): 122.

58. Darnell, Field, and Kidd, *History and Politics of Sport-for-Development*, 4.

59. See Darnell, Field, and Kidd, *History and Politics of Sport-for-Development*, 225-229.

60. Darnell, Field, and Kidd, *History and Politics of Sport-for-Development*, 268.4

Chapter 15

1. For more about Canada's Sports Hall of Fame induction process and the Order of Sport, see www.sportshall.ca/order-of-sport.html?lang=EN.

2. In February 2020, CAAWS rebranded and changed its name to Canadian Women & Sport.

3. An excellent foundational text that engages the use of time in research is Johannes Fabian, *Time and Other: How Anthropology Makes Its Object* (New York: Columbia University Press, 2014).

4. Janice Forsyth, "The Indian Act and the (Re)Shaping of Canadian Aboriginal Sport Practices," *International Journal of Canadian Studies* 35 (2007): 95-111.

5. Katherine Pettipas, *Severing the Ties that Bind: Government Repression of Indigenous Religious Ceremonies on the Prairies* (Winnipeg: University of Manitoba Press, 1994), 107-126.

6. Truth and Reconciliation Commission. *Honoring the Truth, Reconciling for the Future: Summary of the Final Report of the Truth and Reconciliation Commission of Canada* (Ottawa, 2015).

7. Tuck and Yang (2012) make an important point that decolonization is often rendered a discursive and narrative project of progress by settler people and institutions. Thus, focusing our argument here on the reflective practice of fields of study and researchers cannot be understood as the goal or end point but rather a step towards a decolonial transformation of settler colonial societies. See Eve Tuck and K. Wayne Yang, "Decolonization Is Not a Metaphor," *Decolonization: Indigeneity, Education & Society* 1, no. 1 (2012): 2.

8. Bill McKay and Antonia Walmsley. "Maori Time: Notions of Space, Time and Building Form in the South Pacific," *Idea Journal* 4 (2003): 85-95.

9. Leo Killsback, "Indigenous Perceptions of Time: Decolonizing Theory, World History, and the Fate of Human Societies," *American Indian Cultural and Research Journal* 37, no. 4 (2013): 92.

10. Mark Rifkin, *Beyond Settler Time: Temporal Sovereignty and Indigenous Self-Determination* (Durham: Duke University Press, 2017).

11. Don Morrow and Kevin B. Wamsley, *Sport in Canada: A History*, 4th ed. (Don Mills, ON: Oxford University Press, 2016).

12. In a similar vein, Murray et al. ask if "considerations of Indigenous pastimes [in the field of sport history] are relegated to European modernist notions of 'prehistory.'" Murray G. Phillips, Russell Field, Christine O'Bonsawin, and Janice Forsyth, "Indigenous Resurgence, Regeneration, and Decolonization Through Sport History" (special issue), *Journal of Sport History* 46, no. 2 (2019): 143.

13. Phillips et al., "Indigenous Resurgence," 143-324.

14. For an extended analysis, see Malcom Maclean, "Engaging (With) Indigeneity: Decolonization and Indigenous/Indigenizing Sport History" (special issue), *Journal of Sport History* 46, no. 2 (2019): 189-207.

15. Maclean, "Engaging (With) Indigeneity," 204.

16. See Leanne Simpson and Kiera Ladner, *This Is an Honour Song: Twenty Years Since the Blockades* (Winnipeg: APR Books, 2010).

17. "'The terror was brought to us': Memories of Oka Resurface as Rail Blockade Crisis Continues," CBC Radio, February 22, 2020, www.cbc.ca/radio/thehouse/the-terror-was-brought-to-us-memories-of-oka-resurface-as-rail-blockade-crisis-continues-1.5454787, accessed March 15, 2020.

18. Waneek Horn-Miller, "Rally for the Wet'suwet'en," February 24, 2020, www.youtube.com/watch?v=HjGqHXDx9h0, accessed March 15, 2020.

19. Waneek Horn-Miller, "Rally for the Wet'suwet'en."

20. For a broad and comprehensive discussion, see Christine O'Bonsawin's work on colonialism in chapter 13.

21. For a discussion about digital sport history, see Jennifer Guiliano, "Toward a Praxis of Critical Digital Sport History," *Journal of Sport History* 44, no. 2 (2017): 146-159.

22. Jaime Schultz, *Qualifying Times: Points of Change in US Women's Sport* (Chicago: University of Illinois Press, 2014), 187.

INDEX

Note: The italicized *f* and *t* following page numbers refer to figures and tables, respectively.

ABOUT THE EDITOR

Courtesy of University of Lethbridge. Photographer Rob Olson.

Carly Adams, PhD, is a professor in the department of kinesiology and physical education and Board of Governors Research Chair (tier II) at the University of Lethbridge in Alberta, Canada. She teaches courses on sport history, gender, the modern Olympic movement, and oral history. Her research explores sport, recreation, and leisure experiences from the intersections of historical and sociological inquiry, with a focus on gender and community. In collaboration with Dr. Darren Aoki, she is currently working on the Nikkei Memory Capture Project, a community-based oral history project collecting Japanese-Canadian histories in southern Alberta. Her work has appeared in, among others, *Journal of Sport History*, *Journal of Canadian Studies*, *The International Journal of the History of Sport*, and *International Review for the Sociology of Sport*. She is the author of *Queens of the Ice* (published by Lorimer). Dr. Adams is the editor of *Sport History Review*.

ABOUT
THE CONTRIBUTORS

Mary Louise Adams, PhD, is a professor in the School of Kinesiology and Health Studies at Queen's University. Her book *Artistic Impressions: Figure Skating, Sport and the Limits of Masculinity* (2011) has been recognized with the North American Society for Sport History's Book Award and with the Women's and Gender Studies Association's Outstanding Scholarship Prize. Dr. Adams teaches courses on sport and culture, the sociology of fitness and the body, and contemporary issues in sexuality, and she is a three-time recipient of her department's Excellence in Teaching Award. She is currently working on two projects; one examines the feminist implications of women's sporting opportunities, and another focuses on the environmental, industrial, and recreational history of a city park near her home in Kingston, Ontario.

Sarah Barnes, PhD, is a postdoctoral fellow in the sport, society, and technology program in the School of History and Sociology at the Georgia Institute of Technology. Her research interests include issues related to the history and politics of athlete welfare and debates about science and technology in sport. She earned her doctorate in the School of Kinesiology and Health Studies at Queen's University in Kingston, Ontario. Her dissertation, "The Ultimate Performance Enhancer? A History of Ideas About Sleep as an Athletic Training Tool," is the first to study dominant understanding of sleep and sport across the 20th century and early 21st century. Dr. Barnes is working on several manuscripts that explore how sleep-enhancing products and technologies are taken up in high-performance sport settings.

Russell Field, PhD, is an associate professor in the faculty of kinesiology and recreation management at the University of Manitoba. He is the coauthor, with Simon Darnell and Bruce Kidd, of *The History and Politics of Sport-for-Development: Activists, Ideologues and Reformers* (Palgrave Macmillan, 2019). He is a member of the North American Society for Sport History (NASSH) and the International Society for the History of Physical Education and Sport (ISHPES), on whose council he serves. He has been the film and museum reviews editor for the *Journal of Sport History* and is the founder and executive director of the Canadian Sport Film Festival.

Janice Forsyth, PhD, is an award-winning scholar whose research, service, and advocacy focus on Indigenous sport development in Canada. Her publications include *Aboriginal Peoples and Sport in Canada: Historical Foundations and Contemporary Issues* (2013), a popular coedited collection, and the monograph *Reclaiming Tom Longboat: Indigenous Self-Determination in Canada Sport* (2020). The insights generated from her work have shaped federal policies on sport and health while generating critical acclaim and attention from scholars, practitioners, and major media worldwide. The accumulation of her work resulted in her 2019 election to the College of the Royal Society of Canada. She is an associate professor in sociology and the director of Indigenous studies at Western University. She is a member of the Fisher River Cree Nation.

Craig Greenham, PhD, is an assistant professor in the department of kinesiology at the University of Windsor. Educated at the University of Western Ontario, the University of Regina, and Carleton University, his primary research focus is North American team sports—particularly baseball, hockey and Canadian football. Dr. Greenham's writing appears in such publications as the *Journal of Sport History, Sport History Review, International Journal of the History of Sport,* and *Base Ball: New Research on the Early Game.* He is a frequent media source, nationally and internationally, and is a member of the North American Society for Sport History (NASSH).

Robert Kossuth, PhD, is an associate professor in the department of kinesiology and physical education at the University of Lethbridge. His ongoing research examines the history of sport, recreation, and leisure in Canada in the late 19th and early 20th centuries. In 2018 he chaired the North American Society for Sport History (NASSH) Book Award committee. Recent publications have examined physical culture on Canada's prairie frontier, including "Busting Broncos and Breaking New Ground: Reassessing the Legacies of Canadian Cowboys John Ware and Tom Three Persons" (*Great Plains Quarterly,* Spring 2018), and "Indigenous and Colonial Physical Culture in Lethbridge: Sport, Contact, and Settlement on the Prairie Frontier" (*Journal of Sport History,* Summer 2019).

Stacy L. Lorenz, PhD, is a professor in physical education and history at the University of Alberta's Augustana Campus, located in Camrose, Alberta. His research interests include violence and masculinity, newspaper coverage of sport, media experiences of sport, and hockey and Canadian culture. He is the author of *Media, Culture, and the Meanings of Hockey: Constructing a Canadian Hockey World, 1896-1907* (2017), and he has published articles on the sports media in the *Journal of Sport History, Sport History Review, Journal of Canadian Studies,* and *International Journal of the History of Sport.* Dr. Lorenz teaches in the areas of sport history, sport and social issues, and sport and popular culture. He is also a frequent media commentator on issues related to sport, society, and culture.

Courtney W. Mason, PhD, is an associate professor and Canada Research Chair in rural livelihoods and sustainable communities at Thompson Rivers University in British Columbia. His work examines locally driven initiatives in rural and Indigenous communities that enhance regional food security and tourism development. His research on parks and protected areas informs public policy on land use management frameworks and conservation practices. He is the author of *Spirits of the Rockies: Reasserting an Indigenous Presence in Banff National Park* (Toronto: University of Toronto Press, 2014) and the coeditor of *A Land Not Forgotten: Indigenous Food Security and Land-Based Practices of Northern Ontario* (Winnipeg: University of Manitoba Press, 2017).

David McMurray, MA, is an adjunct assistant professor in the department of history at the University of Lethbridge. He is also the manager of applied research in the Centre for Applied Research, Innovation and Entrepreneurship (CARIE) at Lethbridge College. His 2007 MA thesis, "A Rod of Her Own: Women and Angling in Victorian North America" won the prestigious Medal of Merit from the University of Lethbridge School of Graduate Studies. Recent publications examined the sport of lacrosse in early 20th-century western Canada. In addition to academic publications, his research on 19th-century fisherwomen has been highlighted in the *Washington Post* (June 2019) and *Anglers Journal* (Spring 2020).

Ornella Nzindukiyimana, PhD, is an assistant professor of sport history and sociology in the department of human kinetics at St. Francis Xavier University. She has published papers in peer-reviewed journals and is a member of the North American Society for Sport History (NASSH), the International Society for the History of Physical Education and Sport (ISHPES), and the Black Canadian Studies Association. In 2019, she earned the ISHPES Early Career Scholar Award. She was a coeditor for an ISHPES special issue of the *International Journal of the History of Sport* and is on the editorial board of the *Journal of Emerging Sport Studies*. She has also been a keynote speaker at the Telling the Stories of Race and Sports in Canada symposium at the ISHPES Annual Congress.

Christine M. O'Bonsawin, PhD (Abenaki, Odanak Nation), is an associate professor of Indigenous studies and history at the University of Victoria. Her scholarship takes up questions in sport history regarding the rights of Indigenous peoples, particularly as they pertain to the hosting of the Olympic Games and other mega sporting events on unceded Indigenous territories. Dr. O'Bonsawin served as the director of the Indigenous studies program at the University of Victoria from 2007 to 2018 and is the author of several articles and book chapters on Indigenous sport history. She is a coauthor of two recently published special issues: the *Journal of Sport History: Indigenous Resurgence, Regeneration, and Decolonization through Sport History* (2019) and *BC Studies: (Un)Settling the Islands: Race, Indigeneity and the Transpacific* (2020).

Danielle Peers, PhD, is a Canada Research Chair in disability and movement cultures and an assistant professor in the faculty of kinesiology, sport, and recreation at the University of Alberta. Dr. Peers' research builds off of their experiences as a Paralympic athlete as well as a coach, administrator, and athlete leader in the sport of wheelchair basketball. For their doctoral work on disability sport history and its relationship to social justice and injustices, Dr. Peers was awarded the prestigious Vanier Canada Scholarship and Trudeau Foundation Scholarship. Dr. Peers then completed a Banting Postdoctoral Fellowship on flourishing in disability communities (including sporting communities) before beginning their current position.

Jay Scherer, PhD, is a professor in the faculty of kinesiology, sport, and recreation at the University of Alberta, where he has taught a variety of sociology of sport courses over the past 15 years. He has published extensively on the intersections of sport, media, and popular culture and has edited an introductory textbook on the sociology of sport and physical culture. He was named a research fellow by the North American Society for the Sociology of Sport in 2017.

Braden Te Hiwi, PhD, is Māori of Ngāti Raukawa and Rangitāne Iwi (Nations) and is from the Manawatū region of Aotearoa (New Zealand). He is an assistant professor in the Indigenous studies program at the Okanagan Campus of the University of British Columbia, located on the unceded territory of the Okanagan/Syilx Nation. His research and teaching focus on the health and physical activity of Indigenous peoples.

Lisa Tink, MA, is a doctoral candidate in the School of Public Health at the University of Alberta. Prior to returning to academics, Tink worked as a director in the government of Alberta's Recreation and Physical Activity Division and a manager at the Alberta Recreation and Parks Association. Tink's current research highlights how the oppressive and exclusionary practices of the past have been inscribed in our contemporary sport and recreation systems.

Michel Vigneault, PhD, is chargé de cours at Université du Québec à Montréal (UQAM), where he teaches physical activity history. He was the first in Québec to complete a doctoral degree in sport history (Université Laval, 2001); his topic was the beginning of organized hockey in Montréal. He is an original editorial member of the *Sport History Review*. He has received the Brian McFarlane Award from the Society of International Hockey Research (SIHR). He is the author of the chapter "Montreal's Francophone Hockey Beginnings, 1895-1910" in *The Same but Different: Hockey in Quebec*, by Jason Blake and Andrew C. Holman (2017).

Kevin B. Wamsley, PhD, is president and vice-chancellor at St. Francis Xavier University in Nova Scotia, Canada, and a professor of sport history in the department of human kinetics. He has been a member of the North American Society for Sport History (NASSH) since 1987 and has served as its president. He is coauthor of four editions of *Sport in Canada: A History* and coeditor of *Global Olympics: Historical and Sociological Studies of the Modern Games*.